ECCE ROMANI II

A LATIN READING PROGRAM

HOME AND SCHOOL

PASTIMES AND CEREMONIES

SECOND EDITION

Longman

Ecce Romani Student Book II
Home and School and **Pastimes and Ceremonies, second edition**

Longman, 10 Bank Street, White Plains, N.Y. 10606

Associated companies:
Longman Group Ltd., London
Longman Cheshire Pty., Melbourne
Longman Paul Pty., Auckland
Copp Clark Pitman, Toronto

This edition of *Ecce Romani* is based on *Ecce Romani: A Latin Reading Course*, originally prepared by The Scottish Classics Group © copyright The Scottish Classics Group 1971, 1982, and published in the United Kingdom by Oliver and Boyd, a division of Longman Group. It is also based on the 1988 North American edition. This edition has been prepared by a team of American educators.

Photo credits: Credits appear on page 433.

Acknowledgments: Reiterated thanks are due to the consultants who contributed to the 1988 North American edition of *ECCE ROMANI*: Dr. Rudolph Masciantonio, Ronald Palma, Dr. Edward Barnes, and Shirley Lowe. In addition to the authors and consultants who contributed to this new edition and who are listed separately, thanks are due to the following people: to Mary O. Minshall for providing original material for the Frontier Life essays; to Ursula Chen, Julia Gascoyne Fedoryk, and Franklin Kennedy for their help on the Teacher's Guides; and to Marjorie Dearworth Keeley for help with the preparation of the manuscript. Finally, thanks are due to Longman Publishing Group's production team: Janice Baillie and Helen Ambrosio; and its editorial team: Barbara Thayer and Lyn McLean, for all they did.

Executive editor: Lyn McLean
Development editor: Barbara Thayer
Production editor: Janice L. Baillie
Production-editorial and design director: Helen B. Ambrosio
Text design: Creatives NYC, Inc.
Cover design: Circa 86
Cover Illustration: Yao Zen Liu
Text art: Yao Zen Liu
Maps: Laszlo Kubinyi
Photo research: Barbara Thayer
Electronic Production: Function thru Form Inc.

ISBN: 0-8013-1202-7

678910-DOC-9998

REVISION EDITOR: GILBERT LAWALL
University of Massachusetts, Amherst, Massachusetts

AUTHORS AND CONSULTANTS

Peter C. Brush
Deerfield Academy
Deerfield, Massachusetts

Sally Davis
Arlington Public Schools
Arlington, Virginia

Pauline P. Demetri
Cambridge Rindge & Latin School
Cambridge, Massachusetts

Jane Hall
National Latin Exam
Alexandria, Virginia

Thalia Pantelidis Hocker
Old Dominion University
Norfolk, Virginia

Glenn M. Knudsvig
University of Michigan
Ann Arbor, Michigan

Maureen O'Donnell
W.T. Woodson High School
Fairfax, Virginia

Ronald Palma
Holland Hall School
Tulsa, Oklahoma

David J. Perry
Rye High School
Rye, New York

Deborah Pennell Ross
University of Michigan
Ann Arbor, Michigan

Andrew F. Schacht
Renbrook School
West Hartford, Connecticut

Judith Lynn Sebesta
University of South Dakota
Vermillion, South Dakota

The Scottish Classics Group
Edinburgh, Scotland

David Tafe
Rye Country Day School
Rye, New York

Rex Wallace
University of Massachusetts
Amherst, Massachusetts

Allen Ward
University of Connecticut
Storrs, Connecticut

Elizabeth Lyding Will
Amherst College
Amherst, Massachusetts

Philip K. Woodruff
Lake Forest High School
Lake Forest, Illinois

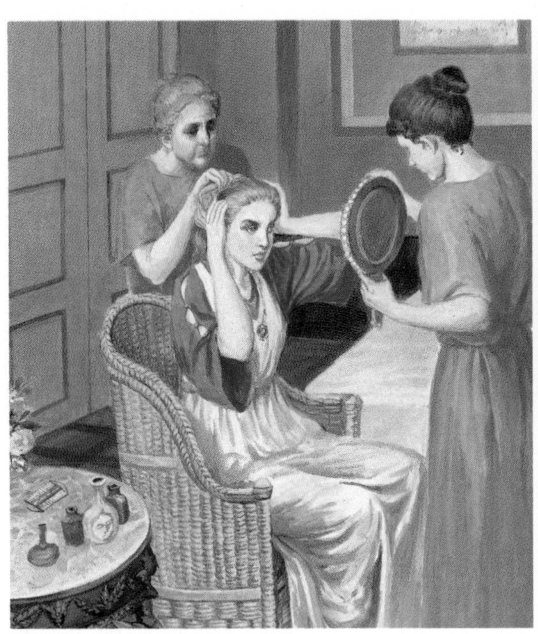

CONTENTS

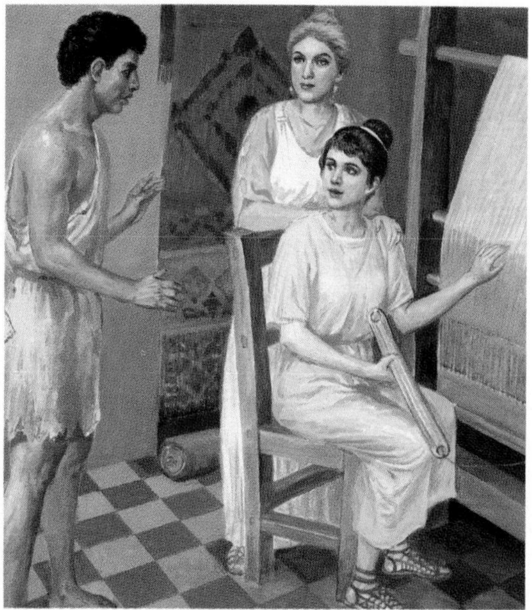

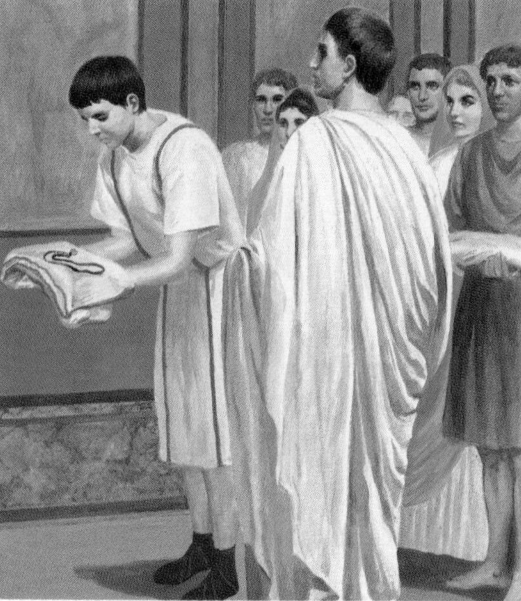

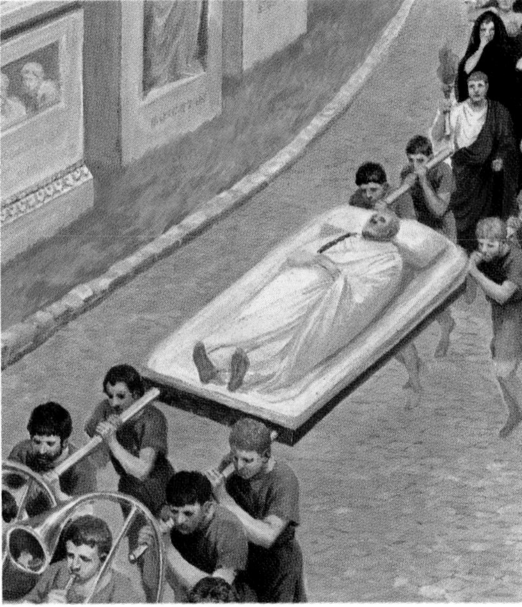

REFERENCE MATERIALS

MAPS

GALLIA
Augusta Praetōria
TRĀNSPADĀNA
VENETIA
Aquileia
Vērōna
Mantua
Hadria
LIGURIA
Genua
GALLIA CISALPĪNA
Ravenna
MARE HADRIĀTICUM
Pīsae
Flōrentia
UMBRIA
ETRŪRIA
Perusia
PĪCĒNUM
Narnia
CORSICA
Aleria
Tarquiniī
Corfīnium
Ōstia
Rōma
LATIUM
SAMNIUM
Asculum
Cannae
Capua
ĀPŪLIA
Venusia
Brundisium
CAMPĀNIA
Puteolī
CALABRIA
MARE
TYRRHĒNICUM
SARDINIA
LŪCĀNIA
Velia
Caralis
BRŪTIĪ
N
Messāna
Rhēgium
SICILIA
Syrācūsae
SCALE of MILES
0
75
150

Italy

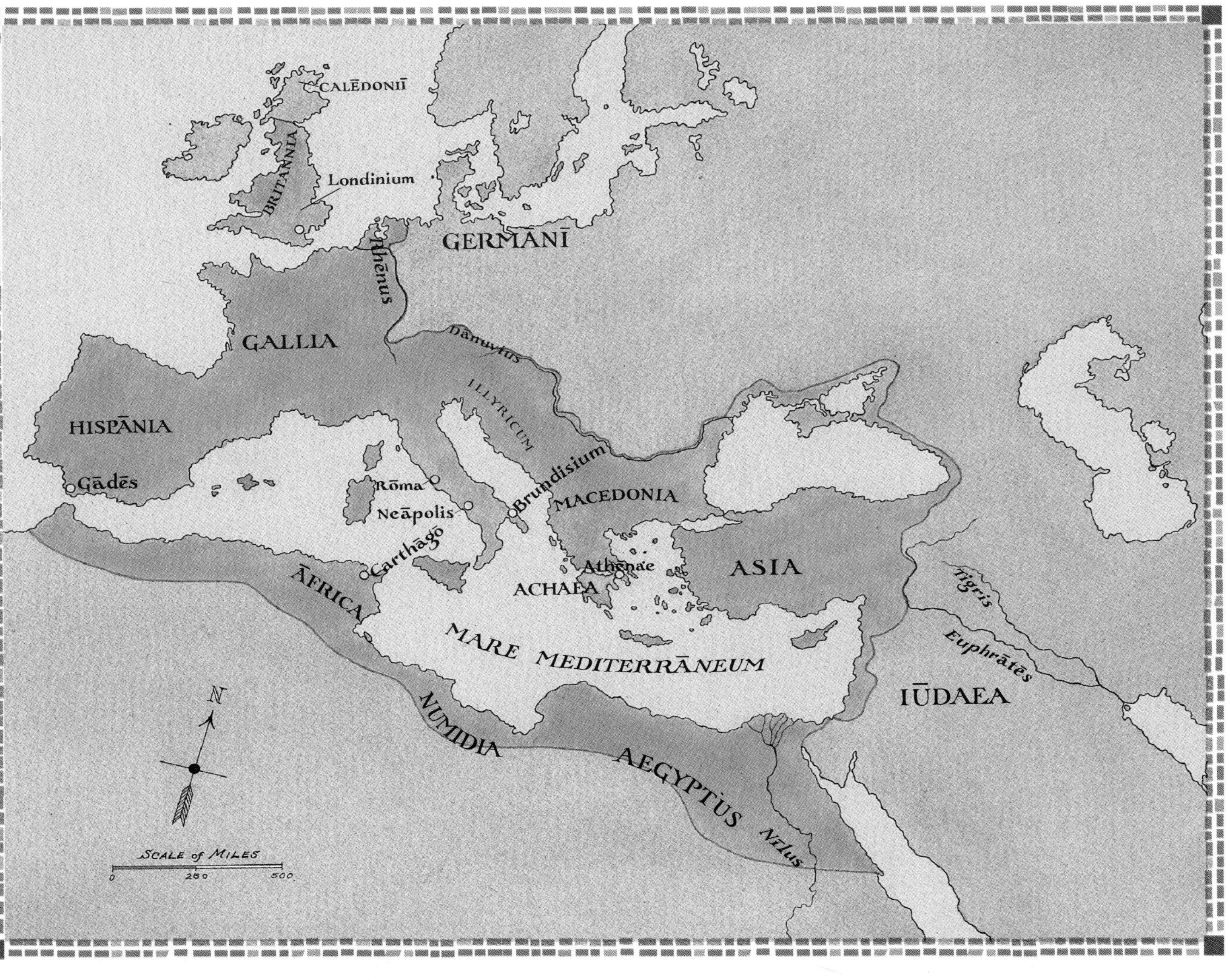

The Roman Empire, A.D. 80

CHAPTER 28

PREPARING TO GO SHOPPING

Māne erat. Aurēlia in cubiculō sedēbat. Crīnēs eius cūrābant duae ancillae, quārum altera speculum tenēbat, altera crīnēs pectēbat. Phrygia, quae crīnēs neglegenter pectēbat, dominam vexābat; Syra, quod manus tremēbat, speculum nōn bene tenēbat. Aurēlia igitur, neglegentiā eārum vexāta, subitō, "Quam neglegentēs estis!" clāmāvit. "Abīte! Abīte! Vocāte Cornēliam! Eam mēcum in urbem dūcere volō."

Statim exiērunt ancillae.

Mox in cubiculum iniit Cornēlia. "Cūr mē vocāvistī, māter?"

Aurēlia respondit, "Pater tuus amīcōs quōsdam, in quibus sunt senātōrēs praeclārī, ad cēnam hodiē invītāvit. Porcum servus iam ēmit, sed ego in animō habeō ipsa in urbem īre ad mercātōrem quendam cuius taberna nōn procul abest, nam glīrēs optimōs ille vēndere solet. Sī tū vīs mēcum īre, mē in ātriō exspectā! Intereā servōs iubēbō sellās ad iānuam ferre."

1 **crīnēs, crīnium,** m. pl., *hair*
2 **speculum, -ī,** n., *mirror*
neglegenter, adv., *carelessly*
4 **vexātus, -a, -um,** *annoyed*
8 **in quibus,** *among whom*
9 **porcus, -ī,** m., *pig*
10 **cuius,** *whose*
glīs, glīris, gen. pl., **glīrium,** m., *dormouse*
11 **sella, -ae,** f., *sedan chair*

2 **pectō, pectere, pexī, pexus,** *to comb*
11 **vēndō, vēndere, vēndidī, vēnditus,** *to sell*

Exercise 28a

Respondē Latīnē:

1. Quid faciēbant duae ancillae?
2. Quam ob causam Phrygia Aurēliam vexābat?
3. Quam ob causam Syra speculum nōn bene tenēbat?
4. Quōcum Aurēlia in urbem īre vult?
5. Quōs ad cēnam Cornēlius invītāvit?
6. Quid servus iam ēmit?
7. Quid Aurēlia emere vult?
8. Quid Aurēlia servōs facere iubēbit?

Quam ob causam...? *For what reason...?* Answer: **Quod...**

BUILDING THE MEANING
Relative Clauses I

A very common type of subordinate clause is the *relative clause.* Relative clauses are descriptive clauses that modify nouns. You have seen clauses of this sort since the very first chapter of this course:

> Cornēlia est puella Rōmāna **quae** in Italiā habitat. (1:1–2)
> *Cornelia is a Roman girl* ***who*** *lives in Italy.*

The relative clause (underlined) gives information about the noun phrase **puella Rōmāna,** describing this Roman girl as one who lives in Italy. Relative clauses are introduced by *relative pronouns* (e.g., **quae,** *who*), which relate or connect the statement made in the subordinate clause to a noun or noun phrase (e.g., **puella Rōmāna,** *a Roman girl*) in the main clause. This noun or noun phrase in the main clause is called the *antecedent* because it goes (Latin **cēdere)** before (Latin **ante-**) the relative clause.

FORMS
Relative Pronouns

Here are all the forms of the relative pronoun:

	Singular			
	Masc.	**Fem.**	**Neut.**	**Meanings**
Nom.	quī	quae	quod	*who, which, that*
Gen.	cuius	cuius	cuius	*whose, of whom, of which*
Dat.	cui	cui	cui	*to whom (which), for whom (which)*
Acc.	quem	quam	quod	*whom, which, that*
Abl.	quō	quā	quō	(see note below)

	Plural			
	Masc.	**Fem.**	**Neut.**	**Meanings**
Nom.	quī	quae	quae	*who, which, that*
Gen.	quōrum	quārum	quōrum	*whose, of whom, of which*
Dat.	quibus	quibus	quibus	*to whom (which), for whom (which)*
Acc.	quōs	quās	quae	*whom, which, that*
Abl.	quibus	quibus	quibus	(see note below)

Be sure to learn these forms thoroughly.

NOTE:

Translation of forms of the relative pronoun in the ablative case will depend on the function of the ablative case in the clause. For example, **quibuscum** means *with whom,* and **quō** could be ablative of means or instrument and mean *with which* or *by which.*

Exercise 28b

On the chart of relative pronouns locate the following forms that appeared in the story at the beginning of this chapter. Some of the forms appear more than once on the chart. Identify all the possibilities that each form could be. Then identify the gender, number, and case of the pronoun as used in the story:

1. quārum (line 1)
2. quae (line 2)
3. quibus (line 8)
4. cuius (line 10)

BUILDING THE MEANING

Relative Clauses II

The form of the relative pronoun that introduces a relative clause depends on two things:

1. the *gender* and *number* of its antecedent
2. the *case* required by the function of the relative pronoun in its own clause

The following passages from the story at the beginning of this chapter illustrate these points:

> ...duae ancillae, **quārum** altera speculum tenēbat.... (28:1–2)

The fact that **quārum** is feminine in gender and plural in number relates it to its antecedent, **duae ancillae** (feminine plural). The fact that **quārum** is genitive shows how it functions in its own clause, namely as a partitive genitive (see Chapter 25) with **altera,** thus *one of whom*.

> Phrygia, **quae** crīnēs neglegenter pectēbat.... (28:2–3)

Here the relative pronoun is feminine singular because of its antecedent **Phrygia,** and it is nominative because it serves as the subject of the verb of its own clause, **pectēbat.**

> ...amīcōs quōsdam, in **quibus** sunt senātōrēs praeclārī.... (28:8)

Here the relative pronoun is masculine plural because of its antecedent **amīcōs quōsdam,** and it is ablative because of its use with the preposition in its own clause.

> ...ad mercātōrem quendam **cuius** taberna nōn procul abest.... (28:10)

Here the relative pronoun is masculine singular because of its antecedent **mercātōrem quendam,** and it is genitive to indicate possession in its own clause (*whose shop*).

Exercise 28c

Here are sentences with relative clauses. Read aloud and translate. Then explain the gender, number, and case of each relative pronoun:

1. Sextus est puer strēnuus **quī** saepe in agrīs et in hortō currit.
2. Dāvus omnēs servōs in āream **quae** est prope vīllam venīre iubet.
3. Aurēlia et Cornēlia spectābant rūsticōs **quī** in agrīs labōrābant.
4. Marcus pede vexābat Cornēliam **quae** dormīre volēbat.
5. "Lectīcāriī, **quōs** vōbīs condūxī, vōs domum ferent," inquit Titus.
6. "Hic est arcus," inquit Titus, "**quem—**"
7. Sextus iam cōgitābat dē omnibus rēbus **quās** Titus heri nārrāverat.
8. Bovēs lapidēs quadrātōs in plaustrō trahēbant ad novum aedificium **quod** Caesar cōnficit.
9. Sunt multī hominēs scelestī **quī** bona cīvium arripiunt.

Exercise 28d

In the following sentences first decide the gender, number, and case required to make a Latin pronoun correspond to the English pronoun in italics. Then locate the correct form of the Latin pronoun on the chart on page 4. Read the sentence aloud with the Latin pronoun and translate:

1. Aurēliae crīnēs, *(which)* duae ancillae cūrābant, pulchrī erant.
2. Syra, *(whose)* manus tremēbat, speculum nōn bene tenēbat.
3. Ancillae, *(whose)* neglegentia Aurēliam vexāverat, ignāvae erant.
4. Mox in cubiculum iniit Cornēlia, *(whom)* Aurēlia vocāverat.
5. Servus, *(to whom)* Aurēlia pecūniam dederat, porcum ēmit.

pulcher, pulchra, pulchrum, *beautiful, pretty*

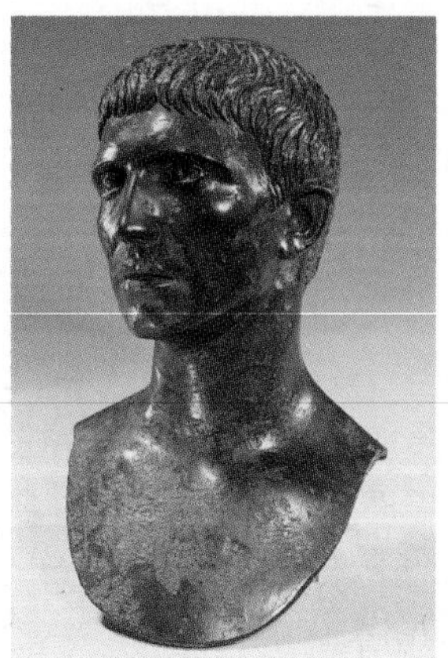

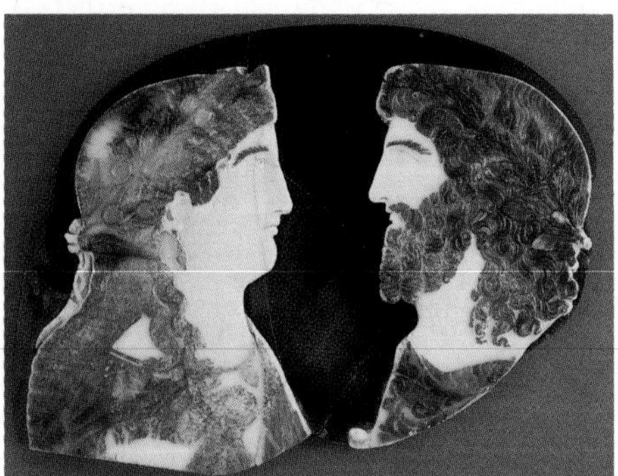

The hairstyles of both men and women varied greatly over time. Men's beards went in and out of fashion. Compare the cameo of Emperor Julian and his wife with the bronze busts of some earlier Romans.

Bronze heads, Louvre, Paris, France; sardonyx cameo, British Museum, London, England

ROMAN LIFE XVII

HAIRSTYLES OF ROMAN GIRLS AND WOMEN

Roman girls and women let their hair grow long. Girls tied it in a bun at the back of the head or wound and knotted it in tresses on the top of the head. Straight hairpins of ivory, silver, or gold were used to hold the hair in place. Woollen fillets (**vittae**) were woven into the tresses as a sign of chastity. Mirrors of polished metal, not glass, were used, and slaves were specially trained to be expert hairdressers (**ōrnātrīcēs**). During some periods and especially at the imperial court and on special occasions some women went to great lengths to arrange their hair in different levels on the top of the head and to supplement their own hair with false hair. Bleaches and dyes were used, as well as

Relief sculpture of a hairdresser, circa A.D. 50
Bas relief, Landesmuseum, Hesse, Germany

A nineteenth century artist's rendition of one hairdo a Roman girl could have worn
Oil on canvas, "A Roman Boat Race" by Sir Edward John Poynter, The Maas Gallery, London, England

lotions to make the hair softer. Styles varied greatly. The poet Ovid recommended that each woman should choose the style that best suited her, and he describes some of them as follows:

> An oval face prefers a parting upon the head left unadorned. Round faces want a small knot left on top of the head, so that the ears show. Let one girl's locks hang down on either shoulder. Let another braid her hair. It is becoming to this one to let her waving locks lie loose; let that one have her tight-drawn tresses closely confined; this one is pleased with an adornment of tortoise-shell; let that one bear folds that resemble waves. I cannot enumerate all the fashions that there are; each day adds more adornments.
>
> Ovid, *Art of Love* III.137–152

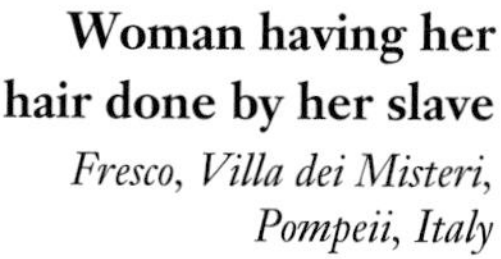

Woman having her hair done by her slave
Fresco, Villa dei Misteri, Pompeii, Italy

The poet Martial describes how a petulant woman named Lalage punished the slave who was dressing her hair because of one curl that went astray:

> A single curl of the whole concoction of hair had strayed, badly fixed in place with an insecure pin. This crime, which she noticed, Lalage avenged with her mirror and Plecusa fell wounded because of these cruel locks of hair. Stop, now, Lalage, to arrange your dire locks and let no maid touch your ill-tempered head.
>
> Martial, *Epigrams* II.66.1–4

GOING TO THE MARKET

Cornēlia summā celeritāte sē parāvit. Brevī tempore māter et fīlia ā servīs per urbem ferēbantur. In viīs erat ingēns multitūdō hominum. Concursābant enim servī, mīlitēs, virī, puerī, mulierēs. Onera ingentia ā servīs portābantur, nam interdiū nihil intrā urbem vehiculō portātur.

Omnia quae videt Cornēlia eam dēlectant. Nunc cōnspicit poētam versūs recitantem, nunc mendīcōs pecūniam petentēs, nunc lectīcam ēlegantissimam quae ab octō servīs portātur. In eā recumbit homō obēsus quī librum legit.

Subitō Cornēlia duōs servōs per viam festīnantēs cōnspicit, quōrum alter porcum parvulum portat. Eō ipsō tempore ē manibus effugit porcus. "Cavēte!" exclāmant adstantēs, sed frūstrā. Homō quīdam, quī per viam celeriter currit, porcum vītāre nōn potest. Ad terram cadit. Paulisper in lutō iacet gemēns. Deinde īrā commōtus servum petit ā quō porcus aufūgit. Est rixa.

Fīnem rixae nōn vīdit Cornēlia quod servī iam sellās in aliam viam tulerant. Tandem advēnērunt ad eam tabernam quam petēbant. Dē sellīs dēscendērunt. Tum Aurēlia, "Vīdistīne," inquit, "illam lectīcam in quā recumbēbat homō obēsus? Ūnus ē lībertīs Caesaris ipsīus—Sed quid accidit? Fūmum videō et flammās."

1 **summā celeritāte,** *with the greatest speed, as fast as possible*
ā servīs ferēbantur, *were being carried by slaves*
2 **concursō, -āre, -āvī -ātus,** *to run to and fro, run about*
4 **portātur,** *is (being) carried*
5 **dēlectō, -āre, -āvī, -ātus,** *to delight, amuse*
6 **mendīcus, -ī,** m., *beggar*
ēlegantissimus, -a, -um, *most elegant*
10 **adstantēs, adstantium,** m. pl., *bystanders*
12 **rixa, -ae,** f., *quarrel*
13 **fīnis, fīnis,** gen. pl., **fīnium,** m., *end*
15 **lībertus, -ī,** m., *freedman*
16 **ipsīus,** gen. sing. of **ipse, ipsa, ipsum**
fūmus, -ī, m., *smoke*

7 **recumbō, recumbere, recubuī,** *to recline, lie down*
12 **aufugiō, aufugere, aufūgī,** *to run away, escape*

Exercise 29a
Respondē Latīnē:

1. Quōmodo Cornēlia sē parāvit?
2. Quid in viīs vidēbant?
3. Cūr onera ā servīs portābantur?
4. Quid faciēbat poēta?
5. Quī festīnābant per viam?
6. Quid portābat alter servōrum?
7. Quis ad terram cadit?
8. Cūr Cornēlia fīnem rixae nōn vīdit?
9. Quō advēnērunt Aurēlia et Cornēlia?
10. Quid ibi vīdit Aurēlia?

The Center of Ancient Rome

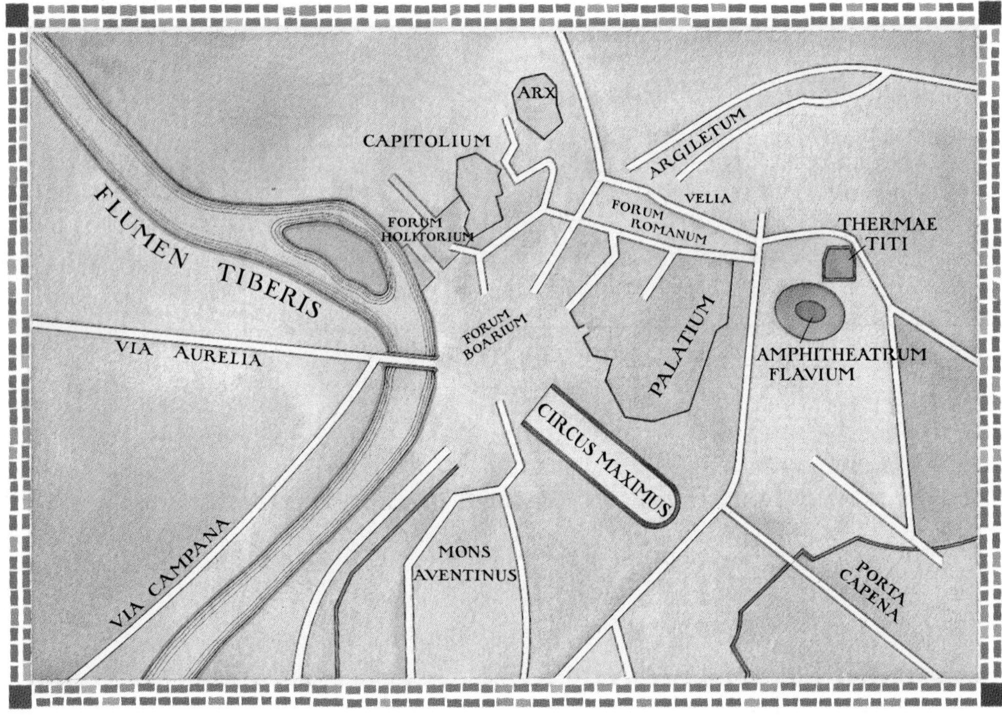

Malum est cōnsilium quod mūtārī nōn potest. *It's a bad plan that can't be changed.* (Publilius Syrus 403)

Hominēs id quod volunt crēdunt. *Men believe what they want to.* (Julius Caesar)

Quī vult dare parva nōn dēbet magna rogāre. *He who wishes to give little shouldn't ask for much.*

Exercise 29b

In the story on page 11, locate eight relative pronouns and explain why the particular gender, number, and case are used. Note that **quīdam, quod,** and **quid** in this passage are not relative pronouns (see below).

Exercise 29c

Read aloud and translate:

1. Servī, quī cistās portābant, hūc illūc concursābant. Cistae, quās servī portābant, plēnae erant vestium.
2. Ancillae, quae Aurēliae crīnēs cūrābant, dominam timēbant. Aurēlia, quae multīs rēbus sollicita erat, ancillās neglegentēs abīre iussit.
3. Servus, ā quō onus portābātur, gemēbat. Onus enim, quod portābat, ingēns erat.

4. Homō obēsus, cuius lectīca erat ēlegantissima, librum legēbat.
5. Porcī, quōs servī portābant, grunniēbant. Adstantēs, quī eōs audiēbant, rīdēbant.

vestis, vestis, gen. pl., **vestium,** f., *clothing, garment*

Exercise 29d

Give the Latin for the relative pronoun (in parentheses) and then read the sentence aloud and translate it:

1. Homō, (*who*) per viam currēbat, ad terram cecidit.
2. Ancilla, (*who*) crīnēs neglegenter pectēbat, Aurēliam vexābat.
3. Homō obēsus, (*whom*) servī portābant, librum legēbat.
4. Aurēlia, (*whom*) ancillae vexābant, speculum ēripuit.
5. Duo servī, (*whom*) Cornēlia cōnspexit, per viam festīnābant.
6. Brevī tempore māter et fīlia in sellās, (*which*) servī tulerant, ascendērunt.
7. Puella, (*to whom*) librum dedī, erat Cornēlia.
8. Servus, (*whose*) dominus erat īrātus, statim aufūgit.

ēripiō, ēripere, ēripuī, ēreptus, *to snatch (from)*

Building The Meaning

Many important Latin words begin with the letters *qu-*. Here are some examples:

1. relative pronouns, which you have studied extensively in Chapters 28 and 29:

   Omnia **quae** videt Cornēlia eam dēlectant. (29:5)
   *All the things **that** Cornēlia sees please her.*

2. the indefinite adjective **quīdam,** *a certain;* pl., *some.*

   Homō **quīdam,**… (29:10)
   ***A certain** man,…*

3. the interrogative pronouns **Quis…?** *Who?* **Quid…?** *What…?*

   Sed **quid** accidit? (29:16)
   *But **what** is happening?*

4. the causal conjunction **quod,** *because.**

   …**quod** servī iam sellās in aliam viam tulerant. (29:13)
   *…**because** the slaves had carried the sedan chairs into another street.*

*Note that **quod** may also be a relative pronoun. When it is, it is preceded by a neuter singular antecedent, e.g., **cisium, quod appropinquābat,…**

5. the exclamatory adverb **Quam...!** *How...!*

> "**Quam** neglegentēs estis!" (28:4)
> *"**How** careless you are!"*

You have seen all of these words a number of times in the readings. There is another important **qu-** word that you will meet, the *interrogative adjective:*

> **Quī** vir est ille?
> ***What** man is that?*
>
> **Quae** fēmina est illa?
> ***What** woman is that?*
>
> **Quem** virum vīdistī?
> ***What** man did you see?*
>
> **Cui** fēminae illud dedistī?
> ***To which** woman did you give that?*

The interrogative adjective modifies a noun and introduces a question. It has exactly the same forms as the relative pronoun.

FORMS

Indefinite Adjectives

The forms of the indefinite adjective **quīdam,** *a certain;* pl., *some,* are the same as those of the relative pronoun plus the letters *-dam,* except for the letters in boldface:

Number Case	Masc.	Fem.	Neut.
Singular			
Nominative	quīdam	quaedam	quo**d**dam
Genitive	cuiusdam	cuiusdam	cuiusdam
Dative	cuidam	cuidam	cuidam
Accusative	que**n**dam	qua**n**dam	quo**d**dam
Ablative	quōdam	quādam	quōdam
Plural			
Nominative	quīdam	quaedam	quaedam
Genitive	quōru**n**dam	quāru**n**dam	quōru**n**dam
Dative	quibusdam	quibusdam	quibusdam
Accusative	quōsdam	quāsdam	quaedam
Ablative	quibusdam	quibusdam	quibusdam

Interrogative Pronouns

In the singular the interrogative pronoun has identical forms in the masculine and feminine; in the plural it is the same as the relative pronoun (see page 4). We give only the singular forms here:

	Singular		
	Masc.	Fem.	Neut.
Nominative	quis	quis	quid
Genitive	cuius	cuius	cuius
Dative	cui	cui	cui
Accusative	quem	quem	quid
Ablative	quō	quō	quō

Learn the forms in the charts above thoroughly.

Exercise 29e

Read aloud and translate. Identify relative pronouns, **quod** causal, **quam** exclamatory, indefinite adjectives, interrogative adjectives, and interrogative pronouns:

1. Aurīgae, quōrum equī sunt celerrimī, nōn semper vincent.
2. Cui mercātōrī Aurēlia pecūniam dabit?
3. Mercātōrī, quī glīrēs vēndit, Aurēlia pecūniam dabit.
4. Quam ingēns est Circus! Quis tantum aedificium umquam vīdit?
5. Hī amīcī, quibuscum ad amphitheātrum crās ībimus, fēriātī erunt.
6. Ancillae quaedam crīnēs Aurēliae cūrābant.
7. Aurēlia īrāta erat quod ancillae neglegenter crīnēs cūrābant.
8. Cīvēs, quōrum clāmōrēs audīvimus, aurīgās spectābant.
9. Quam obēsus est homō quī in lectīcā librum legit!
10. Hanc urbem, in quā habitāmus, valdē amāmus.

celerrimus, -a, -um, *fastest, very fast*

Exercise 29f

Using stories 28 and 29 as guides, give the Latin for:

1. The bedroom, in which the slave-women were taking care of the hair of their mistress, was not large.
2. Syra, whose hand was trembling, was annoying her mistress.
3. No one was able to catch the pig that escaped from the hands of the slave.
4. The fat man, whose litter was most elegant, was reading a book.
5. Aurelia, to whom the merchant sold dormice, was carrying much money.

ROMAN LIFE XVIII

TOWN HOUSE AND APARTMENT

The town house (**domus**) of a wealthy Roman was self-contained and usually built on one level with few, if any, windows on its outside walls. It faced inwards and most of its light came from the opening in the roof of the main hall (**ātrium**) and from the open-colonnaded garden (**peristȳlium**). Grouped around these open areas were the purpose-built rooms of the house: bedrooms (**cubicula**), study (**tablīnum**), kitchen area (**culīna**), and dining room (**trīclīnium**). Decoration and furniture in the **domus** were as splendid as its owner's pocket allowed and in some cases a second story was added. The domus-style house can be identified in towns throughout the Roman world.

A wealthy Roman would normally possess, in addition to his town house (**domus**), at least one country house (**vīlla rūstica** or **vīlla urbāna**). Cicero had several, where he could get away from the city din and summer heat, but even a **domus** provided considerable privacy and seclusion.

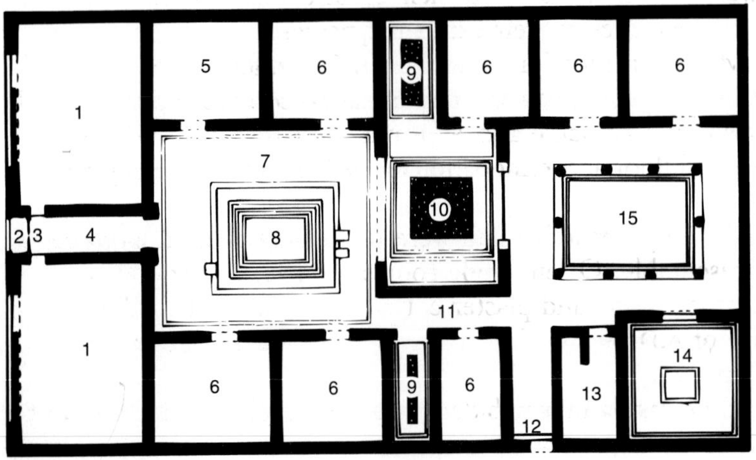

Plan of a domus

1. **tabernae** (shops)
2. **vestibulum** (entrance outside **iānua**)
3. **iānua** (double door)
4. **faucēs** (entrance passage)
5. **cella** (room for doorkeeper)
6. **cubicula** (bedrooms)
7. **ātrium** (hall)
8. **compluvium/impluvium** (roof opening and tank)
9. **āla** (alcove)
10. **tablīnum** (study)
11. **andrōn** (passage)
12. **postīcum** (servants' entrance)
13. **culīna** (kitchen)
14. **trīclīnium** (dining room)
15. **peristȳlium** (garden)

Rooms at the front or the side of a town house (**domus**) often housed shops, in which the owner of the house could conduct his business or which could be rented out. There were bakeries, butcher shops, barber shops, shoe shops, goldsmith shops, textile shops, and fast-food shops where you could get hot and cold food and drink of various sorts. There were also shops for many other kinds of activities such as washing clothes and tanning leather and for many other kinds of merchandise such as olive oil, wine, and knives. Merchants did not restrict themselves to their shops but tended to take over the street in front as well. Martial complained that there were only footpaths left in the middle of the street, that barbers endangered pedestrians with their razors as they shaved their clients, and that the grimy owners of cook-shops took over the whole street. He was happy when the emperor Domitian handed down a ruling requiring shop keepers to limit their activities to their shops. Now, Martial felt, the old Rome had been restored, which previously had become one **magna taberna,** one *huge shop* or shopping mall!

Where building space was at a premium, as in a city like Rome or a commercial town like Ostia, houses tended to grow upwards to accommodate the majority of the inhabitants. These apartment-type houses were called **īnsulae.** Sometimes they stood four or five stories high, and restrictions were introduced as early as the time of the Emperor Augustus to prevent their height exceeding 70 feet or approximately 20 meters.

Brick and concrete were commonly used in their construction, and they often had large windows and doorways enhancing their external appearance. The same rooms in the building tended to serve various functions, and there was a uniformity about the plan of each apartment in the building. Wooden shutters or canvas screens kept out the elements. Running water was rarely available above ground level, so heating and cooking often proved a hazard. Ground floor accommodation in the **īnsulae** was usually the most desirable.

While **īnsulae** could be very attractive and were often built around large central courts, some were less presentable. Often single rooms were let and conditions were cramped. Excessive reliance on wood and plaster construction led to the risk of fire or collapse, and after the fire of A.D. 64 the Emperor Nero introduced tighter control of building materials in the **īnsulae.**

On the ground floor of the **īnsula** in which Seneca, a Roman philosopher and writer, had his apartment there was a small public bath (**balneum**), and he describes some of the noises that disturbed him: the great splash made by the swimmer who likes to dive in as noisily as he can; the slapping sounds as people are being rubbed down; the noises of the man who likes to hear his own voice in the bath; the shouts of the pastrycook and the sausage-maker trying to sell their wares. Martial tells us of a schoolmaster who began shouting at his pupils in the early morning and kept his neighbors from sleeping.

ADDITIONAL READING:

The Romans Speak for Themselves: Book II: "Buildings for Different Ranks of Society," pages 1–11.

FORMS

Prefixes: Compound Verbs II

Some prefixes may undergo a change (often for ease of pronunciation) when they are added to verbs that begin with certain consonants:

1. Prefixes **ad-, con-, dis-, ex-, in-,** and **sub-** may change the final consonant of the prefix to the consonant that follows it. This process is called *assimilation*:

afferō (**ad-** + **ferō**)
attulī (**ad-** + **tulī**)
allātus (**ad-** + **lātus**)
commoveō (**con-** + **moveō**)
differō (**dis-** + **ferō**)
effugiō (**ex-** + **fugiō**)
immittō (**in-** + **mittō**)
succurrō (**sub-** + **currō**)

Note that **in-** and **con-** become **im-** and **com-** before *b* or *p*:

importō (**in-** + **portō**)
compōnō (**con-** + **pōnō**)

2. Prefix **ab-** becomes **au-** in front of verbs beginning with *f*:

aufugiō (**ab-** + **fugiō**)
auferō (**ab-** + **ferō**)

Exercise 29g

Read aloud and translate:

1. Geta effugere nōn potest.
2. Caupō Cornēliam et mātrem ad cubiculum addūxit.
3. Servī cistās in raedam impōnunt.
4. Servī onera ingentia ad vīllam apportābant.
5. Cibum ē vīllā aufert.
6. Aurēlia in cubiculum Marcī subitō irrumpit.
7. Cornēlia librum ē manibus Sextī celeriter abstulit et in hortum aufūgit.
8. Duo canēs ad Cornēliōs subitō accurrunt.
9. Viātōrēs multās fābulās dē caupōnibus scelestīs ad omnēs partēs Italiae differunt.
10. "Nōnne ēsurītis?" inquit caupō. "Mēnsās statim appōnam."

mēnsa, -ae, f., *table*
rumpō, rumpere, rūpī, ruptus, *to burst*

3. Sometimes the verb undergoes a change when a prefix is added:

f*a*cere, *to do* — **perf*i*cere,** *to do thoroughly, accomplish*
ten*ē*re, *to hold* — **cont*i*nēre,** *to hold together, contain*
r*a*pere, *to snatch* — **ēr*i*pere,** *to snatch from, rescue*
c*a*pere, *to take* — **acc*i*pere,** *to take to oneself, receive*
***ia*cere,** *to throw* — **con*i*cere,** *to throw* (emphatic)
cl*au*dere, *to shut* — **incl*ū*dere,** *to shut in*

4. Note that some verbs change conjugation when a prefix is added:

sedeō, sed*ēre*, *to sit* — **cōnsīdō, cōnsīd*ere*,** *to sit down*
dō, d*are*, *to give* — **reddō, redd*ere*,** *to give back*

Exercise 29h

Read aloud and translate. Then tell what the uncompounded verb would be:

1. Servī raedam reficiēbant.
2. Sextus ad terram dēcidit.
3. Subitō Sextus librum arripuit et retinuit.
4. Domina ancillās ā cubiculō īrāta exclūdit.
5. Herculēs multōs labōrēs perfēcit.
6. Servī cistam repetent quod Cornēlia aliam tunicam addere vult.
7. Cornēlius pecūniam caupōnī trādit.
8. Flāvia epistulam ā Cornēliā accipiet.
9. Illī praedōnēs pecūniam surripuērunt.
10. Caupō Cornēliōs cum rīsū excēpit.

FIRE!

Cōnspexerat Aurēlia ingentem īnsulam ē quā ēmittēbātur magna vīs fūmī ac flammārum. Cornēlia iam ad id aedificium summā celeritāte currēbat, cum Aurēlia eī clāmāvit, "Cavē, Cornēlia! Eī incendiō appropinquāre est perīculōsum."

Mox fūmus omnia obscūrābat. Cornēlia aedificium ipsum vix vidēre poterat. Multī hominēs hūc illūc concursābant. Ab incolīs omnia simul aguntur; īnfantēs ex aedificiō ā mātribus efferuntur; īnfirmī ē iānuīs trahuntur; bona ē fenestrīs ēiciuntur; in viā pōnuntur cistae, lectī, ōrnāmenta.

Cornēlia spectāculum tam miserābile numquam anteā vīderat. Lacrimābant mulierēs et līberōs parvōs tenēbant; lacrimābant līberī quī parentēs suōs quaerēbant; clāmābant parentēs quī līberōs suōs petēbant.

Via erat plēna eōrum quī ad spectāculum vēnerant. Aliī ex adstantibus aquam portābant; aliī in īnsulam intrābant et auxilium incolīs miserīs ferēbant. Multī tamen nihil faciēbant. "Nōs certē nihil facere possumus," inquiunt. "In hāc urbe solent esse incendia quae exstinguere nōn possumus. Neque hoc aedificium neque hōs incolās servāre possumus. Ecce! In tertiō tabulātō huius īnsulae est māter cum duōbus līberīs. Hī miserī flammīs paene opprimuntur. Sī incolae sē servāre nōn possunt, quid nōs facere possumus?"

(continued)

1 **īnsula, -ae,** f., *island, apartment building*
vīs, acc., **vim,** abl., **vī,** f., *force, amount*
ac, conj., *and*
3 **incendium, -ī,** n., *fire*
5 **incola, -ae,** m./f., *inhabitant, tenant*
omnia...aguntur, *everything is being done*
6 **īnfirmus, -a, -um,** *weak, shaky, frail*
fenestra, -ae, f., *window*
7 **ōrnāmenta, -ōrum,** n. pl., *furnishings*
8 **tam,** adv., *so*
9 **parvus, -a, -um,** *small*
15 **tabulātum, -ī,** n., *story, floor*
16 **paene,** adv., *almost*
opprimuntur, (they) *are being overwhelmed*

6 **ēiciō, ēicere, ēiēcī, ēiectus,** *to throw out*
9 **quaerō, quaerere, quaesīvī, quaesītus,** *to seek, look for, ask (for)*
16 **opprimō, opprimere, oppressī, oppressus,** *to overwhelm*

Exercise 30a

Respondē Latīnē:

1. Quae ex īnsulā ēmittēbantur?
2. Cui appropinquāre est perīculōsum?
3. Quid agunt incolae?
4. Quid faciēbant līberī?
5. Quid faciēbant parentēs?
6. Quī incolās adiūvērunt?

Subitō exclāmāvit ūnus ex adstantibus, "Cavēte, omnēs! Nisi statim aufugiētis, vōs omnēs opprimēminī aut lapidibus aut flammīs."

Tum Cornēlia, "Ēheu, māter!" inquit. "Ego valdē commoveor cum hōs tam miserōs līberōs videō. Quis eīs auxilium feret? Quōmodo effugient? Quid eīs accidet?"

Cui respondit Aurēlia, "Id nesciō. Sine dubiō iam mortuī sunt. Sed cūr tū ita commovēris? Nōs nihil hīc facere possumus. Nisi statim fugiēmus, nōs ipsae vix servābimur. Satis tamen hodiē vīdistī. Age! Ad Forum ībimus ac glīrēs emēmus."

Illō ipsō tempore parietēs īnsulae magnō fragōre cecidērunt. Nihil manēbat nisi lapidēs ac fūmus.

19 **opprimēminī,** *you will be crushed, overwhelmed*
20 **commoveor,** *I am upset*
22 **dubium, -ī,** n., *doubt*
23 **commovēris,** *you are upset*
24 **servābimur,** *we will be saved*
pariēs, parietis, m., *wall (of a house or room)*

20 **commoveō, commovēre, commōvī, commōtus,** *to move, upset*

Respondē Latīnē:

1. Cūr Cornēlia "Ēheu, māter!" inquit?
2. Quid Aurēlia facere vult?
3. Quōmodo parietēs īnsulae cecidērunt?

Flamma fūmō est proxima. *Flame follows smoke.* (Plautus, *Curculio* I.i.53)
Ubi fūmus, ibi ignis. *Where there's smoke, there's fire.*
Adversus incendia excubiās nocturnās vigilēsque commentus est. *Against the dangers of fires, Augustus conceived of the idea of night guards and watchmen.* (Suetonius, *Life of Augustus* 30)

The danger of fire had prompted Rome's first emperor, Augustus, in A.D. 6 to set up a fire brigade, armed with buckets, axes, and pumps. The effectiveness of this brigade was limited, however, and fire remained a constant threat in Rome. The great fire in A.D. 64 during the reign of Nero devastated half of the city, and a fire raged in the city for three days in A.D. 80, the time of our story, during the reign of Titus.

Life in the city could be dangerous:

> We live in a city largely propped up by slender poles; for this is how the inspector stops the houses falling down and, plastering over old cracks, he bids us sleep secure with disaster hanging over us. We should live where there are no fires, no alarms in the night. By the time the smoke has reached you who are still sleeping on the third floor, Ucalegon on the ground floor is already calling for water and removing his bits and pieces of furniture. For if there is an alarm on the ground floor, the last to burn will be the one protected from the rain only by the tiles where the gentle pigeons lay their eggs.
>
> Juvenal, *Satires* III.193–202

BUILDING THE MEANING

The Vivid or Historic Present

In the story at the beginning of this chapter, the verbs in lines 5–7 switch to the present tense although they describe past events. The effect of this is to make the reader feel personally involved in Cornelia's experience.

This use of the present tense is called the *vivid* or *historic present,* and it adds vividness (as in this story) and, where the story requires it, speed and excitement. Written English normally uses a past tense to describe such actions.

Notice that in the next paragraph, where the narrative resumes, the writer returns to the past tense.

Look back in story 29 and notice how there, too, in the second and third paragraphs the writer switches to the vivid or historic present.

FORMS

Verbs: Active and Passive Voice

Compare the following sentences:

Incolae omnia **agunt.**
*The tenants **are doing** everything.*

Ab incolīs omnia **aguntur.**
*Everything **is being done** by the tenants.*

Mātrēs īnfantēs **efferunt.**
*The mothers **carry out** the babies.*

Īnfantēs ā mātribus **efferuntur.**
*The babies **are carried out** by the mothers.*

Servī onera **portābant.**
*Slaves **were carrying** the loads.*

Onera ā servīs **portābantur.**
*The loads **were being carried** by slaves.*

Flammae vōs **opprīment.**
*The flames **will overwhelm** you.*

Vōs flammīs **opprimēminī.**
*You **will be overwhelmed** by the flames.*

The verbs in the left-hand column are in the *active voice;* in the right-hand column the verbs are in the *passive voice.*

In the active voice the subject performs the action of the verb. In the passive voice the subject receives the action of the verb.

	Singular		Plural
1	míttor, *I am (being) sent*	1	míttimur, *we are (being) sent*
2	mítteris, *you are (being) sent*	2	mittíminī, *you are (being) sent*
3	míttitur, *he, she, it is (being) sent*	3	mittúntur, *they are (being) sent*

The following table gives the forms and meanings of the present passive of **mittere:**

The personal endings above (in bold italics) should be learned thoroughly; they are used on all the passive forms that follow.

The following tables give the forms of the present, imperfect, and future passive of each conjugation. Be sure to learn these forms thoroughly.

Present Passive

		1st Conjugation	2nd Conjugation	3rd Conjugation		4th Conjugation
Singular	1	pórto***r***	móveo***r***	mítto***r***	iácio***r***	aúdio***r***
	2	portā́***ris***	movḗ***ris***	mítte***ris***	iáce***ris***	audī́***ris***
	3	portā́***tur***	movḗ***tur***	mítti***tur***	iáci***tur***	audī́***tur***
Plural	1	portā́***mur***	movḗ***mur***	mítti***mur***	iáci***mur***	audī́***mur***
	2	portā́***minī***	movḗ***minī***	mittí***minī***	iací***minī***	audī́***minī***
	3	portá***ntur***	mové***ntur***	mittú***ntur***	iaciú***ntur***	audiú***ntur***

Imperfect Passive

		1st Conjugation	2nd Conjugation	3rd Conjugation		4th Conjugation
Singular	1	portā́***bar***	movḗ***bar***	mittḗ***bar***	iaciḗ***bar***	audiḗ***bar***
	2	portā***bā́ris***	movē***bā́ris***	mittē***bā́ris***	iaciē***bā́ris***	audiē***bā́ris***
	3	portā***bā́tur***	movē***bā́tur***	mittē***bā́tur***	iaciē***bā́tur***	audiē***bā́tur***
Plural	1	portā***bā́mur***	movē***bā́mur***	mittē***bā́mur***	iaciē***bā́mur***	audiē***bā́mur***
	2	portā***bā́minī***	movē***bā́minī***	mittē***bā́minī***	iaciē***bā́minī***	audiē***bā́minī***
	3	portā***bántur***	movē***bántur***	mittē***bántur***	iaciē***bántur***	audiē***bántur***

Future Passive

		1st Conjugation	2nd Conjugation	3rd Conjugation		4th Conjugation
Singular	1	portā́***bor***	movḗ***bor***	mítt***ar***	iáci***ar***	aúdi***ar***
	2	portā́***beris***	movḗ***beris***	mitt***ḗris***	iaci***ḗris***	audi***ḗris***
	3	portā́***bitur***	movḗ***bitur***	mitt***ḗtur***	iaci***ḗtur***	audi***ḗtur***
Plural	1	portā́***bimur***	movḗ***bimur***	mitt***ḗmur***	iaci***ḗmur***	audi***ḗmur***
	2	portā***bíminī***	movē***bíminī***	mitt***ḗminī***	iaci***ḗminī***	audi***ḗminī***
	3	portā***búntur***	movē***búntur***	mitt***éntur***	iaci***éntur***	audi***éntur***

N.B.: The irregular verbs **esse, posse, velle,** and **nōlle** do not have passive forms. The passive forms of **ferre** are as follows:

		Present	Imperfect	Future
Singular	1	féro***r***	ferḗ***bar***	fér***ar***
	2	fér***ris***	ferē***bā́ris***	fer***ḗris***
	3	fér***tur***	ferē***bā́tur***	fer***ḗtur***
Plural	1	féri***mur***	ferē***bā́mur***	fer***ḗmur***
	2	ferí***minī***	ferē***bā́minī***	fer***ḗminī***
	3	ferú***ntur***	ferē***bántur***	fer***éntur***

Compare the passive forms of **ferre** to the passive forms of **mittere.**

Exercise 30b

Write out in sequence and translate the seven sentences in story 30 that contain passive verbs.

Exercise 30c

Read aloud and translate:

1. Adstantēs auxilium ferēbant; auxilium ab adstantibus ferēbātur.
2. Parentēs nōs ex hōc aedificiō efferunt; nōs ā parentibus ex hōc aedificiō efferimur.
3. Amīcī incolās servābunt; incolae ab amīcīs servābuntur.
4. Flammae tē opprimunt; tū flammīs opprimeris.
5. Lapidēs tē oppriment; tū lapidibus opprimēris.
6. Incolae ōrnāmenta ē fenestrīs ēiciēbant; ōrnāmenta ē fenestrīs ab incolīs ēiciēbantur.
7. Hī līberī miserī mē commovent; ego ab hīs miserīs līberīs commoveor.
8. Ā parentibus servāminī; ab adstantibus servābāminī; ā mātribus servābiminī.
9. Numquam audiar; vix audior; tandem audiēbar.
10. Illō spectāculō commovēbāris; tālibus spectāculīs semper commovēris; crās memoriā commovēberis.
11. Adstantēs removēbuntur; iānuae aperientur; līberī excitantur; nihil agēbātur; fūmus ēmittitur; aqua portābitur.

Exercise 30d

Change each verb from active to passive voice, keeping the same tense, person, and number; translate both verbs:

1. commoveō
2. ēicit
3. quaerēbam
4. fers
5. dūcis
6. trahēs
7. spectāmus
8. custōdiēbant
9. servābis

Exercise 30e

Using story 30 and the charts of passive verb forms as guides, give the Latin for:

1. Everything was being done by the inhabitants at the same time.
2. Their goods were being thrown out of the windows.
3. Water was being brought to the apartment house.
4. The miserable children will be overwhelmed by the flames.
5. Cornelia is very moved when she sees the miserable children.

Trahimur omnēs studiō laudis. ***We are all attracted by the desire for praise.*** **(Cicero, *Pro Archia poeta* XI.26)**

ADDITIONAL READING:

The Romans Speak for Themselves: Book II: "The Vigiles," pages 13–21.

DEADLY STRUGGLES WITHIN THE ROMAN REPUBLIC

When Tiberius Sempronius Gracchus, a tribune of the people, was clubbed to death by a mob of rioters in 133 B.C., Rome witnessed the first of a long series of violent events that marked the conflict between the old guard who ruled the Roman Senate and ambitious individuals who sought to advance their positions in the senatorial aristocracy by courting popular favor through reforms that benefitted different groups within the **populus Rōmānus.**

During the second century B.C., the Roman upper class acquired wealth that many invested in large-scale farming. As their profits grew, they added smaller farms to their holdings. Slaves replaced peasants as the workforce on these large estates. The peasants were driven into the cities where, faced with homelessness and hopeless poverty, they grew desperate and dangerous. Popular reformers, **populārēs,** gathered political strength, especially by seeking to provide displaced farmers and poor urban citizens with land and programs designed to help them. The established leaders, the **optimātēs**, who controlled the Senate, feared and opposed these rival aristocrats, who were trying to gain power at their expense through institutions outside of the Senate. The struggles between **populārēs** and **optimātēs** were marked by much blood and violence. The terms **populārēs** and **optimātēs** did not refer to political parties. They were labels like "leftist" or "right-winger," which were applied to individual aristocrats who tried to gain or retain power in either nontraditional or traditional ways.

THE GRACCHI

The Gracchi brothers became two famous **populārēs**. They were trying to reverse the decline of their family's prestige in the Senate after their father's death. Tiberius Gracchus, as tribune, disregarded the custom of presenting pending legislation to the Senate for review and obtained passage in the popular assembly of a bill distributing portions of public lands to landless peasants. His opponents in the Senate tried to block his plan by refusing to allocate money to put it in operation.

At this same time King Attalus III of Pergamum, a kingdom in Asia Minor, died and in his will bequeathed his kingdom to Rome. At Tiberius' instigation, the popular assembly passed another law that ignored the Senate's traditional control of financial matters and provided that the king's wealth be used to finance the distribution of land to the landless. Then, Tiberius boldly stood for re-election for an unprecedented second consecutive term as tribune so that he could oversee the distribution of lands. To rid themselves of this popular tribune who was undermining their wealth and power in the Senate, his opponents organized a mob that murdered him and 300 of his followers on the Capitoline Hill.

Ten years later Gaius Sempronius Gracchus, Tiberius' younger brother and an eloquent orator, was elected tribune in 123 B.C. Backed by strong popular favor, he expanded his brother's program of land allotments and instituted a program to supply grain at subsidized prices to the poor citizens in Rome. He also engineered a change in the courts that weakened the grip that those who controlled the Senate maintained on the Roman court system: juries were drawn from the class of wealthy non-senators, the equestrian order (**equitēs**), rather than from the Senate. Next, Gaius Gracchus proposed the radical concept of extending Roman citizenship to other Italian cities. Those new citizens would then have become powerful supporters of Gaius in Roman politics. Violent street clashes between supporters of Gaius and mobs incited by his opponents gave his enemies within the Senate an opportunity to declare martial law to keep the peace. One of the consuls surrounded him with a contingent of archers, and he committed suicide with the help of his slave.

GAIUS MARIUS

Gaius Marius, elected consul in 107 B.C., was the next important leader to follow a **populāris** path. A rich equestrian from Arpinum, Marius was a "new man" (**novus homō**), one of the very few Romans who succeeded in senatorial politics without the usual qualification of birth into one of the families of senatorial nobility. His base of power was the military and discontented elements in the populace. He had recruited his legions from the citizenry at large by promising his soldiers pensions of land allotments and a share in the

Marius triumphs over the Cimbri
Oil on canvas by Saverio Altamura, Museo e Gallerie Nazionali di Capodimonte, Naples, Italy

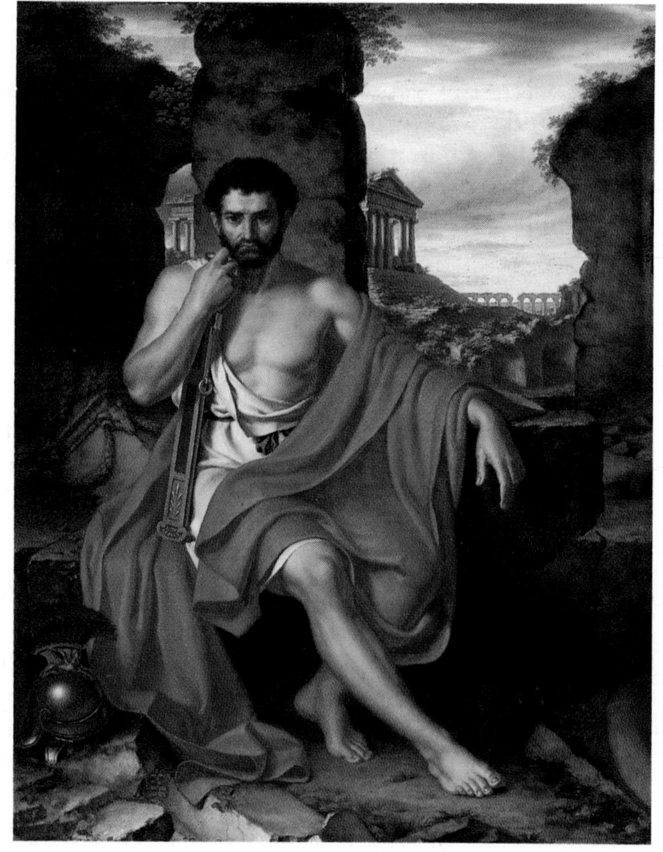

Marius amid the ruins of Carthage
Oil on canvas by John Vanderlyn, Albany Institute of History and Art, Albany, New York

spoils of war. Leading this new kind of army into Africa, Marius was victorious by 105 B.C. over Rome's enemy in North Africa, King Jugurtha.

Next, Marius and his volunteer professional army beat back the Cimbri and Teutones, Germanic tribes threatening Italy's northern borders. But when Marius returned victorious to Rome, many in both the Senate and the popular assembly balked at providing his soldiers the choice lands in Gaul and the western provinces that they had been promised. Marius' soldiers resorted to armed intimidation to get their land grants.

Over the next several years, violent unrest rocked all of Italy, and in Rome bloody power struggles continued between various aristocrats. In 87 B.C. Marius and his **populārēs** seized Rome and conducted a reign of terror against their political enemies, murdering or exiling them and confiscating their property. That reign ended with Marius' death early in his seventh consulship in 86 B.C.

LUCIUS CORNELIUS SULLA

Lucius Cornelius Sulla had become Marius' greatest rival after serving as one of his officers in the war against Jugurtha. He obtained the support of leading **optimātēs** and was elected a consul for 88 B.C. In that year, King Mithridates of Pontus, a land on the south shore of the Black Sea, seized territories under Roman control in Greece and Asia Minor and massacred thousands of Italians and Romans living in those lands. Sulla's supporters in the Senate obtained for him command of the war to punish Mithridates. Marius, however, used popular tribunes to get the command away from Sulla. Sulla unexpectedly captured Rome with his army, drove Marius into exile, killed many of his supporters, and regained the command against Mithridates. While he was gone, Marius returned with an army of his veterans, seized Rome, and was elected to his seventh consulship, during which he died.

Sulla, on his victorious return to Rome, trounced the Marian forces still holding sway there and instituted his own government by terror, as he eliminated his political enemies by a process called proscription. Routinely Sulla posted in the Forum lists of names of his opponents and also of some wealthy equestrians, whose estates might increase the bonus he had promised his troops. Romans who had been thus proscribed were outlaws: a cash reward was paid the murderers who brought in the heads of the proscribed, and Sulla took possession of their property. The Senate granted Sulla the title "dictator for stabilizing the constitution." In exchange, Sulla's reforms did away with the tribunes' power to introduce legislation and thus returned power to his supporters, who had traditionally controlled the Senate. Once he had eliminated his opponents and set in place policies that he believed would assure that **optimātēs** who had supported him would retain firm control of the government, Sulla retired from his dictatorship. He died the next year, 78 B.C., at his villa in Campania.

GNAEUS POMPEIUS

Gnaeus Pompeius (Pompey the Great) had begun his rise to favor and power by lending Sulla the support of his private army of clients for the seizure of Rome in 83 B.C. and then by suppressing Marian forces in Sicily and Africa. For these actions, Sulla reluctantly honored Pompeius with the **cognōmen** "The Great" (**Magnus**). In 77 B.C. the Senate sent Pompey to Spain to put down a rebellion of Marians there. On his triumphant return from that expedition, Pompey's army arrived in Italy in time to cut off any escape for the last of the 70,000 rebellious slaves in the army of the Thracian gladiator Spartacus. For three years (73–71 B.C.), Spartacus had terrorized the wealthy Italian landowners as the leader of a spectacular slave uprising. Pompey's timely arrival ensured the Roman army's victory over Spartacus. Pompey claimed the honor of victory at the expense of Marcus Licinius Crassus, who had done most of the work in defeating Spartacus' uprising. Despite their mutual jealousy, they cooperated on their re-entry to Rome in order to be elected consuls in the face of optimate opposition to their ambitions in the Senate. The co-consuls agreed to support a law rescinding Sulla's removal of the tribune's right to initiate legislation.

In 67 B.C., a tribune proposed a law authorizing Pompey to command a fleet and to suppress the pirates who were at that time disrupting trade in the Mediterranean Sea, a feat he completed in three months. In the following year, a praetor, Marcus Tullius Cicero, the successful orator and an ardent supporter of Pompey, spoke strongly in favor of another tribune's proposal. That one granted Pompey extraordinary powers for tightening Roman control in Asia Minor and meeting the renewed threat of Mithridates. From 66 to 62 B.C. Pompey's military campaigns succeeded in defeating Mithridates once and for all and consolidated Roman domination of the East so that it provided a solid frontier for Rome's empire.

PSEUDOLUS

Quīnta hōra est. Marcus et Sextus per ātrium ambulant, cum subitō ē culīnā cachinnus maximus audītur. Statim in culīnam puerī intrant, ubi Syrum et aliōs servōs vident.

Sextus, "Cūr vōs omnēs rīdētis?" inquit. "Iocumne audīvistis?"

Cui Syrus, "Iocō optimō dēlectāmur, domine. Est in culīnā servus quīdam cui nōmen est Pseudolus. Nōn servus sed mercātor esse vidētur. Heri māne in urbem ad laniī tabernam dēscendit, nam carnem emere volēbat. 'Quantī,' inquit Pseudolus, 'est illa perna?' Ubi pretium audītur, laniō respondet, 'Ego numquam dabō tantum pretium. Praedō quidem mihi vidēris, nōn lanius. Nēmō nisi scelestus tantum petit. Ad aliam tabernam ībō neque umquam—'

"'Procāx es, Pseudole,' interpellat lanius. 'Per iocum sine dubiō hoc dīcis. In hāc viā nēmō carnem meliōrem habet, ut bene scīs. Hoc pretium nōn est magnum. Sī autem multum emēs, pretium fortasse minuētur. Dominus tuus, ut audīvī, crās cēnam amīcīs suīs dabit. Nōnne porcum emēs?'

"Cui Pseudolus, 'Quem porcum mihi vēndere vīs? Ille est pinguis. Da mihi illum!'

(continued)

2 **cachinnus, -ī,** m., *laughter*
5 **optimus, -a, -um,** *best, very good, excellent*
6 **lanius, -ī,** m., *butcher*
7 **carō, carnis,** f., *meat*
Quantī...? *How much...?*
8 **perna, -ae,** f., *ham*
pretium, -ī, n., *price*
9 **quidem,** adv., *indeed*
10 **umquam,** adv., *ever*
11 **procāx, procācis,** *insolent*; as slang, *pushy*
12 **autem,** conj., *however, but*
13 **multus, -a, -um,** *much*
15 **pinguis, -is, -e,** *fat*

13 **minuō, minuere, minuī, minūtus,** *to lessen, reduce, decrease*

Exercise 31a

Respondē Latīnē:

1. Quota hōra est?
2. Ā quibus cachinnus audītur?
3. Quid servōs dēlectat?
4. Cūr Pseudolus ad tabernam laniī dēscendit?
5. Quālis homō lanius vidētur esse?
6. Quid Pseudolus faciet?
7. Estne pretium pernae magnum?
8. Minuēturne pretium?
9. Quālem porcum Pseudolus emere vult?

"'Ille porcus heri in meīs agrīs pascēbātur, meā manū cūrābātur. Nūllum porcum meliōrem in hāc urbe emēs. Senātōrī Rōmānō illum vēndere volō. Itaque tibi decem dēnāriīs eum vēndam.'

"'Decem dēnāriīs? Immō quīnque!'

"'Octō!'

"'Octō, sī ille lepus quoque additus erit grātīs. Sī nōn, nihil emam et ad aliam tabernam ībō.'

"'Nōn sine causā tū vocāris Pseudolus. Vōs servī, nōn nōs laniī, rēctē praedōnēs vocāminī.'

"Multum et diū clāmat lanius, sed Pseudolus nihil respondet. Tandem lanius octō dēnāriōs invītus accipit; porcum et leporem Pseudolō trādit. Iam Pseudolus noster rediit et tōtam fābulam nōbīs nārrāvit. In animō habet leporem amīcō vēndere et pecūniam sibi retinēre."

"Minimē vērō!" clāmāvit Aurēlia, quae ā Forō redierat et omnia audīverat. "Syre, da mihi leporem! Pseudolus ad vīllam rūsticam mittētur. Vōs quoque puniēminī omnēs."

18 **dēnārius, -ī,** m., *denarius (silver coin)*
19 **immō,** adv., *rather, on the contrary*
21 **lepus, leporis,** m., *hare*
additus erit, *(it) will have been added, is added*
grātīs, adv., *free, for nothing*
23 **rēctē,** adv., *rightly, properly*
29 **vērō,** adv., *truly, really, indeed*

16 **pāscō, pāscere, pāvī, pāstus,** *to feed, pasture*
21 **addō, addere, addidī, additus,** *to add*
26 **accipiō, accipere, accēpī, acceptus,** *to receive, get*

Respondē Latīnē:

1. Ubi porcus pascēbātur?
2. Ā quō porcus cūrābātur?
3. Quid faciet Pseudolus sī lepus grātīs nōn additus erit?
4. Quid Pseudolus in animō habet facere?
5. Quis omnia audīverat?

A Roman butcher shop
Stone frieze, 2nd century B.C., Musée de la Civilisation, Paris, France

Exercise 31b

Take parts, read aloud, and translate:

In trīclīniō: Pseudolus, Syrus, aliī servī

SYRUS: Eho! Domina sine dubiō īrāta est hodiē. Ad vīllam mittēris, Pseudole. Ēheu! Nōs quoque puniēmur omnēs.

PSEUDOLUS: Ego nōn commoveor. Sī ad vīllam mittar, multōs leporēs ipse in agrīs capere poterō.

SYRUS: Minimē vērō! In vīllā enim servī semper custōdiuntur neque errāre possunt. Id nescīre vidēris.

PSEUDOLUS: Sine dubiō vōs puniēminī sī nōn statim hōs lectōs movēbitis. Fortasse domina mē ad vīllam mittī iubēbit. Estō! Hīc labōrāre nōlō. Vōs lectōs movēte! Ego fābulam vōbīs nārrābō.

SYRUS: Tacē, Pseudole! Fābulīs tuīs saepe delectāmur, sed sī cachinnus audiētur—

PSEUDOLUS: Nōlīte timēre! Domina fortasse mē reprehendit sed Cornēlius mē ad vīllam mittī nōlet. Hīc certē mē retinērī volet. Saepe enim dominus mē ad Forum mittit ubi aliquid parvō pretiō emī vult.

1 **trīclīnium, -ī**, n., *dining room*
13 **mittī,** *to be sent*
retinērī, *to be held back, kept*
14 **emī,** *to be bought*

12 **reprehendō, reprehendere, reprehendī, reprehēnsus,** *to blame, scold*

FORMS

Verbs: Present Passive Infinitives

Compare these sentences:

1. Aurēlia Pseudolum ad vīllam **mittere** volet.
   *Aurelia will want **to send** Pseudolus to the country house.*

2. Aurēlia Pseudolum ad vīllam ***mittī*** iubēbit.
   *Aurelia will order Pseudolus **to be sent** to the country house.*

In sentence 1, **mittere** is the present *active* infinitive; in sentence 2, **mittī** is the present *passive* infinitive. The table below shows the present active and passive infinitives of each conjugation:

1st Conjugation	2nd Conjugation	3rd Conjugation		4th Conjugation
port***áre***, *to carry* port***ári***, *to be carried*	mov***ére***, *to move* mov***éri***, *to be moved*	mítt***ere***, *to send* mítt***ī***, *to be sent*	iác***ere***, *to throw* iác***ī***, *to be thrown*	aud***íre***, *to hear* aud***íri***, *to be heard*

Exercise 31c

Select, read aloud, and translate:

1. Incolae magna incendia (exstinguī, exstinguere, exstinguit) nōn possunt.
2. Incolae miserī lapidibus et flammīs (opprimere, opprimī, opprimunt) nōlunt.
3. Interdiū nihil intrā urbem vehiculō (portās, portārī, portātur) licet.
4. Cornēliī nūllum vehiculum intrā urbem (vidērī, vident, vidēre) poterant.
5. Syrus cachinnum ā dominā (audīvit, audīre, audīrī) nōn vult.

BUILDING THE MEANING

The Ablative Case (Consolidation)

In Chapter 12, the following uses of the ablative case were formally presented:

1. Ablative of Time When:

    Illō ipsō tempore parietēs īnsulae cecidērunt. (30:25)
    ***At that very moment** the walls of the apartment building fell.*

2. Ablative of Time within Which:

    Brevī tempore māter et fīlia ā servīs per urbem ferēbantur. (29:1–2)
    ***In a short time** the mother and her daughter were being carried through the city by slaves.*

3. Ablative of Instrument or Means (with active verbs):

    Cornēlia Flāviam **complexū** tenet. (9:20)
    *Cornelia holds Flavia **in an embrace**.*

4. Ablative of Manner:

    Parietēs īnsulae **magnō (cum) fragōre** cecidērunt. (30:25)
    *The walls of the apartment building fell **with a great crash**.*

In Chapter 24, the following use of the ablative case was formally presented:

5. Ablative of Cause:

    Tuā culpā raeda est in fossā. (14:7)
    ***Because of your fault** the carriage is in the ditch.*
    It's your fault that the carriage is in the ditch.

In recent chapters you have seen the following uses of the ablative case:

6. Ablative of Price:

    Itaque tibi **decem dēnāriīs** eum vēndam. (31:17–18)
    *Therefore I will sell it to you **for ten denarii**.*

7. Ablative of Personal Agent with Passive Verbs:

Māter et fīlia **ā servīs** per urbem ferēbantur. (29:1–2)
The mother and her daughter were being carried through the city ***by slaves.***

Ab incolīs omnia simul aguntur. (30:5)
Everything is being done at the same time ***by the tenants.***

Note that when the action of the passive verb is carried out by a person (*personal agent*) the preposition **ā** or **ab** is used with the ablative case.

N.B. The ablative of instrument or means is used with both active verbs (see 3 above) and passive verbs (see 8 below).

8. Ablative of Instrument or Means (with passive verbs):

Interdiū nihil intrā urbem **vehiculō** portātur. (29:3–4)
During the day nothing is carried ***by/in a vehicle*** *within the city.*

Iocō optimō dēlectāmur. (31:5) *We are amused* ***by an excellent joke.***

Note that when the action of the passive verb is carried out by a thing (*instrument* or *means*) a preposition is not used with the ablative case.

Exercise 31d

Select the appropriate verb, read aloud, and translate:

1. (a) Puerōs Rōmānōs patrēs saepe ______.
   (b) Puerī Rōmānī ā patribus ______.
   (verberant/verberāmus/verberantur)
2. (a) Uxōrēs Rōmānae ā virīs semper ______.
   (b) Uxōrēs virī Rōmānī semper ______.
   (amābant/amābantur/amātis)
3. (a) Hic liber ā mē tibi ______.
   (b) Hunc librum tibi ______.
   (dabitur/dabit/dabō)
4. (a) Omnēs convīvae cibō magnopere ______.
   (b) Omnēs convīvās cibus magnopere ______.
   (dēlectant/dēlectat/dēlectantur)
5. (a) Mercātor ipse manū porcum ______.
   (b) Porcus manū mercātōris ______.
   (cūrābās/cūrābātur/cūrābat)
6. (a) Lepus ā mercātōre grātīs ______.
   (b) Mercātor leporem grātīs ______.
   (addētur/addent/addet)
7. (a) Domina Pseudolum ad vīllam ______.
   (b) Pseudolus ad vīllam ā dominā ______.
   (mittētur/mittet/mittent)
8. (a) Flammae incolās miserōs ______.
   (b) Incolae miserī flammīs ______.
   (opprimēbantur/opprimēbant/opprimēbātis)
9. (a) Vehicula onera ingentia ______.
   (b) Onera ingentia vehiculīs ______.
   (portantur/portant/portārī)
10. (a) Cornēlia incendiō ______.
    (b) Incendium Cornēliam ______.
    (commōvētur/commōvēre/commōvet)

convīva, -ae, m., *guest (at a banquet)*

magnopere, adv., *greatly*

Exercise 31e

In Exercise 31d, locate the sentences that contain:

1. ablative of personal agent
2. ablative of means or instrument or cause

Laudātur ab hīs, culpātur ab illīs. *He's praised by these and blamed by those.* (Horace)
Avārus animus nūllō satiātur lucrō. *A greedy mind is satisfied with no (amount of) gain.* (Publilius Syrus 55)

FORMS

Demonstrative Adjectives and Pronouns

In Chapter 26 the demonstrative adjectives and pronouns **hic** *this* and **ille** *that* were formally presented. Review them, using the charts at the back of this book. In Chapter 27 the forms of **is, ea, id** were formally presented as a pronoun meaning *he*, *she*, and *it*. Review the forms of this pronoun, using the chart at the back of this book. The forms of **is, ea, id** may also function as adjectives meaning *this* or *that* according to the context, e.g., **eō ipsō tempore**, *at that very moment.*

You have met two other words that may function as either demonstrative adjectives or pronouns:

> **ipse, ipsa, ipsum**, intensive, *himself, herself, itself, themselves, very*
> **īdem, eadem, idem**, *the same*

The forms of these demonstrative adjectives and pronouns are as follows. They should be learned thoroughly:

Number / Case	Masc.	Fem.	Neut.
Singular			
Nominative	ipse	ipsa	ipsum
Genitive	ipsīus	ipsīus	ipsīus
Dative	ipsī	ipsī	ipsī
Accusative	ipsum	ipsam	ipsum
Ablative	ipsō	ipsā	ipsō
Plural			
Nominative	ipsī	ipsae	ipsa
Genitive	ipsōrum	ipsārum	ipsōrum
Dative	ipsīs	ipsīs	ipsīs
Accusative	ipsōs	ipsās	ipsa
Ablative	ipsīs	ipsīs	ipsīs

Compare the forms of **ipse, ipsa, ipsum** above with those of **ille, illa, illud.**

The forms of **īdem**, **eadem**, **idem** are the same as those of **is**, **ea**, **id** plus the letters *-dem*, except for the letters in boldface:

Number Case	Masc.	Fem.	Neut.
Singular			
Nominative	**ī**dem	eadem	idem
Genitive	eiusdem	eiusdem	eiusdem
Dative	eīdem	eīdem	eīdem
Accusative	eu**n**dem	ea**n**dem	idem
Ablative	eōdem	eādem	eōdem
Plural			
Nominative	eīdem	eaedem	eadem
Genitive	eōru**n**dem	eāru**n**dem	eōru**n**dem
Dative	eīsdem	eīsdem	eīsdem
Accusative	eōsdem	eāsdem	eadem
Ablative	eīsdem	eīsdem	eīsdem

Exercise 31f

IN VIĀ SACRĀ

A great man in Rome would normally have men of lower rank (**clientēs**) who looked upon him as their patron (**patrōnus**) and attended him on public occasions. Clients who came along unbidden with their master to a **cēna** were referred to scornfully as **umbrae**, *shadows*. In this conversation, the brothers Vibidius and Servilius discuss how to get Gaius to invite them to his dinner party as members of Messalla's retinue.

Take parts, read aloud, and translate:

VIBIDIUS: Ecce, mī frāter! Vidēsne hanc domum? Est ea dē quā tibi saepe dīxī. Ibi enim multae et optimae cēnae dantur. Eae cēnae sunt per tōtam urbem celebrēs. Hodiē, ut dīcunt omnēs, dominus huius domūs multōs convīvās ad cēnam accipiet. Optima cēna ab illō dabitur. Ab omnibus multum vīnum bibētur et multae fābulae nārrābuntur. Ego et tū invītābimur? Mox sciēmus. Ecce enim appropinquat dominus ipse, Gaius Cornēlius, quī ā quattuor servīs in lectīcā maximā portātur.

SERVĪLIUS: At nōs eī dominō nōn nōtī sumus. Quōmodo ab eō ad cēnam invītābimur?

VIBIDIUS: Sine dubiō is ad Forum portābitur et extrā Cūriam dēpōnētur. Tum in Cūriam intrābit sōlus. Eōdem tempore quō ē lectīcā dēscendet, nōs eī occurrēmus et dīcēmus, "Nōnne tū es Gaius Cornēlius, amīcus nostrī patrōnī Messallae, cuius clientēs fidēlissimī sumus? Numquam sine nōbīs ad cēnam venit Messalla."

SERVĪLIUS: Tum Gaius nōs invītābit ad cēnam?

VIBIDIUS: Fortasse.

SERVĪLIUS: Fortasse? Minimē vēro! Nōs vocābit umbrās, nōn clientēs Messallae.

3 **celeber, celebris, celebre,** *famous*
8 **nōtus, -a, -um,** *known*
12 **fidēlissimus, -a, -um,** *most faithful*

5 **bibō, bibere, bibī,** *to drink*

Exercise 31g

In the story in Exercise 31f above, locate and translate all sentences that contain examples of the demonstrative adjectives and pronouns **hic, haec, hoc; ille, illa, illud; is, ea, id; ipse, ipsa, ipsum**; and **īdem, eadem, idem**. State whether the word is being used as an adjective or a pronoun, and if it is used as an adjective tell what word it modifies.

Exercise 31h

Using story 31 as a guide, give the Latin for:

1. Very loud laughter was heard from the kitchen by the children.
2. The slaves were amused by a very good joke.
3. If Pseudolus buys/will buy a lot, the price will be reduced by the butcher.
4. You slaves are rightly called robbers.
5. That pig and this hare are handed over to Pseudolus.

CHAPTER 32

DINNER PREPARATIONS

The most substantial meal of the day was the dinner (**cēna**), eaten in the late afternoon, while it was still daylight; the richer classes, who could afford lamps or torches, sometimes began later or prolonged the dinner farther into the evening.

Earlier in the day the Romans ate little; in the early morning they took only a drink of water or wine and a piece of bread; this was called **ientāculum**, and was similar to the "continental" rolls and coffee of the present day. The midday meal (**prandium**) would also be cold, possibly something left over from the previous day's **cēna**; this also was merely a snack.

In the early days of Rome, the dinner was eaten in the **ātrium,** but as manners became more sophisticated, a special room was set aside as a dining room. From the second century B.C., the adoption of the Greek custom of reclining at meals demanded a special arrangement of couches and tables that was called in Greek *triklinion* (tri-klin-ion, "three-couch-arrangement"), a word borrowed into Latin as **trīclīnium**. In this arrangement three couches (Latin **lectī**) were set around a table or several small tables, and the name **trīclīnium** came to be used for the dining room itself. At the time of our story, the male diners reclined. The wives who attended the dinner party would sit and not recline. Slaves cut up the food before serving so that the diners could eat with one hand. Though the Romans had spoons and knives, food was generally conveyed to the mouth by the fingers. Napkins (**mappae**) were sometimes provided by the host; guests often brought their own napkins and carried away with them any food they did not eat from their own portions.

Preparations for a banquet

Fragment of mosaic pavement from Carthage, Louvre, Paris, France

Abhinc trēs diēs amīcī quīdam ā Gaiō Cornēliō ad cēnam invītātī erant. Quā dē causā Aurēlia in Forō glīrēs ēmerat. Porcus quoque ā Pseudolō ēmptus erat. Iam diēs cēnae aderat. Māne servī in Forum missī sunt et ibi comparāvērunt holera, pānem, pullōs. Ōva quoque et māla et multa alia comparāta sunt, nam cum senātor Rōmānus amīcōs ad cēnam invītāvit, cēna optima parārī dēbet.

Iam hōra cēnae appropinquābat. Dum in culīnā cibus coquēbātur, ancillae trīclīnium parābant. Mēnsa ā servīs in medium trīclīnium iam allāta erat; trēs lectī circum mēnsam positī erant.

Trīclīnium Cornēliī erat pulcherrimum atque ōrnātissimum. In parietibus erant pictūrae pulcherrimae. In aliā pictūrā canis Cerberus ē rēgnō Plūtōnis extrahēbātur, in aliā Mercurius ad Charōnem mortuōs addūcēbat, in aliā Orpheus ad īnferōs dēscendēbat.

Cornēlius servōs festīnāre iubēbat, nam iam erat nōna hōra. Aurēlia, semper sollicita, ancillās vehementer incitābat. Subitō ancilla quaedam, quae Aurēliam magnopere timēbat, hūc illūc festīnāns ūnum ē candēlābrīs cāsū ēvertit. Candēlābrum in lectum dēiectum est; statim effūsum est oleum in strāta; haec celeriter ignem cēpērunt. Aurēlia īrāta ancillam neglegentem reprehendēbat, sed Cornēlius celeriter palliō ignem exstīnxit.

"Bonō animō es!" inquit Cornēlius. "Ecce! Ignis iam exstīnctus est!" Tum aliae ancillae ab illō vocātae sunt: "Syra! Phrygia! Strāta alia ferte! Necesse est omnia statim reficere, nam convīvae mox aderunt." Omnia Cornēliī iussa facta sunt. (continued)

1 **invītātī erant,** *(they) had been invited*
quā dē causā, *for this reason*
3 **comparō, -āre, -āvī, -ātus,** *to buy, obtain, get ready*
holus, holeris, n., *vegetable*
pānis, pānis, gen. pl., **pānium,** m., *bread*
4 **pullus, -ī,** m., *chicken*
ōvum, -ī, n., *egg*
mālum, -ī, n., *apple*
7 **allāta erat,** *(it) had been brought in*
circum, prep. + acc., *around*
9 **pulcherrimus, -a, -um,** *most/very beautiful*
10 **rēgnum, -ī,** n., *kingdom*
11 **īnferī, -ōrum,** m. pl., *the underworld*
14 **candēlābrum, -ī,** n., *candelabrum, lamp-stand*
cāsū, *by chance, accidentally*
15 **oleum -ī,** n., *oil*
strātum, -ī, n., *sheet, covering*
ignis, ignis, gen. pl., **ignium,** m., *fire*
16 **pallium, -ī,** n., *cloak*
17 **Bonō animō es!/este!** *Be of good mind! Cheer up!*
19 **iussa, -ōrum,** n. pl., *commands, orders*

6 **coquō, coquere, coxī, coctus,** *to cook*
7 **afferō, afferre, attulī, allātus,** irreg., *to bring, bring to, bring in*
14 **ēvertō, ēvertere, ēvertī, ēversus,** *to overturn, upset*
15 **dēiciō, dēicere, dēiēcī, dēiectus,** *to throw down;* pass., *to fall*
effundō, effundere, effūdī, effūsus, *to pour out;* pass., *to spill*

Exercise 32a Respondē Latīnē:

1. Quī ad cēnam invītātī erant?
2. Quid servī in Forō comparāvērunt?
3. Quid ancillae faciēbant?
4. Quae pictūrae in parietibus trīclīniī erant?
5. Quid Aurēlia faciēbat?
6. Quid fēcit ancilla quaedam?
7. Quō īnstrūmentō Cornēlius ignem exstīnxit?

Adveniēbant convīvae, in quibus erant complūrēs clientēs quī ad cēnam invītātī erant. Convīvae mappās sēcum ferēbant, nam cum cēna cōnfecta erit, in mappīs cibum auferre eīs licēbit. Paulisper in ātriō stābant, Cornēlium exspectantēs. Tandem ā Cornēliō ipsō cōmiter salūtātī sunt.

Aberat nēmō nisi Titus Cornēlius, patruus Marcī. Paulisper eum exspectābant omnēs; sed tandem, quamquam ille nōndum advēnerat, convīvae in trīclīnium ductī sunt. Soleae dēpositae ā servīs ablātae sunt. Omnēs in lectīs accubuērunt et cēnam exspectābant.

20 **complūrēs, -ēs, -a,** *several*
21 **cōnfecta erit,** *(it) is/will have been finished*
23 **cōmiter,** adv., *courteously, graciously, in a friendly way*
26 **solea, -ae,** f., *sandal*

21 **auferō, auferre, abstulī, ablātus,** irreg., *to carry away, take away*
26 **accumbō, accumbere, accubuī, accubitūrus,** *to recline (at table)*

Respondē Latīnē:

1. Quid convīvae sēcum ferēbant?
2. Cūr convīvae in ātriō stābant?
3. Quid tandem Cornēlius fēcit?
4. Quis aberat?
5. Quō convīvae ductī sunt?

FORMS

Verbs: Perfect, Pluperfect, and Future Perfect Passive

Look at these sentences with verbs in the passive voice:

Perfect Passive:

Trīclīnium **parātum est.** — *The dining room* ***was prepared/has been prepared.***
Amīcī **invītātī sunt.** — *Friends* ***were invited/have been invited.***

Pluperfect Passive:

Porcus **ēmptus erat.** — *A pig* ***had been bought.***
Trēs lectī **positī erant.** — *Three couches* ***had been placed.***

Future Perfect Passive:

Cēna **cōnfecta erit.** — *Dinner* ***will have been finished.***
Māla **comparāta erunt.** — *Apples* ***will have been bought.***

It is obvious from these examples that the *passive* forms of the *perfect*, *pluperfect*, and *future perfect* tenses are very different from their corresponding active forms. Here are passive forms of these tenses for **portāre**:

		Perfect Passive		Pluperfect Passive		Future Perfect Passive	
Singular	1	portā́tus, -a	sum	portā́tus, -a	éram	portā́tus, -a	érō
	2	portā́tus, -a	es	portā́tus, -a	érās	portā́tus, -a	éris
	3	portā́tus, -a, -um	est	portā́tus, -a, -um	érat	portā́tus, -a, -um	érit
Plural	1	portā́tī, -ae	súmus	portā́tī, -ae	erā́mus	portā́tī, -ae	érimus
	2	portā́tī, -ae	éstis	portā́tī, -ae	erā́tis	portā́tī, -ae	éritis
	3	portā́tī, -ae, -a	sunt	portā́tī, -ae, -a	érant	portā́tī, -ae, -a	érunt

Be sure to learn these forms thoroughly.

NOTES

1. Verbs of all four conjugations and the irregular verb **ferre** follow the same patterns in the perfect, pluperfect, and future perfect passive. They all use forms of the verb **esse** plus the *perfect passive participle*, which you learned in Chapter 20 and which is the fourth principal part of a transitive verb, e.g., **portō, portāre, portāvī, portātus**.
   a. To form the *perfect passive*, use the *present* tense of **esse**, e.g., **portātus *sum*, portātus *es*.**
   b. To form the *pluperfect passive*, use the *imperfect* tense of **esse**, e.g., **portātus *eram*, portātus *erās*.**
   c. To form the *future perfect passive*, use the *future* tense of **esse**, e.g., **portātus *erō*, portātus *eris*.**

2. The perfect passive participle in these verb forms agrees with the subject in gender and number and will always be nominative in case:

Puer laudāt***us*** est.	*The boy was/has been praised.*
Māter laudāt***a*** est.	*The mother was/has been praised.*
Aedificium laudāt***um*** est.	*The building was/has been praised.*
Puerī laudāt***ī*** sunt.	*The boys were/have been praised.*
Mātrēs laudāt***ae*** sunt.	*The mothers were/have been praised.*
Aedificia laudāt***a*** sunt.	*The buildings were/have been praised.*

Exercise 32b

Read aloud and translate:

1. Servus, nōmine Pseudolus, in Forum missus est.
2. Glīrēs ab Aurēliā ēmptī erant.
3. Cum trīclīnium parātum erit, convīvae intrābunt.
4. Servī iocō optimō dēlectātī sunt.
5. Ē culīnā magnus cachinnus audītus erat.
6. Cum lepus ab Aurēliā inventus erit, Pseudolus pūniētur.
7. "Tū, Pseudole," inquit Aurēlia, "leporem emere nōn iussus es."
8. "Ego illō spectāculō miserābilī," inquit Cornēlia, "valdē commōta sum."
9. Octō dēnāriī ā laniō acceptī sunt.
10. "Cum ā Cornēliō salūtātī erimus," inquit ūnus ē convīvīs, "servī eius nōs ad trīclīnium addūcent."

Exercise 32c

Select, read aloud, and translate:

1. ______ ā mātre vocāta erat.
   Ancilla/Līberī/Eucleidēs
2. ______ ex īnsulā ēmissae sunt.
   Fūmus/Ōrnāmenta/Flammae
3. ______ in mēnsā positus erat.
   Pānis/Glīrēs/Mappa
4. ______ ā laniō minūtum est.
   Dēnāriī/Pretium/Porcus
5. ______ in Forō comparātī erant.
   Ōva/Glīrēs/Porcus
6. ______ ā servō allāta erunt.
   Māla/Mappa/Mulier
7. ______ in hāc tabernā ēmpta est.
   Carō/Holera/Lepus
8. ______ ā līberīs petītae sunt.
   Adstantēs/Auxilium/Mātrēs

Exercise 32d

Change each verb from active to passive voice, keeping the same tense, person, and number; translate both verbs. You may use masculine, feminine, or (if appropriate) neuter endings on the perfect passive participles:

1. dūxit
2. portāvistī
3. posuerat
4. oppressimus
5. commōvī
6. accēperit
7. mīserāmus
8. audīverātis
9. tulērunt

Mythological scenes dealing with the underworld, such as those adorning the walls of the Cornelii dining room, have remained popular subjects of art through the ages to this day. Pictured: Charon the Ferryman, who brought souls to the underworld for a fee.

Oil on canvas, "Psyche and Charon" by John Roddam Spencer-Stanhope, Roy Miles Gallery, London

Exercise 32e

Using story 32 and the chart on page 43 as guides, give the Latin for:

1. Vegetables had been bought in the Forum by the slaves.
2. The food was cooked in the kitchen.
3. The table has been brought by the slaves into the middle of the dining room.
4. Cerberus had been dragged from the kingdom of Pluto.
5. When the dinner is finished/will have been finished, the guests will carry food away in napkins.

Ālea iacta est. ***The die has been cast.*** **Said by Julius Caesar at the Rubicon River. (Suetonius, *Caesar* 32)**

WORD STUDY VIII

4th Declension Nouns

Many 4th declension nouns are formed from the stem of the fourth principal part of verbs. For example, **adventus, -ūs,** m., *arrival,* is made from the stem of **adventūrus**, the fourth principal part of **adveniō**. English words are often derived from this kind of 4th declension noun by dropping the ***-us*** ending e.g., *advent,* "an arrival."

Exercise 1

Give the Latin 4th declension noun (nom. sing., gen. sing., and gender) that may be formed from the fourth principal part of each of the following verbs, and give the meaning of the noun:

1. prōcēdere
2. trānsīre
3. habēre
4. agere
5. audīre
6. exīre
7. colere
8. trahere

Exercise 2

Give the English words derived by dropping the ***-us*** ending from each 4th declension noun formed in Exercise 1 above, and give the meaning of each English word.

Exercise 3

Give the Latin verb to which each of these nouns is related, and give the meanings of both verb and noun:

1. **rīsus, -ūs,** m.
2. **lātrātus, -ūs,** m.
3. **reditus, -ūs,** m.
4. **gemitus, -ūs,** m.
5. **cursus, -ūs,** m.
6. **discessus, -ūs,** m.
7. **cōnspectus, -ūs,** m.
8. **aditus, -ūs,** m.
9. **cāsus, -ūs,** m.

More Compound Verbs

The following exercise on compound verbs uses the principles of word formation discussed in Chapter 27, Word Study VII, and Chapter 29.

Exercise 4

After each Latin verb is a group of English words that are derived from compounds of that simple verb. Give the present active infinitive of the compound Latin verb from which each English word is derived, and give the meanings of both the compound Latin verb and the English word:

mittō, mittere, mīsī, missus

1. commit	3. remit	5. admit	7. permit
2. submit	4. transmit	6. emit	8. promise

iaciō, iacere, iēcī, iactus

1. project	3. subject	5. inject	7. conjecture
2. reject	4. eject	6. interject	8. trajectory

faciō, facere, fēcī, factus

1. effect	3. defect	5. infect	7. suffice
2. affect	4. perfect	6. confection	8. affection

trahō, trahere, trāxī, tractus

1. abstract	3. contract	5. distract	7. retract
2. attract	4. detract	6. extract	8. subtract

CHAPTER 33

AT DINNER

Cornēlius ancillīs signum dat. Prīmum aqua ab ancillīs portātur et convīvae manūs lāvant. Dum hoc faciunt, omnibus convīvīs mulsum datur. Deinde fercula ē culīnā efferuntur, in quibus est gustātiō—ōva et olīvae nigrae, asparagus et bōlētī liquāmine aspersī. Intereā ā convīvīs multae fābulae nārrantur, multa dē rēbus urbānīs dīcuntur: alius dē incendiīs nārrat, alius dē pestilentiā in urbe, alius dē amphitheātrō, aedificiō ingentī quod mox dēdicābitur. Aliquid novī audīre omnēs dēlectat. Dum convīvae haec et multa alia nārrant, gustātiō editur, mulsum bibitur.

Tum servī gustātiōnem auferunt; deinde ab eīsdem servīs magnum ferculum in trīclīnium fertur, in mediā mēnsā pōnitur. In eō est porcus ingēns et circum porcum glīrēs quōs Aurēlia ēmerat. Ab aliīs servīs pōcula convīvārum vīnō optimō complentur. Dum convīvae haec spectant extrā trīclīnium magnus tumultus audītur. Subitō in trīclīnium magnō cum strepitū irrumpit Titus Cornēlius.

Mussant convīvae, "Cūr Titus noster sērō venīre solet neque sē umquam excūsat?"

At Titus, ad locum suum lentē ambulāns, "Salvēte, amīcī omnēs!" inquit. "Salvē, mī frāter! Amīcō cuidam in popīnā occurrī."

(continued)

2 **mulsum, -ī,** n., *wine sweetened with honey*
ferculum, -ī, n., *dish, tray*
3 **gustātiō, gustātiōnis,** f., *hors d'oeuvre, first course*
niger, nigra, nigrum, *black*
bōlētus, -ī, m., *mushroom*
liquāmen, liquāminis, n., *garum (a sauce made from fish, used to season food)*
4 **aspersus, -a, -um,** *sprinkled*
rēs urbānae, rērum urbānārum, f. pl., *affairs of the city/town*
5 **pestilentia, -ae,** f., *plague*
10 **pōculum, -ī,** n., *cup, goblet*
14 **locus, -ī,** m., *place*
15 **popīna, -ae,** f., *eating-house, bar*

7 **edō, esse, ēdī, ēsus,** irreg., *to eat*
10 **compleō, complēre, complēvī, complētus,** *to fill*
12 **irrumpō, irrumpere, irrūpī, irruptus,** *to burst in*

Exercise 33a

Respondē Latīnē:

1. Quid prīmum ad convīvās portātur?
2. Quid prīmum ē culīnā effertur?
3. Quibus dē rēbus nārrant convīvae?
4. Quās rēs edunt convīvae dum mulsum bibunt?
5. Quid in mediā mēnsā pōnitur post gustātiōnem?
6. Quōmodo intrat Titus in trīclīnium?
7. Cūr Titus sērō vēnit?

Gaius, quamquam īrātissimus erat, nihil tamen dīxit quod hōc tempore frātrem reprehendere nōlēbat. Statim signum servīs dedit. Tum aliī ex eīs porcum scindēbant, aliī carnem ad convīvās portābant. Nōn omnibus dē porcō datum est: clientibus quidem data sunt pullōrum frusta.

Gaius servō, "Puer," inquit, "da frātrī meō quoque frusta pullī! Nōlī eī dē porcō dare!"

Nunc omnēs cibum atque vīnum habēbant. Omnēs cēnam laudābant. Etiam clientēs, quamquam frusta modo habēbant, ūnā cum cēterīs clāmābant, "Euge! Gaius Cornēlius cēnam optimam dare solet. Nēmō meliōrem coquum habet. Nōnne coquum ipsum laudāre dēbēmus?"

Itaque coquus vocātus ab omnibus laudātus est.

Tandem fercula ā servīs ablāta sunt. Simul Gaius servōs iussit secundās mēnsās in trīclīnium portāre. Servī, quamquam dēfessī erant, hūc illūc currēbant. Ūvae, māla, pira in trīclīnium portāta sunt. Passum quoque in mēnsā positum omnibus est datum.

16 **īrātissimus, -a, -um,** *most/very angry*
18 **dē porcō datum est,** *some pork was given*
19 **frustum, -ī,** n., *scrap*
23 **ūnā,** adv., *together*
cēterī, -ae, -a, *the rest, the others*
Euge! *Hurray!*
24 **coquus, -ī,** m., *cook*
27 **secundae mēnsae, -ārum,** f. pl., *second course, dessert*
28 **ūva, -ae,** f., *grape, bunch of grapes*
pirum, -ī, n., *pear*
29 **passum, -ī,** n., *raisin-wine*

17 **scindō, scindere, scidī, scissus,** *to cut, split, carve*

Respondē Latīnē:

1. Cūr Gaius nihil dīxit?
2. Quibus convīvīs data sunt frusta pullōrum?
3. Quae Titō data sunt?
4. Cūr coquus vocātus est?
5. Quās rēs convīvae postrēmō edunt?

BUILDING THE MEANING

Perfect Passive Participles I

Look at the following sentence:

Coquus **vocātus** ab omnibus laudātus est. (33:26)

In Chapter 32 you learned that perfect passive participles are used with forms of **esse** to produce the passive voice of the perfect, pluperfect, and future perfect tenses, e.g., **laudātus est**.

A different use of the perfect passive participle is shown at the beginning of the sentence above. Here the participle **vocātus** modifies a noun and indicates an action that took place before the action of the main verb: the cook was first summoned and then praised. The sentence can be translated in various ways. The most literal translation is:

*The cook, **having been summoned**, was praised by everyone.*

Any of the following translations might make better English:

After being summoned, the cook was praised by everyone.
When summoned, the cook was praised by everyone.
When the cook had been summoned, he was praised by everyone.
The cook was summoned and praised by everyone.

Similarly, the following sentence can be translated in a variety of ways:

Aurēlia neglegentiā eārum **vexāta** speculum ēripuit.
***Having been annoyed** by their carelessness, Aurelia snatched away the mirror.* (literal translation)
Annoyed by their carelessness, Aurelia snatched away the mirror.
Because/Since Aurelia was annoyed by their carelessness, she snatched away the mirror.
Aurelia, who was annoyed by their carelessness, snatched away the mirror.

Note from the translations offered above that perfect passive participles can often be translated into English as relative clauses or as clauses introduced by conjunctions such as *when*, *after*, *because*, *since*, or *although*.

The perfect passive participle is a verbal adjective that has the endings of an adjective of the 1st and 2nd declensions (like **magnus, -a, -um**). Therefore, it must agree in gender, case, and number with the noun or pronoun it modifies:

Soleae **dēpositae** ā servīs ablātae sunt. (32:26)
*The sandals **having been set down** were carried away by the slaves.*
The sandals, which had been set down, were carried away by the slaves.

Exercise 33b

Give two translations for each of the following sentences: one in which the perfect passive participle is translated literally and the other in which it is translated using a relative clause or a clause introduced by *when*, *after*, *because*, *since*, or *although*:

1. Convīvae ad cēnam invītātī ā Cornēliō ipsō cōmiter salūtātī sunt.
2. Ancillae festīnāre iussae aquam ad convīvās lentē portāvērunt.
3. Convīvae in trīclīnium ductī in lectīs accubuērunt.
4. Magnum ferculum ā servīs ē culīnā lātum in mediā mēnsā positum est.
5. Servī ā Gaiō iussī frusta pullī frātrī eius dedērunt.
6. Porcus ā servīs scissus ad mēnsam portātus est.
7. Ūvae in trīclīnium portātae omnibus convīvīs datae sunt.
8. Cēna optima ā Cornēliō data ab omnibus laudāta est.
9. Coquus ab omnibus laudātus laetus erat.
10. Titus in trīclīnium ductus, "Salvē, mī frāter!" inquit.

Exercise 33c

During the course of Cornelius' dinner party, the guests would have exchanged news or gossip and entertained one another with stories. The Romans enjoyed stories of magic like the following, an adaptation of a tale told by Niceros, a guest at Trimalchio's dinner party in Petronius' *Satyricon*.

Read aloud and translate:

Ubi adhūc servus eram, in urbe Brundisiō habitābāmus. Illō tempore Melissam amābam, ancillam pulcherrimam quae in vīllā rūsticā habitābat. Forte dominus meus ad urbem proximam abierat; ego igitur Melissam vīsitāre cōnstituī, sōlus tamen īre nōluī. Erat autem mihi amīcus quīdam, quī mēcum īre poterat. Mīles erat, homō fortis et temerārius.

Mediā nocte discessimus. Lūna lūcēbat tamquam merīdiē. Vēnimus ad sepulcra prope viam sita. Mīles meus inter sepulcra iit; ego cōnsēdī et stēlās numerābam. Deinde rem mīram vīdī: omnia vestīmenta ab amīcō meō exūta in terrā prope viam dēposita sunt. Dī immortālēs! Nōn per iocum dīcō! Ille subitō lupus factus est! Ego stābam tamquam mortuus. Lupus tamen ululāvit et in silvam fūgit.

Prīmum perterritus eram. Anima mihi in nāsō erat! Deinde ad stēlās prōcessī quod vestīmenta eius īnspicere volēbam. Vestīmenta dēposita tamen lapidea facta erant. Paulisper ibi stābam immōbilis. Gladium tamen strīnxī et umbrās cecīdī dōnec ad vīllam rūsticam pervēnī. Melissa mea ad portam vīllae mihi occurrit. "Dolēmus," inquit, "quod nōn prius vēnistī; auxiliō tuō caruimus. Lupus enim vīllam intrāvit et omnia pecora tamquam lanius necābat. Nec tamen dērīsit. Servus enim noster eum gladiō vulnerāvit."

Ubi haec audīvī, perterritus eram. Neque dormīre neque in vīllā manēre potuī, sed summā celeritāte aufūgī. Postquam vēnī in illum locum in quō vestīmenta lapidea facta erant, invēnī nihil nisi sanguinem. Ubi domum pervēnī, iacēbat mīles meus in lectō tamquam bōs; ā medicō cūrābātur. Tum scīvī mīlitem esse versipellem! Neque posteā potuī aut cum illō pānem esse aut illum amīcum meum vocāre.

2 **forte,** adv., *by chance*
3 **proximus, -a, -um,** *nearby*
6 **lūna, -ae,** f., *moon*
tamquam, conj., *just as if*
merīdiē, adv., *at noon*
7 **situs, -a, -um,** *located, situated*
inter, prep. + acc., *between, among*
stēla, -ae, f., *tombstone*
8 **numerō, -āre, -āvī, -ātus,** *to count*
vestīmentum, -ī, n., *clothing;* pl., *clothes*
9 **Dī immortālēs!** *Immortal gods! Good heavens!*
10 **ululō, -āre, -āvī, -ātus,** *to howl*
12 **anima, -ae,** f., *soul, "heart"*
nāsus, -ī, m., *nose*
13 **lapideus, -a, -um,** *of stone, stony*
14 **umbra, -ae,** f., *shadow, shade (of the dead)*
cecīdī, *I slashed at*
15 **dōnec,** conj., *until*
16 **prius,** adv., *earlier*
17 **pecus, pecoris,** n., *livestock, sheep and cattle*
18 **vulnerō, -āre, -āvī, -ātus,** *to wound*
21 **sanguis, sanguinis,** m., *blood*
22 **medicus, -ī,** m., *doctor*
23 **versipellis, versipellis,** gen. pl., **versipellium (vertō,** *to change* + **pellis,** *skin*), m., *werewolf*
posteā, adv., *afterward*

8 **exuō, exuere, exuī, exūtus,** *to take off*
12 **prōcēdō, prōcēdere, prōcessī, prōcessūrus,** *to go forward*
16 **careō, carēre, caruī, caritūrus** + abl., *to need, lack*
17 **dērīdeō, dērīdēre, dērīsī, dērīsus,** *to laugh at, get the last laugh*

Roman tableware

ROMAN LIFE XIX

RECIPES AND MENUS

The following are recipes from a Roman cookbook of the fourth century A.D. by Apicius.

STUFFED DORMICE

Stuff the dormice with minced pork, the minced meat of whole dormice, pounded with pepper, pine-kernels, asafetida (a kind of garlic), and fish sauce.* Sew up, place on tile, put in oven, or cook, stuffed, in a small oven.

SALT FISH WITHOUT FISH

Cook liver, grind and add pepper and fish sauce or salt. Add oil. Use rabbit, kid, lamb, or chicken liver; shape into a fish in a small mold, if liked. Sprinkle virgin oil over it.

HOMEMADE SWEETS

1. Stone dates, stuff with nuts, pine-kernels, or ground pepper. Roll in salt, fry in cooked honey, and serve.
2. Remove the crust from wheaten loaf, break up in largish morsels. Steep in milk, fry in oil, pour honey over, and serve.

*A staple of Roman cooking, fish sauce (**liquāmen** or **garum**) was made from a mash of finely chopped fish, which had been placed in the sun to ferment.

While menus must have varied very much between rich and poor people, and even between the day-to-day fare and the banquet for a special occasion, all Latin references to the **cēna** suggest that a basic menu was as follows:

1. **gustātiō** (hors d'oeuvre): egg dishes, eaten with **mulsum** (wine sweetened with honey)
2. **cēna** (the main course or courses): fish, game, poultry, pork, with wine
3. **secundae mēnsae** (dessert): usually fruit, with wine

Clientēs were sometimes invited to fill up spare places, but they were not given as good food and wine as the more important guests. Here a "client" expresses his indignation at this treatment:

> If you are asked to dinner by the great man, this is his way of paying you in full for all your services. So if after a couple of months he takes it into his head to invite you, his overlooked client (he can't leave that third place on the lowest couch unoccupied!), you're meant to feel your dearest prayer has been answered.
>
> Oh dear me! what a meal! You are given wine that fresh-clipped wool wouldn't soak up. The great man himself drinks a brand bottled in the days when consuls wore their hair long.
>
> The cup your host is holding is studded with beryl. No one trusts you with gold, or if you are given a precious cup, there's a slave watching you, and all the gems on it have been counted.

Even the water is different for clients; and it will be given you by the bony hand of a fellow you'd rather not meet at midnight among the tombstones of the Via Latina.

All the big houses are full of insolent slaves these days. Another one will grumble as he hands you a morsel of bread you can hardly break, or lumps of dough gone moldy. For your host meanwhile there is kept a tender loaf, snow-white and made from the choicest flour.

You see that huge lobster he's getting now! You'll get a tiny little crab with half an egg around it.

He is served a lamprey. For you—an eel, first cousin to a water-serpent; or maybe a pike that's made its way to Rome up the sewers.

Before the host a huge goose's liver is placed, and a boar piping hot, then truffles. All you can do is sit and watch.

Before the guests will be set some dubious toadstools; before the host a fine mushroom.

Is it the expense he grudges? Not a bit! What he wants is to see you squirm. There's nothing on earth so funny as a disappointed belly!

Juvenal, *Satires V* (extracts)

In Petronius' novel, the *Satyricon*, we are given a glimpse of an elaborate **cēna** given by the wealthy and ostentatious Gaius Trimalchio. The following excerpt illustrates the lengths to which a host might go in order to impress and entertain his dinner guests. A huge roast pig is brought into the dining room, and Trimalchio, eyeing it critically, suddenly becomes angry:

"What? Hasn't this pig been gutted? I swear it has not. Call the cook in here!" The poor cook came and stood by the table and said that he had forgotten to gut it. "What? Forgotten?" shouted Trimalchio. "Off with his shirt!" In a moment the cook was stripped and stood sadly between two torturers. Then everyone began to beg him off, saying: "These things will happen; do let him go; if he does it again none of us will say a word for him." But Trimalchio's face softened into smiles. "Well," he said, "if your memory is so bad, clean him here in front of us." The cook put on his shirt, seized a knife, and carved the pig's belly in various places with a shaking hand. At once the slits widened under the pressure from within, and sausages and black puddings tumbled out. At this the slaves burst into spontaneous applause and shouted, "God bless Gaius!

Petronius, *Satyricon* 49–50 (abridged)

REVIEW VII: CHAPTERS 28–33

Exercise VIIa: Relative Pronouns

Give the Latin for the relative pronoun in italics, and then read the sentence aloud and translate it:

1. Aurēlia, (*whose*) crīnēs Phrygia neglegenter pectēbat, vexāta erat.
2. Līberī, (*whose*) clāmōrēs ab Aurēliā et Cornēliā audiēbantur, flammīs oppressī sunt.
3. Sextus, (*to whom*) Syrus iocum Pseudolī nārrāvit, dēlectābātur.
4. Servī, (*whom*) Aurēlia in urbem mīserat, holera, pānem, pullōs ēmērunt.
5. Magnus tumultus, (*which*) Titus extrā trīclīnium fēcit, ā convīvīs audītus est.
6. Coquus vocātus ā convīvīs (*who*) cēnāverant laudātus est.
7. Pseudolus, ā (*whom*) porcus ēmptus est, mercātor esse vidēbātur.
8. Cēnae (*which*) Cornēlius dare solet optimae sunt.
9. Convīvae, (*whom*) Cornēlius invītāverat, iam domum intrābant.
10. Iocus, (*by which*) servī dēlectābantur, ā Pseudolō nārrātus est.

Exercise VIIb: *is, ea, id*

Supply the correct form of **is**, **ea**, **id** to substitute as a pronoun for the italicized word(s), read aloud, and translate:

1. Audīvistīne *iocum* Pseudolī? ______ nōn audīvī.
2. *Pseudolīne* iocum audīvistī? ______ iocum nōn audīvī.
3. Vīdistisne *flammās* in tertiō tabulātō īnsulae? ______ vīdimus.
4. Trāditne lanius porcum et leporem *Pseudolō?* ______ trādit.
5. Quid post cēnam *convīvīs* licēbit? ______ cibum auferre licēbit.
6. In ferculō erant *olīvae nigrae*. ______ ā convīvīs eduntur.

Exercise VIIc: *hic, haec, hoc*

Supply the correct form of **hic**, **haec**, **hoc**, read aloud, and translate:

1. Aurēlia glīrēs in (*this*) tabernā ēmit.
2. Aurēlia et Cornēlia flammās in tertiō tabulātō (*of this*) īnsulae vīdērunt.
3. Pseudolus octō dēnāriōs (*to this*) laniō dedit.
4. (*This*) magnum ferculum porcum ingentem et multōs glīrēs habet.
5. Ab (*these*) servīs holera, pānis, pullī feruntur.

Exercise VIId: Other Adjectives

In the sentences in Exercise VIIc, supply the correct forms of the following where you previously supplied forms of **hic**, **haec**, **hoc**; then read each new sentence aloud, and translate it:

1. quīdam, quaedam, quoddam
2. ipse, ipsa, ipsum
3. īdem, eadem, idem

Exercise VIIe: Passive Forms of Verbs

Give the requested forms of the following verbs in the present, imperfect, future, perfect, pluperfect, and future perfect. Give all forms in the passive voice:

	Present	Imperfect	Future	Perfect	Pluperfect	Future Perfect
1. ferō *(3rd sing.)*	______	______	______	______	______	______
2. commoveō *(1st pl.)*	______	______	______	______	______	______
3. scindō *(infinitive)*	______					
4. capiō *(2nd sing.)*	______	______	______	______	______	______
5. audiō *(2nd pl.)*	______	______	______	______	______	______
6. commoveō *(infinitive)*	______					
7. incitō *(1st sing.)*	______	______	______	______	______	______
8. addō *(2nd sing.)*	______	______	______	______	______	______
9. inveniō *(infinitive)*	______					
10. accipiō *(3rd pl.)*	______	______	______	______	______	______
11. dēmōnstrō *(infinitive)*	______					
12. dēbeō *(3rd sing.)*	______	______	______	______	______	______

Exercise VIIf: Passive Forms of Verbs

Read aloud and translate:

1. Complūrēs clientēs ā Cornēliō ad cēnam invītātī erant.
2. Soleae ā servīs ablātae sunt.
3. Olīvae et asparagus ab omnibus edēbantur.
4. Coquus ab omnibus convīvīs laudātur.
5. Vīnum allātum omnibus datum est.
6. Illī bōlētī, sī liquāmine aspersī erunt, omnēs convīvās dēlectābunt.
7. Coquus inductus ab omnibus laudātus est.

Exercise VIIg: Passive Forms of Verbs

Complete the following sentences according to the cues provided:

1. Trēs porcī ā Pseudolō ______ ______. (had been bought)
2. Magnum incendium ā praedōnibus ______ ______. (was made)
3. Multae epistulae ā Flāviā ______ ______. (will have been sent)
4. Complūrēs convīvae ā Cornēliō ______ ______. (were invited)
5. Ancilla ab Aurēliā numquam ______ ______. (was praised)
6. Porcus ______ nōn poterat. (to be caught)
7. Coquus ______ vult. (to be praised)

Exercise VIIh: Ablative of Instrument or Means and Ablative of Personal Agent

Identify the phrases that would require the preposition **ā** or **ab**:

1. The first course was carried in by the slaves.
2. Pseudolus was not frightened by Aurelia.
3. The building was overwhelmed by a huge fire.
4. All the guests were delighted by the story.
5. The pig had been raised by the butcher.

Exercise VIIi: Prefixes

Add the given prefixes to the following verbs, and make any necessary changes in the prefix and the verb. Translate the resulting form:

	Compound Verb	Translation
1. re + facimus	______	______
2. ex + fūgistī	______	______
3. ab + ferēbat	______	______
4. in + mīserō	______	______
5. ad + capiēbam	______	______
6. ad + currēbant	______	______
7. con + tenēbās	______	______
8. ab + fugiunt	______	______
9. ad + tulimus	______	______
10. re + ībimus	______	______

Orpheus

Roman mosaic, Blanzy, Musée Municipal, Laon, France

Exercise VIIj: Reading Comprehension

Read the following passage and answer the questions below with full sentences in Latin:

ORPHEUS AND EURYDICE

Multae fābulae nārrantur dē Orpheō quī ā Mūsīs doctus erat citharā lūdere. In pictūrā in trīclīniō Cornēliī sitā Orpheus ad īnferōs dēscendit. Cūr? Dēscendit quod uxor eius Eurydicē morte abrepta iam sub terrā ā Plūtōne tenēbātur. Dolōre oppressus Orpheus cōnstituit Plūtōnī appropinquāre et uxōrem ab eō petere.

Iānua rēgnī Plūtōnis ā Cerberō, cane ferōcī quī tria habēbat capita, custōdiēbātur. Orpheus, quod semper ēsuriēbat Cerberus, frusta cibī ad eum coniēcit et, dum cibus arripitur ā Cerberō, in rēgnum intrāvit. Per umbrās ībat Orpheus; uxōrem diū et dīligenter quaerēbat. Tandem Plūtō dolōre eius commōtus, "Licet tibi," inquit, "uxōrem tuam redūcere, sed hāc condiciōne: Eurydicē exībit ad lūcem tē sequēns; tū vetāris eam respicere. Sī tū respiciēs, ea retrahētur neque umquam iterum ad vīvōs remittētur."

Mox Eurydicē ex umbrīs dūcēbātur. Tum Orpheum sequēns ad lūcem lentē ascendēbat. Orpheus, quamquam uxōrem vidēre valdē dēsīderābat, ascendēbat neque respexit. Iam ad lūcem paene adveniēbant cum Orpheus amōre oppressus est. Respexit. Eurydicē revocāta ad Plūtōnem retracta est neque ad lūcem umquam reddita est.

1 **cithara, -ae,** f., *lyre*
citharā lūdere, *to play (on) the lyre*
3 **dolor, dolōris,** m., *grief*
5 **ferōx, ferōcis,** *fierce*
9 **condiciō, condiciōnis,** f., *condition, stipulation*
11 **vīvus, -a, -um,** *living*
14 **amor, amōris,** m., *love*

3 **abripiō, abripere, abripuī, abreptus,** *to snatch away*
10 **respiciō, respicere, respexī, respectus,** *to look back (at)*

1. By whom was Orpheus taught to play the lyre?
2. What had happened to Eurydice?
3. Where was Pluto holding Eurydice?
4. Why did Orpheus decide to approach Pluto?
5. Who was guarding the kingdom of Pluto?
6. What was Cerberus doing when Orpheus entered the kingdom of Pluto?
7. Was Pluto moved by Orpheus' grief?
8. What was Orpheus forbidden to do?
9. What will happen to Eurydice if Orpheus looks back at her?
10. What overwhelmed Orpheus?

Exercise VIIk: Translation

Translate the following groups of words taken from the story in Exercise VIIj:

1. ā Mūsīs doctus erat (1)
2. uxor eius Eurydicē morte abrepta (3)
3. dolōre oppressus (3–4)
4. Plūtō dolōre eius commōtus (8–9)
5. Eurydicē ex umbrīs dūcēbātur (12)
6. Orpheus amōre oppressus est (14–15)
7. Eurydicē revocāta (15)
8. retracta est (15)
9. reddita est (16)

THE COMMISSATIO

The Roman **cēna** was a major occasion in the daily routine. During the meal wine was drunk, usually mixed with water in the drinking-cup (**pōculum**) to suit the drinker's taste, for undiluted wine (**merum**) was thick and sweet.

Sometimes the dessert course (**secundae mēnsae**) was followed by a drinking party (**commissātiō**) for the male guests who were usually supplied with garlands (**corōnae**) to wear on their heads or around their necks. Originally these were worn not merely for ornament but in the belief that their perfume lessened the effect of the wine. Thus garlands were made with flowers (**flōrēs**), especially roses and violets, and also with herbs, such as parsley (**apium**), and with ivy (**hedera**). Later, and especially in winter, garlands were made with other materials such as copper foil or colored silks. Perfumes (**unguenta**) were also liberally provided at the **commissātiō**. These were applied to the hair and face and even mixed with the wine!

At the **commissātiō** a "master of the drinking" (**arbiter bibendī**) was appointed to determine the strength of wine to be drunk. He was often selected by throwing knucklebones (**tālī**) from a cylindrical box (**fritillus**). The **tālī** were oblong, rounded at the two ends, having four sides with the values 1, 3, 4, and 6 respectively. The highest throw was called **Venus**, when the four **tālī** came up all different; the lowest throw was **canis**—four "ones." Another poor throw was **sēniō**—a combination containing sixes.

The **arbiter bibendī** decided the number of measures (**cyathī**) of water to be added to the wine in the bowl. He might also determine the number and order of the toasts: the formula for the toast was **bene** followed by the dative case, as in a play by Plautus:

Bene mihi, bene vōbīs, bene amīcae meae.
Health to me, to you, and to my girlfriend.

Dice and counting pieces used by Romans in games
Musée Alesia, Alise-Sainte-Reine, France

ADDITIONAL READING:
The Romans Speak for Themselves: Book II: "The Commissatio," pages 23–31.

Cornelius' dinner party continues with a **commissātiō**:

Plūs vīnī est allātum, et omnibus convīvīs corōnae flōrum datae sunt. Aliī corōnās rosārum, aliī hederae corōnās induērunt. Gaius apiō modo sē corōnāvit, sed Titus et rosās et unguenta poposcit, nam in popīnā prope Forum multum vīnum iam biberat.

Ūnus ē convīvīs, cui nōmen erat Messalla, clāmāvit, "Quis creābitur arbiter bibendī?"

"Nōn tū certē, Messalla," inquit alter. "Aliī vīnum sine aquā bibunt, sed tū aquam sine vīnō bibis."

Cui Messalla, "Cūr nōn Gaius ipse? Quis enim est prūdentior quam Gaius? Ille enim aquam et vīnum prūdenter miscēbit, neque sinet convīvās nimis vīnī bibere."

"Minimē!" interpellat Titus magnā vōce. "Hōc modō creāre arbitrum nōn licet. Fer tālōs! Nōn nisi tālīs rēctē creātur arbiter bibendī."

Paulisper tacēbant omnēs. Tum Gaius, "Estō! Fer tālōs! Necesse est omnia rēctē facere."

Statim igitur tālī cum fritillō allātī in mēnsā positī sunt. Ā Gaiō prīmō iactī sunt tālī. "Est seniō!" ab omnibus clāmātum est. Deinde ūnus ē convīvīs tālōs mīsit. "Canis!" omnēs cum rīsū clāmāvērunt. Identidem tālī missī sunt, sed nēmō Venerem iēcit.

Tandem Titus tālōs arripit et in fritillō magnā cum cūrā pōnit. "Meum Herculem," inquit, "invocō." Tum fritillum vehementer movet. Omnēs Titum attentē spectant. Subitō mittuntur tālī.

"Est Venus!" exclāmat Titus. "Vīcī! Vīcī! Herculēs mihi favet! Nunc tempus est bibendī. Iubeō duās partēs aquae et trēs partēs vīnī." Prīmum tamen merum arripit et pōculum suum complet. "Bene tibi, Gaī!" clāmat et pōculum statim haurit. "Bene tibi, Messalla!" clāmat et iterum pōculum haurit. Subitō collāpsus est.

"Non bene tibi, Tite!" inquit Gaius. "Ēheu! Nimis vīnī iam hausistī." Servī Titum vīnō oppressum auferunt. Titus erat bibendī arbiter pessimus omnium.

1 **plūs vīnī,** *more wine*
4 **creō, -āre, -āvī, -ātus,** *to appoint*
7 **prūdentior,** *wiser*
quam, adv., *than*
8 **prūdenter,** adv., *wisely, sensibly*
nimis, adv., *too much*
9 **modus, -ī,** m., *way, method*
16 **cūra, -ae,** f., *care*
17 **invocō, -āre, -āvī, -ātus,** *to invoke, call upon*
22 **collāpsus est,** *he collapsed*
24 **pessimus, -a, -um,** *worst*

3 **poscō, poscere, poposcī,** *to demand, ask for*
8 **misceō, miscēre, miscuī, mixtus,** *to mix*
sinō, sinere, sīvī, situs, *to allow*
21 **hauriō, haurīre, hausī, haustus,** *to drain*

Exercise 34a

Respondē Latīnē:

1. Quālēs corōnās convīvae induērunt?
2. Quid Titus in popīnā fēcerat?
3. Cūr est Gaius prūdentior quam aliī convīvae?
4. Quid Titus poscit?
5. Quis prīmum tālōs iēcit?
6. Quid Titus arripit?
7. Quem Titus invocat?
8. Quantum vīnī Titus hausit?

BUILDING THE MEANING

Adjectives: Positive, Comparative, and Superlative Degrees

Look at these sentences:

Positive:	
Gaius est **laetus**.	*Gaius is **happy**.*
Comparative:	
Messalla est **laet<u>ior</u>** quam Gaius.	*Messalla is **happier** than Gaius.*
Superlative:	
Titus est **laet<u>issimus</u>** omnium.	*Titus is **happiest** of all.*

Adjectives have *positive*, *comparative*, and *superlative degrees*. In the sentences above you can recognize the comparative by the letters ***-ior*** and the superlative by the letters ***-issimus***.

The comparative can have several meanings; for example, **prūdentior** can mean *wiser*, *rather wise*, or *too wise*. In the first sense it is often followed by **quam**, *than*:

Nēmō est **prūdentior** <u>quam</u> Gaius.
*No one is **wiser** <u>than</u> Gaius.*

The superlative can also have several meanings; for example, **prūdentissimus** can mean *wisest* or *very wise*. In the first sense it is often used with a partitive genitive:

Gaius est **prūdentissimus** <u>omnium</u>.
*Gaius is **the wisest** <u>of all</u>.*

The ancient custom of drinking wine was connected to the religious mystery cult of Dionysus, the god of the vine, the grape, and of vegetation in general. Pictured is a detail from a Roman fresco depicting followers of Dionysus.
Fresco, Villa dei Misteri, Pompeii, Italy

Exercise 34b

Locate comparative or superlative forms in the following stories or exercises and translate the sentences in which they occur. Try some of the alternative translations given above:

1. 29:5–7
2. 31f:11–12
3. 33:24
4. 34:7

FORMS

Adjectives: Positive, Comparative, and Superlative

1. Study these further examples of positive, comparative, and superlative adjectives:

Positive	Comparative	Superlative
1st and 2nd declension adjectives:		
molest***us***, ***-a***, ***-um***	molest***ior***, molest***ius***	molest***issimus***, ***-a***, ***-um***
3rd declension adjectives:		
brev***is***, ***-is***, ***-e***, *short*	brev***ior***, brev***ius***	brev***issimus***, ***-a***, ***-um***
fēlīx, fēlīc***is***, *lucky*	fēlīc***ior***, fēlīc***ius***	fēlīc***issimus***, ***-a***, ***-um***
prūdēns, prūdent***is***, *wise*	prūdent***ior***, prūdent***ius***	prūdent***issimus***, ***-a***, ***-um***

2. Note what happens with adjectives that end in ***-er***:

1st and 2nd declension adjectives ending in -er:		
miser, miser***a***, miser***um***	miser***ior***, miser***ius***	miser***rimus***, ***-a***, ***-um***
pulcher, pulchr***a***, pulchr***um***	pulchr***ior***, pulchr***ius***	pulcher***rimus***, ***-a***, ***-um***
3rd declension adjectives ending in -er:		
celer, celer***is***, celer***e***, *swift*	celer***ior***, celer***ius***	celer***rimus***, ***-a***, ***-um***
ācer, ācr***is***, ācr***e***, *keen*	ācr***ior***, ācr***ius***	ācer***rimus***, ***-a***, ***-um***

3. Most 3rd declension adjectives that end in ***-lis*** form their comparatives and superlatives regularly:

fidēl***is***, ***-is***, ***-e***, *faithful*	fidēl***ior***, fidēl***ius***	fidēl***issimus***, ***-a***, ***-um***

Exceptions: six 3rd declension adjectives that end in ***-lis*** form their superlatives irregularly, as does **facilis**:

facil***is***, ***-is***, ***-e***, *easy*	facil***ior***, facil***ius***	facil***limus***, ***-a***, ***-um***

The other adjectives are **difficilis**, *difficult*; **similis**, *similar*; **dissimilis**, *dissimilar*, **gracilis**, *slender*; and **humilis**, *humble*.

4. Note that you can usually recognize the superlative by the endings ***-issimus***, ***-rimus***, or ***-limus***.

Exercise 34c

Form the comparatives and superlatives of the following 1st and 2nd declension adjectives (meanings are given for adjectives you have not yet had):

1. longus, -a, -um
2. asper, aspera, asperum, *rough*
3. īrātus, -a, -um
4. scelestus, -a, -um
5. aeger, aegra, aegrum, *sick*

Exercise 34d

Form the comparatives and superlatives of the following 3rd declension adjectives (meanings are given for adjectives you have not yet had):

1. ēlegāns, ēlegantis
2. pinguis, -is, -e
3. celeber, celebris, celebre
4. difficilis, -is, -e, *difficult*
5. nōbilis, -is, -e, *noble*

Irregular Comparative and Superlative Adjectives

Some very common adjectives are irregular in the comparative and superlative:

Positive	Comparative	Superlative
bonus, -a, -um, *good*	**melior, melius,** *better*	**optimus, -a, -um,** *best*
malus, -a, -um, *bad*	**peior, peius,** *worse*	**pessimus, -a, -um,** *worst*
magnus, -a, -um, *big*	**maior, maius,** *bigger*	**maximus, -a, -um,** *biggest*
parvus, -a, -um, *small*	**minor, minus,** *smaller*	**minimus, -a, -um,** *smallest*
multus, -a, -um, *much*	**plūs,*** *more*	**plūrimus, -a, -um,** *most, very much*
multī, -ae, -a, *many*	**plūrēs, plūra,** *more*	**plūrimī, -ae, -a,** *most, very many*

*Note that **plūs** is not an adjective but a neuter substantive, usually found with a partitive genitive, e.g., Titus **plūs vīnī** bibit. *Titus drank* ***more (of the) wine.***

Exercise 34e

Complete the comparison of the following adjectives by giving the missing items:

Positive	Comparative	Superlative
longus	______	longissimus
______	stultior	stultissimus
______	melior	______
multus	______	______
______	______	maximus
______	ingentior	ingentissimus
______	peior	______
______	pulchrior	pulcherrimus
______	minor	______

Adjectives: Case Endings of Comparatives and Superlatives

All superlatives have the same endings as the 1st and 2nd declension adjective **magn*us*, magn*a*, magn*um***, e.g., **laetissim*us*, laetissim*a*, laetissim*um*.**

The comparatives have endings like those of 3rd declension nouns. Here are the forms of the comparative. Note in particular the neuter nominative and accusative singular form: **laet<u>ius</u>:**

Number Case	Masc.	Fem.	Neut.
Singular			
Nominative	laetior	laetior	laetius
Genitive	laetiōr***is***	laetiōr***is***	laetiōr***is***
Dative	laetiōr***ī***	laetiōr***ī***	laetiōr***ī***
Accusative	laetiōr***em***	laetiōr***em***	laetius
Ablative	laetiōr***e***	laetiōr***e***	laetiōr***e***
Plural			
Nominative	laetiōr***ēs***	laetiōr***ēs***	laetiōr***a***
Genitive	laetiōr***um***	laetiōr***um***	laetiōr***um***
Dative	laetiōr***ibus***	laetiōr***ibus***	laetiōr***ibus***
Accusative	laetiōr***ēs***	laetiōr***ēs***	laetiōr***a***
Ablative	laetiōr***ibus***	laetiōr***ibus***	laetiōr***ibus***

Compare these forms with those of 3rd declension nouns and adjectives. Note the differences from the endings of 3rd declension adjectives.

NOTE:

When given in vocabulary lists, comparatives will be listed as follows: **melior, melior, melius**, gen., **meliōris**, *better*.

Exercise 34f

Change the italicized adjectives to the comparative and then to the superlative. Translate the new sentences. Try some of the alternative translations given above:

1. Gaius, quamquam *īrātus* erat, frātrem nōn reprehendit.
2. Aurēlia, quod erat *sollicita*, ancillās festīnāre iubēbat.
3. Puerī ā Cornēliō vīsī ad cubiculum *parvum* rediērunt.
4. Senātor pecūniam servīs *ignāvīs* nōn dederat.
5. Omnēs convīvae in lectīs *magnīs* accubuērunt.
6. Cēna ā coquō *bonō* parāta ab ancillīs efferēbātur.
7. Ancillae quae hūc illūc currēbant vīnum ad convīvās *fēlīcēs* portāvērunt.
8. Aliī convīvae corōnās rosārum *pulchrārum* induērunt.
9. Plaustrum *novum* ā Cornēliō ēmptum ad vīllam rūsticam missum est.
10. Pater puerī *molestī* mussāvit, "Numquam puerum peiōrem vīdī!"

Exercise 34g

Using story 34 and the presentation of comparative and superlative adjectives as guides, give the Latin for:

1. Titus had already drunk too much wine.
2. No one had drunk more wine.
3. No one is wiser than Gaius, for he always mixes water and wine wisely.
4. Titus was the luckiest when he threw the knucklebones.
5. Titus was very miserable when he collapsed.

Exercise 34h

Take parts, read aloud, and translate:

REFLECTIONS AFTER DINNER

Postquam convīvae discessērunt, nē tum quidem cubitum iērunt Cornēlius et Aurēlia, nam multa dē convīviō inter sē dīcēbant.

AURĒLIA: Placuitne tibi cēna, Gaī?

CORNĒLIUS: Ita vērō! Tū quidem omnia optimē ēgistī. Coquus nōbīs cēnam parāvit optimam quae ab omnibus laudābātur. Quam ingēns erat ille porcus! Maiōrem porcum numquam vīdī. Glīrēs quoque suāviōrēs numquam ēdī.

AURĒLIA: Cūr tam sērō advēnit Titus? Quid eī acciderat?

CORNĒLIUS: Nihil! Amīcō veterī in popīnā occurrerat!

AURĒLIA: In popīnā? Ubi?

CORNĒLIUS: Prope Forum Rōmānum.

AURĒLIA: Omnēs popīnae sunt foedae, sed foedissimae omnium sunt popīnae prope Forum sitae.

CORNĒLIUS: Ita vērō! Iam ēbrius erat cum in trīclīnium irrūpit. Omnēs convīvae erant īrātissimī.

AURĒLIA: Fit in diēs molestior.

CORNĒLIUS: Sed hāc nocte erat molestissimus.

AURĒLIA: Quōmodo?

CORNĒLIUS: Missī sunt tālī; arbiter bibendī creātus est ille; iussit duōs cyathōs aquae et trēs cyathōs vīnī!

AURĒLIA: Paulātim igitur fīēbat magis ēbrius?

CORNĒLIUS: Minimē! Statim factus est maximē ēbrius, nam nīl nisi merum bibit! "Bene tibi, Gaī!" clāmat et, "Bene tibi, Messalla!" tum collāpsus est vīnō oppressus. Hominem magis ēbrium quam Titum numquam vīdī.

AURĒLIA: Quid tum accidit?

CORNĒLIUS: Iussī servōs eum lectīcā portāre domum quam celerrimē.

AURĒLIA: Fortasse crās fīet vir vīnō abstinentissimus!

CORNĒLIUS: Fortasse!

1 **nē...quidem,** *not even*
2 **convīvium, -ī,** n., *feast, banquet*
3 **placeō, -ēre, -uī** + dat., *to please*
4 **optimē,** adv., *very well, excellently*
7 **suāvis, -is, -e,** *sweet, delightful*
9 **vetus, veteris,** *old*
12 **foedus, -a, -um,** *filthy, disgusting*
14 **ēbrius, -a, -um,** *drunk*
16 **in diēs,** *every day, day by day*
20 **cyathus, -ī,** m., *small ladle, measure (of wine)*
21 **paulātim,** adv., *gradually*
magis, adv., *more*
22 **maximē,** adv., *very much, very*
nīl, *nothing*
27 **quam celerrimē,** adv., *as quickly as possible*
28 **vīnō abstinēns,** *refraining from wine, abstemious*

16 **fīō, fierī, factus sum,** irreg., *to become, be made, be done, happen*

Exercise 34i

Here is a famous poem by Catullus (ca. 84–54 B.C.), in which he extends a dinner invitation to his friend Fabullus. This is a piece of original Latin that you can easily read at this stage with the help of the vocabulary given below. After reading the poem consider whether the invitation to dinner is serious or facetious.

Read aloud and translate:

Cēnābis bene, mī Fabulle, apud mē
paucīs, sī tibi dī favent, diēbus,
sī tēcum attuleris bonam atque magnam
cēnam, nōn sine candidā puellā
et vīnō et sale et omnibus cachinnīs.
Haec sī, inquam, attuleris, venuste noster,
cēnābis bene: nam tuī Catullī
plēnus sacculus est arāneārum.
Sed contrā accipiēs merōs amōrēs
seu quid suāvius ēlegantiusvest:
nam unguentum dabo, quod meae puellae
dōnārunt Venerēs Cupīdinēsque,
quod tū cum olfaciēs, deōs rogābis,
tōtum ut tē faciant, Fabulle, nāsum.

—Catullus 13

2 **paucī, -ae, -a,** *few*
4 **candidus, -a, -um,** *white, fair-skinned, beautiful*
5 **sal, salis,** m., *salt, wit*
6 **venuste noster,** *my charming fellow*
8 **sacculus, -ī,** m., *small bag (used for holding money)*
arānea, -ae, f., *cobweb*
9 **contrā,** adv., *in return*
merus, -a, -um, *pure*
10 **seu = sīve,** conj., *or if*
quid suāvius ēlegantiusvest (= ēlegantiusve est), *there is anything sweeter or more elegant*
-ve, enclitic conj., *or*
12 **dōnō, -āre, -āvī, -ātus,** *to give*
dōnārunt = dōnāvērunt
Venus, Veneris, f., *Venus (the goddess of love)*
Cupīdō, Cupīdinis, m., *Cupid (the son of Venus)*
14 **ut tē faciant,** *that they make you*

CRIME

Postquam Aurēlia cubitum iit, Cornēlius adhūc in ātriō manēbat sollicitus. Eucleidēs enim māne ierat domum frātris quī in colle Quirīnālī habitābat. Iam media nox erat neque Eucleidēs domum redierat. Quid eī acciderat?

Tandem intrāvit Eucleidēs, sanguine aspersus. Cornēlius, "Dī immortālēs! Quid tibi accidit?" clāmāvit. Eucleidēs nihil respondit; ad terram ceciderat. Statim servī ad ātrium vocātī celerrimē concurrērunt. Eucleidēs in lectō positus est et vulnera eius lauta atque ligāta sunt. Diū iacēbat immōbilis. Tandem animum recuperāvit et lentē oculōs aperuit. Postquam aliquid vīnī bibit, rem tōtam explicāvit.

"Hodiē māne, dum in urbem dēscendō, poētae cuidam occurrī cui nōmen est Marcus Valerius Mārtiālis. Breviōre itinere mē dūxit ad eam īnsulam in quā habitat frāter meus. Plūrima dē praedōnibus huius urbis mihi nārrāvit. Ego tamen vix eī crēdidī. Sed, ubi īnsulae iam appropinquābāmus, hominēs quōsdam in popīnam intrantēs cōnspeximus.

"'Cavē illōs!' inquit Mārtiālis. 'Illī sunt praedōnēs scelestissimī. Nocte sōlus per hās viās ambulāre nōn dēbēs."

(continued)

2 **collis, collis,** gen. pl., **collium,** m., *hill*
Quirīnālis, -is, -e, *Quirinal (referring to the Quirinal Hill, one of the seven hills of Rome)*
4 **deus, -ī,** m., *god*
6 **vulnus, vulneris,** n., *wound*
7 **ligō, -āre, -āvī, -ātus,** *to bind up*

11 **crēdō, crēdere, crēdidī, crēditus** + dat., *to trust, believe*

Exercise 35a

Respondē Latīnē:

1. Cūr Cornēlius sollicitus in ātriō manēbat?
2. Quō māne ierat Eucleidēs?
3. Quid fēcērunt servī Cornēliī, postquam Eucleidēs cecidit?
4. Quid fēcit Eucleidēs, postquam tandem animum recuperāvit?
5. Cui occurrit Eucleidēs, dum in urbem dēscendit?

"Tōtum diem apud frātrem meum mānsī. Post cēnam optimam domum redīre cōnstituī. Quamquam nox erat, nihil perīculī timēbam. Sēcūrus igitur per Subūram ambulābam cum subitō ē popīnā quādam sē praecipitāvērunt duo hominēs quī fūstēs ferēbant. Timōre affectus, celerius ambulābam. Facile tamen mē cōnsecūtī sunt. Ab alterō percussus sum, sed baculō mē fortissimē dēfendī. Tum ā tergō ab alterō correptus ad terram cecidī. Mihi est adēmptum baculum, adēmpta pecūnia. Abiērunt illī rīdentēs. Diū prōnus in lutō iacēbam. Tandem surrēxī et summā difficultāte domum rediī."

Cornēlius, "Doleō quod vulnera gravia accēpistī. Stultissimus tamen fuistī."

Cui Eucleidēs, "Ita vērō, domine! Sed iam prūdentior sum. Nōn iterum nocte sōlus per viās urbis ambulābō."

16 **sēcūrus, -a, -um,** *carefree, unconcerned*
Subūra, -ae, f., *Subura (a section of Rome off the Forum, known for its night life)*
17 **fūstis, fūstis,** gen. pl., **fūstium,** m., *club, cudgel*
18 **timor, timōris,** m., *fear*
affectus, -a, -um, *affected, overcome*
celerius, adv., *more quickly*
facile, adv., *easily*
cōnsecūtī sunt, *they overtook*
19 **fortissimē,** adv., *most/very bravely*
tergum, -ī, n., *back, rear*
21 **prōnus, -a, -um,** *face down*
summus, -a, -um, *greatest, very great*
22 **gravis, -is, -e,** *heavy, serious*

19 **percutiō, percutere, percussī, percussus,** *to strike*
corripiō, corripere, corripuī, correptus, *to seize, grab*
20 **adimō, adimere, adēmī, adēmptus** + dat., *to take away (from)*

Respondē Latīnē:

1. Quibus occurrit Eucleidēs, dum domum redit?
2. Quid fēcērunt praedōnēs, postquam Eucleidem cōnsecūtī sunt?
3. Quid est perīculōsissimum nocte facere?

BUILDING THE MEANING

Comparisons

Latin sentences in which a direct comparison is made may take one of two patterns:

Sextus est molestior **quam** Marcus.	*Sextus is more annoying* ***than*** *Marcus.*
Sextus est molestior **Marcō.**	

In the first example, **quam** (*than*) is used with the same case on either side of it (i.e., **molestior** and **Marcus** are both nominative). In the second example, no word for "than" is used, and **Marcō** is ablative.

Sometimes an ablative (e.g., **multō**, *much*; **paulō**, *a little*) is used with comparatives to indicate the degree of difference. This is called the *ablative of degree of difference*:

Sextus est **multō** molestior quam Marcus.	*Sextus is more annoying* ***by much*** *than Marcus.*
Sextus est **multō** molestior Marcō.	*Sextus is* ***much*** *more annoying than Marcus.*

Exercise 35b

Using the following lists of names and comparative adjectives, make up pairs of sentences that express comparisons according to the patterns in the discussion above:

Marcus, Sextus, Aurēlia, Cornēlius, Cornēlia, Flāvia, Eucleidēs, Titus, Dāvus, Pseudolus
minor, maior, pulchrior, īrātior, laetior, miserior, scelestior, prūdentior, stultior, dīligentior

dīligēns, dīligentis, *diligent, painstaking, thorough*

Exercise 35c

Using the names and adjectives from Exercise 35b above, and changing each adjective to superlative, make one sentence for each name, according to the following examples:

Dāvus est dīligentissimus omnium.
Flāvia est miserrima omnium.

Exercise 35d

Read aloud and translate:

1. Hic servus est ignāvissimus omnium. Nūllum servum ignāviōrem habet Cornēlius.
2. Cornēliī coquus est optimus omnium. Nēmō meliōrem coquum habet quam Cornēlius.
3. Līberī laetissimī sunt quod crās fēriātī erunt.
4. Mārtiālis Eucleide est multō prūdentior.
5. Ego semper habeō multō minus pecūniae quam tū.
6. Marcus est maximus līberōrum, Sextus est minimus.
7. Flāvia est paulō minor Marcō, sed multō maior Cornēliā.
8. Ad amīcum epistulam longissimam mittam, ad frātrem breviōrem.
9. Dāvus est servus optimus. Sine dubiō nēmō est dīligentior.
10. Coquus plūs cibī in culīnā parābat.

Exēgī monumentum aere perennius. ***I have erected a monument more lasting than bronze.*** **(Horace, *Odes* III.30.1)**

Fāmā nihil est celerius. ***Nothing is swifter than rumor.*** **(adapted from Vergil, *Aeneid* IV.174)**

Mea mihi cōnscientia plūris est quam omnium sermō. ***My conscience is more to me than what the world says.*** **(Cicero, *Letters to Atticus* XII.28.2)**

Adverbs

In Chapter 13, adverbs were presented as words that expand the meaning of a sentence by modifying verbs, other adverbs, or adjectives. Sometimes adverbs are formed from adjectives, but many adverbs are not.

Exercise 35e

In story 35, locate the following adverbs that are not formed from adjectives, and tell what word each modifies:

1. 35:1, adhūc.
2. 35:2, māne.
3. 35:2, iam.
4. 35:4, tandem.
5. 35:5, statim.
6. 35:7, diū.
7. 35:9, hodiē māne.
8. 35:11, vix.
9. 35:14, nōn.
10. 35:23, iterum.

FORMS

Adverbs: Positive

1. Adverbs may be formed from adjectives of the 1st and 2nd declensions by adding ***-ē*** to the base of the adjective:

Adjective	**Adverb**
strēnu***us***, ***-a***, ***-um***	strēnu***ē***, *strenuously, hard*

But note:

bon***us***, ***-a***, ***-um***	ben***e***, *well*
mal***us***, ***-a***, ***-um***	mal***e***, *badly*

2. Adverbs may be formed from adjectives of the 3rd declension by adding ***-iter*** to the base of the adjective or ***-er*** to bases ending in **-nt**:

brev***is***, ***-is***, ***-e***	brev***iter***, *briefly*
prūdēns, prūdent***is***	prūdent***er***, *wisely*

But note:

facil***is***, ***-is***, ***-e***	facil***e***, *easily*.

Exercise 35f

Give the adverbs (and their meanings) that may be formed from these adjectives:

1. **ignāvus, -a, -um,** *lazy*
2. **fortis, -is, -e,** *brave*
3. **lentus, -a, -um,** *slow*
4. **neglegēns, neglegentis,** *careless*
5. **miser, misera, miserum,** *unhappy*
6. **ferōx, ferōcis,** *fierce*
7. **gravis, -is, -e,** *serious*
8. **laetus, -a, -um,** *happy*
9. **vehemēns, vehementis,** *violent*
10. **īrātus, -a, -um,** *angry*
11. **celer, celeris, celere,** *swift*
12. **pulcher, pulchra, pulchrum,** *beautiful*

Adverbs: Comparative and Superlative

Adverbs also have comparative and superlative forms.

The neuter singular comparative adjective (ending in ***-ius***) is used as the comparative adverb.

The superlative adjective ends in ***-us***, ***-a***, ***-um***; the superlative adverb ends in ***-ē***. Study these examples:

laet***ē***, *happily*	laet***ius***	laet***issimē***
fēlīc***iter***, *luckily*	fēlīc***ius***	fēlīc***issimē***
celer***iter***, *quickly*	celer***ius***	celer***rimē***
prūdent***er***, *wisely*	prūdent***ius***	prūdent***issimē***

Note the following as well:

diū, *for a long time*	diūt***ius***	diūt***issimē***
saepe, *often*	saep***ius***	saep***issimē***
sērō, *late*	sēr***ius***	sēr***issimē***

Some adverbs are irregular. Compare these forms with their related adjectives:

bene, *well*	**melius**, *better*	**optimē**, *best*
male, *badly*	**peius**, *worse*	**pessimē**, *worst*
facile, *easily*	**facilius**, *more easily*	**facillimē**, *most easily*
magnopere, *greatly*	**magis**, *more*	**maximē**, *most*
paulum, *little*	**minus**, *less*	**minimē**, *least*
multum, *much*	**plūs**, *more*	**plūrimum**, *most*

Be sure to learn these forms thoroughly.

The comparative adverb, like the comparative adjective, can have several meanings; for example, **lentius** can mean *more slowly*, *rather slowly*, or *too slowly*. In the first sense it may be followed by a comparison using **quam** or the ablative without **quam** (cf. note on comparisons, p. 72):

> Eucleidēs lentius **quam** puerī ambulat.
> Eucleidēs lentius **puerīs** ambulat.
> *Eucleides walks more slowly **than** the boys.*

The ablative of degree of difference may be used with comparative adverbs:

> Eucleidēs **multō** lentius quam puerī ambulat.
> Eucleidēs **multō** lentius puerīs ambulat.
> *Eucleides walks **much** more slowly than the boys.*

The superlative adverb, like the superlative adjective, also has more than one meaning; for example, **lentissimē** can mean *most slowly* or *very slowly*. In the first sense it is often followed by a partitive genitive:

> Dāvus lentissimē **omnium** ambulat.
> *Davus walks most slowly **of all.***

Exercise 35g

Study the forms in the completed columns and then fill in the other columns.
Be sure you can give the meaning of every form:

Adjectives			Adverbs		
longus	longior	longissimus	longē	______	______
lentus	______	______	lentē	lentius	lentissimē
pulcher	pulchrior	pulcherrimus	pulchrē	______	______
fortis	fortior	fortissimus	fortiter	______	______
brevis	brevior	brevissimus	breviter	______	______
facilis	______	______	facile	facilius	facillimē
certus	certior	certissimus	certē	______	______
fidēlis	______	______	fidēliter	fidēlius	fidēlissimē
rēctus	______	______	rēctē	rēctius	rēctissimē
ferōx	ferōcior	ferōcissimus	ferōciter	______	______

longē, adv., *far*
certus, -a, -um, *certain*
rēctus, -a, -um, *right, proper*

Exercise 35h

Read aloud and translate. Try some of the alternative translations suggested above:

1. Diūtius manēre mihi nōn licet. Necesse est mihi celerrimē ad urbem redīre.
2. Hic puer optimē omnium scrībit.
3. Nēmō celerius quam frāter meus currere potest.
4. Sextus paulō celerius Marcō currere potest.
5. Dē perīculīs viārum saepissimē audīvimus.
6. Per viās urbis lentē ambulāre volō.
7. Cornēlius īrātissimus erat quod frāter sērius advēnit.
8. Titus plūrimum bibit.
9. Eucleidī praedōnēs pecūniam adēmērunt atque quam celerrimē discessērunt.
10. Sextus in hortō quam diūtissimē lūdēbat.

quam + a superlative adjective or adverb = *as…as possible*, e.g., **quam celerrimē**, *as quickly as possible*

Exercise 35i

Using story 35 and the presentation of adverbs as guides, give the Latin for:

1. Eucleides returned home very late.
2. He lay motionless a long time and regained his senses rather slowly.
3. Eucleides had walked through the Subura too bravely and had feared no danger.
4. When two men hurled themselves out of a bar, Eucleides ran as quickly as possible.
5. He lay in the mud a very long time.

Canis timidus vehementius lātrat quam mordet. ***A timid dog barks more fiercely than he bites.*** **(adapted from Q. Curtius Rufus, *Exploits of Alexander* VII.4.13)**

ALTIUS, CITIUS, FORTIUS ***Higher, faster, stronger.*** **(Motto of the Olympic Games)**

ADDITIONAL READING:

The Romans Speak for Themselves: Book II: "Violence in the Streets of Rome," pages 33–39.

CICERO, CAESAR, AND THE COLLAPSE OF THE REPUBLIC

Marcus Tullius Cicero reached the peak of his political career in 63 B.C., when he took office as one of the consuls. As an equestrian from Arpinum and a **novus homō**, he had plied his skills as an orator to fuel his rise to the top magistracy. His main opponent in the election had been the ruthless aristocrat Lucius Sergius Catilina, who conspired to assassinate Cicero as part of a plot to overthrow the government and seize power by force. In a series of actions that one can track in Cicero's four famous orations *Against Catiline (In Catilinam)*, the consul drove Catiline out of the city, publicized the details of his plot, and saw to the execution of a group of co-conspirators. Catiline attempted to continue his rebellion from his military base in Etruria. He died, however, in a battle with the Roman army in 62 B.C. Cicero thereafter earnestly advocated a "concord of orders" (**concordia ōrdinum**), the joining together of senators and equestrians to work in support of the republican constitution.

Cicero and the magistrates discovering the tomb of Archimedes

Oil on canvas by Bejamin West, Christie's, London, England

At this point in time, 62 B.C., Pompey returned from his successful campaigns in the East and, contrary to the fears of many, disbanded his army. But many Senators feared the growing power of the popular military hero and refused to approve land grants to Pompey's veterans. He formed a three-man political alliance (**factiō**) with Caesar and Crassus, whose own ambitions were being blocked by the same people. Their alliance is known as the First Triumvirate. Caesar, with the help of Pompey's armed veterans, won passage in 59 B.C. of the veterans' land bill. Caesar's reward for his key effort in this success was a five-year term as proconsular governor of the province of Cisalpine Gaul and Illyricum, which gave him the opportunity to conquer Transalpine Gaul. Crassus obtained financial concessions for wealthy equestrians who backed him.

During the first year of his proconsulship, Caesar led his legions to a rapid succession of victories. By 50 B.C., he had all of Transalpine Gaul under his legions' control and had annexed it as a new province of Rome's empire. Further, he crossed the English Channel and attacked Britain.

While Caesar was away campaigning in Gaul, the political scene in Rome grew violent as **populārēs** and **optimātēs** battled one another for power. One victim who survived physically was Cicero, but his career as a political leader and the moderate voice of the **optimātēs** was destroyed.

The death of Julia, Pompey's wife and Caesar's daughter, weakened the triumvirate in 54 B.C. In the following year, the **factiō** broke apart completely when Crassus was killed in battle against the Parthian Empire in Syria. Violence in the streets escalated as political mobs beset one another, armed factions scuffled, and mass riots erupted. In 52 B.C. the Senate authorized Pompey to quell the rioting in Rome by using his troops and then got him elected sole consul. Leading **optimātēs** in the Senate steadily pressed him to turn against the popular hero Caesar, whom Pompey increasingly viewed as his chief rival now that Crassus was dead.

In January of 49 B.C. the Senate issued a **senātūs cōnsultum ultimum** empowering Pompey to direct Caesar to disband his army. Caesar responded by leading his legions across the Rubicon River, the northern boundary of Italy, and beginning an advance toward Rome. Civil war erupted with Caesar fighting Pompey and the leading **optimātēs**, who were now backing him in the Senate.

As Caesar rapidly advanced toward Rome, Pompey and his allies fled to Greece, where Pompey could recruit and train a new army. His plan, apparently, was to be able to attack Caesar in Italy with both this eastern army and his troops stationed in Spain. Once Pompey had abandoned Italy, Caesar, with almost no opposition, became the master of Rome.

Caesar began to build a fleet so that he could go after Pompey. While his ships were being prepared, he crossed over land into Spain and quickly subdued Pompey's army there. Thus he removed the threat of being surrounded. Then he returned to Rome, secured the consulship, and set sail for Greece. After a nearly disastrous attempt to defeat Pompey in a siege at Dyrrhacchium, Caesar was forced to withdraw to Thessaly, with

Pompey in pursuit. On the plain of Pharsalus in August of 48 B.C., however, Caesar's battle-hardened legions routed Pompey's larger army. Pompey managed to escape and flee to Egypt, in hope of finding refuge there, but the agents of King Ptolemy XIII murdered him and sent his head to Caesar.

Caesar became dictator in October of the same year and followed Pompey's trail to Egypt, where he began a three-year series of campaigns that would finalize his victory as the head of the Roman state. In Alexandria, Caesar fought against King Ptolemy and deposed him. He then set Cleopatra on the throne to assure that Egypt would be friendly to Rome. From there Caesar advanced to Asia Minor and defeated Pharnaces, son of Mithridates, in a war that lasted only days. This victory, the story goes, prompted Caesar's dispatch to Rome, "I came, I saw, I conquered" (**Vēnī, vīdī, vīcī**). In 46 B.C. Caesar celebrated his Gallic, Alexandrian, Pontic, and African triumphs, all in the span of one month. Gigantic parades celebrated Caesar's achievements, displaying the rich spoils from conquered lands and famous prisoners of war and raised his popularity to new heights. The following year, Caesar went once more to Spain, where he wiped out the last of the resistance forces, which were under the command of Pompey's sons.

Territory of the Late Roman Republic

Julius Caesar
Compidoglio, Rome, Italy

In 44 B.C. Caesar was the unchallenged head of the Roman state. He accepted the title "dictator for life" (**dictātor perpetuus**). As dictator Caesar continued his program of reforms. He granted Roman citizenship to people in Gallia Narbonensis and sent Romans from the city to create colonies in the provinces, thus increasing his number of clients. There was also a public works program: expanding the Forum, building the Basilica Julia and the temple of Venus Genetrix, and rebuilding the Curia. Through the so-called Julian reform, Caesar adapted an Egyptian solar calendar, which we still use today in modified form, for use in Rome.

Caesar made it increasingly clear that he intended to rule Rome himself and not to bring back the Senate-dominated republican constitution. He weakened the old guard's power in the Senate by appointing a diverse group of new senators from the equestrian order and from cities in other parts of Italy. The **optimātēs** resented Caesar's evident desire to be king, especially when they saw him put on a purple robe and sit on a golden chair. Romans had hated the title "king" (**rēx**) since the ouster of Tarquinius Superbus and could not easily accept the thought that one man might change the government of the free city-state of Rome into a monarchy, although the old form of government was ill-suited for ruling an empire. On the Ides of March, 44 B.C., a group of Roman senators, armed with daggers and led by Gaius Cassius and Marcus Brutus, assassinated Caesar under the gaze of Pompey's statue. By their plot they hoped to rescue the Republic from the threat of the would-be tyrant.

WORD STUDY IX

Adjective Suffixes *-ōsus, -idus,* and *-bilis*

When added to the base of a Latin noun, the suffix ***-ōsus***, ***-ōsa***, ***-ōsum*** creates an adjective meaning *full of…*:

> **fābula, -ae,** f., *story*
> base: **fābul-** + ***-ōsus*** = **fābulōsus, -a, -um,** *"full of story," legendary*

English words derived from these adjectives commonly end in *-ous* (sometimes *-ious*, *-eous*, or *-ose*), e.g., *fabulous*, which means "astonishing" (as in legend or myth).

Exercise 1

Give the Latin adjective ending in ***-ōsus*** for each of the nouns below and give its English derivative. Give also the meaning of the Latin adjective and its English derivative. Is the meaning of the English derivative the same as that of the Latin adjective?

1. **numerus, -ī,** m.
2. **onus, oneris,** n.
3. **pretium, -ī,** n. (*in the derivative* t *changes to* c)
4. **glōria, -ae,** f.
5. **cūra, -ae,** f.
6. **labor, labōris,** m.
7. **tumultus, -ūs,** m. (*add* u *to base:* **tumultu-**)
8. **iocus, -ī,** m. (*derivative begins with* j *and ends in* -ose)
9. **perīculum, -ī,** n. (*derivative drops* -cu- *from* **perīculum**)
10. **verbum, -ī,** n., *word*

The addition of the suffix ***-idus, -ida, -idum*** to the base of the present infinitive of a Latin verb (often of the 2nd conjugation) creates a Latin adjective meaning *tending to…* or *inclined to…*:

> **timēre,** *to fear*
> infinitive base: **tim-** + ***-idus*** = **timidus, -a, -um,** *"tending to fear," afraid*

Exercise 2

For each Latin verb below, give the Latin adjective ending in ***-idus*** and give its English derivative. Use the English derivative in a sentence that illustrates its meaning:

1. **sordēre,** *to be dirty*
2. **stupēre,** *to be astonished*
3. **placēre,** *to please, to be agreeable*
4. **vīvere,** *to be alive, to live*
5. **valēre,** *to be strong*
6. **rapere,** *to seize, to tear away*
7. **lūcēre,** *to be light, to shine*
8. **frīgēre,** *to be cold*

The suffix ***-bilis, -bilis, -bile***, when added to the base of the present infinitive (sometimes the perfect passive participial stem) of a Latin verb, creates an adjective that usually means *able to be....* In adjectives formed from 1st conjugation verbs, the suffix is preceded by **-ā-**; in adjectives formed from verbs of other conjugations, the suffix is preceded by **-i-**:

laudāre, *to praise*
infinitive base: **laud-** + **-ā-** + ***-bilis*** = **laudābilis, -is, -e,** *"able to be praised," praiseworthy*

reprehendere, *to scold*
perfect passive participial stem: **reprehēns-** + **-i-** + ***-bilis*** = **reprehēnsibilis, -is, -e,** *"able to be scolded," blameworthy*

English words derived from these Latin adjectives generally end in *-ble*, e.g., *laudable* and *reprehensible.*

Note that whether the English word ends in *-able* or *-ible* is usually determined by the conjugation of the original Latin verb: *-able* usually comes from a Latin verb of the 1st conjugation and *-ible* from a verb of one of the other conjugations.

Exercise 3

For each of the following Latin verbs, give the adjective ending in ***-bilis***, and give the English derivative and its meaning. Use the infinitive base in Nos. 1–9, and the perfect passive participial stem in No. 10.

1. audīre
2. crēdere
3. excūsāre
4. habitāre
5. legere
6. portāre
7. revocāre
8. vincere
9. vulnerāre
10. vidēre

N.B.: On some Latin adjectives (and their English derivatives), the suffix ***-bilis*** means *able to....* rather than *able to be....* The following verbs produce adjectives of this type:

11. dēlectāre
12. stāre
13. terrēre

Latin in the Law

One of the greatest achievements of the Romans was the spread of the rule of law throughout their empire. From its first codification in the Law of the Twelve Tables in the fifth century B.C. to its ultimate expression in the *Corpus iuris civilis* of the emperor Justinian in the sixth century A.D., Roman law formed the foundation for the development of modern legal systems. The rights of inheritance, the notion of private property, the sanctity of contracts—these and many other common legal concepts have their origins in Roman law.

It is not surprising, therefore, that Latin words and phrases are still in use in the practice of law today. Some of these Latin legal expressions have been incorporated into everyday English. For example, an *alibi* (Latin for *elsewhere*) in law is a claim that the accused was not at the scene of the crime and is therefore not guilty; in everyday language, however, the word refers to any sort of excuse.

Exercise 4

Look up the italicized expressions in an English dictionary (or a law dictionary) and explain the meaning of each of the following phrases:

1. a *prima facie* case
2. a plea of *nolo contendere*
3. to serve a *subpoena*
4. the *onus probandi* of the prosecution
5. a writ of *habeas corpus*
6. the responsibility of the school *in loco parentis*
7. the necessary *corpus delicti*
8. an *ex post facto* law
9. a *bona fide* (*mala fide*) offer
10. an offense *malum in se* (*malum prohibitum*)
11. *de facto* (*de jure*) segregation
12. testimony of an *amicus curiae*
13. caught *in flagrante delicto*
14. a claim that the accused is *non compos mentis*

Exercise 5

Give an example to illustrate each of these Latin legal maxims:

1. Ignorantia legis neminem excusat. *Ignorance of the law is no excuse.*
2. Caveat emptor. *Let the buyer beware.*
3. Res ipsa loquitur. *The matter speaks for itself.*
4. De minimis non curat lex. *The law does not concern itself with trifles.*
5. Nemo est supra leges. *No one is above the law.*
6. Publicum bonum privato est praeferendum. *Public good is to be preferred over private.*
7. Potior est conditio possidentis. *Possession is nine-tenths of the law.*
8. Qui tacet consentire videtur. *Silence is taken as consent.*
9. Qui facit per alium, facit per se. *He who acts through another acts by himself.*
10. Nemo debet bis vexari pro una et eadem causa. *No one ought to be tried twice for one and the same reason.*

CHAPTER 36

A LETTER

Cornēlia Flāviae S.D.

Hodiē Nōnīs Novembribus illam epistulam accēpī quam tū scrīpsistī Kalendīs Novembribus. Eam iterum iterumque lēgī, quod tē maximē dēsīderō. Quam celeriter tua epistula hūc advēnit! Quīnque modo diēbus! Heri aliam epistulam Brundisiī scrīptam accēpit pater meus. Haec epistula ā Valeriō prīdiē Īdūs Octōbrēs scrīpta Rōmam post vīgintī diēs advēnit!

Valerius, ut scīs, est adulēscēns pulcher et strēnuus quī cum patre suō diū in Bīthȳniā morātus est. Nunc in Italiam Brundisium regressus est. Brundisiō Īdibus Novembribus proficīscētur et Rōmam a.d. iii Kal. Dec. adveniet.

Quam libenter eum rūrsus vidēbō! Sānē tamen multō libentius tē vidēbō ubi tū Rōmam veniēs! Tum tē libentissimē nōs omnēs accipiēmus!

(continued)

Note that the Romans did not start a letter with "Dear So-and-So." They put the name of the person sending it (in the nominative case) followed by the name of the person to whom it was sent (in the dative case), and after that the letters **S.D.** (**salūtem dīcit,** *sends greetings*) or **S.P.D.** (**salūtem plūrimam dīcit,** *sends fondest greetings*). There was no signature at the end, but simply the word **valē**.

2 **Nōnīs Novembribus,** *on November 5*
Kalendīs Novembribus, *on November 1*
3 **-que,** enclitic conj., *and*
4 **hūc,** adv., *here, to here*
Brundisiī, *at Brundisium*
5 **prīdiē,** adv. + acc., *on the day before*
prīdiē Īdūs Octōbrēs, *on October 14*
6 **vīgintī,** *twenty*
7 **adulēscēns, adulēscentis,** m., *young man*
8 **morātus est,** *he has stayed*
regressus est, *he has returned*
Īdibus Novembribus, *on November 13*
9 **proficīscētur,** *he will set out*
a.d. iii Kal. Dec. = ante diem tertium Kalendās Decembrēs, *on November 29*
10 **libenter,** adv., *gladly*
rūrsus, adv., *again*
sānē, adv., *certainly, of course*

Exercise 36a
Respondē Latīnē:

1. Quō diē Cornēlia epistulam Flāviae accēpit?
2. Quis epistulam ad patrem Cornēliae mīsit?
3. Ubi nunc est Valerius?
4. Quem Cornēlia libentissimē vidēbit?

In epistulā tuā multa rogābās dē perīculīs urbānīs. Abhinc trēs diēs in īnsulā quādam magnum incendium vīdimus. Nihil miserābilius umquam vīdī. Quamquam enim maior pars incolārum ē perīculō effūgit, māter et duo līberī quōs in tertiō tabulātō cōnspeximus effugere nōn poterant. Ēheu! Hī miserī flammīs oppressī sunt. Ubi dē illā mātre et līberīs cōgitō, valdē commoveor.

Heri vesperī Eucleidēs noster, ab urbe domum rediēns, duōs hominēs ē popīnā quādam exeuntēs vīdit. Quī hominēs, ubi Eucleidem cōnspexērunt, statim eum secūtī sunt. Eucleidēs effugere cōnātus est, sed frūstrā. Quō celerius currēbat ille, eō celerius currēbant hominēs. Facile eum cōnsecūtī sunt. Ō miserrimum Eucleidem! Ā praedōnibus correptus ac fūstibus percussus, gravissimē vulnerātus est. Vix quidem sē domum trāxit.

Sed dē perīculīs satis! Hodiē māter pulcherrimam mihi pallam ēmit, quae mihi valdē placuit. Sed trīstis sum quod lānam semper trahō. Trīstissima autem sum quod tē nōn videō. Fortasse tū Rōmam cum patre veniēs. Nōnne tū patrī hoc persuādēbis? Tē plūrimum dēsīderō. Scrībe, sīs, quam saepissimē. Valē!

18 **quī hominēs,** *which/those men*
secūtī sunt, *(they) followed*
19 **cōnātus est,** *(he) tried*
quō celerius...eō celerius..., *the faster...the faster...*
23 **trīstis, -is, -e,** *sad*
25 **sīs = sī vīs,** *if you wish, please*

24 **persuādeō, persuādēre, persuāsī, persuāsus,** *to make something* (acc.) *agreeable to someone* (dat.); *to persuade someone of something*

Respondē Latīnē:

1. Dē quibus rēbus Flāvia in epistulā rogābat?
2. Quid Cornēlia in īnsulā quādam vīdit?
3. Quid Cornēliae placuit?
4. Cūr est Cornēlia trīstis?

FORMS

Dates

In each month there were three special days from which Romans calculated all dates:

The Kalends (**Kalendae, -ārum,** f. pl.) were always on the 1st of the month.
The Nones (**Nōnae, -ārum,** f. pl.) usually fell on the 5th of the month.
The Ides (**Īdūs, Īduum,** f. pl.) usually fell on the 13th of the month.

But in March, May, July, and October, the Nones were on the 7th and the Ides were on the 15th.

Actual dates were expressed in the following ways:

1. The ablative of time when indicates that the date coincides with one of the special days:

Kalendīs Aprīlibus, *on April 1*
Nōnīs Februāriīs, *on February 5*
Īdibus Mārtiīs, *on March 15*

Compare **eō diē,** *on that day.*

2. The word **prīdiē** + *accusative* indicates the day before one of the special days:

   prīdiē Kalendās Maiās (lit., *on the day before May 1*), *on April 30*
   prīdiē Īdūs Octōbrēs, *on October 14.*

3. A phrase beginning **ante diem (a.d.)** is used to express all other dates:

   ante diem iv Kalendās Decembrēs (lit., *on the fourth day before December 1*), *on November 28*. (When calculating, you should include the special day and count backwards, e.g., Dec. 1, Nov. 30, Nov. 29, Nov. 28.)

   ante diem viii Īdūs Mārtiās (lit., *on the eighth day before the Ides of March*), *on March 8.*

   Here are the Latin names for the months, expressed as adjectives:

   Iānuārius, -a, -um
   Februārius, -a, -um
   Mārtius, -a, -um
   Aprīlis, -is, -e
   Maius, -a, -um
   Iūnius, -a, -um
   Iūlius, -a, -um
   Augustus, -a, -um
   September, Septembris, Septembre
   Octōber, Octōbris, Octōbre
   November, Novembris, Novembre
   December, Decembris, Decembre

4. The Romans designated years by the names of the consuls, the chief Roman magistrates, who were elected annually. The ablative case is used: **Antoniō et Cicerōne cōnsulibus** = 63 B.C.

   cōnsul, cōnsulis, m., *consul*

5. They also designated years by counting from the foundation of Rome, which was set at a year corresponding to 753 B.C. These dates were expressed with the initials A.U.C. (**ab urbe conditā,** *from the foundation of the city*).

   condō, condere, condidī, conditus, *to found*

   To convert a Roman year to our system, follow these rules:

   a. If the A.U.C. date is 753 or less, subtract it from 754 and you will obtain a B.C. date.
   b. If the A.U.C. date is 754 or greater, subtract 753 from it and you will obtain an A.D. date.

   Examples:

   691 A.U.C. (less than 753)

   $$\begin{array}{r} 754 \\ -\ 691 \\ \hline 63 \end{array}$$

   63 B.C. (the year of Cicero's consulship)

833 A.U.C. (greater than 754)

```
 833
-753
  80 A.D. (the year of our story)
```

To convert a year designated according to our system to a Roman year, follow these rules:

a. If the year is B.C., subtract it from 754.
b. If the year is A.D., add it to 753.

Examples:

```
 754
 -63 B.C. (the year of Cicero's consulship)
 691 A.U.C.

 753
 +80 A.D. (the year of our story)
 833 A.U.C.
```

Exercise 36b

Give English equivalents for the following dates:

1. Kalendīs Iānuāriīs
2. Kalendīs Decembribus
3. Kalendīs Iūniīs
4. Nōnīs Augustīs
5. Nōnīs Octōbribus
6. Īdibus Mārtiīs
7. Īdibus Maiīs
8. Īdibus Septembribus
9. prīdiē Kalendās Februāriās
10. prīdiē Kalendās Iūliās
11. prīdiē Nōnās Augustās
12. prīdiē Īdūs Iānuāriās
13. prīdiē Īdūs Novembrēs
14. ante diem iv Kalendās Iūniās
15. ante diem iii Nōnās Iūliās
16. a.d. vi Kal. Apr.
17. a.d. xviii Kal. Maiās
18. a.d. xii Kal. Feb.
19. a.d. vi Nōn. Mārt.
20. a.d. iv Īd. Feb.

Roman girl reading a letter
Oil on canvas, "Neaera Reading a Letter from Catullus" by Henry J. Hudson, Bradford Art Galleries and Museums, England

Exercise 36c
Give Roman equivalents for the following dates:

1. Today's date
2. Your own birthday
3. The foundation of Rome (April 21)
4. Cicero's birthday (January 3, 106 B.C.)
5. The date of the assassination of Julius Caesar (March 15, 44 B.C.)
6. Martial's birthday (March 1, A.D. 40)
7. The date of the Emperor Titus' accession to power (June 23, A.D. 79).
8. The date of the eruption of Mount Vesuvius (August 24, A.D. 79)

Exercise 36d
Using story 36 and the discussion of Roman dates above as guides, give the Latin for:

1. Cornelia received a letter on October 10 that Flavia had written on October 5.
2. On November 3 Cornelia and her mother saw a great fire.
3. On November 4 Eucleides was struck and very seriously wounded by robbers.
4. On November 5 Aurelia bought a very beautiful palla for Cornelia.
5. On November 29 Valerius will arrive at Rome.

ad Kalendās Graecās, ***until the Greek Kalends*** (Since there were no Kalends in the Greek calendar, this phrase means the event will never happen.)

BUILDING THE MEANING
Translating *quam*

You have now met several uses of **quam**. The following clues should help you choose the correct meaning:

1. In a comparison:
   clue: *comparative adjective or adverb before* **quam**—translate *than*:

   Marcus est prūdent**ior quam** Sextus.
   Marcus is wiser ***than*** *Sextus.*

2. In a phrase with a superlative:
   clue: *superlative adjective or adverb after* **quam**—translate the phrase *as…as possible*:

   Scrībe **quam** saep**issimē**. (36:25)
   Write ***as often as possible.***

3. In an exclamation:
clue: *adjective or adverb after* **Quam**—translate *How…!* or *What a…!*

Quam molestus puer est Sextus!
What a troublesome *boy Sextus is!*

Quam celeriter tua epistula hūc advēnit! (36:3–4)
How quickly *your letter arrived here!*

4. In a question:
clue: *adjective or adverb after* **Quam** *and question mark at the end of the sentence*—translate *How…?*

Quam molestus est Sextus? Sextus est molestior quam Marcus.
How troublesome *is Sextus? Sextus is more troublesome than Marcus.*

5. In a relative clause:
clue: *singular feminine noun as antecedent of* **quam**—translate *whom*, *which*, or *that*:

Illam epistulam accēpī **quam** tū scrīpsistī Kal. Nov. (36:2–3)
I have received that letter ***that*** *you wrote on November 1.*

Cornēlia dē Flāviā **quam** Baiīs relīquerat saepe cōgitābat.
Cornelia often used to think about Flavia, ***whom*** *she had left behind in Baiae.*

Exercise 36e
Read aloud and translate:

1. Quam pulcher adulēscēns est Valerius! Libentissimē eum accipiēmus.
2. Nihil miserābilius quam illud incendium vīdī.
3. Mulier illa miserrima quam Cornēlia in tertiō tabulātō sitam cōnspexit ex incendiō effugere nōn poterat.
4. Nēmō erat magis ēbrius quam Titus, nam plūs vīnī quam cēterī biberat.
5. Quam pulchra est illa palla quam māter mihi ēmit! Mihi valdē placet.
6. Mīlitēs Rōmānī quī audācissimī erant semper quam fortissimē sē dēfendēbant.
7. Quamquam celerius ambulābat Eucleidēs, praedōnēs eum mox cōnsecūtī sunt.
8. Quam graviter vulnerātus est!
9. Quam celeriter praedōnēs currere possunt? Celerius quam Eucleidēs currere possunt.

audāx, audācis, *bold*

HELGE'S SPINNING

Chapter 6 told how the slave-women in the Cornelius household were spinning wool into strands of yarn at the country house in Baiae, and Cornelia in her letter to Flavia complains of constantly spinning wool at home in Rome. In fact, all women in the ancient world spun and wove, from the humblest peasant to the wife of the emperor. Helge, the Ubian woman you met in previous Frontier Life sections was no exception, having learned the craft as a child from her mother.

The region around Ara Ubiorum was noted for its sheep. The sheep, in fact, was probably one of the very first animals domesticated by man, its fleece used for weaving cloth for clothing and blankets since prehistoric times. The story that follows takes us back to the first year of Helge's marriage to Lucius.

As is done today, the sheep were sheared in the spring so they would not suffer through the summer in their heavy fleeces. Helge's father had sheared sheep, and so had

Penelope, wife of Ulysses, working at her loom

Oil on canvas, "Penelope and Her Suitors" by J.W. Waterhouse, City of Aberdeen Art Gallery and Museums Collections, Scotland

Lucius on the farm in Italy where he was raised. The shears used by both Lucius and Helge's father were identical to those used in modern times until the invention of electric clippers, and it was with a pair of these shears that, in the spring, Lucius and his companions sheared the sheep owned by Numistronius, their centurion, who had a farm near Ara Ubiorum.

Lucius began the shearing with a particularly large ram. With the help of two of his fellow legionaries, he wrestled the ram to the ground and tied its front and back feet so the animal could not run away. Grasping the shears directly above the two blades, Lucius straddled the ram and applying gentle, oblique pressure removed the entire fleece at once, flipping the heavy animal over on one side or the other as necessary. As the lanolin, the natural oil in the sheep's fleece, built up on Lucius' shears, he dipped them into a bucket of water to clean them as he worked.

After all the sheep were sheared, each fleece was spread out and cut apart, and the wool was separated into grades according to its quality. The thickest and strongest fleece came from the sheep's back, and the next thickest came from the sides. The fleece from the belly was soft and airy—just right for tunics. The worst wool came from the legs and tail, where it was apt to be encrusted with dirt. The wool was carefully placed into bags, each marked as to the quality of fleece it contained.

Helge and her friend, Helena Favonia, who also lived in the area surrounding the military camp, were now ready to convert the wool into tunics and cloaks for the legionaries. First, the wool was washed in cold water and beaten with sticks to remove dirt, leaves, and thorns and to detach fibers for easier carding. Then Helge and Helena carded the wool, a task that meant working it through the teeth of flat iron combs with their fingers over and over, separating the fibers from one another.

Finally, after washing the carded wool, this time in warm soapy water, Helge and Helena were ready to dye it. For the cloaks, the wool would be left the natural color of the sheep or dyed brown. However, the tunics had to be a red color by legion order, and it was this color that Helge prepared by filling a pot with water, scraps of iron from the legion armory, and the sour red wine (**posca**) issued to Roman legionaries. To enhance the reddish color, she added some dry stalks of a plant called madder. Letting the pot sit over the fire until just warm, Helge dumped the wool into the mixture and stirred it until it was thoroughly saturated with the dye. Lifting it out, she wrung out the wool and rinsed it in plain water. Wringing it out again, she dipped it into water that had been poured through wood ashes to fix the color. She repeated this process over and over until she had wool of just the right hue.

Helge knew the art of creating good dyes of many bright colors created by using native plants and metals. But the Romans scorned those bright colors for clothing, considering them barbarian.

The washed, correctly colored, and dry wool, placed in baskets, was now ready for spinning. A simple spindle with a circular whorl mounted on it was used throughout the ancient world. The Roman poet Catullus describes how the Fates spun the threads of destiny by twirling this very same instrument with skillful movements of their fingers:

> The right hand lightly drawing out the thread shaped it with fingers turned upwards and then with a twisting movement of the thumb turned downwards twirled the spindle balanced by the circular whorl.

So Helge spun the brick-red wool into strands of yarn.

As the yarn became longer, Helge wound it on the shaft of her spindle. She and Helena continued to spin until the baskets of wool were empty.

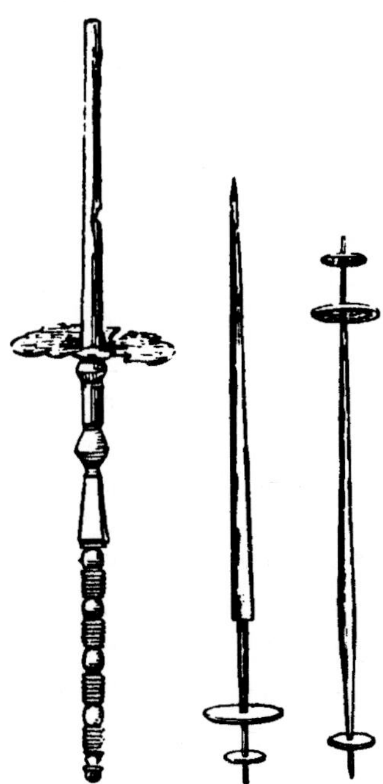

Spindles with circular whorls

CHAPTER 37

OFF TO SCHOOL

Māne in urbe fuit strepitus maximus; canēs lātrābant, servī per viās currēbant, sed neque Marcus neque Sextus sē mōvit. Adhūc in lectō iacēbat Sextus et sēcum cōgitābat: "Quis est mē miserior? Cotīdiē ante lūcem mihi necesse est ad lūdum proficīscī. Sed ad lūdum īre vereor. In lūdō numquam laudor; semper castīgor. Illōs versūs Vergiliī memoriā tenēre nōn possum. Ille grammaticus mē experītur, et cotīdiē eadem dīcit: 'Tū, Sexte, nihil scīs quod semper loqueris,' vel 'Es puer pessimus,' vel 'Nisi dīligentius labōrābis, verberāberis.' Itaque domī manēre volō."

Ita cōgitābat Sextus cum Eucleidēs paedagōgus in cubiculum ingressus est. "Surgite, puerī!" inquit. "Nōlīte diūtius in lectō manēre! Est enim tempus ad lūdum proficīscī, ubi Palaemōn, grammaticus ille ērudītissimus, vōs laetus accipiet. Vōs docēbit plūrima quae vōbīs erunt ūtilissima."

Nihil respondērunt puerī; invītī ē lectō surrēxērunt, vestēs induērunt, ē domō ēgressī sunt. Nōndum lūcēbat, sed cum Eucleide in viās urbis profectī sunt. Lanternam eīs praeferēbat Eucleidēs.

Subitō cōnspexit Marcus tabernam quandam. "Ecce, Eucleidēs!" clāmāvit Marcus. "Vidēsne illam tabernam? Est pīstrīnum. Licetne nōbīs aliquid cibī emere?"

(continued)

3 **cotīdiē,** adv., *daily, every day*
lūdus, -ī, m., *school*
proficīscī, *to set out*
4 **vereor,** *I am afraid*
castīgō, -āre, –āvī, -ātus, *to rebuke, reprimand*
Vergilius, -ī, m., *Vergil (Roman poet)*
5 **grammaticus, -ī,** m., *secondary school teacher*
experītur, *(he) tests*
6 **loqueris,** *you are talking*
vel, conj., *or*
8 **paedagōgus, -ī,** m., *tutor*
ingressus est, *(he) entered*
10 **ērudītus, -a, -um,** *learned, scholarly*
11 **ūtilis, -is, -e,** *useful*
12 **ēgressī sunt,** *(they) went out*
13 **profectī sunt,** *(they) set out*
16 **pīstrīnum, -ī,** n., *bakery*

14 **praeferō, praeferre, praetulī, praelātus,** irreg., *to carry X* (acc.) *in front of Y* (dat.)

Exercise 37a

Respondē Latīnē:

1. Cūr miser est Sextus?
2. Quandō necesse est ad lūdum proficīscī?
3. Cūr Sextus in lūdō semper castīgātur?
4. Quālis grammaticus (ut dīcit Eucleidēs) est Palaemōn?
5. Quid Palaemōn puerōs docēbit?
6. Cūr necesse erat Eucleidī lanternam puerīs praeferre?

"Estō," respondit Eucleidēs. "Nōn sērō est. Etiamsī nōs aliquid cibī edēmus, tamen ad tempus ad lūdum perveniēmus."

Puerī igitur scriblītās emunt, Eucleidēs pānem et paulum vīnī. Dum ientāculum dēvorant, Marcus et Sextus inter sē loquuntur. Tandem iterum profectī mox lūdō appropinquābant.

17 **etiamsī,** conj., *even if*
18 **ad tempus,** *on time*
19 **scriblīta, -ae,** f., *tart or pastry with cheese filling*
paulum, -ī, n., *a small amount, a little*
ientāculum, -ī, n., *breakfast*
20 **loquuntur,** *(they) talk*

Respondē Latīnē:

1. Ubi Eucleidēs et puerī ientāculum emunt?
2. Quid emunt puerī? Quid Eucleidēs?

FORMS

Deponent Verbs

Look at these sentences:

Eucleidēs effugere **cōnātus est.**	*Eucleides* ***tried*** *to escape.*
Praedōnēs eum **cōnsecūtī sunt.**	*The robbers* ***overtook*** *him.*
Sed ad lūdum īre **vereor**.	*But* ***I am afraid*** *to go to school.*
Semper **loqueris**.	***You are*** *always* ***talking***.
Grammaticus mē **experītur**.	*The teacher* ***tests*** *me.*
Brundisiō **proficīscētur**.	***He will set out*** *from Brundisium.*
Tempus est **proficīscī**.	*It is time* ***to set out***.

In each of the above examples, the Latin verb in boldface has a *passive* ending but its meaning is *active*. Verbs that behave in this way are called *deponent verbs*.

NOTES:

1. Deponent verbs occur in all four conjugations and are conjugated the same as *passive* forms of regular verbs. Deponents are *translated* with *active* meanings:

Regular Verb: Passive	**Deponent Verb**
Laudātur. *He is praised.*	**Cōnātur.** *He tries.*
Laudārī potest. *He is able to be praised.*	**Cōnārī** potest. *He is able to try.*

2. Deponent verbs have only *three* principal parts:
   1st: 1st person singular, present tense: **cōnor**, *I try, I am trying, I do try*
   2nd: present infinitive: **cōnārī**, *to try, to be trying*
   3rd: 1st person singular, perfect tense: **cōnātus sum**, *I tried, I have tried*

	Present	Infinitive	Perfect	Meaning
1st Conj.	cṓnor	cōnā́rī	cōnā́tus sum	*to try*
2nd Conj.	véreor	verḗrī	véritus sum	*to be afraid*
3rd Conj.	lóquor	lóquī	locū́tus sum	*to speak*
(-*iō*)	regrédior	régredī	regréssus sum	*to go back*
4th Conj.	expérior	experī́rī	expértus sum	*to test*

3. The *perfect participle* of a deponent verb, although passive in form, is translated *actively*:

   Puerī in viās urbis **ēgressī** mox lūdō appropinquābant.
   The boys, ***having gone out*** *into the streets of the city, soon were approaching the school.*

Here is a chart showing sample forms of deponent verbs. Note that the singular imperatives have forms identical to the present active infinitive of non-deponent verbs. In the future and imperfect tenses only the singular forms are shown. In the perfect, pluperfect, and future perfect tenses only the 1st person singular forms are shown.

			1st Conjugation	2nd Conjugation	3rd Conjugation		4th Conjugation
Present Infinitive			cōn***ā́rī***	ver***ḗrī***	lóqu***ī***	régred***ī***	exper***ī́rī***
Imperative			cōn***ā́re***	ver***ḗre***	lóqu***ere***	regréd***ere***	exper***ī́re***
			cōn***ā́minī***	ver***ḗminī***	loqu***íminī***	regred***íminī***	exper***ī́minī***
Present	**Singular**	1	cṓno***r***	véreo***r***	lóquo***r***	regrédio***r***	expério***r***
		2	cōnā́***ris***	verḗ***ris***	lóque***ris***	regréde***ris***	experī́***ris***
		3	cōnā́***tur***	verḗ***tur***	lóqui***tur***	regrédi***tur***	experī́***tur***
	Plural	1	cōnā́***mur***	verḗ***mur***	lóqui***mur***	regrédi***mur***	experī́***mur***
		2	cōnā́***minī***	verḗ***minī***	loquí***minī***	regredí***minī***	experī́***minī***
		3	cōnā́***ntur***	verḗ***ntur***	loquú***ntur***	regrediú***ntur***	experiú***ntur***
Imperfect	**Singular**	1	cōnā́***bar***	verḗ***bar***	loquḗ***bar***	regrediḗ***bar***	experiḗ***bar***
		2	cōnā***bā́ris***	verē***bā́ris***	loquē***bā́ris***	regrediē***bā́ris***	experiē***bā́ris***
		3	cōnā***bā́tur***	verē***bā́tur***	loquē***bā́tur***	regrediē***bā́tur***	experiē***bā́tur***
Future	**Singular**	1	cōnā́***bor***	verḗ***bor***	lóqua***r***	regrédia***r***	expéria***r***
		2	cōnā́***beris***	verḗ***beris***	loquḗ***ris***	regrediḗ***ris***	experiḗ***ris***
		3	cōnā́***bitur***	verḗ***bitur***	loquḗ***tur***	regrediḗ***tur***	experiḗ***tur***
Perfect		1	cōnā́tus sum	véritus sum	locū́tus sum	regréssus sum	expértus sum
Pluperfect		1	cōnā́tus éram	véritus éram	locū́tus éram	regréssus éram	expértus éram
Future Perfect		1	cōnā́tus erō	véritus érō	locū́tus érō	regréssus érō	expértus érō

You have met forms of the following deponent verbs so far (listed by conjugation):

1st: **cōnor, cōnārī, cōnātus sum,** *to try* (36:19)
moror, morārī, morātus sum, *to delay, remain, stay* (36:8)
2nd: **vereor, verērī, veritus sum,** *to be afraid, fear* (37:4)

3rd:	**collābor, collābī, collāpsus sum,** *to collapse* (34:22)
	cōnsequor, cōnsequī, cōnsecūtus sum, *to catch up to, overtake* (35:18)
	loquor, loquī, locūtus sum, *to speak, talk* (37:6)
	proficīscor, proficīscī, profectus sum, *to set out, leave* (36:9)
	sequor, sequī, secūtus sum, *to follow* (36:18)
(*-iō*)	**ēgredior, ēgredī, ēgressus sum,** *to go out, leave* (37:12)
	ingredior, ingredī, ingressus sum, *to go in, enter* (37:8)
	regredior, regredī, regressus sum, *to go back, return* (36:8)
4th:	**experior, experīrī, expertus sum,** *to test, try* (37:5)

Exercise 37b

Here are some forms of deponent verbs. Translate them into English:

1. proficīscuntur
2. experientur
3. secūtī erāmus
4. morātae sunt
5. verēbimur
6. ēgrederis
7. profectī eritis
8. sequere
9. collābī
10. cōnsequēbātur

Exercise 37c

Refer to the principal parts of the verbs listed above and say the following in Latin:

1. We have tried.
2. You (*sing.*) enter.
3. They had set out.
4. Speak, boys!
5. I will test.
6. She was following.
7. You (*pl.*) collapsed.
8. Don't be afraid, Sextus!
9. They will have returned.
10. We were delaying.
11. He has gone out.
12. I will try to overtake you.

Exercise 37d

Read aloud and translate:

1. Quid puellae facere cōnantur? Puellae pallam facere cōnantur. Quid tū facere cōnāris? Ego labōrāre cōnor. Quid vōs facere cōnāminī? Nōs dormīre cōnāmur.
2. Quandō nōs vīsitāre cōnāberis? Ego mox vōs vīsitāre cōnābor. Amīcī meī quoque vōs vīsitāre cōnābuntur. Nōs omnēs eōdem diē vōs vīsitāre cōnābimur.
3. Quis loquitur? Ego nōn loquēbar. Nōs cum magistrō loquēbāmur.
4. Quō puerī proficīscuntur? Rōmam proficīscuntur. Nōs cum eīs proficīscēmur. Nōnne vōs quoque proficīscī vultis?
5. Quandō puerī ē lūdō ēgredientur? Puerī ē lūdō ēgredientur sextā hōrā. Ēgrediēturne cum puerīs magister? Minimē vērō! Magister in lūdō morābitur.
6. Quandō tū proficīscēris? Ubi māter domum regressa erit, ego proficīscar. Puer prīmā lūce proficīscētur. Servī nunc proficīscī nōn possunt. Mox sequentur.

7. Paulisper in urbe morātī sumus. Cūr morātī estis? Ego morātus sum quod patrem vidēre volēbam. Amīcī meī morātī sunt quod aedificia urbis vidēre volēbant.
8. Prīmā lūce servī Cornēliī in viās ēgressī sunt. Illōs praedōnēs scelestōs sequī cōnātī sunt sed eōs cōnsequī nōn potuērunt.
9. Nōlī in lectō diūtius morārī, Sexte. Cōnāre illōs versūs Vergiliī memoriā tenēre. Fortasse ā grammaticō hodiē laudāberis sī nōn nimis loquēris.
10. Cornēlius convīvīs, "Intrāte, amīcī!" inquit. "Ingrediminī domum meam! Vōs libentissimē excipiō." Convīvae quam celerrimē ingressī inter sē magnō cum strepitū in ātriō colloquēbantur.

sextus, -a, -um, *sixth* **magister, magistrī,** m., *schoolmaster*

Exercise 37e

In each sentence below, replace the verb in italics with the appropriate form of the deponent verb in parentheses, keeping the same tense, person, and number; then translate the new sentence:

1. Valerius Brundisiō Īdibus Novembribus *discessit.* (proficīscor)
2. Ā grammaticō laudātī sumus quod versūs memoriā tenēre *potuerāmus.* (cōnor)
3. Tabellārius ex urbe quam celerrimē *exībit.* (ēgredior)
4. Māter et Cornēlia in illā tabernā diūtissimē *manēbant.* (moror)
5. "Hīc *sedē,* Marce," inquit Eucleidēs. (moror) "Nōlī mē *vexāre*!" (sequor)
6. Eucleidēs per urbis viās nocte ambulāre *nōn vult.* (vereor)
7. "Ego prīmus," inquit Marcus, "in lūdum *intrāvī.*" (ingredior)

Exercise 37f

Using story 37 and the information on deponent verbs as guides, give the Latin for the following. Use deponent verbs whenever possible:

1. Marcus and Sextus were staying in their beds.
2. Marcus and Sextus set out for school before dawn every day.
3. Why are you afraid to go to school, Sextus?
4. The teacher will test Sextus.
5. Sextus always talks in school, never works diligently, and is often beaten by the teacher.

Forsan miserōs meliōra sequentur. *For those in misery perhaps better things will follow.* (Vergil, *Aeneid* XII.153)
Multī fāmam, cōnscientiam paucī verentur. *Many fear their reputation, few their conscience.* (Pliny, *Letters* III.20)
Vir sapit quī pauca loquitur. *It is a wise man who speaks little.* (*Anonymous*)

ROMAN LIFE XX

ROMAN EDUCATION I

THE EARLIEST YEARS: EDUCATION IN THE HOME

Little is known about the early training of Roman boys and girls, but certainly the home played the most important part. During the first seven years education was chiefly in the hands of the mother:

> In the good old days, every citizen's son was brought up, not in the chamber of some hired nurse, but in his mother's lap. Thus we are told Cornelia, the mother of the Gracchi, directed their upbringing. The same was true of Aurelia, the mother of Caesar, and of Atia, the mother of Augustus.
>
> Tacitus, *Dialogue* 28

This was not the time of formal instruction; it was the influence of the home on the child that was the greatest at this stage:

> In ancient times it was the established custom that Romans should learn from their elders not only by watching but also by listening. The father of each one served as his teacher.
>
> Pliny, *Letters* VIII.14

The home was always considered the natural place for early training, and the practice of sending children to school away from their home town, although it increased in later years, was looked upon with suspicion by some:

> Surely it is a matter of great importance that your children should study here rather than anywhere else. Where can they live more happily than in their native town, or be more strictly brought up than under their parents' eye, or be educated at less expense than at home? What an easy matter it would be to hire teachers and add to their salaries the money you now spend on lodgings, traveling, and all you have to purchase away from home.
>
> Pliny, *Letters* IV.13

Roman classroom scene

THE PRIMARY SCHOOL

At the age of seven, if their fathers could afford it, children were sent to school—the **lūdus litterārius**—to be taught their "letters" by a schoolmaster, generally called **litterātor** or **magister lūdī**. (Note that the Romans used the same word **lūdus** for both *play* and *school*.) The teacher's pay was small, for teaching was not considered very highly as a profession. The curriculum at this stage was limited to three subjects—reading, writing, and arithmetic.

Education at home, however, was not unusual, for there was no state education. It was usually in the hands of a tutor—most often a Greek slave or freedman.

Occasionally, we read of fathers who themselves looked after the education of their sons. This was true of Cato and Aemilius Paulus, but note their different ideas and ideals:

> As soon as Cato's son began to learn with understanding, his father took him in charge and taught him to read, although he had a very good slave, called Chilo, who was a schoolteacher and was already teaching many boys. But Cato did not think it right, as he himself says, that his son should be scolded by a slave or pulled by the ear when slow to learn, nor that such an important thing as education should be left to a slave. He himself therefore taught him reading, law, and gymnastics and also gave him instruction in how to throw a javelin, to fight in armor, to ride and box, to endure both heat and cold, and to swim.
>
> —Plutarch, *Cato the Elder* 20

> Aemilius Paulus himself looked after the education of his children. He brought them up in the old-fashioned Roman way as he himself had been brought up, but he was even more enthusiastic about Greek education. For this reason their teachers of grammar, logic, and rhetoric, their teachers of sculpture and drawing, those in charge of their dogs and horses, and those who taught them how to hunt, were all Greeks.
>
> Plutarch, *Aemilius Paulus* 6

In schools, discipline was generally very strict. Martial, speaking of one schoolmaster as "a person hated by both girls and boys," continues:

> The crested cocks have not yet broken the silence of the night, but you are making a noise by roaring savagely and thrashing your pupils.
>
> Martial, *Epigrams* IX.68

Many Romans followed the Greek custom of sending their children to school accompanied by a slave (**paedagōgus**) to look after their conduct, manners, and morals:

> It is the job of the **paedagōgus** to make the boy learn what his teacher has taught him by encouraging and shouting at him, by fetching out the strap, and by using the cane. He makes him do his work by driving every lesson into his head.
>
> Libanius, *Orations* 58.8

REVIEW VIII: CHAPTERS 34–37

Exercise VIIIa: Comparative and Superlative of Adjectives and Adverbs

Supply in the blanks comparative and superlative adjectives or adverbs corresponding to the positive forms in the original statements. Read aloud and translate:

1. Messalla coquum *bonum* habet. Titus coquum ______ habet quam Messalla. Cornēlius coquum ______ omnium habet.
2. Messalla tālōs *dīligenter* iacit. Cornēlius tālōs ______ iacit Messallā. Titus tālōs ______ omnium iacit.
3. Eucleidēs ad lūdum *lentē* proficīscitur. Marcus ad lūdum ______ proficīscitur quam Eucleides. Sextus ad lūdum ______ omnium proficīscitur.
4. Marcus *bene* scrībit. Eucleidēs ______ Marcō scrībit. Grammaticus ______ omnium scrībit.
5. Messalla ē poculō *pulchrō* bibit. Titus ē poculō ______ bibit quam Messalla. Cornēlius ē poculō omnium ______ bibit.
6. Coquus Messallae cēnam *celeriter* parat. Coquus Titī cēnam ______ parat quam coquus Messallae. Coquus Cornēliī cenam ______omnium parat.
7. Eucleidēs ē lectō *sērō* surgit. Marcus ē lectō ______ surgit quam Eucleidēs. Sextus ē lectō ______ omnium surgit.
8. Messalla *multum* vīnī bibit. Cornēlius ______ vīnī bibit Messallā. Titus omnium ______ vīnī bibit.
9. Cornēlius *magnā* vōce clāmat. Messalla ______ vōce clāmat quam Cornēlius. Titus omnium ______ vōce clāmat.
10. Praedōnēs tabernārium *ferōciter* verberāvērunt. Praedōnēs lanium ______ verberāvērunt quam tabernārium. Praedōnēs Eucleidem ______ omnium verberāvērunt.

Exercise VIIIb: Forms of Deponent Verbs

Give the requested forms of the following deponent verbs:

	Present	Imperfect	Future	Perfect	Pluperfect	Future Perfect
1. sequor *(3rd sing.)*	______	______	______	______	______	______
2. loquor *(1st pl.)*	______	______	______	______	______	______
3. vereor *(3rd pl.)*	______	______	______	______	______	______
4. cōnor *(1st sing.)*	______	______	______	______	______	______
5. collābor *(2nd sing.)*	______	______	______	______	______	______
6. regredior *(3rd pl.)*	______	______	______	______	______	______
7. moror *(2nd pl.)*	______	______	______	______	______	______
8. experior *(3rd sing.)*	______	______	______	______	______	______

Exercise VIIIc: Imperatives of Deponent Verbs

Give the singular and plural imperatives of the following deponent verbs:

	Singular	Plural
1. cōnor	______	______
2. loquor	______	______
3. regredior	______	______
4. experior	______	______
5. vereor	______	______

Exercise VIIId: Active Forms of Non-deponent Verbs

Give the requested forms of the following verbs in the active voice:

	Present	Imperfect	Future	Perfect	Pluperfect	Future Perfect
1. vincō *(2nd sing.)*	______	______	______	______	______	______
2. compleō *(1st sing.)*	______	______	______	______	______	______
3. hauriō *(2nd pl.)*	______	______	______	______	______	______
4. excitō *(1st pl.)*	______	______	______	______	______	______
5. percutiō *(3rd pl.)*	______	______	______	______	______	______
6. crēdō *(3rd sing.)*	______	______	______	______	______	______

Exercise VIIIe: Passive Forms of Non-deponent Verbs

Repeat Exercise VIIId, but give the requested forms of the verbs in the passive voice.

Exercise VIIIf: Imperatives of Non-deponent Verbs

Give the singular and plural active imperatives of the verbs in Exercise VIIId.

Exercise VIIIg: Reading Comprehension

Read the following passage and answer the questions below with full sentences in Latin:

THE TROJAN HORSE

Graecī, quī iam decem annōs Troiam obsidēbant, domum regredī valdē cupiēbant. Mussābant igitur, "Quōmodo Troiānī vincentur? Cōnsilium novum et melius capiēmus. Equum ligneum aedificābimus quem extrā mūrōs urbis relinquēmus. In eō pōnentur fortissimī ē mīlitibus nostrīs. Deinde ad īnsulam vīcīnam ipsī proficīscēmur et nōs ibi cēlābimus. Fortasse equus in urbem ā Troiānīs trahētur."

Postquam Graecī abiērunt, laetissimī ex urbe ēgressī sunt Troiānī. Equum ligneum spectant. "Quid est hoc?" rogant. "Cūr equus tantus ē lignō factus est? Cūr Graecī hunc equum relīquērunt?"

Aliī, "Cavēte Graecōs!" inquiunt. "Nōlīte eīs crēdere." Aliī, "Gaudēte!" inquiunt. "Equus, sī intrā mūrōs ductus erit, urbem nostram custōdiet et dēfendet."

Itaque maximō gaudiō equum intrā mūrōs trahere cōnstituērunt. Nox erat. Troiānī somnō vīnōque oppressī per tōtam urbem dormiēbant. Ecce! Dē equō dēscendērunt Graecī. Intereā cēterī ex īnsulā regrediēbantur et urbem quam celerrimē petēbant. Eī quī in equō cēlātī erant portās Graecīs aperuērunt. Magnō cum strepitū irrūpērunt. Undique clāmor et tumultus, undique incendia et caedēs. Mātrēs sollicitae cum līberīs per viās currēbant; flammae omnia dēlēbant. Urbs tandem capta est.

1 **annus, -ī,** m., *year*
2 **cōnsilium capere,** *to form a plan*
3 **ligneus, -a, -um,** *wooden*
18 **caedēs, caedis,** gen. pl., **caedium,** f., *slaughter*

1 **obsideō, obsidēre, obsēdī, obsessus,** *to besiege*
2 **cupiō, cupere, cupīvī, cupītus,** *to desire, want*
18 **dēleō, dēlēre, dēlēvī, dēlētus,** *to destroy*

1. For how many years had the Greeks been besieging Troy?
2. What kind of plan did the Greeks want to adopt?
3. What did they build?
4. Where did they put it?
5. Where did the other Greeks hide?
6. What did the Trojans do after the Greeks left?
7. What were the Trojans saying who did not trust the Greeks?
8. When did the Trojans drag the horse within the walls?
9. Why didn't the Trojans see the Greeks when they descended from the horse?
10. What were the other Greeks doing at this very time?
11. Who opened the gates to the Greeks?

Exercise VIIIh: Discriminating between Deponent Verbs and Passive Forms of Regular Verbs

The verbs below are taken from the story in Exercise VIIIg. Say whether the verb is a deponent verb or a passive form of a regular verb. Then give a translation of the verb that would fit the context in the story.

1. regredī (1)
2. vincentur (2)
3. pōnentur (4)
4. proficīscēmur (5)
5. trahētur (6)
6. ēgressī sunt (7)
7. factus est (8)
8. regrediēbantur (15)
9. cēlātī erant (16)
10. capta est (19)

CHAPTER

38

THE LESSONS BEGIN

Omnēs puerī in lūdum vix ingressī erant cum grammaticus ita coepit: "Abhinc trēs mēnsēs prīmus liber Aenēidis ā vōbīs lēctus est. Quis ē vōbīs dē Aenēā mihi nārrāre potest?"

Cui ūnus ē discipulīs respondit: "Urbs Troia ā Graecīs decem annōs obsidēbātur, sed tandem capta et incēnsa est. Effūgit ē ruīnīs illīus urbis Aenēās, et ūnā cum patre fīliōque suō et complūribus amīcīs ex Asiā nāvigāvit, nam terram petēbat quae Hesperia vocāta est. Postquam multa terrā marīque passus est, ad Siciliam vix vēnit. Atque ubi ē Siciliā profectus est, maxima tempestās nāvēs complūrēs dēlēvit. Aenēās ipse, ad Āfricam tempestāte āctus, cum septem modo nāvibus ad urbem quandam advēnit ubi ā rēgīnā Dīdōne cōmiter acceptus ad convīvium invītātus est."

(continued)

1 **coepit,** *(he) began*
2 **mēnsis, mēnsis,** m., *month*
Aenēis, Aenēidis, f., *the* Aeneid *(an epic poem by Vergil)*
Aenēās, Aenēae, m., *Aeneas (son of Venus and Anchises and legendary ancestor of the Romans)*
4 **discipulus, -ī,** m., *pupil*
annus, -ī, m., *year*
5 **ruīna, -ae,** f., *collapse, ruin*
6 **nāvigō, -āre, -āvī, -ātus,** *to sail*
terra, -ae, f., *earth, ground, land*
Hesperia, -ae, f., *Hesperia (the land in the West, Italy)*
7 **mare, maris,** abl. sing., **marī,** gen. pl., **marium,** n., *sea*
8 **tempestās, tempestātis,** f., *storm*
nāvis, nāvis, gen. pl., **nāvium,** f., *ship*
9 **rēgīna, -ae,** f., *queen*
10 **Dīdō, Dīdōnis,** f., *Dido (queen of Carthage)*

4 **obsideō, obsidēre, obsēdī, obsessus,** *to besiege*
5 **incendō, incendere, incendī, incēnsus,** *to burn, set on fire*
7 **patior, patī, passus sum,** *to suffer; endure*
8 **dēleō, dēlēre, dēlēvī, dēlētus,** *to destroy*

Exercise 38a

Respondē Latīnē:

1. Quī urbem Troiam obsidēbant?
2. Quis ē ruīnīs urbis effūgit?
3. Quibuscum ex Asiā nāvigāvit?
4. Quam terram petēbat Aenēās?
5. Quid passus est?
6. Quō īnstrūmentō nāvēs complūrēs dēlētae sunt?
7. Quot nāvēs ad terram advēnērunt?
8. Ā quō Aenēās in Āfricā acceptus est?

Tum grammaticus, “Rēs optimē nārrāta est. Sed quid in convīviō factum est?”

Cui alter discipulus, “Rēgīna plūrima rogābat dē urbe Troiā, dē rēbus Troiānīs, dē perīculīs itineris. Tandem omnēs convīvae tacuērunt et Aenēās multa et mīra nārrāre coepit.”

Hoc respōnsum grammaticō maximē placuit; quī, “Nunc,” inquit, “nōs ipsī audiēmus ea quae ab Aenēā nārrāta sunt. Nunc legēmus aliquōs versūs ē secundō librō Aenēidis. Age, Marce! Mihi recitā illōs versūs!”

Marcus igitur ita recitāre coepit:

> Conticuēre omnēs intentīque ōra tenēbant.
> Inde torō pater Aenēās sīc orsus ab altō:
> “Īnfandum, rēgīna, iubēs renovāre dolōrem.”
> *They all fell silent and were eager to listen.*
> *Then from his lofty couch Father Aeneas thus began:*
> *“Unspeakable, O Queen, is the grief you bid me revive.”*

16 **aliquī, -ae, -a,** *some*

Optimum est patī quod ēmendāre nōn possīs. ***It is best to endure what you cannot change.*** **(Seneca, *Moral Epistles* CVII.9)**

Caelum, nōn animum, mūtant, quī trāns mare currunt. ***Those who run off across the sea change their climate but not their mind.*** **(Horace, *Epistles* I.II.27)**

Like Dido in the *Aeneid* or Ariadne in earlier myth, a woman might help a hero only to be abandoned. *“Ariadne in Naxos,” oil on canvas, Evelyn de Morgan, The de Morgan Foundation, London*

FORMS
Numbers in Latin

	Cardinal	Ordinal
I	**ūnus, -a, -um,** *one*	**prīmus, -a, -um,** *first*
II	**duo, -ae, -o,** *two*	**secundus, -a, -um,** *second*
III	**trēs, trēs, tria,** *three*	**tertius, -a, -um,** *third*
IV	**quattuor,** *four*	**quārtus, -a, -um**
V	**quīnque,** *five*	**quīntus, -a, -um**
VI	**sex,** *six*	**sextus, -a, -um**
VII	**septem,** *seven*	**septimus, -a, -um**
VIII	**octō,** *eight*	**octāvus, -a, -um**
IX	**novem,** *nine*	**nōnus, -a, -um**
X	**decem,** *ten*	**decimus, -a, -um**
XI	**ūndecim,** *eleven*	**ūndecimus, -a, -um**
XII	**duodecim,** *twelve*	**duodecimus, -a, -um**
XIII	**tredecim,** *thirteen*	**tertius decimus, -a, -um**
XIV	**quattuordecim,** *fourteen*	**quārtus decimus, -a, -um**
XV	**quīndecim,** *fifteen*	**quīntus decimus, -a, -um**
XVI	**sēdecim,** *sixteen*	**sextus decimus, -a, -um**
XVII	**septendecim,** *seventeen*	**septimus decimus, -a, -um**
XVIII	**duodēvīgintī,** *eighteen*	**duodēvīcēsimus, -a, -um**
XIX	**ūndēvīgintī,** *nineteen*	**ūndēvīcēsimus, -a, -um**
XX	**vīgintī,** *twenty*	**vīcēsimus, -a, -um**
L	**quīnquāgintā,** *fifty*	**quīnquāgēsimus, -a, -um**
C	**centum,** *a hundred*	**centēsimus, -a, -um**
D	**quīngentī, -ae, -a,** *five hundred*	**quīngentēsimus, -a, -um**
M	**mīlle,** *a thousand*	**mīllēsimus, -a, -um**

N.B. The cardinal numbers from **quattuor** to **centum** do not change their form to indicate case and gender.

The question word **Quot...?** requires an answer from the *cardinal* column:

Quot līberōs habēbat lībertus? Septem habēbat.
How many children did the freedman have? He had seven.

The word **Quotus...?** requires an answer from the *ordinal* column:

Quota hōra est? Est nōna hōra.
What time is it? It is the ninth hour.

Exercise 38b

Read aloud and translate:

1. Puerī novem hōrās dormīvērunt. Tempus est eōs excitāre.
2. Convīvae sex hōrās morābantur. Cēna Cornēliī erat optima.
3. Ulixēs multa terrā marīque passus domum decimō annō pervēnit.
4. Quot librī Aenēidis sunt? Duodecim sunt librī Aenēidis.
5. Quota hōra est? Est sexta hōra.
6. Quotus mēnsis annī est Aprīlis? Aprīlis mēnsis annī est quārtus.
7. Ōlim Mārtius mēnsis erat prīmus annī, et septimus vocātus est mēnsis September, octāvus mēnsis Octōber, nōnus mēnsis November, decimus mēnsis December. Nunc mēnsis Iānuārius est prīmus annī.
8. Quot sorōrēs habēbat Dīdō? Ūnam sorōrem Annam nōmine habēbat Dīdō.
9. Marcus ā grammaticō rogātus aliquōs versūs ē secundō librō Aenēidis bene recitāvit.
10. Aenēās, ut in sextō Aenēidis librō legimus, in Plūtōnis rēgnum dēscendit.

Ulixēs, Ulixis, m., *Ulysses, Odysseus (Greek hero of the Trojan War)*

Exercise 38c

Give equivalents for the following in Arabic numerals:

1. XXX
2. XXIV
3. XVII
4. XIX
5. LX
6. CV
7. DXC
8. MDCCLXXVI
9. XLIV
10. CLIX.

Exercise 38d

Give the Latin for each of the following questions (each of your questions should expect a numerical answer), and then give an appropriate answer:

1. What hour is it?
2. What month is it?
3. How many months are there in a year?
4. How many brothers and how many sisters do you have?
5. How many books have you read today?

ROMAN LIFE XXI

ROMAN EDUCATION II

THE SECONDARY SCHOOL: THE GRAMMATICUS

After five years at a **lūdus litterārius**, children were sent to a **grammaticus**, a grammarian. Secondary education was more restricted, for only the wealthy could send their children to these schools. Here they studied both Latin and Greek literature. In addition, the **grammaticus** would teach mathematics, natural science, astronomy, philosophy, and music, but only in so far as these subjects were relevant to understanding the works of Greek and Latin literature that were read in the schools.

Students had to learn to read aloud books in which there was no punctuation or even spaces between words, and to recite them. They also had to be able to answer very detailed questions on every word of the books they were reading. A favorite author, from the end of the first century B.C. onwards, was Publius Vergilius Maro, whom we call Vergil. He had written a great poem called the *Aeneid* (because its hero was Aeneas) about the origins of the Romans.

We can get some idea of what a lesson in the school of a **grammaticus** might have been like from a grammarian called Priscian who lived in the sixth century A.D. Here is part of a series of questions and answers that he gives on the first line of the second book of Vergil's *Aeneid*.

Conticuēre omnēs intentīque ōra tenēbant.

"Partēs ōrātiōnis quot sunt?"	*"How many parts of speech are there?"*
"Sex."	*"Six."*
"Quot nōmina?"	*"How many nouns?"*
"Duo. *Omnēs* et *ōra*."	*"Two.* **omnēs** *and* **ōra**."
"Quot verba?"	*"How many verbs?"*
"Duo. *Conticuēre* et *tenēbant*."	*"Two.* **conticuēre** *and* **tenēbant**."
"Quid aliud habet?"	*"What else does it have?"*
"Participium *intentī* et coniūnctiōnem *-que*."	*"A participle* **intentī** *and a conjunction* **-que**."
"*Conticuēre* —quae pars ōrātiōnis est?"	*"What part of speech is* **conticuēre**?"
"Verbum."	*"A verb."*
"Quāle?"	*"What tense?"*
"Perfectum"	*"The perfect."*
"Quōmodo dictum?"	*"How is it described?"*
"Indicātīvō coniugātiōnis secundae."	*"Indicative, of the second conjugation."*
"Cuius significātiōnis?"	*"What voice is it?"*
"Actīvae."	*"Active."*
"Dīc passīvum."	*"Tell me the passive."*

And so it goes on for many more questions, each word being treated in the same way.

HIGHER EDUCATION

After assuming the **toga virīlis** at age sixteen, a boy was ready for the most advanced stage of Roman education—that of the teacher of rhetoric (**rhētor**). From the **rhētor** he learned the art of public speaking, a necessary qualification for anyone aspiring to high office in law or politics.

A few favored youths completed their education by further study of rhetoric and philosophy at Athens or some other foreign city.

ATTITUDES TO EDUCATION

Horace's father, though a freedman of moderate means, did not consider it too great a sacrifice to give his son the best possible education. Horace recalls his father's efforts with pride and gratitude:

> My father refused to send me to Flavius' (the local) school where the big sons of the local gentry went, with school-bag and writing-tablets over their left shoulders, bringing their school fees of eight **asses*** on the Ides of each month. He dared to take me to Rome.
>
> Horace, *Satires* I.6.71–76

Pliny, who showed his interest in a practical way by contributing money to found a school in his native town of Comum, was also concerned that education should be more than book-learning:

> But now the most important thing is who gives him his instruction. Up to the present he has been at home and has had teachers there. At home there is little or no opportunity for going astray. Now his studies must be carried away from home, and we must find a teacher of Latin rhetoric in whose school we shall find a strict training along with good manners and moral standards.
>
> Pliny, *Letters* III.3

A character in a novel of Petronius deplores the acceptance of lax standards of discipline in schools:

> What's to be done? It's the parents who are to blame for refusing to let their children benefit by severe discipline. But now boys play in school, young men are laughing-stocks in public and, what is worse than either, they refuse to admit in old age the mistakes they learned at school.
>
> Petronius, *Satyricon* 4

*about 19 cents

Quintilian, a famous "professor" of rhetoric in Rome at the period of our story, has a very different attitude from that of the cruel schoolmaster about whom Martial wrote (see above, page 104):

> The teacher should adopt before all things the attitude of a parent toward his pupils and consider that he is taking the place of those by whom their children have been entrusted to him. He should not have faults himself, nor should he allow his pupils to have any. He should be strict but not harsh, courteous but not lax, lest the former breed hatred, the latter contempt. He should not be bad-tempered, but neither should he pass over what requires correction. When praising the speeches of his pupils, he should be neither grudging nor effusive, for the one will lead to distaste for the work, the other to over-confidence.
>
> Quintilian, *Institutio oratoria* II.4–8

ST. AUGUSTINE AND PLINY ON EDUCATION

The following passages give two very personal and sharply contrasting views of education. St. Augustine, writing in the late fourth century A.D., looks back on his school days with horror. Pliny, on the other hand, writing in the early second century A.D., remembers his schooling with great fondness:

> Then I was put into school to get learning, in which I (poor wretch) did not know what use there was. And yet, if sluggish in my learning, I was beaten. What miseries and mockeries did I experience then!
>
> St. Augustine, *Confessions* I.9

> Thanks to you, I am returning to school and (as it were) taking up again the sweetest part of my life; I take my seat, as I used to, with the youngsters and I experience how much respect my learning has among them.
>
> Pliny, *Letters* II.18

ADDITIONAL READING:
The Romans Speak for Themselves: Book II: "Early Education in Rome," pages 41–49.

CHAPTER 39

A Lesson for Sextus

Postquam Marcus fīnem recitandī fēcit, grammaticus, "Illī versūs bene recitātī sunt. Nunc dīc mihi hoc! Quot sunt verba in prīmō versū?" "Quīnque." "Sed quot in secundō versū?" "Octō." "Quid dē verbō *conticuēre* mihi dīcere potes?" "*Conticuēre* est idem ac *conticuērunt*. Sīc verbum saepe scrībunt poētae."

"Bene respondistī. Et tū, Aule, dīc mihi hoc! Quī sunt 'omnēs'?" "Troiānī ūnā cum rēgīnā et comitibus." "Ubi sunt hī omnēs?" "In Āfricā." "Quō in locō?" "Carthāginī." "Unde vēnit Aenēās?" "Troiā." "Quō itinere Troiā nāvigāvit?" "Prīmum ad Siciliam vēnit; deinde tempestāte Carthāginem āctus est."

"Multa tamen dē hāc fābulā omittis, nam Aenēās comitēsque multōs annōs errābant antequam ad Siciliam advēnērunt. Prīmum ad Thrāciam, deinde Dēlum, tum ad Crētam nāvigāvērunt. Cūr nusquam morātus est Aenēās, Marce?" "Monitus ā dīs, Aenēās semper Hesperiam petēbat. Volēbat enim novam condere Troiam."

Omnēs discipulī grammaticum attentē audiēbant—praeter Sextum quī dormitābat. Quem ubi animadvertit grammaticus, "Sexte," clāmāvit, "Expergīscere! Dīc mihi! Ubi est Hesperia?"

(continued)

1 **fīnem recitandī fēcit,** *(he) made an end of reciting, (he) stopped reciting*
2 **verbum, -ī,** n., *word, verb*
3 **idem ac,** *the same as*
4 **sīc,** adv., *thus, in this way*
6 **comes, comitis,** m./f., *companion*
8 **Carthāgō, Carthāginis,** f., *Carthage (city on the northern coast of Africa)*
10 **antequam,** conj., *before*
Thrācia, -ae, f., *Thrace (country northeast of Greece)*
Dēlos, Dēlī, f., *Delos (small island off the eastern coast of Greece)*
Crēta, -ae, f., *Crete (large island southeast of Greece)*
11 **nusquam,** adv., *nowhere*
moneō, -ēre, -uī, -itus, *to advise, warn*
deus, -ī, nom. pl., **dī,** dat., abl. pl., **dīs,** m., *god*
13 **dormitō, -āre, -āvī,** *to be sleepy*

3 **conticēscō, conticēscere, conticuī,** *to become silent*
14 **animadvertō, animadvertere, animadvertī, animadversus,** *to notice*
expergīscor, expergīscī, experrēctus sum, *to wake up*

Exercise 39a

Respondē Latīnē:

1. Quid Marcus grammaticō dīcit dē verbō *conticuēre*?
2. Quō errābat Aenēās antequam ad Siciliam advēnit?
3. Cūr Aenēās Hesperiam semper petēbat?
4. Quid faciēbat Sextus, dum cēterī discipulī grammaticum audiēbant?

"Hesperia? Nōnne est Graecia?" "Minimē, ō puer abōminande! Hesperia est Italia." "Nīl interest," mussāvit Sextus.

"At maximē interest," respondit grammaticus, īrā maximā commōtus. Ferulam sūmpsit et vōce terribilī, "Extende manum, Sexte!" clāmāvit. Cēterī discipulī conticuērunt. At Sextus grammaticō nōn pāruit. "Nōn extendam," inquit. Stupuit grammaticus. Longum fuit silentium. Tandem, "Abī, puer!" clāmat. "Vocā Eucleidem paedagōgum! Ille tē domum dūcet. Satis procācitātis tuae passus sum. Tē hūc redīre vetō, nisi labōrāre volēs. Nunc abī!"

Cēterī discipulī verbīs grammaticī territī erant. Numquam anteā puer domum missus erat.

17 **interest,** *it is important*
18 **ferula, -ae,** f., *cane*
19 **extendō, extendere, extendī, extentus,** *to hold out*
20 **pāreō, -ēre, -uī** + dat., *to obey*

Respondē Latīnē:

1. Quid respondit Sextus dē Hesperiā rogātus?
2. Quid sūmpsit grammaticus?
3. Quōmodo grammaticus "Extende manum!" dīcit?
4. Cūr Sextus ā grammaticō domum missus est?

BUILDING THE MEANING

Place Clues

Look at the following sentences:

Ad Forum festīnant.	*They hurry* ***to the Forum.***
Rōmam festīnāvit.	*He hurried* ***to Rome.***
Ē lūdō venit Eucleidēs.	*Eucleides comes* ***from the school.***
Brundisiō discesserat Pūblius.	*Publius had departed* ***from Brundisium.***
Cornēlius **in ātriō** amīcōs exspectat.	*Cornelius waits for his friends* ***in the atrium.***
Pūblius **Baiīs** morābātur.	*Publius was staying* ***in Baiae.***

In the first sentence of each pair, the preposition and the case of the noun give clues to the meaning of the phrase. In the second sentence of each pair, there is no preposition. This is normal with names of cities, towns, and small islands.

NOTES

1. With names of cities, towns, and small islands, the *accusative case* without a preposition indicates place *to which*:

Rōmam festīnāvit.	*He hurried **to Rome.***
Dēlum nāvigāvit.	*He sailed **to Delos.***

2. With names of cities, towns, and small islands, the *ablative case* without a preposition may indicate place *from which:*

Brundisiō discesserat Pūblius.	*Publius had gone **from Brundisium.***
Dēlō abiit.	*He went away **from Delos.***
Baiīs profectus est.	*He set out **from Baiae.***

With names of cities, towns, and small islands, the *locative case* without a preposition indicates place *in which*. The endings of the locative case are as follows:

a. singular nouns of the 1st and 2nd declensions: identical in spelling to the *genitive*:

Rōm***ae*** manēbat.	*He was remaining **in Rome.***
Brundisi***ī*** habitat.	*He lives **in Brundisium.***

b. singular nouns of the 3rd declension: same as *ablative* (sometimes *dative*):

Sīdōn***e*** multa ēmit.	*He bought many things **in Sidon.***
Carthāgin***ī*** cōmiter acceptus est.	*He was received graciously **at Carthage.***

c. plural nouns: same as *ablative*:

Bai***īs*** vīllam habet.	*He has a farm **in Baiae.***
Gād***ibus*** morābātur.	*He was staying **at Gades.***

3. When a noun has the same endings for both place *from which* and place *in which*, the verb will help with the meaning:

Bai***īs*** manēbat.	*He was remaining **in Baiae.***
Bai***īs*** profectus est.	*He set out **from Baiae.***

4. The words **domus**, *home*, and **rūs**, *country*, *country estate*, behave in a similar way:

Accusative of place to which:

Domum iit.	*He went **home.***
Rūs iit.	*He went **to the country/to his country estate.***

Ablative of place from which:

Domō profectus est.	*He set out **from home.***
Rūre rediit.	*He returned **from the country/from his country estate.***

Locative of place where:

Domī est.	*He is **at home.***
Rūrī est.	*He is **in the country/on his country estate.***

The word **rūs, rūris** is a regular 3rd declension neuter noun; its locative is **rūrī**. The feminine noun **domus** appears as a 4th declension noun (see the forms at the left below), but some of its cases have 2nd declension alternatives (at the right below), of which the locative is one:

	Singular		Plural	
Nominative	dom***us***		dom***ūs***	
Genitive	dom***ūs***	dom***ī*** (locative)	dom***uum***	dom***ōrum***
Dative	dom***uī***	dom***ō***	dom***ibus***	
Accusative	dom***um***		dom***ūs***	dom***ōs***
Ablative	dom***ū***	dom***ō***	dom***ibus***	
Vocative	dom***us***		dom***ūs***	

Omnia Rōmae cum pretiō. *Everything is available in Rome—for a price!* (Juvenal, *Satires* III.183–184)

Exercise 39b

Use each place name listed below to replace the italicized words in the following sentences. Use the prepositions **ab, in,** or **ad** *only where necessary*:

1. Mox *ad urbem* veniam.
2. Iam *ab urbe* discessī.
3. Diū *in urbe* morābar.

Āfrica, -ae, f.
Athēnae, -ārum, f. pl., *Athens*
Baiae, -ārum, f. pl.
Brundisium, -ī, n.
Carthāgō, Carthāginis, f.
Dēlos, Dēlī, f.
domus, -ūs, f.
Gādēs, Gādium, f. pl.
Gallia, -ae, f., *Gaul*
Philippī, -ōrum, m. pl.
Rōma, -ae, f.
rūs, rūris, n.
Sīdōn, Sīdōnis, f.

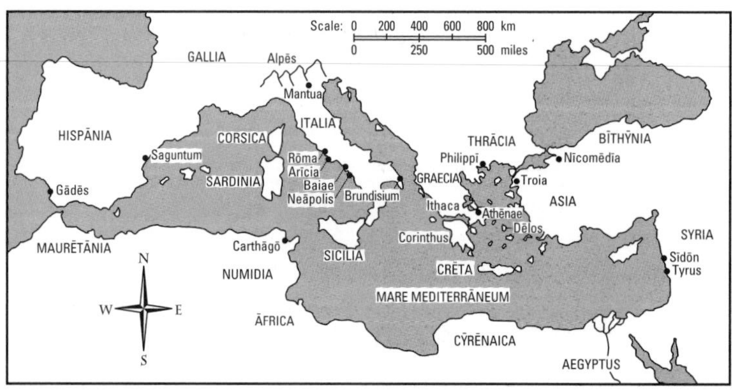

Exercise 39c

Read aloud and translate:

1. Ubi Graecī fīnem bellī fēcērunt, Ulixēs cum comitibus Troiā profectus est.
2. Domum redīre et uxōrem suam vidēre volēbat.
3. Multīs post annīs Ithacam pervēnit.
4. Cornēliī aestāte Baiīs, hieme Rōmae habitant. Nunc autem Cornēliī domī Rōmae sunt.
5. Aestāte Cornēliī domō proficīscuntur; Baiās eunt; rūrī habitant.
6. Aenēās, quī ē Siciliā profectus erat, magnā tempestāte iactātus, Carthāginem tandem advēnit.
7. Carthāginī Aenēās breve modo tempus morābātur; Carthāgine discessit quod novam urbem in Italiā condere volēbat.
8. Hannibal, ubi Saguntum, oppidum Hispāniae, cēpit, iter longum per Galliam et trāns Alpēs in Italiam fēcit.
9. Mox Quīntus Valerius, amīcus Cornēliōrum, ē Bīthȳniā Rōmam regrediētur. Tribus mēnsibus domum perveniet.

bellum, -ī, n., *war*
multīs post annīs, *many years afterward*
hiems, hiemis, f., *winter*
iactō, -āre, -āvī, -ātus, *to toss about, drive to and fro*
oppidum, -ī, *n., town*
Hispānia, -ae, f., *Spain*
trāns, prep. + acc., *across*

Time Clues

1. Prepositions will be found introducing some expressions of time:

post multōs annōs	***after*** *many years*
ante prīmam lūcem	***before*** *dawn*

2. Words or phrases in the accusative or ablative cases without prepositions are found expressing other ideas of time:

a. *Accusative of duration of time:*

mult***ōs*** ann***ōs***	*throughout many years, for many years*
tōt***um*** di***em***	*throughout the whole day, for the whole day*

b. *Ablative of time when* and *ablative of time within which*:

aestāt***e***	*in summer*
e***ō*** tempor***e***	*at that time*
prīm***ā*** lūc***e***	*at dawn*
Īd***ibus*** Mārti***īs***	*on the Ides of March*
brev***ī*** tempor***e***	*within a short time, in a short time, soon*
tr***ibus*** mēns***ibus***	*in three months*

3. Adverbs are found in some expressions of time:

a. You have seen adverbs such as the following very frequently (see Chapter 13 of Level I): **crās,** *tomorrow*; **hodiē,** *today*; **iam,** *now*, *already*; **iterum,** *again*, *a second time*; **nunc,** *now*; etc. These cause no problems, but note the following:

b. **abhinc,** *back from this point in time, ago* + accusative of duration of time:

abhinc trēs diēs	***back from the present*** *for three days = three days* ***ago***

c. **post,** *after(ward)* + ablative
ante, *previously, before* + ablative:

tribus **post** diēbus	***afterward*** *by three days = three days* ***later***
tribus **ante** diēbus	***previously*** *by three days = three days* ***before***

Note that **post** and **ante** may be either prepositions with the accusative or adverbs with the ablative.

Exercise 39d

Select, read aloud, and translate:

1. Puerī ē lūdō (sextā hōrā/paucīs mēnsibus/decem hōrās) rediērunt.
2. Hodiē, Marce, (trēs hōrās/aestāte/ante prīmam lūcem) surrēxistī.
3. Graecī Troiam (quīnque mēnsēs/tribus annīs/decem annōs) obsidēbant.
4. Nōs apud Cornēlium (ūnum mēnsem/nōnā hōrā/tōtum diem) cēnābimus.
5. Ad vīllam (tōtum diem/duōs mēnsēs/aestāte) profectī estis.
6. Ego ad urbem (abhinc trēs diēs/octō mēnsēs/ūnō annō) advēnī.
7. Aenēās comitēsque (duōbus diēbus/multōs annōs/septem annīs) errābant.
8. Sextus iam (ūnō annō/trēs mēnsēs/quīnque hōrīs) in urbe habitat.
9. Discipulī versūs Vergiliī (tōtum diem/brevī tempore/ūnō diē) legēbant.
10. Convīvae ad domum Cornēliānam (brevī tempore/quattuor hōrās/ūnam noctem) advenient.

Exercise 39e

Using story 39 and the information on place and time clues as guides, give the Latin for:

1. When did Aeneas and his companions sail from Troy?
2. Many years later they came to Sicily.
3. They were driven to Carthage by a storm.
4. For many months they remained in Carthage; finally they returned to Sicily.
5. After a long journey they arrived at Hesperia.

Exercise 39f

Read this story of Vergil's life aloud and answer in English the questions that follow:

Pūblius Vergilius Marō, maximus poētārum Rōmānōrum, nātus est Īdibus Octōbribus prope Mantuam, quod est oppidum Italiae septentriōnālis. Puer Cremōnam missus, ab optimīs magistrīs ibi doctus, sextō decimō annō togam virīlem sūmpsit. Paulisper domī in patris fundō morātus, profectus est adulēscēns Mediolānum. Paucōs annōs et litterīs et linguae Graecae dīligentissimē studēbat. Mox tamen, quod pater post bellum ē fundō suō expulsus erat, Vergilius Rōmam cum patre migrāvit. Dum Rōmae habitat, versūs multīs dē rēbus scrīpsit et mox praeclārus factus est poēta. In numerō amīcōrum et poētam Horātium et prīncipem Augustum ipsum habēbat; sed (ēheu!) saepe aegrōtābat et semper īnfirmā erat valētūdine. Interdum Neāpolī in sōlitūdine vīvēbat. Iam quīnquāgintā annōs nātus dum in Graeciā iter facit, prīncipī occurrit Athēnīs. Quī, ad Italiam rediēns, Vergilium sēcum dūxit. Athēnīs profectī ad Italiam nāvigāvērunt. In terram ēgressus Brundisium, Vergilius aegerrimus fīēbat et in eō oppidō mortuus est. Corpus Neāpolim lātum ab amīcīs trīstissimīs est sepultum.

2 **Mantua, -ae,** f., *Mantua* (*town in northern Italy*)
septentriōnālis, -is, -e, *northern*
3 **Cremōna, -ae,** f., *Cremona* (*town in northern Italy*)
4 **fundus, -ī** m., *farm*
5 **Mediolānum, -ī,** n., *Milan*
litterae, -ārum, f. pl., *letters, literature*
lingua, -ae, f., *tongue, language*
studeō, -ēre, -uī + dat., *to study*
7 **migrō, -āre, -āvī, -ātūrus,** *to move one's home*
8 **Horātius, -ī,** m., *Horace* (*Roman poet*)
9 **Augustus, -ī,** m., *Augustus* (*first Roman emperor*)
aegrōtō, -āre, -āvī, -ātūrus, *to be ill*
10 **īnfirmā...valētūdine,** *in poor health*
interdum, adv., *from time to time*
12 **rediēns,** *returning*
13 **in terram ēgressus,** *having disembarked*
aeger, aegra, aegrum, *ill*

1 **nāscor, nāscī, nātus sum,** *to be born*
6 **expellō, expellere, expulī, expulsus,** *to drive out, expel*
10 **vīvō, vīvere, vīxī, vīctūrus,** *to live*
14 **morior, morī, mortuus sum,** *to die*
sepeliō, sepelīre, sepelīvī, sepultus, *to bury*

1. When and where was Vergil born?
2. Where was he sent as a boy?
3. At what age did he take up the **toga virīlis?**
4. How long did he stay in Milan?
5. What did he study while in Milan?
6. Why did he move to Rome with his father?
7. Who were among his friends in Rome?
8. At what age did he take his fatal trip to Greece?
9. With whom did he return from Greece?
10. Where did Vergil die and where was he buried?

AUGUSTUS

The assassination of Julius Caesar on the Ides of March, 44 B.C., inaugurated a struggle for power in Rome that took fourteen years of war and intrigue to resolve. The ultimate struggle lay between the consul at the time of Caesar's murder, Marcus Antonius (Mark Antony), and Caesar's principal heir, adopted son, and grandnephew, Octavian. The struggle encompassed such drama and such fervor that subsequent ages have drawn upon it repeatedly for great works of art and literature. Early on in the struggle Cicero fell victim to proscriptions instituted by the Second Triumvirate, a coalition of Octavian, Antony, and Caesar's old lieutenant Lepidus, to fight their common political enemies in the name of avenging Caesar. At Antony's insistence, Cicero's severed head and hands were put on display on the Rostra in the Forum. The conclusion of the struggle was marked by Octavian's victory over Antony at the naval battle of Actium in 31 B.C. and the suicides of Antony and Cleopatra. Octavian was eighteen years old when the struggle began and thirty-two when he finally prevailed. He showed himself to be a ruthless military and political strategist and leader, but his great contributions were to begin when he took the helm in Rome in 30 B.C.

Antony and Cleopatra as the subjects of Shakespeare's tragedy
Antony and Cleopatra by American artist Rockwell Kent

PAX ROMANA

After more than 100 years of political turmoil and civil wars, it seemed that a chance for a lasting peace had come to Rome. In 27 B.C., after adjusting the membership of the Senate and laying other groundwork, Octavian proclaimed the Restoration of the Republic. On the surface he appeared to have put the old constitution back in place: the Senate regained its role of leadership; the popular assemblies met as before to pass laws and elect magistrates to the offices of the **cursus honōrum**. It was in gratitude for this "restoration" that the senators awarded him the title **Augustus,** *Venerable,* by which title he is principally remembered today. In fact, however, it was he who ruled the Empire as its first emperor, and certain powers the Senate granted him assured his authority (**auctoritās**). He had the right to propose legislation in the assemblies as well as decrees in the Senate, where he ranked as senior senator, a position that allowed him to speak first with the consequence of encouraging subsequent speakers to support his proposals. He held guaranteed control over the armies, foreign affairs, and the provinces. The title he preferred for himself, however, was not **imperātor,** *commander,* hence, "emperor," but simply **prīnceps,** *first citizen,* hence, "prince." More important than any titles was his talent for convincing people to do what he wanted without seeming to order their actions.

Later in his life, Augustus personally recorded his accomplishments in his official memoirs, *The Deeds of the Deified Augustus (Res gestae Divi Augusti).* His account was published on inscriptions that were placed at his tomb in Rome and elsewhere in the empire. One inscription, which survived on the walls of a temple in Ankara, Turkey, is called, because of its location, the **Monumentum Ancyrānum**. In the text Augustus lists the offices and honors he held, his private funding of public works, and his achievements in war and peace. He also stresses that he was just in his treatment of his enemies and always acted within the legal guidelines of the republican constitution that he restored.

The remarkable **auctoritās** that Augustus possessed enabled him to lay the foundation of imperial government. Throughout the empire, professional armies loyal to the emperor enforced the **pāx Rōmāna** that he had established. In the *Res gestae* Augustus indicates his own pride in the peace when he mentions the consecration of the Altar of Augustan Peace (**Āra Pācis Augustae**) on the Campus Martius and the ceremonial closing of the doors of the Shrine of Janus Quirinus three times during his principate, a symbolic gesture of peace for Rome that had occurred only twice before since the founding of the city in 753 B.C.

On those occasions when Augustus did order the doors of the Shrine of Janus opened, the armies under his **imperium** extended the northern frontiers to the Rhine and Danube Rivers, so that communication between the eastern and western provinces was firmly protected. Late in his principate Augustus suffered one military defeat. In A.D. 9, Quinctilius Varus led three legions into a trap in the Teutoberger Forest, where the Germans slaughtered them. Augustus thereupon gave up his attempt to conquer and Romanize Germany. He expressed his displeasure by banging his head against a door in the palace and crying out, "Quinctilius Varus, give me back my legions!"

Augustus realized that he could not direct everything in the empire single-handedly; he therefore created an imperial bureaucracy, staffed by members of the senatorial and equestrian classes, to whom he delegated the responsibility of administering law and order in the provinces and in the city. The **lēgātī** who served as governors in Augustus' proconsular provinces were paid well enough so that they stayed at their posts for years and administered their duties knowledgeably and efficiently. Within the city of Rome **praefectī** and **cūrātōrēs** managed public works and agencies concerned with the citizens' welfare. The superintendent of aqueducts (**cūrātor aquārum**), for example, was in charge of the aqueducts and water supply, and the commander of watchmen (**praefectus vigilum**) commanded the companies of **vigilēs**, who dealt with fire-fighting and minor criminals.

The Roman Empire in the Age of Augustus

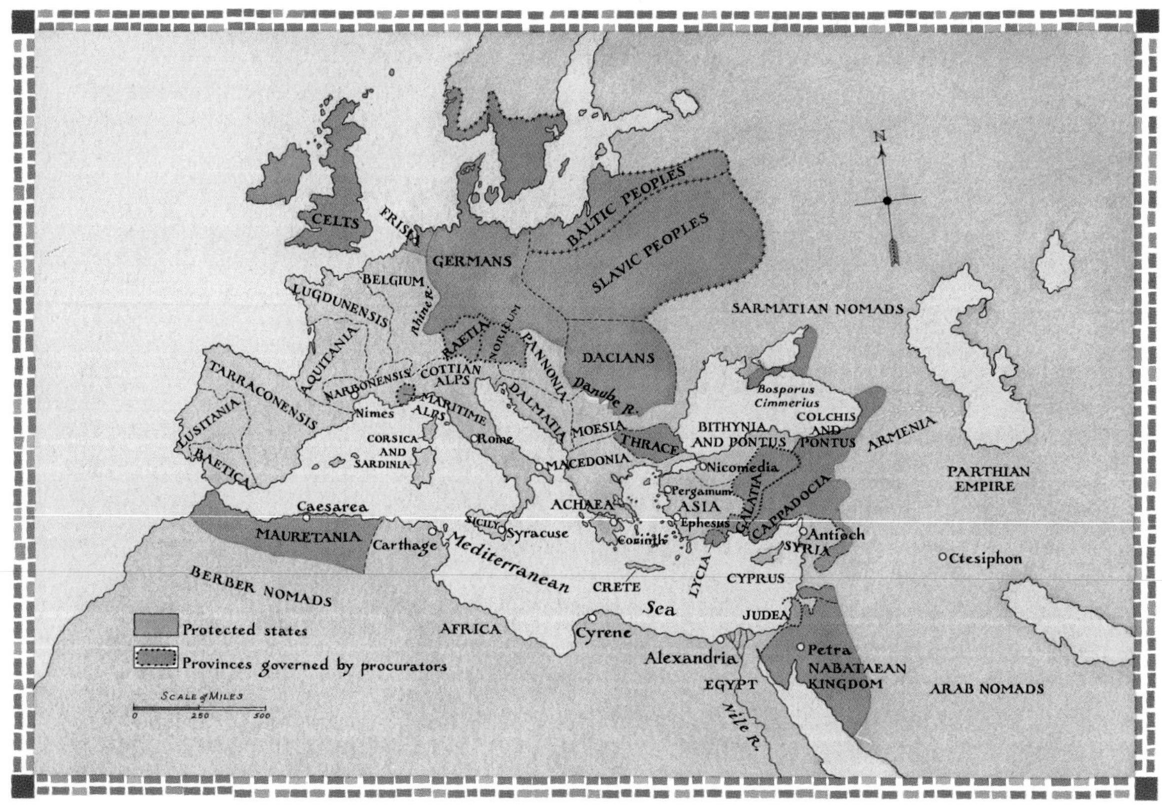

Under Augustus' influence, then, the Roman Empire enjoyed a sound economy, marked by increased trade and prosperity and by solvent state finances. To sense that Rome was becoming more prosperous, the citizens of Rome had only to look about them and observe the ambitious building program directed by Augustus and Marcus Agrippa, his right-hand man and son-in-law: the renovation of many old buildings, the completion of the Basilica Julia, and the construction of a new Forum. In addition, to make sure that everyone realized how great Rome, Italy, and their **prīnceps** were, the writers of the Augustan age concentrated on literary themes that glorified the Romans and their nation. Livy's impressive books on the history of Rome supported the idea that Roman character, as displayed by heroes of the past, was the source of Roman greatness. Gaius Maecenas, a wealthy equestrian businessman and a friend of Augustus, was a patron who supported several poets who helped propagandize Augustan nationalism. Horace owed him his Sabine villa and the leisure to explore patriotic themes in his *Odes* as well as the traditional topics of lyric poetry. Vergil dedicated to Maecenas his *Georgics*, poems that praised the Italian landscape and country life, where the Italian peasant farmer flourished.

Even more stirring was Vergil's epic, the *Aeneid*, in which, long before Rome was founded, Jupiter told his daughter Venus that he had granted the Romans "rule without limit" (**imperium sine fine**) and that a Caesar, descended from the Trojans, would rise to power after many centuries and that the gates of war of the Shrine of Janus would be closed. Later in the epic, when the hero, Aeneas, visits the underworld, his father, Anchises, foretells the future greatness of Rome and specifically points out the spirit of Augustus Caesar, son of a god, who will establish again for Latium a Golden Age (**Aurea Saecula**).

Augustus and Livia
Marble statues, Ephesus Museum, Turkey

At the climax of his predictions, Anchises instructs Aeneas:

> "Tū regere imperiō populōs, Rōmāne, mementō
> (hae tibi erunt artēs) pācisque impōnere mōrem,
> parcere subiectīs et dēbellāre superbōs."

Aeneid VI.851–853

> "You, Roman, remember to rule nations with power
> (these will be your skills) and to impose the conditions of peace,
> to spare the conquered and to conquer the arrogant."

That, Anchises tells both Aeneas and, through Vergil's epic, the Romans of Augustus' generation, is Rome's mission.

Exercise 39g

Here are the first seven lines of Vergil's *Aeneid.* Read them aloud and translate them:

> Arma virumque canō, Troiae quī prīmus ab ōrīs
> Ītaliam fātō profugus Lāvīniaque vēnit
> lītora, multum ille et terrīs iactātus et altō
> vī superum, saevae memorem Iūnōnis ob īram,
> multa quoque et bellō passus, dum conderet urbem
> īnferretque deōs Latiō, genus unde Latīnum
> Albānīque patrēs atque altae moenia Rōmae.

1 **arma, -ōrum,** n. pl., *arms, weapons*
ōra, -ae, f., *shore*
2 **fātum, -ī,** n., *fate*
profugus, -a, -um, *exiled, fugitive*
Lāvīnius, -a, -um, *of Lavinium (name of the town where the Trojans first settled in Italy)*
3 **lītus, lītoris,** n., *shore*
altum, -ī, n., *the deep, the sea*
4 **superī, -ōrum,** m. pl., *the gods above*
superum = superōrum
saevus, -a, -um, *fierce, savage*
memor, memoris, *remembering, mindful, unforgetting*
Iūnō, Iūnōnis, f. *Juno (queen of the gods)*
ob, prep. + acc., *on account of*
5 **dum conderet…īnferretque,** *until he could found…and bring…into*
6 **Latium, -ī,** n., *Latium (the area of central Italy that included Rome)*
genus, generis, n., *race, stock, nation*
7 **Albānus, -a, -um,** *of Alba Longa (city founded by Aeneas' son, Ascanius)*
moenia, moenium, n. pl., *city walls*

1 **canō, canere, cecinī, cantus,** *to sing*

Mantua mē genuit, Calabrī rapuēre, tenet nunc
Parthenopē: cecinī pascua, rūra, ducēs.
Mantua gave me life, Calabria took it away, now
Naples holds me: I sang of pastures, fields, and heroes.
(Inscription on the tomb of Vergil)

Vergil reading the *Aeneid* to Augustus and his sister, Octavia, memorialized here by Ingres. Legend has it that Octavia fainted when Vergil reached the verses about the death of her son.
Watercolor and graphite drawing, the Fogg Art Museum, Harvard University, Cambridge. Bequest of Grenville L. Winthrop

CHAPTER 40

TO FATHER FROM SEXTUS

Sextus patrī suō S.P.D.

Avē, mī pater! Sī tū valēs, ego gaudeō. Sed nēmō est mē miserior. Māter mea Pompeiīs mortua est. Tū mē in Italiā relīquistī, cum in Asiam profectus es. O mē miserum!

Prīmō quidem Baiīs habitāre mē dēlectābat. Ibi ad lītus īre, in marī natāre, scaphās spectāre solēbam. In silvīs quoque cum Marcō cotīdiē ambulābam; inde regressus, cum vīlicō Dāvō, quī mē maximē amat, in hortō labōrābam.

Ōlim, dum prope rīvum in silvīs ambulāmus, Cornēliam et Flāviam magnā vōce clāmantēs audīvimus. Statim accurrimus et lupum ingentem puellās petentem cōnspeximus. Tum Marcus, maximō terrōre affectus, arborem ascendit neque dēsilīre ausus est. Ego tamen magnō rāmō lupum reppulī et puellās servāvī sōlus.

At abhinc paucōs mēnsēs nōs omnēs, Baiīs profectī, maximō itinere Rōmam pervēnimus. Dum autem Rōmae habitō, mē dēlectat ad Circum Maximum īre. Russātīs ego faveō quī semper vincunt.

(continued)

2 **Avē!/Avēte!** *Greetings!*
valeō, -ēre, -uī, -itūrus, *to be strong, be well*
5 **prīmō,** adv., *first, at first*
natō, -āre, -āvī, -ātūrus, *to swim*
scapha, -ae, f., *small boat*
6 **inde,** adv., *from there, then*

10 **dēsiliō, dēsilīre, dēsiluī,** *to leap down*
11 **audeō, audēre, ausus sum,** semi-deponent + infin., *to dare (to)*
repellō, repellere, reppulī, repulsus, *to drive off, drive back*

Exercise 40a
Respondē Latīnē:

1. Ubi nunc est Sextī pater?
2. Quid Sextus Baiīs facere solēbat?
3. Quis Sextum maximē amābat?
4. Dīcitne Sextus vēra?
5. Dīcitne Sextus vēram fābulam dē puellīs et lupō?
6. Quid Sextum Rōmae facere dēlectat?
7. Cūr Sextus russātīs favet?

vērus, -a, -um, *true*
vēra dīcere, *to tell the truth*

Nunc tamen miserrimus sum propter īrācundiam Palaemonis magistrī nostrī. Ille enim homō īrācundissimus mē, quamquam discere semper cupiō, saepe ferulā ferōciter verberat. Cotīdiē dē Aenēae itineribus multa mē rogat. Eī rogantī respondēre semper cōnor. Cēterōs tamen puerōs semper facillima, mē semper difficillima rogat. Heri quidem dē Hesperiā loquēbātur, dē quā neque ego neque cēterī puerī quidquam sciunt. Immō vērō, etiam Aenēās ipse ignōrābat ubi esset Hesperia! Grammaticus tamen, cum ego ignōrārem, īrā commōtus, ferulam rapuit et mē crūdēlissimē verberāvit. Deinde domum statim ab Eucleide ductus sum. Cum prīmum domum advēnimus, ā Cornēliō arcessītus sum. Eī rem tōtam explicāre cōnābar, sed mē nē loquī quidem sīvit. Iterum igitur poenās dedī.

Ō pater, regredere, obsecrō, quam prīmum in Italiam! Ego sum miser et valdē aegrōtō. Amā mē et valē!

15 **īrācundia, -ae,** f., *irritability, bad temper*
19 **neque...neque...quidquam,** *neither...nor...anything*
20 **immō vērō,** adv., *on the contrary, in fact*
ignōrō, -āre, -āvī, -ātus, *to be ignorant, not to know*
cum, conj., *since*
21 **crūdēlis, -is, -e,** *cruel*
22 **cum prīmum,** conj., *as soon as*
24 **poena, -ae,** f., *punishment, penalty*
poenās dare, *to pay the penalty, be punished*
25 **obsecrō, -āre, -āvī, -ātus,** *to beseech, beg*
quam prīmum, adv., *as soon as possible*

16 **discō, discere, didicī,** *to learn*
cupiō, cupere, cupīvī, cupītus, *to desire, want*
21 **rapiō, rapere, rapuī, raptus,** *to snatch, seize*
23 **arcessō, arcessere, arcessīvī, arcessītus,** *to summon, send for*

Respondē Latīnē:

1. Estne Palaemōn magister vērō īrācundissimus?
2. Estne rogātiō dē Hesperiā vērō facilis vel difficilis?
3. Aegrōtatne vērō Sextus?

rogātiō, rogātiōnis, f., *question*

FORMS

Semi-deponent Verbs

Some Latin verbs have regular active forms with active meanings in the present, imperfect, and future tenses but have passive forms with active meanings in the perfect, pluperfect, and future perfect:

audeō, audēre, ausus sum + infin., *to dare (to)*
gaudeō, gaudēre, gāvīsus sum, *to be glad, rejoice*
soleō, solēre, solitus sum + infin., *to be accustomed (to), be in the habit of*

These are called *semi-deponent verbs* because they are deponent (i.e., they have passive forms with active meanings) only in the perfect, pluperfect, and future perfect tenses, those made from the third principal part.

Exercise 40b

Read aloud and translate:

1. audet
2. audēbis
3. ausus sum
4. audēbāmus
5. ausī erāmus
6. audētis
7. ausae erunt
8. ausī sunt
9. gaudēmus
10. gāvīsae sumus
11. gaudēbāmus
12. gāvīsī eritis
13. gāvīsus es
14. gāvīsa eris
15. gaudēbunt
16. gāvīsus eram
17. solent
18. solitī sumus
19. solēbāmus
20. solitī eritis
21. solētis
22. solitae erāmus
23. solēbam
24. solēbitis

BUILDING THE MEANING

Present Participles

Look at the following sentence:

Cornēliam et Flāviam **clāmantēs** audīvimus. (40:8–9)
We heard Cornelia and Flavia ***shouting.***

The word **clāmantēs** is a *present active participle*. As you learned in Chapter 33, participles are *verbal adjectives*, that is, adjectives made from the stems of verbs. The participle **clāmantēs** is a verbal adjective describing **Cornēliam et Flāviam.**

Here are some further examples:

Cornēliam et Flāviam magnā vōce **clāmantēs** audīvimus. (40:8–9)
We heard Cornelia and Flavia ***shouting*** *with a loud voice/loudly.*

Lupum ingentem puellās **petentem** cōnspeximus. (40:9–10)
We caught sight of a huge wolf ***attacking*** *the girls.*

Since participles are *verbal* adjectives, they can be modified by ablatives such as **magnā vōce**, and they can take direct objects such as **puellās**, as seen in the sentences above.

Translating Present Participles:

The present participle describes an action going on *at the same time* as the action of the main verb in the clause. Translation of the participle will vary according to the tense of the main verb:

Puellās **clāmantēs** audīmus. (main verb present tense)
We hear the girls ***shouting.***
We hear the girls ***who are shouting.***

(continued)

Puellās **clāmantēs** audīvimus. (main verb perfect tense)
We heard the girls ***shouting****.*
We heard the girls ***who <u>were</u> shouting.***

Present participles can sometimes best be translated into English as relative clauses (see the examples just above). Sometimes they can best be translated as clauses introduced by subordinating conjunctions:

Puerī **currentēs** dēfessī fīunt.
The boys ***when/while running*** *become tired.*
The boys ***because/since they are running*** *become tired.*

Puerī **currentēs** tamen dēfessī nōn fīunt.
The boys, ***although they are running****, nevertheless do not become tired.*

Present Participles as Substantives:

Since participles are adjectives, they can also be used *substantively*, i.e., as words that function as nouns. In Chapter 23 you learned that adjectives may be used substantively, i.e., that **multa et mīra** (neuter plural adjectives) can mean *many wonderful things*. Participles may also be used substantively:

Subitō exclāmāvit ūnus ex **adstantibus**, "Cavēte, omnēs!" (30:18)
Suddenly one of [those] ***standing near*** *shouted, "Watch out, everyone!"*
Suddenly one of ***the bystanders....***

Here the participle **adstantibus** is used as a noun meaning *bystanders*.

Exercise 40c

In your reading you have already met these sentences with present participles. The participles are in boldface. Read the sentences aloud and translate them. When participles are being used as adjectives, tell what noun they modify:

1. "Cavēte!" exclāmant **adstantēs**, sed frūstrā.
2. Subitō Cornēlia duōs servōs per viam **festīnantēs** cōnspicit.
3. Nunc Cornēlia cōnspicit poētam versūs **recitantem**, nunc mendīcōs pecūniam **petentēs**.
4. Convīvae paulisper in ātriō stābant, Cornēlium **exspectantēs**.
5. Titus, ad locum suum lentē **ambulāns**, "Salvēte, amīcī omnēs!" inquit.
6. Ubi īnsulae iam appropinquābāmus, hominēs quōsdam in popīnam **intrantēs** cōnspeximus.
7. Heri vesperī Eucleidēs noster, ab urbe domum **rediēns**, duōs hominēs ē popīnā quādam **exeuntēs** vīdit.

FORMS
Present Participles

Here are the nominative and genitive singular forms of present participles of all four conjugations:

1st:	**parāns, parantis,** *preparing*	*-iō:*	**iaciēns, iacientis,** *throwing*
2nd:	**habēns, habentis,** *having*	4th:	**audiēns, audientis,** *hearing*
3rd:	**mittēns, mittentis,** *sending*		

The participles of deponent verbs have similar active forms and are active in meaning:

1st:	**cōnāns, cōnantis,** *trying*	*-iō:*	**regrediēns, regredientis,** *returning*
2nd:	**verēns, verentis,** *fearing*		
3rd:	**loquēns, loquentis,** *speaking*	4th:	**experiēns, experientis,** *testing*

NOTES
1. The nominative ends in ***-ns***, and the stem, which is found by dropping the ending from the genitive singular, ends in ***-nt-***.
2. The vowel preceding the letters ***-ns*** is always long.
3. The vowel preceding the letters ***-nt-*** is always short.

Present participles have 3rd declension endings. Compare the endings of present participles with those of 3rd declension nouns and adjectives and of comparative adjectives:

When the participle is used as a simple *adjective*, the ablative singular ends in ***-ī***, just as do 3rd declension adjectives; when the participle is used as a true *verbal adjective* or as a *substantive*, the ablative singular ends in ***-e***, just as do 3rd declension nouns, thus:

Number / Case	Masc.	Fem.	Neut.
Singular			
Nominative	parāns	parāns	parāns
Genitive	parant***is***	parant***is***	parant***is***
Dative	parant***ī***	parant***ī***	parant***ī***
Accusative	parant***em***	parant***em***	parāns
Ablative	parant***ī/e***	parant***ī/e***	parant***ī/e***
Plural			
Nominative	parant***ēs***	parant***ēs***	parant***ia***
Genitive	parant***ium***	parant***ium***	parant***ium***
Dative	parant***ibus***	parant***ibus***	parant***ibus***
Accusative	parant***ēs***	parant***ēs***	parant***ia***
Ablative	parant***ibus***	parant***ibus***	parant***ibus***

Eucleidēs ā praedōne **currentī** cōnsecūtus est. (simple adjective)
Eucleides was overtaken by the ***running*** *robber.*

Eucleidēs ā praedōne **celerrimē currente** cōnsecūtus est. (verbal adjective)
Eucleides was overtaken by the robber ***that was running very quickly.***

(continued)

Aqua ab **adstante** ad incendium portāta est. (substantive)
*Water was brought to the fire by **a bystander**.*

The present participle of the verb **īre,** *to go*, is **iēns, euntis.** There is no present participle of the verb **esse,** *to be.*

Exercise 40d

Read aloud and translate. Locate three examples of participles used as substantives. Try translating the other participles with relative clauses or with clauses introduced by *when*, *while*, or *although:*

1. Aenēās Hesperiam petēns Carthāginem advēnit.
2. Marcus patrem epistulās in tablīnō scrībentem invēnit.
3. Adstantēs rogāvī ubi esset incendium.
4. Eucleidēs nocte per viās domum rediēns ā praedōnibus percussus est.
5. Dāvō in hortō labōrantī molestī erant puerī.
6. Mihi rogantī puellae nihil respondērunt.
7. Plūrimī natantium scaphās lītorī appropinquantēs vīdērunt.
8. Audīta est vōx magistrī puerōs reprehendentis.
9. Cornēlius in ātriō Eucleidem exspectāns cēterōs servōs in culīnā colloquentēs audīvit.
10. Cornēliō domō ēgredientī occurrit Titus, frāter eius.
11. Clāmōrēs gaudentium in viīs audītī sunt.
12. Cornēlius servīs fercula in triclīnium portantibus signum dedit.
13. Cornēliī in caupōnā pernoctantēs mortem timēbant.
14. Mulierēs ad templum prōcēdentēs cōnspeximus.
15. Puellae inter sē colloquentēs multa et mīra dē puerīs nārrābant.
16. Nōs domō ēgredientēs mātrem in ātriō sedentem vīdimus.
17. Sextum arborem ascendentem dēsilīre iussī.

Quidquid id est, timeō Danaōs et dōna ferentēs. ***Whatever it is, I fear the Greeks, even bearing gifts.*** **(Vergil, *Aeneid* II.49)**

Venientī occurrite morbō! ***Meet the malady as it comes!*** **(Persius, *Satires* III.64)**

Rīdentem dīcere vērum quid vetat? ***What prevents me from speaking the truth with a smile?*** **(Horace, *Satires* I.I.24–25)**

ROMAN LIFE XXII

WRITING, LETTERS, AND BOOKS

The letter that Cornelia wrote to Flavia in Chapter 36 and the one that Sextus wrote to his father in Chapter 40 would have been written either on tablets (**tabellae** or **cērae**) or on sheets of material made from papyrus. Tablets made of sheets of wood with the surface hollowed out and filled with wax **(cēra)** were widely used for everyday writing needs and in the schools. Two or more tablets could be fastened together with leather thongs laced through holes, and writing was done on the wax surfaces with a stylus (**stilus**) that was pointed at one end for writing and flat at the other end for erasing mistakes by smoothing the wax.

Letters could also be written on sheets of material made from Egyptian papyrus. This material was manufactured in Egypt and exported throughout the Mediterranean world. It was made from the pith of the triangular stalks of the papyrus plant that grew to be four or five inches thick and up to fourteen feet tall. Strips of the pith were laid out side by side, and another layer of strips was placed over them at right angles. When pressed together the papyrus strips released an adhesive agent that bonded them. The resulting sheets of material were then dried in the sun and smoothed with pumice stone as necessary. Sheets could be glued together as needed, and writing was done with pens (**pennae**) made from reeds or metal with ink made from lamp soot and vegetable gum.

If the letter was written on a pair of tablets, they could be folded together with the writing on the inside and bound with a cord that could be sealed with wax and stamped by the letter writer with his or her signet ring. The papyrus paper could be rolled up, bound, and sealed in the same way.

Books were usually produced by gluing sheets of papyrus side by side into a long strip of material that was then rolled up into what was called a **volūmen**, *roll.* The writing was usually done only on the side of the material that was rolled up inside, and it was done in columns perpendicular to the length of the material. To read a papyrus roll you would hold the roll in your right hand and unroll it with your left, rolling it up again at the left hand as you read the successive columns of text as they appeared from the roll at the right. When finished, one would rewind the material to the right so that it would be ready for the next reader to unroll it. A strip of material called a **titulus** was often attached to the edge of the last sheet of papyrus on the roll and would protrude from the roll. On it would be written the author and title of the book. Knobs might also be attached to the top and bottom of the last sheet of the roll to make it easier to roll it up. Since papyrus rolls were relatively fragile, they were often slipped into cases (**capsae** or **capsulae**) and stored in round wooden boxes or cabinets.

In the third century B.C. great libraries flourished in the centers of Greek civilization in the East, with the most famous one being in Alexandria in Egypt. In the late Republic Romans began to collect books in private libraries in their homes. Cicero, for example, had several libraries, both in his town house and at his country estates. During the reign of Augustus public libraries were established in Rome, and by the time of our story libraries were available in some of the great bathing establishments, where one could also hear recitations of literary works.

In an age before printing, copies of books were created by a scribe, shown here as later centuries pictured him.

Oil on canvas, "A Roman Scribe" by Sir Lawrence Alma-Tadema, private collection

Rather than writing themselves, well-to-do Romans would usually have highly trained slaves take dictation. Copies of books could be made by individual slaves copying by sight from an original onto a new papyrus roll or by groups of slaves simultaneously taking dictation from one master reader. The book trade was only loosely organized, but by the time of our story there were book shops in Rome where one could buy books or have copies made. The poet Martial referred to the district in Rome called the Argiletum as a place where his poetry could be bought:

> Of course you often go down to the Argiletum. There is a shop opposite Caesar's Forum with its door-posts from top to bottom bearing advertisements, so that you can in a moment read through the list of poets. Look for me in that quarter. No need to ask Atrectus (that is the name of the shopkeeper): out of the first or second pigeon-hole he will offer you Martial smoothed with pumice and smart with purple, for five **dēnāriī**.
>
> Martial, *Epigrams* I.117.9–17

WORD STUDY X

The Present Participial Stem

The stem of the present participle of a Latin verb sometimes becomes an English noun or adjective with a meaning closely related to that of the Latin verb. The stem of the present participle is found by dropping the ending ***-is*** from the genitive singular, e.g., **laudantis**, stem **laudant-**. The English word *agent* is derived from the Latin **agēns, agentis** (stem: **agent-**), the present participle of **agere**, *to do, drive*. Similarly, the English word *vigilant* is derived from **vigilāns, vigilantis** (stem: **vigilant-**), the present participle of **vigilāre**, *to stay awake*.

Whether the English word ends in *-ant* or *-ent* usually depends on the spelling of the Latin participle from which it is derived, as the above examples show. There are a few exceptions to this rule: they are words that came from Latin into English through Old French, which regularly changed all Latin present participial stems to *-ant*. Such English words end in *-ant*, regardless of the spelling of the original Latin participle. For example, the English word *dormant*, from Old French *dormant*, is derived from **dormiēns, dormientis** (stem: **dormient-**), the present participle of **dormīre**, *to sleep*. To be sure of the correct spelling, always consult an English dictionary.

Exercise 1

Give the English word made from the present participial stem of each of the following Latin verbs. Give the meaning of the English word, and check in a dictionary for its correct spelling:

1. servāre
2. recipere
3. exspectāre
4. accidere
5. patī
6. studēre
7. occupāre
8. dēfendere
9. repellere

Present Participial Stem + Suffix *-ia*

The suffix ***-ia*** may be added to the stem of the present participle of some Latin verbs. The addition of this suffix forms a first declension noun that designates the "state of," "quality of," or "act of" the meaning of the verb:

Latin Verb	Pres. Part.	P. P. Stem	Suffix	Latin Noun
convenīre, *to come together*	**conveniēns, convenientis**	**convenient-**	+ *-ia*	**convenientia, -ae,** f., *agreement, harmony*
cōnstāre, *to stand firm*	**cōnstāns, cōnstantis**	**cōnstant-**	+ *-ia*	**cōnstantia, -ae,** f., *steadiness*

When nouns formed in this way come into English, the letters **-tia** become *-ce* or *-cy*, e.g., *convenience, constancy*.

Exercise 2

For each English word below, give the Latin present participle (nom. sing.) and the meaning of the Latin verb from which it is derived. Give the meaning of the English word. Consult an English dictionary, as necessary:

1. audience
2. currency
3. stance
4. cadence
5. science
6. ambulance
7. sequence
8. eloquence
9. credence

Suffixes *-īnus* and *-(i)ānus*

Some Latin adjectives are formed by adding either the suffix ***-īnus***, ***-a***, ***-um*** or ***-(i)ānus***, ***-a***, ***-um*** to the base of a noun. Such adjectives mean *of* or *pertaining to* the word to which the suffix is attached:

Latin Noun	Base		Suffix		Latin Adjective
Rōma, -ae, f.	**Rōm-**	+	***-ānus***	=	**Rōmānus, -a, -um,** *Roman, of Rome*
mare, maris, n.	**mar-**	+	***-īnus***	=	**marīnus, -a, -um,** *marine, of the sea*

English words derived from this kind of Latin adjective generally end in *-ine* or *-an* (occasionally *-ane*), e.g., *marine, Roman.*

Exercise 3

For each Latin word below, give the Latin adjective ending in ***-(i)ānus***. Give the English derivative and its meaning:

1. **Āfrica, -ae,** f.
2. **silva, -ae,** f.
3. **merīdiēs, -ēī,** m.
4. **Troia, -ae,** f.
5. **vetus, veteris**
6. **urbs, urbis,** f. (two English words)

The suffix ***-īnus*** is commonly found on Latin words for animals, e.g., **canīnus, -a, -um,** *of dogs*. The English derivative is *canine*.

Exercise 4

For each of the following animals, give the Latin adjective ending in ***-īnus***. Give the English derivative and its meaning:

1. **lupus, -ī,** m.
2. **porcus, -ī,** m.
3. **equus, -ī,** m.
4. **bōs, bovis,** m./f.

Latin in Medicine

The roots of modern medicine go back to ancient Greece and Rome. The Greek physician, Hippocrates, who lived in the fifth century B.C., is considered the "father of medicine." In Roman times it was Galen, doctor to the emperor Marcus Aurelius (ruled A.D. 161–180), who expanded the frontiers of medical knowledge. His writings formed the foundation of medical science for centuries. It is no wonder that Latin and Greek are fundamental to the vocabulary of medicine.

Some Latin medical terms have become common English words, e.g., *abdomen* (belly), *cancer* (crab), *virus* (poison). Others are more obscure, e.g., *angina pectoris* (chest pain), *vena cava* ("hollow vein," vein entering the right *atrium* of the heart). Further evidence of medical Latin may be found in doctors' prescriptions, many of which use Latin abbreviations:

Rx (Recipe)	*Take*
c̄ (cum)	*with*
p.c. (post cibum)	*after eating*
t.i.d. (ter in diē)	*3 times a day*
non rep. (nōn repetātur)	*Do not repeat*

Knowledge of Latin (and Greek) can be very helpful in solving the mystery that often surrounds medical language.

Exercise 5

Replace the italicized words in each sentence with a Latin medical term of equivalent meaning, chosen from the pool below. Consult an English dictionary (or medical dictionary) for the meanings of the terms in the pool.

1. The kick Eucleides received was strong enough to break his *shinbone*.
2. Sometimes a doctor will prescribe a *substance containing no medication* in order to humor a patient whose illness is imaginary.
3. The doctor's prescription read, "Take *at bedtime*."
4. The heartbeat of the *unborn child* was normal.
5. The *small piece of tissue* that hangs down at the back of the throat is a Latin word meaning "little grape."
6. The backbone is made up of several *disk-shaped bones*.
7. The doctor wrote "*before meals*" on the prescription.
8. The *brain* is protected by the skull.
9. The ulcer was located in the *intestine measuring twelve fingers long*.
10. The *outer layer* of the adrenal gland produces important substances.
11. Lifting requires contraction of the *two-headed muscle* of the upper arm.
12. The doctor's abbreviation read, "Take *twice a day*."

biceps	vertebrae	H.S. (hōrā somnī)
cerebrum	placebo	duodenum
tibia	a.c. (ante cibum)	b.i.d. (bis in diē)
fetus	uvula	cortex

Exercise 6

Using reference material from a library or from your science teacher, make a diagram of the human skeleton, and label the bones that have Latin or Greek names.

DRAMATIC NEWS

Māne erat. Iam puerī ad lūdum profectī erant. Cornēlia sōla in domō sedēns tēlam sine studiō texēbat. Īrācunda erat quod Baiās regredī atque Flāviam amīcam suam vidēre cupiēbat. Dē multīs rēbus cōgitābat trīstis, cum māter ingressa est.

"Trīstis vidēris, Cornēlia. Aegrane es?"

"Urbs Rōma mihi nōn placet, māter," respondit Cornēlia. "Tōtum diem sōla domī maneō. Mihi nōn licet forās īre. Hīc ego labōrō sōla, sed Marcus et Sextus ūnā cum multīs aliīs in lūdō student. Hīc nūllās amīcās habeō. Hīc nē canem quidem habeō. Cūr nōn Baiās regredī licet? Meam enim Flāviam rūrsus vidēre cupiō."

"Cūr Baiās regredī vīs, Cornēlia? Quīntus Valerius, adulēscēns ille optimus, hūc paucīs diēbus veniet. Nōnne eum vidēre vīs? Diū in Bīthȳniā, ut bene scīs, āfuit sed nunc in Italiam regressus est. Nāve ēgressus, paulisper Brundisiī est morātus. Inde abhinc trēs diēs discessisse dīcitur; paucīs diēbus hūc adveniet. Pater tuus diū loquēbātur cum illō servō quī epistulam attulit. Quī ūnā cum dominō suō ē Bīthȳniā profectus, ē multīs itineris perīculīs vix effūgit atque, ut ipse dīcit, dominum ex hīs perīculīs ēripuit."

Cornēlia, cum hoc audīvisset, maximē gaudēbat quod Valerium vidēre valdē cupiēbat. "Quantum mē dēlectat tālia audīre!" inquit. "Arcesse, obsecrō, māter, illum servum! Ipsa cum eō loquī cupiō et dē hīs perīculīs audīre."

Itaque arcessītus servus rem tōtam eīs nārrāvit.

(continued in Chapter 42)

1 **tēla, -ae,** f., *web, fabric*
2 **studium, -ī,** n., *enthusiasm*
6 **forās,** adv., *outside*
12 **discessisse,** *to have departed*
dīcitur, *(he) is said*
16 **Quantum...!** adv., *How much...!*
tālia, tālium, n. pl., *such things*

2 **texō, texere, texuī, textus,** *to weave*

Exercise 41a

Respondē Latīnē:

1. Quid faciēbat Cornēlia sōla sedēns?
2. Cūr trīstis Cornēlia vidētur?
3. Ubi tōtum diem manet Cornēlia?
4. Puerīne quoque ibi manent?
5. Habetne in urbe amīcās Cornēlia?
6. Quem Cornēlia rūrsus vidēre cupit?
7. Quō Cornēlia regredī cupit?
8. Quis est Valerius?
9. Quandō Rōmam adveniet Valerius?
10. Ubi morātus est Valerius?
11. Unde in Italiam est Valerius regressus?
12. Quōcum Valerius iter fēcit?
13. Quis epistulam ab hōc servō accēpit?
14. Quid necesse fuit Valeriī servō in itinere facere?
15. Cūr servum Valeriī arcessī Cornēlia vult?

FORMS

Verbs: Perfect Active Infinitive

The form **discessisse**, *to have departed*, which you met in line 12 of story 41, is a *perfect active infinitive*. First look at the principal parts of this verb:

discēdō, discēdere, discessī, discessūrus

Two clues will help you recognize the perfect active infinitive:

the perfect stem, **discess-**, formed by dropping the ***-ī*** from the third principal part

the ending ***-isse***

The perfect active infinitive expresses an action that was completed *before* the action of the main verb:

Inde abhinc trēs diēs **discessisse** dīcitur. (41:11–12)
He is said ***to have departed*** *from there three days ago.*

Exercise 41b

Read aloud and translate (note that the verbs in this exercise and the next are all taken from story 41):

1. trāxisse
2. fuisse
3. cupīvisse
4. cōgitāvisse
5. placuisse
6. respondisse
7. mānsisse
8. vīdisse
9. texuisse

Exercise 41c

Give the Latin for:

1. He is said to have studied diligently.
2. . . . to have had a dog.
3. . . . to have seen Valerius in Brundisium.
4. . . . to have wanted to see him.
5. . . . to have come from Bithynia.
6. . . . to have arrived home.
7. . . . to have brought a letter.
8. . . . to have escaped from many dangers.
9. . . . to have snatched his master from these dangers.
10. . . . to have told the whole thing.

FRONTIER LIFE V

WEAVING THE TUNIC

In the previous Frontier Life section, you read how Helge and her friend Helena spun wool into yarn for weaving. In the story at the beginning of this chapter you saw Cornelia weaving fabric while daydreaming of returning to Baiae and seeing her friend Flavia. We resume our story of frontier life with a description of how Helge wove her yarn into a tunic for her husband Lucius.

To weave the wool into a tunic (Helena was making a cloak), Helge used an upright loom with the warp threads weighted down by stones with holes drilled in them. Before she could string the warp, she had to weave the starting border, which would be attached to the top bar of the loom, for the threads extending from this border would be the warp. Using the pegs of the hand loom, Helge measured off from her strongest, stoutest yarn the exact length she would need for the warp, and she then wove a short border, one finger joint wide.

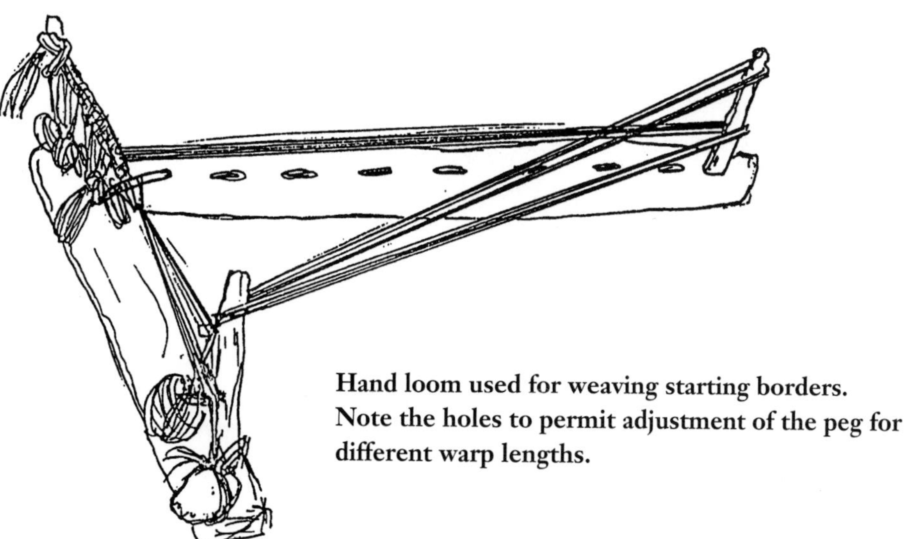

Hand loom used for weaving starting borders. Note the holes to permit adjustment of the peg for different warp lengths.

Her starting border finished, Helge was ready to begin warping her big loom. She attached the border to the round bar that was the top of her loom, taking care that none of the threads became tangled, and she took the warp-weights and arranged them in a row at the base of the loom. She tied the threads to the weights with about six threads to a stone. Weighting all the threads and preparing her loom for the weaving was a painstaking process that took skill and patience. Only then could the weaving of the cloth itself actually begin.

The poet Ovid (*Metamorphoses* VI.55–58) describes the weaving as follows:

> A reed separates the threads of the warp, and the woof is inserted through them with sharp shuttles passed quickly by the fingers, and the notched teeth of the comb pound the woof passed through the warp into place.

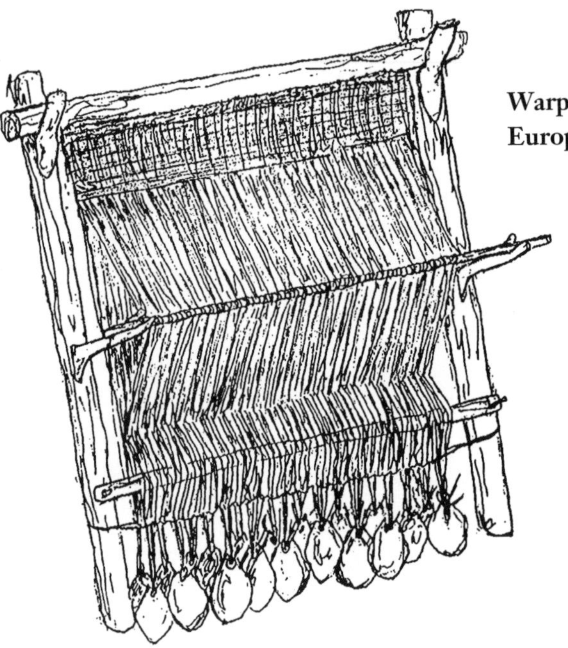

Warp weighted loom of northern Europe, first century A.D.

Since neither Helge nor her mother knew how to read or write, the way that they remembered the patterns of their complicated tartans was by verses of song, handed down from generation to generation. Although Helge was now weaving cloth of a solid color, out of habit she sang a song that told her the instructions and the colors for one of the beautiful clan plaids:

> Red, red for the color of the sun, two strands of red.
> Blue, blue, twenty strands of blue, the color of my eyes.
> Green, five strands of green, the color of the leaves of the oak.
> Red, again red, two strands.
> Yellow, the color of the sun, five strands of yellow, the color of my hair.

Helge continued singing and weaving until the tunic length was finished.

Taking a bone needle, she threaded it with the same red yarn used for the cloth, and passing it in and out she sewed a border at the bottom. She removed the starting border from the pegs at the top of the loom. Carefully folding the tunic length over her arm, she knelt on the floor and untied the warp weights. Then she repeated the whole process and wove another rectangle of material.

In comparison with the weaving, the actual sewing of the tunic was easy. Helge could not help but notice that the amount of fabric needed was just right for a tunic for her younger brother of thirteen but much, much too small for her father or any other grown man of her people; the Romans were that much smaller than the Ubians and other northern clans. Helge hemmed the two rectangles of fabric together, leaving a neck hole, and at the sides leaving openings for the arms. Looking at the finished tunic, she smiled. "Won't my soldier be pleased with his new tunic," she thought as she carefully folded it.

A SLAVE TO THE RESCUE

Quīntus Valerius, dominus meus, abhinc duōs mēnsēs ē Bīthȳniā Rōmam ā patre missus est epistulās ferēns. Ego ūnā cum dominō profectus sum. Cum quattuor diēs nāvigāvissēmus, subitō maxima tempestās coorta est. Nāvis hūc illūc ventīs iactāta in ingentī erat perīculō. Tandem cum undae et ventī nāvem ad īnsulam quandam ēgissent, nōs in terram vix ēvāsimus. Tōtam noctem in lītore morātī, prīmā lūce, quod iam vīs tempestātis cecidisse vidēbātur, in nāvem regressī sumus.

Subitō complūrēs scaphās hominum plēnās cōnspeximus. Magister nāvis nostrae, cum hās scaphās cōnspexisset, "Prō dī immortālēs!" exclāmāvit. "Hī hominēs sunt pīrātae. Ēheu! effugere nōn poterimus."

Cui dominus meus, "Sī mē servāveris," inquit, "pater meus, quī est vir dīves et praeclārus, magnam tibi pecūniam dabit. Haec nāvis est illīs scaphīs celerior. Pīrātae, etiam sī sequentur, nōs nōn capient."

Effugere cōnātī sumus, sed frūstrā. Pīrātae enim, cum nōs effugere cōnantēs cōnspexissent, nāvem nostram adortī sunt. Dominus meus statim gladium strīnxit et mihi clāmāns "Mē sequere!" in scapham dēsiluit.

Ego quidem secūtus dominum meum dēfendere coepī, nam vulnus grave accēpisse vidēbātur. Magister nāvis, cum valdē timēret, suōs vetuit nōs adiuvāre. "Sī pīrātīs resistēmus," inquit, "nōs omnēs sine dubiō necābimur."

(continued)

3 **ventus, -ī,** m., *wind*
4 **unda, -ae,** f., *wave*
7 **scapha, -ae,** f., *small boat, ship's boat*
magister, magistrī, m., *schoolmaster; master, captain*
8 **Prō dī immortālēs!** *Good heavens!*
10 **dīves, dīvitis,** *rich*

3 **coorior, coorīrī, coortus sum,** *to rise up, arise*
5 **ēvādō, ēvādere, ēvāsī, ēvāsus,** *to escape*
14 **adorior, adorīrī, adortus sum,** *to attack*
18 **resistō, resistere, restitī** + dat., *to resist*

Exercise 42a
Respondē Latīnē:

1. Quis Quīntum Valerium ē Bīthȳniā mīsit?
2. Quot diēs nāvigāverant?
3. Quid nāvem iactāvit?
4. Quem ad locum nāvis ācta est?
5. Quō in locō Valerius et servus noctem morātī sunt?
6. Quid magister nāvis prīmā lūce cōnspexit?
7. Quid pīrātae fēcērunt cum nāvem fugientem cōnspexissent?
8. Quid servus facere coepit cum dominus vulnus accēpisset?

Tum pīrātae, cum nōs superāvissent, arma nōbīs adēmērunt et nōs ad lītus addūxērunt. Cum prīmum in terrā fuimus, pīrātae circum nōs stantēs rogābant quī essēmus, unde vēnissēmus, quō iter facerēmus. Omnēs tacēbant praeter dominum meum. Ille enim, "Sī pecūniam vultis," inquit, "nūllam pecūniam hīc inveniētis. Nōs omnēs pauperēs sumus. At nisi nōs abīre sinētis, vōs omnēs poenās certē dabitis. Cīvis sum Rōmānus."

Rīsērunt pīrātae, et ūnus ex eīs exclāmāvit, "Rōmānōs nōn amō. Sī vōs nūllam pecūniam habētis, vōs certē necābimus." Tum magister nāvis metū commōtus, "Hic adulēscēns," inquit, "vēra nōn dīcit. Pater eius est vir dīvitissimus. Ille magnam vōbīs pecūniam dabit." Itaque pīrātārum aliī dominum meum in casam suam trāxērunt, aliī nōs cēterōs in nāvem redūxērunt et ibi custōdiēbant.

Nocte, cum omnēs dormīrent, ego surrēxī, pūgiōne modo armātus. Clam in mare dēsiluī, ad lītus natāvī, casam pīrātārum summā celeritāte petīvī. Cum casae fūrtim appropinquāvissem, per fenestram vīdī dominum meum in lectō iacentem ac duōs custōdēs vīnum bibentēs. Paulisper nihil faciēbam. Mox tamen alter ē custōdibus ē casā exiit, alter cum dominō meō manēbat. Tum ego silentiō ingressus hunc custōdem pūgiōne percussī. Deinde ē casā ēgressus ad lītus dominum portāvī, nam ille propter vulnus aegrōtābat neque ambulāre poterat. Ibi scapham invēnī quam pīrātae nōn custōdiēbant. Ita ā lītore profectī ex īnsulā ēvāsimus.

Iam multōs diēs in scaphā erāmus cum ā mercātōribus quibusdam inventī sumus. Quoniam neque cibum neque aquam habēbāmus, graviter aegrōtābāmus. Sed mercātōrēs nōs cūrāvērunt et Brundisium attulērunt. Ibi dominus meus multōs diēs morātus iam convaluit et paucīs diēbus aderit.

19 **superō, -āre, -āvī, -ātus,** *to overcome*
23 **pauper, pauperis,** *poor*
28 **casa, -ae,** f., *hut, cottage*
30 **pūgiō, pūgiōnis,** m., *dagger*
clam, adv., *secretly*
39 **quoniam,** conj., *since*
41 **convalēscō, convalēscere, convaluī,** *to grow stronger, get well*

Respondē Latīnē:

1. Quō pīrātae superātōs addūxērunt?
2. Quid pīrātae facient sī Valerius pecūniam nōn habet?
3. Quid servus nocte fēcit?
4. Quōmodo Valerius et servus ex īnsulā ēvāsērunt?

Fortī et fidēlī nihil est difficile. ***Nothing is difficult for a brave and trustworthy man.***

BUILDING THE MEANING
Subordinate Clauses with the Subjunctive I

Since Chapter 40 you have been meeting subordinate clauses with their verbs in the *subjunctive*. The subjunctive (Latin, **sub-**, *under* + **iūnct-**, *joined*) is a set of Latin verb forms that are often used in subordinate clauses. Here are examples from the story at the beginning of this chapter:

1. Magister nāvis, cum valdē **timēret**, suōs vetuit nōs adiuvāre. (42:17)
   The captain of the ship, since/because ***he was*** *very* ***frightened****, forbade his own men to help us.*

2. Cum quattuor diēs **nāvigāvissēmus**, subitō maxima tempestās coorta est. (42:2–3)
   When ***we had sailed*** *four days, suddenly a very great storm arose.*

The verb **timēret** in the first sentence above is an *imperfect subjunctive* and is translated *was*....

The verb **nāvigāvissēmus** in the second sentence above is a *pluperfect subjunctive* and is translated *had*....

Exercise 42b
Read aloud and translate these two sentences from story 42, both of which contain verbs in the subjunctive (in boldface):

1. Nocte, cum omnēs **dormīrent**, ego surrēxī, pūgiōne modo armātus.
2. Cum casae fūrtim **appropinquāvissem**, per fenestram vīdī dominum meum in lectō iacentem ac duōs custōdēs vīnum bibentēs.

FORMS
Verbs: Imperfect and Pluperfect Subjunctive Active
Imperfect Subjunctive Active

The imperfect subjunctive active is formed by adding the personal endings to the present active infinitive:

Active Voice

		1st Conjugation	2nd Conjugation	3rd Conjugation		4th Conjugation
Singular	1	portáre***m***	movére***m***	míttere***m***	iácere***m***	audíre***m***
	2	portárē***s***	movérē***s***	mítterē***s***	iácerē***s***	audírē***s***
	3	portáre***t***	movére***t***	míttere***t***	iácere***t***	audíre***t***
Plural	1	portāré***mus***	movēré***mus***	mitteré***mus***	iaceré***mus***	audīré***mus***
	2	portāré***tis***	movēré***tis***	mitteré***tis***	iaceré***tis***	audīré***tis***
	3	portáre***nt***	movére***nt***	míttere***nt***	iácere***nt***	audíre***nt***

		ésse
Singular	1	éssem
	2	éssēs
	3	ésset
Plural	1	essḗmus
	2	essḗtis
	3	éssent

So also the irregular verbs **posse**, **velle**, **nōlle**, **īre**, and **ferre**.

Be sure to learn these forms thoroughly.

Note that the *e* at the end of the infinitive lengthens to *ē* except before ***-m***, ***-t***, and ***-nt***.

Pluperfect Subjunctive Active

The pluperfect subjunctive active is formed by adding the personal endings to the perfect active infinitive:

		1st Conjugation	2nd Conjugation	3rd Conjugation		4th Conjugation
Singular	1	portāvíssem	mōvíssem	mīsíssem	iēcíssem	audīvíssem
	2	portāvíssēs	mōvíssēs	mīsíssēs	iēcíssēs	audīvíssēs
	3	portāvísset	mōvísset	mīsísset	iēcísset	audīvísset
Plural	1	portāvissḗmus	mōvissḗmus	mīsissḗmus	iēcissḗmus	audīvissḗmus
	2	portāvissḗtis	mōvissḗtis	mīsissḗtis	iēcissḗtis	audīvissḗtis
	3	portāvíssent	mōvíssent	mīsíssent	iēcíssent	audīvíssent

		ésse
Singular	1	fuíssem
	2	fuíssēs
	3	fuísset
Plural	1	fuissḗmus
	2	fuissḗtis
	3	fuíssent

So also the irregular verbs **posse (potuisse*m*)**, **velle (voluisse*m*)**, **nōlle (nōluisse*m*)**, **īre (īsse*m*)**, and **ferre (tulisse*m*)**.

Note again that the *e* at the end of the infinitive lengthens to *ē* except before ***-m***, ***-t***, and ***-nt***. Be sure to learn these forms thoroughly.

Exercise 42c

In story 42, locate four verbs in the imperfect subjunctive and seven in the pluperfect subjunctive.

Exercise 42d

Give the imperfect and pluperfect subjunctives, 3rd person plural, of the following verbs:

1. superō, -āre, -āvī, -ātus
2. ēvādō, ēvādere, ēvāsī, ēvāsus

BUILDING THE MEANING
Subordinate Clauses with the Subjunctive II

1. **Cum** Causal Clauses
   Subordinate clauses that are introduced by the conjunction **cum** may be ***cum*** *causal clauses*; **cum** is translated as *since* or *because*. Such clauses state the reason for the action of the main clause:

   Magister nāvis, cum valdē **timēret**, suōs vetuit nōs adiuvāre. (42:17)
   *The captain of the ship, since/because **he was** very **frightened**, forbade his own men to help us.*

2. **Cum** Circumstantial Clauses

   Subordinate clauses that are introduced by the conjunction **cum** may also be ***cum*** *circumstantial clauses*; **cum** is translated as *when*. Such clauses describe the circumstances that accompanied or preceded the action of the main clause:

   Cum quattuor diēs **nāvigāvissēmus**, subitō maxima tempestās coorta est. (42:2–3)
   *When **we had sailed** four days, suddenly a very great storm arose.*

   Often only the context and sense will tell you whether **cum** is to be translated *since/because* or *when*.

3. Indirect Questions

   Pīrātae rogābant quī **essēmus**, unde **vēnissēmus**, quō iter **facerēmus**. (42:20–21)
   *The pirates were asking who **we were**, from where **we had come**, [and] to where **we were making** a journey.*

   Look at these pairs of sentences:

   a. Direct question: Quī estis?
   Who are you?

   b. Indirect question: Pīrātae rogābant quī **essēmus.**
   *The pirates were asking who **we were**.*

   a. Direct question: Unde vēnistis?
   From where have you come?

   b. Indirect question: Pīrātae rogābant unde **vēnissēmus**.
   *The pirates were asking from where **we had come**.*

(continued)

a. Direct question: Quō iter facitis?
To where are you making a journey?

b. Indirect question: Pīrātae rogābant quō iter **facerēmus**.
*The pirates were asking to where **we were making a journey**.*

After the introductory words **Pīrātae rogābant**, the direct questions (a) are stated indirectly in subordinate clauses (b, underlined), and their verbs are in the subjunctive. These subordinate clauses are called *indirect questions.*

Exercise 42e

Read aloud and translate; be sure to decide whether **cum** clauses are circumstantial or causal and be sure that your translation reflects the tense of each verb in the subjunctive:

1. Cum prope rīvum ambulārēmus, Cornēliam et Flāviam clāmantēs audīvimus.
2. Grammaticus Marcum rogāvit unde vēnisset Aenēās.
3. Grammaticus Sextum rogāvit ubi esset Hesperia.
4. Grammaticus mē, cum dē Hesperiā ignōrārem, verberāvit.
5. Pīrātae Valerium rogāvērunt quis esset.
6. Magister nāvis, cum pīrātās timēret, dē patre Valeriī vēra dīcere cōnstituit.
7. Servus, cum in mare dēsiluisset, ad lītus celeriter natāvit.
8. Cum casae appropinquāvissem, dominum vīdī.
9. Cum casam intrāvisset, custōdem pūgiōne percussit.
10. Cum neque cibum neque aquam habērent, aegerrimī erant.

Exercise 42f

Using story 42 and the material above on the subjunctive as guides, give the Latin for the following (use subjunctives in all subordinate clauses):

1. When the force of the storm had subsided, we returned onto the ship.
2. Since the men were pirates, we were afraid to resist.
3. When my master had drawn his sword, he leaped down into the boat.
4. We asked why the pirates had captured us poor men.
5. Since my master was ill on account of his wound, he was not able to walk.

ROMAN LIFE XXIII

PIRACY

Piracy was a constant threat to travel and trade by sea in the ancient world. Merchant ships were often seized by pirates and their goods sold, and sailors and travelers caught by pirates would be sold as slaves at the great slave markets such as that on the island of Delos in the Aegean Sea. Pirates would also attack coastal towns and coastal roads, ruthlessly killing or capturing men, women, and children to ransom or to sell as slaves.

In 74 B.C. Julius Caesar was captured by pirates. The historian Suetonius tells the story:

> While crossing to Rhodes, after the winter season had already begun, he was taken by pirates near the island of Pharmacussa and remained in their custody for nearly forty days in a state of intense vexation, attended only by a single physician and two body-servants; for he had sent off his traveling companions and the rest of his attendants at the outset, to raise money for his ransom. Once he was set on shore on payment of fifty talents, he did not delay then and there to launch a fleet and pursue the departing pirates, and the moment they were in his power to inflict on them the punishment which he had often threatened when joking with them.
>
> Suetonius, *Julius Caesar* 4.1–2

In 66 B.C., Cicero enumerated the troubles that pirates had caused the Romans in the recent past, claiming that the sea had been virtually closed to Rome's allies, that envoys had been captured, that ransom had been paid for Rome's ambassadors, that the sea had been unsafe for merchants, that Roman lictors had been captured by pirates, that whole cities had fallen into their hands, that the harbors of the Romans and their trading partners had been held by pirates, and that a fleet commanded by a Roman had been captured and destroyed by pirates. Cicero reported that all of these troubles had been ended the previous year, when the Roman general Pompey the Great (**Pompeius Magnus**) was given a fleet and empowered to rid the sea of pirates. Cicero tells what happened:

> Pompeius, though the sea was still unfit for navigation, visited Sicily, explored Africa, sailed to Sardinia and, by means of strong garrisons and fleets, made secure those three sources of our country's grain supply. After that he returned to Italy, secured the two provinces of Spain together with Transalpine Gaul, dispatched ships to the coast of the Illyrian Sea, to Achaea and the whole of Greece, and so provided the two seas of Italy with mighty fleets and strong garrisons; while he himself, within forty-nine days of starting from Brundisium, added all

> Cilicia to the Roman Empire. All the pirates, wherever they were, were either captured or put to death; or they surrendered to his power and authority and to his alone.
>
> Cicero, *On the Manilian Law* 12.34–35

Augustus established a permanent fleet to keep the seas safe from pirates, but the menace remained, and a traveler such as Valerius in our story could easily be captured by pirates while sailing from Asia Minor to Brundisium.

REVIEW IX: CHAPTERS 38–42

Exercise IXa: Place

Select, read aloud, and translate:

1. Mercātōrēs Rōmānī ______ morābantur.	Gādēs/Gādium/Gādibus
2. Cornēliī ______ profectī sunt.	Rōma/Rōmae/Rōmā
3. Cornēliī ______ sērō advēnērunt.	Baiae/Baiārum/Baiās
4. Cornēliī ______ profectī sunt.	domus/domī/domō
5. Mīles Rōmānus ______ discessit.	Carthāginī/Carthāginem/Carthāgine
6. Amīcus mīlitis adhūc ______ habitat.	Carthāginī/Carthāginem/Carthāgō
7. Cornēlia ______ manet.	domī/domum/domō
8. Cornēliī ______ diū manēbant.	Rōmae/Rōmam/Rōmā
9. Cornēliī ______ diū manēbunt.	rūs/rūrī
10. Cornēliī ______ semper aestāte redeunt.	rūs/rūrī

Exercise IXb: Time

Read aloud, supplying the Latin words for the English cues, and translate:

1. Cornēliī in vīllā rūsticā ______ ______ morābantur. (for many months)
2. Ad urbem Rōmam ______ ______ regredientur. (in a few days)
3. Pseudolus ______ ______ ______ porcum ēmit. (three days ago)
4. Cornēliī ad vīllam rūsticam______ ______ ______ regressī sunt. (after a few months)
5. Puerī in lūdō______ ______ sedēbant. (for the whole day)
6. Valerius Brundisiō ēgressus Rōmam ______ ______ ______ adveniet. (several days later)

Exercise IXc: Present Participles

Read aloud and translate. Identify all present participles and tell what word they modify, unless they are being used as substantives:

1. Valerius iter ad Italiam faciēns tempestāte ad īnsulam āctus est.
2. Pīrātae celeriter sequentēs nāvem Valeriī cōnsecūtī sunt.
3. Nāvis Valeriī ā sequentibus capta est.
4. Servus Valeriī pīrātās in casā dormientēs adortus est.
5. Custōs ā servō Valeriī in casam ingrediente pugiōne percussus est.
6. Graviter aegrōtantēs ā mercātōribus inveniuntur.

Exercise IXd: Present Participles

Select, read aloud, and translate:

1. Sextum domum ______ audīvit Cornēlius.	intrantī/intrante/intrantem
2. Nāvis Valeriī pīrātās ______ effugere nōn poterat.	sequentēs/sequentibus/sequentium
3. Magistrō ______ ūnus ē discipulīs bene respondit.	rogantem/rogantī/rogantis
4. Aenēās Hesperiam ______ tempestāte Carthāginem āctus est.	petentem/petente/petēns
5. Cornēlius ā frātre nimis vīnī ______ vexātus est.	bibentem/bibentis/bibente

Exercise IXe: Numbers

Match the cardinal numbers at the left with the corresponding ordinal numbers at the right and give the meaning of the numbers in each pair:

1. quīnque	a. octāvus
2. octō	b. duodecimus
3. duo	c. quīngentēsimus
4. quīngentī	d. secundus
5. duodecim	e. quīntus
6. centum	f. septimus
7. trēs	g. quīnquāgēsimus
8. novem	h. tertius
9. quīnquāgintā	i. centēsimus
10. septem	j. nōnus

Exercise IXf: Semi-deponent Verbs

Translate into Latin, using semi-deponent verbs:

1. You (sing.) dare.
2. You (sing.) will be glad.
3. You (sing.) were daring.
4. You (sing.) dared.
5. You (sing.) had been glad.
6. You (sing.) will have dared.
7. We are accustomed.
8. We will dare.
9. We were daring.
10. We dared.
11. We had been accustomed.
12. We will have been glad.

Exercise IXg: Perfect Active Infinitives

Give and translate the present and perfect active infinitives of the following verbs:

1. laudō
2. habeō
3. currō
4. iaciō
5. dormiō

Exercise IXh: Imperfect and Pluperfect Subjunctives

Give the imperfect and pluperfect subjunctives of the verbs in Exercise IXg in the following persons and numbers:

1. Second person singular
2. First person plural

Exercise IXi: Subordinate Clauses with the Subjunctive

Read aloud and translate. Identify the tense of each verb in the subjunctive, and identify **cum** causal clauses, **cum** circumstantial clauses, and indirect questions:

1. Cum Vergilius Cremōnam advēnisset, ab optimīs magistrīs doctus est.
2. Scīvistīne ubi Vergilius togam virīlem sūmpsisset?
3. Cum Vergilius Mediolānum vēnisset, litterīs et linguae Graecae dīligentissimē studēbat.
4. Cum mīlitēs patrem Vergiliī ē fundō expulissent, Vergilius et pater Rōmam migrāvērunt.
5. Cum Vergilius Rōmae optimōs versūs scrīberet, poēta praeclārus factus es.
6. Cum Vergilius Rōmae habitāret, saepe aegrōtābat.
7. Cum in Graeciā iter faceret, prīncipī occurrit Athēnīs.
8. Cum prīnceps ad Italiam redīret, Vergilium sēcum dūxit.
9. Cum Brundisium advēnissent, Vergilius aegerrimus factus est.
10. Scīvistīne ubi amīcī Vergilium sepelīvissent?

Exercise IXj: Reading Comprehension

Read the following passage and answer the questions below in English:

LIFE OF AUGUSTUS

A.d. ix Kal. Oct., M. Cicerōne et C. Antōniō cōnsulibus, nātus est C. Octāvius, quī posteā prīmus prīnceps Rōmānus factus est. Cum quattuor annōs complēvisset, pater mortuus est; Gaius igitur a mātre Atiā alēbātur. Avunculus magnus quoque, C. Iūlius Caesar, eum multa docuisse dīcitur.

Ubi Caesar ā coniūrātīs necātus est, Octāvius iam XVIII annōs nātus aberat in Īllyricō. Rōmam quam celerrimē regressus, hērēs Caesaris testāmentō adoptātus est atque, cum cognōvisset quī Caesarem necāvissent, statim cōnstituit avunculum mortuum, ut patrem, ōlim ulcīscī. Eō tempore tamen, quod nūllum exercitum habēbat, nihil facere poterat.

Intereā, quod M. Antōnius populum Rōmānum excitāverat, coniūrātī ex urbe fugere coāctī sunt. Dum tamen Antōnius coniūrātōs per Italiam persequēbātur, M. Tullius Cicerō, ōrātor ille praeclārissimus, ōrātiōnēs habuit in quibus dīcēbat Antōnium esse hostem reī pūblicae. Tum Octāvius, dīvitiīs ūsus quās testāmentō Caesaris accēperat, senātuī persuāsit ut sē cōnsulem creāret. Eōdem tempore nōminātus est Gaius Iūlius Caesar Octāviānus. Volēbant senātōrēs Octāviānum contrā Antōnium, quem iam timēbant, urbem Rōmam dēfendere. Octāviānus tamen cum Antōniō se coniūnxit.

Prīmō Octāviānus et Antōnius ūnā coniūrātōs in Graeciā cōnsecūtī, proeliō dēbellāvērunt. Deinde, cum coniūrātōs superāvissent, cōnstituērunt Octāviānus et Antōnius imperium Rōmānum inter sē dīvidere. Rōmam regressus est Octāviānus; ad Aegyptum profectus est Antōnius. Rēgīna autem Aegyptiōrum erat Cleopatra, quam pulcherrimam statim amāvit Antōnius. Mox Antōnius et Cleopatra tōtum imperium Rōmānum regere volēbant. Quae cum ita essent, Octāviānō necesse fuit bellum Antōniō īnferre. Proelium ad Actium factum est; Cleopatra Antōniusque victī sē necāvērunt. Octāviānus tōtam Aegyptum bellō captam imperiō Rōmānō addidit. Tum Iānum Quirīnum clausit atque pācem tōtum per imperium prōnūntiāvit. Ipse prīnceps Rōmānōrum factus est.

Multa et optima et ūtilissima populō Rōmānō ab eō īnstitūta sunt atque imperium Rōmānum auctum stabilītumque est. Multī etiam poētae—Vergilius, Horātius, Propertius, Ovidius—rēs Rōmānās versibus laudābant. Inter multōs honōrēs quōs senātus eī dedit maximus certē erat cognōmen Augustus, quod eī dēlātum est a.d. XVII Kal. Feb. anno DCCXXVII, A.U.C. Ex hōc tempore mēnsis Sextīlis nōminātus est Augustus.

Bis uxōrem dūxit sed nūllum fīlium habēbat. Generum autem Marcellum in animō habēbat hērēdem adoptāre. Hic tamen annō DCCXXXI A.U.C. trīstissimē morbō mortuus est. Augustus igitur Tiberium, fīlium Līviae uxōris secundae, hērēdem adoptāvit.

Cum annum septuāgēsimum sextum paene complēvisset, dum iter in Campāniā facit, trīstissimē morbō a.d. XIV Kal. Sept. mortuus est. Corpus Rōmam relātum ingentī in sepulcrō sepultum est atque ūnō post mēnse senātus, quī Augustum iam dīvīnum esse prōnūntiāverat, eum cum avunculō inter deōs numerāvit.

1 **M. = Marcus**
C. = Gaius
3 **avunculus, -ī,** m., *maternal uncle*
5 **coniūrātus, -ī,** m., *conspirator*
6 **hērēs, hērēdis,** m., *heir*
8 **ōlim,** adv., *at some future time, one day*
exercitus, -ūs, m., *army*
10 **populus, -ī,** m., *people*
13 **hostis, hostis,** gen. pl., **hostium,** m., *enemy*
rēs pūblica, reī pūblicae, f., *republic, the state*
dīvitiae, -ārum, f. pl., *riches*
14 **ut sē cōnsulem creāret,** *to make him consul*
15 **contrā,** prep. + acc., *against*
16 **coniungō, coniungere, coniūnxī, coniūnctus,** *to join*
17 **proelium, -ī,** n., *battle*
18 **dēbellō, -āre, -āvī, -ātus,** *to defeat*
19 **imperium, -ī,** n., *power, empire*
20 **Aegyptus, -ī,** f., *Egypt*
22 **bellum īnferre** + dat., *to make war upon*
24 **Iānus Quirīnus, -ī,** m., *shrine of Janus Quirinus*
25 **pāx, pācis,** f., *peace*
prōnūntiō, -āre, -āvī, -ātus, *to proclaim*
27 **stabiliō, -īre, -īvī, -ītus,** *to steady, make firm*
32 **bis,** adv., *twice*
uxōrem dūcere, *to marry*
gener, generī, m., *son-in-law*
33 **morbus, -ī,** m., *illness*
39 **numerō, -āre, -āvī, -ātus,** *to number, include*

2 **compleō, complēre, complēvī, complētus,** *to fill, complete*
3 **alō, alere, aluī, altus,** *to rear*
7 **cognōscō, cognōscere, cognōvī, cognitus,** *to learn*
8 **ulcīscor, ulcīscī, ultus sum,** *to avenge*
11 **cōgō, cōgere, coēgī, coāctus,** *to compel, force*
persequor, persequī, persecūtus sum, *to pursue*
13 **ūtor, ūtī, ūsus sum** + abl., *to use*
22 **regō, regere, rēxī, rēctus,** *to rule*
26 **īnstituō, īnstituere, īnstituī, īnstitūtus,** *to establish*
27 **augeō, augēre, auxī, auctus,** *to increase*
29 **dēferō, dēferre, dētulī, dēlātus,** irreg., *to award, grant*
37 **referō, referre, retulī, relātus,** irreg., *to bring back*

1. On what day of what month was Gaius Octavius born?
2. How old was he when his father died?
3. Who were responsible for his rearing and education?
4. Where was Octavius when Caesar was assassinated?
5. What did Octavius decide to do when he learned who had assassinated Caesar?
6. Why was he unable to do anything at the time?
7. Why were the conspirators forced to flee from Rome?
8. Who pursued them?
9. What attitude did Cicero take toward Antony?
10. How did Octavius persuade the Senate to make him consul?

(continued)

11. Who overtook the conspirators in Greece and defeated them?
12. Where did the victors go?
13. What were Antony and Cleopatra's plans?
14. Who defeated whom at the battle of Actium?
15. What new province did Octavian add to the Roman empire?
16. What kind of a ruler was Octavian?
17. What was the greatest honor that the Senate gave him?
18. Whom did he want to succeed him as ruler?
19. Why was that not possible?
20. What honor did the Senate confer upon Augustus after his death?

At the Baths

One of the main entertainments of the Romans was their daily visit to the baths — either to the public **thermae** or to the smaller, private **balneae**. They would expect to find three basic rooms: a warm room (**tepidārium**), which one would enter after undressing in the changing-room (**apodytērium**); a hot room (**caldārium**), where hot water would be provided in a specially heated room, which might also incorporate a steam bath; and a cold room (**frīgidārium**), where one could plunge into a cold bath after the heat of the **caldārium**.

In the big public bathing establishments one would also expect to find an exercise ground (**palaestra**), often in the open air, with a covered portico around it, where one might engage in a variety of exercises. There were various types of ball games, including a game involving the "snatching" (**rapere**) of a heavy ball (**harpastum**) and **trigōn**, a throwing and catching game played by three people with a ball also called **trigōn** from the name of the game. Men might engage in wrestling (**lūctārī**), fencing at a post (**pālus**), or weightlifting. After exercising, the Roman would be rubbed down with oil (**unguentum**), which cleansed and refreshed the skin. The excess oil was then removed with a special metal instrument (**strigilis**). Then the skin would be rubbed down with a towel (**linteum**).

In Rome the baths opened at noon and remained open till dusk. The opening and closing times were indicated by the striking of a gong.

Many establishments had separate facilities for men and women bathers; others fixed different hours for the two sexes.

The baths were regarded as social clubs, and people went there to exercise, play games, meet each other, and share gossip and news, as well as to bathe.

Iam hōra sexta erat. Titus Cornēlius, ut cōtīdiē solēbat, domō ēgressus, in Campum Mārtium ad Thermās Nerōnēās dēscendit, nam eō amīcī eius conveniēbant et dē rēbus urbānīs colloquēbantur.

Quō cum Titus pervēnisset, pecūniā datā, in vestibulum ingressus est. Ibi complūrēs ex amīcīs eum salūtāvērunt atque ūnā in apodytērium iniērunt. Vestīmenta exūta trādidērunt servīs suīs, quī unguenta et strigilēs portābant.

Iam ūnctī in palaestram exiērunt ubi multī cīvēs variīs modīs sē exercēbant. Aliī harpastum rapiēbant, aliī trigōne lūdēbant, aliī lūctābantur, aliī pālum gladiō petēbant. Titus cum duōbus amīcīs trigōne lūdēbat. Cum satis sē ita exercuissent, ā servīs plūs unguentī poposcērunt et strigilibus dēfrictī sunt. Mox tepidārium, deinde caldārium iniērunt. Hīc, cum calōrem et vapōrem vix patī possent, haud multum morābantur. Cum in tepidārium regressī essent, statim inde frīgidārium intrāvērunt et in aquam frīgidam dēsiluērunt. Posteā linteīs tersī, vestīmenta rūrsus induērunt.

Nē tum quidem domum discessērunt sed, vīnō sūmptō, inter sē colloquī coepērunt. Titum, cum ille semper vidērētur omnia audīvisse et vīdisse, dē rēbus urbānīs omnēs rogābant. Maximē enim cupiēbant cognōscere quid in senātū agerētur, quid ā prīncipe contrā incendia factum esset, quī hominēs praeclārī iam in urbe adessent.

(continued)

1 **Campus Mārtius, -ī,** m., *the Plain of Mars on the outskirts of Rome*
2 **Nerōnēus, -a, -um,** *of Nero*
4 **quō,** adv., *there, to that place*
Quō cum, *When…there*
pecūniā datā, *with his money having been given, after paying his entrance fee*
vestibulum, -ī, n., *entrance passage*
7 **exerceō, -ēre, -uī, -itus,** *to exercise, train*
11 **calor, calōris,** m., *heat*
haud, adv., *not*
14 **vīnō sūmptō,** *with wine having been taken, after a drink of wine*
17 **contrā,** prep. + acc., *against*

7 **unguō, unguere, ūnxī, ūnctus,** *to anoint, smear with oil*
10 **dēfricō, dēfricāre, dēfricuī, dēfrictus,** *to rub down*
13 **tergeō, tergēre, tersī, tersus,** *to dry, wipe*
16 **cognōscō, cognōscere, cognōvī, cognitus,** *to find out, learn*

Exercise 43a
Respondē Latīnē:

1. Quō Titus cōtīdiē ībat?
2. Quid Titus prīmum in thermīs fēcit?
3. Quibus trādidit vestīmenta sua?
4. Quid cīvēs in palaestrā faciēbant?
5. Quid Titus cum duōbus amīcīs faciēbat?
6. Cum satis sē exercuissent, quō iniērunt?
7. Cūr in caldāriō haud multum morābantur?
8. Postquam vestīmenta induērunt, quid sūmpsērunt?
9. Cūr omnēs Titum dē rēbus urbānīs rogābant?

"Nīl magnī," respondit Titus, "sed heri in Balneīs Palātīnīs rem rīdiculam vīdī; senex calvus, tunicā russātā indūtus, inter puerōs capillātōs pilā lūdēbat. Eās pilās quae ad terram ceciderant nōn repetēbat, nam servus follem habēbat plēnum pilārum, quās lūdentibus dabat. Tandem hic senex digitōs concrepuit et aquam poposcit. Tum, cum manūs lāvisset, in capite ūnīus ē puerīs tersit!"

18 **senex, senis,** m., *old man*
19 **calvus, -a, -um,** *bald*
indūtus, -a, -um, *clothed*
capillātus, -a, -um, *with long hair*
20 **follis, follis,** gen. pl., **follium,** m., *bag*
21 **digitus, -ī,** m., *finger*

20 **repetō, repetere, repetīvī, repetītus,** *to pick up, recover*
21 **concrepō, concrepāre, concrepuī,** *to snap (the fingers)*

Respondē Latīnē:

1. Quālem fābulam Titus nārrāvit?
2. Quid faciēbat senex quem Titus in Balneīs Palātīnīs vīdit?
3. Cūr servus pilās lūdentibus dabat?
4. Quid senex in capite puerī capillātī fēcit?

BUILDING THE MEANING

Subordinate Clauses with the Subjunctive (Review)

In Chapter 42 you learned about three kinds of subordinate clauses that have their verbs in the subjunctive. Here are examples from the story at the beginning of the present chapter:

1. **Cum** Causal Clauses:

   Hīc, **cum** calōrem et vapōrem vix patī **possent**, haud multum morābantur. (43:11)
   Here, ***since they were*** *scarcely* ***able*** *to endure the heat and the steam, they did not stay a long time.*

2. **Cum** Circumstantial Clauses:

   Quō **cum** Titus **pervēnisset,** in vestibulum ingressus est. (43:4)
   When *Titus* ***had arrived*** *there, he entered the entrance passage.*

3. Indirect Questions:

   Maximē enim cupiēbant cognōscere **quī** hominēs praeclārī iam in urbe **adessent.** (43:16–17)
   They especially wanted to learn ***what*** *famous men* ***were*** *now* ***present*** *in the city.*

Note that clauses with the imperfect subjunctive describe actions that were going on at the same time as the action of the main clause (translate *was.../were...*) and that clauses with the pluperfect subjunctive describe actions that had been completed before the action of the main clause (translate *had...*).

In Chapter 42 you learned the forms of the imperfect and pluperfect *active* subjunctives. In the current chapter you have also met the three kinds of subordinate clauses illustrated above with *passive* forms of the subjunctive:

1. **Cum** Causal Clauses:

   ...cum ille semper **vidērētur** omnia audīvisse et vīdisse,... (43:15)
   *...since he **seemed** always to have heard and seen everything,...*

2. **Cum** Circumstantial Clauses:

   Cum in tepidārium **regressī essent,**...(43:11–12)
   *When **they had returned** into the warm room,...*

3. Indirect Questions:

   ...quid in senātū **agerētur,**...(43:16)
   *...what **was being done** in the Senate,...*

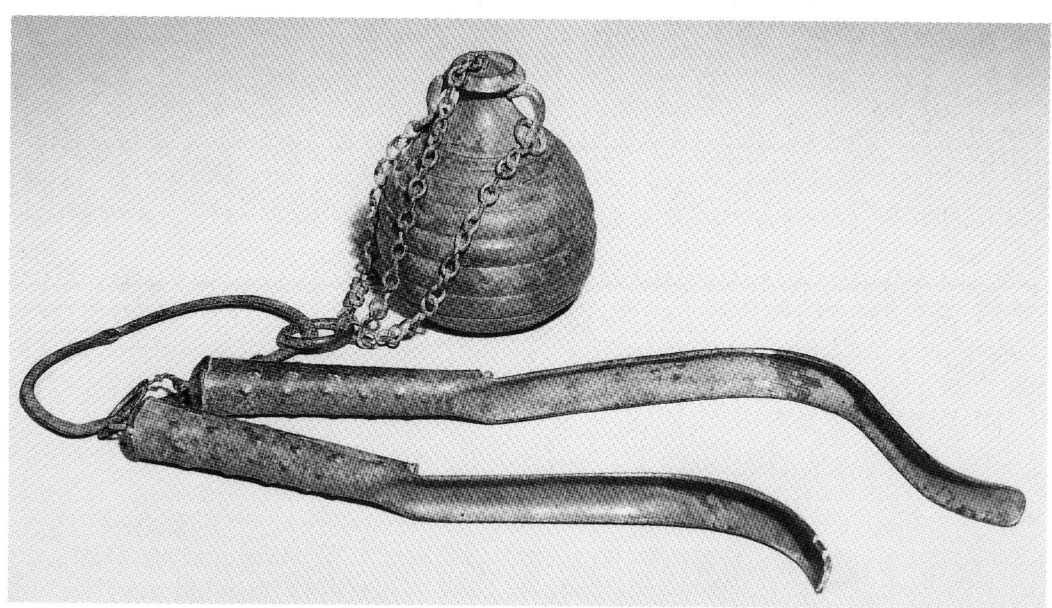

Oil flask and strigil

Forms

Verbs: Imperfect and Pluperfect Subjunctive Passive

Imperfect Subjunctive Passive

The imperfect subjunctive passive is formed by adding the passive personal endings to the present active infinitive. Here are the imperfect active and passive subjunctive forms:

Active Voice

		1st Conjugation	**2nd Conjugation**	**3rd Conjugation**		**4th Conjugation**
	1	portā́re***m***	movḗre***m***	míttere***m***	iácere***m***	audī́re***m***
S	2	portā́rē***s***	movḗrē***s***	mítterē***s***	iácerē***s***	audī́rē***s***
	3	portā́re***t***	movḗre***t***	míttere***t***	iácere***t***	audī́re***t***
	1	portārḗ***mus***	movērḗ***mus***	mitterḗ***mus***	iacerḗ***mus***	audīrḗ***mus***
P	2	portārḗ***tis***	movērḗ***tis***	mitterḗ***tis***	iacerḗ***tis***	audīrḗ***tis***
	3	portā́re***nt***	movḗre***nt***	míttere***nt***	iácere***nt***	audī́re***nt***

Passive Voice

	1	portā́re***r***	movḗre***r***	míttere***r***	iácere***r***	audī́re***r***
S	2	portārḗ***ris***	movērḗ***ris***	mitterḗ***ris***	iacerḗ***ris***	audīrḗ***ris***
	3	portārḗ***tur***	movērḗ***tur***	mitterḗ***tur***	iacerḗ***tur***	audīrḗ***tur***
	1	portārḗ***mur***	movērḗ***mur***	mitterḗ***mur***	iacerḗ***mur***	audīrḗ***mur***
P	2	portārḗ***minī***	movērḗ***minī***	mitterḗ***minī***	iacerḗ***minī***	audīrḗ***minī***
	3	portāré***ntur***	movēré***ntur***	mitteré***ntur***	iaceré***ntur***	audīré***ntur***

For the imperfect subjunctive of deponent verbs, first form what would be the present active infinitive if the verb had one (which, of course, deponent verbs do not!) and then add the passive personal endings. These forms are, as usual, passive in form but active in meaning:

Deponent

S	1	cōnā́re***r***	verḗre***r***	lóquere***r***	regrédere***r***	experī́re***r***
		etc.	etc.	etc.	etc.	etc.

Pluperfect Subjunctive Passive

The pluperfect subjunctive passive is made in the same way as the pluperfect indicative passive, except that **essem,** the imperfect subjunctive, is substituted for **eram.** On the following page, on the left are the pluperfect active forms, in the middle are the pluperfect passive forms, and at the right are the pluperfect forms of a deponent verb.

		Active Voice	Passive Voice		Deponent Verb	
S	1	audīvísse***m***	audī́tus, -a	éssem	cōnā́tus, -a	éssem
	2	audīvíssē***s***	audī́tus, -a	éssēs	cōnā́tus, -a	éssēs
	3	audīvísse***t***	audī́tus, -a, -um	ésset	cōnā́tus, -a, -um	ésset
P	1	audīvissé***mus***	audī́tī, -ae	essḗmus	cōnā́tī, -ae	essḗmus
	2	audīvissé***tis***	audī́tī, -ae	essḗtis	cōnā́tī, -ae	essḗtis
	3	audīvísse***nt***	audī́tī, -ae, -a	éssent	cōnā́tī, -ae, -a	éssent

Exercise 43b

In story 43, locate five verbs in the imperfect or pluperfect subjunctive active and locate four passive subjunctive forms. Identify the tense, person, and number of each form.

Exercise 43c

Here are sample forms of the imperfect and pluperfect subjunctives, active and passive, of a regular verb and sample forms of the imperfect and pluperfect subjunctives of a deponent verb:

Regular Verb:

Imperfect Active **parārem**	*Imperfect Passive* **parārer**
Pluperfect Active **parāvissem**	*Pluperfect Passive* **parātus essem**

Deponent Verb:

Imperfect
cōnārer

Pluperfect
cōnātus essem

Give imperfect and pluperfect subjunctive forms of the following verbs in the designated person and number, following the pattern above. For deponent verbs give only passive forms:

1. dēfricō, dēfricāre, dēfricuī, dēfrictus: 3rd sing.
2. tergeō, tergēre, tersī, tersus: 1st pl.
3. repetō, repetere, repetīvī, repetītus: 1st pl.
4. colloquor, colloquī, collocūtus sum: 3rd pl.
5. regredior, regredī, regressus sum: 2nd pl.

Exercise 43d

Read aloud and translate each sentence, and then identify each subordinate clause by type (**cum** causal, **cum** circumstantial, or indirect question). Tell if the action in the subordinate clause was happening at the same time as the action of the main clause or had been completed before the action of the main clause:

1. Cum prīmā lūce profectī essēmus, iam dēfessī erāmus.
2. Ego nesciēbam cūr Rōmam proficīscerēmur.
3. Hodiē cum Titus domō ēgressus esset, ad thermās dēscendit.
4. Cum pecūnia data esset, Titus in vestibulum ingressus est.
5. Cum caldārium calidissimum esset, Titus ibi nōn diū morātus est.
6. Amīcī Titum rogāvērunt quid māne fēcisset.
7. Nēmō cognōvit quid heri in senātū āctum esset.
8. Cum senex calvus pilā lūderet, nūllam pilam ā terrā repetēbat.
9. Cum servus follem plēnum pilārum habēret, necesse nōn erat pilās ā terrā repetere.
10. Titus nārrāvit quōmodo digitī senis in capite puerī tersī essent.

Excercise 43e

Using story 43 and the sets of forms of the imperfect and pluperfect subjunctive as guides, give the Latin for:

1. When Titus had descended to the Campus Martius, he entered the Baths of Nero.
2. There his friends asked him what had been done in the Senate today.
3. Since he had been present in the Senate, he was able to tell everything.
4. When Titus was in the Palatine Baths yesterday, he saw a bald old man.
5. He did not know who the old man was.

ROMAN LIFE XXIV

THE BATHS

In addition to the many references to baths in Roman literature, much information about the **balneae** and **thermae** can be deduced from the archaeological remains of bathing establishments still evident today. In Rome, the great Thermae of Diocletian now house the National Museum, its extensive grounds having been laid out by Michelangelo centuries after the baths were built. Grand opera is performed during the summer months in the Baths of Caracalla.

At Pompeii, both public and private bathing establishments have been found, and even in many of the houses there are full suites of bathrooms—warm, hot, and cold rooms—which were apparently used only by the family. On country estates and in town houses, in addition to the suites of baths for the owner, there were bath houses for slaves.

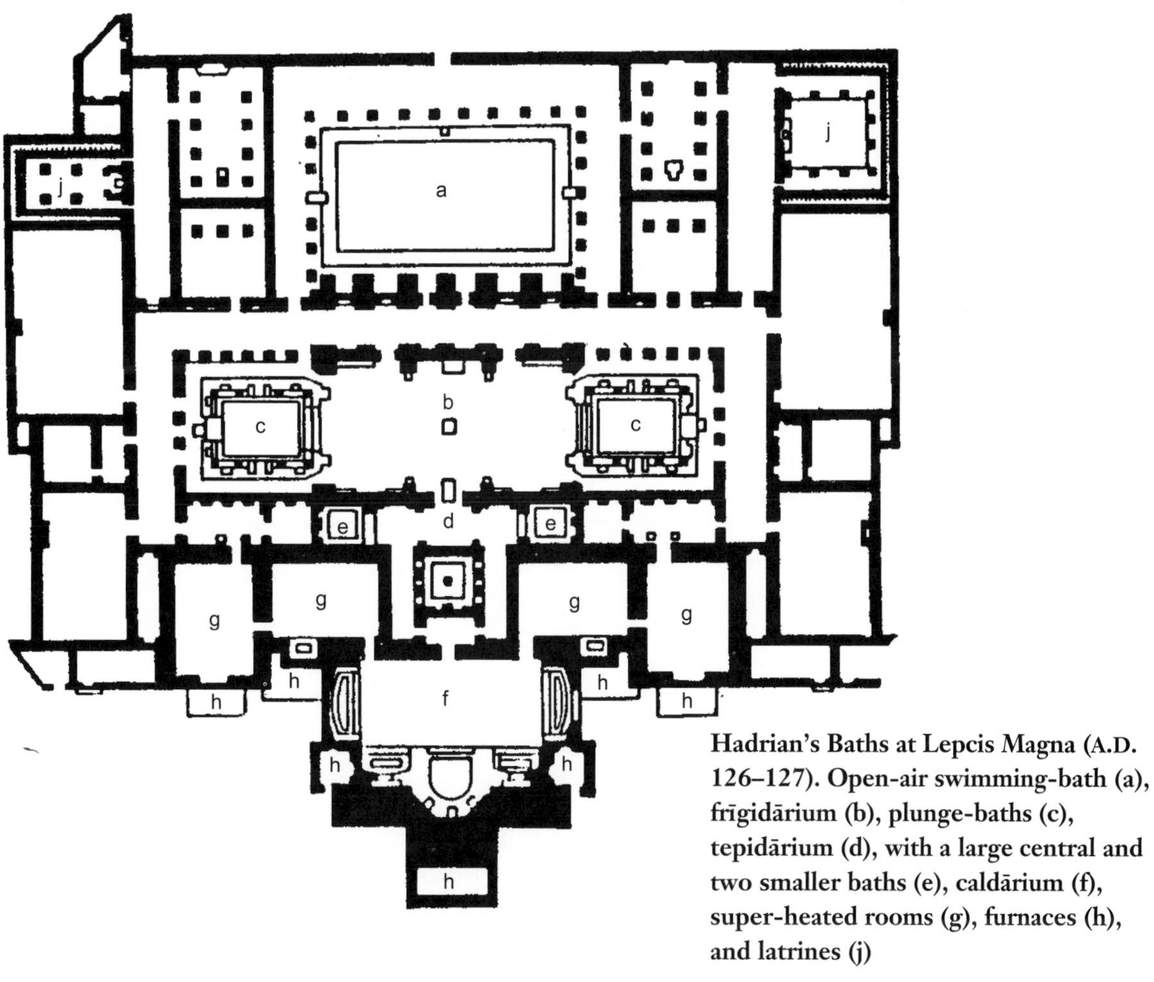

Hadrian's Baths at Lepcis Magna (A.D. 126–127). Open-air swimming-bath (a), frīgidārium (b), plunge-baths (c), tepidārium (d), with a large central and two smaller baths (e), caldārium (f), super-heated rooms (g), furnaces (h), and latrines (j)

The first public baths in Rome were built in the second century B.C.; they were small, practical wash-houses for men only. Later, bathing establishments called **balneae** began to be built at private expense and run for profit by individuals or a consortium. As the practice of bathing became more and more popular, huge baths (**thermae**) were built by the state. These were increased in size and splendor under the emperors, e.g., the Thermae of Caracalla (A.D. 217) and of Diocletian (A.D. 303).

Romans of all social classes could spend an hour or more in the luxury of such complexes for only a **quadrāns**, the smallest Roman coin. Children were admitted free. The management of the state **thermae** was awarded for a fixed sum to a contractor. Sometimes a rich citizen or magistrate undertook to pay him the equivalent of the total entrance fees for a certain period, during which entry to the baths was entirely free.

So attached were the Romans to their daily hot steam-bath that they built baths in most communities throughout their Empire. Where there were hot springs, as in Bath, England, they used these and built gymnasia and dressing-rooms around them. Where there were no hot springs, they heated the air by a hypocaust (**hypocauston,** a Greek term meaning literally, "burning underneath"), a system whereby hot air from a furnace circulated under the raised floor and through ducts and vents in the walls. The fuel for the furnace, which was stoked by slaves, was wood and charcoal. Huge reservoirs were built near the baths to provide a constant and plentiful supply of water.

Bathers would take various articles with them to the baths, including towels, bottles of oil, and strigils. All but the poor would bring their own slaves to attend them, but it was possible to hire the services of others at the baths (e.g., masseur, barber). Attendants would guard clothes for a small fee.

Roman baths varied considerably in size and layout, but in all of them the following series of rooms was to be found:

1. **apodytērium:** a changing room with stone benches and rows of deep holes in the walls for holding clothes.

2. **frīgidārium:** cold room, with cold plunge bath at one side.

3. **tepidārium:** warm room, to acclimatize bathers to the difference in temperature between the cold and hot rooms.

4. **caldārium:** hot room, with hot bath and hot air like the modern Turkish bath. It was the best-lit room and was equipped with basins and tubs. Its ceiling was usually domed to allow condensation to run off.

The bathers could take the three stages of bathing in any order, but it was usual to end up with a cold plunge. Medicinal and perfumed baths were also available.

The baths became a suitable place for taking exercise. A large complex would have a court for ball games and an area for gymnastics and wrestling, in addition to the swimming pool. There were various ball games, each using a different type of ball and sometimes a racquet as well. Hoops or a dumbbell were also used for exercising.

The Roman baths were centers for recreation and relaxation in the fullest sense, and in the largest establishments the amenities could include gardens, reading rooms, and even libraries. "Snack-bars" (**popīnae**) were numerous inside the building or nearby, while vendors of every type advertised their wares on all sides.

A GRAFFITO FROM THE BATHS AT ROME

Balnea, vīna, Venus corrumpunt corpora nostra;
at vītam faciunt—balnea, vīna, Venus.

balnea = **balneae** **Venus** = **amor**

corrumpō, corrumpere, corrūpī, corruptus, *to spoil, harm, ruin*

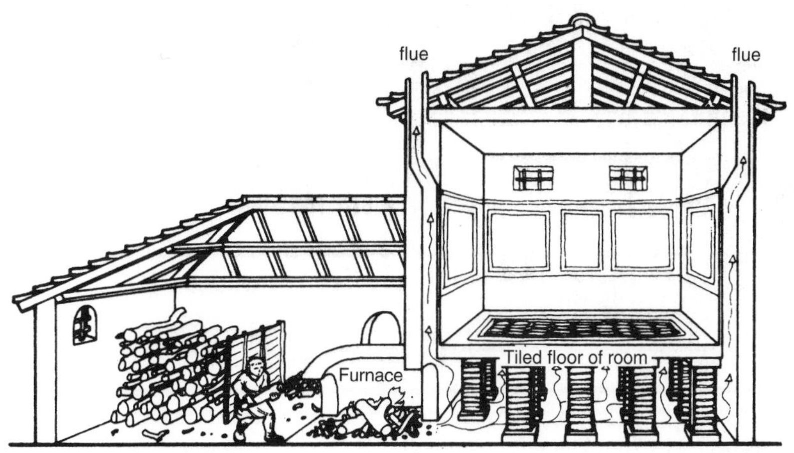

Diagram of a Hypocaust

ADDITIONAL READING:
The Romans Speak for Themselves: Book II: "An Unexpected Bath at Trimalchio's," pages 51–61.

CHAPTER 44

Stop Thief!

Marcus et Sextus ē lūdō ēgressī ūnā cum Eucleide et alterō servō domum ībant. Subitō Eucleidēs puerīs, "Vultisne ad thermās īre?" inquit.

Quibus verbīs audītīs, puerī maximē gaudēbant. Mox ad thermās advēnērunt et in apodytērium intrāvērunt, quod iam erat plēnum puerōrum quī ē lūdō ēgressī eō cum paedagōgīs vēnerant. Ibi vestīmenta exuēbant.

Marcus, vestīmentīs exūtīs, "Nunc in palaestram exeāmus," inquit. At Eucleidēs, "Minimē!" inquit. "Pater tuus mē iussit vōs ante nōnam hōram redūcere." Deinde alterī servō, cui nōmen erat Asellus, "Hīc manē!" inquit. "Vestīmenta dīligenter custōdī! Hīc enim solent esse multī fūrēs quī vestīmenta surrepta in urbe vēndunt."

Cui Asellus respondit, "Ego semper vestīmenta dīligenter custōdiō. Nēmō vestīmenta, mē custōde, surripere potest."

Tum puerī, vestīmentīs trāditīs, in tepidārium intrāvērunt et inde in caldārium, ubi erat magna turba hominum. Subitō tamen exclāmāvit Sextus, "Aeger sum. Hunc calōrem patī nōn possum. Exībō et ad apodytērium regrediar."

Dum ē tepidāriō exit, Asellum prope vestīmenta sedentem cōnspexit. Dormiēbat Asellus. Eō ipsō tempore vestīmenta ā servō quōdam surripiēbantur. Quod ubi vīdit Sextus, "Prehende fūrem!" exclāmāvit. Simul fūr clāmōrem Sextī audīvit, simul Asellus ē sellā exsiluit, simul Sextus ad iānuam cucurrit. Fūr in palaestram cōnfūgit, nam sē in turbā cēlāre in animō habēbat. Cum tamen inde in viam ēvādere nōn posset, in frīgidārium fūgit.

(continued)

3 **quibus verbīs audītīs,** *with which words having been heard, when they had heard this*
6 **exeāmus,** *let us go out*
9 **fūr, fūris,** m., *thief*
11 **mē custōde,** *with me on guard, while I am on guard*
18 **sella, -ae,** f., *sedan-chair; seat, chair*

9 **surripiō, surripere, surripuī, surreptus,** *to steal*
17 **prehendō, prehendere, prehendī, prehēnsus,** *to seize*
18 **exsiliō, exsilīre, exsiluī,** *to leap out*
cōnfugiō, cōnfugere, cōnfūgī, *to flee for refuge*

Exercise 44a

Respondē Latīnē:

1. Cūr puerī maximē gaudēbant?
2. Ubi vestīmenta exuēbant?
3. Cūr vestīmenta dīligenter custōdīrī dēbent?
4. Quid Sextus patī nōn potest?
5. Ubi sedēbat Asellus et quid faciēbat?
6. Cūr fūr in frīgidārium fūgit?

Sextus tamen fūrem cōnspectum subsequēbātur. Fūr, Sextō vīsō, iam valdē timēbat. In pavīmentō lāpsus in aquam frīgidam cecidit. Statim in aquam dēsiluit Sextus. Fūrem ex aquā trahere cōnābātur; sed frūstrā. Cum tamen adiūvissent adstantēs, fūr ā Sextō captus ex aquā extractus est. Quem captum Sextus dominō trādidit.

22 **pavīmentum, -ī,** n., *tiled floor*

21 **subsequor, subsequī, subsecūtus sum,** *to follow (up)*
22 **lābor, lābī, lāpsus sum,** *to slip, fall*

Respondē Latīnē:

1. Quī fūrem ā Sextō captum ex aquā extrāxērunt?
2. Cui trāditus est fūr?

BUILDING THE MEANING

Verbs: Perfect Passive Participles II

In Chapter 33 you saw the following sentence with a perfect passive participle:

Coquus **vocātus** ab omnibus laudātus est. (33:26)
*The cook, **having been summoned,** was praised by everyone.*
After being summoned, the cook was praised by everyone.
When summoned, the cook was praised by everyone.
When the cook had been summoned, he was praised by everyone.
The cook was summoned and praised by everyone.

Here the perfect passive participle modifies the subject of the sentence.
A perfect passive participle may also modify the direct or indirect object:

Coquum **vocātum** omnēs laudāvērunt.
*They all praised the cook **having been summoned.***
They all praised the cook who had been summoned.
When the cook had been summoned, they all praised him.

Coquō **vocātō** omnēs grātiās ēgērunt.
*They all gave thanks to the cook **having been summoned.***
They all gave thanks to the cook who had been summoned.
When the cook had been summoned, they all gave thanks to him.

Exercise 44b

Read aloud and translate the following sentences. Identify the case of all perfect passive participles and tell what they modify:

1. Amīcī Titum cōnspectum salūtāvērunt.
2. Titus rogātus quid in senātū agerētur, "Nīl magnī," respondit.
3. Vestīmenta exūta Marcus servō trādidit.
4. Strigilibus dēfrictī tepidārium ingressī sunt.
5. Vestīmenta dominō vocātō trādita sunt.

Ablatives Absolute

Another arrangement is also possible:

> Coquō **vocātō,** omnēs cēnam laudāvērunt.
> *The cook* ***having been summoned,*** *they all praised the dinner.*
> *When the cook* ***had been summoned,*** *they all praised the dinner.*

Here the participle does not agree with the subject of the sentence or with a direct or indirect object but rather with another word, **coquō,** which is in the ablative case. The two words taken together, **coquō vocātō,** make a construction known as the *ablative absolute,* in which a noun (or pronoun) and a participle are in the ablative case and make up a phrase that is separate from the rest of the sentence (Latin **absolūtus,** *complete in itself, self-contained*) and is usually set off by commas.

In addition to the translations given above, the ablative absolute **coquō vocātō** could be translated *after the cook had been summoned.* Some ablatives absolute may best be translated with *because, since, although,* or *if,* depending on the context.

The participle of an ablative absolute may also be in the present tense:

> Fūre vestīmenta **surripiente**, Sextus in apodytērium ingreditur.
> *While the thief* ***is stealing*** *the clothes, Sextus enters the changing room.*

Note that the ablative singular ending of present participles used in ablatives absolute is ***-e,*** not ***-ī*** (see Chapter 40, page 135).

The present active participle is used for an action going on at the same time as the action of the main verb of the sentence; the perfect passive participle is used for an action that was completed before the action of the main verb.

Often the present participle will be translated with a past tense in English because it describes an action going on in the past at the same time as the action of the main verb in a past tense:

> Fūre vestīmenta **surripiente,** Sextus in apodytērium ingrediēbātur.
> *While the thief* ***was stealing*** *the clothes, Sextus was entering the changing room.*

Since classical Latin has no present participle for the verb **esse,** ablatives absolute sometimes consist only of two nouns in the ablative case, e.g., **mē custōde,** *with me (being) a guard, as long as I'm on guard* (44:11), or of a noun and an adjective, e.g., **Sextō aegrō,** *since Sextus is (was) sick.*

Exercise 44c

Locate five examples of ablatives absolute in story 44. Translate the sentences in which they occur.

Iūs et fūrī dīcitur. ***Justice is granted even to the thief.*** **(Seneca,** ***On Benefits*** **IV.28)**
lapsus calami ***a slip of the pen***
lapsus linguae ***a slip of the tongue***

Exercise 44d

Read aloud and translate each sentence, and then identify the ablatives absolute. Comment on the temporal relationship between the participle of the ablative absolute and the action of the verb in the main clause:

1. Puerīs in lūdō clāmantibus, magister īrātus fit.
2. Magistrō īrātō, puerī ē lūdō missī sunt.
3. Lūdō relictō, puerī ad thermās iērunt.
4. Titō salūtātō, puerī in apodytērium iniērunt.
5. Vestīmentīs Asellō trāditīs, in palaestram iniērunt.
6. Lūdīs in palaestrā cōnfectīs, in tepidārium intrāvērunt.
7. Marcō in caldāriō morante, Sextus ad apodytērium regressus est.
8. Asellō custōde, fūr vestīmenta surripuit.
9. Fūre cōnspectō, Sextus magnā vōce clāmāvit.
10. Vestīmentīs ā fūre trāditīs, puerī domum iērunt.

Exercise 44e

Using story 44 and the information on ablatives absolute as guides, give the Latin for the following. Use ablatives absolute to translate subordinate clauses:

1. When they had taken off their clothes, they entered the warm room.
2. While Asellus was sleeping, a certain slave was stealing the clothes.
3. The thief, when he had seen Sextus, was very afraid.
4. While Sextus was trying to drag the thief out of the water, the bystanders were doing nothing.
5. When the thief had been handed over to his master, Sextus was happy.

BUILDING THE MEANING

Linking *quī*

In story 44 you met the following:

Quibus verbīs audītīs.... (3)	*When they heard* **these** *words....*
Cui Asellus respondit.... (10)	*Asellus replied* **to him**....
Quod ubi vīdit.... (16)	*When he saw* **this**....
Quem captum.... (24)	*Now that he had caught* **him**....

A linking **quī** is translated in English as either a demonstrative pronoun (*these*, *this*, etc.) or a personal pronoun (*him*, etc.), not as a relative pronoun (*which*, *whom*, etc.).

The relative pronoun at the beginning of a sentence provides a link with a person, thing, or action in the previous sentence:

Quibus verbīs refers to what Eucleides said in the previous sentence.
Cui refers to Eucleides, who had just finished speaking.
Quod refers to the theft Sextus had just seen.
Quem refers to the thief mentioned in the previous sentence.

ROMAN LIFE XXV

THIEVES AT THE BATHS

Even as early as the time of the comic playwright Plautus (ca. 254–184 B.C.), Romans knew how difficult it was to guard their clothes at the baths:

> Even one who goes to the baths to bathe and watches his clothes carefully there has them stolen all the same, since he's confused as to which of the crowd to watch. The thief easily sees the one who's watching; the guard doesn't know who the thief is.
>
> Plautus, *Rudens* 382–385 (adapted)

Scene from a Roman comedy
Mosaic, Museo Nazionale di San Martino, Naples, Italy

The following story was told by a guest at Trimalchio's dinner party:

> We were just about to step into the dining room when a slave, utterly naked, landed on the floor in front of us and implored us to save him from a whipping. He was about to be flogged, he explained, for a trifling offense. He had let someone steal the steward's clothing, worthless stuff really, in the baths. Well, we pulled back our right feet, faced about and returned to the entry where we found the steward counting a stack of gold coins. We begged him to let the servant off. "Really, it's not the money I mind," he replied with enormous condescension, "so much as the idiot's carelessness. It was my dinner-suit he lost, a birthday present from one of my dependents. Expensive too, but then I've already had it washed. Well, it's a trifle. Do what you want with him." We thanked him for his gracious kindness, but when we entered the dining room up ran the same slave whom we'd just begged off. He overwhelmed us with his thanks and then, to our consternation, began to plaster us with kisses. "You'll soon see whom you've helped," he said. "The master's wine will prove the servant's gratitude."

Petronius, *Satyricon* 30–31

CHAPTER 45

PYRAMUS AND THISBE

In ancient Rome, the first contact the public was likely to have with a new poem or a completed section of a longer poem would be not through reading it in a book but through listening to it at a public reading (**recitātiō**) given by the poet in a private house or theater or recital room. Some enterprising poets even tried to gather an audience in the Forum, at the Circus, or in the public baths. The large public baths often contained, in fact, libraries and reading rooms and thus catered to the minds as well as the bodies of their patrons. Martial complained of a boorish poet who pursued him wherever he went, reciting his verses: "I flee to the baths; you echo in my ear. I seek the swimming pool; you don't allow me to swim."

After the adventure with the thief, Marcus, Sextus, and Eucleides relax in the library at the baths and enjoy listening to a recitation of one of the most famous love stories of the ancient world. The story of Pyramus and Thisbe, set in ancient Babylon and made familiar to English readers by Shakespeare's *Romeo and Juliet* and *A Midsummer Night's Dream*, was originally part of a long narrative poem, the *Metamorphoses*, by the Latin poet Ovid (43 B.C.–A.D. 17).

Legendary lovers of antiquity
Illustration by Mahmoud Sayah

Olim Babylōne habitābat adulēscēns quīdam pulcherrimus, nōmine Pȳramus. In vīcīnā domō habitābat virgō cui nōmen erat Thisbē. Pȳramus hanc virginem in viā forte cōnspectam statim amāvit. Et Thisbē, Pȳramō vīsō, amōre capta est. Sed ēheu! Parentēs et virginis et adulēscentis, quoniam multōs iam annōs inter sē rixābantur, eōs convenīre vetuērunt. Pȳramō Thisbēn nē vidēre quidem licēbat. Valdē dolēbant et adulēscēns et virgō.

Erat pariēs domuī utrīque commūnis. Parva tamen rīma, ā nūllō anteā vīsa, ab amantibus inventa est. (Quid nōn sentit amor?) Quam ad rīmam sedentēs inter sē sēcrētō colloquēbantur, alter alterī amōrem exprimēns. Sed mox, ōsculīs parietī datīs, valedīcēbant invītī.

Tandem novum cōnsilium cēpērunt. Cōnstituērunt enim, parentibus īnsciīs, domō nocte exīre, in silvam convenīre, sub arbore quādam cōnsīdere. Itaque Thisbē silentiō noctis, cum vultum vēlāmine cēlāvisset, fūrtim ēgressa ad silvam festīnāvit. Quō cum advēnisset, sub illā arbore cōnsēdit. Ecce tamen vēnit leō saevus, ōre sanguine bovis aspersō. Quō cōnspectō, Thisbē perterrita in spēluncam, quae prope erat, cōnfūgit. Et dum fugit, vēlāmen relīquit. Quod vēlāmen leō ōre sanguineō rapuit, sed mox dēposuit.

Haud multō post Pȳramus ex urbe ēgressus, dum ad arborem eandem prōgreditur, vēstīgia leōnis vīdit. Subitō puellae vēlāmen sanguine aspersum cōnspexit. Timōre tremēns, "Quid accidit?" clāmāvit.

(continued)

1 **Babylōn, Babylōnis,** f., *Babylon*
Pȳramus, -ī, m., *Pyramus*
2 **virgō, virginis,** f., *maiden*
Thisbē, Thisbēs, f., *Thisbe*
4 **rixor, -ārī, -ātus sum,** *to quarrel*
7 **uterque, utraque, utrumque,** *each (of two), both*
rīma, -ae, f., *crack*
9 **ōsculum, -ī,** n., *kiss*
11 **cōnsilium, -ī,** n., *plan*
cōnsilium capere, *to adopt a plan*
īnscius, -a, -um, *not knowing*
13 **vultus, -ūs,** m., *face*
vēlāmen, vēlāminis, n., *veil, shawl*
14 **ōre sanguine aspersō,** *his mouth spattered with blood*
15 **spēlunca, -ae,** f., *cave*

8 **sentiō, sentīre, sēnsī, sēnsus,** *to feel, notice*
9 **exprimō, exprimere, expressī, expressus,** *to press out, express*
valedīcō, valedīcere, valedīxī, valedictūrus, *to say goodbye*
15 **aspergō, aspergere, aspersī, aspersus,** *to sprinkle, splash, spatter*
17 **prōgredior, prōgredī, prōgressus sum,** *to go forward, advance*

Exercise 45a

Respondē Latīnē:

1. Ubi habitābant Pȳramus et Thisbē?
2. Quandō Pȳramus Thisbēn amāvit?
3. Placuitne amor Pȳramī et Thisbēs parentibus?
4. Quid erat inter duās domūs?
5. Quid faciēbant amantēs ad rīmam parietis sedentēs?
6. Quid fēcerat Thisbē antequam ad silvam festīnāvit?
7. Quid Thisbē in silvā vīdit?
8. Quid vīdit Pȳramus ex urbe ēgressus?

"Ēheu! Ego tē occīdī, mea Thisbē, quod tē iussī in silvam noctū sōlam venīre, nec prior vēnī. Sine tē vīvere nōlō." Gladiō igitur strictō, sē vulnerāvit atque ad terram cecidit moriēns.

Ecce! Metū nōndum dēpositō, Thisbē ē spēluncā timidē exit, Pȳramum quaerit. Subitō corpus eius humī iacēns cōnspicit; multīs cum lacrimīs, "Pȳrame," clāmat, "quis hoc fēcit?" Deinde, suō vēlāmine cōnspectō, iam moritūra, "Ō mē miseram!" clāmat. "Vēlāmen meum tē perdidit. Sine tē vīvere nōlō." Et gladiō Pȳramī ipsa sē occīdit.

Parentēs, dolōre commōtī, eōs in eōdem sepulcrō sepelīvērunt.

20 **nec,** conj., *and...not*

21 **prior, prior, prius,** gen., **priōris,** *first (of two), previous*

25 **moritūra,** *intending to die, determined to die*

20 **occīdō, occīdere, occīdī, occīsus,** *to kill*

26 **perdō, perdere, perdidī, perditus,** *to destroy*

Respondē Latīnē:

1. Cūr Pȳramus sē occīdit? Cūr Thisbē?
2. Cūr parentēs Pȳramum Thisbēnque in eōdem sepulcrō sepelīvērunt?

FORMS

Verbs: Future Active Participles

Since Chapter 20 you have seen the future active participle as the fourth principal part of intransitive verbs, e.g., **veniō, venīre, vēnī, ventūrus.**

Transitive verbs form their future active participles by adding ***-ūrus, -a, -um*** to the perfect passive participial stem, e.g., **portātus;** stem, **portāt-**; future active participle, **portātūrus, -a, -um**.

Deponent verbs form their future active participles by adding ***-ūrus, -a, -um*** to the perfect participial stem, e.g., perfect participle, **cōnātus;** stem **cōnāt-**; future active participle, **cōnātūrus, -a -um.**

The future active participle of some verbs ends instead in ***-itūrus, -a, -um***, e.g., **moritūrus, -a, -um** (from **morior, morī, mortuus sum**):

> Thisbē...iam **moritūra**, "Ō mē miseram!" clāmat. (45:23–25)
> *Thisbe...now **about to die,** cries, "Poor me!"*

The following is a tabulation of the participles of non-deponent verbs in conjugations 1–4:

Tense	Active Voice	Passive Voice
Present	1. portāns, portantis *carrying* 2. movēns, moventis *moving* 3. mittēns, mittentis *sending* iaciēns, iacientis *throwing* 4. audiēns, audientis *hearing*	
Perfect		1. portātus, -a, -um *(having been) carried* 2. mōtus, -a, -um *(having been) moved* 3. missus, -a, -um *(having been) sent* iactus, -a, -um *(having been) thrown* 4. audītus, -a, -um *(having been) heard*
Future	1. portātūrus, -a, -um *about to carry* 2. mōtūrus, -a, -um *about to move* 3. missūrus, -a, -um *about to send* iactūrus, -a, -um *about to throw* 4. audītūrus, -a, -um *about to hear*	

NOTES

1. The present and future participles are active in form and meaning.
2. The perfect participle is passive in form and meaning.
3. The present participle of **īre** (*to go*) is **iēns**, **euntis**. The participles of the other irregular verbs are formed regularly, e.g., **volēns**, **volentis**. There is no present participle of **esse** (*to be*).
4. The future participle of **īre** is **itūrus**, **-a**, **-um**.
5. The future participle of **esse** is **futūrus**, **-a**, **-um**.
6. Other possible translations of the future participle include: *going to*, *likely to*, *intending to*, *determined to*, *on the point of…-ing*.

7. Although the participles of deponent verbs have the same endings as those of non-deponent verbs, all the meanings are active:

Present Participle	1. cōnāns, cōnantis, *trying* 2. verēns, verentis, *fearing* 3. loquēns, loquentis, *speaking* ēgrediēns, ēgredientis, *going out* 4. experiēns, experientis, *testing*
Perfect Participle	1. cōnātus, -a, -um, *having tried* 2. veritus, -a, -um, *having feared* 3. locūtus, -a, -um, *having spoken* ēgressus, -a, -um, *having gone out* 4. expertus, -a, -um, *having tested*
Future Participle	1. cōnātūrus, -a, -um, *about to try* 2. veritūrus, -a, -um, *about to fear* 3. locūtūrus, -a, -um, *about to speak* ēgressūrus, -a, -um, *about to go out* 4. expertūrus, -a, -um, *about to test*

Exercise 45b

Give the present, perfect, and future participles of the following verbs in the nominative feminine singular. Translate each form you give:

1. amō
2. moneō
3. aspergō
4. cōnspiciō
5. sentiō
6. rixor
7. polliceor
8. sequor
9. prōgredior
10. experior

polliceor, pollicērī, pollicitus sum, *to promise*

Exercise 45c

Read aloud and translate. Then identify each participle, give its tense, gender, case, and number, say whether it is active or passive in meaning, and tell what it modifies:

1. Multīs hominibus subsequentibus, fūr effugere nōn potuit.
2. Sextus fūrem effugere cōnantem subsequēbātur.
3. Puerī calōrem breve modo tempus passī ē caldāriō exiērunt.
4. Sextus domum profectūrus ab omnibus laudātus est.
5. Thisbē moritūra ad terram cecidit.
6. Fūr vestīmenta surreptūrus in thermās ingressus est.
7. Pȳramus ad illam arborem prōgrediēns vēstīgia leōnis vīdit.
8. Vēlāmine relictō, Thisbē in spēluncam cōnfūgit.
9. Ad rīmam inter sē sēcrētō colloquentēs amōrem exprimēbant.
10. Pȳramus Thisbēn secūtūrus ex urbe profectus est.
11. Sōle oriente, mercātōrēs profectī sunt ad Āfricam nāvigātūrī.
12. Multa virginī pollicitus, Pȳramus eī valedīxit.

orior, orīrī, ortus sum, *to rise*

OVID'S *METAMORPHOSES*

The title of Ovid's great poem, the *Metamorphoses*, is Greek for *changes of form*. In this highly original poem in fifteen books, Ovid describes or alludes to a change in form of a god or a human being in every story from the creation of the universe to the deification of Julius Caesar in 42 B.C. It has been one of the most important sources of mythology for all writers since Ovid's time. These stories have delighted readers for over 2,000 years. Here are four of these stories told briefly in English.

BAUCIS AND PHILEMON

Baucis and Philemon, an aged couple who did not have much in the way of worldly goods, welcomed Jupiter and Mercury, who were traveling on earth disguised as mortals. One thousand homes had turned the gods away and would not grant them hospitality, but this pious couple prepared a meal for their guests with the very best that they had and shared everything with these strangers—the epitome of hospitality. In return Jupiter granted their wish to die at the same moment, when their time had come, by turning them into two trees growing from one trunk.

ACTAEON

Actaeon and his friends had been hunting one morning with great success. At noon, since it was very hot, Actaeon urged his friends to go home with their spoils and return the next morning.

In a secret glade through which ran a sparkling stream, the goddess Diana used to bathe when she was tired of hunting. On this day she had given her bow and arrows, her

Ovid among the Scythians, by Delacroix
Oil on canvas, National Gallery, London, England

robe, and her sandals to her attendant nymphs, let down her hair, and stepped into the pool. Actaeon, wandering through the unfamiliar woods, came upon the goddess as she was bathing. As he gazed awestruck at her, she splashed water into his face and said, "Now you are free to tell anyone that you have seen me undressed—if you can." As she spoke, Actaeon was changed into a spotted stag with fear in his heart. He fled but his own hounds caught his scent and gave chase. He tried to cry out, "I am your master, Actaeon," but he no longer had a human voice. He was finally caught, and his pack of hounds killed him. The goddess Diana had no pity for him until the hounds had torn his life out.

NIOBE

Niobe, the daughter of Tantalus, refused to honor Latona, mother of Apollo and Diana, and insulted her by ridiculing the fact that Latona only had two children while she herself had fourteen—seven boys and seven girls. Latona was angry and asked her children, Apollo and Diana, to make Niobe pay for insulting her divinity. Immediately Apollo and Diana went to Thebes and with bow and arrow killed the seven sons of Niobe. Niobe's grief-stricken husband, Amphion, killed himself with a dagger. In spite of all this, Niobe still insisted that she had triumphed over Latona as she still had more children than the goddess. At once as the daughters stood grieving for their brothers, they were killed one by one by the arrows of Apollo and Diana. Finally realizing the enormity of her crime, Niobe sat among the bodies of her children and slowly changed into stone. She was taken by a whirlwind to Maeonia, her native land, where she became part of the rocky mountains from which a trickling stream of tears flows eternally.

CALLISTO

Callisto was a beautiful nymph of Arcadia and a follower of the goddess Diana. When Jupiter caught sight of her wandering in the woods, he desired her very much. He assumed the dress and form of the goddess Diana and so was able to overcome her fear of men and then force her to his will. Her shame and fear of her secret becoming known by Diana and the other nymphs made her flee away from them deeper into the woods. When her son Arcas was born, Juno was no longer able to contain her jealousy and took revenge by taking away Callisto's human form and changing her into a huge black bear. Because she still had human feelings, Callisto fled both the hunters and the other bears and wandered lonely through the woods. Out hunting one day, Arcas, now fifteen years old, happened upon his mother in the forest. As he was about to kill her with his spear, Jupiter stopped him, snatched them both up, and placed them in the sky as Ursa Major and Ursa Minor. Juno was even more angry at seeing Callisto and Arcas so honored and went straight to Tethys and Oceanus, gods of the sea, and asked them to bar these two from ever coming into the stream of Ocean. The gods assented, and Ursa Major and Ursa Minor move constantly around the pole but are never allowed to go below the horizon into the stream of Ocean.

LOVERS' GRAFFITI

I

Rōmula hīc cum Staphylō morātur.
Romula hangs around here with Staphylus.

II

Restitūtus multās saepe dēcēpit puellās.
Restitutus has often deceived many girls.

III

Vibius Restitūtus hīc sōlus dormīvit et Urbānam suam dēsīderābat.
Vibius Restitutus slept here—alone—and longed for his Urbana.

IV

Successus textor amat caupōniae ancillam, nōmine Hīredem, quae quidem illum nōn cūrat. Sed ille rogat illa commiserētur. Scrībit rīvālis. Valē.
Successus the weaver is in love with the hostess's maid, Iris by name, who of course doesn't care about him. But he asks that she take pity (on him). His rival is writing (this). Farewell.

V

Quisquis amat, valeat; pereat quī nescit amāre!
    Bis tantō pereat, quisquis amāre vetat!
Whoever's in love, may he succeed; whoever's not, may he perish!
    Twice may he perish, whoever forbids me to love!

A FAMOUS POEM OF CATULLUS

Odī et amō. Quare id faciam, fortasse requīris.
    Nesciō, sed fierī sentiō et excrucior.

LXXXV

I love and I hate. Perhaps you ask why I do this.
    I do not know, but I feel it happening and I am tormented.

WORD STUDY XI

Diminutive Suffixes

When added to the base (occasionally the nominative singular) of a Latin noun or adjective, the suffixes ***-ulus*** (***-olus*** after a vowel), ***-(i)culus***, and ***-ellus*** (sometimes ***-illus***) alter the meaning of the word by diminishing its size or importance:

Noun or Adjective	Base (or Nom. Sing.)		Suffix		Diminutive
puer, -ī, m., *boy*	**puer-**	+	***-ulus***	=	**puerulus, -ī,** m., *little boy, young slave boy*
parvus, -a, -um, *small*	**parv-**	+	***-ulus***	=	**parvulus, -a, -um,** *little, tiny*

Diminutives were sometimes used affectionately:

fīlia, -ae, f., *daughter*	**fīli-**	+	***-ola***	=	**fīliola, -ae,** f., *little daughter, darling daughter*

but they could also be disparaging:

mulier, mulieris, f., *woman*	**mulier-**	+	***-cula***	=	**muliercula, -ae,** f., *a little, weak, foolish woman*

Some diminutives had special meanings:

ōs, ōris, n., *mouth*	**ōs-**	+	***-culum***	=	**ōsculum, -ī,** n., *a kiss*

Adjectives formed with diminutive suffixes have endings of the 1st and 2nd declensions; diminutive nouns are in either the 1st or 2nd declension, and the gender is usually the same as that of the original noun:

novus, -a, -um, *new*	**nov-**	+	***-ellus***	=	**novellus, -a, -um,** *young, tender*
pars, partis, f., *part*	**part-**	+	***-icula***	=	**particula, -ae,** f., *a little part*

English words derived from these Latin diminutives usually end in *-le*, *-ule*, *-ole*, *-cle*, *-cule*, *-el*, or *-il*, e.g., *particle*, *novel.*

Exercise 1

Give the meaning of the following Latin diminutives. Consult a Latin dictionary to determine what (if any) special meanings these diminutives may have had for the Romans:

1. **servulus, -ī,** m.
2. **oppidulum, -ī,** n.
3. **amīcula, -ae,** f.
4. **lectulus, -ī,** m.
5. **capitulum, -ī,** n.
6. **cistella, -ae,** f.
7. **ancillula, -ae,** f.
8. **libellus, -ī,** m.
9. **lapillus, -ī,** m.
10. **puellula, -ae,** f.

Exercise 2

Give the English word derived from each of the following Latin diminutives:

1. **mūsculus, -ī,** m., *little mouse*
2. **circulus, -ī,** m., *a round figure*
3. **corpusculum, -ī,** n., *a little body*
4. **rīvulus, -ī,** m., *a little stream*
5. **minusculus, -a, -um,** *somewhat small*
6. **tabernāculum, -ī,** n., *tent*

Exercise 3

Look up the Roman emperor Caligula in an encyclopedia and find out why he was known by this diminutive nickname.

Frequentative Verbs

Frequentative verbs are formed from other Latin verbs and denote repeated or intensified action. (They are also called intensive verbs.) They are usually in the first conjugation, e.g., **dictō, -āre,** *to say often, repeat* (from **dīcō, -ere,** *to say*). Often the special frequentative meaning has been lost and the frequentative verb has nearly the same meaning as the original verb, e.g., **cantō, -āre,** *to sing* (from **canō, -ere,** *to sing*). Frequentative verbs are formed from other verbs in one of two ways:

1. by adding ***-ō*** to the stem of the fourth principal part, e.g., **acceptō, -āre,** *to receive* (from **acceptus**, perfect passive participle of **accipiō**)
2. by adding ***-itō*** to the base of the present infinitive (occasionally to the stem of the fourth principal part), e.g., **rogitō, -āre,** *to ask frequently or earnestly* (from **rogāre**), and **ēmptitō, -āre,** *to buy up* (from **ēmptus**, perfect passive participle of **emō**)

Exercise 4

Give the original Latin verb to which each of the following frequentative verbs is related:

1. iactō, -āre
2. cessō, -āre
3. habitō, -āre
4. ventitō, -āre
5. haesitō, -āre
6. cursō, -āre
7. vīsitō, -āre
8. scrīptitō, -āre
9. exercitō, -āre
10. dormitō, -āre
11. clāmitō, -āre
12. ductō, -āre
13. tractō, -āre
14. agitō, -āre

Exercise 5

Look up each of the frequentative verbs in Exercise 4 in a Latin dictionary. Identify each frequentative verb whose meaning differs significantly from the meaning of the original verb.

Exercise 6

Form a frequentative verb from each of the following Latin verbs by adding ***-ō*** to the stem of the fourth principal part. Look up the frequentative verb in a Latin dictionary and compare its meaning with that of the original verb:

1. excipiō
2. reprehendō
3. olfaciō
4. expellō
5. adiuvō
6. terreō
7. gerō
8. capiō

REVIEW X: CHAPTERS 43–45

Exercise Xa: Imperfect and Pluperfect Subjunctives

Give the imperfect and pluperfect subjunctives of the following verbs in the third person singular (give both active and passive forms for numbers 1–5):

1. amō
2. moneō
3. dūcō
4. capiō
5. inveniō
6. moror
7. vereor
8. sequor
9. ingredior
10. experior

Exercise Xb: Participles

Give the present, perfect, and future participles of the verbs in Exercise Xa in the nominative and accusative singular feminine.

Exercise Xc: Translation

Read aloud and translate:

CAESAR VISITS BRITAIN

Gaius Iūlius Caesar, dux praeclārus Rōmānōrum, in Galliā pugnāns multa dē Britanniā cognōvit. Mercātōrēs enim ē Britanniā ad Galliam trānsgressī multa emēbant ac vēndēbant; et Britannī auxilium Gallīs Caesarī resistentibus semper mittēbant. Caesar igitur, Gallīs victīs et nāvibus parātīs, in Britanniam trānsgredī cōnstituit. Profectūrī tamen mīlitēs, magnā tempestāte coortā, nāvēs cōnscendere vix poterant. Complūribus post diēbus, cum tempestāte nāvēs paene dēlētae essent, Rōmānī Britanniae appropinquantēs incolās in omnibus collibus īnstructōs cōnspexērunt. Ēgredientēs Rōmānōs Britannī, pīlīs coniectīs, dēpellere cōnātī sunt; sed, quamquam multōs Rōmānōrum vulnerāvērunt, tandem superātī sunt.

1 **dux, ducis,** m., *general*
pugnō, -āre, -āvī, -ātūrus, *to fight*

6 **cōnscendō, cōnscendere, cōnscendī, cōnscēnsus,** *to board (ship)*

8 **īnstructus, -a, -um,** *drawn up, deployed*
pīlum, -ī, n., *javelin*

9 **dēpellō, dēpellere, dēpulī, dēpulsus,** *to drive away*

Exercise Xd: Identification

In the story in Exercise Xc, identify the following in sequence:

1. a present active participle
2. a perfect participle of a deponent verb
3. a present active participle
4. an ablative absolute
5. a future active participle
6. an ablative absolute
7. a **cum** circumstantial clause
8. a present active participle
9. a perfect passive participle
10. a present participle of a deponent verb
11. an ablative absolute

Exercise Xe: Substitution

Choose the phrase or clause that could be substituted for the words quoted from the story in exercise Xc and that would keep the same sense. Then translate the sentence, substituting the new phrase or clause for the original words:

1. **in Galliā pugnāns**
   a. in Galliā pugnātūrus
   b. quī in Galliā pugnābat
   c. in Galliā pugnant
2. **ē Britanniā ad Galliam trānsgressī**
   a. quī ē Britanniā ad Galliam trānsgredientur
   b. ē Britanniā ad Galliam trānsgressūrī
   c. quī ē Britanniā ad Galliam trānsgressī erant
3. **Gallīs victīs et nāvibus parātīs**
   a. cum Gallī victī essent et nāvēs essent parātae
   b. Gallōs victūrus et nāvēs parātūrus
   c. Gallōs vincēns et nāvēs parāns
4. **profectūrī tamen mīlitēs**
   a. profectīs tamen mīlitibus
   b. mīlitēs tamen quī proficīscī in animō habēbant
   c. mīlitēs tamen quī profectī essent
5. **cum tempestāte nāvēs paene dēlētae essent**
   a. tempestāte nāvēs paene dēlente
   b. quod tempestāte nāvēs paene dēlētae sunt
   c. nāvibus tempestāte paene dēlētīs
6. **quamquam multōs Rōmānōrum vulnerāvērunt**
   a. multīs Rōmānīs vulnerātīs
   b. multōs Rōmānōrum vulnerātūrī
   c. multī Rōmānōrum vulnerātī

Exercise Xf: Reading Comprehension

Read the following story from Ovid and answer the questions with full sentences in English:

ARACHNĒ ET MINERVA

Lȳdia Arachnē, perītissima omnium puellārum quae tēlās texēbant, per urbēs Lȳdiās arte suā erat praeclārissima. Iter ex urbibus vīcīnīs faciēbant multī, quī cūriōsī Arachnēn tēlās texentem spectāre volēbant. Etiam nymphae, silvīs et montibus et undīs relictīs, ad casam Arachnēs veniēbant. Omnēs mīrābantur nōn modo tēlās textās sed etiam artem quā texēbat. Minerva ipsa Arachnēn docuisse dīcēbātur, sed puella hoc vehementer negāvit. "Nūlla dea," inquit, "mihi magistra fuit! Sī dea ipsa advēnerit, certāmen nōn vītābō!"

Quō audītō, Minerva Arachnēn vīsitātūra anum simulāvit et baculō innixa ad puellam superbam vēnit. In casam ingressa sīc locūta est: "Audī mē monentem! Fāmam pete inter mortālēs sed cēde deae veniamque tuīs dictīs, temerāria, rogā! Veniam dabit dea rogantī."

"Abī, anus!" clāmāvit Arachnē. "Nōlī mē monēre!" Mīrāta tamen est cūr dea ipsa nōn vēnisset, cūr certāmen vītāret. Tum dea, "Vēnī!" inquit et fōrmam simulātam dēposuit. Quamquam dea sē ostenderat, puella tamen nōn timuit, immō certāmen prōposuit.

Tum ambae, cum ad tēlās cōnsēdissent, pictūrās pulcherrimās texere coepērunt. Operibus cōnfectīs, tēla Minervae nūllō modō melior erat tēlā Arachnēs. Minerva autem rēs ā dīs bene gestās texuerat, Arachnē rēs male gestās. Quō vīsō, īrātissima facta est dea. Arachnē, ferōciter ā deā castīgāta, sē laqueō suspendit.

Puellae pendentis miserita est Minerva, quae sīc locūta est: "Vīve, superba! Sed vīve, fōrmā arāneae sūmptā!"

Arachnē, capite statim dēminūtō, ipsa tōtō corpore parva facta est. Adhūc tamen fīlum dēdūcēns arānea tēlam texit.

1 **Lȳdius, -a, -um,** *from Lydia (a country in Asia Minor), Lydian*
perītus, -a, -um, *skilled*
tēla, -ae, f., *web, fabric, loom*
2 **cūriōsus, -a, -um,** *curious*
3 **nympha, -ae,** f., *nymph, nature spirit*
4 **mīror, -ārī, -ātus sum,** *to admire, wonder at, wonder*
6 **negō, -āre, -āvī, -ātus,** *to deny*
7 **certāmen, certāminis,** n., *contest*
8 **anus, -ūs,** f., *old woman*
simulō, -āre, -āvī, -ātus, *to pretend, take the form of*
innixus, -a, -um +abl., *leaning on*
9 **superbus, -a, -um,** *proud, arrogant*
10 **venia, -ae,** f., *pardon, forgiveness*
dicta, -ōrum, n. pl., *words*
16 **ambō, ambae, ambō,** *both*
17 **opus, operis,** n., *work, product*
19 **laqueus, -ī,** m., *noose*
20 **misereor, -ērī, -itus sum** + gen., *to pity*
21 **arānea, -ae,** f., *spider*
23 **fīlum, -ī,** n., *thread*
dēdūcēns, *drawing out, spinning*

10 **cēdō, cēdere, cessī, cessūrus** + dat., *to yield to, give in to*
14 **ostendō, ostendere, ostendī, ostentus,** *to show*
18 **gerō, gerere, gessī, gestus,** *to wear; to carry on, perform, do*
19 **suspendō, suspendere, suspendī, suspēnsus,** *to suspend, hang*
20 **pendeō, pendēre, pependī,** *to be suspended, hang*
22 **dēminuō, dēminuere, dēminuī, dēminūtus,** *to reduce in size*

1. For what was Arachne most famous?
2. What did curious people do?
3. What did the nymphs do?
4. What did they admire?
5. Who was said to have taught Arachne?
6. What challenge to the goddess did Arachne make?
7. What form did the goddess assume?
8. What advice did she give?
9. What did Arachne say in reply?
10. Who proposed the contest?
11. Whose woven fabric was better?
12. What had Minerva and Arachne woven?
13. Why did Arachne hang herself?
14. How did Minerva react?
15. What does Arachne continue to do in her transformed state?

Minerva

A Rainy Day

Many of the games that children play today were also played by Roman children. They built toy houses and rode on long sticks; they had spinning tops, hoops that they bowled along with a stick, and dolls (**pūpae**); they tossed coins, calling out "heads or ships" (**capita aut nāvia**); and they played at being soldiers or judges or consuls. They also harnessed mice to toy carts.

Several children's games used nuts. In one a nut was balanced on three others, and children competed at knocking them down with a fruit pit. The winner got all the nuts. They also competed at tossing nuts into a narrow-necked vase placed some distance away. A very popular game was to ask your partner to guess whether the number of nuts (or pebbles or other similar objects) hidden in your hand was odd or even (**pār impār**). In another popular game two players each showed (or "flashed") a number of fingers on their right hands (**digitīs micāre**) and simultaneously called out how many fingers altogether they believed had been shown. The round was won by the player who first guessed correctly five times. This game is still played in Italy under the name of *morra*.

Both adults and children played a game that resembled checkers or chess (**lūdus latrunculōrum,** *game of bandits*), in which they moved two sets of pieces on a checkered board. They also played a game of chance with knucklebones (**tālī**). Older children and young men took exercise on the Campus Martius—wrestling, riding, and driving chariots—followed possibly by a swim across the Tiber.

As we rejoin our story, Marcus, Cornelia, and Sextus are spending a rainy day at home.

Roman children at play

"Ēheu!" mussāvit Marcus. "Cūr 'ēheu'?" rogāvit Sextus.

"Semper pluit!" respondit Marcus. "Ego in animō habēbam ad Campum Mārtium hodiē dēscendere et ad palaestram īre, sed pater nōs domī manēre iussit. Putō patrem esse crūdēlem."

Eō ipsō tempore Eucleidēs ingressus puerōs rogāvit cūr tam trīstēs essent. "In palaestram īre cupiēbāmus," inquit Marcus, "sed pater hoc vetuit."

Cui Eucleidēs, "Bonō animō este!" inquit. "Ego vōs docēbō latrunculīs lūdere. Putō hunc lūdum esse optimum."

Duās ferē hōrās ita lūdēbant. Postrēmō Sextus exclāmāvit, "Hic lūdus mē nōn iam dēlectat. Ego putō hunc lūdum esse pessimum. Age, Marce! Nōnne vīs pār impār lūdere vel digitīs micāre?"

Statim clāmāre coepērunt ambō. Simul Marcus, "Quīnque!" simul Sextus, "Novem!" Deinde Marcus, "Octō!" Sextus, "Sex!"

"Tacēte, puerī!" interpellāvit Eucleidēs. "Nolīte clāmōribus vestrīs vexāre mātrem et Cornēliam! Putō vōs esse molestissimōs hodiē." At puerī eī nōn pārēbant. Itaque Cornēlia, clāmōribus audītīs, in ātrium ingressa rogāvit quid facerent.

"Nōlī nōs vexāre!" inquit Sextus. "Abī! Sed cūr pūpam in manibus habēs? Num pūpā lūdis?"

(continued)

3 **putō, -āre, -āvī, -ātus,** *to think, consider*
8 **lūdus, -ī,** m., *school, game*
9 **ferē,** adv., *almost, approximately*
postrēmō, adv., *finally*
12 **ambō, ambae, ambō,** *both*
17 **pūpa, -ae,** f., *doll*
Num...? *Surely...not...?* (introduces a question that expects the answer "no")

Exercise 46a

Respondē Latīnē:

1. Cūr erat Marcus trīstis?
2. Cūr Marcus patrem crūdēlem esse putat?
3. Quid Eucleidēs puerōs docuit?
4. Quid Sextus post duās hōrās facere voluit?
5. Quōs Marcus et Sextus clāmōribus vexābant?
6. Quis in ātrium ingressa est?
7. Quid in manibus habuit?

"Stultus es, Sexte! Pūpa nōn est mea. Num crēdis mē pūpā lūdere? Hanc pūpam, quam ego ipsa fēcī, fīliae Dāvī dōnō dabō. Hodiē est diēs nātālis eius."

Subitō Sextus, pūpā abreptā, in peristȳlium aufūgit. Quō vīsō, Eucleidēs Sextō clāmāvit, "Nōlī pūpam laedere! Statim eam refer!"

Eō ipsō tempore ingressus est Cornēlius. Cum audīvisset quid Sextus fēcisset, "Sexte!" clāmāvit. "Venī hūc!" Puer, iam timidus, in ātrium regressus pūpam Cornēliae reddidit. Tum Cornēlius Sextum sēcum ex ātriō ēdūxit.

Quō factō, Marcus rogāvit, "Quid pater faciet? Quid Sextō fīet?"

Cui Cornēlia, "Putō," inquit, "patrem in animō habēre Sextum verberāre."

20 **dōnum, -ī,** n., *gift*
dōnō (dat.) **dare,** *to give as a gift*
diēs nātālis, diēī nātālis, m., *birthday*

21 **peristȳlium, -ī,** n., *peristyle, (courtyard surrounded with a colonnade)*

26 **Quid Sextō fīet?** *What will happen to Sextus?*

21 **abripiō, abripere, abripuī, abreptus,** *to snatch away*
22 **laedō, laedere, laesī, laesus,** *to harm*

Respondē Latīnē:

1. Lūdēbatne pūpā Cornēlia?
2. Cuius erat diēs nātālis?
3. Quid Sextus, pūpā vīsā, fēcit?
4. Cui Sextus pūpam reddidit?
5. Quid Cornēlius factūrus erat?

BUILDING THE MEANING

Accusative and Infinitive (Indirect Statement) I

The following sentences occurred in the story:

Putō **hunc lūdum esse** optimum. (46:7–8)
*I think **that this game is** very good.*

Putō **vōs esse** molestissimōs. (46:15)
*I think **that you are** very annoying.*

Num crēdis **mē** pūpā **lūdere**? (46:19)
*Surely you do not believe **that I am playing** with a doll?*

In such sentences, you are being given two pieces of information:

(1) I think	(2) what I think
Putō	hunc lūdum esse optimum.
	(that) this game is very good.

You will see that, in the second part, the Latin subject is expressed in the *accusative* case and the verb is in the *infinitive*, where English says *that this game* and *is*. Similarly:

Sciō		**vōs esse** molestissimōs.
I know	*that*	***you are*** *very troublesome.*
Vidēmus		**Dāvum** in agrīs **labōrāre.**
We see	*that*	***Davus is working*** *in the fields.*
Audiō		**eum** domī **morārī.**
I hear	*that*	***he is staying*** *at home.*

Other verbs that may be followed by the *accusative and infinitive* construction include **dīcō** (*I say*), **spērō** (*I hope*), and **sentiō** (*I feel*).

Sextus sentit **sē** aegrum **esse.**
Sextus feels ***that he is*** *ill.*

In translating this Latin construction, the next English word after verbs such as *I think*, *I know*, *I see*, *I hear*, and *I feel* will most often be *that*.

This accusative and infinitive construction in which something is being reported indirectly is known as *indirect statement.*

Exercise 46b

Read aloud and translate:

1. Eucleidēs dīcit lūdum latrunculōrum esse optimum.
2. Sciō Cornēlium esse senātōrem Rōmānum.
3. Nōs omnēs scīmus Cornēliam esse puellam Rōmānam.
4. Putō Sextum puerum temerārium esse.
5. Audiō Cornēlium ad Cūriam festīnāre.
6. Scit ancillās cēnam parāre.
7. Videō haud longam esse viam.
8. Audiō caupōnem esse amīcum Eucleidis.
9. Putāmus in agrīs labōrāre servōs.
10. Crēdō Aurēliam in urbem dēscendere.
11. Dīcunt Marcum dormīre.
12. Scīmus semper ēsurīre puerōs.
13. Audiō Titum mappam nōn habēre.
14. Cornēlia putat pūpam esse pulcherrimam.

Exercise 46c

Select, read aloud, and translate:

1. Aliī putant (Sextus/Sextum) esse bonum, aliī putant eum (est/erat/esse) molestum.
2. Dāvus quidem scit omnēs (puerōs/puerum/puerī) saepe esse (molestum/molestī/molestōs).
3. At Aurēlia putat Marcum et Sextum semper bonōs (sunt/esse/erant).
4. Sextus Marcō dīcit Dāvum (esse/est/sum) īrācundum.
5. Respondet Marcus (Dāvī/Dāvō/Dāvum) nōn semper (esse/est) īrācundum.
6. Dīcit Dāvum in agrīs strēnuē (labōrāre/labōrāvit/labōrat).
7. Sextus respondet Dāvum sub arbore cotīdiē post merīdiem (dormīs/dormiēbat/dormīre).
8. Cornēlia putat (puerī/puerīs/puerōs) haud strēnuē (labōrāvērunt/labōrant/labōrāre).
9. Dīcit Cornēlia Marcum et (Sextī/Sextum/Sextus) saepe in lectīs diū (iacēre/iacent/iacēmus).
10. Flāvia, amīca Cornēliae, putat (Cornēlia/Cornēliam/Cornēliae) puellam pulcherrimam (esse/sunt/est).

Exercise 46d

Using story 46 and the information on indirect statement as guides, give the Latin for:

1. Marcus says that his father is cruel.
2. Eucleides says that the game of bandits is the best, but Sextus thinks it is the worst.
3. Eucleides says that the children are very annoying today.
4. Sextus believes that Cornelia is playing with the doll.
5. Eucleides thinks that Sextus is harming the doll.

ROMAN LIFE XXVII

GAMES PLAYED BY CHILDREN AND ADULTS

Descriptions of games played by Roman children are preserved in the writings of ancient authors. They are often difficult for us to interpret, although they were probably perfectly clear to ancient readers who would have been familiar with the games and their rules. In the following passage the poet Ovid describes games boys played with nuts (**nucēs**). See if you can figure out how many games Ovid describes and how they were played. We give both the Latin and an English translation of each couplet. You may want to look up some of the Latin words in a dictionary:

Hās puer aut certō rēctās dīlāminat ictū
  aut prōnās digitō bisve semelve petit.
These (nuts), as they stand upright, a boy splits with certain aim,
  or, as they lie on their side, strikes with his finger once or twice.

Quattuor in nucibus, nōn amplius, ālea tōta est,
  cum sibi suppositīs additur ūna tribus.
In four nuts, and no more, is all his hazard,
  when one is added to the three beneath it.

Per tabulae clīvum lābī iubet alter et optat
  tangat ut ē multīs quaelibet ūna suam.
Another has them roll down a sloping board, and prays
  that one out of many, whichever it may be, may touch his own.

Est etiam, pār sit numerus quī dīcat an impār,
  ut dīvīnātās auferat augur opēs.
Then there is (a boy) who guesses whether the number be odd or even,
  that the augur may bear away the wealth he has divined.

Fit quoque dē crētā, quālem caeleste figūram
  sīdus et in Graecīs littera quarta gerit.
Then too there is drawn in chalk a shape, such as a heavenly
  constellation or the fourth Greek letter bears.

Haec ubi distīncta est gradibus, quae cōnstitit intus
  quot tetigit virgās, tot capit ipsa nucēs.
When this has been marked with stages, the nut that stops within it
  gains itself as many nuts as it has touched lines.

Vās quoque saepe cavum spatiō distante locātur,
 in quod missa levī nux cadat ūna manū.
Often too a hollow vessel is placed at a distance,
 into which a nut flung by a skillful hand may fall.

—Ovid, *Nux* 73–86

The next two passages refer to playing **pār impār** by flashing the fingers (**micāre**):

When they praise a man's honesty, they say, "He is a man with whom you can safely play at odd and even in the dark."

Cicero, *De officiis* III. 77

"Suppose there were two men to be saved from a sinking ship—both of them wise men—and only one small plank. Should both seize it to save themselves? Or should one give way to the other?"

"Why, of course one should give way to the other, but that other must be the one whose life is more valuable, either for his own sake or for that of his country."

"But what if these considerations are of equal weight in both?"

"Then there will be no contest, but one will give place to the other, as if the point were decided by lot or at a game of odd and even."

Cicero, *De officiis* III. 90

GAMBLING WITH KNUCKLEBONES

From a personal letter of the Emperor Augustus:

I dined, dear Tiberius, with the same company; we had besides as guests Vinicius and the elder Silius. We gambled like old men during the meal both yesterday and today. When the knucklebones were thrown, whoever turned up the "dog" or the six put a denarius in the pool for each one of the knucklebones and the whole was taken by anyone who threw the "Venus."

From a personal letter of the Emperor Augustus to his daughter:

I send you two hundred and fifty denarii, the sum that I gave each of my guests, in case they wished to play at knucklebones or at odd and even during the dinner.

Suetonius, *Augustus* LXXI.2, 4

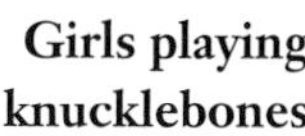

Girls playing knucklebones

THE LAST MOVE IN A GAME OF CHESS

Julius Canus, after a long dispute with the Emperor Caligula, was ordered by the capricious emperor to be executed. Seneca the moralist praises the bravery of Canus under sentence of death:

> Will you believe that Canus spent the ten intervening days before his execution in no anxiety of any sort? What the man said, what he did, how tranquil he was, passes all credence. He was playing chess when the centurion who was dragging off a whole company of victims to death ordered that he also be summoned. Having been called, he counted the pawns and said to his partner: "See that after my death you do not claim falsely that you won." Then nodding to the centurion, he said, "You will bear witness that I am one pawn ahead."
>
> Seneca, *De tranquillitate* XIV 6–7

Quid est tam incertum quam tālōrum iactus? *What is so uncertain as a cast of dice?* (Cicero, *De divinatione* II.121)

nucēs relinquere *to leave childhood behind* (Persius, *Satires* I.10)

FORMS

The Irregular Verb *fīō, fierī, factus sum*

This irregular verb, meaning *to become, be made*, or *happen*, serves as the passive of **faciō.** Note that the verb has only three principal parts: **fīō,** *I become;* **fierī,** *to become*, and **factus sum**, *I became*. Some of its forms were introduced in Exercise 34h. You saw an example in the story at the beginning of this chapter:

"Quid pater faciet? Quid Sextō **fīet**?" (46:26)
*"What will father do? What **will happen** to Sextus?"*

Its forms in the present, imperfect, and future tenses are as follows:

		Present	Imperfect	Future
	1	fī*ō*	fīḗ*bam*	fī*am*
S	2	fī*s*	fīḗ*bās*	fī*ēs*
	3	fi*t*	fīḗ*bat*	fī*et*
	1	fī*mus*	fīē*bā́mus*	fī*ḗmus*
P	2	fī*tis*	fīē*bā́tis*	fī*ḗtis*
	3	fī*unt*	fīḗ*bant*	fī*ent*

Learn the above forms thoroughly.

Exercise 46e

Read aloud and translate:

1. Titus vīnum bibit et paulātim ēbrius fit.
2. Sī Titus plūs vīnī bibet, magis ēbrius fīet.
3. Aurēlia Titum in diēs molestiōrem fierī putat.
4. Quid Titō fīet sī etiam plūs vīnī nunc bibet?
5. Aliquid malī certē eī fīet.

THE EARLY EMPIRE

Augustus died at the age of seventy-six in A.D. 14, in the month named for him in 27 B.C. At the time of his death, the mood in Rome was one of contentment. The frontiers of the empire were secure, the state bureaucracy was operating well, the **equitēs** were satisfied with the expansion of trade and the new careers that were open to them in political and military service, and the urban population was happy to have enough food and entertainment. Augustus had also left behind a strong national consciousness of the strength and glorious achievements of the Roman Empire, a perception that the *Aeneid* and other works of literature had helped to create.

Growth of the Roman Empire, 44 B.C.–A.D. 180

At death of Caesar, 44 B.C.
To death of Augustus, A.D. 14
To death of Marcus Aurelius, A.D. 180
Battle sites

For almost half a century, the Roman world had been ruled by a single master who held all real authority in his own hands, despite the trappings of republican government. Only an extraordinary individual could maintain that kind of control. Inevitably, upon his death, trouble was bound to come. What made matters even worse was that Augustus intended the office of emperor to be hereditary, but in order to maintain the illusion of republicanism it could not officially be made hereditary. Unfortunately, he had failed to produce a son of his own, whom he could have maneuvered into a position to be accepted as emperor after his death. Therefore, Augustus had to use the children and grandchildren of his sister, Octavia; his daughter, Julia; and his wife's first husband, T. Claudius Nero, as substitutes. That is why the dynasty of emperors who ruled the first century of the Roman Empire is called the Julio-Claudian dynasty. Because of Augustus' maneuverings to procure an heir from his own family, many different people could claim a right to succeed to Augustus' principate. Therefore, family intrigue and murder were prominent in the history of this dynasty.

THE JULIO-CLAUDIAN DYNASTY

The personal lives of the Julio-Claudian dynasty inspired much scandal and malicious rumor that were gleefully reported by ancient writers such as the biographer Suetonius. Much of it has been dramatized in modern novels and films such as Robert Graves' *I Claudius* and *Claudius the God.* Even after the falsehoods have been eliminated, the truth still sometimes sounds like a soap opera.

The man who ultimately succeeded Augustus was his stepson Tiberius, who had been a loyal and effective subordinate in military and political affairs. Unfortunately, he had never been Augustus' first choice as a successor, and he was old and disillusioned by the time Augustus had no one else old enough left to succeed him. Tiberius' biggest problems were that he instinctively disdained many of the old families in the Senate and let himself be too influenced by Sejanus, corrupt head of the Praetorian Guard. Sejanus had tried to eliminate other members of the Julio-Claudian family and take control through marrying Tiberius' niece. By the time Tiberius found out about Sejanus' plottings and had him executed, only his nephew Caligula was in a position to succeed.

Caligula had suffered a very abnormal childhood. At first he was spoiled by his father, Germanicus, who had been in line to succeed Tiberius. When Gaius was a small boy, his father's soldiers had made him their mascot dressed in a soldier suit and had named him Caligula, "Little Boot," after the tiny army boots (**caligae**) he wore. When he arrived in Rome to head the state, his personality and generosity made a good first impression: He gave the praetorians a large cash bonus, provided the people with grand spectacles, and even displayed interest in the government. He had no real training for the job, however, and before long began to show bad temper, arrogance, and irrational fear of plots against him. As emperor he lived in terror of losing his life in palace intrigue, and he finally ended up in Tiberius' eccentric refuge on the Isle of Capri. Despite a promising start, he quickly proved unfit to rule and was assassinated in A.D. 41.

The Praetorian Guard proclaimed Caligula's uncle Claudius as the new emperor. Born prematurely with mental and physical infirmities, Claudius had not previously been seen as suited to rule. He was more able than many had realized, however. Unfortunately, lack of affection as a child made him easily susceptible to scheming wives who tried to use him to promote their family interests. His fourth wife, Agrippina the Younger, probably killed him with poisoned mushrooms in order to obtain the throne for her son, Nero, after she had brought about the murder of Claudius' own son, Britannicus.

Claudius
Marble head, Louvre, Paris, France

Nero Claudius Caesar was sixteen years old when he became emperor. Agrippina encouraged him to devote himself to music, drama, and chariot races so that she could be the power behind the throne. Eventually, he tired of her dominance and had her murdered. He spent more and more time and money on the circus, theater, and musical contests while he neglected the finances and the provincial armies. After a great fire destroyed much of Rome in A.D. 64, he rebuilt the city and erected a new palace called the **Domus Aurea** *(Golden House)*, on such a lavish scale that he was accused of starting the fire to have the chance of showing off. He deflected attention to the Christians in Rome by accusing them and condemning many to horrible deaths. His cowardice and brutality alienated many Romans, but the final straw was a costly tour of Greece, where he competed as a performing artist in public competitions in A.D. 67 and 68. When Nero returned to Rome, he faced a thoroughly hostile Senate and armies who were rebelling because they had not been paid. Under the threat of troops coming to carry out the Senate's decree of execution, Nero took his own life.

Despite their personal deficiencies and their inability to get along with the Senate, which resented the increasingly centralized power of the emperor, the Julio-Claudians had provided the Roman Empire with two generations of peace and prosperity. Tiberius promoted public careers for the **equitēs** and consolidated the military gains of Augustus, while Claudius added the province of Britain through conquest in 43. Claudius further professionalized the imperial bureaucracy by using loyal freedmen and promoted economic growth by building roads, bridges, and harbors. During most of Nero's reign, capable advisors such as the philosopher Seneca kept things outside of Rome on an even keel.

THE FLAVIAN DYNASTY

Powerful generals from the provinces had already begun to maneuver against Nero before his death. The years A.D. 68 and 69 saw the rapid succession of four emperors in a series of assassinations and civil wars: Galba, Otho, Vitellius, and Vespasian. Fortunately for Rome and the empire, Vespasian was able to stop the slide into chaos and establish his own Flavian dynasty firmly in power. Vespasian was an **eques** of Sabine origin who had become a successful general in the conquest of Britain and in subduing a major insurrection by the Jews of Judaea. He quickly restored the principate on the model of Augustus. To show the new direction of his reign, he tore down Nero's **Domus Aurea** and began construction of the Flavian Amphitheater (the Colosseum) on part of the site for the benefit of the public.

Vespasian's elder son, Titus, who had captured Jerusalem in A.D. 70, had served as his father's loyal Praetorian prefect until Vespasian died in A.D. 79. Titus' popularity grew during his brief reign when he promptly provided relief to the victims of Mt. Vesuvius' eruption in A.D. 79 and of a plague and great fire at Rome in A.D. 80. He completed the Flavian Amphitheater and dedicated it with magnificent games. His death from a fever caused great mourning. He was honored by the Arch of Titus in the Forum, which depicts his triumph over Judaea.

Titus' younger brother, Domitian, had always resented his more popular brother and used his own power as emperor to settle the score for real or imagined hurts earlier in life. His autocratic behavior and paranoid treatment of "enemies" unleashed a cycle of assassination plots and oppression among the senatorial class that finally resulted in his murder in A.D. 96. Despite his bad points, however, Domitian had followed many of the successful policies of his father and brother. Like them, he had kept the support of the lower classes through generous treatment, preserved peace on the frontier, and kept a good surplus in the treasury.

Trajan
Marble bust, Ephesus Museum, Turkey

THE FIVE GOOD EMPERORS

The senators who had plotted against Domitian had tried to break the pattern of dynastic succession established by Augustus and Vespasian. They elected as emperor a childless and elderly senator named Nerva. To protect himself against being overthrown by the Praetorian Guard and provincial armies, however, Nerva had to create a dynastic heir by adopting Trajan, the powerful general of Lower Germany. Before Trajan could even get to Rome to greet his new father, Nerva died.

Trajan showed great respect for the Senate, and grateful senators gave him the title **Optimus Prīnceps**. He revived the expansionism of the old republic by conquering Dacia, Armenia, Mesopotamia, and Assyria. Dacia was rich in gold, but Trajan's rapid expansion dangerously overextended the empire's borders and exhausted him. Just before his heart failed in 177, he adopted his son-in-law Hadrian as his heir.

Hadrian upset many senators when he concluded that it was necessary to abandon most of Trajan's conquests except Dacia. He concentrated his efforts on building strong, fixed defensive boundaries such as his famous wall in Britain. His one major war was fought in Judaea against a new rebellion. After his victory, he founded a Roman colony on the site of Jerusalem and further scattered the Jewish people from their ancient home. Hadrian had taken more power away from the Senate, and when he suppressed a senatorial plot near the end of his life, he alienated the Senate even more. When he died, the senators tried to withhold the honor of deification.

Since Hadrian had no children, he had adopted Titus Aurelius Antoninus as his heir. Antoninus earned the **cognōmen** Pius by persuading hostile senators to deify Hadrian in return for concessions that would restore some of the Senate's lost prestige. Antoninus ruled benignly and lived a simple life of Roman modesty. The momentum that had been built up by Trajan and Hadrian carried the empire safely through his long and peaceful reign, and he left the biggest surplus that the treasury had ever seen. Unfortunately, while he was content to stay in Italy and tend his country estate, hostile forces were massing just beyond the imperial frontiers. His son-in-law and adopted son Marcus Aurelius had to deal with the first in a series of unprecedented military crises that almost led to the empire's destruction during the third century A.D.

During the reign of the Five Good Emperors, the Roman Empire reached the height of its peace and prosperity under rulers who promoted the public welfare and patronized literature and the arts: Nerva and Trajan established the **alimenta,** a welfare program for orphans that also provided investment for agricultural development. Trajan and Hadrian founded and beautified cities all over the empire. Many monuments such as Trajan's Column, which depicts the Dacian War, Trajan's Market, Hadrian's villa at Tivoli, his domed Pantheon, his temple to Venus and Rome, and his tomb, the Castel Sant' Angelo, still stand. The emperors' concerns for good government are revealed in the letters of Pliny the Younger, who was favored by Trajan. Marcus Aurelius was devoted to Stoic philosophy, and in his *Meditations* he left behind a much-admired testament to his fortitude and commitment to a moral life in the face of continuous warfare against barbarian enemies, a disastrous plague, court intrigue, and treachery.

Marcus Aurelius
Gold aureus, private collection

CHAPTER
47

LOOKING FORWARD TO THE GAMES

Postrīdiē, dum Gaius Cornēlius in tablīnō scrībit, subitō intrāvit Titus, frāter eius.

"Salvē, Gaī!" clāmāvit Titus. "Quid agis?"

"Bene!" respondit Cornēlius. "Sed semper sum, ut vidēs, negōtiōsus."

Cui Titus, "Prō certō habeō tē crās nōn labōrātūrum esse. Omnēs enim cīvēs Rōmānī ad mūnera itūrī sunt. Spērō tē quoque ad mūnera itūrum esse."

At Cornēlius, "Mūnera?" inquit. "Quid dīcis, mī Tite?"

"Prō dī immortālēs!" exclāmāvit Titus. "Crās Caesar amphitheātrum aperiet novum. Tū tamen rogās quid dīcam?"

Cornēlius autem cum rīsū, "Nōnne sentīs mē per iocum hoc dīxisse? Certē hic diēs maximē omnium memorābilis erit. Cōnstat servōs strēnuē labōrāvisse et amphitheātrum summā celeritāte cōnfēcisse. Mārtiālis epigrammata dē spectāculīs iam scrībit. Plūrimī gladiātōrēs mox clāmābunt, 'Avē, imperātor, moritūrī tē salūtant!' "

Cui Titus, "Mehercule! Tōtum populum continēbit hoc amphitheātrum. Crās māne viae erunt plēnae hominum quī ab omnibus partibus ad spectāculum congredientur."

"Ita!" inquit Cornēlius. "Putō tamen Aurēliam eō nōn itūram esse. Scīs enim Aurēliam neque mūnera neque sanguinem amāre. Aurēlia domī manēre māvult. Marcum tamen mēcum sum ductūrus. Iam adulēscēns est et mox togam virīlem sūmet. Sextus autem, quod adhūc puer est, domī manēbit; nam, ut docet Seneca, 'Quō maior populus, eō plūs perīculī.' Quotā hōrā tū ad amphitheātrum crās māne es itūrus?"

(continued)

3 **negōtiōsus, -a, -um,** *busy*
4 **prō certō habēre,** *to be sure*
5 **mūnera, mūnerum,** n. pl., *games*
spērō, -āre, -āvī, -ātus, *to hope*
10 **cōnstat,** *it is agreed*
11 **epigramma, epigrammatis,** n., *epigram*
12 **imperātor, imperātōris,** m., *commander, emperor*
16 **māvult,** *(she) prefers*
18 **quō maior…, eō plūs…,** *the greater…, the more…*

13 **contineō, continēre, continuī, contentus,** *to confine, hold*
16 **mālō, mālle, māluī,** irreg., *to prefer*

Exercise 47a

Respondē Latīnē:

1. Quandō intrāvit Titus tablīnum Gaiī?
2. Quālis vir est Cornēlius?
3. Quō cīvēs Rōmānī crās ībunt?
4. Quid Caesar crās faciet?
5. Quālis diēs erit crās?
6. Quid servī aedificāvērunt?
7. Unde hominēs ad spectāculum congredientur?
8. Cūr Aurēlia domī manēre māvult?
9. Quis cum Cornēliō ad mūnera ībit?
10. Cūr Sextus domī manēbit?

"Prīmā lūce," respondit Titus, "nam mātūrē advenīre in animō habeō. Quandō tū et Marcus eō perveniētis?"

"Haud mātūrē," inquit Cornēlius, "sed prō certō habeō nōs tē in amphitheātrō vīsūrōs esse. Nunc haec epistula est cōnficienda. Valē!"

"Valē!" inquit Titus. "Nōs abitūrī tē salūtāmus!"

20 **mātūrē,** adv., *early*

23 **epistula est cōnficienda,** *the letter must be finished*

Respondē Latīnē:

1. Quotā hōrā Titus ad amphitheātrum crās ībit?
2. Quem putat Cornēlius sē in amphitheātrō crās vīsūrum esse?
3. Quid Cornēlius nunc cōnficere vult?

BUILDING THE MEANING

Accusative and Infinitive (Indirect Statement) II

The future infinitive and the perfect infinitive are also used in indirect statements. Look at the following examples:

> Putō Aurēliam eō nōn **itūram esse.** (47:15)
> *I think that Aurelia* ***will*** *not* ***go*** *there.*

> Prō certō habeō nōs tē **vīsūrōs esse.** (47:22–23)
> *I am sure that we* ***will see*** *you.*

The phrases **itūram esse** and **vīsūrōs esse** are *future active infinitives*. You will recognize this form as **esse** with the future participle, which appears in the accusative case agreeing with the subject of the infinitive clause in gender, case, and number. (For the future participle, see Chapter 45.)

> Cōnstat servōs strēnuē **labōrāvisse** et amphitheātrum summā celeritāte **cōnfēcisse.** (47:10–11)
> *It is agreed that slaves* ***worked*** *hard and* ***finished*** *the amphitheater very quickly.*

The *perfect active infinitive* of non-deponent verbs (e.g., **labōrāvisse** and **cōnfēcisse** above) can be recognized by the ending **-isse**, which is added to the perfect stem. (See Chapter 41.)

The *perfect infinitive* of deponent verbs consists of the perfect participle plus the infinitive of the verb *to be*, **esse**. The perfect infinitive of deponent verbs is active in meaning:

locūtus esse, *to have spoken*
secūtus esse, *to have followed*

Thus:

Titus dīcit hominēs ab omnibus partibus Rōmam **congressōs esse.**
Titus says that men from all regions ***have come together*** *to Rome.*

Note that the participle **congressōs** agrees with the subject of the indirect statement, **hominēs**.

When **sē** is used in the accusative and infinitive construction in indirect statements, it is translated *he*, *she*, or *they* and refers to the subject of the verb of *saying*, *thinking*, or *hearing*:

Titus dīxit **sē** ad amphitheātrum itūrum esse.
Titus said that ***he*** *would go to the amphitheater.*

The use of **sē** in this sentence shows that *he* refers to Titus. If the *he* had referred to someone else, **eum** would have been used instead of **sē**.

Adulēscēns spērat sē diū vīctūrum esse; senex potest dīcere sē diū vīxisse. ***A young man hopes that he will live a long time; an old man is able to say that he has lived a long time.*** **(adapted from Cicero, *On Old Age* XIX.68)**

Exercise 47b

Read aloud and translate:

1. Putāmus servōs strēnuē labōrātūrōs esse.
2. Putāsne patruum tuum ad amphitheātrum pervēnisse?
3. Cōnstat illum diem memorābilem fuisse.
4. Scīs Cornēliam domī mānsūram esse.
5. Cornēlius audit Titum domum nōn vēnisse.
6. Cornēlius putat Aurēliam in peristȳlium ingressam esse.
7. Scīmus Sextum ad patrem suum epistulam mīsisse.
8. Audīmus Caesarem amphitheātrum novum aperuisse.
9. Scīmus omnēs cīvēs Rōmānōs ad mūnera itūrōs esse.
10. Spērat Aurēlia Cornēlium domum festīnātūrum esse.

Exercise 47c

Select, read aloud, and translate:

1. Prō certō habeō puerum (locūtus esse/locūtum esse/locūtūrōs esse).
2. Putāmus mīlitēs tribus diēbus (adventūrōs/adventūrās/adventūram) esse.
3. Spērō tē, Cornēlia, mox (reditūrus/reditūram/reditūrum) esse.
4. Scīmus (eam/eōs/eum) mox ingressūram esse.
5. Putat (omnēs/nēminem/paucōs) discessūrum esse.
6. Sciō (eōs/eum/eam) nōs secūtōs esse.
7. Putō puellās heri (ēgredī/ēgressās esse/ēgressūrās esse).
8. Audīvī servōs paucīs diēbus amphitheātrum (cōnficere/cōnfectūrum esse/cōnfectūrōs esse).
9. Respondent servī sē heri quam celerrimē (currere/cucurrisse/cursūrōs esse).
10. Eucleidēs dīcit sē epistulam crās (cōnficere/cōnfēcisse/cōnfectūrum esse).

Exercise 47d

Using story 47 and the information on indirect statement as guides, give the Latin for:

1. I know that all the Roman citizens will go to the games tomorrow.
2. Titus says that Caesar will open the new amphitheater tomorrow.
3. Cornelius says that slaves worked hard and finished the amphitheater very quickly.
4. Titus says that the amphitheater will hold the whole population (people).
5. Cornelius says that he has not yet finished his letter.

CIRCUS AND ARENA

The Romans did not have regular sporting events as we have on weekends or organized entertainment available every day as we have in the theater or movies. Instead, to celebrate religious festivals, commemorate great national victories, or honor the emperor, there were public holidays. These lasted a varying number of days, during which entertainments were presented in the circus and the arena. The number of these festivals increased as time went on until, by the reign of Claudius, 159 days of the year were holidays.

Admission to the shows was free, and all the emperors made sure there was plenty of entertainment. According to Fronto:

> Trajan sensibly always paid attention to the idols of the theater, the circus, or the arena because he knew that the entertainment of the people was very important to the government; doling out corn or money might keep individuals quiet, but shows were necessary to keep the mob happy.
>
> Fronto, *Preamble to History* 17

The Colosseum as it looks today

Juvenal, too, refers to the demand of the Roman mob for **pānem et circēnsēs**—the bread-dole and games in the circus.

The cost of the public games was met by the state. Often, magistrates added to the grant from their own pockets in order to increase their popularity and the chance of success in their careers. To do this they even ran into debt:

> Julius Caesar spent money so recklessly that many thought he was paying a high price to create a short-lived sensation, but really he was buying very cheaply the most powerful position in the world. Before entering politics he was thirteen hundred talents in debt. As aedile he staged games with 320 pairs of gladiators fighting in single combat. In this and his other extravagance in presenting theatrical performances, processions, and public banquets, he completely outdid all previous efforts to obtain publicity in this way.
>
> Plutarch, *Caesar* 5

THE COLOSSEUM

When the family of Cornelius returned to Rome, the great building of the Colosseum was nearing completion. Until this time, Rome's amphitheaters had usually been temporary wooden structures, and these caused some frightful disasters, as at Fidenae near Rome in A.D. 27, when a wooden amphitheater collapsed, killing or maiming 50,000 people. Wooden structures continued to be built even after the completion of the magnificent architectural monument known to its contemporaries as the **Amphitheātrum Flāvium** but familiar to us as the Colosseum, so named from the nearby colossal statue of Nero, converted by Vespasian into a statue of the sun-god.

Begun by Vespasian, the Colosseum was dedicated in A.D. 80 by his son Titus, who, to speed up its construction, had used Jewish prisoners taken in the capture of Jerusalem ten years before. The massive elliptical building rose in four tiers and measured overall 620 x 512 feet or 189 x 156 meters. With seating space estimated at 45,000, it could be covered over by a massive awning in excessive heat or rain—though Gaius Caligula is said to have taken delight in opening such awnings of earlier wooden amphitheaters in times of extreme heat and forbidding anyone to leave! It took 1,000 sailors of the imperial fleet to raise the awning over the Colosseum.

Admission was free and open to men, women, and children, slave or free, so long as places were available. Women were confined to the topmost area, and their view must certainly have been restricted.

The floor of the Colosseum was of timber, strewn with sand, and had numerous trapdoors. Under the arena, and extending beyond it, was a vast complex of subterranean cells and passages, which now lie open and exposed to view. Remains can be seen of lifts and machinery (worked by counterweights) used to raise, at various points in the arena, caged animals, scenery, and other apparatus needed for wild beast hunts.

On the occasion of the dedication of the Colosseum, Titus held a festival for 100 days and during the celebrations staged a very lavish gladiatorial show.

For more than 1900 years, the Colosseum has stood as the most imposing monument in the city of Rome and has been almost synonymous with the city itself. A medieval writer, the Venerable Bede (c. A.D. 673–735), quoted the following pilgrims' proverb or prophecy linking the fate of the Colosseum with that of Rome and of the world:

Quam diū stat Colyssaeus, stābit et Rōma.
Quandō cadet Colyssaeus, cadet et Rōma.
Quandō cadet Rōma, cadet et mundus.

While stands the Coliseum, Rome shall stand;
When falls the Coliseum, Rome shall fall;
And when Rome falls—the World.

translated by Lord Byron

MARTIAL'S EPIGRAMS

Born in Bilbilis, Spain, about A.D. 40, Martial went to Rome in A.D. 64, the year of the Great Fire, when Nero was emperor. His fame as a keen observer of life in the city and as a composer of biting, satirical epigrams **(epigrammata)** rests on poems he published in great numbers between A.D. 86 and 98. In A.D. 80, the year in which the Flavian Amphitheater was dedicated, Martial wrote a group of epigrams that he published under the title *De spectaculis*, in which he describes many of the memorable combats that took place in the arena that year. Translations of the first three poems in the collection are given below. In the first, Martial tries to assess the importance of the Amphitheater as an architectural monument. In the second he describes the joy of the Roman people in the building program of Vespasian and Titus that replaced the hated **Domus Aurea** of Nero with structures of more use to the people. In the third he pictures the influx of people from all over the Roman world who came to the dedication ceremonies.

(I)

Do not let barbarian Memphis tell of the wonder of her Pyramids, nor Assyrian toil vaunt its Babylon; let not the soft Ionians be praised for Trivia's temple; let the altar built of many horns keep its Delos hidden; let not Carians exalt to the skies with excessive praise the Mausoleum poised on empty air. The results of all these labors of man yield to Caesar's Amphitheater. One work in place of all shall Fame rehearse.

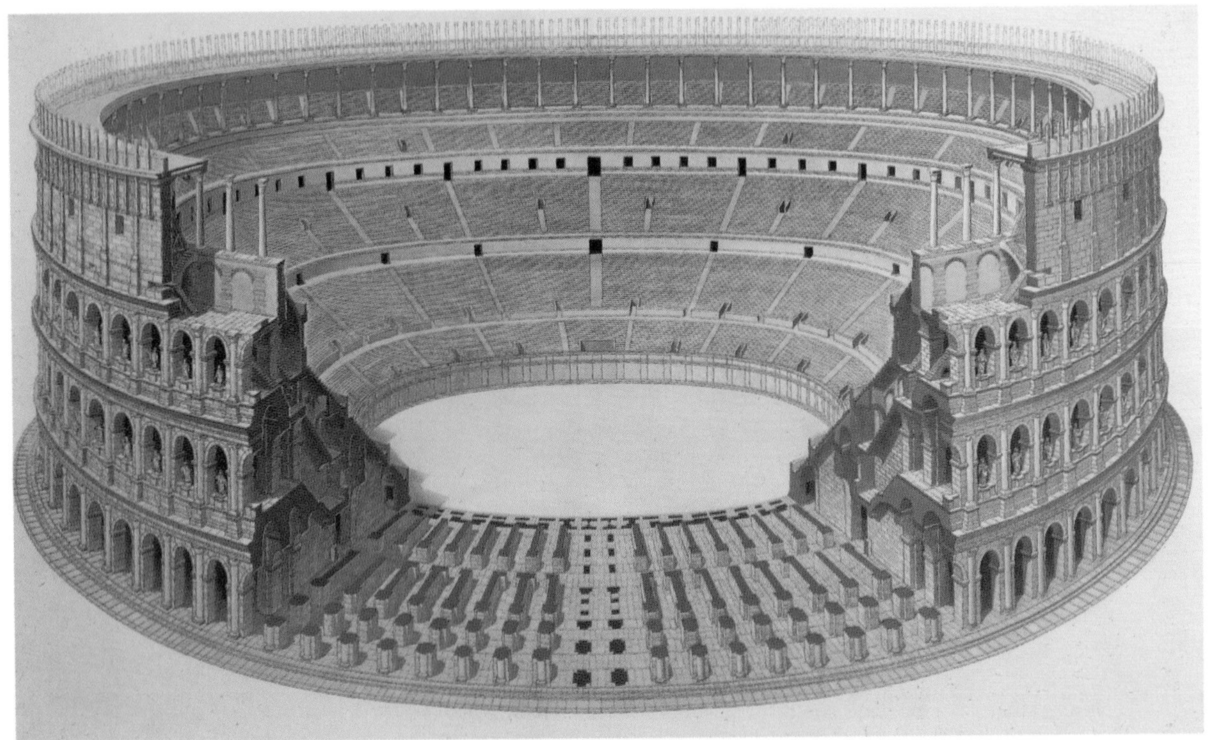

Reconstruction of the Colosseum

(II)

Here where, rayed with stars, the Colossus has a close view of heaven, and in the middle of the way tall scaffolds rise, hatefully gleamed the palace of a savage king, and only a single House then stood in all the City. Here, where the far-seen Amphitheater lifts its mass august, was Nero's lake. Here where we admire the warm baths, a gift swiftly built, a proud domain had robbed the poor of their dwellings. Where the Claudian Colonnade extends its outspread shade, the Palace ended in its farthest part. Now Rome is restored to itself, and under your rule, Caesar, what had been the delight of a tyrant is now the delight of the people.

(III)

What nation is so far distant, what people so barbarous, Caesar, that a spectator has not come from one of them to your city? A farmer of Rhodope has come from Orphic Haemus; a Sarmatian fed on draughts of horses' blood has come; and he who drinks at its source the stream of first-found Nile, and he whose shore the wave of farthest Tethys beats; the Arab has hurried here, Sabaeans have hurried, and Cilicians have here been drenched in their own saffron dew. With hair twined in a knot Sygambrians have come, and Aethiopians with their locks twined in other ways. The languages of the peoples are varied, yet they are one when you are acclaimed your country's true father.

FORMS

The Irregular Verb *mālō, mālle, māluī*

The verb **mālō** is a compound of the adverb **magis** and the irregular verb **volō**, and it means *to wish more, wish rather,* or *prefer*. It has no imperative. In the story at the beginning of this chapter, you saw:

> Aurēlia domī manēre **māvult.** (47:16)
> *Aurelia* ***prefers*** *to stay at home.*

The forms of this verb in the present, imperfect, and future tenses are as follows:

		Present	Imperfect	Future
	1	mā́l***ō***	mālḗ***bam***	mā́l***am***
S	2	mā́vī***s***	mālḗ***bās***	mā́l***ēs***
	3	mā́vul***t***	mālḗ***bat***	mā́l***et***
	1	mā́lu***mus***	mālē***bā́mus***	māl***ḗmus***
P	2	māvúl***tis***	mālē***bā́tis***	māl***ḗtis***
	3	mā́lu***nt***	mālḗ***bant***	mā́l***ent***

Learn the above forms thoroughly.

Note carefully when the third letter is *l* and when it is *v* in the present tense. The imperfect, future, and the tenses formed from the perfect stem are regular.

Review the forms of **volō** and **nōlō** in the Forms section at the end of this book before doing the following exercise.

Exercise 47e

Read aloud and translate. Then for each form of the verb **volō**, substitute the corresponding form of the verb **nōlō**, read aloud, and translate. Then substitute the corresponding forms of **mālō**, read aloud, and translate:

1. Titus trigōne lūdere volēbat.
2. Puerī ad thermās īre volunt.
3. "In silvam convenīre volumus," inquiunt Pȳramus et Thisbē.
4. "Ad amphitheātrum crās īre volam," inquit Marcus.
5. Titus prīmā lūce ad amphitheātrum īre vult.
6. Sciō puerōs prīmā lūce surgere velle.
7. Cūr pār impār lūdere vīs, Marce?
8. "Vultisne latrunculīs lūdere, puerī?" inquit Eucleidēs.
9. "Dormīre volō," inquit Sextus.
10. Cornēliī ad vīllam rūsticam mox redīre volent.
11. Sciō Aurēliam heri domī manēre voluisse.

Dīmidium dōnāre Linō quam crēdere tōtum
quī māvult, māvult perdere dīmidium.
Whoever prefers to give Linus half rather than trust him with the whole, prefers to lose the half. (Martial, *Epigrams* I.75)

CHAPTER 48

A Day at the Colosseum

A day at the Colosseum was a great occasion. Tickets (**tesserae**), shown to the gate-keepers (**appāritōrēs**), were numbered according to the seating areas in the amphitheater. Seventy-six main entrances and numerous marble plaques illustrating the seating areas enabled the spectators to move swiftly and efficiently through a network of passages, stairs, and ramps to their correct place. The officiating magistrate, usually the emperor in Rome, would go to the imperial seat of honor (**pulvīnar**), and then the show could begin. The gladiators would parade and stop before the **pulvīnar**; they would greet the emperor with the words: "Hail, emperor, those about to die salute you!" (**Avē, imperātor, moritūrī tē salūtant.**) Next the trumpet-players and horn-players (**tubicinēs** and **cornicinēs**) would strike up. Then came the games. Pairs (**paria**) of gladiators would fight, urged on by the trainers (**lanistae**). The people joined in with roars of "Thrash him!" (**Verberā!**), "Murder him!" (**Iugulā!**), "He's hit!" (**Hoc habet!**), "Let him go!" (**Mitte!**). The savagery reached a peak with the midday fighters (**merīdiānī**), usually condemned criminals.

Avē, imperātor, moritūrī tē salūtant, depicted by Jean Leon Gerome
Yale University Art Gallery, New Haven, Connecticut, Gift of C. Ruxton Love, Jr.

Marcus and his father go to the amphitheater early in the morning as planned:

Prope amphitheātrum omnēs viae erant plēnae hominum quī ad spectāculum veniēbant. Undique clāmor ac strepitus; undique cīvēs, fēminae, servī. Multī tōtam noctem extrā amphitheātrī portās morātī erant. Nunc adfuit hōra spectāculī.

Cornēlius, cum tesserās appāritōribus ostendisset, ad locum senātōribus reservātum cum Marcō ā servō ductus est. Marcus tot et tam variōs hominēs numquam vīderat. Dum attonitus circumspicit, subitō vīdit Titum iam cōnsēdisse. Patruum rogāre cupiēbat quandō pervēnisset, nam sciēbat Titum sērō ē lectō surgere solēre. Sed, quod pater aderat, Marcus nihil dīxit. Quam ingēns erat amphitheātrum! Quanta erat spectātōrum turba! Marcus coniciēbat quot spectātōrēs amphitheātrō continērī possent cum subitō fuit silentium. Omnēs ad pulvīnar oculōs convertērunt.

"Ecce!" clāmāvit Titus. "Iam intrat Caesar, amor ac dēliciae generis hūmānī!"

Tum, clāmōre sublātō, spectātōrēs prīncipem ūnā vōce salūtāvērunt. Stupuit Marcus, admīrātiōne captus. Iam gladiātōrēs cūnctī contrā pulvīnar cōnstiterant. "Avē, imperātor!" clāmāvērunt. "Moritūrī tē salūtant." Exiērunt gladiātōrēs. Mox tubicinēs et cornicinēs. Postrēmō gladiātōrum paria in arēnam intrāvērunt.

(continued)

5 **tot,** indecl. adj., *so many*
11 **dēliciae, -ārum,** f. pl., *delight*
13 **admīrātiō, admīrātiōnis,** f., *amazement*
contrā, prep. + acc., *against, opposite, in front of, facing*

4 **ostendō, ostendere, ostendī, ostentus,** *to show, point out*
9 **coniciō, conicere, coniēcī, coniectus,** *to throw, throw together; to figure out, guess*
10 **convertō, convertere, convertī, conversus,** *to turn (around)*
12 **tollō, tollere, sustulī, sublātus,** irreg., *to lift, raise*
13 **cōnsistō, cōnsistere, cōnstitī,** *to halt, stop, stand*

Exercise 48a
Respondē Latīnē:

1. Quō hominēs veniēbant?
2. Quid Cornēlius appāritōribus ostendit?
3. Quō Cornēlius ductus est?
4. Quid Marcus coniciēbat?
5. Quid spectātōrēs fēcērunt postquam Caesar intrāvit?
6. Quid gladiātōrēs clāmāvērunt?

Nunc undique erat clāmor, tumultus, furor. Lanistae hūc illūc concursantēs, "Verberā!" "Iugulā!" clāmābant; turba, "Hoc habet!" aut, "Mitte!" aut, "Iugulā!" Marcus nihil tāle prius vīderat. Complūrēs hōrās ācriter pugnābātur; haud minus ferōciter ā spectātōribus clāmābātur.

Subitō Cornēlius, "Nunc," inquit, "domum nōbīs redeundum est. Mox enim pugnābunt merīdiānī, quōs aliās tū, Marce, vidēbis."

"Nōnne tū quoque discēdere vīs, patrue?" clāmāvit Marcus.

Cui respondit Titus sē discēdere nōlle; sē nōndum satis vīdisse; merīdiānōs mox in arēnam ventūrōs esse. Brevī tempore Marcus cum Cornēliō in lectīcā per urbem portābātur et sēcum cōgitābat, "Quid ego prīmum Sextō nārrābō?"

16 **furor, furōris,** m., *frenzy*
18 **ācriter,** adv., *fiercely*
pugnābātur, *the fighting went on*
20 **nōbīs redeundum est,** *we must return*
21 **aliās,** adv., *at another time*
24 **arēna, -ae,** f., *sand, arena*

Respondē Latīnē:

1. Quid clāmābant lanistae?
2. Quōmodo pugnābātur?
3. Quōmodo ā spectātōribus clāmābātur?
4. Quōs gladiātōrēs Marcus aliās vidēbit?
5. Quid Marcus in lectīcā cōgitābat?

Quot hominēs, tot sententiae. ***Everyone has his own opinion.*** **(Terence, *Phormio* 454)**

Exercise 48b

Read aloud and translate:

1. Titus respondet sē domum redīre nōlle.
2. Nōs omnēs scīmus Marcum ad amphitheātrum īsse.
3. Prō certō habēmus Titum sērō perventūrum esse.

BUILDING THE MEANING

Accusative and Infinitive (Indirect Statement) III

So far, the verbs of *thinking, knowing, saying,* and *seeing* introducing indirect statements have usually been in the present tense. Now look carefully at these sentences and compare them with the three sentences in Exercise 48b:

Titus respondit sē domum redīre **nōlle.**
*Titus replied that he **was unwilling** to return home.*

Nōs omnēs sciēbāmus Marcum ad amphitheātrum **īsse.**
We all knew that Marcus ***had gone*** *to the amphitheater.*

Prō certō habēbāmus Titum sērō **perventūrum esse.**
We were sure that Titus ***would arrive*** *late.*

After the past tenses **respondit, sciēbāmus,** and **habēbāmus,** although the accusative and infinitive clauses are exactly the same in Latin as they were in Exercise 48b, in English

the present infinitive is translated by *was unwilling,*
the perfect infinitive is translated by *had gone,* and
the future infinitive is translated by *would arrive.*

In all indirect statements, whether introduced by verbs in the present or a past tense,

the present infinitive = action going on at the *same time* as the action of the main verb;
the perfect infinitive = action that was completed *before* the action of the main verb;
the future infinitive = action that will take place *after* the action of the main verb.

Exercise 48c

Read aloud and translate each sentence, with the main verb first in the present tense and then in the past tense:

1. Titus spērat (spērāvit) puerōs ad mūnera itūrōs esse.
2. Marcus dīcit (dīxit) patrem epistulam cōnfēcisse.
3. Audiō (audīvī) Cornēlium ad Cūriam festīnāre.
4. Cornēlius dīcit (dīxit) sē Marcum sēcum ductūrum esse.
5. Num crēdis (crēdidistī) Cornēliam pūpā lūdere?
6. Prō certō habeō (habēbam) Aurēliam nōbīscum nōn itūram esse.
7. Aurēlia scit (sciēbat) Cornēliam pūpam fīliae Dāvī dedisse.
8. Patruus meus respondet (respondit) sē manēre mālle.
9. Sextus dīcit (dīxit) Marcum domum mātūrē reditūrum esse.
10. Marcus putat (putāvit) sē numquam tot et tam variōs hominēs vīdisse.

Sōcratēs tōtīus mundī sē incolam et cīvem arbitrābātur. ***Socrates thought himself an inhabitant and a citizen of the whole world.*** **(Cicero, *Tusculan Disputations* 5.108)**

Exercise 48d

MARCUS REPORTS BACK

Read the following passage aloud and answer the questions that follow with full sentences in Latin:

Marcus iam domum regressus omnia quae vīderat Sextō nārrābat:

"Cum amphitheātrō appropinquārēmus, vīdimus magnam hominum multitūdinem per portās intrāre. Nōs ipsī ingressī vīdimus multa mīlia cīvium iam consēdisse. Ego nōn crēdidissem tot hominēs amphitheātrō continērī posse. Patruum exspectāre voluī, sed pater mihi dīxit Titum sine dubiō iam adesse. Et rēctē dīxit; nam cum ad locum senātōribus reservātum vēnissēmus, vīdimus Titum eō iam ductum esse.

Subitō undique clāmātum est. Deinde vīdī imperātōrem ā gladiātōribus salūtārī. Quam fortiter incēdēbant hī gladiātōrēs! Multī tamen eōrum moritūrī erant. Ubi pugnam commīsērunt, spectābam obstupefactus. Nihil tāle prius vīderam. Vīdī multōs vulnerārī atque complūrēs quidem occīdī. Quam fortēs erant gladiātōrēs!

Maximē dolēbam quod ante merīdiem domum nōbīs redeundum erat. Titus dīxit sē mālle manēre, cum cuperet merīdiānōs vidēre. Spērō patrem mē ad amphitheātrum iterum ductūrum esse. Fortasse tē quoque dūcet."

3 **mīlia, mīlium,** n. pl., *thousands*
4 **crēdidissem,** *I would have believed*
8 **clāmātum est,** *there was shouting*
10 **pugna, -ae,** f., *fight, battle*
pugnam committere, *to join battle*
obstupefactus, -a, -um, *astounded*

9 **incēdō, incēdere, incessī,** *to go in, march in*

Exercise 48e

Respondē Latīnē:

1. Quandō Marcus hominum multitūdinem vīdit?
2. Quid Marcus vīdit postquam amphitheātrum intrāvit?
3. Quid Marcus nōn crēdidisset?
4. Quid Cornēlius Marcō dīxit?
5. Quem ad locum Marcus vīdit Titum ductum esse?
6. Quōmodo Marcus pugnam spectābat?
7. Quid Marcus in gladiātōrum pugnā fierī vīdit?
8. Cūr Marcus dolēbat?
9. Quid Titus dīxit?
10. Quid Marcus spērat?

Accusative and Infinitive (Indirect Statement) IV

Passive infinitives and infinitives of deponent verbs are also used in this construction:

Vīdī multōs **vulnerārī** atque complūrēs quidem **occīdī.** (48d:11)
*I saw that many **were being wounded** and several actually **were being killed.***

Titus dīxit omnēs Rōmānōs dē amphitheātrō **loquī.**
*Titus said that all the Romans **were talking** about the amphitheater.*

The present passive infinitive is already familiar from Chapter 31. It can be recognized by the ending ***-rī*** in the 1st, 2nd, and 4th conjugations and the ending ***-ī*** in the 3rd conjugation.

For the perfect tense, the passive infinitive consists of the perfect participle and **esse:**

Vīdimus Titum eō iam **ductum esse.** (48d:6–7)
*We saw that Titus **had** already **been taken** there.*

Audīvimus omnēs Rōmānōs dē amphitheātrō **locūtōs esse.**
*We heard that all the Romans **had been talking** about the amphitheater.*

Note that the perfect participle agrees in gender, case, and number with the subject of the infinitive.

Exercise 48f

Form the present passive and the perfect passive infinitives of the following verbs. For the perfect passive infinitives, make the participles feminine accusative singular:

1. salūtō, -āre, -āvī, -ātus
2. videō, vidēre, vīdī, vīsus
3. ostendō, ostendere, ostendī, ostentus
4. coniciō, conicere, coniēcī, coniectus
5. sepeliō, sepelīre, sepelīvī, sepultus

Exercise 48g

Form the perfect infinitives of these deponent verbs. Make the participles masculine accusative singular:

1. moror, -ārī, -ātus sum
2. vereor, -ērī, -itus sum
3. loquor, loquī, locūtus sum
4. ingredior, ingredī, ingressus sum
5. experior, experīrī, expertus sum

Exercise 48h

Read aloud and translate:

1. Eucleidēs vīdit Cornēliam ā puerīs vexārī.
2. Sextus nescit vōcem suam audītam esse.
3. Vīdimus complūrēs nāvēs nōs sequī.
4. Putātis vestīmenta ā servō custōdīrī.
5. Scīvī mīlitēs in Britanniam profectōs esse.
6. Scīvī fūrēs in apodytērium ingressōs esse.
7. Cornēlius vīdit pūpam ā Sextō abreptam esse.
8. Cornēlius scīvit fīliam ā Sextō saepe vexārī.
9. Cōnstat amphitheātrum celeriter ā servīs cōnfectum esse.
10. Marcus Sextō dīcit sē ā patre ad amphitheātrum ductum esse.

One type of gladiator was the *net man*, who fought using only a net and trident.

FORMS
Verbs: Infinitives (Consolidation)

You have now met the following forms of the infinitive:

	Present		Perfect		Future
	Active	Passive	Active	Passive	Active
1	portā́re	portā́rī	portāvísse	portā́tus, -a, -um ésse	portātū́rus, -a, -um ésse
2	movḗre	movḗrī	mōvísse	mṓtus, -a, -um ésse	mōtū́rus, -a, -um ésse
3	míttere	míttī	mīsísse	míssus, -a, -um ésse	missū́rus, -a, -um ésse
-iō	iácere	iácī	iēcísse	iáctus, -a, -um ésse	iactū́rus, -a, -um ésse
4	audī́re	audī́rī	audīvísse	audī́tus, -a, -um ésse	audītū́rus, -a, -um ésse

Deponent Verbs

The present and perfect infinitives of deponent verbs are passive in form; the future infinitive is active in form:

Present	Perfect	Future
cōnā́rī	cōnā́tus, -a, -um ésse	cōnātū́rus, -a, -um ésse
séquī	secū́tus, -a, -um ésse	secūtū́rus, -a, -um ésse

NOTES

1. The future passive infinitive rarely appears in Latin and will not be taught in this book.
2. Translations of the various forms of the infinitive are not given in the charts above because they will vary according to the use of the infinitive in the sentence. The infinitives of deponent verbs in all three tenses are active in meaning.

Exercise 48i

Using the story in Exercise 48d and the information in this chapter on indirect statement as guides, give the Latin for:

1. Marcus said that a great multitude of men had entered through the gates. (Use **ingredior**.)
2. Marcus said that he had seen nothing of this sort before.
3. Marcus said that many gladiators had been wounded.
4. Marcus said that Titus stayed and saw the midday fighters.
5. Marcus hopes that his father will take him to the amphitheater again.

ROMAN LIFE XXIX

GLADIATORS

Criminals sentenced to death could be purchased cheaply and thrown to the beasts or made to fight to the death, unarmed, in the arena. But those convicted of lesser crimes, for which the mines or deportation was the penalty, might instead go to a gladiatorial school. Slaves acquired through war or piracy were another source of recruitment, and occasionally volunteers, including Roman citizens, actually took up the gladiatorial trade. All gladiators bound themselves to their trade by an oath that laid down the severest penalties for backsliders or runaways: "to be burnt with fire, shackled with chains, beaten with rods, and killed with steel" (**ūrī, vincīrī, verberārī, ferrōque necārī**).

After thorough training in the barracks, the gladiator was ready for the arena. Successful gladiators, like chariot drivers, were popular heroes. This is an inscription from Pompeii:

> The girls' heart-throb, the Thracian Celadus, (property) of Octavius, three wins out of three.

Victorious gladiators were richly rewarded and, after a period of service, might win the wooden sword of freedom, even if slaves. Veteran gladiators could also be employed as overseers in the gladiatorial schools.

The fate of a defeated gladiator rested with the spectators. If he had won favor, the spectators might wave their handkerchiefs, and the emperor or presiding magistrate might then signal for his release. Otherwise, a turn of the thumb indicated that the fallen gladiator should speedily be killed.

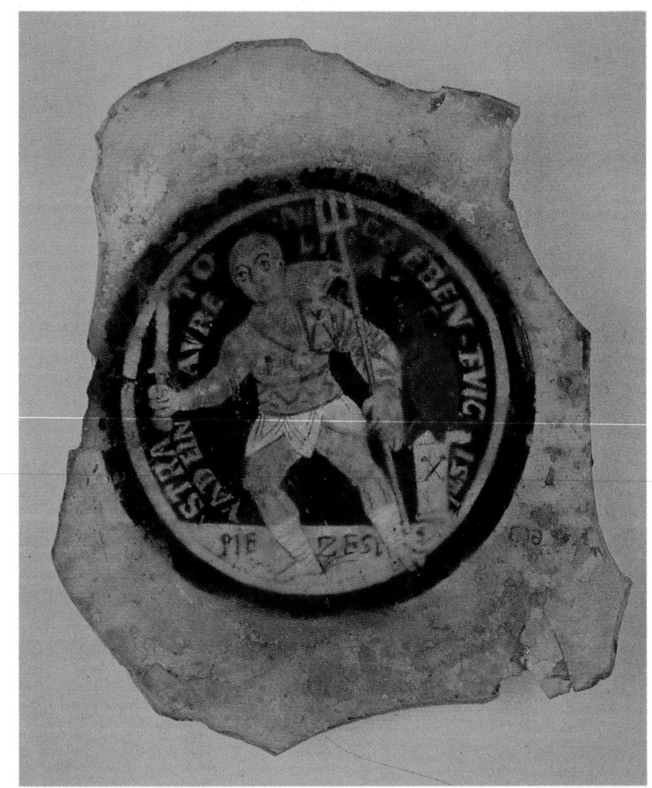

Gilded glass fragment showing a gladiator
British Museum, London, England

There were various classes of gladiators—these included the heavily armed Samnite with oblong shield, visored helmet, and short sword; the Thracian carrying a small round shield and curved scimitar; the **murmillō**, or *fish man*, who wore a helmet with a fish emblem on it and was armed with a sword and large shield; and the **rētiārius,** or *net man*, who was unarmed but for a great net and sharp trident. Each had his own supporters: the Emperor Titus, for example, supported the Thracians, as did Caligula. Local rivalry, too, was common, as is borne out by this inscription from Pompeii:

> Luck to the people of Puteoli and all those from Nuceria; down with the Pompeians.

Such rivalry could lead to trouble, as this incident in the reign of Nero illustrates:

> About this time there was a serious riot involving the people of Pompeii and Nuceria. It started with a small incident at a gladiatorial show. Insults were being exchanged, as often happens in these disorderly country towns. Abuse changed to stone-throwing, and then swords were drawn. The games were held in Pompeii and the locals came off best. Many badly wounded Nucerians were taken to their city. Many parents and children were bereaved. The Emperor ordered the Senate to inquire into the matter, and the Senate passed it on to the consuls. As a result of their report, the Senate banned Pompeii from holding any similar event for ten years.

Tacitus, *Annals* XIV.17

Gladiators were not used to fight animals (**bēstiae**) in the wild-beast hunts. For this, special fighters, **bēstiāriī**, were employed. In these shows, such animals as lions, tigers, bears, bulls, hippopotami, elephants, crocodiles, deer, pigs, and even ostriches were made to fight each other or the **bēstiāriī** or else driven to attack condemned criminals, who were sometimes chained or nailed to stakes. When Trajan held four months of festivities to celebrate his Dacian wars, some 10,000 gladiators and over 11,000 animals appeared in the arena over this period.

Even before the time of the emperors we read of the provinces being scoured for animals for these shows. Caelius, in a letter to his friend Cicero, wrote:

> Curio is very generous to me and has put me under an obligation; for if he had not given me the animals which had been shipped from Africa for his own games, I would not have been able to continue with mine. But, as I must go on, I should be glad if you would do your best to let me have some animals from your province—I am continually making this request.

Cicero, *Letters to His Friends* VIII.8

OTHER SHOWS IN THE ARENA

While dedicating the Amphitheater, the Emperor Titus also held a sea fight (**naumachia**) on the old artificial lake of Augustus and afterwards used the empty basin of the lake for still more gladiatorial bouts and a wild-beast hunt (**vēnātiō**) in which over 5,000 animals of different kinds died in a single day. His brother and imperial successor, Domitian, was not to be outdone; he even used the Amphitheater itself as a lake! Suetonius, in his life of Domitian, writes:

> Domitian constantly gave lavish entertainments both in the Amphitheater and in the Circus. As well as the usual races with two-horse and four-horse chariots, he put on two battles, one with infantry and one with cavalry; he also exhibited a naval battle in his amphitheater. He gave hunts of wild beasts and gladiatorial fights at night by torchlight, and even fights between women.
>
> He staged sea battles with almost full-sized fleets. For these he had a pool dug near the Tiber and seats built around it. He even went on watching these events in torrential rain.
>
> Suetonius, *Domitian* 4

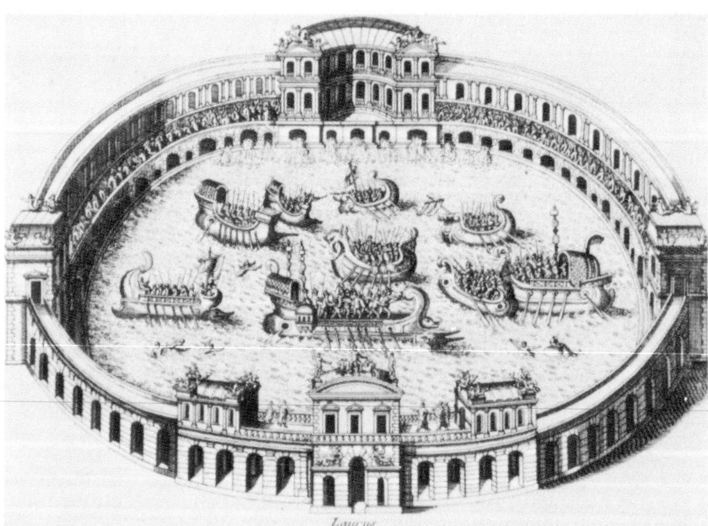

A drawing of a sea fight staged in an arena. Notice the rams on the front of the boats.

GRAFFITI AND INSCRIPTIONS

Written at night on the facade of a private house in Pompeii:

D. Lucrētī Satrī Valentis flāminis Nerōnis Caesaris Aug. fīlī perpetuī gladiātōrum paria XX et D. Lucrētī Valentis fīlī glad. paria X, pug. Pompēīs VI V IV III pr. Īdūs Apr. Vēnātiō legitima et vēla erunt.
Twenty pairs of gladiators provided by Decimus Lucretius Satrius Valens priest for life of Nero, son of Caesar Augustus, and ten pairs of gladiators provided by the son of Decimus Lucretius Valens, will fight at Pompeii on April 8, 9, 10, 11, and 12. There will be a regular hunt and awnings.

Scratched on the columns in the peristyle of a private house in Pompeii:

Suspīrium puellārum Tr. Celadus Oct. III III.
The girls' heart-throb, the Thracian Celadus, (property) of Octavius, three wins out of three.

A curse against a **bēstiārius:**

Occīdite extermināte vulnerāte Gallicum, quem peperit Prīma, in istā hōrā in amphiteātrī corōnā. Oblīgā illī pedēs membra sēnsūs medullam; oblīgā Gallicum, quem peperit Prīma, ut neque ursum neque taurum singulīs plāgīs occīdat neque bīnīs plāgīs occīdat neque ternīs plāgīs occīdat taurum ursum; per nōmen deī vīvī omnipotentis ut perficiātis; iam iam citō citō allīdat illum ursus et vulneret illum.
Kill, destroy, wound Gallicus whom Prima bore, in this hour, in the ring of the amphitheater. Bind his feet, his limbs, his senses, his marrow; bind Gallicus whom Prima bore, so that he may slay neither bear nor bull with single blows, nor slay (them) with double blows, nor slay with triple blows bear (or) bull; in the name of the living omnipotent god may you accomplish (this); now, now, quickly, quickly let the bear smash him and wound him.

Sepulchral inscription of a **rētiārius:**

D. M. Vītālis invictī rētiārī, nātiōne Bataus, hīc suā virtūte pariter cum adversāriō dēcidit, alacer fu. pugnīs III. Convīctor eius fēcit.
To the deified spirits of Vitalis, a net-fighter who was never beaten; a Batavian by birth, he fell together with his opponent as a result of his own valor; he was a keen competitor in his three fights. His messmate erected (this monument).

Exercise 48j

The poet Martial, whose epigrams you have already met, found much to write about in the contests taking place in the Amphitheater. In the following poem he praises the gladiator Hermes, who excelled in no fewer than three fighting roles: as a **vēles** lightly armed with a spear, as a **rētiārius** with net and trident, and as a **Samnīs** heavily armed with visored helmet. This explains why he is called **ter ūnus** in the last line. The meter is hendecasyllabic.

Read aloud and translate:

Hermēs Mārtia saeculī voluptās,
Hermēs omnibus ērudītus armīs,
Hermēs et gladiātor et magister,
Hermēs turba suī tremorque lūdī,
Hermēs quem timet Hēlius, sed ūnum,
Hermēs cui cadit Advolāns, sed ūnī,
Hermēs vincere nec ferīre doctus,
Hermēs suppositīcius sibi ipse,
Hermēs dīvitiae locāriōrum,
Hermēs cūra laborque lūdiārum,
Hermēs belligerā superbus hastā,
Hermēs aequoreō mināx tridente,
Hermēs casside languidā timendus,
Hermēs glōria Mārtis ūniversī,
Hermēs omnia sōlus, et ter ūnus.

—Martial, *Epigrams* V.24

1 **Hermēs:** the gladiator has adopted the name of the Greek god Hermes (= Mercury, the messenger god who conducts souls of the dead to the underworld)
Mārtius, -a, -um, *connected with Mars (the god of war and combat)*
saeculum, -ī, n., *age, era*
voluptās, voluptātis, f., *pleasure, delight*

4 **turba, -ae,** f., *crowd; cause of confusion/turmoil*
suī...lūdī, *of his school (of gladiators)*
tremor, tremōris, m., *cause of fright, terror*

5 **Hēlius,** Greek word for *Sun*, and **Advolāns,** literally, *Flying to (the Attack)*—two distinguished gladiators
sed ūnum, *but the only one*

7 **feriō, -īre, -īvī, -ītus,** *to strike, kill*

8 **suppositīcius sibi ipse,** *himself his only substitute*

9 **dīvitiae, -ārum,** f. pl., *wealth, riches*
locārius, -ī, m., *scalper (a person who buys up seats,* ***loca,*** *in the amphitheater and then sells them for as high a price as he can get)*

10 **cūra, -ae,** f., *care;* here, *the favorite*
labor, labōris, m., *work, toil;* here, *a cause of suffering/distress, "heart-throb"*
lūdia, -ae, f., *female slave attached to a gladiatorial school*

11 **belliger, belligera, belligerum** (cf. the phrase **bellum gerere,** *to wage war*), *warlike*
superbus, -a, -um, *proud, arrogant*
hasta, -ae, f., spear

12 **aequoreō...tridente** (cf. **aequor, aequoris,** n., *the sea*), *with his sea trident*
minax, minācis, *menacing*

13 **cassis, cassidis,** f., *plumed metal helmet*
languidus, -a, -um, *drooping (describing the crest of the helmet drooping down over the eyes)*
timendus, -a, -um, *to be feared*

14 **Mārtis ūniversī,** *of every kind of combat*

15 **ter,** adv., *three times*

Gladiātor in arēnā cōnsilium capit. ***The gladiator adopts a plan in the arena.*** **(Seneca, *Epistulae Morales* XXII)**
Nōn tē petō, piscem petō. Quid mē fugis, Galle? ***It is not you I am aiming at, but the fish. Why do you flee from me, Gallus?*** **(spoken by the adversary of a murmillō; quoted by Festus, 285M, 358L)**

CHAPTER 49

ANDROCLES AND THE LION

Ōlim in Circō Maximō lūdus bēstiārius populō dabātur. Omnēs spectātōribus admīrātiōnī fuērunt leōnēs, sed ūnus ex eīs vidēbātur saevissimus. Ad pugnam bēstiāriam intrōductus erat inter complūrēs servus quīdam cui Androclēs nōmen fuit. Quem cum ille leō procul vīdisset, subitō quasi admīrāns stetit ac deinde lentē et placidē hominī appropinquābat. Tum caudam clēmenter et blandē movēns, manūs hominis, prope iam metū exanimātī, linguā lambit. Androclēs, animō iam recuperātō, leōnem attentius spectāvit. Tum, quasi mūtuā recognitiōne factā, laetī ibi stābant et homō et leō.

Ea rēs tam mīrābilis turbam maximē excitāvit. Androclem ad pulvīnar arcessītum rogāvit Caesar cūr ille saevissimus leō eī sōlī pepercisset. Tum Androclēs rem mīrābilem nārrāvit:

"Dum ego in Āfricā cum dominō meō habitō," inquit, "propter eius crūdēlitātem fugere coāctus in spēluncam cōnfūgī. Haud multō post ad eandem spēluncam vēnit hic

(continued)

2 **admīrātiōnī esse,** *to be a source of amazement (to)*
3 **Androclēs, Androclis,** m., *Androcles*
4 **quasi,** adv., *as if*
admīror, -ārī, -ātus sum, *to wonder (at)*
placidē, adv., *gently, peacefully, quietly, tamely*
5 **clēmenter,** adv., *in a kindly manner*
blandē, adv., *in a coaxing/winning manner*
6 **exanimātus, -a, -um,** *paralyzed*
7 **mūtuus, -a, -um,** *mutual*
11 **crūdēlitās, crūdēlitātis,** f., *cruelty*

6 **lambō, lambere, lambī,** *to lick*
9 **parcō, parcere, pepercī** + dat., *to spare*
12 **cōgō, cōgere, coēgī, coāctus,** *to compel, force*

Exercise 49a

Respondē Latīnē:

1. Quālis vidēbātur ūnus ē leōnibus?
2. Quis ad pugnam intrōductus erat?
3. Quid fēcit leō cum hominem vīdisset?
4. Quid leō linguā lambit?
5. Quōmodo Androclēs leōnem spectāvit?
6. Quid Caesar fēcit?
7. Ubi Androclēs habitābat?
8. Quālem dominum habēbat?
9. Quō cōnfūgit?

leō gemēns et dolēns, ūnō pede claudus. Atque prīmō quidem terrōris plēnus latēbam. Sed leō, cum mē cōnspexisset, mītis et mānsuētus appropinquāvit atque pedem mihi ostendit, quasi auxilium petēns. Stirpem ingentem, quae in eius pede haerēbat, ego extrāxī ac iam sine magnō timōre vulnus lāvī. Tum ille, pede in manibus meīs positō, recubuit et dormīvit.

"Trēs annōs ego et leō in eādem spēluncā habitābāmus, eōdem cibō vēscentēs. Posteā captus ā mīlitibus, reductus sum ad dominum quī mē statim ad bēstiās condemnāvit."

Prīnceps, fābulā servī audītā, maximē admīrābātur. Androclēs omnium cōnsēnsū līberātus est, datusque eī leō.

13 **doleō, -ēre, -uī, -itūrus,** *to be sorry, be sad, be in pain*
claudus, -a, -um, *lame*
lateō, -ēre, -uī, *to lie in hiding*
14 **mītis, -is, -e,** *gentle*
mānsuētus, -a, -um, *tame*
15 **stirps, stirpis,** gen. pl., **stirpium,** f., *thorn*
20 **cōnsēnsus, -ūs,** m., *agreement*

18 **vēscor, vēscī** + abl., *to feed (on)*

Respondē Latīnē:

1. Quālis erat leō?
2. Quid leō hominī ostendit?
3. Quid in pede leōnis haerēbat?
4. Quam diū Androclēs et leō in eādem spēluncā habitābant?
5. Quis Androclem ad bēstiās condemnāvit?
6. Quid Androclēs omnium cōnsēnsū accēpit?

BUILDING THE MEANING
What to Expect with the Verb *audiō*

Look at the following sentences:

Audīvit cūr pater advēnisset.
He heard why his father had arrived.

Clāmōrēs servōrum audīvit.
He heard the shouts of the slaves.

Audīvit patrem ad urbem advēnisse.
He heard that his father had reached the city.

You will see that the sense after *heard* can develop in three different ways:

He heard why, who, what, how....	*indirect question* (with verb in the subjunctive)
He heard something/someone.	*direct object* (accusative case)
He heard that....	*indirect statement* (with accusative and infinitive)

When you meet **audiō**, you must expect one of these three possibilities:

1. **Audiō cūr, quis, quid, quōmodo...:** translate straight on:

   Audīvī quid dīcerēs.
   I heard what you were saying.

2. **Audiō** *accusative*...: wait to see if there is also an *infinitive*. If there is no infinitive, the accusative is the direct object of **audiō**:

   Audiō servōs.
   I hear the slaves.

   Audiō servōs in viīs clāmantēs.
   I hear the slaves shouting in the streets.

3. If there is an infinitive, insert *that* and continue with the translation of the accusative:

   Audiō servōs cēnam parāvisse.
   I hear (that) the slaves have prepared dinner.

The following verbs have to be treated in the same way:

sciō, *I know*
intellegō, *I understand, realize*
videō, *I see*
sentiō, *I feel, notice, realize*

Exercise 49b

Read aloud and translate:

1. Puerī audīvērunt gladiātōrēs prīncipem salūtantēs.
2. Eucleidēs nōn sēnsit ubi essent puerī.
3. Marcus vīdit gladiātōrēs iam in arēnam intrāvisse.
4. Spectātōrēs nōn intellēxērunt cūr leō manūs servī lamberet.
5. Cornēlius sciēbat locum senātōribus reservātum esse.
6. Androclēs dīxit sē stirpem ē pede leōnis extrāxisse.
7. Pȳramus crēdēbat Thisbēn ā leōne occīsam esse.
8. Nōnne audīs illōs leōnēs strepitum maximum facientēs?
9. Ita vērō! Leōnēs audiō; sed cīvēs maiōrem strepitum facere videntur.
10. Cīvēs intellegēbant servōs saepe fugere cōgī.

Exercise 49c

Read aloud and translate:

1. Puer nesciēbat quot gladiātōrēs vulnerātī essent.
2. Androclēs dīxit leōnem ūnō pede claudum ad spēluncam vēnisse.
3. Scīvistīne bēstiās sub arēnā continērī? Ipse eās audīvī.
4. Cīvēs prō certō habēbant nūllōs gladiātōrēs effugere cōnātūrōs esse.
5. Spectātōrēs vīdērunt leōnem caudam clēmenter moventem.

Exercise 49d

Using story 49 and the information on **audiō** and other verbs as guides, give the Latin for:

1. We have never heard that a lion had spared a man.
2. No one understood why the lion was licking the man's hand.
3. Androcles suddenly realized that he had lived with this lion in Africa.
4. He saw that a huge thorn was sticking in its foot.
5. Everyone knew why the lion had been given to him.

The legend of overpowering a lion was an important one throughout antiquity. Pictured: the nymph Cyrene taming a lion and being crowned by Libya
British Museum, London, England

quid pro quo literally, *"something for something," one thing in exchange for another.*
Manus manum lavat. *One hand washes the other* **or** *One good turn deserves another.*
Ab aliō expectēs alterī quod fēceris. *Expect (the same treatment from another) that you give to your neighbor.* **(Publilius Syrus 2)**

How do these sayings fit the moral of the story of Androcles and the lion?

Exercise 49e Take parts, read aloud, and translate:

Scene I: In the Amphitheater

(Licinius Caeliusque, duo spectātōrēs in amphitheātrō sedentēs, inter sē loquuntur.)

LICINIUS: Ecce! In arēnam veniunt bēstiāriī! Scīsne quot sint?

CAELIUS: Minimē vērō! Scīsne tū quot leōnēs, quot tigrēs adsint? Ego audīvī multōs leōnēs ingentēs ab Āfricā allātōs esse et sub arēnā in caveīs tenērī.

(Intrat Postumius quī sērō venīre solet.)

POSTUMIUS: Videō prīncipem iam advēnisse et ā cīvibus salūtārī.

CAELIUS: Ecce! Iam bēstiāriī eum salūtant! Ēheu! Sciunt sē moritūrōs esse.

POSTUMIUS: Tacēte! Audiō bēstiās! Vidētisne leōnēs in arēnam immittī?

LICINIUS: Ecce bēstia immānis! Servō illī parvō numquam parcet! Iam pugnāre incipiunt. Euge!

POSTUMIUS: Euge! At cōnstitit leō! Mīror cūr leō cōnstiterit!

CAELIUS: Num crēdis eum rē vērā cōnstitisse? Prō certō habeō eum mox impetum ferōciter factūrum esse.

LICINIUS: At videō leōnem lentē et placidē hominī appropinquantem. Mehercule! Vidēsne eum manūs hominis linguā lambentem? Sciō leōnem esse saevissimum. Nesciō cūr hominem nōn occīdat.

CAELIUS: Vidēsne servum leōnem spectantem? Timēre nōn vidētur.

POSTUMIUS: Videō servum ā prīncipe arcessītum esse. Mīror quid dīcat.

Scene II: Leaving the Amphitheater

LICINIUS: Nōn poteram intellegere cūr leō impetum nōn faceret. Mīrum quidem erat spectāculum.

CAELIUS: Audīvī leōnem ā prīncipe hominī darī.

POSTUMIUS: Ita vērō! Sed ecce! Paetus venit. Salvē, Paete!

PAETUS: Cūr hunc tantum clāmōrem facitis?

CAELIUS: Hoc vix crēdēs! Vīdimus leōnem, bēstiam saevissimam, servī manūs lambentem! Nescīmus cūr manūs nōn dēvorāverit.

PAETUS: Quid? Nōnne audīvistis causam? Leō ille sēnsit sē hominem anteā vīdisse. Homō prīncipī nārrāvit quōmodo stirpem ōlim ē pede leōnis extrāxisset. Nārrāvit sē et leōnem in Āfricā in eādem spēluncā trēs annōs habitāvisse. Ubi captus est, putāvit sē numquam iterum leōnem vīsūrum esse. Nesciēbat quō leō īsset.

POSTUMIUS: Agite! Sērō est. Ēsuriō! Domum redeāmus. Fortasse vidēbimus servum leōnem per viās dūcentem.

4 **cavea, -ae,** f., *cage*
9 **immānis, -is, -e,** *huge*
11 **mīror, -ārī, -ātus sum,** *to wonder*
12 **rē vērā,** *really, actually*
impetus, -ūs, m., *attack*
31 **redeāmus,** *let us return*

8 **immittō, immittere, immīsī, immissus,** *to send in, release*
10 **incipiō, incipere, incēpī, inceptus,** *to begin*
19 **intellegō, intellegere, intellēxī, intellēctus,** *to understand, realize*

ROMAN LIFE XXX

OPPOSITION TO THE GAMES

Sometimes high-born Romans were so enthusiastic about the combats in the arena that they took part themselves as gladiators. The Roman poet Juvenal, and Romans generally, strongly disapproved:

> There in the arena you have a disgrace to the city: Gracchus fighting not in the arms of a **murmillō** with shield and saber, for he scorns and rejects such equipment; nor does he hide his face with a visor. Look! It's a trident he sports; he shakes his trailing net in his right hand, casts, and misses. Then he holds up his naked face for all to see and runs frantically around the whole arena, easily recognizable!
>
> Juvenal, *Satires* VIII.199–206

Some Romans protested the brutality of gladiatorial shows. Seneca writes about the midday "interval" between the morning and afternoon sessions. In this interval criminals were forced to fight in the arena until everyone was dead:

> By chance I attended a midday exhibition, expecting some fun, wit, and relaxation—an exhibition at which men's eyes have respite from the slaughter of their fellow-men. But it was quite the reverse. The previous combats were the essence of compassion; but now all the trifling is put aside and it is pure murder. The men have no defensive armor. They are exposed to blows at all points, and no one ever strikes in vain. Many persons prefer this program to the usual pairs and to the bouts "by request." Of course they do; there is no helmet or shield to deflect the weapon. What is the need of defensive armor, or of skill? All these mean delaying death. In the morning they throw men to the lions and the bears; at noon, they throw them to the spectators. The spectators demand that the slayer shall face the man who is to slay him in his turn; and they always reserve the latest conqueror for another butchering. The outcome of every fight is death, and the means are fire and sword.
>
> Seneca, *Epistulae morales* VII

After Seneca, others came out against the institution of the games. Among those were Christian writers such as Tertullian and Augustine. The Emperor Constantine made a decree of abolition, but this seems not to have been enforced. Gladiatorial shows were finally suppressed by Honorius (Emperor of the West, A.D. 395–423), though other blood-sports in the arena continued for several centuries after this.

FRONTIER LIFE VI

TRIER

The story of Lucius and Helge is a fictional account of the very real and significant historic process of Romanization in northern Europe. The history of the city of Trier, situated in what is now Rheinland-Pfalz, Germany, testifies eloquently to the factual record of that process.

Situated on a broad expanse of lush meadow in the Moselle valley, the city had its origins as the tribal capital of the Treveri, a Celtic clan. The Roman beginnings date from the time of Julius Caesar, to whom the Treveri supplied cavalry troops. A civilian settlement grew up around the small Roman fort. The actual Roman city dates from the reign of Augustus, who founded Augusta Treverorum to establish a supply base for the armies on the Rhine, and to spread urban civilization to the frontier of northern Europe by establishing a model city there.

Trier

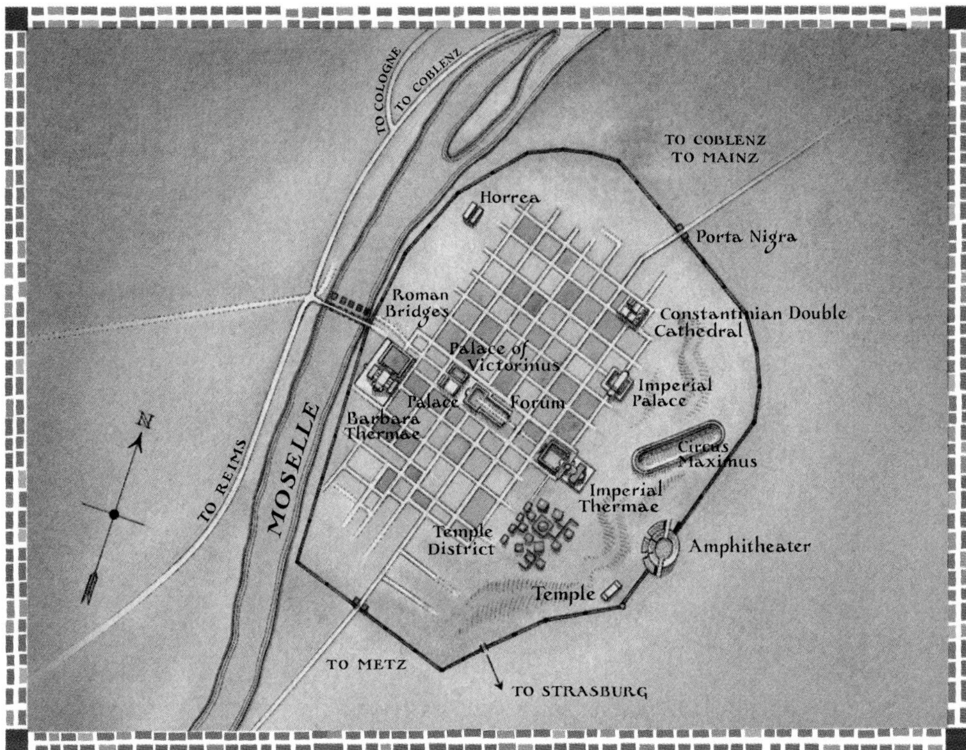

Located at a crossroads, the city became a commercial center for trade in food, wine, textiles, leather goods, pottery, and building materials. In time, it began to possess all the characteristics of a Roman city. The grid of cross-streets intersecting at a forum was probably laid out during the reign of Claudius (A.D. 41–54). There were baths, a residence for the Roman procurator, and an amphitheater, built around A.D. 100, with a seating capacity of about 20,000. That amphitheater, a smaller version of the Flavian Amphitheater in Rome, was a hallmark of Trier's Romanization. At the same time, a bathing complex was constructed, and temples were built, not only to gods the Romans brought with them, such as Mithras, the Indo-Iranian god so popular with Roman soldiers, but also to Lenus Mars, a local deity who combined a Celtic god with the Roman Mars.

The peaceful development of the city was interrupted a number of times in its Roman history, but it always recovered. Tragedy struck when the Alemanni crossed the Rhine and sacked the city and other centers of urban civilization about 275. However, Probus (reigned 276–282) drove the barbarians back over the Rhine and restored order.

In A.D. 293 the Emperor Diocletian made sweeping changes in the administrative structure of the Roman empire. There were to be two emperors, **Augustī:** Maximian in the West and Diocletian himself in the East. Each **Augustus** was to have a co-regent, a **Caesar,** thus forming a tetrarchy or rule of four princes. Constantius Chlorus, father of Constantine the Great, was named by Diocletian to be **Caesar** of the West and took up residence at Augusta Treverorum, now called Treveri. Recovering from the destruction eighteen years earlier, it became a capital city again. Twelve years later Constantius became the **Augustus** of the West.

As befits a capital city, unprecedented building took place. The magnificent Imperial Baths, equalled only by the baths of Caracalla and Diocletian at Rome, and a circus for chariot races were built, and the amphitheater was repaired and enlarged. Constantine, who succeeded his father as Caesar of the West and who resided from time to time at Treveri, built a monumental gateway and completed one of the most impressive building complexes, the Aula Palatina, a law-court (**basilica**). Later when Constantine became sole Augustus, he founded Constantinople in the East as the new capital of the Empire.

Constantine the Great died in 337. Valentinian (reigned 364–375) left his brother to rule in Constantinople and took up his own residence at Treveri. His son, Gratian (reigned 367–383), also resided there. He renovated the baths; a new sewage system was built, the streets were repaved and lined with porticos, and the double church that forms the ancient nucleus of the present-day cathedral was constructed.

Treveri was also a center of learning. In 365 Valentinian engaged Decimus Magnus Ausonius, a professor of rhetoric at the University of Burdigala (Bordeaux), to serve as tutor to his son, Gratian. Gratian maintained a lifelong friendship with Ausonius, elevating him to a consulship. Ausonius is the author of a poem extolling the beauty of the Moselle and another in which he acknowledges Treveri as a city that "feeds, clothes, and arms the empire's troops."

In 383 Gratian was slain by a usurper to the throne, and his brother, Valentinian II, was the last ruler to reside at Treveri. Roman troops were withdrawn from the Rhine, and Treveri went into a state of decline, finally being overrun by Franks.

What is especially noteworthy about the many years of prestige and prosperity that Trier enjoyed (as Augusta Treverorum and as Treveri), is that most of its inhabitants were not Italians or Romans but Celts, a proud people native to that area of northern Europe. The Celts, who had their own traditions, engaged at times in rebellion against Roman rule. However, once they accepted the benefits of Roman urban civilization, the people of Treveri thrived in the prosperity of the Pax Romana for over four hundred years.

ADDITIONAL READING:

The Romans Speak for Themselves: Book II: "Alypius Catches Gladiator Fever," pages 63–71.

WORD STUDY XII

Suffixes *-ārium* and *-ōrium*

The addition of the suffix ***-ārium*** (neuter form of the adjectival suffix ***-ārius***; see Word Study V) to the base of a Latin noun or adjective creates a 2nd declension neuter noun meaning *a place for…*, e.g., **libr-** (base of **liber**, *book*) + ***-ārium*** = **librārium**, **-ī**, n., *a place for books* or *a bookcase*. English sometimes uses this Latin suffix to create new words, such as *aquarium* (literally, "a place for water," from Latin **aqua**), but most English words derived from Latin words with the suffix ***-ārium*** end in *-ary*, e.g., *library*.

Similarly, the suffix ***-ōrium*** (neuter form of ***-ōrius***, an adjectival suffix similar to ***-ārius***), when added to the stem of the fourth principal part of a Latin verb, forms a 2nd declension neuter noun that denotes a place where the action of the verb takes place, e.g., **audīt-** (perfect passive participial stem of **audīre**, *to hear*) + ***-ōrium*** = **auditōrium**, **-ī**, n., *a place for listening, lecture-room.*

Exercise 1

Give the meaning of each of the following Latin nouns, using the words in parentheses as guides. Confirm the meanings in a Latin dictionary:

1. caldārium (**calidus**)
2. repositōrium (**repōnere**)
3. armārium (**arma**)
4. aviārium (**avis**, *bird*)
5. sōlārium (**sōl**, *sun)*
6. Tabulārium (**tabula,** *tablet, record*)

Exercise 2

Give the meaning of each of the following English nouns, and give the Latin root word from which each is derived:

1. dormitory
2. infirmary
3. lavatory
4. terrarium
5. laboratory
6. diary

Suffix *-ūra*

The suffix ***-ūra*** may be added to the stem of the fourth principal part of a Latin verb to form a 1st declension noun that means the *act of* or *result of...*, e.g., **scrīpt-** (perfect passive participial stem of **scrībere,** *to write*) + ***-ūra*** = **scrīptūra, -ae,** f., *a writing*. English words derived from these nouns generally end in *-ure*, e.g., *scripture*.

Exercise 3

Give the Latin noun ending in ***-ūra*** that is formed from the stem of the fourth principal part of each of the following verbs. Give the English derivative of each noun formed. Consult an English dictionary as needed:

1. colō
2. coniciō
3. adveniō
4. stō
5. pōnō
6. capiō
7. misceō
8. nāscor

Exercise 4

Give the meaning of each of the following English nouns and give the Latin verb from which each is derived. Consult an English dictionary as needed:

1. lecture
2. creature
3. pasture
4. aperture
5. rupture
6. stricture

Suffix *-mentum*

When the suffix ***-mentum*** is added to the present stem of a Latin verb, a 2nd declension neuter noun is formed that means the *result of* or *means of* the action of the verb, e.g., **impedī-** (pres. stem of **impedīre,** *to hinder*) + ***-mentum*** = **impedīmentum, -ī,** n., *a hindrance;* pl., *baggage*. English derivatives of these nouns end in *-ment*, e.g., *impediment*. Latin nouns ending in ***-mentum*** frequently alter the spelling of the present stem of the root verb, e.g., **documentum**, from **docēre**.

Exercise 5

Give the Latin noun ending in ***-mentum*** formed from the present stem of each of the following verbs. Give the meaning of the noun and of its English derivative:

1. compleō
2. ligō
3. paviō, -īre, *to pound, tamp down*

Exercise 6

Give the meaning of each of the following English words and give the Latin root verb from which each is derived. Consult an English dictionary as needed:

1. sediment
2. monument
3. sentiment
4. regiment
5. momentum
6. augment

Inceptive Verbs

Latin verbs that end in ***-scō*** are called *inceptive* (from **incipiō**, *to begin*) since they denote an action in its beginning stages, e.g., **conticēscō**, *to become silent.* Compare the simple verb, **taceō**, *to be silent.* Inceptive verbs belong to the 3rd conjugation. Often the inceptive is related to a noun or adjective rather than to another verb, e.g., **advesperāscit**, *it grows dark*, from **vesper,** *evening.*

Exercise 7

Using the words in parentheses as guides, give the meaning of each of the following inceptive verbs:

1. quiēscō (**quiēs, quiētis**, f., *rest, quiet)*
2. convalēscō (**valeō**, *to be strong*)
3. senēscō (**senex**, *old*)
4. ingravēscō (**ingravō**, *to burden;* cf. **gravis**, *heavy*)
5. aegrēscō (**aeger**, *sick*)
6. stupēscō (**stupeō**, *to be amazed*)
7. proficīscor (**faciō**, *to make, do*)
8. adolēscō (**adulēscēns**, *a young man*)

Exercise 8

The present participial stem of an inceptive verb often becomes an English word. Give the meaning of the following English words, derived from inceptive verbs in Exercise 7. Consult an English dictionary as needed:

1. convalescent
2. quiescent
3. adolescent
4. senescent

REVIEW XI: CHAPTERS 46-49

Exercise XIa: The Irregular Verb *fīō, fierī, factus sum*

Give the forms of this verb in the second person singular in each of the following tenses. Translate each form you give:

1. Present
2. Imperfect
3. Future
4. Perfect
5. Pluperfect
6. Future Perfect

Exercise XIb: The Irregular Verb *mālō, mālle, māluī*

Give the forms of this verb in the third person singular in the tenses listed above. Translate each form you give.

Exercise XIc: Infinitives

Give the present active and passive, the perfect active and passive, and the future active infinitives of the following verbs. Translate each form you give:

1. amō
2. moneō
3. dūcō
4. iaciō
5. inveniō

Exercise XId: Infinitives

Give the present, perfect, and future infinitives of the following deponent verbs. Translate each form you give:

1. moror
2. vereor
3. loquor
4. ingredior
5. experior

Exercise XIe: Translation and Identification

Read aloud and translate. Identify each indirect statement, indirect question, ablative absolute, and **cum** circumstantial clause:

1. Aurēlia servōs in culīnā loquentēs audīvit.
2. Cornēlia Valerium ad Italiam regressum esse nōn audīverat.

3. Spectātōrēs nōn audīverant cūr servus līberātus esset.
4. Stirpe ē pede extractā, leō recubuit et dormīvit.
5. Prīnceps, fābulā audītā, cōnstituit servō parcere. Negāvit enim sē umquam prius tālem fābulam audīvisse.
6. Audīvimus spectātōrēs, cum leōnem hominis manūs lambentem vidērent, attonitōs esse.
7. Cornēlius putāvit Titum domum sē secūtum esse; sed mox intellēxit eum in amphitheātrō morātum esse.
8. Sextō vīsō, fūr effugere cōnāns in pavīmentō lāpsus est.
9. "Ēheu!" inquit Thisbē. "Putō meum vēlāmen tē perdidisse." Quibus verbīs dictīs, sē occīdere cōnāta est.
10. Dīcitur duōs amantēs in eōdem sepulcrō sepultōs esse.

negō, -āre, -āvī, -ātus, *to say that...not*

Exercise XIf: Translation and Identification

Read aloud and translate. Identify the tense and voice of each participle and of each infinitive:

1. Sciēbāmus multōs fūrēs vestīmenta ē balneīs surrepta in urbe vēndere.
2. Pȳramus, vēstīgiīs leōnis vīsīs, putāvit puellam necātam esse.
3. Thisbē, corpore Pȳramī vīsō, dīcit ipsam sē occīsūram esse.
4. Ex urbe profectūrī audīvimus viam Appiam clausam esse. Nesciēbāmus quandō Baiās perventūrī essēmus.
5. Puerī ex ātriō ēgredientēs, vōce Eucleidis audītā, sē in cubiculum cōnfugitūrōs esse mussāvērunt.
6. Sextus ē lūdō domum missus sciēbat Cornēlium sē pūnītūrum esse.
7. Titō rogantī Cornēlius respondit Aurēliam ad amphitheātrum nōn itūram esse; eam domī manēre mālle.
8. Marcus Titum cōnspectum rogāvit quot spectātōrēs amphitheātrō continērī possent.
9. Gladiātōrēs pugnātūrī Caesarem salūtāre solent. Sciunt multōs moritūrōs esse.
10. Post pugnās in amphitheātrō factās spectātōrēs multōs gladiātōrēs occīsōs esse vīdērunt.

Exercise XIg: Reading Comprehension

THE SIEGE OF JERUSALEM

In A.D. 69, Vespasian was forced to withdraw from suppressing a growing rebellion in Judea to return to Rome and assert his claims to the imperial throne. The next year, however, he sent his son Titus back to Judea to end the revolt by whatever means necessary. Titus besieged the city of Jerusalem for four months before it was finally captured and destroyed. Many Jews were taken prisoner and sent back to Rome in slavery. Now, forty years after the destruction of the city, a young Jewish boy from the city of Caesarea has written a letter to his grandfather, who was captured during the siege and taken to Rome as a slave. The grandfather, now a **lībertus**, writes a letter back with his memories of the siege of Jerusalem.

Read the following letter and answer the questions in English:

Appius Iūlius Giora nepōtī suō S. P. D.:

Salvē, Simōn! Quam laetus epistulam tuam accēpī. Gaudeō quod valēs. Spērō etiam valēre et patrem tuum et mātrem et sorōrēs et omnēs quī tēcum Caesarēae habitent. In epistulā tuā multa dē Hierosolymīs ā Titō imperātōre obsessīs rogābās. Difficile est mihi hās trīstissimās rēs referre sed, cum omnia cognōscere velīs, ut poēta ille dīxit, "Quamquam animus meminisse horret lūctūque refūgit, incipiam."

Quōmodo nōs Iūdaeī abhinc quadrāgintā annōs, rebelliōne contrā Rōmānōs factā, Gessium Flōrium, prōcūrātōrem illum Iūdaeae pessimum, ex urbe Hierosolymīs expulerimus, iam bene scīs. Ego ipse forte Hierosolyma paulō ante advēneram, nam diēbus fēstīs sānctissimīsque rem dīvīnam facere volēbam. Cum scīrēmus, Gessiō expulsō, Rōmānōs regressūrōs esse, urbem dēfendere parābāmus.

Urbs autem Hierosolyma nātūrā arteque mūnītissima erat: moenia enim ab Hērōde aedificāta erant, templum ā Solomōne rēge, arx ā Rōmānīs ipsīs. Sed ēheu! Eō tempore Iūdaeī sibi paene exitiō erant. Mīlitēs enim nostrī in trēs dīversās factiōnēs dīvidēbantur, quārum ducēs inter sē cotīdiē rixābantur, nam aliī alia cōnsilia capere volēbant. Itaque, antequam Rōmānī regressī sunt, multī Iūdaeī iam necātī erant, multum cibī dēlētum erat.

T. Flāvius Vespāsiānus, prīnceps Rōmānōrum, quod urbem recipere cōnstituerat, Titum fīlium cum quattuor legiōnibus mīsit. Castrīs extrā Hierosolyma positīs, Rōmānī quattuor mēnsēs urbem mūrō circumdatam obsidēbant. Tandem, multīs proeliīs factīs multīsque utrimque necātīs, Iūdaeī cibō carēbant. Multīs famē pereuntibus, Iūdaeī tamen sē nōn trādidērunt. Titus igitur urbem summīs vīribus adortus est: arce dēlētā, templō incēnsō, omnēs cīvēs aut captī aut necātī sunt.

Ego ipse, prīmō mēnse ā Rōmānīs proeliō captus, nōn necātus sum. In servitūtem tamen abstractus sum, neque fīnem obsidiōnis ipse vīdī. Dīcitur Titus urbī populōque Iūdaeō parcere voluisse. Ferunt quoque templum Titō invītō dēlētum esse. Id tamen vix crēdere possum. Rōmānī enim nec mōrēs nostrōs nec sacra ūllō modō intellēxērunt, immō semper reprehendērunt. Sēnsit tamen Titus templum esse sēdem sēditiōnis atque prō certō habēbat, templō dēlētō, Iūdaeōs mox arma trāditūrōs esse.

Aliter autem rem nārrant sapientēs nostrī, apud quōs legimus Deum, īrātum quod Iūdaeī nōn iam piī essent, eōs pūnīre cōnstituisse. Itaque et urbem et templum dēlēre Rōmānōs sīvit, immō adiūvit! Sīc pūnīvit Deus populum suum. Valē!

1 **nepōs, nepōtis,** m., *grandson*
3 **Caesarēa, -ae,** f., *Caesarea (a town in Palestine, on the Mediterranean Sea)*
4 **Hierosolyma, -ōrum,** n. pl., *Jerusalem*
6 **meminisse,** *to remember*
horreō, -ēre, -uī, *to shudder, be unwilling*
lūctus, -ūs, m., *grief, mourning*
7 **Iūdaeī, Iūdaeōrum,** m. pl., *the Jews*
quadrāgintā, *forty*
8 **prōcūrātor, prōcūrātōris,** m., *procurator, governor*
Iūdaea, -ae, f., *Judaea*
9 **paulō,** adv., *a little*
10 **fēstus, -a, -um,** *festival/feast (day)*
sānctus, -a, -um, *holy, sacred*
rēs dīvīna, reī dīvīnae, f., *religious rite*
12 **mūnītus, -a, -um,** *fortified*
Hērōdēs, Hērōdis, m., *Herod (the Great, king of Judaea, 40–4 B.C.)*
13 **Solomōn, Solomōnis,** m., *Solomon (son of David and third king of Israel)*
arx, arcis, f., *citadel, fortress*
14 **exitiō esse,** *to be a source of destruction*
dīversus, -a, -um, *different, opposed*
15 **dux, ducis,** m., *leader*
18 **legiō, legiōnis,** f., *legion (a division of the Roman army)*
castra pōnere, *to pitch camp*
19 **proelium, -ī,** n., *battle*
20 **utrimque,** adv., *on both sides*
famēs, famis, abl., **famē,** f., *hunger, starvation*
21 **vīrēs, vīrium** (pl. of **vīs**), f. pl., *military forces*
24 **obsidiō, obsidiōnis,** f., *siege*
25 **ferunt,** *they say*
26 **mōs, mōris,** m., *custom;* pl., *character*
sacra, -ōrum, n. pl., *religious rites*
ūllus, -a, -um, *any*
27 **sēdēs, sēdis,** gen. pl., **sēdium,** f., *seat, center (of some activity)*
sēditiō, sēditiōnis, f., *political strife, rebellion*
29 **aliter,** adv., *differently*
sapiēns, sapientis, m., *wise man*
30 **pius, -a, -um,** *dutiful, worshipful*

5 **referō, referre, rettulī, relātus,** *to bring back, report, write down*
6 **refugiō, refugere, refūgī,** *to shrink back, recoil*
17 **recipiō, recipere, recēpī, receptus,** *to receive, recapture*
19 **circumdō, circumdare, circumdedī, circumdatus,** *to surround*
20 **pereō, perīre, periī, peritūrus,** *to perish, die*
24 **abstrahō, abstrahere, abstrāxī, abstractus,** *to drag away, carry off*

1. Who is writing to whom?
2. What had Simon asked about?
3. When had the Jews revolted?
4. Who was expelled from Jerusalem?
5. Why was the author in Jerusalem?
6. How well was Jerusalem fortified?
7. How were the Jews almost destroyed?
8. What did the Jewish factions do?
9. Who was sent against the city?
10. How long was the city besieged?
11. Did the Jews surrender?
12. Why was the author not killed?
13. What is said about Titus?
14. Why did Titus destroy the Temple?

NOTHING EVER HAPPENS

Sōl caelō serēnō lūcēbat. Cantābant avēs. Nātūra ipsa gaudēre vidēbātur. Trīstī vultū tamen sedēbat Cornēlia sōla in peristȳliō. Sēcum cōgitābat: "Mē taedet sōlitūdinis. Cūr nēmō mē observat? Cūr mēcum nēmō loquitur? Pater tantum temporis in tablīnō agit ut eum numquam videam. Māter tam occupāta est ut mēcum numquam loquātur. Marcus et Sextus suīs lūdīs adeō dēditī sunt ut nihil aliud faciant. Nōn intellegō cūr nūper etiam servae mē neglēxerint, cūr Eucleidēs ille verbōsus verbum nūllum mihi dīxerit. Ō mē miseram!"

Cornēliae haec cōgitantī, "Heus tū, Cornēlia!" clāmāvit Marcus quī tum intrāvit in peristȳlium. "Pater iubet tē in tablīnō statim adesse. Festīnāre tē oportet."

Cornēlia, cum in tablīnum intrāvisset, vīdit adesse et patrem et mātrem, id quod erat eī admīrātiōnī et cūrae.

(continued)

1 **sōl, sōlis,** m., *sun*
serēnus, -a, -um, *clear, bright*
avis, avis, gen. pl., **avium,** m./f., *bird*
3 **observō, -āre, -āvī, -ātus,** *to watch, pay attention to*
5 **adeō,** adv., *so much, to such an extent*
dēditus, -a, -um, *devoted, dedicated*
nūper, adv., *recently*
8 **Heus!** *Hey there!*
10 **id quod,** *that/a thing which*
11 **cūrae esse,** *to be a cause of anxiety (to)*

1 **lūcet, lūcēre, lūxit,** *it is light, it is day; (it) shines*
2 **taedet, taedēre, taesum est,** *it bores, makes one* (acc.) *tired of something* (gen.)
Mē taedet sōlitūdinis, *It tires me of…, I am tired of/bored with…*
6 **neglegō, neglegere, neglēxī, neglēctus,** *to neglect, ignore*
9 **oportet, oportēre, oportuit,** *it is fitting; ought*
Festīnāre tē oportet, *That you hurry is fitting, You ought to hurry.*

Exercise 50a
Respondē Latīnē:

1. Cūr Cornēlia trīstis est?
2. Ubi pater multum temporis agit?
3. Quam occupāta est Aurēlia?
4. Quibus rēbus sunt Marcus et Sextus dēditī?
5. Loquunturne aut servae aut Eucleidēs cum Cornēliā?
6. Quis Cornēliae clāmāvit?
7. Quō Cornēliam īre oportet?

Tum pater gravī vultū, "Ōlim, Cornēlia," inquit, "Pūblius Cornēlius Scīpiō Āfricānus, vir praeclārissimus gentis nostrae, dīcitur inter epulās senātōrum fīliam suam Tiberiō Gracchō dēspondisse. Post epulās, cum Scīpiō domum regressus uxōrī dīxisset sē fīliam dēspondisse, illa maximā īrā erat commōta. 'Nōn decet patrem,' inquit, 'dēspondēre fīliam, īnsciā mātre.' At pater tuus nōn est Pūbliō Cornēliō similis, nam ūnā cōnstituimus et ego et māter tua iuvenī cuidam nōbilī tē dēspondēre. Quīntus Valerius, adulēscēns ille optimus, vult tē in mātrimōnium dūcere, id quod nōbīs placet. Placetne tibi, Cornēlia?"

Cornēlia adeō perturbāta erat ut vix loquī posset, sed tandem submissā vōce, "Mihi quoque placet," respondit.

Cui Cornēlius, "Estō! Crās aderit Valerius ipse."

13 **gēns, gentis,** gen. pl., **gentium,** f., *family, clan*
epulae, -ārum, f. pl., *banquet, feast*
16 **similis, -is, -e** + dat., *similar (to), like*
17 **iuvenis, iuvenis,** m., *young man*
20 **submissus, -a, -um,** *quiet, subdued, soft*

14 **dēspondeō, dēspondēre, dēspondī, dēspōnsus,** *to betroth, promise in marriage*
15 **decet, decēre, decuit,** *it is becoming, fitting; should*
Nōn decet patrem dēspondēre fīliam, *That a father should betroth his daughter is not fitting, A father should not betroth his daughter.*

Respondē Latīnē:

1. Quō in locō Pūblius Cornēlius Scīpiō fīliam suam dēspondisse dīcitur?
2. Quōmodo uxor eius commōta erat?
3. Cūr commōta erat?
4. Quid Cornēlius et Aurēlia facere cōnstituerant?
5. Quis Cornēliam in mātrimōnium dūcere vult?
6. Placetne ille Cornēliō et Aurēliae?
7. Placetne ille Cornēliae?

BUILDING THE MEANING

Result Clauses

When you meet these words—

adeō, adv., *so much, to such an extent*
ita, adv., *thus, in such a way*
sīc, adv., *thus, in this way*
tālis, -is, -e, *such*
tam, adv., *so*
tantus, -a, -um, *so great*
tantum, adv., *so much*
tot, indecl. adj., *so many*

—you will often find the word **ut** later in the sentence meaning *that*, followed by a clause indicating *result*:

> **Adeō** perturbāta erat **ut** vix loquī posset. (50:20)
> *She was **so** confused **that** she could hardly speak.*
>
> **Tam** occupāta est **ut** mēcum numquam loquātur. (50:4)
> *She is **so** busy **that** she never speaks to me.*

If the result clause is negative, **ut** is followed by **nōn:**

> **Adeō** perturbāta est **ut** loquī **nōn** possit.
> *She is **so** confused **that** she **cannot** speak.*

The verb in the result clause is in the subjunctive and is translated into the equivalent tense of the English indicative. The verbs **loquātur** and **possit** in the examples above are *present subjunctives.*

FORMS

Verbs: Present and Perfect Subjunctive

The imperfect and pluperfect subjunctives were tabulated in the Forms section of Chapter 43. The following is the tabulation of the other two tenses of the subjunctive, the present and perfect:

Present Subjunctive

Active Voice

		1st Conjugation	2nd Conjugation	3rd Conjugation		4th Conjugation
S	1	pórt***em***	móve***am***	mítt***am***	iáci***am***	aúdi***am***
	2	pórt***ēs***	móve***ās***	mítt***ās***	iáci***ās***	aúdi***ās***
	3	pórt***et***	móve***at***	mítt***at***	iáci***at***	aúdi***at***
P	1	port***ḗmus***	move***ā́mus***	mitt***ā́mus***	iaci***ā́mus***	audi***ā́mus***
	2	port***ḗtis***	move***ā́tis***	mitt***ā́tis***	iaci***ā́tis***	audi***ā́tis***
	3	pórt***ent***	móve***ant***	mítt***ant***	iáci***ant***	aúdi***ant***

Passive Voice

		1st Conjugation	2nd Conjugation	3rd Conjugation		4th Conjugation
S	1	pórt***er***	móve***ar***	mítt***ar***	iáci***ar***	aúdi***ar***
	2	port***ḗris***	move***ā́ris***	mitt***ā́ris***	iaci***ā́ris***	audi***ā́ris***
	3	port***ḗtur***	move***ā́tur***	mitt***ā́tur***	iaci***ā́tur***	audi***ā́tur***
P	1	port***ḗmur***	move***ā́mur***	mitt***ā́mur***	iaci***ā́mur***	audi***ā́mur***
	2	port***ḗminī***	move***ā́minī***	mitt***ā́minī***	iaci***ā́minī***	audi***ā́minī***
	3	port***éntur***	move***ántur***	mitt***ántur***	iaci***ántur***	audi***ántur***

Deponent Verbs

S	1	cṓn***er*** etc.	vére***ar*** etc.	lóqu***ar*** etc.	regrédi***ar*** etc.	expéri***ar*** etc.

Irregular Verbs

ésse		
	1	s***im***
S	2	s***īs***
	3	s***it***
	1	s***ī́mus***
P	2	s***ī́tis***
	3	s***int***

So also **póss*im*, vél*im*, nṓl*im*, mā́l*im***

ī́re		
	1	é***am***
S	2	é***ās***
	3	é***at***
	1	e***ā́mus***
P	2	e***ā́tis***
	3	é***ant***

So also **fér*am*, fī́*am***

Perfect Subjunctive

Active Voice

	1	portā́v***erim***	mṓv***erim***	mī́s***erim***	iḗc***erim***	audī́v***erim***
S	2	portā́v***eris***	mṓv***eris***	mī́s***eris***	iḗc***eris***	audī́v***eris***
	3	portā́v***erit***	mṓv***erit***	mī́s***erit***	iḗc***erit***	audī́v***erit***
	1	portāv***érimus***	mōv***érimus***	mīs***érimus***	iēc***érimus***	audīv***érimus***
P	2	portāv***éritis***	mōv***éritis***	mīs***éritis***	iēc***éritis***	audīv***éritis***
	3	portā́v***erint***	mṓv***erint***	mī́s***erint***	iḗc***erint***	audī́v***erint***

Passive Voice

S	1	portā́tus sim etc.	mṓtus sim etc.	míssus sim etc.	iáctus sim etc.	audī́tus sim etc.

Deponent Verbs

S	1	cōnā́tus sim etc.	véritus sim etc.	locū́tus sim etc.	regréssus sim etc.	expértus sim etc.

Irregular Verbs

ésse		
S	1	fú***erim*** etc.

So also **potú*erim*, volú*erim*, nōlú*erim*, mālú*erim*, *íerim***, and **túl*erim***. The perfect subjunctive of **fī́ō** is **fáctus sim**.

Be sure to learn the above forms thoroughly.

Exercise 50b

Here are sample forms of all the tenses of the subjunctive, active and passive, of a regular verb and sample forms of the subjunctives of a deponent verb:

Regular Verb:

Present Active	*Present Passive*
parem	**parer**
Perfect Active	*Perfect Passive*
parāverim	**parātus sim**
Imperfect Active	*Imperfect Passive*
parārem	**parārer**
Pluperfect Active	*Pluperfect Passive*
parāvissem	**parātus essem**

Deponent Verb:

Present
cōner

Perfect
cōnātus sim

Imperfect
cōnārer

Pluperfect
cōnātus essem

Give subjunctive forms of the following verbs in the designated person and number, following the pattern above. For deponent verbs give only passive forms:

1. observō, -āre, -āvī, -ātus: 3rd pl.
2. dēspondeō, dēspondēre, dēspondī, dēspōnsus: 1st sing.
3. neglegō, neglegere, neglēxī, neglēctus: 1st pl.
4. proficīscor, proficīscī, profectus sum: 3rd sing.
5. ēgredior, ēgredī, ēgressus sum: 2nd pl.

A betrothal ring

BUILDING THE MEANING

Sequence of Tenses

Compare the following pairs of sentences containing indirect questions:

1. a. Nōn intellegō cūr servae mē **neglegant.**
   I do not understand why the slave-girls ***neglect*** *me.*

   b. Nōn intellegō cūr servae mē **neglēxerint.**
   I do not understand why the slave-girls ***neglected*** *me.*

2. a. Nōn intellēxī cūr servae mē **neglegerent.**
   I did not understand why the slave-girls ***were neglecting*** *me.*

   b. Nōn intellēxī cūr servae mē **neglēxissent.**
   I did not understand why the slave-girls ***had neglected*** *me.*

When the verb in the main clause is in the *present tense* (as in 1a and 1b above), a *present subjunctive* in the indirect question (as in 1a above) indicates an action going on at the same time as (or after) that of the main verb, and a *perfect subjunctive* in the indirect question (as in 1b above) indicates an action that took place before that of the main verb.

When the verb in the main clause is in a *past tense* (as in 2a and 2b above), an *imperfect subjunctive* in the indirect question (as in 2a above) indicates an action going on at the same time as (or after) that of the main verb, and a *pluperfect subjunctive* in the indirect question (as in 2b above) indicates an action that took place before that of the main verb.

This relationship between the tense of the verb in the main clause and the tense of the subjunctive in the subordinate clause is called *sequence of tenses.* The sequence is said to be *primary* when the verb in the main clause is in a primary tense, i.e., *present* or *future* or *future perfect*, as in 1a and 1b above. The sequence is said to be *secondary* when the verb in the main clause is in a secondary tense, i.e., *imperfect* or *perfect* or *pluperfect*, as in 2a and 2b above.

SEQUENCE OF TENSES		
	Main Clause Indicative	**Subordinate Clause** Tense of Subjunctive *Time of Action* *Relative to Main Clause*
Primary Sequence	Present Future Future Perfect	Present = *Same time or after* Perfect = *Time before*
Secondary Sequence	Imperfect Perfect Pluperfect	Imperfect = *Same time or after* Pluperfect = *Time before*

Exercise 50c

Read aloud and translate each sentence, and then explain the sequence of tenses between the main and the subordinate clauses:

1. Tam laetae cantant avēs ut nātūra ipsa gaudēre videātur.
2. Tam laetae cantābant avēs ut nātūra ipsa gaudēre vidērētur.
3. Tot spectātōrēs ad lūdōs conveniunt ut Circus vix omnēs contineat.
4. Tot spectātōrēs ad lūdōs convēnerant ut Circus vix omnēs continēret.
5. Cornēlia nōn rogat cūr pater sē Valeriō dēsponderit.
6. Cornēlia nōn rogāvit cūr pater sē Valeriō dēspondisset.

Sequence of Tenses in Result Clauses

In result clauses a present subjunctive will usually be used in primary sequence and an imperfect or perfect subjunctive in secondary sequence. The imperfect subjunctive in result clauses is used to emphasize the natural or logical connection between the main clause and the result:

> Leō tantus et tam ferōx erat ut servus metū exanimātus **caderet.**
> *The lion was so large and so fierce that the slave (as could be expected)* ***fell down*** *paralyzed with fear.*

The perfect subjunctive would emphasize the fact that the result actually did take place:

> Leō tantus et tam ferōx erat ut servus metū exanimātus **ceciderit.**
> *The lion was so large and so fierce that the slave (actually)* ***fell down*** *paralyzed with fear.*

Exercise 50d

Read aloud and translate each sentence, and make your translations show the difference in meaning between the use of the imperfect and the perfect subjunctives:

1. Tanta tempestās coorta erat ut sērō Brundisium advenīrēmus.
2. Tanta tempestās coorta erat ut sērō Brundisium advēnerimus.
3. Pater tam gravī vultū locūtus est ut Cornēlia mīrārētur quid accidisset.
4. Pater tam gravī vultū locūtus est ut Cornēlia mīrāta sit quid accidisset.
5. Cornēlia Flāviae scrīpsit: "Tam laeta eram ut vix loquī possem."
6. Cornēlia Flāviae scrīpsit: "Tam laeta eram ut vix loquī potuerim."

ROMAN LIFE XXXI

ROMAN WEDDINGS

When a Roman girl reached marriageable age—somewhere between twelve and fourteen—her father set about finding her a husband.

When a friend asked the writer Pliny to help him find a suitable match for his niece, Pliny wrote back to say that a certain Acilianus would be just the man. After speaking highly of Acilianus' father, his grandmother on his mother's side, and his uncle, he describes the prospective bridegroom as follows:

> Acilianus himself is a person of very great energy and application, but at the same time exceedingly modest. He has held the offices of quaestor, tribune, and praetor with very great distinction, and this relieves you of the need to canvass

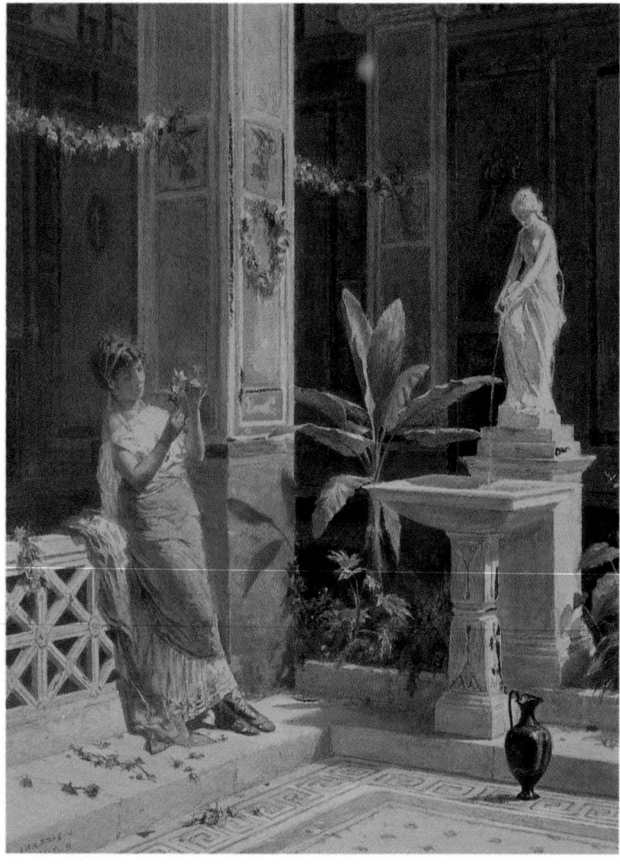

A girl of marriageable age in a courtyard in Pompeii

Oil on canvas "In a Courtyard in Pompeii" by Luigi Bazzani, Waterhouse and Dodd, London, England

on his behalf. His expression is frank and open; his complexion is fresh and he has a healthy color; his whole bearing is noble and handsome, with the dignity of a senator. I don't know whether I should add that his father has ample means; for, when I picture you and your brother for whom we are seeking a son-in-law, I think there is no need for me to say more on that subject; and yet, when I consider the attitudes of people nowadays and even the laws of the country, which judge a man's income as of primary importance, I'm probably right in thinking that even a reference to his father's means should not be omitted. Certainly, if one thinks of the children of the marriage and their children, one must take the question of money into account when making a choice.

Pliny, *Letters* I.14

When we remember that a Roman would be nearly forty before he attained the praetorship, Pliny's candidate (if we read between the lines) was probably red-faced, stout, and middle-aged, but Pliny seems to consider these points less important than having good family connections and plenty of money.

So our thirteen-year-old Cornelia might find herself engaged to a mere boy (minimum age fourteen) or to someone three times her age, but she was not expected to raise any objections to what was simply a legal contract between families.

Before the actual wedding, a betrothal ceremony (**spōnsālia**) often took place, witnessed by relatives and friends. The father of the girl was asked formally if he "promised" his daughter and replied that he did. (Question: **Spondēsne?** Answer: **Spondeō.**) Gifts were then given to the bride-to-be, including a ring (**ānulus**) either of gold or of iron set in gold. This was worn on the third finger of the left hand, from which it was believed a nerve ran straight to the heart. Aulus Gellius, a Roman scholar and writer of the second half of the second century A.D., explains:

I have heard that the ancient Greeks wore a ring on the finger of the left hand which is next to the little finger. They say, too, that the Roman men commonly wore their rings in that way. Apion in his *Egyptian History* says that the reason for this practice is that, upon cutting into and opening human bodies, it was found that a very fine nerve proceeded from that finger alone of which we have spoken, and made its way to the human heart; that it therefore seemed quite reasonable that this finger in particular should be honored with such an ornament, since it seems to be joined, and as it were united, with that supreme organ, the heart.

Aulus Gellius, *Attic Nights* X.10

Before the betrothal ceremony, the two families had usually already discussed the terms of the dowry (**dōs**), a sum of money or property given by the bride's father along with his daughter. The dowry was returnable in the event of a divorce.

Exercise 50e

Read aloud and translate:

Omnia iam diū ad spōnsālia parāta erant, īnsciā Cornēliā. Valerius enim, cum prīmum Brundisiī ē nāve ēgressus est, ad Cornēlium scrīpserat sē velle Cornēliam in mātrimōnium dūcere; deinde Cornēlius rescrīpserat sē libenter fīliam Valeriō dēspōnsūrum esse; tum Aurēlia Vīniam, mātrem Flāviae, invītāverat ut prōnuba esset. Ad spōnsālia igitur Valerius et Vīnia et Flāvia Rōmam iam advēnerant.

Aderat diēs spōnsālium. Quīntā hōrā omnēs Cornēliī atque propinquī amīcīque in ātrium convēnērunt. Deinde, silentiō factō, Cornēlia vultū dēmissō ingressa in ātrium dēducta est. Tum Valerius, quī contrā Cornēlium in mediō ātriō stābat, eī, "Spondēsne," ait, "tē fīliam tuam mihi uxōrem datūrum esse?"

Cui Cornēlius, "Spondeō."

Quō dictō, Valerius ad Cornēliam conversus ānulum aureum tertiō digitō sinistrae manūs eius aptāvit. Tum ōsculum eī dedit. Omnēs spōnsō et spōnsae grātulātī sunt.

1 **spōnsālia, spōnsālium,** n. pl., *betrothal ceremony*
  ad spōnsālia, *for the betrothal*
5 **prōnuba, -ae,** f., *bride's attendant*
7 **propinquus, -ī,** m., *relative*
10 **ait,** *(he/she) says, said*
12 **conversus, -a, -um,** *having turned, turning*
  ānulus, -ī, m., *ring*
13 **sinister, sinistra, sinistrum,** *left*
  aptō, -āre, -āvī, -ātus, *to place, fit*
14 **grātulor, -ārī, -ātus sum** + dat., *to congratulate*

8 **dēmittō, dēmittere, dēmīsī, dēmissus,** *to let down, lower*
10 **spondeō, spondēre, spopondī, spōnsus,** *to promise solemnly, pledge*

Sīqua volēs aptē nūbere, nūbe parī. ***If you wish a suitable marriage, marry an equal.*** (Ovid, *Heroides* IX.32)

CHAPTER 51

MARCUS COMES OF AGE

Coming of age was an important occasion for a Roman boy, and it was marked both by an official ceremony (**officium togae virīlis**) and by family celebrations. The ceremony usually took place when the boy had reached the age of sixteen but not on his birthday. It was common for it to be celebrated at the **Līberālia** (the festival of Liber or Bacchus, the god of wine) on March 17. It began with the boy dedicating (**cōnsecrāre**) the luck-charm (**bulla**) which he had worn since he was a baby and the toga with the purple edge (**toga praetexta**). These he placed before the shrine of the household gods (**larārium**), which was usually in the **ātrium** of the house. From this time on he wore the plain white toga (**toga virīlis** or **toga pūra**) indicating that he was no longer a boy but a man. After the ceremony members of his family and friends escorted him to the Forum (**in Forum dēdūcere**). There, in the building where the public records were housed (**Tabulārium**), his name was entered in the records (**tabulae,** literally, *tablets*). The official ceremony was now completed, and the family entertained their friends at a private celebration.

The time has now come for Marcus to assume the **toga virīlis.**

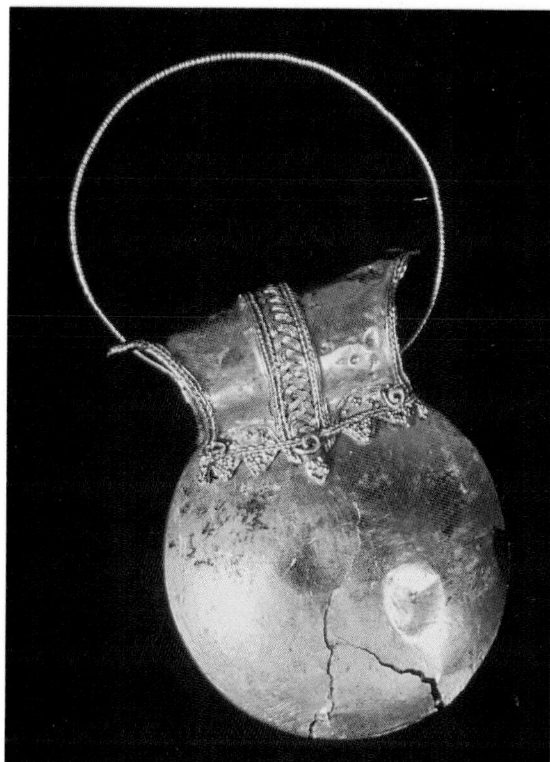

Gold bulla
Museo e Gallerie Nazionali di Capodimonte, Naples, Italy

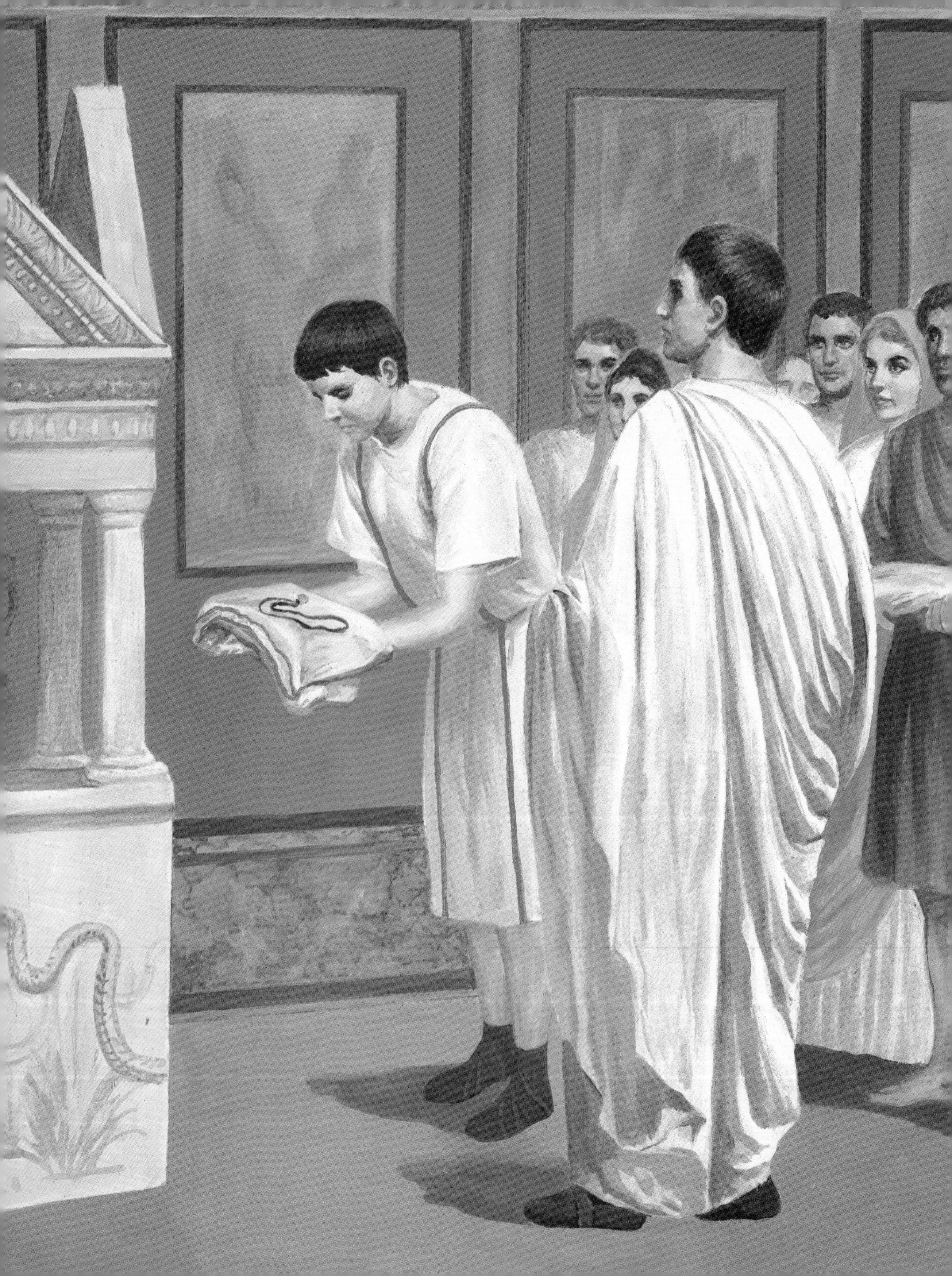

Iam aderat mēnsis Mārtius. Erat diēs Līberālium quō diē adulēscentēs Rōmānī togam pūram sūmere solēbant. Abhinc complūrēs mēnsēs Marcus sēdecim annōs complēverat; nunc togam virīlem sumptūrus erat. Itaque Cornēlius amīcōs clientēsque omnēs invītāverat ut eō diē apud sē convenīrent. Omnēs sciēbant patrem Marcī dīvitissimum esse; omnēs prō certō habēbant eum optimam cēnam amīcīs datūrum esse.

Domus Gaiī Cornēliī plēna erat tumultūs, strepitūs, clāmōris. Tot et tam variī hominēs eō conveniēbant ut iānitor, ab iānuā prōgressus, in ipsō līmine sollicitus stāret. Sī quis appropinquābat, eum magnā vōce rogābat quis esset et quid vellet. Aliōs rogābat ut in domum prōcēderent, aliīs praecipiēbat ut in viā manērent. Nōnnūllī autem, quī neque amīcī Cornēliī erant neque clientēs, domuī appropinquāvērunt, quod spērābant Cornēlium sē ad cēnam invītātūrum esse. Hī iānitōrem ōrābant nē sē dīmitteret; ille autem eīs imperābat ut statim discēderent.

Tandem, omnibus rēbus parātīs, Cornēlius tōtam familiam rogāvit ut in ātrium convenīrent. Aderant propinquī; aderant multī amīcī; aderant plūrimī clientium; aderant omnēs servī lībertīque Cornēliōrum. Cūnctī inter sē colloquēbantur, cūnctī gaudēbant quod ad hoc officium togae virīlis invītātī erant.

In ātriō ante larārium stābat Marcus togam praetextam bullamque auream in manibus tenēns. Sēnsit oculōs omnium in sē conversōs esse. Conticuērunt omnēs. Marcus prīmum togam praetextam atque bullam ante larārium dēpositās Laribus familiāribus cōnsecrāvit. "Nunc," inquit, "hās rēs puerīlēs hīc dēpōnō. Nunc vōbīs, ō Larēs familiārēs, haec libenter cōnsecrō."

(continued)

2 **pūrus, -a, -um,** *spotless, clean, plain white*
sūmere, *to assume (i.e., put on for the first time)*
4 **invītāverat ut,** *he had invited (them) to*
7 **līmen, līminis,** n., *threshold, doorway*
8 **sī quis,** *if anyone*
9 **nōnnūllī, -ae, -a,** *some*
11 **ōrō, -āre, -āvī, -ātus,** *to beg*
nē sē dīmitteret, *not to send them away*
12 **imperō, -āre, -āvī, -ātus** + dat., *to order*
19 **Larēs, Larum,** m. pl., *household gods*
20 **familiāris, -is, -e,** *belonging to the family/household*

9 **praecipiō, praecipere, praecēpī, praeceptus** + dat., *to instruct, order*
11 **dīmittō, dīmittere, dīmīsī, dīmissus,** *to send away*

Exercise 51a Respondē Latīnē:

1. Quī mēnsis erat?
2. Quot annōs complēverat Marcus?
3. Quid hodiē factūrus erat?
4. Quid omnēs amīcī clientēsque Cornēliī prō certō habēbant?
5. Cūr iānitor sollicitus erat?
6. Quid iānitor rogābat appropinquantēs?
7. Quid iānitor rogābat ut quīdam ex appropinquantibus facerent?
8. Quid aliīs praecipiēbat?
9. Quid iānitor iubēbat eōs facere quī neque amīcī Cornēliī neque clientēs erant?
10. Quō tōta familia convēnit?
11. Cūr cūnctī gaudēbant?
12. Quid Marcus Laribus familiāribus cōnsecrāvit?

Quō factō, pater servō cuidam imperāvit ut togam virīlem Marcō indueret. Deinde parentēs eum amplexī sunt et cēterī eī grātulātī sunt. Nunc Marcus, multīs comitantibus, in Forum ā patre est dēductus.

Quō cum pervēnissent, Marcō ad Tabulārium ductō, pater eōs quī comitābantur rogāvit ut extrā Tabulārium manērent. Ipse ūnā cum fīliō et paucīs propinquīs in Tabulārium ingressus est, nam ibi nōmen Marcī in tabulīs pūblicīs erat īnscrībendum.

Quibus rēbus cōnfectīs, omnēs adstantēs Marcum iam ēgressum magnō clāmōre salūtāvērunt. Deinde cum Marcus omnibus grātiās ēgisset propter tantam ergā sē benevolentiam, omnēs domum Cornēliōrum rediērunt, nam Cornēlius multōs invītāverat ut apud sē eō diē cēnārent.

23 **comitor, -ārī, -ātus sum,** *to accompany*

27 **erat īnscrībendum,** *had to be registered*

29 **grātiās agere** + dat., *to thank*

ergā, prep. + acc., *toward*

benevolentia, -ae, f., *kindness*

23 **amplector, amplectī, amplexus sum,** *to embrace*

Respondē Latīnē:

1. Quid Cornēlius servō cuidam imperāvit ut faceret?
2. Quō est Marcus dēductus?
3. Quī in Tabulārium ingressī sunt?
4. Quid in Tabulāriō factum est?
5. Quid ut facerent Cornēlius multōs invītāverat?

Building the Meaning

Telling to, Asking to: Indirect Commands

Compare the following pairs of sentences:

1. a. Aliōs rogat **ut** in domum **prōcēdant**. (cf. 51:8–9)
   *He asks some **to go forward** into the house.*

   b. Aliōs rogāvit **ut** in domum **prōcēderent**. (cf. 51:8–9)
   *He asked some **to go forward** into the house.*

2. a. Hī iānitōrem ōrant **nē** sē **dīmittat**. (cf. 51:11)
   *They keep begging the doorkeeper **not to send** them **away**.*

   b. Hī iānitōrem ōrābant **nē** sē **dīmitteret**. (51:11)
   *They kept begging the doorkeeper **not to send** them **away**.*

In these sentences **ut** is translated by *to*; **nē** is translated by *not to*. The subordinate clauses in the sentences above, introduced by **ut** or **nē** and with their verbs in the subjunctive, are called *indirect commands.*

A *present subjunctive* will be found in primary sequence (examples 1a and 2a above), and an *imperfect subjunctive* will be found in secondary sequence (examples 1b and 2b above).

Verbs such as the following may introduce indirect commands:

hortor, *to encourage, urge*
imperō, *to order*
invītō, *to invite*
obsecrō, *to beseech, beg*
ōrō, *to beg*
rogō, *to ask*
moneō, *to advise, warn*
persuādeō, *to persuade*
praecipiō, *to instruct, order*

Note that most of the verbs that introduce indirect commands take a direct object in the accusative case:

Aliōs rogābat ut in domum prōcēderent. (51:8–9)
He was asking ***some*** *to go forward into the house.*

The verbs **imperō, praecipiō,** and **persuādeō**, however, take the dative case:

Coquō imperāvit (praecēpit/persuāsit) ut in ātrium venīret.
He ordered (instructed/persuaded) ***the cook*** *to come into the atrium.*

Another arrangement is also possible:

Imperāvit ut coquus in ātrium venīret.
He ordered that the cook come into the atrium.

Here the order was issued not to the cook but to someone else (not specified).

Exercise 51b

In story 51, locate nine subordinate clauses that express indirect commands.

1. Translate the sentences in which these indirect commands occur.
2. Tell in English what the direct command (or request) was or would have been that is being reported indirectly in each case.
3. Locate one example of a subordinate clause with *indirect questions* (rather than indirect commands or requests) in story 51, and tell in English what the direct questions were that are here being reported indirectly.

Ego vōs hortor ut amīcitiam omnibus rēbus hūmānīs anteponātis.
I urge you to set friendship before all other human affairs. **(Cicero, *On Friendship* V.17)**

Exercise 51c

Read aloud and translate each sentence, identify the type of each subordinate clause, and then identify the tense of each verb in the subjunctive:

1. Cornēlius convīvās omnēs invītat ut in ātrium prōcēdant.
2. Tum Cornēlius Marcō imperāvit ut rēs puerīlēs Laribus cōnsecrāret.
3. Cornēlius Marcum togā pūrā indūtum rogāvit ut ad Forum sēcum proficīscerētur.
4. In Tabulāriō pater rogat ut nōmen Marcī in tabulīs pūblicīs īnscrībātur.
5. Cornēlius omnēs convīvās invītāvit ut apud sē cēnārent.
6. Tē ōrō atque obsecrō ut domum veniās.
7. Iānitor iam iānuam claudēbat: tam dēfessus erat ut dormīre cuperet.
8. Asellus iānitōrem vīsum rogāvit quid eō diē fēcisset.
9. "Tibi dīcō," inquit iānitor, "plūrimōs hominēs ā mē aut ad iānuam acceptōs esse aut dīmissōs."
10. "Nōlī ibi morārī," inquam, "nam dominus imperāvit ut iānua claudātur."

Note that in sentence 10 present time is clearly in the speaker's mind when using the verb **imperāvit,** *has ordered.* When the perfect tense is used in this way, the sequence is primary, and therefore a present subjunctive is used in the indirect command.

Exercise 51d

Select, read aloud, and translate:

1. Nōlī mē hortārī ut ad illam urbem (īrem/eam).
2. Tē semper moneō nē in mediā viā (ambulēs/ambulārēs).
3. Abhinc multōs mēnsēs Valerius Cornēliō persuāsit ut Cornēliam sibi (spondēret/spondeat).
4. Plūrimī hominēs cum ad domum Cornēliī pervēnissent rogābant ut intrāre (liceat/licēret).
5. Prīmō omnēs hominēs hortor ut in viā (maneant/manērent).
6. Deinde amīcōs propinquōsque Cornēliī rogāvī ut (intrārent/intrent).
7. Clientibus praecēpī nē statim in domum (prōcēderent/prōcēdant).
8. Nōnnūllī, quōs nōn prius vīdī, mē ōrant nē sē (dīmitterem/dīmittam).
9. Eōs monuī nē ad iānuam (morārentur/morentur).
10. Tandem coāctus sum servōs rogāre ut eōs baculīs (repellant/repellerent).

Exercise 51e

Using story 51 and the information on indirect commands as guides, give the Latin for the following. Use present subjunctives in all of the indirect commands:

1. Cornelius is inviting all his friends and clients to come together at his house.
2. The doorkeeper asks some people to go forward into the house.
3. Others he orders to stay in the street.
4. Others he orders to depart immediately.
5. Cornelius orders a certain slave to put a toga of manhood on Marcus.

ROMAN LIFE XXXII

COMING-OF-AGE CEREMONIES

When Cicero, the great statesman and orator (106–43 B.C.), was governor of Cilicia, an area of southern Asia Minor, he wrote the following in a letter to his friend Atticus (50 B.C.) about his nephew Quintus and his son Marcus:

> Cicerōnēs puerī amant inter sē, discunt, exercentur, sed alter frēnīs eget, alter calcāribus. Quīntō togam pūram Līberālibus cōgitābam dare; mandāvit enim pater.
>
> My son and nephew are fond of one another, learn their lessons, and take their exercise together; but the one needs the rein and the other the spur. I intend to celebrate Quintus' coming of age on the feast of Bacchus. His father asked me to do this.
>
> Cicero, *Letters to Atticus* VI.1

The following year Cicero planned to give the **toga pūra** to his own son, Marcus, in his hometown of Arpinum to the southeast of Rome:

> Volō Cicerōnī meō togam pūram dare, Arpīnī putō.
>
> I wish to celebrate my son's coming of age. Arpinum, I think, will be the place.
>
> Cicero, *Letters to Atticus* IX.17

On 31 March, 49 B.C., Cicero, barred from Rome for political reasons, wrote with pride from Arpinum:

> Ego meō Cicerōnī, quoniam Rōmā carēmus, Arpīnī potissimum togam pūram dedī, idque mūnicipibus nostrīs fuit grātum.
>
> Since Rome was out of bounds, I celebrated my son's coming of age at Arpinum in preference to any other place, and so doing delighted my fellow townsmen.
>
> Cicero, *Letters to Atticus* IX.19

THE LATE EMPIRE

The Late Empire was beset with enormous problems that were political, administrative, economic, financial, and military all at once. Throughout this period the matter of succession between one emperor and the next was a bloody one. The frontiers of the empire were under attack everywhere by encroaching barbarian tribes. The Roman economy was in decline, overburdened by the enormous combined costs of maintaining continuous wars of defense along all the frontiers and dealing with uprisings in many provinces, supporting an enormous slave population, and paying the salaries and expenses of a huge administrative bureaucracy that had spread to every corner of the empire. In addition, former provinces and allies were developing into economic centers that competed with rather than supported Rome.

Below are brief descriptions of some of the emperors who tried to rule the empire and hold it together.

CARACALLA, A.D. 211–217

Caracalla enacted a measure that granted full Roman citizenship to all freeborn people throughout the empire. His motive was a practical one: Since all citizens were subject to inheritance taxes, increasing their numbers increased the revenues of the state. Caracalla was such a ruthless tyrant, however, that his Praetorian prefect had him put to the sword.

DIOCLETIAN, A.D. 284–305

Diocletian, who claimed Jupiter as his protector, formed a tetrarchy, a government ruled by four leaders. He assumed the title **Augustus** for himself and took charge of the eastern provinces. He named Maximian the **Augustus** in command of Italy and Africa. The two **Augustī,** in turn, appointed two **Caesarēs** as their junior partners: Galerius looked after the Danube provinces and Constantius the western districts. This restructuring was an effort to deal with the fact that the empire had become too large for a single

Caracalla—Roman marble bust

Marble cuirassed bust, Louvre, Paris, France

Amethyst cameo of Constantine II

Carved amethyst cameo, British Museum, London, England

ruler to control. Each member of the tetrarchy achieved military success in his own realm, while Diocletian took the lead in creating new laws that made the state more important than the individual citizen. The emperor was no longer a **prīnceps** working along with others, but a **dominus** surrounded by a royal court, who dictated his orders to a bureaucracy reorganized into four prefectures, twelve dioceses, and about 100 provinces. In addition, there was a gradual move to tie people by heredity to specific trades and tracts of land, as well as an unsuccessful attempt at price-fixing, a measure by which Diocletian hoped to improve the poor economic conditions in the empire.

CONSTANTINE, A.D. 324–337

In A.D. 305, Diocletian and Maximian, the two **Augustī,** abdicated, and the rival **Caesarēs**, Galerius and Constantius Chlorus, became the two new **Augustī.** Constantine, the son of Constantius, was then a hostage in Galerius' court. Constantine escaped, however, and went to Eboracum (York) in England and joined his father shortly before Constantius died. After the troops in England proclaimed Constantine their new leader, Galerius allowed him to remain in power as **Caesar** of Britain and Gaul. Driven by an ambition to acquire even greater power, Constantine waited for the right moment and then invaded Italy. On his way to Rome in A.D. 312, as the Christian historian Eusebius tells the story, Constantine saw the symbol of the cross in the sky together with the words, **In hōc signō vincēs** *(Under this sign you will win).* This apparition inspired him to order his soldiers to mark this Christian emblem on their shields. Shortly thereafter Constantine defeated Maxentius, the self-proclaimed **Augustus** of the West, in a pitched battle at the Mulvian Bridge outside Rome and became lord of the western half of the empire. Convinced that the Christian God had granted him his victory, Constantine persuaded the Augustus of the East, Licinius, to join him in issuing the Edict of Milan, which gave Christians the right to worship as they chose and thus ended their years of persecution.

After sharing the rule of the empire for a time, however, the two **Augustī,** Constantine and Licinius, went to war against each other. In A.D. 324, Constantine defeated Licinius and became the one and only leader of the reunified Roman Empire. For the rest of his reign, Constantine worked to further the reforms of Diocletian, displaying even more fully his talents as general, administrator, and legislator. Because of the accomplishments of these two emperors, the Roman Empire would continue to exist for more than another century. Constantine was responsible, however, for a truly dramatic break from Roman traditions. To carry out his idea that unity could be reinforced through the influence of the Christian church, he founded a Christian city, Constantinople, and proclaimed it the new capital city of the empire. When he died in A.D. 337, baptized at last in his final hours, one suspects that he actually did believe that the Christian God had chosen him to lead Rome on a new path of glory.

WORD STUDY XIII

Latin and the Romance Languages

Although Latin has influenced the development of many languages (including English, of course), there are five modern languages that are so universally derived from Latin as to be called "Romance" (i.e., Roman) languages. These languages are Italian, French, Spanish, Portuguese, and Rumanian. The following examples show clearly the relationship of the Romance languages to Latin:

Latin	French	Italian	Spanish	Portuguese	Rumanian
arbor, *tree*	arbre	albero	árbol	árvore	arbore
dulcis, *sweet*	doux	dolce	dulce	doce	dulce

Rome's conquering legions brought Latin to lands as far apart as Britain and Egypt. In those places with well-established civilizations, such as Egypt, Latin did not displace the native languages; when the Romans left, Latin left with them. However, in areas such as Gaul (France) where civilization in Roman times was relatively primitive, Latin took hold and became the language of the people. The Romans also sent many colonists to these less-developed and less-populated provinces, further ensuring the dominance of Latin as the accepted tongue in these lands.

In the evolution of provincial Latin into the Romance languages, these major developments (as well as many others) took place:

1. In general, the importance of word endings (inflection) in classical Latin was greatly reduced in the Romance languages. Nouns were usually reduced to two forms: a singular and a plural, e.g., the French *homme*, *hommes*, from the Latin **hominem**; and endings such as those of the comparative and superlative of adjectives were often replaced by words meaning "more" and "most," e.g., the Latin **dīligentior** became in Italian, *più diligente*. (*Più* is derived from the Latin **plūs**.)
2. The definite article developed from the demonstrative pronoun and adjective **ille**. For example, the Latin **ille lupus** became "the wolf" in each of the Romance languages, as follows:

French	Italian	Spanish	Portuguese	Rumanian
le loup	il lupo	el lobo	o lobo	lupul*

(*The article is attached as a suffix in Rumanian.)

3. Pronunciation developed separately in each language, diverging greatly from that of classical Latin, e.g., the Latin word **caelum** (*c* pronounced *k*) became *cielo* in Italian (*c* pronounced *ch*), and *ciel* in French (*c* pronounced *s*).

Exercise 1

Next to each number below are words of equivalent meaning from each of three Romance languages. Give the Latin word from which each trio of Romance language words is derived and give the English meaning. Consult an Italian, Spanish, or French dictionary, as needed:

	Italian	Spanish	French	Latin	Meaning
			Nouns		
1.	acqua	agua	eau	______	______
2.	amico	amigo	ami	______	______
3.	libro	libro	livre	______	______
4.	lingua	lengua	langue	______	______
5.	madre	madre	mère	______	______
6.	ora	hora	heure	______	______
7.	pane	pan	pain	______	______
8.	tempo	tiempo	temps	______	______
9.	terra	tierra	terre	______	______
			Verbs		
10.	abitare	habitar	habiter	______	______
11.	amare	amar	aimer	______	______
12.	dormire	dormir	dormir	______	______
13.	scrivere	escribir	écrire	______	______
			Adjectives		
14.	buono	bueno	bon	______	______
15.	breve	breve	bref	______	______
16.	fàcile	fácil	facile	______	______
17.	male	malo	mal	______	______
			Numbers		
18.	quattro	cuatro	quatre	______	______
19.	sette	siete	sept	______	______
20.	dieci	diez	dix	______	______

Exercise 2

In which of the following places is French spoken? In which is Spanish spoken? In which is Portuguese spoken? Consult an encyclopedia as needed:

1. Brazil
2. Haiti
3. Guatemala
4. Belgium
5. Madagascar
6. Angola
7. Quebec
8. Argentina
9. Switzerland
10. Mexico

CHAPTER 52

PAPIRIUS PRAETEXTATUS

Now that Marcus has assumed the **toga virīlis**, Cornelius will begin to consider his public career. In the early Republic, boys began their training for public life when they were much younger than Marcus is now. In those days fathers took their sons with them while they carried out their public duties. This story shows that Papirius, though still wearing the **toga praetexta**, had already learned how to be discreet.

Mōs anteā senātōribus Rōmae fuit in Cūriam cum praetextātīs fīliīs introīre. Ōlim in senātū rēs maior agēbātur et in diem posterum prōlāta est. Placuit nē quis eam rem ēnūntiāret. Māter Papīriī, puerī quī cum parente suō in Cūriā fuerat, rogāvit fīlium quid in senātū patrēs ēgissent. Puer tamen respondit nōn licēre eam rem ēnūntiāre. Eō magis mulier audīre cupiēbat; silentium puerī animum eius adeō incitāvit ut vehementius quaereret.

Tum puer, mātre urgente, prūdēns cōnsilium cēpit. Dīxit āctum esse in senātū utrum ūnus vir duās uxōrēs habēret an ūna uxor duōs virōs. Hoc ubi illa audīvit, domō trepidāns ēgressa est. Ad cēterās mātrōnās rem pertulit.

Vēnit ad senātum postrīdiē mātrōnārum caterva. Lacrimantēs atque obsecrantēs ōrāvērunt ut ūna uxor duōs virōs habēret potius quam ut ūnus vir duās uxōrēs. Senātōrēs ingredientēs in Cūriam mīrābantur quid mātrōnae vellent.

(continued)

1 **mōs, mōris,** m., *custom;* pl., *character*
2 **posterus, -a, -um,** *next, following*
placuit, *it was decided*
nē quis, *that no one*
3 **ēnūntiō, -āre, -āvī, -ātus,** *to reveal, divulge*
4 **patrēs, patrum,** m. pl., *senators*
eō magis, adv., *all the more*
7 **dīxit āctum esse,** *he said that there had been a debate*
utrum...an..., conj., *whether...or...*
8 **habēret,** *should have*
trepidāns, trepidantis, *in a panic*
10 **caterva, -ae,** f., *crowd*
11 **potius quam,** *rather than*

2 **agō, agere, ēgī, āctus,** *to do, drive;* here, *to discuss, debate*
prōferō, prōferre, prōtulī, prōlātus, irreg., *to carry forward, continue*
7 **urgeō, urgēre, ursī,** *to press, insist*

Exercise 52a

Respondē Latīnē:

1. Quī mōs senātōribus Rōmae fuit?
2. Quālis rēs in senātū agēbātur?
3. Quid senātōribus placuit?
4. Quid māter Papīrium rogāvit?
5. Quid puer respondit?
6. Quid mulier vehementius faciēbat?
7. Quid puer prūdēns dīxit?
8. Quid māter fēcit?

Puer Papīrius in medium prōgressus nārrāvit quid māter audīre cupīvisset et quid ipse mātrī dīxisset. Senātus fidem atque ingenium puerī laudāvit ac cōnsultum fēcit nē posteā puerī cum patribus in Cūriam introīrent praeter illum ūnum Papīrium. Puerō posteā cognōmen honōris causā Praetextātus datum est quod tantam prūdentiam praebuerat.

14 **fidēs, fideī,** f., *good faith, reliability, trust*
ingenium, -ī, n., *intelligence, ingenuity*
cōnsultum, -ī, n., *decree*
16 **cognōmen, cognōminis,** n., *surname (third or fourth name of a Roman)*
honōris causā, *for the sake of an honor, as an honor*
17 **praebeō, -ēre, -uī, -itus,** *to display, show*

Respondē Latīnē:

1. Quid Papīrius senātōribus nārrāvit?
2. Quod cōnsultum senātus fēcit?
3. Cūr cognōmen Papīriō datum est?

BUILDING THE MEANING

Impersonal Verbs I

You have seen the following impersonal verbal phrases and impersonal verbs since early in this course (for discussion, see Chapter 20):

1. **necesse est,** *it is necessary*
   Nōbīs **necesse est** statim discēdere. (9:13–14)
   *To leave immediately **is necessary** for us.*
   ***It is necessary** for us to leave immediately.*

2. **licet, licēre, licuit** + dat., *it is allowed*
   Vōbīs **licet** hīc cēnāre. (cf. 20:8)
   *To dine here **is allowed** for you.*
   ***It is allowed** for you to dine here.*
   *You **are allowed** to dine here.*
   *You **may** dine here.*

   The underlined infinitives are the subjects of the impersonals, but other translations, as suggested above, make better English.

   You have seen **licet** used in the infinitive:

   Puer tamen respondit nōn **licēre** eam rem ēnūntiāre. (52:4)
   *The boy replied that **it was** not **permitted** to reveal the matter.*

Here is another verb that may be used impersonally:

3. **placeō, placēre, placuī-** + dat., *to please*

This verb can be used with a noun as its subject:

Placuitne tibi cēna, Gaī? (34h:3)
***Did** the dinner **please** you, Gaius?*
Did you like the dinner, Gaius?

Or it may be used with an impersonal subject (expressed or unexpressed):

"Quīntus Valerius vult tē in mātrimōnium dūcere, id quod nōbīs **placet.** **Placet**ne tibi, Cornēlia?" "Mihi quoque **placet,**" respondit. (50:17–21)
*"Quintus Valerius wishes to marry you, that which **is pleasing** to us. **Is it pleasing** to you, Cornelia?" **"It is** also **pleasing** to me," she replied.*

This verb is often used impersonally in the perfect tense, meaning not *it pleased* but *it was decided*, with a clause in the subjunctive as its subject:

Placuit nē quis eam rem ēnūntiāret. (52:2–3)
*That no one should reveal the matter **was decided.***
***It was decided** that no one should reveal the matter.*

You have seen these other impersonal verbs:

4. **decet, decēre, decuit**, *it is becoming, fitting; should*

Nōn **decet** patrem dēspondēre fīliam, īnsciā mātre. (50:15–16)
*That a father betroth his daughter without the mother knowing **is** not **fitting.***
***It is** not **fitting** that a father betroth his daughter without the mother knowing.*
*A father **should** not betroth his daughter without the mother knowing.*

Here the accusative and infinitive serve as the subject of the impersonal verb.

5. **oportet, oportēre, oportuit**, *it is fitting; ought*

Festīnāre tē **oportet.** (50:9)
*That you hurry **is fitting.***
***It is fitting** that you hurry.*
You ought to hurry.

6. **taedet, taedēre, taesum est,** *it bores, makes one* (acc.) *tired of something* (gen.)

Mē **taedet** sōlitūdinis. (50:2)
***It tires** me of loneliness.*
I am tired of/bored with loneliness.

Exercise 52b

Read aloud and translate:

1. Papīriō nōn licuit rem ēnūntiāre.
2. Papīriī respōnsum mātrī nōn placuit.
3. Papīriō tamen necesse erat rem cēlāre.
4. Puerō nōn decuit rem mātrī ēnūntiāre.
5. Mātrem taesum est silentiī Papīriī.
6. "Loquī tē oportet," inquit māter.
7. Papīriō placuit ut aliam rem mātrī nārrāret.

Exercise 52c

Read aloud and translate. Identify the type of subordinate clause in each sentence:

1. Senātōrēs Papīriō imperāvērunt nē rem ēnūntiāret.
2. Māter Papīriī rogāvit fīlium quid ā senātōribus āctum esset.
3. Puer respondit sē eam rem nōn ēnūntiātūrum esse.
4. Silentium puerī mātrem adeō incitāvit ut vehementius quaereret.
5. Cum māter respōnsum audīvisset, domō ēgressa est.
6. Māter mātrōnās hortāta est ut ad senātum postrīdiē īrent.
7. Trepidantēs ōrāvērunt ut ūna uxor duōs virōs habēret potius quam ut ūnus vir duās uxōrēs.
8. Senātōrēs mīrābantur cūr mātrōnae hoc dīcerent.
9. Papīrius ēnūntiāvit quid ipse mātrī dīxisset.
10. Ingenium puerī senātōrēs adeō incitāvit ut eī cognōmen dederint.

mōs maiōrum *literally, "the custom of the ancestors," inherited custom, tradition*
mōs prō lēge *A long established custom has the force of law.*
mōre suō *in one's own way*
nūllō mōre *without precedent, unparalleled*

Mōribus antīquīs rēs stat Rōmāna virīsque. *On customs and men of olden times the Roman state stands firm.* (Ennius)
Ō tempora! Ō mōrēs! *How times and customs have changed!*
(Cicero, *Orations against Catiline* I.2)

ROMAN RELIGION

In Chapter 51 you saw how important it was for Marcus to dedicate his **bulla** and **toga praetexta** at the shrine of the household gods (**larārium**). In order to understand this ritual and the rites that will take place at Cornelia's wedding in the next chapter, you need to know something about Roman religion.

When Romans said they believed in gods, they were saying that gods were everywhere at work in the ordinary events of nature. Their religious activity therefore consisted of trying to make these unseen forces work for them rather than against them. Sometimes they gave them names and fashioned images of them, such as Mars, Jupiter, and Venus, whom they visualized in human form, godlike in power but otherwise all too human. Sometimes they gave them names but no precise form, such as Vesta, goddess of the hearth, and the peasant-farmer gods, Pomona (fruit), Robigus (blight), and Ceres (growth). This idea that each god had a particular domain was worked out in great detail. For example, since the security of a house depended on the security of its door, there was thought to be a god (Janus Patulcius) in charge of opening doors and another (Janus Clusivius) to see that they were properly closed.

Melitene, priestess of the Mother of the Gods. Roman marble bust, consecrated A.D. 162
Louvre, Paris, France

Sacrifice to Apollo

Detail from "Landscape with the Father of Psyche Sacrificing to Apollo," oil on canvas by Claude Lorrain, National Trust, Fairhaven

Religious observances that could harness the power of these beings were prayer and sacrifice. These could be offered together, or prayer could be used to ask for something, and a sacrifice made if the request were granted. For instance, we have the inscription **servus vōvit, līber solvit** (*a slave made the vow, a free man carried it out*), showing that the slave had promised a gift to a god if he became free and that he had kept his promise when he got his freedom.

Essentially, a sacrifice had to embody life in some form, since life is energy, and divine energy is necessary to answer the prayer. Animals were therefore generally used for sacrifice, but small cakes, flour mixed with salt, flowers, honey, cheese, fruit, wine, and milk were all employed, especially in domestic rites, at the **larārium** in the **ātrium**, for example. In fact, it was thought that these gifts kept up the vitality of the gods, enabling them to put forth the power required to grant the request. Accordingly, when an animal was sacrificed, the most vital parts (the heart, liver, entrails, etc.) were burnt upon the altar, and the rest of the carcass, fortunately the more appetizing part, was eaten at the time by those present at the sacrifice. The sacrificial procedure was as follows: Suppliants chose the deity appropriate to the request they had in mind and went along to that god's temple with a sacrifice, which had to be the proper animal for the god in question. For instance, black animals were correct for the underworld gods, white animals for gods in the upper world, and no one would have dreamed of offering a male animal to a female deity, or vice versa. While the rite was in progress, a flute player played to drown out any ill-omened sounds. If the flute player stopped playing or a mistake was made in the ceremony, the whole process had to be repeated from the beginning!

The sacrifice took place on a large altar in front of the temple in the open air. The temple itself, consisting of a walled chamber surrounded by a colonnade, contained no seats and only a small altar on which incense was burned. It was not used for religious services but for housing the image of the god, which was made on the grandest scale and of the most precious materials. Often the only light in the building fell upon the statue from the doorway, so that the worshiper, who came in from the blinding sun to the half-gloom of the shrine, would indeed feel the presence of the god.

A worshiper making a vow would advance to the image and fasten to its legs waxen tablets inscribed with prayers and details of the promised sacrifice. Then, standing erect, and with arms outstretched to the god, the worshiper reverently prayed aloud.

In addition, the Romans, like the Etruscans, laid great stress upon augury, the "science" of "taking the omens." They would not contemplate taking any important step until it was clear from the omens that the gods were in favor of it.

First of all, they would offer a sacrifice to some appropriate god or gods. For example, for an important family event, they would offer a sacrifice to their household gods, called the **Larēs** and **Penātēs**, at the family shrine in the **ātrium**; someone planning to go on a journey might offer a sacrifice to Mercury, a soldier going into battle a sacrifice to Mars or Mithras, and a young man in love an offering to Venus or Fortuna.

At home, the sacrifice could be small cakes, honey, cheese, or fruit, which would be burned upon the altar. At a temple, an animal such as a pig, a sheep, or a bull (or all three, the **suovetaurīlia**) would be sacrificed.

In the latter case, once the animal had been killed, the vital organs—heart, liver, and intestines—were inspected by the **haruspicēs**, who claimed to be able to tell from the spots or marks on these organs whether the omens were favorable or not. If the omens were bad, the ordinary Roman simply put off the undertaking to another day. More sceptical Romans usually dismissed all this as mumbo-jumbo and, in fact, the Elder Cato said, "How can one **haruspex** look at another without laughing?" Yet Julius Caesar, though a confessed atheist, held the office of Pontifex Maximus, the chief priest who was in charge of all public religious observances.

The most popular form of augury, **auspicium** (*taking the auspices*), can be described quite accurately as "bird watching" (from **avis,** *bird*, and **spectāre**, *to watch*). The **auspex** based his predictions upon the number of birds seen at a particular time, the direction of flight, and so on. Astrology, dreams, thunder and lightning, and strange events of any kind were all taken very seriously by those engaged in augury.

There was no creed in which people were expected to believe. For ideas of this kind we have to turn to Stoic and Epicurean philosophy, and for religion in our sense to the Eastern cults of Isis and Mithras, Isis being originally an Egyptian goddess and Mithras a Persian god.

The Romans continued to worship the **Larēs** and **Penātēs** in their own homes and the great gods in the temples of their cities, and, since the emperor stood for the continuity of household and city and wielded so much power, he too began to be worshiped as a god.

Many legends about auguries surround the early kings of Rome.
"Tarquin the Elder Consulting Attus Navius the Augur," oil on canvas by Sebastiano Ricci, Sotheby's, London

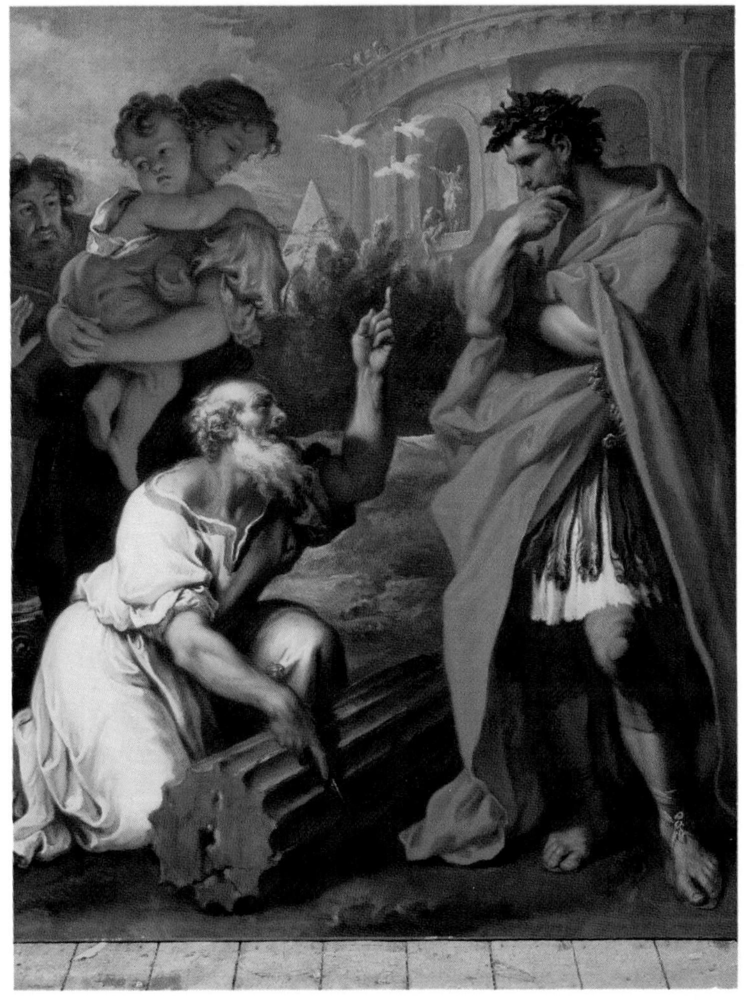

In A.D. 80 the Romans regarded Christianity as eccentric superstition. They could hardly have foreseen that a little over two centuries later it would oust other religions and, though it was the religion of the common man, that it would make a convert of the emperor himself.

CORNELIA'S WEDDING

In spite of the unromantic pre-arrangements, the wedding itself was celebrated with great festivity by the families and guests. The second half of June was considered to be the luckiest time for a wedding.

On the evening before her marriage, the girl dedicated her toys to the household gods and her **toga praetexta** to the goddess Fortuna Virginalis in the city, just as a boy dedicated his **toga praetexta** and **bulla** at the coming-of-age ceremony. At the same time, she received her **mundus muliebris**—the jewelry, perfumes, toilet articles, and attire of the grown-up woman.

On her wedding day, the bride wore a white tunic (**tunica alba**) and white shoes. Her hair was specially styled for the occasion with a yellow hairnet (**rēticulum**), and over it she wore a bright orange veil (**flammeum**). Her attendant was a married woman (**prōnuba**). The bride's house, where the wedding ceremony (**nūptiae**) was performed, was also decorated for the occasion.

The bride and her family and friends assembled in the **ātrium** and received the bridegroom and his guests. The ceremony began with a sacrifice, usually of a pig, the entrails of which were carefully examined by the **auspex** to make sure that the omens were favorable. If they were unfavorable, the marriage was postponed. The ceremony also included the signing of the marriage contract (**tabulās nūptiālēs obsignāre**) by ten witnesses, the joining of the couple's right hands (**dextrās iungere**) by the **prōnuba**, and the repetition of the formula **Ubi tū Gaius, ego Gaia** by the bride. Then the guests all shouted, "Good luck!" (**Fēlīciter!**).

The ceremony was followed by a banquet, and then, after nightfall, the couple prepared to go to their new home. The bridegroom pretended to carry off the bride by force just as the Romans once carried off the Sabine women. Then the bride and groom were escorted home by a procession of guests (**dēductiō**) carrying torches (**taedae**) and singing songs to Hymen, god of marriage. Some guests threw nuts (**nucēs**) to children for luck. On arrival at the house, the bride was carried over the threshold (**super līmen tollere**) to avoid an unlucky stumble.

Ubi diēs nūptiālis vēnit, omnēs mātūrē surrēxērunt. Aurēlia Marcum Sextumque hortābātur ut festīnārent. Ancillae hūc illūc concursābant ut omnia parārent.

Flāvia et Vīnia, māter eius, iam diū aderant. Mox adveniēbant cēterī amīcī et propinquī. Appropinquantēs laetī vīdērunt iānuam et postēs vittīs et corōnīs myrtī laurīque ōrnātōs esse. Domum ingressī in ātrium ductī sunt ubi Cornēlia, tunicā albā indūta, flammeum gerēns, eōs exspectābat. Paulō post clāmor rīsusque maximus audītus est. Valerius cum propinquīs amīcīsque suīs intrābat.

Cornēlia cum prōnubā ad āram stābat. Sacrīs rīte parātīs, auspex prōcessit ut porcum sacrificāret. Cum exta īnspexisset, "Ōmina," inquit, "bona sunt." Deinde tabulae nūptiālēs obsignātae sunt. Vīnia prōnuba dextrās Valeriī et Cornēliae iūnxit. Valeriō rogantī, "Quid nōmen tibi est?" Cornēlia, "Ubi tū Gaius, ego Gaia," respondit. Quō factō, cūnctī, "Fēlīciter!" exclāmābant.

Cēnā iam parātā, omnēs convīvae accubuērunt, atque optimam post cēnam cōnsecūta est commissātiō hilaritātis plēna.

Iam advesperāscēbat. Cornēlia ad mātrem haerēbat; Valerius simulābat sē eam ē manibus mātris vī abripere. Mox illa domum novam multīs comitantibus dēdūcēbātur. Praecēdēbant quīnque puerī quī taedās ārdentēs ferēbant; subsequēbantur cēterī rīdentēs et cantantēs; nucēs ad līberōs, quī undique concurrerant, coniciēbant. Cum domum vēnissent, nova nūpta super līmen sublāta est nē lāberētur.

"Quam fēlīx est Cornēlia!" exclāmāvit Flāvia.

4 **vitta, -ae,** f., *ribbon*
myrtus, -ī, f., *myrtle*
5 **laurus, -ī,** f., *bay (tree), laurel*
ōrnō, -āre, -āvī, -ātus, *to decorate*
8 **āra, -ae,** f., *altar*
sacra, -ōrum, n. pl., *religious rites, sacrifice*
rīte, adv., *properly*
auspex, auspicis, m., *augur; officiating priest*
9 **exta, -ōrum,** n. pl., *the inner organs of sacrificial animals (heart, lungs, liver)*
10 **dextra, -ae,** f., *right hand*
19 **nova nūpta, -ae,** f., *bride*
nē lāberētur, *so she wouldn't stumble*

10 **iungō, iungere, iūnxī, iūnctus,** *to join*
17 **ārdeō, ārdēre, ārsī, ārsūrus,** *to burn, blaze*

Exercise 53a

Respondē Latīnē:

1. Cūr ancillae hūc illūc concursābant?
2. Quandō clāmor rīsusque maximus audītus est?
3. Quandō prōcessit auspex?
4. Cūr auspex prōcessit?
5. Quid Valerius rogāvit cum dextrae iūnctae essent?
6. Quid Cornēlia respondit?
7. Quid Valerius simulābat?
8. Cūr nova nūpta super līmen sublāta est?

Building the Meaning

Purpose Clauses

In addition to the uses of the subjunctive described in Chapter 43 (causal and circumstantial clauses and indirect questions), Chapter 50 (result), and Chapter 51 (indirect commands), the subjunctive is used with **ut** to express *purpose*. Here, it is usually most naturally translated as *to* or *so that*. The corresponding negative, **nē**, can be translated in various ways, e.g., *lest*, *so that...not*, *in case*, *to avoid*, or *to prevent*:

> Ancillae hūc illūc concursābant ut omnia **parārent**. (53:2)
> *The slave-women were running about here and there to prepare everything.*
>
> Super līmen sublāta est **nē lāberētur**. (53:19)
> *She was carried over the threshold so she wouldn't stumble/to avoid stumbling.*

The imperfect subjunctive is used in secondary sequence (as in the examples above). The present subjunctive is used in primary sequence (as below):

> Ancillae hūc illūc concursant **ut** omnia **parent**.
> *The slave-women are running about here and there to prepare everything.*
>
> Super līmen tollētur **nē lābātur**.
> *She will be carried over the threshold to avoid stumbling.*

Exercise 53b

Read aloud and translate each sentence, identify the tenses of all verbs, and determine whether the subordinate clauses are in primary or secondary sequence:

1. Multī amīcī convēnērunt ut novae nūptae grātulārentur.
2. Iānitor baculum habet ut eōs quī neque amīcī neque propinquī sint repellat.
3. Marcus ante larārium stābat ut bullam Laribus cōnsecrāret.
4. Cavēte nē cadātis, amīcī!
5. Ancilla in cubiculum festīnāvit ut Cornēliae speculum daret.
6. Servus vestīmenta custōdit nē quis ea surripiat.
7. Flāvia Rōmam veniet ut Cornēliam adiuvet.
8. Eucleidēs per viās festīnāvit nē ā praedōnibus caperētur.
9. Pater Sextī Rōmam redībit ut fīlium sēcum domum dūcat.
10. Marcus ad Tabulārium dēductus est ut nōmen eius in tabulīs pūblicīs īnscrīberētur.

Exercise 53c

There is much evidence to show that husbands and wives loved each other and lived as happily as if they had themselves chosen each other. When a bride repeated the words **Ubi tū Gaius, ego Gaia** at the wedding ceremony, she was promising to be a faithful wife. The following story, adapted from Pliny (*Letters* III.16), tells us how Arria, during the illness of her husband, concealed the death of her son from him to avoid aggravating his illness.

Read the paragraph aloud and translate it:

Aegrōtābat Caecina Paetus, marītus Arriae; aegrōtābat et fīlius, uterque mortiferē, ut vidēbātur. Fīlius dēcessit, puer eximiā pulchritūdine et parentibus cārissimus. Huic Arria ita fūnus parāvit, ita dūxit exsequiās ut ignōrāret marītus. Praetereā cum cubiculum eius intrāverat, simulābat vīvere fīlium atque etiam convalēscere; ac Paetō saepe interrogantī quid ageret puer, respondēbat, "Bene quiēvit; libenter cibum sūmpsit." Deinde cum lacrimae prōrumperent, ē cubiculō ēgrediēbātur. Tum sē dolōrī dabat. Tandem siccīs iam oculīs, vultū iam compositō redībat; atque dum marītus aegrōtābat, sīc lacrimās retinēbat, dolōrem operiēbat.

1 **marītus, -ī,** m., *husband*
2 **mortiferē,** adv., *mortally, critically*
eximius, -a, -um, *outstanding*
3 **cārus, -a, -um,** *dear, beloved*
fūnus, fūneris, n., *funeral*
dūxit exsequiās, *(she) carried out the funeral rites*
4 **cum...intrāverat,** *whenever she entered*
5 **quid ageret,** *how he was*
7 **siccus, -a, -um,** *dry*

2 **dēcēdō, dēcēdere, dēcessī, dēcessūrus,** *to die*
8 **operiō, operīre, operuī, opertus,** *to hide, cover*

Exercise 53d

Using story 53 as a guide, give the Latin for the following. Use subordinate clauses with the subjunctive in each sentence:

1. When the pig had been sacrificed, the nuptial tablets were signed.
2. Vinia went forward to join the right hands of Valerius and Cornelia.
3. The cook went into the kitchen to prepare dinner.
4. Cornelia was clinging to Aurelia lest she be snatched away by Valerius.
5. The bride was carried across the threshold with such great care that she did not stumble.

Exercise 53e

The following is part of a longer poem by Catullus (c. 84–54 B.C.). It is to be sung as the bride is accompanied on the evening of her wedding from her father's house to her new home. The bride's name is Aurunculeia. In the first two stanzas she is told to dry her tears. After all, she is very beautiful!

Read the stanzas and translate them:

Flēre dēsine! Nōn tibi, Aurunculeia, perīculum est
nē qua fēmina pulchrior
clārum ab Ōceanō diem
  vīderit venientem.

Tālis in variō solet
dīvitis dominī hortulō
stāre flōs hyacinthinus.
Sed morāris! Abit diēs!
  Prōdeās, nova nūpta!

At last the chorus see the bright veil of the bride appearing. It is time for the hymn and the distribution of nuts:

Tollite, ō puerī, facēs!
Flammeum videō venīre.
Īte, concinite in modum
"Iō Hymēn Hymenaee iō,
  iō Hymēn Hymenaee!"

Da nucēs puerīs, iners
concubīne: satis diū
lūsistī nucibus. Lubet
iam servīre Talassiō.
  Concubīne, nucēs da!

—Catullus LXI. 86–95, 121–125, and 131–135

---

1 **nōn...perīculum est nē qua,** *there is no danger that any*
4 **clārus, -a, -um,** *bright*
Ōceanus, -ī, m., *Ocean*
6 **varius, -a, -um,** *different, varied, many-hued*
7 **hortulus, -ī,** m., *small garden*
11 **fax, facis,** f., *wedding-torch*
13 **modus, -ī,** m., *way, method;* here, *rhythmic/harmonious manner*

14 **Iō!**: a ritual exclamation; the *-i* is consonantal, and the word is pronounced as one syllable

Hymēn!: an exclamation chanted at weddings; later thought of as the god of weddings

Hymenaee! = Hymēn!

16 **iners, inertis,** *lazy*

17 **concubīnus, -ī,** m., *bridegroom*

19 **serviō, -īre, -īvī, -ītūrus** + dat., *to serve*

Talassius, -ī, m., *Talassius (god of marriage)*

1 **fleō, flēre, flēvī, flētus,** *to weep, cry*

dēsinō, dēsinere, dēsiī, dēsitus, *to stop*

10 **prōdeō, prōdīre, prōdiī, prōditūrus,** irreg., *to come forth*
The present subjunctive **prōdeās** expresses a command.

13 **concinō, concinere, concinuī,** *to sing together*

18 **lubet = libet, libēre, libuit** or **libitum est,** *it is pleasing to someone* (dat.) *to do something* (infin.). Supply **tibi.**

Aurelius Hermia and his wife, a freedwoman

Exercise 53f

The culmination of Arria's devotion is described in the following story of her death, also told in the letter of Pliny (III.16) from which the passage in Exercise 53c is adapted.

Read this portion of the letter:

> Many years later Scribonianus in Illyria took up arms against the emperor Claudius, and Paetus took part in the revolt. Scribonianus was killed, and Paetus was captured and put on board a ship to be taken to Rome. When he was about to go on board, Arria pleaded with the soldiers to be allowed to go with him. "Surely a man of senatorial rank is entitled to have some slaves to prepare his food, dress him, and put on his shoes? I will do all of these tasks on my own." Her request was refused, however. She therefore hired a small fishing boat and followed the larger vessel. When they reached Rome, Paetus was condemned to death, but he was told that he might take his own life, if he wished. At that point, Arria, who had no desire to go on living after the death of her husband, drew a dagger, plunged it into her breast, drew it out, and, as she held it out to her husband, uttered the immortal words, **"Paete, nōn dolet"** (*"Paetus, it does not hurt"*).

Martial wrote the following epigram on Arria's death. Read it aloud and translate it:

> Casta suō gladium cum trāderet Arria Paetō
>   quem dē visceribus trāxerat ipsa suīs,
> "Crēde mihī, vulnus quod fēcī nōn dolet," inquit.
>   "Sed quod tū faciēs, hoc mihi, Paete, dolet."
>
> —Martial, *Epigrams* I.13

1 **castus, -a, -um,** *virtuous, chaste*
2 **dē,** prep. + abl., *down from, concerning, about*; here, *from*
viscera, viscerum, n. pl., *vital organs*
4 **quod,** *(the one) that*

ADDITIONAL READING:
The Romans Speak for Themselves: Book II: "The Wedding of Cato and Marcia," pages 73–80.

A Sad Occasion

When a death occurred in a Roman family, it was the custom to display grief. Tears and lamentation were expected, and it was usual, for female mourners at least, to beat the breast (**pectus plangere**) and go about with torn clothing (**scissā veste**) and dishevelled hair (**capillīs solūtīs**). Some families even hired professional mourners to do this for them.

In the case of an important family, like the Cornelii in our story, the actual funeral procession (**pompa**) was a very elaborate affair. After the body had lain in state, feet toward the door, in the **ātrium** of the house surrounded by lamps (**lucernae**) and candles (**candēlae**), there would be a procession through the city to the Forum and then on to the family tomb. For the procession, the deceased was placed on a litter with face uncovered. Musicians playing pipes, horns, and trumpets headed the procession, which would include torchbearers, professional mourners, and singers of dirges (**nēniae**), as well as members of the mourning family and household (including freedmen and slaves), friends, and buffoons, who would jestingly mock the dead person. Also in the procession would be actors wearing masks of the dead person's ancestors and appropriate clothing and, in the case of a magistrate or ex-magistrate, public attendants (**līctōrēs**) carrying the symbols of office, bundles of rods (**fascēs**).

A halt was made in the Forum where a speech of praise (**laudātiō**) was made in honor of the deceased.

At the family tomb outside the walls, the body was usually placed on a funeral pyre (**rogus**), which was set alight by a member of the family after some of the deceased's possessions had been placed on it. Flowers and spices were also thrown on the fire.

After the body had been cremated, the ashes were cooled with wine and were collected with the bones in an urn and placed in the family tomb. The last farewell was then uttered, and after nine days of mourning a food offering was made at the tomb to the spirit of the dead man (**mānēs**).

Slaves and the very poor, who could not afford even to hire bearers to carry the bier, were usually buried in public cemeteries in simple coffins. Some, however, would join one of the guilds or societies that were formed to ensure a respectable funeral for their members and spare them the indignity of being flung into a common grave. The poor were buried on the day they died, and their funerals, like those of children, usually took place after dark with a minimum of ceremony. Death among children was common, both in the early vulnerable years and in later childhood, as is proved by many inscriptions found on tombstones in various parts of the Roman world.

Mēnse Iūliō tantus erat calor in urbe ut omnēs ad vīllam īre vellent. Gaius Cornēlius igitur omnia parāre coepit ut Baiās īrent. Antequam profectī sunt, accidit rēs trīstissima.

Cornēlius, ut solēbat, cum Titō frātre ad balneās ierat. Per tōtam domum erat silentium. Subitō audītae sunt vōcēs atque clāmor. Cornēlius servōs hortābātur ut lectīcam in domum maximā cum cūrā ferrent. Aurēlia, vōcibus audītīs, in ātrium irrūpit. "Quid factum est, Gaī? Cūr servōs iubēs lectīcam in domum ferre?" Cui Cornēlius, "Titus noster aliquid malī accēpit. Frīgidāriī pavīmentum tam lēve et lūbricum erat ut ille lāpsus ceciderit. Putō eum coxam frēgisse. Medicus statim est arcessendus."

Multōs diēs Titus in lectō iacēbat. Prīmō convalēscere vidēbātur; mox tamen fīēbat īnfirmior, nam in febrem subitō inciderat. In diēs morbus ingravēscēbat.

Tandem tam īnfirmus erat ut vix loquī posset. Haud multō post ē vītā excessit. Cornēlius maximō dolōre affectus est. Tōta domus sē dolōrī dedit. Aurēlia et Cornēlia et omnēs ancillae, scissā veste capillīsque solūtīs, pectora plangēbant. Corpus Titī in ātriō in lectō fūnebrī positum est. Circum lectum ardēbant lucernae et candēlae.

Postrīdiē corpus Titī summō honōre ēlātum est. Praecēdēbant tībīcinēs, cornicinēs, tubicinēs. In pompā erant virī taedās tenentēs, mulierēs nēniās cantantēs, āctōrēs imāginēs et vestīmenta maiōrum gerentēs, mīmī, līctōrēs fascēs ferentēs, familiārēs, amīcī plōrantēs.

(continued)

5 **hortor, -ārī, -ātus sum,** *to encourage, urge*
8 **lēvis, -is, -e,** *smooth*
9 **coxa, -ae,** f., *hipbone*
est arcessendus, *must be sent for*
11 **febris, febris,** gen. pl., **febrium,** f., *fever*
morbus, -ī, m., *illness*
15 **fūnebris, -is, -e,** *funeral*
16 **tībīcen, tībīcinis,** m., *piper*
18 **imāgō, imāginis,** f., *likeness, mask*
maiōrēs, maiōrum, m. pl., *ancestors*
mīmus, -ī, m., *actor of mime, buffoon*
familiārēs, familiārium, m. pl., *members of the household*
19 **plōrō, -āre, -āvī, -ātus,** *to lament, mourn*

9 **frangō, frangere, frēgī, frāctus,** *to break*
11 **ingravēscō, ingravēscere,** *to grow worse*
14 **scindō, scindere, scidī, scissus,** *to cut, split, carve, tear*
solvō, solvere, solvī, solūtus, *to loosen, untie, dishevel*

Exercise 54a

Respondē Latīnē:

1. Quō erant Cornēliī itūrī?
2. Quālis rēs accidit?
3. Quō ierant Cornēlius et Titus?
4. Quid Cornēlius servōs hortābātur ut facerent?
5. Quis in ātrium irrūpit?
6. Cūr Titus cecidit?
7. Quid Cornēlius eum frēgisse putat?
8. Quis arcessendus est?
9. Cūr Titus īnfirmior fīēbat?
10. Quam īnfirmus fīēbat Titus?
11. Quōmodo affectus est Cornēlius?
12. Quid faciēbant Aurēlia et Cornēlia et omnēs ancillae?
13. Quī in pompā fūnebrī erant?

Cum in Forum vēnissent, Gaius Cornēlius prōcessit ut frātrem mortuum laudāret. Commemorāvit quālis vir Titus fuisset, quot merita in prīncipem cīvēsque contulisset.

Quō factō, corpus Titī ad sepulcra Viae Flāminiae in pompā lātum est. Ibi rogus exstrūctus erat. In rogum impositum est corpus et super corpus vestēs atque ōrnāmenta. Appropinquāvit Gaius Cornēlius taedam manū tenēns. Quam taedam oculīs āversīs in rogum iniēcit.

Exsequiīs cōnfectīs, Cornēliī trīstēs domum regressī sunt. Multa dē Titō loquēbantur. Commemorābant quam hilaris fuisset, quantum līberōs amāvisset. "Maximē," inquiunt, "nōs omnēs eum dēsīderābimus."

21 **commemorō, -āre, -āvī, -ātus,** *to mention, comment on, recount*
merita cōnferre, *to render services (to)*

22 **Via Flāminia, -ae,** f., *Via Flaminia (a road from Rome leading through the Campus Martius and north to Ariminum on the Adriatic Sea)*

27 **hilaris, -is, -e,** *cheerful*

23 **exstruō, exstruere, exstrūxī, exstrūctus,** *to build*

Respondē Latīnē:

1. Quid Cornēlius in Forō fēcit?
2. Ubi rogus exstrūctus erat?
3. Quō īnstrūmentō Cornēlius rogum accendit?
4. Quālis vir fuerat Titus?

accendō, accendere, accendī, accēnsus, *to set on fire*

BUILDING THE MEANING

Translating *ut*

You have now met the following uses of **ut**:

A. With an indicative verb:

Semper sum, **ut** vidēs, negōtiōsus. (47:3)
As *you see, I am always busy.*

Sextus, **ut** lupum cōnspexit, arborem ascendit.
When *Sextus caught sight of the wolf, he climbed the tree.*

Clue: **ut** followed by an indicative verb should be translated by *as* or *when.*

B. With a subjunctive verb:

1. To indicate *result*:

   Tam īnfirmus erat **ut** vix loquī posset. (54:12)
   *He was **so** weak **that** he could scarcely speak.*

   Clue: a word like **tam**, **tantus**, **tālis**, **tot**, or **adeō** suggests that the translation will be *so...that*.

2. In an *indirect command*:

   Cornēlius servōs hortābātur **ut** lectīcam maximā cum cūrā ferrent. (54:5–6)
   Cornelius was urging the slaves to carry the litter very carefully.

   Ōrāvērunt **ut** ūna uxor duōs virōs habēret. (52:11)
   *They begged **that** one wife should have two husbands.*

   Clue: the **ut** clause depends on a verb of *telling*, *ordering*, *begging*, *urging*, *persuading*, etc.

3. To indicate *purpose*:

   Gaius Cornēlius prōcessit **ut** frātrem mortuum laudāret. (54:20)
   Gaius Cornelius came forward to praise his dead brother.

   This type of **ut** clause is very common after verbs that suggest that someone went somewhere *to do* something.

Exercise 54b

Read aloud and translate each of the following sentences, and then identify each use of **ut** and explain the sequence of tenses for all subjunctives:

1. Magister Sextō imperāvit ut domum statim redīret.
2. Sextus, ut imperāverat magister, domum statim rediit.
3. Marcus nōs rogat ut sēcum ad Campum Mārtium eāmus.
4. Titus tam īnfirmus erat ut surgere nōn posset.
5. Amīcō meō persuāsī ut mēcum ad Circum venīret.
6. Cum Titus mortuus esset, Marcus et Sextus tam trīstēs erant ut lacrimārent.
7. Servō imperāvistī ut pānem emeret.
8. Cornēliī ex urbe Rōmā discēdent ut Baiās eant.
9. In balneīs diū morābāmur ut cum amīcīs colloquerēmur.
10. Eucleidēs, "Ut fēriātī estis," inquit, "vōs moneō ut multōs librōs legātis."

Exercise 54c

Complete the following sentences and explain the use of **ut** in each:

1. Cornēlius Cornēliae praecēpit ut…
2. Tantus erat terror in urbe ut…
3. Marcus, ut tū…, est fīlius senātōris.
4. Iānitor servīs imperāvit ut…
5. In urbem dēscendit ut…
6. Aurēlia tam īrāta erat ut…
7. Puerī, ut vōcem patris…, in tablīnum intrāvērunt.
8. Senātōrēs nūntium mīsērunt ut…
9. Sextus adeō ēsuriēbat ut…
10. Eucleidēs, ut nōs omnēs…, est ērudītissimus.

Exercise 54d

Using story 54 as a guide, give the Latin for the following. Use **ut** clauses in each sentence:

1. There is such great heat in the city that the Cornelii wish to go to Baiae.
2. Cornelius, as he is accustomed, goes to the baths with Titus.
3. Cornelius urges the slaves to carry the litter into the house with great care.
4. Cornelius orders a doctor to be summoned.
5. Cornelius approaches to throw a torch onto the pyre.

Funeral procession of a warrior

Engraving by Joseph Charles Barrow, Victoria and Albert Museum, London, England

ROMAN LIFE XXXIV

ROMAN FUNERALS

The following account of Roman funerals was given by Polybius, a historian of the second century B.C.:

> Whenever an important citizen dies, they have a funeral procession, in which his body is carried into the Forum to the Rostra, sometimes upright so as to be conspicuous, less often in a reclining position. There, surrounded by the whole populace, a grown-up son mounts the rostrum and delivers a speech about the virtues and achievements of the deceased. As a result, the majority of those present are so deeply affected that the loss seems not merely a private one affecting the relatives only, but a public loss involving everyone.
>
> Then, after he is buried with the usual ceremonies, they place a likeness of the deceased in a part of the house where everyone can readily see it, and they enclose it in a little wooden shrine. This likeness is a mask that reproduces with remarkable faithfulness the features and complexion of the deceased.
>
> On the death of any important member of the family, these likenesses are taken to the Forum, worn by those members of the family who seem most nearly to resemble them in height and bearing. These people wear togas with a purple border if the deceased was a consul or praetor, totally purple if he was a censor, and edged with gold if he had celebrated a triumph or had any similar distinction. They all ride in chariots preceded by the **fascēs**, axes, and other emblems appropriate to the official positions held by each during his life; and when they arrive at the Rostra, they all sit down in their proper order on chairs of ivory.
>
> It would be difficult to imagine a sight more inspiring to an ambitious young man than to see the likenesses of men who had once been famous for their goodness all together and as if alive and breathing. What sight could be finer than this?
>
> Besides, the person who makes the speech over the deceased, after speaking of the deceased himself, goes on to tell of the successful exploits of the other ancestors whose likenesses are present, beginning from the earliest. In this way, by constantly refreshing their memories about the fame of good men, the glory of those who performed noble deeds becomes immortal, and the fame of those who served their country well is passed on to future generations.
>
> Polybius, *Histories* VI.3

TWO LAWS CONCERNING BURIAL

Law of the XII Tables:

> Hominem mortuum in urbe nē sepelītō nēve ūritō.
> *Let no one bury or burn a dead man in the city.*

Law of the Colony of Julia Genetiva in Spain:

> No person shall bring a dead person or bury one or burn one inside the boundaries of the town or the area marked around by the plough or build a monument to a dead person there. Any person breaking this law shall be fined 5,000 sesterces.

THE CRIER'S WORDS AT A CEREMONIAL FUNERAL

_______*, a citizen, has died; it is now time for those for whom it is convenient to go to his funeral. _______* is being brought from his house for burial.

(*name of deceased)

EPITAPHS

Roman tombs ranged from the very simple to the extremely elaborate. There was usually an inscription on the tomb, and many of these have survived. The following five are in some cases slightly modified.

(i)

Pontia Prīma hīc est sita. Nōlī violāre!

situs, -a, -um, *located, situated, buried*
violō, -āre, -āvī, -ātus, *to do harm*

(ii)

Est hoc monumentum Marcī Vergileī Eurysacis pīstōris redēmptōris appāritōris.

pīstor, pīstōris, m., *baker*
redēmptor, redēmptōris, m., *contractor*
appāritor, appāritōris, m., *gate-keeper, public servant*

(iii)

Carfinia Marcī līberta vīxit annōs XX. Iūcunda suīs, grātissima amīcīs, omnibus officiōsa fuit.

iūcundus, -a, -um, *pleasant, delightful*
grātus, -a, -um + dat., *loved (by), pleasing (to), dear (to)*
officiōsus, -a, -um + dat., *ready to serve, obliging*

(iv)

Dīs mānibus. C. Tullius Hesper āram fēcit sibi ubi ossa sua coniciantur. Quae sī quis violāverit aut inde exēmerit, optō eī ut cum dolōre corporis longō tempore vīvat et, cum mortuus fuerit, īnferī eum nōn recipiant.

dīs mānibus, *to the spirits of the dead*
os, ossis, n., *bone*
optō, -āre, -āvī, -ātus, *to wish*

eximō, eximere, exēmī, exēmptus, *to remove*

(v)

Hospes, quod dīcō paullum est; adstā ac perlege.
Hīc est sepulcrum haud pulchrum pulchrae fēminae:
nōmen parentēs nōminārunt Claudiam.
Suum marītum corde dīlēxit suō:
nātōs duōs creāvit: hōrum alterum
in terrā linquit, alium sub terrā locat.
Sermōne lepidō, tum autem incessū commodō,
domum servāvit. Lānam fēcit. Dīxī. Abī.

1 **paul(l)us, -a, -um,** *little, small*
3 **nōminārunt = nōmināvērunt**
4 **cor, cordis,** n., *heart*
5 **nātus, -ī,** m., *son*
7 **sermō, sermōnis,** m., *conversation, talk*
lepidus, -a, -um, *charming*
incessus, -ūs, m., *bearing, walk(ing)*
commodus, -a, -um, *pleasant*

4 **dīligō, dīligere, dīlēxī, dīlēctus,** *to love, have special regard for*
6 **linquō, linquere, līquī,** *to leave*

Exercise 54e

The poet Catullus was very devoted to his brother, who died far away from home in Asia Minor. Catullus visited the tomb and wrote these lines. He does not tell us what he sees for his brother beyond the grave. He merely seeks comfort from the age-old Roman ritual for the dead.

Read aloud and translate:

Multās per gentēs et multa per aequora vectus,
  adveniō hās miserās, frāter, ad īnferiās,
ut tē postrēmō dōnārem mūnere mortis
  et mūtam nēquīquam alloquerer cinerem.
Quandoquidem fortūna mihī tētē abstulit ipsum,
  heu miser indignē frāter adēmpte mihi,
nunc tamen intereā haec, prīscō quae mōre parentum
  trādita sunt trīstī mūnere ad īnferiās,
accipe frāternō multum mānantia flētū,
  atque in perpetuum, frāter, avē atque valē!

1 **gens, gentis,** gen. pl., **gentium,** f., *family, clan;* pl., *peoples*
aequor, aequoris, n., *sea*
vectus, -a, -um, *having been carried, having traveled*
2 **īnferiae, -ārum,** f. pl., *offerings and rites in honor of the dead at the tomb*
3 **dōnō, -āre, -āvī, -ātus,** *to give; to present somebody* (acc.) *with something* (abl.)
mūnus, mūneris, n., *gladiatorial show;* here, *gift, service*
4 **mūtus, -a, -um,** *silent*
nēquīquam, adv., *in vain*
cinis, cineris, m., *ashes, dust (of the cremated body)*
5 **quandōquidem,** adv., *since*
tētē = emphatic **tē**
6 **indignē,** adv., *undeservedly*
7 **prīscus, -a, -um,** *of olden times, ancient*
prīscō...mōre, *by the ancient custom*
8 **trīstī mūnere,** *as a sad service (to the dead)*
ad īnferiās, *for (these) rites in honor of the dead*
9 **mānō, -āre, -āvī,** *to flow*
flētus, -ūs, m., *weeping, tears*
10 **in perpetuum,** *forever*

1 **vehō, vehere, vexī, vectus,** *to carry;* pass., *to be carried, travel*
4 **alloquor, alloquī, allocūtus sum,** *to speak to, address*

Exercise 54f

Read and translate these humorous epigrams of Martial:

(i)

Doctor and Undertaker: Same Trade

Nūper erat medicus, nunc est vispillo Diaulus:
  quod vispillo facit, fēcerat et medicus.

I.47

vispillō, vispillōnis, m., *undertaker*

(ii)

Symmachus Takes the Students Around

Languēbam: sed tū comitātus prōtinus ad mē
    vēnistī centum, Symmache, discipulīs.
Centum mē tetigēre manūs aquilōne gelātae;
    nōn habuī febrem, Symmache: nunc habeō.

V.9

langueō, -ēre, *to be ill in bed*
comitātus, -a, -um, *accompanied*
prōtinus, adv., *immediately*
tangō, tangere, tetigī, tāctus, *to touch*
    tetigēre = tetigērunt
aquilōne gelātae, *chilled by the north wind*

(iii)

Hermocrates, Who Cures All

Lōtus nōbīscum est, hilaris cēnāvit, et īdem
    inventus māne est mortuus Andragorās.
Tam subitae mortis causam, Faustīne, requīris?
    In somnīs medicum vīderat Hermocratem!

VI.53

lōtus = lautus, perfect passive participle of **lavō**
    lōtus est, *he bathed*
subitus, -a, -um, *sudden*

requīrō, requīrere, requīsīvī, requīsītus,
    to ask, inquire

(iv)

Epitaph with a Difference!

Sit tibi terra levis, mollīque tegāris harēnā
    nē tua nōn possint ēruere ossa canēs!

IX.29.11–12

sit, *may (it) be*
levis, -is, -e, *light*
mollis, -is, -e, *soft*
tegāris, *may you be covered*
harēna, -ae, f., *sand*
nē...nōn possint, *so that (they) may not be unable*

ēruo, ēruere, ēruī, ērutus, *to dig up*

REVIEW XII: CHAPTERS 50-54

Exercise XIIa: Subjunctives

Give the present, perfect, imperfect, and pluperfect active and passive subjunctives of the following verbs in the first person plural:

1. amō
2. moneō
3. dūcō
4. cōnspiciō
5. inveniō

Exercise XIIb: Subjunctives

Give the present, perfect, imperfect, and pluperfect subjunctives of the following deponent verbs in the third person plural:

1. moror
2. vereor
3. loquor
4. ingredior
5. experior

Exercise XIIc: Subjunctives

Give the present, perfect, imperfect, and pluperfect subjunctives of the following irregular verbs in the second person plural:

1. sum
2. possum
3. volō
4. nōlō
5. mālō
6. eō
7. ferō
8. fīō

Exercise XIId: Translation and Identification

Read aloud and translate. Identify each result clause, indirect command, purpose clause, and indirect question:

1. Cornēlia tam dēfessa est ut paene lacrimet.
2. Cornēlius Sextum monuit nē iterum in lūdō tam ignāvus esset.
3. Iānitor eīs imperat ut statim abeant.

4. Matrōnae ad senātum lacrimantēs vēnērunt ut senātōribus persuādērent.
5. Servus in aquam dēsilit nē fūr effugiat.
6. Eucleidēs puerīs persuāsit ut vēra dīcerent.
7. Cornēlia nescit cūr pater sē adesse in tablīnō iusserit.
8. Puerōs rogāvit ut extrā tablīnum manērent.
9. Gaius puerōs monet nē ē cubiculō exeant.
10. Ancillae in cubiculum festīnant ut crīnēs Aurēliae cūrent.
11. Servus arborem ascendit nē caperētur.
12. Ille liber est tālis ut Aurēlia eum legere nōlit.

Exercise XIIe: Translation and Identification

Read aloud and translate. Identify the tense and voice of each verb in the subjunctive and tell whether each subordinate clause is in primary or secondary sequence:

1. Tanta multitūdō ad domum convenit ut omnibus intrāre nōn liceat.
2. Tam longum erat iter ut Valerius dēfessus esset.
3. Cornēlius Valerium rogat quid in itinere factum sit.
4. Sextus Marcum rogat ut sibi nārret quid in amphitheātrō āctum sit.
5. Cīvēs in palaestram excēdunt ut sē exerceant.
6. Aenēās ad Hesperiam nāvigābat ut urbem novam conderet.
7. Servus casam pīrātārum celerrimē petīvit ut dominum servāret.
8. Grammaticus Sextum rogat unde Aenēās nāvigāverit.
9. Praedōnēs tam celeriter currunt ut Eucleidem facile cōnsequantur.
10. Tot et tanta erant incendia ut cīvēs aedificia servāre nōn possent.
11. Tanta tempestās coorta est ut mīlitēs nāvem cōnscendere vix possent.
12. Eucleidēs Sextō imperat nē pūpam laedat.

Exercise XIIf: Impersonal Verbs

Read aloud and translate:

1. Gaiō et Aurēliae placuit ut Valerius Cornēliam in mātrimōnium dūceret.
2. Valeriō placet Cornēliam in mātrimōnium dūcere.
3. Hodiē Marcō togam virīlem gerere licet.
4. Sextō nōn iam decet togam virīlem gerere.
5. Cornēliam diē nūptiālī tunicam albam gerere oportet.
6. Nunc Cornēlia ūnā cum Valeriō vīvit. Valdē occupāta est; eam nōn iam taedet sōlitūdinis.

Exercise XIIg

Read the following passage and answer the questions below in English.

CONSTANTINE

Annō MXLVI A.U.C. imperium Rōmānum multās per prōvinciās patēbat. Eō tempore tot gentēs, tot nātiōnēs regēbant Rōmānī ut placuerit summum imperium inter quattuor imperātōrēs, duōs Augustōs et duōs Caesarēs, dīvidī. Inde alter Augustus Nīcomēdīae regēbat, alter Mediōlānī. Duodecim post annīs Galērius, ut Augustus, imperium Nīcomēdīae, Cōnstantius, alter Augustus, Trēverīs imperium obtinēbat.

Cōnstantiī fīlius erat Cōnstantīnus, iuvenis summī ingeniī et reī mīlitāris perītissimus. Galērius autem, cum tōtō imperiō Rōmānō potīrī vellet, Cōnstantīnum sēcum Nīcomēdīae dētinēbat nē iuvenis ille mīlitibus patris grātus fieret. Cōnstantīnus tamen, cum cognōvisset patrem iam in Britanniā bellum gerentem morbō affectum esse, ā custōdibus effūgit, atque summā celeritāte in Britanniam festīnāvit. Patrī occurrit Eborācī. Haud multō post Cōnstantius mortuus est.

Tum Cōnstantīnus ut Augustus ā mīlitibus salūtātus est. Cum autem multī eī invidērent, imperium armīs cōnfirmandum erat. Dum per Italiam iter Rōmam cum mīlitibus facit, vīdit Cōnstantīnus signum mīrum: in caelō appāruit crux flammea et super crucem haec verba: IN HOC SIGNO VINCES. Quō vīsō, Cōnstantīnus statim mīlitibus imperāvit ut signum crucis scūtīs galeīsque impōnerent. Deinde proeliō ad Rōmam ad pontem Mulvium factō hostēs vīcit. Quam propter victōriam tam grātus fuit Cōnstantīnus ut semper posteā crucem prō signō suō retinēret atque paucīs post mēnsibus annō MLXVI A.U.C. ēdictum Mediōlānī prōnūntiāverit nē Chrīstiānī diūtius vexārentur. Ipse autem nōndum Chrīstiānus factus est.

Itaque Cōnstantīnus post victōriam Mulviānam in potestāte redēgit illam partem imperiī Rōmānī ad occidentem sitam; alteram quoque partem, quae ā Liciniō regēbātur, bellō capere in animō habēbat. Putābat enim imperium Rōmānum ab ūnō prīncipe regī dēbēre. Itaque post ūndecim annōs maximum exercitum contrā Licinium dūxit. Liciniō multīs proeliīs victō, Cōnstantīnus summō imperiō potītus prīnceps sōlus rēgnābat.

Iam intellegēbat Cōnstantīnus Byzantium, nōn Rōmam, orbis terrārum caput esse dēbēre. Cum enim mercātōrēs iter ad orientem iam saepe facerent, Byzantium aptius ad mercātūram quam Rōma situm erat. Sēdem igitur imperiī Rōmā Byzantium mōvit, quō in locō aedificāvit urbem novam et pulcherrimam quam ā suō nōmine Cōnstantīnopolem nōminārī iussit. Haud multō antequam mortuus est, Cōnstantīnus ipse Chrīstiānus factus est.

1 **imperium, -ī,** n., *empire, power*
pateō, -ēre, -uī, *to extend*
2 **summus, -a, -um,** *highest, supreme*
4 **Nīcomēdīa, -ae,** f., *Nicomedia (a city in Bithynia)*
5 **Trēverī, -ōrum,** m. pl., *Treveri (the modern city of Trier)*
6 **rēs mīlitāris, reī mīlitāris,** f., *military affairs*
7 **perītus, -a, -um** + gen., *skilled (in), expert (in)*
potior, -īrī, -ītus sum + abl., *to obtain, seize*
9 **bellum gerere,** *to wage war*

11 **Eborācum, -ī,** n., *York (in Britain)*
13 **cōnfirmō, -āre, -āvī, -ātus,** *to strengthen, make secure*
cōnfirmandum erat, *had to be...*
14 **crux, crucis,** f., *cross*
16 **scūtum, -ī,** n., *shield*
galea, -ae, f., *helmet*
proelium, -ī, n., *battle*
17 **hostis, hostis,** gen. pl., **hostium,** m., *enemy*
grātus, -a, -um + dat., *loved (by), pleasing (to), dear (to);* here, *grateful, thankful*
18 **prō,** prep. + abl., *as*
19 **ēdictum, -ī,** n., *edict*
prōnūntiō, -āre, -āvī, -ātus, *to give out, proclaim*
21 **potestās, potestātis,** f., *control, power*
22 **occidēns, occidentis,** m., *the west*
24 **exercitus, -ūs,** m., *army*
25 **rēgnō, -āre, -āvī, -ātus,** *to rule*
26 **Byzantium, -ī,** n., *Byzantium (the modern Constantinople)*
orbis, orbis, gen. pl., **orbium,** m., *circle*
orbis terrārum, *the circle of the lands, the whole earth*
27 **oriēns, orientis,** m., *the east, the orient*
aptus, -a, -um + **ad** + acc., *suitable (for), favorable (to)*
28 **mercātūra, -ae,** f., *trade, trading*
sēdēs, sēdis, gen. pl., **sēdium,** f., *seat*

2 **regō, regere, rēxī, rēctus,** *to rule*
5 **obtineō, obtinēre, obtinuī, obtentus,** *to hold*
8 **dētineō, dētinēre, dētinuī, dētentus,** *to detain, hold as a prisoner*
13 **invideō, invidēre, invīdī, invīsus** + dat., *to envy, be jealous of*
21 **redigō, redigere, redēgī, redāctus,** *to bring*
in potestātem redigere, *to bring under the control/power (of)*

1. In what year, according to our reckoning, does our story begin?
2. What decision was made?
3. Who were the two Augusti in A.D. 305?
4. Where and by whom was Constantius' son being held?
5. What did he do?
6. How did he become Augustus?
7. Why did he have to take up arms?
8. What did he see when marching to Rome?
9. What order did Constantine then give?
10. Where did he conquer his enemies?
11. What two things did he do that showed his gratitude for his victory?
12. Why did he wish to conquer the other half of the Empire?
13 What new city did he found and why?
14. What did he do before he died?

THE FUTURE LIVES OF OUR CHARACTERS

Unfortunately for Gaius Cornelius, the Emperor Titus, whose favor he had enjoyed, died in September, A.D. 81. Distrustful of his brother Domitian's ambition, Titus had not given him any active role in government, and Domitian, who became emperor on September 14, was in turn distrustful of anyone Titus had favored. After a rebellion by Antonius Saturninus, governor of the province of Upper Germany, failed in A.D. 89, Domitian was relentless in punishing anyone who had participated or seemed to have participated in the rebellion. Cornelius was fortunate in having only to give up his estate at Baiae.

Domitian was assassinated on September 18, A.D. 96, by a conspiracy led by his own wife and two praetorian prefects, and the next emperor, Nerva, recalled those who had been exiled by Domitian and tried to undo the damage Domitian had caused. He therefore rewarded and honored a number of able senators, whom Domitian had ignored or exiled, including Cornelius, by appointing them to serve as consul for one month. Nerva returned the estate at Baiae to Cornelius and helped him be named by the Senate to be proconsular governor in Africa for A.D. 98. Upon his return to Rome, Cornelius from time to time served in a number of positions such as curator to prevent flooding by the Tiber (**cūrātor rīpārum Tiberis**). He died in A.D. 112, at age seventy-two.

Aurelia also had some property of her own taken by Domitian, but it was restored to her by Nerva. She accompanied Cornelius to Africa and upon his death lived with Marcus. Wishing to assist her native town of Narnia in Umbria (where Nerva also had been born), she endowed a school for orphan girls, where they learned to read and write, were trained in a trade, and were given a dowry upon reaching age fifteen. She died in A.D. 123, at age seventy-six.

Because of Domitian's dislike of Gaius Cornelius, Marcus' early career suffered. He served for three years as officer of an auxiliary infantry unit (**praefectus cohortis peditum**) in Lower Germany, due to the influence of Valerius' father. Upon returning to Rome, he began to plead cases in the civil court at Rome. In A.D. 92, Marcus married a distant cousin, Cornelia Hispulla, and they eventually had three daughters and two sons. Again, through the influence of the Valerii, he served from time to time on the staff of various governors of the provinces of Bithynia and Asia, until Nerva's accession.

Marcus' career advanced steadily under Nerva and his excellent successor, Trajan. Marcus was appointed in A.D. 97 as an official in charge of keeping the streets clean (**quattuorvir viīs in urbe pūrgandīs**) and in the next year became quaestor at age forty-three. Four years later, he was elected praetor, and two years later he became governor (**lēgātus**) of Further Spain. His appointment as a consul designate for A.D. 113 was made just before

Roman soldiers destroying a German camp

his father died; Marcus was very happy that his father knew of this honor to the family. His last honor, before his accidental death in A.D. 120, was to be appointed augur.

Quintus Valerius, age twenty-six when he married Cornelia, was already well started on his political career. He had served as officer of an auxiliary infantry unit and as officer of a legion (**tribūnus legiōnis**) in Upper Germany, and as an official in charge of the mint (**triumvir monētālis**) in Rome. Just prior to his return to Rome for the marriage, he had been on the staff of the governor of Bithynia. In A.D. 83, he and Cornelia rejoiced at the birth of the first of their three sons, and the next year he became quaestor. From A.D. 85 to 87, he furthered his military experience in Lower Germany as officer of an auxiliary cavalry unit (**praefectus ālae equitum**); because of Sextus' ties with the Cornelius family, Valerius took Sextus along.

Upon his return to Rome, Valerius resumed his career as a lawyer in Rome's courts and held the position of **praetor urbānus** before Domitian, who favored Valerius despite his marriage ties with the Cornelii, appointed him as administrator (**prōcūrātor**) of his imperial estates in Bithynia in A.D. 95. Under Nerva, who admired Valerius both for his ability and his loyalty to the Cornelii, he served as governor of Galatia. In all his posts outside Rome, Cornelia accompanied him, but she particularly enjoyed Ancyra, the capital of Galatia. After a lesiurely sight-seeing trip back to Rome, Valerius and Cornelia collaborated in writing a history of Galatia and Bithynia. They lived long enough to see their great-grandchildren and died within two days of each other in A.D. 135.

When Sextus arrived in Lower Germany, Valerius helped him become one of the 120 young men of equestrian rank attached to a legion as an aide-de-camp to learn military leadership. In three years' time Sextus became an officer of an auxiliary infantry unit and gradually advanced through the ranks. His unit, the **āla Gallōrum et Thrācum,** was transferred to Britain in the early years of Trajan's reign. Sextus enjoyed military life. He held the rank of **tribūnus legiōnis** when he bravely died at age forty-nine trying to rally his panicked *Legio IX* stationed at York (**Eboracum**) during a native revolt early in Hadrian's reign.

When Domitian seized the villa at Baiae, he sold a number of slaves, including Davus. The Cornelii were unable to find out what happened to Davus, but they freed his daughter. After Sextus rejoined his own father, Eucleides became Gaius' secretary and steward. He accompanied Cornelius to Africa but fell ill with a fever and died there.

Roman Britain

The sons of Lucius the legionary participated in the Roman invasion of Britain in A.D. 43 under the Emperor Claudius and helped establish a Roman presence in Britain. The *Legio XX* suppressed the wild cult of the Druids, helped defeat Boudicca the rebellious queen of the native tribe of the Iceni, established a base at Virconium and built towns and roads to link the towns together. Under the legate Agricola, the *Legio XX* campaigned in the far north against the Pictish tribes and defeated Calgacus, chief of the Caledonians. After retreating from the north, Roman legions at the behest of the Emperor Hadrian built a wall across the island of Britain, eight feet thick, sixteen feet high, and seventy-five miles long with a **castra** for an auxiliary cohort every six miles and a fortress (**castellus**) every mile. But then the empire was divided into two halves, and the strength of the legions declined. Eventually the legions were withdrawn from Britain to protect Italy and Rome itself from barbarian attacks.

At the beginning of the fifth century A.D., the Alemanni and other barbarian hordes were massing on the Rhine, Alaric the Visigoth was threatening Rome, and Flavius Stilicho, the Roman general and ruler of the Western Empire, needed reinforcements. He recalled the *Legio XX* from Britain. Under the capable leadership of Stilicho, the *Legio XX* defeated Alaric in a battle fought Easter Sunday, A.D. 403, at Pollentia, Italy. The legion was probably later posted to the frontier along the Rhine. In A.D. 406, the Alemanni and other tribes massed on the eastern bank of the river. That winter the river froze and on New Year's day, A.D. 407, the hordes crossed, destroying everything and everyone in their path. The *Legio XX* disappears from history, probably destroyed in that battle.

In 410 Alaric the Visigoth sacked Rome; in 455 Gaeseric the Vandal sacked the city again. In 476 Odoacer the German deposed the last Roman Emperor of the West, Romulus Augustulus. Odoacer was in turn overthrown by Theodoric the Ostrogoth in 493, who established an Ostrogothic kingdom in Italy, ushering in the Middle Ages.

THE MULTICULTURAL TRADITION

In the streets of Rome or in any of the cities and towns of the empire, one would meet people from all areas of the Roman world, which, by the time of the Cornelii, encompassed a variety of European, Mid-Eastern, and African lands and peoples (see map below). While some of the inhabitants of these lands had gained Roman citizenship and the right to wear the toga, most had not, and their various native costumes and languages must have made the streets and forums of Rome a fascinating, ever-changing scene. The very household of Cornelius reflected the multicultural Roman Empire. Eucleides, of course, was a Greek, Davus a Briton captured in Boudicca's rebellion. To judge from their names, Syria, Phrygia, and Geta were originally from Syria, Phrygia (a region in modern Turkey), and Thrace (roughly modern Bulgaria).

The Roman Empire, A.D. 80

THE ANCIENT MULTICULTURAL TRADITION

Multiculturalism was a basic aspect of ancient Mediterranean life. Rome, like other ancient civilizations, owed much of its culture to civilizations that preceded it, including Eygpt, Greece, Persia (modern Iran), Palestine, North Africa (northern parts of modern Morocco, Algeria, and Libya), and perhaps even India. The Roman alphabet, for instance, came from the Etruscans, who had modified the Greek alphabet, and the Greeks in turn had modified the alphabet of the Phoenicians (a maritime culture inhabiting the coast of Syria and Lebanon). The papyrus scrolls the **grammaticus** Palaemon read from were an Egyptian invention.

Rome also borrowed freely from its various provinces, and through trade cultural exchanges became easier than ever before. From the provinces of Gaul, Germany, and Britain, for instance, the Romans and the peoples of the empire adopted various kinds of warm, water-proof cloaks, such as the **cucullus,** and soldiers' warm pants, **brācae.** The bright plaids that Helge and her friends wove proved so popular that weavers in the eastern provinces began to imitate them. The Romans brought to Italy and to their European provinces the cherry and the peach (**persica,** *Persian fruit*) among other Oriental, Arabic, and African foods and spices. The culture of imperial Rome was such an amalgam of cultures that "Roman" signifies a great deal more than "pertaining to the people of the city of Rome."

The Greek philosopher, Socrates
Marble statue, British Museum, London

For example, many of Rome's most famous literary figures were neither born in Rome themselves, nor were they even of Roman/Italian descent. Vergil, Rome's "national poet laureate" was born of a father who had a small farm near Mantua in northern Italy. His **cognōmen**, Maro, suggests that his family was of Celtic descent, perhaps from the Gauls who ravaged Italy and even sacked Rome in 390 B.C. The satiric poet Martial was from Spain, as was the philosopher Seneca, tutor of the Emperor Nero. And, of course, the Romans, tutored by the Greeks, were well read in the works of ancient Greece, from the philosophers, poets, and lofty dramatists to the immensely popular fable-teller, Aesop.

Likewise, beginning with the Emperor Trajan, a number of emperors were not born in Rome or even in Italy. Trajan and Hadrian, for example, were born in the Roman colony Italica, near Seville, Spain. Septimius Severus, emperor from A.D. 193–211, was born in North Africa near Leptis Magna in Libya, and the Emperor Constantine in the province of **Moesia superior** (modern West-Central Balkans).

Much of the strength and vitality of the empire was due to the willingness of its various inhabitants to adopt, adapt, and develop ideas, inventions, customs, religions, and philosophies from other provinces and a willingness to tolerate differences. If it is true that in the eastern Mediterranean an earlier melding of cultures called "Hellenistic" was inherited by the Romans when they conquered this area, it was the Romans who spread multiculturalism out of the Mediterranean basin into northern Europe and, in turn, enabled the northern European cultures to influence those of the Mediterranean more strongly than they had before. And it was only the Romans who became willing to extend their citizenship to those of other tribes and nations. The Emperor Claudius, who was born in Lugdunum (Lyons) in Gaul, enrolled some Gallic nobles in the Senate, opened the public magistracies to all Roman citizens in Gaul, and began to extend a limited form of citizenship to urban communities in Romanized provinces. Under the Flavian emperors this policy of granting citizenship was systematized and expanded until finally the Emperor Caracalla (also born in Lugdunum) in A.D. 212 conferred Roman citizenship on all free residents of the empire who had not yet received it. Such a willingness to extend citizenship found support and reinforcement in the tradition of the "unity of mankind" of the Hellenistic Stoic philosophy, which was embraced by many prominent Romans.

Roman depicted as Egyptian pharoah
Egyptian marble bust, Louvre, Paris

AVENUES OF MULTICULTURAL INFLUENCE

In antiquity one culture might receive and absorb cultural influences from another in several ways. One way—but not the main way—was through conquest of a town or nation and the enslavement of the conquered inhabitants. (The hero ancestor of the Romans, Aeneas, and his band of Trojans, is one example of a people fleeing death and enslavement by defeat in war.) Often, however, such military conquest might result in the enslavement of only a small percentage of the conquered population (if at all). Instead, the majority of the conquered people and territory would become a source of economic advantage to the victors through payment of money (taxes) or of raw goods. The troubles in Africa, over which Cornelius was recalled to the Senate in Rome, originated because of this kind of economic exploitation of defeated peoples.

More frequently, however, societies in the ancient world came into contact through expansion of trading relationships along new land, and, even more often, along new sea routes. Many times such trading ventures were primarily seeking more abundant supplies of minerals, food stuffs, or other raw materials, but, as merchants traveled to new places, they also came across new materials, technologies, and luxury goods.

Warship

Merchant ship

Slavery as an Avenue of Multicultural Influence

Such merchants also engaged in the trade of slaves. A person might become a slave in various ways in addition to being enslaved as a result of defeat in war. Areas and periods of political unrest saw increased piracy: individual pirate ships might land on an unprotected coastal estate, while flotillas of pirate ships might have enough manpower to raid an unsuspecting town and take away many inhabitants. Illegal kidnapping continued despite any measures a city or town might take. Parents who felt they could not raise an additional child would "expose" the child. Anyone who found the child could raise it as a family member or as a slave. It was also legal in many societies to sell a child into slavery or to sell oneself to raise money to pay off a debt. Slaves also had children, who were automatically slaves. Even such "hereditary" slaves, however, could earn or be awarded freedom.

Slaves could be members of any race or any culture. Slaves from societies such as existed in the Near East were often skilled at some craft and were especially in demand by owners of workshops making pottery, weapons, jewelry, and woven goods. Slaves not so skilled were used as agricultural laborers. If they proved talented at learning the master's language and were obedient, they might become domestic servants, such as maids, grooms, gardeners, and, in time, overseers of slaves. Those Greek slaves who were educated and literate were particularly prized by the Roman elite as tutors, doctors, secretary-accountants, and teachers. Slaves from northern provinces were usually untrained in any skill in demand by Mediterranean cultures and often proved (or were regarded as) very stubborn but physically strong and so were often used in situations where strength was required. The Athenians, for example, used enslaved Scythian archers as a kind of security force in Athens; among the Romans, male barbarian slaves were often placed in the training schools for gladiators or used as personal bodyguards by emperors. People showed off their wealth and social status by giving slaves specialized duties and by having numerous slaves attend them in the street, Forum, and law courts. State or local governments also owned slaves who did the manual labor required for street repair and the building of walls, sewers, and aqueducts. Slavery was so basic a part of ancient societies that even freedmen would own slaves, and a slave like Davus, before his own captivity, might have owned a slave or two himself.

The cultural influence a slave might have could be considerable. The earliest author in Roman literature, known to us as L. Livius Andronicus, had become a slave after the Romans took the Greek city Tarentum in 272 B.C. His Roman master established him in Rome as a teacher of Greek; when manumitted the freed slave took his master's name. Not only did Andronicus translate Homer's *Odyssey* into Latin (this became almost immediately one of the standard texts read in Roman schools), but he became the first author-actor in Rome, adapting Greek comedies to Roman taste. Doubtless these comedies were read by the later playwright, P. Terentius Afer (190?–159 B.C.), himself a slave, brought to Rome from North Africa. His **cognōmen** suggests that his family might have been from some Berber tribe conquered by the Carthaginians; he came to Rome as a slave in the house of Terentius Lucanus, a Senator. Having learned Latin, his intelligence, African origin, and skill as a comic writer brought him to the notice of Scipio Africanus the Younger and his literary circle. Though Terence died young, his six surviving plays have for centuries continued to influence playwrights of the world, including Shakespeare and Molière. The great Roman poet Horace (65–8 B.C.) was the son of a freedman father who is thought to have been a public slave owned by a town. Horace's poetic genius and insightful observations about human nature not only gained him the patronage of Augustus himself, but also endure to this day for their wit and accuracy.

MULTICULTURAL ORIGINS OF MEDICINE

The whole discipline and art of medicine is a legacy of cross-cultural origin that passed to and through Rome. The **medicus** treating Titus before he died relied on a wide range of drugs, ointments, and salves that evolved out of the medical treatments of the Mesopotamians, Egyptians, and Hebrews, as well as the Greeks. His close observation of the symptoms of Titus' fatal illness derived from the principles established by the Greek physician, Hippocrates, whose analytic, scientific observation of disease earned him the title "Father of Medicine." The physician Galen began his practice at a training school for gladiators in Pergamum (modern Turkey) and later went to Rome to teach medicine and become the personal physician of the emperor Commodus. Galen's main work on therapy, *Ars magna*, was used by physicians until the last century. Most medical books in the empire, however, were written in Greek, and after the fall of the empire the Jewish physicians living in the Mediterranean countries now ruled by the Arabs were the

"Visit of a sick child to the temple of Asclepius"
Oil on canvas by John William Waterhouse, The Fine Art Society, London

main translators in the East of the Greek texts into Syriac and Arabic and, much later, in the West from Arabic into Latin for European doctors. In fact, one of the most important medical centers, especially for surgery, was Spain under Arabic (Moorish) rule because Arabic and Jewish doctors there had access to Greco-Roman texts in both Greek and Latin. In former Roman Gaul, however, the Greek medical texts were not available, and medical practice and knowledge regressed with the decline of imperial Roman culture, so that Charlemagne, emperor of the Holy Roman Empire, had to request help from the Caliph (ruler) of Bagdad (modern Iran) in improving the knowledge of his doctors. The continued importance of imperial Roman medical knowledge for the modern European, American, and Arabic cultures is reflected in today's scientific and medical vocabulary, which is ninety percent or more drawn from Greek and Latin roots.

Asclepius, son of Apollo, god of medicine

MULTICULTURAL SPREAD OF THE LATIN LANGUAGE

Like medical knowledge and other aspects of imperial Roman culture, the survival of Latin varied from province to province. The Latin used by the common people of Rome was quite different from the Latin used by the wealthy, aristocratic elite. Widely spoken throughout the European provinces by common Roman citizens (called in Latin **vulgus**), vulgar Latin gradually developed into the various Romance languages of French, Spanish, Portuguese, Italian, Catalan, Romansch, and Rumanian. Even though subsequent invasions by various barbarian peoples brought new languages into these provinces, Latin remained the basic language, though undergoing local changes in grammar and pronunciation over time.

In the Germanic territory, Germanic dialects, rather than Latin, predominated as the basis of communication, but these dialects absorbed Latin vocabulary. For example, the German word *Pfund* ("pound") is derived from the Latin **pondus** (*weight*), and the German noun for innkeeper, *Kaufmann*, is a compound of the German word *Mann* ("man") and the Latin noun **caupō** (*innkeeper*). English developed from Germanic dialects and was strongly influenced by Latin over the centuries. The use today of English as a worldwide language continues to sustain and spread elements of Latin to every corner of the world.

MULTICULTURAL SPREAD OF ROMAN LAW

The discipline of law has also gone through very interesting multicultural transformations while perpetuating Rome's legacy. The system of Roman law, a reasoned, consistent body of practices resolving the inevitable conflicts arising in daily life, was one of the benefits perceived by the peoples whom the Romans conquered. In general, the written Roman code of law remained an important basis for law of various countries, though beginning in the eleventh century it began to be interpreted, developed, and adapted to existing conditions. For example, "Roman-Dutch" law, as developed and adapted by jurists of the Netherlands, is used not only in the Netherlands but also in countries once part of the Dutch Empire, such as South Africa and Ceylon.

Lictor

The barbarians who invaded Roman Germany, Gaul, and Spain (Visigoths, Burgundians, and Franks) generally wished to maintain the existing Roman administrative system, including its law. In Gaul, men of Roman descent remained under Roman law, but the barbarian invaders had the right to be tried by the customs of the tribe they belonged to. In imitation of the Roman code of law these barbarian customs were also written down and codified, assimilating some of the Roman law in the process. Over the centuries France continued to use this adaptation of Roman law for situations affecting the individual, tenure of real property, order of inheritance, and system of mortgages but used common or "customary" law for other legal problems until the French Revolution instituted a very radical system of law. Finding this system too radical, the emperor Napoleon decided to systematize French law, and he united in the Napoleonic *Code Civile* what in Roman law and in customary law was now best suited to France in its new conditions. Given the political and cultural importance of France in the 1800s, which paralleled the Roman Empire, this civil code became the model for countries reforming their legal codes or new countries instituting a legal code. The Canadian province of Quebec uses a French-derived law code built largely on Roman law, and the state of Louisiana (acquired by purchase from Napoleon in 1803) continues to use a civil code deriving from both the modified Roman law that was in effect when Spain owned this territory and from the Napoleonic code.

Likewise in Germany during the Middle Ages, both Roman law and tribal customary law were in force, Roman law being applied in cases where it was not excluded by contrary local (customary) provisions. This situation changed when, in 1900, a common code for the whole German empire was adopted. A different situation occurred in Spain, where, under the Romans, Roman magistrates were expected to defer to the established law of the district (**mūnicipium**). This municipal system of law, along with Roman law, was continued by the Visigothic and the Arabic kingdoms of Spain and became part of the Spanish legal system when Spain came to be ruled by its own kings. As part of Napoleon's empire, Spain, too, adopted the Napoleonic Code.

Roman culture did not survive extensively in what is now the United Kingdom (Great Britain) after the Angles, Saxons, and Jutes invaded that region in the 400s. Roman culture had not been planted as deeply there as on the continent. So many Roman Britons fled to Gaul that the area they settled was named after them, Brittany. Nonetheless, Roman law influenced Anglo-Saxon tribal law indirectly through the Church. The Anglo-Saxon law of property was modified by Roman legal conceptions concerning ownership, donations, wills, and rights of women. After the Norman Conquest this modification continued as Britain was opened to contact with France and Italy. Today, in both England and the United States, Roman law is the source of doctrines, principles, and rules, some of which—for example, the law of gifts—remain virtually unchanged from the days of Rome.

TRACING THE SPREAD OF ROMAN INFLUENCE

The way the Roman inheritance was passed down among the cultures of the former provinces of the Roman Empire is a fascinating process. Consider, for example, how the Roman legacy traveled via **Hispānia** (modern Spain). The earliest inhabitants of **Hispānia** were **Hiberēs**, who migrated from northern Africa, and Celts, who entered the region by crossing the Pyrenees. In the 800s B.C., they began trading with the Phoenicians, who were an ancient maritime culture spread over southwest Asia and the eastern Mediterranean. The peoples of **Hispānia** thus came into contact with the cultures of the eastern Mediterranean and the Orient, who brought them new foods, such as wine and olive oil in exchange for gold and metals. Later, when the Greeks settled colonies on Spain's coasts in the 500s B.C., they introduced the natives to the use of coinage. When Spain became part of the Roman Empire, after the Second Punic War, the Romans established many **colōniae** of Roman citizens there who helped develop the two Spanish provinces into two of the most prosperous of Roman lands. Some of the emperors and writers who came from **Hispānia** to become leading Romans were mentioned above and included the philosopher Seneca, the satiric poet Martial, and the Emperors Trajan and Hadrian.

After the fall of the Roman Empire, Spain was ultimately taken over by Arabs who invaded from Morocco in A.D. 711. These Moroccan Arabs (Moors) brought to Spain their own adaptations of Roman imperial culture. When the Arabs began invading the former eastern provinces of Rome and taking over their cities, they were impressed, among other things, by the buildings and architecture. These they adapted to their own use. Building walls among the colonnaded avenues of the former classical cities, the Arabs created their characteristic linear markets (*suqs*). The Arabs found they also enjoyed baths and kept the entire Roman bath complex save for the **tepidārium;** as it was for the Romans, bathing became for the Arabs a social occasion, and the bath complex of the Caliph's palace included a state room. The palaces kept the axial arrangement of Roman palaces. Imperial Roman cer-

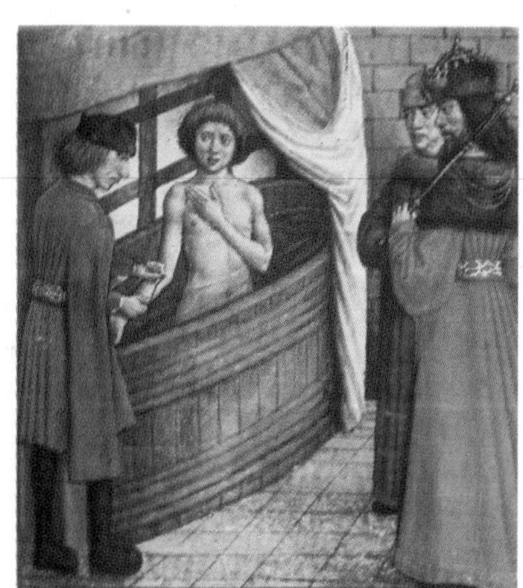

Seneca, who suffered all his life from serious ill health, spoke out against the murderous entertainment staged in the Colosseum. A medieval artist depicts him here in a medicinal bath, attended by doctors.

"Seneca Bleeding in Bath," Roman de la Rosa, British Library, London, England

emony was adapted as well: the axis of the Caliph's main palace led to a triple arched facade and entrance gate. The entrance ceremony of the Caliph was inspired by the **adventus** (*arrival*) ceremony of the Roman emperor.

ROMAN ARCHITECTURE IN AMERICA

When the Spaniards came to the two American continents, they in turn brought their adaptations of Roman imperial architecture. Behind the typical layout of the cities that they established it is easy to discern the basic Roman plan. The center of a Spanish city was the rectangular plaza (from Latin **platea**, *wide street*, which itself is from the Greek *plateia*, "wide"), which corresponded to the **forum**, the center of a Roman town. Four principal streets led to the plaza from the north, south, east, and west, analogous to the main Roman streets, the **cardō maximus** and **decumānus maximus**. Like the Roman streets, these four principal streets were lined with arcades and shops.

But it is due to a most curious twist of history that the style of many of the public and governmental buildings of the United States is based on Roman imperial architecture. Former provinces of the Roman Empire had evolved into modern European nations, each with its own architectural "look" and style for their governmental buildings. By the time of the American Revolution, European public buildings were not constructed in a Roman style. Thomas Jefferson, who was himself an architect, argued that his new country should not use the architectural style then current in Britain and Europe. He was instrumental in developing the American Federal style of architecture, which was used for the Capitol Building in Washington, D.C., state capitols, public museums, and non-public buildings such as banks. A basic model for that style was a small Roman temple, the Maison Carrée in Nîmes, France, with which Jefferson had become entranced while he was ambassador to France. Jefferson also designed the campus of the University of Virginia to recreate a Roman villa with linked porticos, enclosed spaces, and pillared buildings. For his own home of Monticello, Jefferson drew on the Pantheon in Rome. The Pantheon also inspired the president of the Girard Trust of Philadelphia when he made a tour of Europe early in this century. Upon his return, he ordered that his new bank building be modeled on this second century A.D. Roman temple.

CONCLUSION

Acquiring facility with the Latin language and familiarity with Roman culture is actually, then, a starting point for lifelong enrichment along multicultural lines. With this learning we reach far back into history and keep contact with a fascinating, vital process of the world's development and our own. Our food and our drink, our clothing and our embellishments, our sports and our games, our literature and all our arts, our medicine and our law, the buildings and libraries and schools of our society, our political and military theories, our philosophies and our sciences, our history and our languages—all of these are an inherited, shared legacy, that we continuously modify, add to, and use in the real, living world with all its variety and all its common ground.

Philosophy (literally "love of wisdom") is a multicultural legacy from antiquity.
Woodcut by Albrecht Dürer

Forms

The following charts show the forms of typical Latin nouns, adjectives, pronouns, and verbs. As an aid in pronunciation, markings of long vowels and of accents are included.

I. Nouns

Number Case	1st Declension	2nd Declension				3rd Declension		
	Fem.	Masc.	Masc.	Masc.	Neut.	Masc.	Fem.	Neut.
Singular								
Nominative	puélla	sérvus	púer	áger	báculum	páter	vōx	nṓmen
Genitive	puéllae	sérvī	púerī	ágrī	báculī	pátris	vṓcis	nṓminis
Dative	puéllae	sérvō	púerō	ágrō	báculō	pátrī	vṓcī	nṓminī
Accusative	puéllam	sérvum	púerum	ágrum	báculum	pátrem	vṓcem	nṓmen
Ablative	puéllā	sérvō	púerō	ágrō	báculō	pátre	vṓce	nṓmine
Vocative	puélla	sérve	púer	áger	báculum	páter	vōx	nṓmen
Plural								
Nominative	puéllae	sérvī	púerī	ágrī	bácula	pátrēs	vṓcēs	nṓmina
Genitive	puellā́rum	servṓrum	puerṓrum	agrṓrum	baculṓrum	pátrum	vṓcum	nṓminum
Dative	puéllīs	sérvīs	púerīs	ágrīs	báculīs	pátribus	vṓcibus	nōmínibus
Accusative	puéllās	sérvōs	púerōs	ágrōs	bácula	pátrēs	vṓcēs	nṓmina
Ablative	puéllīs	sérvīs	púerīs	ágrīs	báculīs	pátribus	vṓcibus	nōmínibus
Vocative	puéllae	sérvī	púerī	ágrī	bácula	pátrēs	vṓcēs	nṓmina

Number Case	4th Declension		5th Declension	
	Masc.	Neut.	Masc.	Fem.
Singular				
Nominative	árcus	génū	díēs	rēs
Genitive	árcūs	génūs	diḗī	réī
Dative	árcuī	génū	diḗī	réī
Accusative	árcum	génū	díem	rem
Ablative	árcū	génū	díē	rē
Vocative	árcus	génū	díēs	rēs
Plural				
Nominative	árcūs	génua	díēs	rēs
Genitive	árcuum	génuum	diḗrum	rḗrum
Dative	árcibus	génibus	diḗbus	rḗbus
Accusative	árcūs	génua	díēs	rēs
Ablative	árcibus	génibus	diḗbus	rḗbus
Vocative	árcūs	génua	díēs	rēs

II. Adjectives

Number / Case	1st and 2nd Declension			3rd Declension		
	Masc.	Fem.	Neut.	Masc.	Fem.	Neut.
Singular						
Nominative	mágn***us***	mágn***a***	mágn***um***	ómn***is***	ómn***is***	ómn***e***
Genitive	mágn***ī***	mágn***ae***	mágn***ī***	ómn***is***	ómn***is***	ómn***is***
Dative	mágn***ō***	mágn***ae***	mágn***ō***	ómn***ī***	ómn***ī***	ómn***ī***
Accusative	mágn***um***	mágn***am***	mágn***um***	ómn***em***	ómn***em***	ómn***e***
Ablative	mágn***ō***	mágn***ā***	mágn***ō***	ómn***ī***	ómn***ī***	ómn***ī***
Vocative	mágn***e***	mágn***a***	mágn***um***	ómn***is***	ómn***is***	ómn***e***
Plural						
Nominative	mágn***ī***	mágn***ae***	mágn***a***	ómn***ēs***	ómn***ēs***	ómn***ia***
Genitive	magn***ṓrum***	magn***ā́rum***	magn***ṓrum***	ómn***ium***	ómn***ium***	ómn***ium***
Dative	mágn***īs***	mágn***īs***	mágn***īs***	ómn***ibus***	ómn***ibus***	ómn***ibus***
Accusative	mágn***ōs***	mágn***ās***	mágn***a***	ómn***ēs***	ómn***ēs***	ómn***ia***
Ablative	mágn***īs***	mágn***īs***	mágn***īs***	ómn***ibus***	ómn***ibus***	ómn***ibus***
Vocative	mágn***ī***	mágn***ae***	mágn***a***	ómn***ēs***	ómn***ēs***	ómn***ia***

III. Comparative Adjectives

Number / Case	Masc.	Fem.	Neut.
Singular			
Nominative	púlchrior	púlchrior	púlchrius
Genitive	pulchriṓr***is***	pulchriṓr***is***	pulchriṓr***is***
Dative	pulchriṓr***ī***	pulchriṓr***ī***	pulchriṓr***ī***
Accusative	pulchriṓr***em***	pulchriṓr***em***	púlchrius
Ablative	pulchriṓr***e***	pulchriṓr***e***	pulchriṓr***e***
Vocative	púlchrior	púlchrior	púlchrius
Plural			
Nominative	pulchriṓr***ēs***	pulchriṓr***ēs***	pulchriṓr***a***
Genitive	pulchriṓr***um***	pulchriṓr***um***	pulchriṓr***um***
Dative	pulchriṓr***ibus***	pulchriṓr***ibus***	pulchriṓr***ibus***
Accusative	pulchriṓr***ēs***	pulchriṓr***ēs***	pulchriṓr***a***
Ablative	pulchriṓr***ibus***	pulchriṓr***ibus***	pulchriṓr***ibus***
Vocative	pulchriṓr***ēs***	pulchriṓr***ēs***	pulchriṓr***a***

Adjectives have *positive*, *comparative*, and *superlative* forms. You can usually recognize the comparative by the letters **-ior(-)** and the superlative by ***-issimus***, ***-errimus***, or ***-illimus***:

ignā́vus, -a, -um, *lazy*	**ignā́vior, ignā́vius**	**ignāvíssimus, -a, -um**
púlcher, púlchra, púlchrum, *beautiful*	**púlchrior, púlchrius**	**pulchérrimus, -a, -um**
fácilis, -is, -e, *easy*	**facílior, facílius**	**facíllimus, -a, -um**

Some very common adjectives are irregular in the comparative and superlative:

Positive	Comparative	Superlative
bónus, -a, -um, *good*	**mélior, mélius,** *better*	**óptimus, -a, -um,** *best*
málus, -a, -um, *bad*	**péior, péius,** *worse*	**péssimus, -a, -um,** *worst*
mágnus, -a, -um, *big*	**máior, máius,** *bigger*	**máximus, -a, -um,** *biggest*
párvus, -a, -um, *small*	**mínor, mínus,** *smaller*	**mínimus, -a, -um,** *smallest*
múltus, -a, -um, *much*	**plūs,*** *more*	**plū́rimus, -a, -um,** *most, very much*
múltī, -ae, -a, *many*	**plū́rēs, plū́ra,** *more*	**plū́rimī, -ae, -a,** *most, very many*

*Note that **plūs** is not an adjective but a neuter substantive, usually found with a partitive genitive, e.g., Titus **plūs vīnī** bibit. *Titus drank* ***more (of the) wine***.

IV. Present Participles

Number / Case	Masc.	Fem.	Neut.
Singular			
Nominative	párāns	párāns	párāns
Genitive	paránt***is***	paránt***is***	paránt***is***
Dative	paránt***ī***	paránt***ī***	paránt***ī***
Accusative	paránt***em***	paránt***em***	párāns
Ablative	paránt***ī/e***	paránt***ī/e***	paránt***ī/e***
Plural			
Nominative	paránt***ēs***	paránt***ēs***	paránt***ia***
Genitive	paránt***ium***	paránt***ium***	paránt***ium***
Dative	paránt***ibus***	paránt***ibus***	paránt***ibus***
Accusative	paránt***ēs***	paránt***ēs***	paránt***ia***
Ablative	paránt***ibus***	paránt***ibus***	paránt***ibus***

V. Numbers

Case	Masc.	Fem.	Neut.	Masc.	Fem.	Neut.	Masc.	Fem.	Neut.
Nom.	ū́n**us**	ū́n**a**	ū́n**um**	dú**o**	dú**ae**	dú**o**	tr**ēs**	tr**ēs**	tr**ía**
Gen.	ūn**ī́us**	ūn**ī́us**	ūn**ī́us**	du**ṓrum**	du**ā́rum**	du**ṓrum**	tr**íum**	tr**íum**	tr**íum**
Dat.	ū́n**ī**	ū́n**ī**	ū́n**ī**	du**ṓbus**	du**ā́bus**	du**ṓbus**	tr**íbus**	tr**íbus**	tr**íbus**
Acc.	ū́n**um**	ū́n**am**	ū́n**um**	dú**ōs**	dú**ās**	dú**o**	tr**ēs**	tr**ēs**	tr**ía**
Abl.	ū́n**ō**	ū́n**ā**	ū́n**ō**	du**ṓbus**	du**ā́bus**	du**ṓbus**	tr**íbus**	tr**íbus**	tr**íbus**

	Cardinal	Ordinal
I	**ū́nus, -a, -um,** *one*	**prī́mus, -a, -um,** *first*
II	**dúo, -ae, -o,** *two*	**secúndus, -a, -um,** *second*
III	**trēs, trēs, tría,** *three*	**tértius, -a, -um,** *third*
IV	**quáttuor,** *four*	**quā́rtus, -a, -um**
V	**quī́nque,** *five*	**quī́ntus, -a, -um**
VI	**sex,** *six*	**séxtus, -a, -um**
VII	**séptem,** *seven*	**séptimus, -a, -um**
VIII	**óctō,** *eight*	**octā́vus, -a, -um**
IX	**nóvem,** *nine*	**nṓnus, -a, -um**
X	**décem,** *ten*	**décimus, -a, -um**
XI	**ū́ndecim,** *eleven*	**ūndécimus, -a, -um**
XII	**duódecim,** *twelve*	**duodécimus, -a, -um**
XIII	**trédecim,** *thirteen*	**tértius décimus, -a, -um**
XIV	**quattuórdecim,** *fourteen*	**quā́rtus décimus, -a, -um**
XV	**quī́ndecim,** *fifteen*	**quī́ntus décimus, -a, -um**
XVI	**sḗdecim,** *sixteen*	**séxtus décimus, -a, -um**
XVII	**septéndecim,** *seventeen*	**séptimus décimus, -a, -um**
XVIII	**duodēvīgíntī,** *eighteen,*	**duodēvīcḗsimus, -a, -um**
XIX	**ūndēvīgíntī,** *nineteen,*	**ūndēvīcḗsimus, -a, -um**
XX	**vīgíntī,** *twenty*	**vīcḗsimus, -a, -um**
L	**quīnquāgíntā,** *fifty*	**quīnquāgḗsimus, -a, -um**
C	**céntum,** *a hundred*	**centḗsimus, -a, -um**
D	**quīngéntī, -ae, -a,** *five hundred*	**quīngentḗsimus, -a, -um**
M	**mī́lle,** *a thousand*	**mīllḗsimus, -a, -um**

N.B. The cardinal numbers from **quattuor** to **centum** do not change their form to indicate case and gender.

VI. Personal Pronouns

Number Case	1st Declension	2nd Declension	3rd Declension Masc.	Fem.	Neut.
Singular					
Nominative	égo	tū	is	éa	id
Genitive	méī	túī	éius	éius	éius
Dative	míhi	tíbi	éī	éī	éī
Accusative	mē	tē	éum	éam	id
Ablative	mē	tē	éō	éā	éō
Plural					
Nominative	nōs	vōs	éī	éae	éa
Genitive	nóstrī	véstrī	eṓrum	eā́rum	eṓrum
	nóstrum	véstrum			
Dative	nṓbīs	vṓbīs	éīs	éīs	éīs
Accusative	nōs	vōs	éōs	éās	éa
Ablative	nṓbīs	vṓbīs	éīs	éīs	éīs

Note: The forms of **is, ea, id** may also serve as demonstrative adjectives.

VII. Reflexive Pronoun

Singular	
Nominative	——
Genitive	súī
Dative	síbi
Accusative	sē
Ablative	sē
Plural	
Nominative	——
Genitive	súī
Dative	síbi
Accusative	sē
Ablative	sē

VIII. Relative Pronoun

	Masc.	Fem.	Neut.
Singular			
Nominative	quī	quae	quod
Genitive	cúius	cúius	cúius
Dative	cui	cui	cui
Accusative	quem	quam	quod
Ablative	quō	quā	quō
Plural			
Nominative	quī	quae	quae
Genitive	quṓrum	quā́rum	quṓrum
Dative	quíbus	quíbus	quíbus
Accusative	quōs	quās	quae
Ablative	quíbus	quíbus	quíbus

IX. Interrogative Pronoun

Number Case	Masc.	Fem.	Neut.
Singular			
Nominative	quis	quis	quid
Genitive	cúius	cúius	cúius
Dative	cui	cui	cui
Accusative	quem	quem	quid
Ablative	quō	quō	quō
Plural	Same as the plural of the relative pronoun above.		

X. Indefinite Adjective

Number Case	Masc.	Fem.	Neut.
Singular			
Nominative	quídam	quaédam	quóddam
Genitive	cuiúsdam	cuiúsdam	cuiúsdam
Dative	cúidam	cúidam	cúidam
Accusative	quéndam	quándam	quóddam
Ablative	quṓdam	quā́dam	quṓdam
Plural			
Nominative	quídam	quaédam	quaédam
Genitive	quōrúndam	quārúndam	quōrúndam
Dative	quibúsdam	quibúsdam	quibúsdam
Accusative	quṓsdam	quā́sdam	quaédam
Ablative	quibúsdam	quibúsdam	quibúsdam

XI. Demonstrative Adjectives and Pronouns

Number Case	Masc.	Fem.	Neut.	Masc.	Fem.	Neut.
Singular						
Nominative	hic	haec	hoc	ílle	ílla	íllud
Genitive	húius	húius	húius	illī́us	illī́us	illī́us
Dative	húic	húic	húic	íllī	íllī	íllī
Accusative	hunc	hanc	hoc	íllum	íllam	íllud
Ablative	hōc	hāc	hōc	íllō	íllā	íllō
Plural						
Nominative	hī	hae	haec	íllī	íllae	ílla
Genitive	hṓrum	hā́rum	hṓrum	illṓrum	illā́rum	illṓrum
Dative	hīs	hīs	hīs	íllīs	íllīs	íllīs
Accusative	hōs	hās	haec	íllōs	íllās	ílla
Ablative	hīs	hīs	hīs	íllīs	íllīs	íllīs

Number Case	Masculine	Feminine	Neuter
Singular			
Nominative	ípse	ípsa	ípsum
Genitive	ipsī́us	ipsī́us	ipsī́us
Dative	ípsī	ípsī	ípsī
Accusative	ípsum	ípsam	ípsum
Ablative	ípsō	ípsā	ípsō
Plural			
Nominative	ípsī	ípsae	ípsa
Genitive	ipsṓrum	ipsā́rum	ipsṓrum
Dative	ípsīs	ípsīs	ípsīs
Accusative	ípsōs	ípsās	ípsa
Ablative	ípsīs	ípsīs	ípsīs

Number Case	Masc.	Fem.	Neut.	Masc.	Fem.	Neut.
Singular						
Nominative	is	éa	id	ī́dem	éadem	ídem
Genitive	éius	éius	éius	eiúsdem	eiúsdem	eiúsdem
Dative	éī	éī	éī	eī́dem	eī́dem	eī́dem
Accusative	éum	éam	id	eúndem	eándem	ídem
Ablative	éō	éā	éō	eṓdem	eā́dem	eṓdem
Plural						
Nominative	éī	éae	éa	eī́dem	eaédem	éadem
Genitive	eṓrum	eā́rum	eṓrum	eōrúndem	eārúndem	eōrúndem
Dative	éīs	éīs	éīs	eī́sdem	eī́sdem	eī́sdem
Accusative	éōs	éās	éa	eṓsdem	eā́sdem	éadem
Ablative	éīs	éīs	éīs	eī́sdem	eī́sdem	eī́sdem

XII. Adverbs

Latin adverbs may be formed from adjectives of the 1st and 2nd declensions by adding ***-ē*** to the base of the adjective, e.g., **strēnu*ē***, *strenuously*, from **strēnuus, -a, -um**. To form an adverb from a 3rd declension adjective, add ***-iter*** to the base of the adjective or ***-er*** to bases ending in **-nt-**, e.g., **brev*iter***, *briefly*, from **brevis, -is, -e**, and **prūdent*er***, *wisely*, from **prūdēns, prūdentis**.

láet*ē*, *happily*	laét***ius***	laet***íssimē***
fēlī́***citer***, *luckily*	fēlī́c***ius***	fēlīc***íssimē***
celé***riter***, *quickly*	celér***ius***	celér***rimē***
prūdént***er***, *wisely*	prūdént***ius***	prūdent***íssimē***

Note the following as well:

díū, *for a long time*	diū́t***ius***	diūt***íssimē***
saépe, *often*	saép***ius***	saep***íssimē***
sḗrō, *late*	sḗr***ius***	sēr***íssimē***

Some adverbs are irregular:

béne, *well*	**mélius**, *better*	**óptimē**, *best*
mále, *badly*	**péius**, *worse*	**péssimē**, *worst*
fácile, *easily*	**facílius**, *more easily*	**facíllimē**, *most easily*
magnópere, *greatly*	**mágis**, *more*	**máximē**, *most*
paúlum, *little*	**mínus**, *less*	**mínimē**, *least*
múltum, *much*	**plūs**, *more*	**plū́rimum**, *most*

XIII. Regular Verbs Active: Infinitive, Imperative, Indicative

			1st Conjugation	2nd Conjugation	3rd Conjugation		4th Conjugation
	Infinitive		par***ā́re***	hab***ḗre***	mítt***ere***	iác***ere*** (***-iō***)	aud***ī́re***
	Imperative		pár***ā***	háb***ē***	mítt***e***	iác***e***	aúd***ī***
			par***ā́te***	hab***ḗte***	mítt***ite***	iác***ite***	aud***ī́te***
Present	Singular	1	pár***ō***	hábe***ō***	mítt***ō***	iáci***ō***	aúdi***ō***
		2	párā***s***	hábē***s***	mítti***s***	iáci***s***	aúdī***s***
		3	pára***t***	hábe***t***	mítti***t***	iáci***t***	aúdi***t***
	Plural	1	parā́***mus***	habḗ***mus***	mítti***mus***	iáci***mus***	audī́***mus***
		2	parā́***tis***	habḗ***tis***	mítti***tis***	iáci***tis***	audī́***tis***
		3	pára***nt***	hábe***nt***	míttu***nt***	iáciu***nt***	aúdiu***nt***
Imperfect	Singular	1	parā́***bam***	habḗ***bam***	mittḗ***bam***	iaciḗ***bam***	audiḗ***bam***
		2	parā́***bās***	habḗ***bās***	mittḗ***bās***	iaciḗ***bās***	audiḗ***bās***
		3	parā́***bat***	habḗ***bat***	mittḗ***bat***	iaciḗ***bat***	audiḗ***bat***
	Plural	1	parā***bā́mus***	habē***bā́mus***	mittē***bā́mus***	iaciē***bā́mus***	audiē***bā́mus***
		2	parā***bā́tis***	habē***bā́tis***	mittē***bā́tis***	iaciē***bā́tis***	audiē***bā́tis***
		3	parā́***bant***	habḗ***bant***	mittḗ***bant***	iaciḗ***bant***	audiḗ***bant***
Future	Singular	1	parā́***bō***	habḗ***bō***	mítt***am***	iáci***am***	aúdi***am***
		2	parā́***bis***	habḗ***bis***	mítt***ēs***	iáci***ēs***	aúdi***ēs***
		3	parā́***bit***	habḗ***bit***	mítt***et***	iáci***et***	aúdi***et***
	Plural	1	parā́***bimus***	habḗ***bimus***	mitt***ḗmus***	iaci***ḗmus***	audi***ḗmus***
		2	parā́***bitis***	habḗ***bitis***	mitt***ḗtis***	iaci***ḗtis***	audi***ḗtis***
		3	parā́***bunt***	habḗ***bunt***	mítt***ent***	iáci***ent***	aúdi***ent***
Perfect	Singular	1	parā́v***ī***	hábu***ī***	mī́s***ī***	iḗc***ī***	audī́v***ī***
		2	parāv***ístī***	habu***ístī***	mīs***ístī***	iēc***ístī***	audīv***ístī***
		3	parā́v***it***	hábu***it***	mī́s***it***	iḗc***it***	audī́v***it***
	Plural	1	parā́v***imus***	habú***imus***	mī́s***imus***	iḗc***imus***	audī́v***imus***
		2	parāv***ístis***	habu***ístis***	mīs***ístis***	iēc***ístis***	audīv***ístis***
		3	parāv***ḗrunt***	habu***ḗrunt***	mīs***ḗrunt***	iēc***ḗrunt***	audīv***ḗrunt***
Pluperfect	Singular	1	parā́v***eram***	habú***eram***	mī́s***eram***	iḗc***eram***	audī́v***eram***
		2	parā́v***erās***	habú***erās***	mī́s***erās***	iḗc***erās***	audī́v***erās***
		3	parā́v***erat***	habú***erat***	mī́s***erat***	iḗc***erat***	audī́v***erat***
	Plural	1	parāv***erā́mus***	habu***erā́mus***	mīs***erā́mus***	iēc***erā́mus***	audīv***erā́mus***
		2	parāv***erā́tis***	habu***erā́tis***	mīs***erā́tis***	iēc***erā́tis***	audīv***erā́tis***
		3	parā́v***erant***	habú***erant***	mī́s***erant***	iḗc***erant***	audī́v***erant***
Future Perfect	Singular	1	parā́v***erō***	habú***erō***	mī́s***erō***	iḗc***erō***	audī́v***erō***
		2	parā́v***eris***	habú***eris***	mī́s***eris***	iḗc***eris***	audī́v***eris***
		3	parā́v***erit***	habú***erit***	mī́s***erit***	iḗc***erit***	audī́v***erit***
	Plural	1	parāv***érimus***	habu***érimus***	mīs***érimus***	iēc***érimus***	audīv***érimus***
		2	parāv***éritis***	habu***éritis***	mīs***éritis***	iēc***éritis***	audīv***éritis***
		3	parā́v***erint***	habú***erint***	mī́s***erint***	iḗc***erint***	audī́v***erint***

XIV. Regular Verbs Passive: Infinitive, Imperative, Indicative

			1st Conjugation	2nd Conjugation	3rd Conjugation		4th Conjugation
Present	Infinitive	1	portā́rī	movḗrī	míttī	iácī	audī́rī
	Imperative	1	portā́re	movḗre	míttere	iácere	audī́re
		2	portā́minī	movḗminī	mittíminī	iacíminī	audī́minī
	Singular	1	pórtor	móveor	míttor	iácior	aúdior
		2	portā́ris	movḗris	mítteris	iáceris	audī́ris
		3	portā́tur	movḗtur	míttitur	iácitur	audī́tur
	Plural	1	portā́mur	movḗmur	míttimur	iácimur	audī́mur
		2	portā́minī	movḗminī	mittíminī	iacíminī	audī́minī
		3	portántur	movéntur	mittúntur	iaciúntur	audiúntur
Imperfect	Singular	1	portā́bar	movḗbar	mittḗbar	iaciḗbar	audiḗbar
		2	portābā́ris	movēbā́ris	mittēbā́ris	iaciēbā́ris	audiēbā́ris
		3	portābā́tur	movēbā́tur	mittēbā́tur	iaciēbā́tur	audiēbā́tur
	Plural	1	portābā́mur	movēbā́mur	mittēbā́mur	iaciēbā́mur	audiēbā́mur
		2	portābā́minī	movēbā́minī	mittēbā́minī	iaciēbā́minī	audiēbā́minī
		3	portābántur	movēbántur	mittēbántur	iaciēbántur	audiēbántur
Future	Singular	1	portā́bor	movḗbor	míttar	iáciar	aúdiar
		2	portā́beris	movḗberis	mittḗris	iaciḗris	audiḗris
		3	portā́bitur	movḗbitur	mittḗtur	iaciḗtur	audiḗtur
	Plural	1	portā́bimur	movḗbimur	mittḗmur	iaciḗmur	audiḗmur
		2	portābíminī	movēbíminī	mittḗminī	iaciḗminī	audiḗminī
		3	portābúntur	movēbúntur	mitténtur	iaciéntur	audiéntur

		Perfect Passive		Pluperfect Passive		Future Perfect Passive	
Singular	1	portā́tus, -a	sum	portā́tus, -a	éram	portā́tus, -a	érō
	2	portā́tus, -a	es	portā́tus, -a	érās	portā́tus, -a	éris
	3	portā́tus, -a, -um	est	portā́tus, -a, -um	érat	portā́tus, -a, -um	érit
Plural	1	portā́tī, -ae	súmus	portā́tī, -ae	erā́mus	portā́tī, -ae	érimus
	2	portā́tī, -ae	éstis	portā́tī, -ae	erā́tis	portā́tī, -ae	éritis
	3	portā́tī, -ae, -a	sunt	portā́tī, -ae, -a	érant	portā́tī, -ae, -a	érunt

XV. Regular Verbs Active: Subjunctive

			1st Conjugation	2nd Conjugation	3rd Conjugation		4th Conjugation
Present	Singular	1	pórt***em***	móve***am***	mítt***am***	iáci***am***	aúdi***am***
		2	pórt***ēs***	móve***ās***	mítt***ās***	iáci***ās***	aúdi***ās***
		3	pórt***et***	móve***at***	mítt***at***	iáci***at***	aúdi***at***
	Plural	1	port***ḗmus***	move***ā́mus***	mitt***ā́mus***	iaci***ā́mus***	audi***ā́mus***
		2	port***ḗtis***	move***ā́tis***	mitt***ā́tis***	iac***ā́tis***	audi***ā́tis***
		3	pórt***ent***	móve***ant***	mítt***ant***	iáci***ant***	aúdi***ant***
Imperfect	Singular	1	portā́re***m***	movḗre***m***	míttere***m***	iácere***m***	audī́re***m***
		2	portā́rē***s***	movḗrē***s***	mítterē***s***	iácerē***s***	audī́rē***s***
		3	portā́re***t***	movḗre***t***	míttere***t***	iácere***t***	audī́re***t***
	Plural	1	portārḗ***mus***	movērḗ***mus***	mitterḗ***mus***	iacerḗ***mus***	audīrḗ***mus***
		2	portārḗ***tis***	movērḗ***tis***	mitterḗ***tis***	iacerḗ***tis***	audīrḗ***tis***
		3	portā́re***nt***	movḗre***nt***	mittere***nt***	iā́cere***nt***	audī́re***nt***
Perfect	Singular	1	portā́v***erim***	mṓv***erim***	mī́s***erim***	iḗc***erim***	audī́v***erim***
		2	portā́v***eris***	mṓv***eris***	mī́s***eris***	iḗc***eris***	audī́v***eris***
		3	portā́v***erit***	mṓv***erit***	mī́s***erit***	iḗc***erit***	audī́v***erit***
	Plural	1	portāv***érimus***	mōv***érimus***	mīs***érimus***	iēc***érimus***	audīv***érimus***
		2	portāv***éritis***	mōv***éritis***	mīs***éritis***	iēc***éritis***	audīv***éritis***
		3	portā́v***erint***	mṓv***erint***	mī́s***erint***	iḗc***erint***	audī́v***erint***
Pluperfect	Singular	1	portāvísse***m***	mōvísse***m***	mīsísse***m***	iēcísse***m***	audīvísse***m***
		2	portāvíssē***s***	mōvíssē***s***	mīsíssē***s***	iēcíssē***s***	audīvíssē***s***
		3	portāvísse***t***	mōvísse***t***	misísse***t***	iēcísse***t***	audīvísse***t***
	Plural	1	portāvissḗ***mus***	mōvissḗ***mus***	mīsissḗ***mus***	iēcissḗ***mus***	audīvissḗ***mus***
		2	portāvissḗ***tis***	mōvissḗ***tis***	mīsissḗ***tis***	iēcissḗ***tis***	audīvissḗ***tis***
		3	portāvísse***nt***	mōvísse***nt***	mīsísse***nt***	iēcísse***nt***	audīvísse***nt***

XVI. Regular Verbs Passive: Subjunctive

			1st Conjugation	2nd Conjugation	3rd Conjugation		4th Conjugation
Present	Singular	1	pórt***er***	móve***ar***	mítt***ar***	iáci***ar***	aúdi***ar***
		2	port***ḗris***	move***ā́ris***	mitt***ā́ris***	iaci***ā́ris***	audi***ā́ris***
		3	port***ḗtur***	move***ā́tur***	mitt***ā́tur***	iaci***ā́tur***	audi***ā́tur***
	Plural	1	port***ḗmur***	move***ā́mur***	mitt***ā́mur***	iaci***ā́mur***	audi***ā́mur***
		2	port***ḗminī***	move***ā́minī***	mitt***ā́minī***	iaci***ā́minī***	audi***ā́minī***
		3	port***éntur***	move***ántur***	mitt***ántur***	iaci***ántur***	audi***ántur***
Imperfect	Singular	1	portā́re***r***	movḗre***r***	míttere***r***	iácere***r***	audī́re***r***
		2	portārḗ***ris***	movērḗ***ris***	mitterḗ***ris***	iacerḗ***ris***	audīrḗ***ris***
		3	portārḗ***tur***	movērḗ***tur***	mitterḗ***tur***	iacerḗ***tur***	audīrḗ***tur***
	Plural	1	portārḗ***mur***	movērḗ***mur***	mitterḗ***mur***	iacerḗ***mur***	audīrḗ***mur***
		2	portārḗ***minī***	movērḗ***minī***	mitterḗ***minī***	iacerḗ***minī***	audīrḗ***minī***
		3	portārḗ***ntur***	movērḗ***ntur***	mitterḗ***ntur***	iacerḗ***ntur***	audīrḗ***ntur***
Perfect		1	portā́tus sim etc.	mṓtus sim etc.	míssus sim etc.	iáctus sim etc.	audī́tus sim etc.
Pluperfect		1	portā́tus éssem etc.	mṓtus éssem etc.	míssus éssem etc.	iáctus éssem etc.	audī́tus éssem etc.

XVII. Deponent Verbs: Infinitive, Imperative, Indicative

			1st Conjugation	2nd Conjugation	3rd Conjugation		4th Conjugation
Present Infinitive			cōn***ā́rī***	ver***ḗrī***	lóqu***ī***	régred***ī***	exper***ī́rī***
Imperative			cōn***ā́re*** cōn***ā́minī***	ver***ḗre*** ver***ḗminī***	lóqu***ere*** loqu***íminī***	regréd***ere*** regred***íminī***	exper***ī́re*** exper***ī́minī***
Present	Singular	1	cṓno***r***	véreo***r***	lóquo***r***	regrédio***r***	expério***r***
		2	cōnā́***ris***	verḗ***ris***	lóque***ris***	regréde***ris***	experī́***ris***
		3	cōnā́***tur***	verḗ***tur***	lóqui***tur***	regrédi***tur***	experī́***tur***
	Plural	1	cōnā́***mur***	verḗ***mur***	lóqui***mur***	regrédi***mur***	experī́***mur***
		2	cōnā́***minī***	verḗ***minī***	loquí***minī***	regredí***minī***	experī́***minī***
		3	cōnā́***ntur***	verḗ***ntur***	loquú***ntur***	regrediú***ntur***	experiú***ntur***
Imperfect	Singular	1	cōnā́***bar***	verḗ***bar***	loquḗ***bar***	regrediḗ***bar***	experiḗ***bar***
		2	cōnā***bā́ris***	verē***bā́ris***	loquē***bā́ris***	regrediē***bā́ris***	experiē***bā́ris***
		3	cōnā***bā́tur***	verē***bā́tur***	loquē***bā́tur***	regrediē***bā́tur***	experiē***bā́tur***
Future	Singular	1	cōnā́***bor***	verā́***bor***	lóqua***r***	regrédia***r***	expéria***r***
		2	cōnā́***beris***	verḗ***beris***	loquḗ***ris***	regrediḗ***ris***	experiḗ***ris***
		3	cōnā́***bitur***	verḗ***bitur***	loquḗ***tur***	regrediḗ***tur***	experiḗ***tur***
Perfect		1	cōnā́tus sum	véritus sum	locū́tus sum	regréssus sum	expértus sum
Pluperfect		1	cōnā́tus éram	véritus éram	locū́tus éram	regréssus éram	expértus éram
Future Perfect		1	cōnā́tus érō	véritus érō	locū́tus érō	regréssus érō	expértus érō

XVIII. Deponent Verbs: Subjunctive

			1st Conjugation	2nd Conjugation	3rd Conjugation		4th Conjugation
Present	Singular	1	cṓn***er***	vére***ar***	lóqu***ar***	regrédi***ar***	expéri***ar***
		2	cōn***ḗris***	vere***ā́ris***	loqu***ā́ris***	regredi***ā́ris***	experi***ā́ris***
		3	cōn***ḗtur***	vere***ā́tur***	loqu***ā́tur***	regredi***ā́tur***	experi***ā́tur***
	Plural	1	cōn***ḗmur***	vere***ā́mur***	loqu***ā́mur***	regredi***ā́mur***	experi***ā́mur***
		2	cōn***ḗminī***	vere***ā́minī***	loqu***ā́minī***	regredi***ā́minī***	experi***ā́minī***
		3	cōn***éntur***	vere***ántur***	loqu***ántur***	regredi***ántur***	experi***ántur***
Imperfect	Singular	1	cōnā́re***r***	verḗre***r***	lóquere***r***	regrēdere***r***	experī́re***r***
		2	cōnārḗ***ris***	verērḗ***ris***	loquerḗ***ris***	regrederḗ***ris***	experīrḗ***ris***
		3	cōnārḗ***tur***	verērḗ***tur***	loquerḗ***tur***	regrederḗ***tur***	experīrḗ***tur***
	Plural	1	cōnārḗ***mur***	verērḗ***mur***	loquerḗ***mur***	regrederḗ***mur***	experīrḗ***mur***
		2	cōnārḗ***minī***	verērḗ***minī***	loquerḗ***minī***	regrederḗ***minī***	experīrḗ***minī***
		3	cōnārḗ***ntur***	verērḗ***ntur***	loquerḗ***ntur***	regrederḗ***ntur***	experīrḗ***ntur***
Perfect		1	cōnā́tus sim etc.	véritus sim etc.	locū́tus sim etc.	regréssus sim etc.	expértus sim etc.
Pluperfect		1	cōnā́tus éssem etc.	véritus éssem etc.	locū́tus éssem etc.	regréssus éssem etc.	expértus éssem etc.

XIX. Irregular Verbs: Infinitive, Imperative, Indicative

Infinitive			ésse	pósse	vélle	nṓlle	mā́lle
Imperative			es	——	——	nṓl**ī**	——
			és**te**	——	——	nōl**ī́te**	——
Present	**Singular**	1	su**m**	pós**sum**	vól**ō**	nṓl**ō**	mā́l**ō**
		2	e**s**	pót**es**	vī**s**	nōn vī**s**	mā́vī**s**
		3	es**t**	pót**est**	vul**t**	nōn vul**t**	mā́vul**t**
	Plural	1	sú**mus**	pós**sumus**	vólu**mus**	nṓlu**mus**	mā́lu**mus**
		2	és**tis**	pot**éstis**	vúl**tis**	nōn vúl**tis**	māvúl**tis**
		3	su**nt**	pós**sunt**	vólu**nt**	nṓlu**nt**	mā́lu**nt**
Imperfect	**Singular**	1	éra**m**	pót**eram**	volḗ**bam**	nōlḗ**bam**	mālḗ**bam**
		2	erā**s**	pót**erās**	volḗ**bās**	nōlḗ**bās**	mālḗ**bās**
		3	éra**t**	pót**erat**	volḗ**bat**	nōlḗ**bat**	mālḗ**bat**
	Plural	1	erā́**mus**	pot**erā́mus**	volē**bā́mus**	nōlē**bā́mus**	mālē**bā́mus**
		2	erā́**tis**	pot**erā́tis**	volē**bā́tis**	nōlē**bā́tis**	mālē**bā́tis**
		3	éra**nt**	pót**erant**	volḗ**bant**	nōlḗ**bant**	mālḗ**bant**
Future	**Singular**	1	ér**ō**	pót**erō**	vōl**am**	nṓl**am**	mā́l**am**
		2	ér**is**	pót**eris**	vól**ēs**	nṓl**ēs**	mā́l**ēs**
		3	ér**it**	pót**erit**	vól**et**	nṓl**et**	mā́l**et**
	Plural	1	éri**mus**	pot**érimus**	vol**ḗmus**	nōl**ḗmus**	māl**ḗmus**
		2	éri**tis**	pot**éritis**	vol**ḗtis**	nōl**ḗtis**	māl**ḗtis**
		3	éru**nt**	pót**erunt**	vól**ent**	nṓl**ent**	mā́l**ent**

Infinitive			férre	férrī	fíerī	ī́re
Imperative			fer	férre	——	ī
			fér**te**	ferí**minī**	——	ī́**te**
Present	**Singular**	1	fér**ō**	féro**r**	fī́**ō**	é**ō**
		2	fer**s**	fér**ris**	fī**s**	ī**s**
		3	fer**t**	fér**tur**	fi**t**	i**t**
	Plural	1	féri**mus**	féri**mur**	fī́**mus**	ī́**mus**
		2	fér**tis**	ferí**minī**	fī́**tis**	ī́**tis**
		3	féru**nt**	ferú**ntur**	fī́u**nt**	éu**nt**
Imperfect	**Singular**	1	ferḗ**bam**	ferḗ**bar**	fīḗ**bam**	ī́**bam**
		2	ferḗ**bās**	ferē**bā́ris**	fīḗ**bās**	ī́**bās**
		3	ferḗ**bat**	ferē**bā́tur**	fīḗ**bat**	ī́**bat**
	Plural	1	ferē**bā́mus**	ferē**bā́mur**	fīē**bā́mus**	ī**bā́mus**
		2	ferē**bā́tis**	ferē**bā́minī**	fīē**bā́tis**	ī**bā́tis**
		3	ferḗ**bant**	ferē**bántur**	fīḗ**bant**	ī́**bant**
Future	**Singular**	1	fér**am**	fér**ar**	fī́**am**	ī́**bō**
		2	fér**ēs**	fer**ḗris**	fī́**ēs**	ī**bis**
		3	fér**et**	fer**ḗtur**	fī́**et**	ī**bit**
	Plural	1	fer**ḗmus**	fer**ḗmur**	fī**ḗmus**	ī**bimus**
		2	fer**ḗtis**	fer**ḗminī**	fī**ḗtis**	ī́**bitis**
		3	fér**ent**	fer**éntur**	fī́**ent**	ī́**bunt**

XX. Irregular Verbs: Perfect, Pluperfect, Future Pefect Indicative

Full charts are not supplied for these forms because (except for the perfect of **eō**, for which see below) they are not irregular in any way. They are made in the same way as the perfect, pluperfect, and future perfect tenses of regular verbs, by adding the perfect, pluperfect and future perfect endings to the perfect stem. The perfect stem is found by dropping the ***-ī*** from the third principal part. The first three principal parts of the irregular verbs are as follows:

sum, esse, fu***ī***
possum, posse, potu***ī***
volō, velle, volu***ī***
nōlō, nōlle, nōlu***ī***
mālō, mālle, mālu***ī***
ferō, ferre, tul***ī***
eō, īre, i*ī* or īv***ī***

Examples:

Perfect: fuistī, voluērunt, tulimus
Pluperfect: fueram, potuerant, nōluerāmus
Future Perfect: fuerō, volueris, tulerimus

The perfect forms of **eō** made from the stem **i-** are as follows:

Singular: iī, īstī, iit
Plural: iimus, īstis, iērunt

Note that the stem vowel (**i-**) contracts with the *-i* of the endings ***-istī*** and ***-istis*** to give **ī-** (**īstī, īstis**). Thus also the perfect infinitive: **īsse** (for **iisse**).

The perfect forms of **eō** made from the stem **īv-** are regular, as follows:

Singular: īvī, īvistī, īvit
Plural: īvimus, īvistis, īvērunt

XXI. Irregular Verbs: Subjunctive

Present	Singular	1	s***im***	póss***im***	vél***im***	nṓl***im***	mā́l***im***
		2	s***īs***	póss***īs***	vél***īs***	nṓl***īs***	mā́l***īs***
		3	s***it***	póss***it***	vél***it***	nṓl***it***	mā́l***it***
	Plural	1	s***ī́mus***	poss***ī́mus***	vel***ī́mus***	nōl***ī́mus***	māl***ī́mus***
		2	s***ī́tis***	poss***ī́tis***	vel***ī́tis***	nōl***ī́tis***	māl***ī́tis***
		3	s***int***	póss***int***	vél***int***	nōl***int***	mā́l***int***
Imperfect	Singular	1	ésse***m***	pósse***m***	vélle***m***	nṓlle***m***	mā́lle***m***
		2	éssē***s***	póssē***s***	véllē***s***	nṓllē***s***	mā́llē***s***
		3	ésse***t***	pósse***t***	vélle***t***	nṓlle***t***	mā́lle***t***
	Plural	1	essḗ***mus***	possḗ***mus***	vellḗ***mus***	nōllḗ***mus***	māllḗ***mus***
		2	essḗ***tis***	possḗ***tis***	vellḗ***tis***	nōllḗ***tis***	māllḗ***tis***
		3	ésse***nt***	pósse***nt***	vélle***nt***	nṓlle***nt***	mā́lle***nt***
Perfect	Singular	1	fú***erim***	potú***erim***	volú***erim***	nōlú***erim***	mālú***erim***
		2	fú***eris***	potú***eris***	volú***eris***	nōlú***eris***	mālú***eris***
		3	fú***erit***	potú***erit***	volú***erit***	nōlú***erit***	mālú***erit***
	Plural	1	fu***ḗrimus***	potu***ḗrimus***	volu***ḗrimus***	nōlu***ḗrimus***	mālu***ḗrimus***
		2	fu***ḗritis***	potu***ḗritis***	volu***ḗritis***	nōlu***ḗritis***	mālu***ḗritis***
		3	fú***erint***	potú***erint***	volú***erint***	nōlú***erint***	mālú***erint***
Pluperfect	Singular	1	fuísse***m***	potuísse***m***	voluísse***m***	nōluísse***m***	māluísse***m***
		2	fuíssē***s***	posuíssē***s***	voluíssē***s***	nōluíssē***s***	māluíssē***s***
		3	fuísse***t***	potuísse***t***	voluísse***t***	nōluísse***t***	māluísse***t***
	Plural	1	fuissḗ***mus***	potuissḗ***mus***	voluissḗ***mus***	nōluissḗ***mus***	māluissḗ***mus***
		2	fuissḗ***tis***	potuissḗ***tis***	voluissḗ***tis***	nōluissḗ***tis***	māluissḗ***tis***
		3	fuísse***nt***	potuísse***nt***	voluísse***nt***	nōluísse***nt***	māluísse***nt***

Present	Singular	1	fér***am***	fér***ar***	fī́***am***	é***am***
		2	fér***ās***	fer***ā́ris***	fī́***ās***	é***ās***
		3	fér***at***	fer***ā́tur***	fī́***at***	é***at***
	Plural	1	fer***ā́mus***	fer***ā́mur***	fī***ā́mus***	e***ā́mus***
		2	fer***ā́tis***	fer***ā́minī***	fī***ā́tis***	e***ā́tis***
		3	fér***ant***	fer***ántur***	fī́***ant***	é***ant***
Imperfect	Singular	1	férre***m***	férre***r***	fíere***m***	ī́re***m***
		2	férrē***s***	ferrḗ***ris***	fíerē***s***	ī́rē***s***
		3	férre***t***	ferrḗ***tur***	fíere***t***	ī́re***t***
	Plural	1	ferrḗ***mus***	ferrḗ***mur***	fierḗ***mus***	īrḗ***mus***
		2	ferrḗ***tis***	ferrḗ***minī***	fierḗ***tis***	īrḗ***tis***
		3	férre***nt***	ferré***ntur***	fíere***nt***	ī́re***nt***
Perfect	Singular	1	túl***erim***	lā́tus sim	fáctus sim	í***erim***
		2	túl***eris***	lā́tus sīs	fáctus sīs	í***eris***
		3	túl***erit***	lā́tus sit	fáctus sit	í***erit***
	Plural	1	tul***ḗrimus***	lā́tī sī́mus	fáctī sī́mus	i***ḗrimus***
		2	tul***ḗritis***	lā́tī sī́tis	fáctī sī́tis	i***ḗritis***
		3	túl***erint***	lā́tī sint	fáctī sint	í***erint***
Pluperfect	Singular	1	tulísse***m***	lā́tus éssem	fáctus éssem	ī́sse***m***
		2	tulíssē***s***	lā́tus éssēs	fáctus éssēs	ī́ssē***s***
		3	tulísse***t***	lā́tus ésset	fáctus ésset	ī́sse***t***
	Plural	1	tulissḗ***mus***	lā́tī essḗmus	fáctī essḗmus	īssḗ***mus***
		2	tulissḗ***tis***	lā́tī essḗtis	fáctī essḗtis	īssḗ***tis***
		3	tulísse***nt***	lā́tī éssent	fáctī éssent	ī́sse***nt***

Note: the perfect subjunctive of **eō** may be **ierim,** etc., as above, or **īverim.** The pluperfect subjunctive of **eō** may be **īssem,** etc., as above, or **īvissem.**

XXII. Participles of Non-deponent Verbs

		Active	Passive
Present	1	párāns, parántis	
	2	hábēns, habéntis	
	3	míttēns, mitténtis	
	-iō	iáciēns, iaciéntis	
	4	aúdiēns, audiéntis	
Perfect	1		parā́tus, -a, -um
	2		hábitus, -a, -um
	3		míssus, -a, -um
	-iō		iáctus, -a, -um
	4		audī́tus, -a, -um
Future	1	parātū́rus, -a, -um	
	2	habitū́rus, -a, -um	
	3	missū́rus, -a, -um	
	-iō	iactū́rus, -a, -um	
	4	audītū́rus, -a, -um	

XXIII. Participles of Deponent Verbs

Present Participle	1	cṓnāns, cōnántis
	2	vérēns, veréntis
	3	lóquēns, loquéntis
	-iō	ēgrédiēns, ēgrediéntis
	4	expériēns, experiéntis
Perfect Participle	1	cōnā́tus, -a, -um
	2	véritus, -a, -um
	3	locū́tus, -a, -um
	-iō	ēgréssus, -a, -um
	4	expértus, -a, -um
Future Participle	1	cōnātū́rus, -a, -um
	2	veritū́rus, -a, -um
	3	locūtū́rus, -a, -um
	-iō	ēgressū́rus, -a, -um
	4	expertū́rus, -a, -um

XXIV. Infinitives of Non-deponent Verbs

		Active	Passive
Present	1	paráre	parárī
	2	habére	habérī
	3	míttere	míttī
	-iō	iácere	iácī
	4	audíre	audírī
Perfect	1	parāvísse	parátus, -a, -um ésse
	2	habuísse	hábitus, -a, -um ésse
	3	mīsísse	míssus, -a, -um ésse
	-iō	iēcísse	iáctus, -a, -um ésse
	4	audīvísse	audítus, -a, -um ésse
Future	1	parātúrus, -a, -um ésse	
	2	habitúrus, -a, -um ésse	
	3	missúrus, -a, -um ésse	
	-iō	iactúrus, -a, -um ésse	
	4	audītúrus, -a, -um ésse	

XXV. Infinitives of Deponent Verbs

Present	1	cōnárī
	2	verérī
	3	lóquī
	-iō	égredī
	4	experírī
Perfect	1	cōnátus, -a, -um ésse
	2	véritus, -a, -um ésse
	3	locútus, -a, -um ésse
	-iō	ēgréssus, -a, -um ésse
	4	expértus, -a, -um ésse
Future	1	cōnātúrus, -a, -um ésse
	2	veritúrus, -a, -um ésse
	3	locūtúrus, -a, -um ésse
	-iō	ēgressúrus, -a, -um ésse
	4	expertúrus, -a, -um ésse

REFERENCE GRAMMAR

I. NOUNS

A. Nominative Case

1. Subject
   A noun or pronoun in the nominative case may be the subject of a verb:

   In pictūrā est **puella....** (1:1)
   *A **girl** is in the picture....*

2. Complement
   A linking verb may be accompanied by a complement in the nominative case:

   Cornēlia est **puella....** (1:1)
   *Cornelia is a **girl**....*

   Cornēlia est **laeta....** (1:2–3)
   *Cornelia is **happy**....*

   While the verb **esse** is the most common linking verb, the verbs in the following sentences are also classed as linking verbs and have complements in the nominative case:

   "Quam **scelestus** ille caupō <u>vidētur</u>!" (21:22)
   *"How **wicked** that innkeeper <u>seems</u>!"*

   "'Nōn sine causā tū <u>vocāris</u> **Pseudolus**.'" (31:23)
   *"'Not without reason <u>are</u> you <u>called</u> **Pseudolus**.'"*

   "Quis <u>creābitur</u> **arbiter** bibendī?" (34:4)
   *"Who <u>will be chosen</u> **master** of the drinking?"*

   <u>Fit</u> in diēs **molestior**. (34h:16)
   *"He <u>becomes</u> **more troublesome** every day."*

B. Genitive Case (see Book I, page 80)

The genitive case usually relates or attaches one noun to another.

1. Genitive of Possession

   ...vīlicus ipse <u>vīllam</u> **dominī** cūrat. (11:3)
   *...the overseer himself looks after the <u>country house</u> **of the master**.*

2. Genitive with Adjectives
   Words or phrases in the genitive case may be found with certain adjectives, especially those having to do with fullness:

   Brevī tempore ārea est <u>plēna</u> **servōrum** et **ancillārum....** (11:4)
   *In a short time the threshing-floor is <u>full</u> **of slaves and slave-women....***

3. Partitive Genitive
A word or phrase in the genitive case may indicate the whole of which something is a part (see Book I, page 229):

"<u>Nihil</u> **malī**," inquit. (21:7)
"<u>Nothing</u> ***of a bad thing***,*" he said.*
"*Nothing bad*" or "*There is nothing wrong.*"

Crās <u>satis</u> **temporis** habēbimus. (23f:14)
Tomorrow we will have <u>enough</u> ***(of) time***.

With numbers and the words **paucī,** *a few*, **quīdam,** *a certain*, and **nūllus,** *no*, *no one*, the preposition **ex** or **dē** with the ablative is used:

<u>ūnus</u> **ē praedōnibus** (26:24)
<u>one</u> ***of the robbers***

The partitive genitive is used with superlative adjectives and adverbs (see Book II, pages 64 and 76):

Titus erat bibendī arbiter <u>pessimus</u> **omnium**. (34:24)
Titus was the <u>worst</u> master of the drinking ***of all***.

Hic puer <u>optimē</u> **omnium** scrībit. (35h:2)
This boy writes <u>best</u> ***of all***.

4. Genitive of Indefinite Value
The genitive case may be found in statements or questions of the general value of something (compare this with the ablative of price, below):

"'**Quantī**,' inquit Pseudolus, 'est illa perna?'" (31:7–8)
"'***How much***,' *says Pseudolus, 'is that ham?'*"

C. Dative Case

1. Indirect Object of Transitive Verbs
A word or phrase in the dative case may indicate the indirect object of transitive verbs, especially verbs of "giving," "telling," or "showing" (see Book I, pages 186–187 and 189 and Exercise 22d):

...servī cistās Cornēliōrum **raedāriō** <u>trādidērunt</u>. (22:2)
...the slaves <u>handed</u> the chests of the Cornelii <u>over</u> ***to the coachman.***

2. Dative with Intransitive Verbs
Intransitive verbs and verbs that may be transitive but are used without a direct object may be accompanied by words or phrases in the dative case (see Book I, page 189):

Aulus **Septimō** <u>clāmāvit</u>. (21:8–9)
Aulus <u>shouted</u> ***to Septimus***.

3. Dative with Intransitive Compound Verbs
   Many intransitive compound verbs are accompanied by words or phrases in the dative case (see Book I, page 212):

   Iam **urbī** <u>appropinquābant</u>. (22:12)
   *Already <u>they were coming near to/approaching</u> **the city**.*

4. Dative with Special Intransitive Verbs (see Book I, page 253)
   The dative case is used with special intransitive verbs such as **cōnfīdere**, *to trust*, **favēre**, *to (give) favor (to), to (give) support (to)*, **nocēre**, *to do harm (to)*, and **placēre**, *to please*:

   Ego **russātīs** <u>favēbō</u>. (27:25)
   *I <u>will give favor</u> **to the reds**.*
   *I <u>will favor</u> **the reds**.*

5. Dative with Impersonal Verbal Phrases and Impersonal Verbs
   The dative case is found with impersonal verbal phrases such as **necesse est** and with impersonal verbs (see Book I, page 190):

   "**Nōbīs** <u>necesse est</u> statim discēdere." (9:13–14)
   *"<u>It is necessary</u> **for us** to leave immediately."*

   "<u>Licet</u>ne **nōbīs**," inquit Marcus, "hīc cēnāre?" (20:7)
   *"<u>Is it allowed</u> **for us**," said Marcus, "to dine here?"*
   "May we dine here?"

6. Dative with Verbs of Taking Away or Depriving
   A word in the dative case sometimes denotes the person or thing from which something is taken:

   Mihi <u>est adēmptum</u> baculum…. (35:20)
   *(My) stick <u>was taken away</u> **from me**….*

7. Dative of Possession
   When found with a form of the verb **esse,** the dative case may indicate possession; the thing possessed is the subject of the clause and the person who possesses it is in the dative:

   …servus quīdam **cui** nōmen <u>est</u> Pseudolus. (31:5–6)
   *…a certain slave, **to whom** the name <u>is</u> Pseudolus.*
   …whose name is Pseudolus.
   …who has the name Pseudolus.

8. Dative of Purpose
   A noun in the dative case may express purpose:

   Hanc pūpam fīliae Dāvī **dōnō** dabō. (46:19–20)
   *I will give this doll to the daughter of Davus **to serve as a gift**.*
   *I will give this doll **as a gift** to the daughter of Davus.*

9. Double Dative
Two datives may be used together in what is called the double dative construction. One of the datives is a dative of reference, denoting the person or thing concerned, and the other is a dative of purpose:

Omnēs **spectātōribus admīrātiōnī** fuērunt leōnēs. (49:1–2)
All the lions were ***a source of amazement with reference to the spectators.***
All the lions were ***a source of amazement to the spectators.***

10. Dative of Agent
With the passive periphrastic conjugation (see V. D, Gerundive or Future Passive Participle, below), consisting of the gerundive and a form of the verb **esse**, the person by whom the thing is to be done is regularly denoted by the dative, not by **ab** and the ablative:

"Nunc...domum **nōbīs** redeundum est." (48:20)
"Now...there must be a returning home ***by us.***"
"Now...we must return home."

D. Accusative Case

1. Direct Object
A word or phrase in the accusative case may be the direct object of a transitive verb (see Book I, pages 20 and 40–41):

Sextus...semper **Cornēliam** vexat. (4:1)
Sextus...is always annoying ***Cornelia.***

2. Double or Predicate Accusative
Verbs of naming, electing, making, and asking often take two accusatives, the first the direct object and the second a predicate to that object:

Cēterōs...puerōs semper **facillima, mē** semper **difficillima** rogat. (40:18)

He always (asks) ***the other boys very easy things, me*** *he always asks* ***very difficult things.***

3. Accusative with Prepositions
The accusative case is used with certain prepositions, especially those expressing motion toward or into or through (see Book I page 64):

ad **vīllam**, *to/toward* ***the country house*** (2:7)
in **piscīnam**, *into* ***the fishpond*** (3:8)
per **agrōs**, *through* ***the fields*** (9:1)

Prepositional phrases with the accusative case may also indicate the vicinity in which someone or something is located:

<u>prope</u> **rīvum** (5:3)
*<u>near</u> **the stream***
...iānitor <u>ad</u> **iānuam** vīllae dormit. (9:3)
*...the doorkeeper sleeps <u>near/at</u> **the door** of the country house.*

4. Accusative of Place to Which without a Preposition
   With names of cities, towns, small islands, and the words **domus** and **rūs**, the idea of place to which is expressed by the accusative case without a preposition (see Book II, pages 118–120):

   Rōmam festīnāvit.
   *He hurried **to Rome**.*

   Domum iit.
   *He went **home**.*

   Rūs proficīscitur.
   *He sets out **for the country**.*

5. Accusative of Duration of Time
   Words or phrases in the accusative case without a preposition may indicate duration of time (see Book II, page 121):

   Iam **multōs diēs** in scaphā erāmus.... (42:38)
   *We had already been in the boat **for many days**....*

6. Adverbial Accusative
   A word in the accusative case may be used as an adverb:

   Multum et diū clāmat lanius, sed Pseudolus **nihil** respondet. (31:25)
   *The butcher shouts **a lot** and for a long time, but Pseudolus makes **no** reply.*

7. Exclamatory Accusative
   The accusative case is used in exclamations:

   "**Ō mē miseram!**" (9:18) ***"Poor me!"***

8. For the accusative and infinitive, see IX.D–F below.

E. Ablative Case

1. Ablative of Respect
   A noun or phrase in the ablative may denote that with respect to which something is or is done:

   In pictūrā est puella, **nōmine** Cornēlia. (1:1)
   *In the picture is a girl, Cornelia **with respect to her name**.*
   *In the picture is a girl, Cornelia **by name/called** Cornelia.*

2. Ablative of Time When
   A noun or phrase in the ablative case without a preposition may indicate time when:

   Etiam in pictūrā est vīlla rūstica ubi Cornēlia **aestāte** habitat. (1:2)
   Also in the picture is the country house and farm where Cornelia lives ***in summer***.

3. Ablative of Time within Which
   A noun or phrase in the ablative case without a preposition may indicate time within which:

   Brevī tempore Cornēlia est dēfessa. (2:4–5)
   In/Within a short time *Cornelia is tired.*

4. Ablative of Instrument, Means, or Cause
   A word or phrase in the ablative case without a preposition may indicate the means by which, the instrument with which, or the cause on account of which an action is carried out or a person or thing is in a certain state (see Book I, page 91, Book I, page 213, and Book II, pages 34–35):

   Dāvus eum **tunicā** <u>arripit</u> et **baculō** <u>verberat</u>. (means, instrument, 12:17–18)
   Davus <u>grabs hold of</u> him ***by the tunic*** *and <u>beats</u> him* ***with his stick***.

   Tuā culpā raeda <u>est in fossā</u>. (cause, 14:7)
   Because of your fault *the carriage <u>is in the ditch</u>.*
   It's your fault that the carriage is in the ditch.

   The ablative of instrument, means, or cause is often used with passive verbs (see Book II, page 35):

   ...nam interdiū nihil intrā urbem **vehiculō** <u>portātur</u>. (29:3–4)
   ...for during the day nothing <u>is carried</u> ***by a vehicle*** *within the city.*

5. Ablative of Agent
   If the action of a passive verb is carried out by a person, the ablative of agent is used, consisting of the preposition **ā** or **ab** with the ablative case (see Book II, page 35):

   ...māter et fīlia **ā servīs** per urbem <u>ferēbantur</u>. (29:1–2)
   ...the mother and her daughter <u>were being carried</u> through the city ***by slaves***.

6. Ablative of Manner
   A phrase consisting of a noun and adjective in the ablative case may be used with or without the preposition **cum** to indicate how something happens or is done (see Book II, page 34):

   Tum venit Dāvus ipse et, "Tacēte, omnēs!" **magnā vōce/magnā cum vōce** clāmat. (11:6)
   *Then Davus himself comes, and he shouts **in a loud voice**, "Be quiet, everyone!"*

   The ablative of manner may consist of a single noun with **cum**:

   Caupō iam **cum rīsū** clāmāvit.... (19:17)
   *Now **with a laugh/jokingly** the innkeeper shouted....*

   Occasionally the ablative of manner may consist of a noun in the ablative case without an accompanying adjective or **cum**:

   Tum ego **silentiō** ingressus.... (42:34)
   *Then I having entered **silently**....*

7. Ablative of Price
   The ablative case is used to refer to the specific price of something (compare this with the genitive of indefinite value, above):

   "'Itaque tibi **decem dēnāriīs** eum vēndam.'" (31:17–18)
   *"'Therefore I will sell it to you **for ten denarii**.'"*

8. Ablative of Comparison
   The ablative of comparison may be found with comparative adjectives and adverbs (see Book II, pages 72 and 76):

   Mārtiālis **Eucleide** est multō prūdentior. (35d:4)
   *Martial is much wiser **than** Eucleides.*

   Sextus paulō celerius **Marcō** currere potest. (35h:4)
   *Sextus can run a little faster **than** Marcus.*

9. Ablative of Degree of Difference
   The ablative case is used to express the degree of difference with comparative adjectives, adverbs, and other words implying comparison (see Book II, pages 72 and 76):

   "Quam libenter eum rūrsus vidēbō! Sānē tamen **multō** libentius tē vidēbō ubi tū Rōmam veniēs!" (36:10–11)
   *"How gladly I will see him again! But of course I will see you **much** more gladly/more gladly **by much** when you come to Rome!"*

   Multīs post **annīs**...pervēnit. (39c:3)
   *"He arrived...**many years** later/later **by many years**.*

10. Ablative of Separation
Verbs or adjectives implying separation are often accompanied by words or phrases in the ablative, sometimes with **ab** or **ex** and sometimes without a preposition, to express the thing from which something is separated or free:

...vir **vīnō** abstinentissimus! (34h:28)
...a man most abstinent ***from wine!***

11. Ablative with Prepositions
The ablative case is used with certain prepositions, especially those expressing motion from or out of, place where, and accompaniment (see Book I, pages 64 and 90):

ab **urbe**, *from* ***the city*** (13:12)
ē **silvā**, *out of* ***the woods*** (5:12)
ex **agrīs**, *out of* ***the fields*** (2:7)
in **pictūrā**, *in* ***the picture*** (1:1)
sub **arbore**, *under* ***the tree*** (1:3)
cum **canibus**, *with* ***dogs*** (12:9)

12. Ablative of Place from Which without a Preposition
With names of cities, towns, small islands, and the words **domus** and **rūs**, the idea of place from which is expressed by the ablative case without a preposition (see Book II, page 119):

Brundisiō...proficīscētur.... (36:8–9)
He will set out ***from Brundisium****....*

Domō/Rūre profectus est.
He set out ***from home/from the country****.*

13. Ablative of Description
A noun and adjective in the ablative case may be used without a preposition to describe another noun:

[Vergilius] semper **īnfirmā** erat **valētūdine**. (39f:9–10)
[Vergil] was always ***of weak health****.*

14. Ablative Absolute
A noun (or pronoun) and a participle in the ablative case form an ablative absolute, an adverbial phrase separate from the rest of the sentence and often set off with commas (see Book II, page 177). Ablatives absolute are best translated in English with clauses introduced by *when*, *although*, *since*, or *if*.

Titus..., **pecūniā datā,** in vestibulum ingressus est. (43:4)
Titus..., ***with his money having been given,*** *entered the vestibule.*
*...**after paying his entrance fee**,...*

Fūre vestīmenta **surripiente,** Sextus in apodytērium ingrediēbātur.
While the thief was stealing *the clothes, Sextus was entering the changing room.*

Since classical Latin has no present participle for the verb **esse,** ablatives absolute sometimes consist only of two nouns in the ablative case or a noun and an adjective:

Titō prīncipe....	**Sextō aegrō....**
Titus (being) Emperor....	***Sextus (being) sick....***
When Titus is (was) Emperor....	***Since Sextus is (was) sick....***

F. Vocative Case
The vocative case is used when addressing a person or persons directly (see Book I, page 56):

"Dēscende, **Sexte**!" (4:6)
"Come down, ***Sextus!****"*

"Abīte, **molestī**!" (3:8–9)
"Go away, ***pests!****"*

G. Locative Case
The locative case is used to indicate place where with names of cities, towns, small islands, and the words **domus** and **rūs** (see Book II, pages 119–120):

Rōmae *at Rome*, **Brundisiī** *at Brundisium*, **Carthāginī** *at Carthage*, **Baiīs** *at Baiae*, **domī** *at home*, and **rūrī** *in the country*

II. ADJECTIVES

A. Agreement
Adjectives agree with the nouns they modify in gender, number, and case (see Book I, pages 139–140).

B. Adjectives Translated as Adverbs
Adjectives may sometimes best be translated as adverbs:

Brevī tempore, ubi Marcus advenit, eum **laetae** excipiunt. (5:12–13)
In a short time, when Marcus arrives, they welcome him ***happily****.*

C. Adjectives as Substantives
Adjectives may be used as substantives, i.e., as nouns (see Book I, page 200):

"Abīte, **molestī**!" (3:8–9)
"Go away, ***pests!****"*

Multa et **mīra** vidēbunt puerī. (23:12)
The boys will see ***many*** *(and)* ***wonderful (things)****.*

D. Comparison of Adjectives

Adjectives occur in positive, comparative, and superlative degrees (see Book II, pages 64 and 65). For an example of a comparative adjective, see **prūdentior** in I.E.8 above, and for an example of a superlative adjective, see **pessimus** in I.B.3 above.

Instead of following the rules given in Book II, page 65, a few adjectives form their comparative and superlative degrees with the adverbs **magis** and **maximē:**

Paulātim igitur fīēbat **magis ēbrius?** (34h:21)
*Did he therefore gradually become **more drunk?***

Statim factus est **maximē ēbrius**.... (34h:22)
*Suddenly he became **very drunk.***

Comparative adjectives may be used with **quam** or with the ablative case to express the comparison (see Book II, pages 64 and 72):

"Quis enim est prūdentior **quam** Gaius?" (34:7)
"Quis enim est prūdentior **Gaiō**?"
*"For who is wiser **than** Gaius?"*

Mārtiālis est multō prūdentior **quam** Eucleidēs.
Mārtiālis **Eucleide** est multō prūdentior. (35d:4)
*Martial is much wiser **than** Eucleides.*

Superlative adjectives may be used with the partitive genitive, see I.B.3 above.

III. ADVERBS

A. Adverbs may modify verbs, other adverbs, or adjectives (see Book I, pages 100–101):

Laeta est Flāvia quod Cornēlia **iam** in vīllā habitat. (1:5)
*Flavia is happy because Cornelia is **now** living in the country house.*

Scrībe **quam** saepissimē. (36:25)
*Write **as** often **as possible.***

"**Valdē** dēfessī," respondit Cornēlius. (23:9)
*"**Very** tired," replied Cornelius.*

B. Comparison of Adverbs

Adverbs occur in positive, comparative, and superlative degrees (see Book II, pages 74–76). For an example of a comparative adverb, see **celerius** in I.E.8 above, and for an example of a superlative adverb, see **optimē** in I.B.3 above.

The comparative adverb may be used with **quam** or with the ablative case:

Nēmō celerius **quam** frāter meus currere potest. (35h:3)
*No one is able to run faster **than** my brother.*

Sextus celerius **Marcō** currere potest. (35h:4)
*Sextus is able to run faster **than** Marcus.*

The superlative adverb may be used with a partitive genitive, see I.B.3 above.

IV. VERBS

A. Function

Verbs may be divided into three types according to their function in the sentence or clause:

1. Linking verbs connect a subject with a predicate noun or adjective:

   <u>Cornēlia</u> **est** <u>puella Rōmāna</u>. (1:1) *<u>Cornelia</u> **is** <u>a Roman girl</u>.*

   For other examples, see I.A.2 above.

2. Intransitive verbs describe actions that do not take direct objects:

   Cornēlia...in Italiā **habitat**. (1:1–2) *Cornelia **lives** in Italy.*

3. Transitive verbs describe actions that take direct objects:

   Sextus...semper <u>Cornēliam</u> **vexat**. (4:1)
   *Sextus...always **annoys** <u>Cornelia</u>.*

B. Voice

1. Active and Passive

   Verbs may be either active or passive in voice. In the active voice the subject performs the action of the verb; in the passive voice the subject receives the action of the verb (see Book II, pages 23–24, 33, and 42–43):

   <u>Incolae</u> omnia **agunt**. (active, Book II, page 23)
   *<u>The tenants</u> **are doing** everything.*

   Ab incolīs <u>omnia</u> **aguntur**. (passive, Book II, page 23)
   *<u>Everything</u> **is being done** by the tenants.*

2. Deponent Verbs

   Some verbs, called deponent, are passive in form but active in meaning (see Book II, pages 98–100):

   Subitō **collāpsus est.** (34:22) *Suddenly **he collapsed.***

3. Semi-deponent Verbs

   Some verbs, such as **audeō, audēre, ausus sum**, have regular active forms with active meanings in the present, imperfect, and future tenses but have passive forms with active meanings in the perfect, pluperfect, and future perfect tenses (see Book II, pages 132–133):

   Tum Marcus arborem ascendit neque dēsilīre **ausus est**. (40:10–11)
   *Then Marcus climbed a tree and **did** not **dare** jump down.*

4. Impersonal Passive

   Verbs may be used impersonally in the passive to place emphasis on the action itself rather than on any of the participants in it:

   Complūrēs hōrās ācriter **pugnābātur**.... (48:18)
   ***The fighting went on** fiercely for several hours....*

5. Impersonal Verbs

   See Book II, pages 278–279, and IX.c, Uses of the Infinitive, below.

C. Tenses of the Indicative

1. Present

   The present tense describes an action or a state of being in present time (see Book I, page 73):

   In pictūrā **est** puella...quae in Italiā **habitat**. (1:1–2)
   *In the picture **is** a girl...who **lives** in Italy.*

2. Vivid or Historic Present

   Sometimes a writer will switch to the present tense while describing past events; this is called the vivid or historic present and helps make the reader feel personally involved in the narrative (see Book II, page 23).

3. Imperfect

   The imperfect tense (see Book I, page 106) describes a continuing, repeated, or habitual action or state of being in past time:

   Ego et Marcus **spectābāmus** cisium. (continuing action, 14:10)
   *Marcus and I **were watching** the carriage.*

   Cornēlius...Syrum identidem **iubēbat** equōs incitāre. (repeated action, 13:1–2)
   *Cornelius **kept ordering** Syrus again and again to spur on the horses.*

   Dāvus in Britanniā **habitābat**. (habitual action)
   *Davus **used to live** in Britain.*

The imperfect tense may also indicate the beginning of an action in past time (see Book I, page 107):

Equōs ad raedam nostram **dēvertēbat**. (14:11)
*He **began to turn** the horses **aside** in the direction of our carriage.*

The imperfect tense with **iam** and an expression of duration of time is often best translated in English with a pluperfect:

Iam <u>multōs diēs</u> in scaphā **erāmus** cum ā mercātōribus quibusdam inventī sumus. (42:38)
*We **had already been** in the boat <u>for many days</u> when we were found by certain merchants.*

4. Future
   The future tense indicates an action that will take place at some time subsequent to the present (see Book I, page 201):

   "Brevī tempore ad Portam Capēnam **adveniēmus**...." (22:26)
   *"In a short time **we will arrive** at the Porta Capena...."*

5. Perfect System
   The perfect, pluperfect, and future perfect tenses are formed from the perfect stem, which is derived from the third principal part of the verb.

   a. The perfect tense refers to an action that happened or that someone did in past time or to an action completed as of present time (see Book I, pages 150–151):

      Eō ipsō tempore ad iānuam caupōnae **appāruit** homō obēsus... (18:12)
      *At that very moment a fat man **appeared** at the door of the inn....*

      "Servī meī alium lectum tibi **parāvērunt**." (19:17–18)
      *"My slaves **have prepared** another bed for you."*

   b. The pluperfect tense describes an action that was completed prior to some other action in the past (see Book I, page 213):

      Titus in itinere mōnstrāvit puerīs mīra aedificia quae prīncipēs in Palātīnō **aedificāverant**. (24:19–20)
      *Along the way Titus showed the boys the wonderful buildings that the emperors **had built** on the Palatine.*

   c. The future perfect tense describes an action that will have been completed before another action in future time begins (see Book I, page 218):

      "Cum **intrāverimus**, tandem aurīgās ipsōs spectābimus." (26:17–18)
      *"When we **enter/will have entered**, we will finally watch the charioteers themselves."*

D. Mood

1. Indicative Mood

   The term *indicative mood* refers to a set of verb forms that are used to express statements or questions of fact in main clauses and statements of fact in many subordinate clauses:

   "Cum **intrāverimus**, tandem aurīgās ipsōs **spectābimus**." (26:17–18)
   *"When **we enter/will have entered**, we **will** finally **watch** the charioteers themselves."*

2. Imperative Mood

   The imperative mood is used to express a command (see Book I, page 74):

   "**Abīte**, molestī!" (3:8–9)
   *"**Go away**, pests!"*

   A negative command is expressed by **nōlī/nōlīte** and the infinitive:

   "**Nōlī** servōs **excitāre**!" (9:9)
   *"**Don't wake up** the slaves!"*

3. Subjunctive Mood

   The term *subjunctive mood* refers to a set of verb forms that you have seen used in certain types of subordinate clauses: **cum** causal clauses, **cum** circumstantial clauses, indirect questions, result clauses, purpose clauses, and indirect commands (see below). This mood gets its name from the Latin elements **sub-**, *under*, and **iūnct-**, *joined*, because verbs in this mood are often found in subordinate clauses, i.e., clauses that are "joined under" the main clause. In such clauses the subjunctive is often not translated any differently from the way a verb in the corresponding tense of the indicative would be translated. (For examples, see below.)

4. Subjunctive in Main Clauses

   a. Hortatory Subjunctive

      The present subjunctive may be used in main clauses for a variety of purposes. One is to issue commands. When commands are addressed by speakers to themselves and those with them, we call them exhortations, and we label the subjunctive hortatory:

      "Nunc in palaestram **exeāmus**," inquit. (44:6)
      *"Now **let us go out** into the exercise-ground," he said.*

b. Potential Subjunctive
The subjunctive may be used in a main clause that stands by itself but implies a larger sentence in the form of a condition that would require the subjunctive:

"Ego nōn **crēdidissem** tot hominēs amphitheātrō continērī posse." (48d:4)
*"I **would** not **have believed** that so many men could be held (in) the amphitheater."*

The larger conditional sentence would have been: *If I had not seen it for myself, I would not have believed....*

V. PARTICIPLES

A. Present Participles (see Book II, pages 133–134)

1. Participles as Verbal Adjectives
Participles are verbal adjectives and may modify nouns:

Nunc cōnspicit <u>poētam</u> versūs **recitantem**. (29:5)
*Now she catches sight of a <u>poet</u> **reciting** verses.*

Since the participle is a verbal adjective, it may take a direct object of its own; in the sentence above **versūs** is the object of the participle **recitantem**.

2. Participles as Substantives
Present active participles are frequently used as substantives (nouns) (see Book II, page 134):

"Cavēte!" exclāmant **adstantēs**.... (29:9–10)
*"Watch out!" shout **the bystanders**....*

B. Perfect Participles as Adjectives
Perfect participles often modify the subject of the verb of the clause (see Book II, pages 50–51):

Itaque coquus **vocātus** ab omnibus laudātus est. (33:26)
*Therefore the cook, **having been summoned**, was praised by everyone.*
See Book II, page 51 for alternative translations.

...inde **regressus**...in hortō labōrābam. (40:6–7)
*...**having returned** from there...I worked in the garden.*

Perfect participles may also modify other elements in the sentence, for example, the direct object (see Book II, page 176):

Coquum vocātum omnēs laudāvērunt.
*They all praised <u>the cook</u> **who had been summoned.***
When the cook had been summoned, they all praised him.

C. Future Active Participles
The future active participle, translated *going to, likely to, intending to, determined to, on the point of...-ing,* may modify a noun (see Book II, page 184):

Thisbē, iam moritūra, "Ō mē miseram!" clāmat. (45:25)
Thisbe, now ***about to die,*** *cries, "Poor me!"*

It may also be used in a verbal phrase with any tense of the verb **esse**; this is called the active periphrastic:

Marcum tamen mēcum **sum ductūrus.** (47:16–17)
However, ***I am intending to take*** *Marcus with me.*

D. Gerundive or Future Passive Participle
The gerundive is a verbal adjective that appears in all genders, numbers, and cases. It is future and passive in meaning and is often called a future passive participle. It will be formally introduced in Book III.
Sometimes it is used as a simple adjective:

"Minimē, ō puer **abominande**! Hesperia est Italia." (39:16)
"No, ***horrible*** *child! Hesperia is Italy."*

Sometimes it is used with some form of the verb **esse** to express obligation or necessity. This is called the passive periphrastic. In the following sentence **cōnficienda** is the gerundive of **cōnficere**.

"Nunc haec epistula **est cōnficienda.**" (47:23)
"Now this letter ***must be finished."***

VI. GERUNDS
The gerund is a neuter verbal noun that appears in the genitive, dative, accusative, and ablative singular only. It will be formally introduced in Book III. Gerunds are translated as verbal nouns in English:

"Quis creābitur arbiter **bibendī**?" (34:4)
"Who will be made master ***of the drinking****?"*

VII. SENTENCES

A. Agreement
The subject and verb of a sentence must agree in number; a singular subject takes a singular verb, and a plural subject, a plural verb:

Cornēlia est puella Rōmāna.... (1:1)
Cornelia *is a Roman girl....*

Cornēlia et Flāvia sunt puellae Rōmānae.... (2:1–2)
Cornelia and Flavia *are Roman girls....*

B. Questions

1. Questions may be introduced by many interrogative words:

   Quid facit Cornēlia? — ***What** is Cornelia doing?*

2. Questions may also be introduced by the particle **-ne** attached to the end of the first word (often the verb) of the question:

   Est**ne** puer ignāvus? (5:4) — *Is the boy cowardly?*

3. Questions that expect the answer "yes" are introduced with **nōnne**:

   "**Nōnne** cēnāre vultis?" (19:2) — "***Surely** you want to eat, **don't you**?*"

C. Coordinating Conjunctions

Conjunctions are words that join together (Latin **con-,** *together* + **iungere,** *to join*) sentences or elements within a sentence. Coordinating conjunctions join elements that are simply added to one another and are of equal grammatical importance (Latin **co-,** *together, same* + **ōrdō,** *order, rank*):

Cornēlia sedet **et** legit. (1:3)
*Cornelia sits **and** reads.*

Etiam Sextus dormit **neque** Cornēliam vexat. (6:2)
*Even Sextus is sleeping **and** is **not** annoying Cornelia.*

Marcus **neque** ignāvus **neque** temerārius est. (5:5–6)
*Marcus is **neither** cowardly **nor** rash.*

Hodiē puellae nōn sedent **sed** in agrīs ambulant. (2:2–3)
*Today the girls are not sitting **but** are walking in the fields.*

Servī in vīllā sedent, **nam** dēfessī sunt. (8c:8)
*The slaves are sitting in the country house, **for** they are tired.*

Sextus est puer molestus quī semper Cornēliam vexat. Cornēlia **igitur** Sextum nōn amat. (4:1–2)
*Sextus is an annoying boy who always annoys Cornelia. Cornelia, **therefore**, does not like Sextus.*

VIII. SUBORDINATE CLAUSES

A clause is a group of words containing a verb. The following sentence contains two clauses, each of which is said to be a main clause because each could stand by itself as a complete sentence:

Rīdent Marcus et Cornēlia, sed nōn rīdet Sextus. (4:10–11)
Marcus and Cornelia laugh, but Sextus does not laugh.

Subordinate (Latin **sub-**, *below* + **ōrdō**, *order, rank*) clauses are clauses that are of less grammatical importance than the main clause in a sentence. They are sometimes called dependent (Latin **dē-**, *down from* + **pendēre**, *to hang*) clauses because they hang down from the main clause and cannot stand by themselves. They are joined to the main clause by pronouns, adverbs, or subordinating conjunctions.

A. Adjectival Subordinate Clauses vith Verbs in the Indicative

Subordinate clauses are modifiers. They may be descriptive, like adjectives, and modify nouns:

Cornēlia est puella Rōmāna **quae** in Italiā habitat. (1:1–2)
Cornelia is a Roman girl, ***who*** *lives in Italy.*

Etiam in pictūrā est vīlla rūstica **ubi** Cornēlia aestāte habitat. (1:2)
Also in the picture is a country house and farm ***where*** *Cornelia lives in the summer.*

The relative pronoun (**quī**, **quae**, **quod**) introduces relative clauses, as in the first example above, and agrees with its antecedent in number and gender; its case depends on its use in its own clause (see Book II, pages 4–5):

Deinde īrā commōtus servum petit ā **quō** porcus aufūgit. (29:11–12)
Then in a rage he goes after the slave from ***whom*** *the pig escaped.*

The relative pronoun **quō** is masculine and singular because of the gender and number of its antecedent, **servus**; it is ablative because of its use with the preposition **ā** in its own clause.

Omnia **quae** videt Cornēlia eam dēlectant. (29:5)
Everything ***that*** *Cornelia sees pleases her.*

The relative pronoun **quae** is neuter and plural because of the gender and number of its antecedent, **omnia**; it is accusative because of its use as the direct object of **videt** in its own clause.

"...īre ad mercātōrem quendam **cuius** taberna nōn procul abest...." (28:10)
"*...to go to a certain merchant* ***whose*** *shop is not far away....*"

The relative pronoun **cuius** is masculine and singular because of the gender and number of its antecedent, **mercātōrem quendam**; it is genitive because of its use as a possessive within its own clause (*whose shop*).

B. Adverbial Subordinate Clauses with Verbs in the Indicative
In contrast to adjectival subordinate clauses described above, most subordinate clauses are adverbial, that is, they modify the verb of the main clause or the action of the main clause as a whole and are introduced by subordinating conjunctions that express ideas such as the following:

sī, condition:

Sī tū puer strēnuus es, ascende arborem!
If *you are an energetic boy, climb a tree!*

quamquam, concession:

Quamquam dominus abest, necesse est nōbīs strēnuē labōrāre. (11:7)
Although *the master is away, it is necessary for us to work hard.*

dum, **ubi**, **cum**, etc., time:

Dum Cornēlia legit, Flāvia scrībit. (1:4–5)
While *Cornelia reads, Flavia writes.*

Dum per viam ībant, Aurēlia et Cornēlia spectābant rūsticōs quī in agrīs labōrābant. (13:3–4)
(**Dum** with the imperfect tense = *while/as long as.*)
While/As long as *they were going along the road, Aurelia and Cornelia were looking at the peasants who were working in the fields.*

Dum puerī cibum dēvorant, subitō intrāvit mīles quīdam. (20:13)
While *the boys were devouring their food, a certain soldier suddenly entered.*
(Here the present tense verb in the **dum** clause is to be translated with the English past tense that describes ongoing action.) (See Book I, page 161.)

Puerī, **ubi** clāmōrem audiunt, statim ad puellās currunt. (5:10)
The boys, ***when*** *they hear the shout, immediately run to the girls.*

Crās, **ubi surgētis**, puerī, clāmōrem et strepitum audiētis.
Tomorrow ***when*** *you get up/will get up, boys, you will hear shouting and noise.*

Cum intrāverimus, tandem aurīgās ipsōs spectābimus. (26:17–18)
When *we enter/will have entered, we will finally watch the charioteers themselves.*

(While the verbs of the subordinate clauses are in the future, **surgētis**, and future perfect, **intrāverimus**, we translate them into English as presents; see Book I, page 218. The use of the tenses is more exact in Latin.)

quod, cause:

Cornēlia est laeta **quod** iam in vīllā habitat. (1:2–3)
Cornelia is happy ***because*** *she now lives in the country house.*

Conjunctions you have met that may introduce adverbial subordinate clauses with their verbs in the indicative are:

dum, *as long as* (15:1)
dum, *while* (20:13)
nisi, *if not, unless* (18:16)
postquam, *after* (21:10)
quamquam, *although* (11:7)
quod, *because* (1:3)
simulac, *as soon as* (24:1)
sī, *if* (5:1)
ubi, *when* (5:10)
ut, *as* (16:17)

C. Subordinate Clauses with Verbs in the Subjunctive
If a subordinate clause has its verb in the subjunctive, the tense of the subjunctive is determined by the following rules for the sequence of tenses (see Book II, pages 260–261):

When the verb in the main clause is in the present or a future tense (primary sequence), a present subjunctive in the subordinate clause indicates an action going on at the same time as (or after) that of the main verb, and a perfect subjunctive in the subordinate clause indicates an action that took place before that of the main verb.

When the verb in the main clause is in a past tense (secondary sequence), an imperfect subjunctive in the subordinate clause indicates an action going on at the same time as (or after) that of the main verb, and a pluperfect subjunctive indicates an action that took place before that of the main verb.

For examples, see Indirect Questions below.

Note that sometimes the perfect tense describes an action completed as of present time (e.g., *I have ordered*) instead of a simple past action (*I ordered*). In this case, primary sequence is followed:

"Dominus imperāvit ut iānua **claudātur.**" (51c:10)
"The master has ordered that the door ***be closed.****"*

Here the present instead of the imperfect subjunctive is used after the main verb in the perfect tense, because the perfect tense here clearly implies present time (*The master has ordered*).

D. Adverbial Subordinate Clauses with Verbs in the Subjunctive

1. **Cum** Causal Clauses
   Subordinate clauses that are introduced by the conjunction **cum** and have their verbs in the subjunctive may be **cum** causal clauses; **cum** is translated as *since* or *because.* Such clauses are adverbial and state the reason for the action of the main clause (see Book II, page 153):

   Magister nāvis, **cum** valdē **timēret**, suōs vetuit nōs adiuvāre. (42:17)
   *The captain of the ship, **since/because he was** very **frightened**, forbade his own men to help us.*

   Cum prīmā lūce **profectī essēmus**, iam dēfessī erāmus (43d:1).
   ***Since we had set** out at dawn, we were now tired.*

2. **Cum** Circumstantial Clauses
   Subordinate clauses that are introduced by the conjunction **cum** and have their verbs in the subjunctive may also be **cum** circumstantial clauses; **cum** is translated as *when.* Such clauses are adverbial and describe the circumstances that prevailed at the time of the action of the main clause (see Book II, page 153):

   Cum omnēs dormīrent, ego surrēxī. (42:30)
   ***When** all **were sleeping**, I got up.*

   Quō cum Titus **pervēnisset**, in vestibulum ingressus est. (43:4)
   ***When** Titus **had arrived** there, he entered the entrance hall.*

   Often only the context and sense will tell you whether **cum** is to be translated *since/because* or *when.*

3. Result Clauses
   The result of an action described in the main clause of a sentence may be expressed by an adverbial subordinate clause introduced by **ut** (positive) or **ut nōn** (negative); the present subjunctive is used in primary sequence and the imperfect subjunctive (or sometimes the perfect subjunctive) in secondary sequence. Result clauses are usually anticipated in the main clause by a word such as **adeō,** *so*, **sīc**, *thus, in this way*, **tālis,** *such*, **tam,** *so*, and **tantum,** *so, so much* (see Book II, pages 256–257 and 261 and the examples on the next page).

a. Primary sequence:

"Pater tantum temporis in tablīnō agit ut eum numquam videam." (50:3–4)
"Father spends so much time in the study ***that I never see him.****"*

b. Secondary sequence with imperfect subjunctive, emphasizing the natural or logical connection between the main clause and the result (see Book II, page 261):

Cornēlia adeō perturbāta erat **ut** vix loquī **posset**. (50:20)
Cornelia was so confused ***that she was*** *scarcely* ***able*** *to speak.*

c. Secondary sequence with perfect subjunctive, emphasizing the fact that the result actually did take place:

Leō tantus et tam ferōx erat **ut** servus metū exanimātus **ceciderit.**
The lion was ***so large*** *and* ***so*** *fierce* ***that*** *the slave* ***fell down****, paralyzed with fear.*

d. Negative with **ut...nōn** (see Book II, page 257):

Adeō perturbāta est **ut** loquī **nōn possit.**
She is so confused ***that she cannot*** *speak.*

4. Purpose Clauses
The purpose for which the action described in the main clause of a sentence is undertaken may be expressed by an adverbial subordinate clause introduced by **ut** (positive) or **nē** (negative). Purpose clauses are sometimes translated with infinitives in English (see Book II, page 288):

Iānitor baculum habet **ut** clientēs **repellat.** (53b:2)
The doorkeeper has a stick to drive off clients.

Nova nūpta super līmen sublāta est **nē lāberētur**. (53:19)
The bride was carried over the threshold ***so she would not stumble.***

E. Substantive Subordinate Clauses with Verbs in the Subjunctive

1. Indirect Questions (see Book II, pages 153–154, 166–167, and 260)
Indirect questions are substantive or noun clauses that may serve as the object of the main verb of the sentence; their verbs are in the subjunctive. The examples on the next page illustrate the sequence of tenses (see C above) and show how direct questions become indirect:

Primary Sequence:

Direct question (present tense):

Cūr servae mē **neglegunt**?
*Why do the slave girls **neglect** me?*

Indirect question:

Nōn intellegō cūr servae mē **neglegant**.
*I do not understand why the slaves girls **neglect** me.*

Direct question (past tense):

Cūr servae mē **neglēxērunt**?
*Why **did** the slave girls* **neglect** *me?*

Indirect Question:

Nōn intellegō cūr servae mē **neglēxerint**.
*I do not understand why the slave girls **neglected** me.*

Secondary Sequence:

Direct question (present tense):

Cūr servae mē **neglegunt**?
*Why **do** the slave girls **neglect** me?*

Indirect question:

Nōn intellēxī cūr servae mē **neglegerent.**
*I didn't understand why the slave girls **were neglecting** me.*

Direct question (past tense):

Cūr servae mē **neglēxērunt**?
*Why **did** the slave girls **neglect** me?*

Indirect question:

Nōn intellēxī cūr servae mē **neglēxissent.**
*I didn't understand why the slave girls **had neglected** me.*

2. Telling to, Asking to: Indirect Commands
Direct requests or commands such as **In ātrium procēdite!** *Step forward into the atrium!* may be stated indirectly in substantive clauses introduced by **ut** for a positive command or **nē** for a negative command, with the verb in the subjunctive. Indirect commands are usually translated with infinitives in English (see Book II, pages 268–269):

Cornēlius convīvās omnēs invītat **ut** in ātrium **prōcēdant.** (51c:1)
*Cornelius invites all the guests **to go forward** into the atrium.*

Hī iānitōrem ōrābant **nē** sē **dīmitteret**. (51:11)
*These kept begging the doorkeeper **not to send** them **away**.*

IX. USES OF THE INFINITIVE

A. Complementary Infinitive
The meaning of verbs and verbal phrases such as **velle**, **nōlle**, **posse**, **parāre**, **solēre**, **timēre**, and **in animō habēre** is often completed by a complementary infinitive (see Book I, page 26):

Cūr Marcus arborēs **ascendere** nōn vult? (5:4)
*Why does Marcus not want **to climb** trees?*

B. Infinitive as Subject
The infinitive may be used as the subject of the verb **est**, with a neuter singular complement (see Book I, page 162):

"Etiam in caupōnā **pernoctāre** saepe est perīculōsum." (20:19)
*"**To spend the night** in an inn is also often dangerous."*
*"It is also often dangerous **to spend the night** in an inn."*

C. Infinitive with Impersonal Verbal Phrases and Impersonal Verbs
Impersonal verbal phrases and impersonal verbs are often used with infinitives (see Book I, page 162, and Book II, pages 278–279):

Nōbīs igitur necesse est statim **discēdere**. (9:13–14)
***To leave** immediately is necessary for us.*
*It is necessary for us **to leave** immediately.*

"Licetne nōbīs," inquit Marcus, "hīc **cēnāre**?" (20:7)
*"Is it allowed for us," Marcus said, "**to dine** here?"*
"May we dine here?"

Strictly speaking, the infinitive is the subject of the impersonal verbal phrase or impersonal verb, but we usually supply *it* as the subject in English and translate the infinitive after the verb.

D. Accusative and Infinitive as Subject (see Book II, page 279)
An accusative and infinitive phrase may serve as the subject of an impersonal verb:

Nōn decet **patrem dēspondēre fīliam,** insciā mātre. (50:15–16)
***That a father betroth his daughter** without the mother knowing is not fitting.*
*It is not fitting **that a father betroth his daughter** without the mother knowing.*
A father should not betroth his daughter without the mother knowing.

Festīnāre tē oportet. (50:9)
***That you hurry** is fitting.*
*It is fitting **that you hurry.***
You ought to hurry.

E. Accusative and Infinitive as Object (see Book I, pages 72 and 162):

The verbs **docēre**, *to teach*, **iubēre**, *to order*, and **vetāre**, *to forbid*, are used with an accusative and infinitive as object:

> Aurēlia **Cornēliam** docet vīllam **cūrāre**. (6:11)
> *Aurelia teaches **Cornelia** (how) **to take care of** the country house.*

> **Ancillam** iubet aliās tunicās et stolās et pallās in cistam **pōnere**. (10:2)
> *She orders **the slave woman to put** other tunics and stolas and pallas into a chest.*

> Cūr pater meus **nōs exīre** vetat? (26:12)
> *Why does my father forbid **us to go out**?*

Note, however, that the verb **imperō,** *to order*, is used with the dative case and an indirect command:

> Coquō **imperāvit** ut in ātrium venīret.
> ***He ordered** the cook to come into the atrium.*

F. Accusative and Infinitive: Indirect Statement
A number of verbs of saying, hoping, thinking, perceiving, and feeling may be found with an accusative and infinitive construction (indirect statement). The tense of the infinitive in the indirect statement is the same as the tense of the verb in the original, direct statement.

When translating into English, the present infinitive in the indirect statement will be translated with the same tense as that of the verb in the main clause; a future infinitive will be translated to show action after that of the verb in the main clause; and a perfect infinitive will be translated to show time before that of the verb in the main clause.

The following examples show direct statements (active and passive, present, future, and perfect tenses) being changed into indirect statements:

1. Verb of main clause in **present** tense:

    a. Pater **est** crūdēlis.

    Putō **patrem esse** crūdēlem. (46:3–4)
    *I think that **father is** cruel.*

    Present infinitive replaces present indicative of the original statement (see Book II, pages 200–201). Note the agreement of **patrem** and **crūdēlem**.

b. Leōnēs in arēnam **immittuntur**.

Vidētisne **leōnēs** in arēnam **immittī**? (49e:8)
Do you see that ***the lions are being sent*** *into the arena?*

Present passive infinitive replaces present passive indicative of the original statement (see Book II, page 229).

c. Tū crās nōn **labōrābis**.

Prō certō habeō **tē** crās nōn **labōrātūrum esse**. (47:4)
I am certain that ***you will*** *not* ***work*** *tomorrow.*

Future active infinitive replaces future active indicative of the original statement (see Book II, page 214).

d. Hoc per iocum **dīxī**.

Nōnne sentīs **mē** per iocum hoc **dīxisse**? (47:9)
Surely you realize that ***I said*** *this as a joke, don't you?*

Perfect active infinitive replaces perfect active indicative of the original statement (see Book II, page 214).

e. Servus ā prīncipe **arcessītus est**.

Videō **servum** ā prīncipe **arcessītum esse**. (49e:18)
I see that ***the slave was summoned*** *by the emperor.*

Perfect passive infinitive replaces perfect passive indicative of the original statement (see Book II, page 229).

2. Verb of main clause in **past** tense:

a. Discēdere nōlō.

Respondit Titus **sē** discēdere **nōlle**. (48:23)
Titus replied that ***he did not want*** *to leave.*

Present active infinitive replaces present active indicative of the original statement (see Book II, pages 226–227).

b. Imperātor ā gladiātōribus **salūtātur**.

Vīdī **imperātōrem** ā gladiātōribus **salūtārī.** (48d:8–9)
I saw ***the emperor being greeted*** *by the gladiators.*

Present passive infinitive replaces present passive indicative of the original statement (see Book II, page 229).

c. Merīdiānī mox in arēnam **venient.**

Respondit Titus **merīdiānōs** mox in arēnam **ventūrōs esse**. (48:23–24)
Titus replied that ***the midday fighters would*** *soon* ***come*** *into the arena.*

Future active infinitive replaces future active indicative of the original statement (see Book II, pages 226–227).

d. Titus iam **cōnsēdit**.

Subitō vīdit **Titum** iam **cōnsēdisse.** (48:6)
Suddenly he saw that ***Titus had*** *already* ***taken his seat.***

Perfect active infinitive replaces perfect active indicative of the direct statement (see Book II, pages 226–227).

e. Titus eō iam **ductus est**.

Vīdimus **Titum** eō iam **ductum esse**. (48d:6–7)
We saw that ***Titus had*** *already* ***been led*** *to that place.*

Perfect passive infinitive replaces perfect passive indicative of the original statement.

3. A reflexive pronoun or adjective in an indirect statement refers to the subject of the verb in the main clause that introduces the indirect statement (see Book II, page 215):

Puellae puerīs dīxērunt **sē** eōs adiūtūrās esse.
The girls told the boys that ***they*** *would help them.*

Puerī dīxērunt puellās **sē** adiūtūrās esse.
The boys said that the girls would help ***them.***

LATIN TO ENGLISH VOCABULARY

Numbers in parentheses at the end of entries refer to the chapters in which the words appear in vocabulary entries or in Building the Meaning or Forms sections. Roman numerals refer to Review chapters.

A

ā or **ab**, prep. + abl., *from, by* (13, 29, 31)
ábeō, abī́re, ábiī or **abī́vī, abitū́rus**, irreg., *to go away* (3, 9)
abhínc, adv., *ago, previously* (25, 39)
abōminándus, -a, -um, *detestable, horrible* (39)
abrípiō, abrípere, abrípuī, abréptus, *to snatch away* (46)
ábstinēns, abstinéntis + abl., *refraining from* (34)
ábstulī (see **aúferō**)
ábsum, abésse, ā́fuī, āfutū́rus, irreg., *to be away, be absent, be distant* (11, 25)
ac, conj., *and* (30)
ī́dem ac, *the same as* (39)
accéndō, accéndere, accéndī, accḗnsus, *to set on fire* (54)
áccidit, accídere, áccidit, *it happens* (14, 26)
accípiō, accípere, accḗpī, accéptus, *to receive, get, welcome* (31)
accúmbō, accúmbere, accúbuī, accubitū́rus, *to recline (at table)* (32)
accúrrō, accúrrere, accúrrī, accursū́rus, *to run toward/up to* (29)
accū́sō, -ā́re, -ā́vī, -ā́tus, *to accuse* (21)
ā́cer, ā́cris, ā́cre, *keen* (34)
ā́criter, adv., *fiercely* (48)
ā́ctor, āctṓris, m., *actor* (54)
ad, prep. + acc., *to, toward, at, near* (2, 9)
ad témpus, *on time* (37)
áddō, áddere, áddidī, ádditus, *to add* (31)
addū́cō, addū́cere, addū́xī, addúctus, *to lead on, bring* (29)
adḗmpte (from **adḗmptus**, see **ádimō**)
ádeō, adv., *so much, to such an extent* (50)
ádeō, adī́re, ádiī, áditus, irreg., *to come to, approach*
adhū́c, adv., *still, as yet* (5, 13)
ádimō, adímere, adḗmī, adḗmptus + dat., *to take away (from)* (35)
ádiuvō, adiuvā́re, adiū́vī, adiū́tus, *to help* (6, 21)
admīrā́tiō, admīrātiṓnis, f., *amazement* (48)
admīrātiṓnī ésse, *to be a source of amazement (to)* (49)
admī́ror, -ā́rī, -ā́tus sum, *to wonder (at)* (49)
admóveō, admovḗre, admṓvī, admṓtus, *to move toward* (22)
adóptō, -ā́re, -ā́vī, -ā́tus, *to adopt* (IX)
adórior, adorī́rī, adórtus sum, *to attack* (42)
ádstō, adstā́re, ádstitī, *to stand near, stand by* (54)
adstántēs, adstántium, m. pl., *bystanders* (29)
ádsum, adésse, ádfuī, adfutū́rus, irreg., *to be present, be near* (26)
adulḗscēns, adulēscéntis, m., *young man, youth* (36)
advéniō, advenī́re, advḗnī, adventū́rus, *to reach, arrive (at)* (5, 23)
advesperā́scit, advesperā́scere, advesperā́vit, *it gets dark* (17)
aedifícium, -ī, n., *building* (17)
aedíficō, -ā́re, -ā́vī, -ā́tus, *to build* (24)
aéger, aégra, aégrum, *ill* (39)
aegrṓtō, -ā́re, -ā́vī, -ātū́rus, *to be ill* (39)
Aenḗās, Aenḗae, m., *Aeneas (son of Venus and Anchises and legendary ancestor of the Romans)* (38)
Aenḗis, Aenḗidis, f., *the* Aeneid (38)
aéquor, aéquoris, n., *sea* (54)
aequóreus, -a, -um, *of/belonging to the sea* (48)
aéstās, aestā́tis, f., *summer* (1, 12)
aéstus, -ūs, m., *heat* (24, 25)
áfferō, afférre, áttulī, allā́tus, irreg., *to bring, bring to, bring in* (29, 32)
affíciō, affícere, affḗcī, afféctus, *to affect* (54)
afféctus, -a, -um, *affected, overcome* (35)

Ā́frica, -ae, f., *Africa* (38)
áger, ágrī, m., *field, territory, land* (2)
agnṓscō, agnṓscere, agnṓvī, ágnitus, *to recognize* (18)
ágō, ágere, ḗgī, ā́ctus, *to do, drive; discuss, debate* (8, 14, 23, 52)
  Áge!/Ágite! *Come on!* (8)
  grā́tiās ágere + dat., *to thank* (26, 51)
  Quid ágis? *How are you?* (18)
áit, *he/she says, said* (50)
Albā́nus, -a, -um, *of Alba Longa (city founded by Aeneas' son, Ascanius)* (39)
albā́tus, -a, -um, *white* (27)
álbus, -a, -um, *white* (53)
áliās, adv., *at another time* (48)
áliquī, -ae, -a, *some* (38)
áliquis, áliquid, *someone, something* (25, 51)
  áliquid málī, *some harm* (46)
  nē quis (quis = áliquis), *that no one* (52)
  sī quis (quis = áliquis), *if anyone* (51)
áliter, adv., *otherwise* (26)
álius, ália, áliud, *another, other, one... another* (10)
  áliī...áliī..., *some...others...* (9)
álloquor, álloquī, allocū́tus sum, *to speak to, address* (54)
Álpēs, Álpium, f. pl., *the Alps* (39)
álter, áltera, álterum, *a/the second, one (of two), the other (of two), another* (1)
  álter...álter, *the one...the other* (16)
áltus, -a, -um, *tall, high, deep* (38)
  áltum, -ī, n., *the deep, the sea* (39)
ámbō, ámbae, ámbō, *both* (46)
ámbulō, -ā́re, -ā́vī, -ātū́rus, *to walk* (2)
amī́ca, -ae, f., *friend* (2)
amī́cus, -ī, m., *friend* (3)
ámō, -ā́re, -ā́vī, -ā́tus, *to like, love* (4)
ámor, amṓris, m., *love* (34)
amphitheā́trum, -ī, n., *amphitheater* (25)
ampléctor, ampléctī, ampléxus sum, *to embrace* (51)
an, conj., *or* (52)
  útrum...an..., conj., *whether...or...* (52)
ancílla, -ae, f., *slave-woman* (6)
Ándroclēs, Ándroclis, m., *Androcles* (49)
ánima, -ae, f., *soul, "heart"* (33)
animadvértō, animadvértere, animadvértī, animadvérsus, *to notice* (39)
ánimus, -ī, m., *mind* (16)
  ánimum recuperā́re, *to regain one's senses, be fully awake* (21)
  Bónō ánimō es!/éste! *Be of good mind! Cheer up!* (32)
  in ánimō habḗre, *to intend* (16)
ánnus, -ī, m., *year* (38)
  múltīs post ánnīs, *many years afterward* (39)
ánte, prep. + acc., *before, in front of* (36, 39)
ánte, adv., *previously, before* (39)
ánteā, adv., *previously, before* (20)
ántequam, conj., *before* (39)
antī́quus, -a, -um, *ancient* (26)
ā́nulus, -ī, m., *ring* (50)
apériō, aperī́re, apéruī, apértus, *to open* (16, 26)
ápium, -ī, n., *parsley* (34)
apodytḗrium, -ī, n., *changing-room* (43)
appā́reō, -ḗre, -uī, -itū́rus, *to appear* (15, 18)
appā́ritor, appāritṓris, m., *gatekeeper, public servant* (48, 54)
appéllō, -ā́re, -ā́vī, -ā́tus, *to call, name* (21)
appropínquō, -ā́re, -ā́vī, -ātū́rus + dat. or **ad** + acc., *to approach, come near (to)* (4, 22)
Aprī́lis, -is, -e, *April* (36)
áptō, -ā́re, -ā́vī, -ā́tus, *to place, fit* (50)
ápud, prep. + acc., *with, at the house of, in front of, before* (16, 26)
áqua, -ae, f., *water* (6)
aquaedúctus, -ūs, m., *aqueduct* (23, 25)
áquilō, aquilṓnis, m., *north wind* (54)
ā́ra, -ae, f., *altar* (53)
arā́nea, -ae, f., *cobweb* (34)
árbiter, árbitrī, m., *master* (34)
  árbiter bibéndī, *master of the drinking* (34)
árbor, árboris, f., *tree* (1)
arcéssō, arcéssere, arcessī́vī, arcessī́tus, *to summon, send for* (40, 54)
árcus, -ūs, m., *arch* (24, 25)

árdeō, ārdḗre, ā́rsī, ārsū́rus, *to burn, blaze* (53)
ā́rea, -ae, f., *open space, threshing-floor* (11)
arḗna, -ae, f., *sand, arena* (48)
árma, -ṓrum, n. pl., *arms, weapons* (39)
armā́tus, -a, -um, *armed* (42)
arrípiō, arrípere, arrípuī, arréptus, *to grab hold of, snatch, seize* (5, 19, 26)
ars, ártis, gen. pl., **ártium**, f., *skill* (14)
ascéndō, ascéndere, ascéndī, ascēnsū́rus, *to climb, climb into (a carriage)* (4, 22)
Ásia, -ae, f., *Asia Minor* (21)
aspáragus, -ī, m., *asparagus* (33)
aspérgō, aspérgere, aspérsī, aspérsus, *to sprinkle, splash, spatter* (45)
  aspérsus, -a, -um, *sprinkled, spattered* (33)
at, conj. *but* (23)
Athḗnae, -ā́rum, f. pl., *Athens* (39)
átque, conj., *and, also* (22)
ā́trium, -ī, n., *atrium, main room* (26)
atténtē, adv., *attentively, closely* (20)
attónitus, -a, -um, *astonished, astounded* (24)
aúdāx, audā́cis, *bold* (36)
aúdeō, audḗre, aúsus sum, semi-deponent + infin., *to dare (to)* (40)
aúdiō, -ī́re, -ī́vī, -ī́tus, *to hear, listen to* (4, 20)
aúferō, auférre, ábstulī, ablā́tus, irreg., *to carry away, take away* (29, 32)
aufúgiō, aufúgere, aufū́gī, *to run away, escape* (29)
Augústus, -a, -um, *August* (36)
Augústus, -ī, m., *Augustus (first Roman emperor)* (39)
aúreus, -a, -um, *golden* (25)
aurī́ga, -ae, m., *charioteer* (13)
aúrum, -ī, n., *gold* (21)
aúspex, aúspicis, m., *augur, officiating priest* (53)
aut, conj., *or* (26)
  aut...aut, conj., *either...or* (26)
aútem, conj., *however, but, moreover* (31)
auxílium, -ī, n., *help* (5, 15)
  Fer/Férte auxílium! *Bring help! Help!* (5)
Ávē!/Avḗte! *Hail! Greetings!* (40, 48)
āvértō, āvértere, āvértī, āvérsus, *to turn away, divert* (54)
ávis, ávis, gen. pl., **ávium**, m./f., *bird* (50)

B

Bábylōn, Babylṓnis, f., *Babylon* (45)
báculum, -ī, n., *stick, staff* (10, 15)
Báiae, -ā́rum, f. pl., *Baiae*
bálneae, -ā́rum, f. pl., *baths* (41)
bélliger, bellígera, bellígerum, *warlike* (48)
béllum, -ī, n., *war* (39)
béne, adv., *well* (22, 35)
benevoléntia, -ae, f., *kindness* (51)
bḗstia, -ae, f., *beast* (49)
bēstiā́rius, -a, -um, *involving wild beasts* (49)
bēstiā́rius, -ī, m., *a person who fights wild beasts in the arena* (49)
bíbō, bíbere, bíbī, *to drink* (31)
Bīthȳ́nia, -ae, f., *Bithynia (province in Asia Minor)* (39)
blándē, adv., *in a coaxing/winning manner* (49)
bōlḗtus, -ī, m., *mushroom* (33)
bónus, -a, -um, *good* (12, 34)
  bóna, -ṓrum, n. pl., *goods, possessions* (26)
  Bónō ánimō es!/éste! *Be of good mind! Cheer up!* (32)
bōs, bóvis, m./f., *ox, cow* (15)
brévis, -is, -e, *short* (2, 34)
  bréviter, *briefly* (35)
Británnī, -ṓrum, m. pl., *Britons* (X)
Británnia, -ae, f., *Britain* (8)
Británnicus, -a, -um, *British* (3)
Brundísium, -ī, n., *Brundisium* (36)
  Brundísiī, *at Brundisium* (36)
  Brundísiō, *from Brundisium* (36)
  Brundísium, *to Brundisium* (36)
búlla, -ae, f., *luck-charm, locket* (51)

C

cachínnus, -ī, m., *laughter* (30)
cádō, cádere, cécidī, cāsū́rus, *to fall* (3, 22)
caélum, -ī, n., *sky, heaven* (17)
Caésar, Caésaris, m., *Caesar, emperor* (27)
caldā́rium, -ī, n., *hot room (at baths)* (43)
cálidus, -a, -um, *warm* (5)
Calígula, -ae, m., *Caligula (emperor A.D. 37–41)* (27)
cálor, calṓris, m., *heat* (43)

cálvus, -a, -um, *bald* (43)
cámpus, -ī, m., *plain, field* (43)
Cámpus Mā́rtius, -ī, m., *the Plain of Mars on the outskirts of Rome* (43)
candḗla, -ae, f., *candle* (54)
candēlā́brum, -ī, n., *candelabrum, lamp-stand* (32)
cándidus, -a, -um, *white, fair-skinned, beautiful* (34)
cánis, cánis, m./f., *dog, the lowest throw of the knucklebones* (12, 34)
cánō, cánere, cécinī, cántus, *to sing* (39)
cántō, -ā́re, -ā́vī, -ā́tus, *to sing* (21)
capillā́tus, -a, -um, *with long hair* (43)
capíllī, -ṓrum, m. pl., *hair* (54)
cápiō, cápere, cḗpī, cáptus, *to take, catch, capture, seize* (21)
cōnsílium cápere, *to adopt a plan* (45)
captī́vus, -ī, m., *captive, prisoner* (26)
cáput, cápitis, n., *head* (25)
cáreō, carḗre, cáruī, caritū́rus + abl., *to need, lack* (33)
cárō, cárnis, f., *meat, flesh* (31)
Carthā́gō, Carthā́ginis, f., *Carthage (city on the north coast of Africa)* (39)
cā́rus, -a, -um, *dear, beloved* (53)
cása, -ae, f., *hut, cottage* (42)
cássis, cássidis, f., *plumed metal helmet* (48)
castī́gō, -ā́re, -ā́vī, -ā́tus, *to rebuke, reprimand* (37)
cástus, -a, -um, *virtuous, chaste* (53)
cā́sū, *by chance, accidentally* (32)
catérva, -ae, f., *crowd* (52)
caúda, -ae, f., *tail* (18)
caúpō, caupṓnis, m., *innkeeper* (17)
caupṓna, -ae, f., *inn* (17, 20)
caúsa, -ae, f., *reason* (25)
genitive + **caúsā**, *for the sake of, as* (52)
honṓris caúsā, *for the sake of an honor, as an honor* (52)
quā dē caúsā, *for this reason* (32)
Quam ob caúsam...? *For what reason...?* (28)
cávea, -ae, f., *cage* (49)
cáveō, cavḗre, cā́vī, caútus, *to be careful, watch out for, beware* (4, 13, 23)
céleber, célebris, célebre, *famous* (31)
céler, céleris, célere, *swift* (34)
celériter, adv., *quickly* (8, 13, 35)
celérius, adv., *more quickly* (35)
celérrimē, adv., *very fast, very quickly* (14)
celérrimus, -a, -um, *fastest, very fast* (29)
quam celérrimē, adv., *as quickly as possible* (34)
celéritās, celeritā́tis, f., *speed* (29)
súmmā celeritā́te, *with the greatest speed, as fast as possible* (29)
cḗlō, -ā́re, -ā́vī, -ā́tus, *to hide, conceal* (11)
cḗna, -ae, f., *dinner* (19)
cḗnō, -ā́re, -ā́vī, -ā́tus, *to dine, eat dinner* (19)
centḗsimus, -a, -um, *hundredth* (38)
céntum, *a hundred* (15, 38)
Cérberus, -ī, m., *Cerberus (three-headed dog guarding the underworld)* (32)
cértus, -a, -um, *certain* (35)
cértē, adv., *certainly* (19, 35)
prō cértō habḗre, *to be sure* (47)
céssō, -ā́re, -ā́vī, -ātū́rus, *to be idle, do nothing, delay* (14)
cḗterī, -ae, -a, *the rest, the others* (33)
Chárōn, Charṓnis, m., *Charon (ferryman in the underworld)* (32)
Chrīstiā́nus, -a, -um, *Christian* (XII)
Chrīstiā́nī, -ṓrum, m. pl., *the Christians* (XII)
cíbus, -ī, m., *food* (6)
cínis, cíneris, m., *ashes, dust (of the cremated body)* (54)
circḗnsis, -is, -e, *in the circus* (27)
lū́dī circḗnsēs, lūdṓrum circḗnsium, m. pl., *chariot-racing* (27)
círcum, prep. + acc., *around* (32)
circúmeō, circumī́re, circúmiī or **circumī́vī, circúmitus**, irreg., *to go around* (24)
circumspíciō, circumspícere, circumspéxī, circumspéctus, *to look around* (48)
Círcus Máximus, -ī, m., *Circus Maximus (a stadium in Rome)* (23)
císium, -ī, n., *light two-wheeled carriage* (14, 15)
císta, -ae, f., *trunk, chest* (10)
cī́vis, cī́vis, gen. pl., **cī́vium**, m./f., *citizen* (13)
clam, adv., *secretly* (42)
clā́mō, -ā́re, -ā́vī, -ātū́rus, *to shout* (3)

clámor, clāmṓris, m., *shout, shouting* (5)
clā́rus, -a, -um, *bright* (53)
claúdō, claúdere, claúsī, claúsus, *to shut* (26)
claúsus, -a, -um, *shut, closed* (24)
claúdus, -a, -um, *lame* (49)
clēménter, adv., *in a kindly manner* (49)
clíēns, cliéntis, gen. pl., **cliéntium**, m., *client, dependent* (25)
coépī, *I began* (38)
cṓgitō, -ā́re, -ā́vī, -ā́tus, *to think* (21)
cognṓmen, cognṓminis, n., *surname (third or fourth name of a Rome)* (IX, 52)
cognṓscō, cognṓscere, cognṓvī, cógnitus, *to find out, learn* (43)
cṓgō, cṓgere, coḗgī, coā́ctus, *to compel, force* (49)
collā́bor, collā́bī, collā́psus sum, *to collapse* (34, 37)
cóllis, cóllis, gen. pl., **cóllium**, m., *hill* (35)
collóquium, -ī, n., *conversation* (26)
cólloquor, cólloquī, collocū́tus sum, *to converse, speak together* (37)
cólō, cólere, cóluī, cúltus, *to cultivate* (23)
cómes, cómitis, m./f., *companion* (39)
cṓmiter, adv., *courteously, graciously, in a friendly way* (32)
cómitor, -ā́rī, -ā́tus sum, *to accompany* (51)
comitā́tus, -a, -um, *accompanied* (54)
commémorō, -ā́re, -ā́vī, -ā́tus, *to mention, comment on, recount* (54)
commissā́tiō, commissātiṓnis, f., *drinking party* (34)
commíttō, commíttere, commī́sī, commíssus, *to bring together, entrust* (48)
púgnam commíttere, *to join battle* (48)
cómmodus, -a, -um, *pleasant* (54)
commóveō, commovḗre, commṓvī, commṓtus, *to move, upset* (29, 30)
commṓtus, -a, -um, *moved, excited* (14)
commū́nis, -is, -e, *common* (45)
cómparō, -ā́re, -ā́vī, -ā́tus, *to buy, obtain, get ready* (32)
cómpleō, complḗre, complḗvī, complḗtus, *to fill, complete* (33)
compléxus, -ūs, m., *embrace* (9, 25)
complū́rēs, -ēs, -a, *several* (32)
compṓnō, compṓnere, compósuī, compósitus, *to compose* (53)
cóncidō, concídere, cóncidī, *to fall down* (14)
cóncinō, concínere, concínuī, *to sing together* (53)
cóncrepō, concrepā́re, concrépuī, *to snap (the fingers)* (43)
concubī́nus, -ī, m., *bridegroom* (53)
concúrrō, concúrrere, concúrrī, concursū́rus, *to run together, rush up* (35)
concúrsō, -ā́re, -ā́vī, -ā́tus, *to run to and fro, run about* (29)
condémnō, -ā́re, -ā́vī, -ā́tus, *to condemn* (49)
cóndō, cóndere, cóndidī, cónditus, *to found, establish* (36, 39)
condū́cō, condū́cere, condū́xī, condúctus, *to hire* (23)
cṓnferō, cōnférre, cóntulī, collā́tus, irreg., *to confer, bestow* (54)
mérita cōnférre, *to render services (to)* (54)
cōnfíciō, cōnfícere, cōnfḗcī, cōnféctus, *to accomplish, finish* (25, 32)
cōnfī́dō, cōnfī́dere, cōnfī́sus sum + dat., *to give trust (to), trust* (26)
cōnfúgiō, cōnfúgere, cōnfū́gī, *to flee for refuge* (44)
congrédior, cóngredī, congréssus sum, *to come together* (47)
coníciō, conícere, coniḗcī, coniéctus, *to throw, throw together; to figure out, guess* (21, 48)
cóniūnx, cóniugis, m./f., *husband, wife* (26)
cṓnor, -ā́rī, -ā́tus sum, *to try* (36, 37)
cṓnsecrō, -ā́re, -ā́vī, -ā́tus, *to dedicate* (51)
cōnsḗnsus, -ūs, m., *agreement* (49)
cṓnsequor, cṓnsequī, cōnsecū́tus sum, *to catch up to, overtake* (35, 37)
cōnsī́dō, cōnsī́dere, cōnsḗdī, *to sit down* (23)
cōnsílium, -ī, n., *plan* (45)
cōnsílium cápere, *to adopt a plan* (45)
cōnsístō, cōnsístere, cṓnstitī, *to halt, stop, stand* (48)
cōnspíciō, cōnspícere, cōnspéxī, cōnspéctus, *to catch sight of* (4, 21)
cṓnstat, *it is agreed* (47)

cōnstítuō, cōnstitúere, cōnstítuī, cōnstitū́tus, *to decide* (23)
cṓnsul, cṓnsulis, m., *consul* (36)
cṓnsulō, cōnsúlere, cōnsúluī, cōnsúltus, *to consult* (7)
cōnsúltum, -ī, n., *decree* (52)
conticḗscō, conticḗscere, contícuī, *to become silent* (38, 39)
contíneō, continḗre, contínuī, conténtus, *to confine, hold* (47)
cóntrā, adv., *in return* (34)
cóntrā, prep. + acc., *against, opposite, in front of, facing* (43, 48)
convalḗscō, convalḗscere, conváluī, *to grow stronger, get well* (42)
convéniō, convenī́re, convḗnī, conventū́rus, *to come together, meet, assemble* (43)
convértō, convértere, convértī, convérsus, *to turn (around)* (48)
  convérsus, -a, -um, *having turned, turning* (50)
convī́va, -ae, m., *guest (at a banquet)* (31)
convī́vium, -ī, n., *feast, banquet* (34)
cónvocō, -ā́re, -ā́vī, -ā́tus, *to call together* (12)
coórior, coorī́rī, coórtus sum, *to rise up, arise* (42)
cóquō, cóquere, cóxī, cóctus, *to cook* (6, 32)
cóquus, -ī, m., *cook* (33)
cor, córdis, n., *heart* (54)
Cornēliā́nus, -a, -um, *belonging to Cornelius* (10)
Cornḗliī, -ṓrum, m. pl., *the members of the family of Cornelius* (22)
córnicen, cornícinis, m., *horn-player* (48)
corṓna, -ae, f., *garland, crown* (34)
corṓnō, -ā́re, -ā́vī, -ā́tus, *to crown* (34)
córpus, córporis, n., *body* (21)
corrípiō, corrípere, corrípuī, corréptus, *to seize, grab* (35)
cotī́diē, adv., *daily, every day* (37)
cóxa, -ae, f., *hipbone* (54)
crās, adv., *tomorrow* (10, 13)
crḗdō, crḗdere, crḗdidī, crḗditus + *dat., to trust, believe* (35)
Cremṓna, -ae, f., *Cremona (town in northern Italy)* (39)
créō, -ā́re, -ā́vī, -ā́tus, *to appoint, create* (34, 54)
Crḗta, -ae, f., *Crete (large island southeast of Greece)* (39)
crī́nēs, crī́nium, m. pl., *hair* (28)
crótalum, -ī, n., *castanet* (21)
crūdḗlis, -is, -e, *cruel* (40)
crūdḗlitās, crūdēlitā́tis, f., *cruelty* (49)
cubículum, -ī, n., *room, bedroom* (8, 15)
cúbitum ī́re, *to go to bed* (19)
Cúius...? *Whose...?* (22)
culī́na, -ae, f., *kitchen* (21)
cúlpa, -ae, f., *fault, blame* (14)
cum, prep. + abl., *with* (12)
cum, conj., *when, since, whenever* (22, 40)
  cum prī́mum, *as soon as* (40)
cū́nctī, -ae, -a, *all* (14)
Cupī́dō, Cupī́dinis, m., *Cupid (the son of Venus)* (34)
cúpiō, cúpere, cupī́vī, cupī́tus, *to desire, want* (40)
Cūr...? *Why...?* (1)
cū́ra, -ae, f., *care* (34, 48)
  cū́rae ésse, *to be a cause of anxiety (to)* (50)
Cū́ria, -ae, f., *Senate House* (23)
cū́rō, -ā́re, -ā́vī, -ā́tus, *to look after, take care of* (6)
currículum, -ī, n., *race track* (27)
cúrrō, cúrrere, cucúrrī, cursū́rus, *to run* (2, 23)
custṓdiō, -ī́re, -ī́vī, -ī́tus, *to guard* (17)
cústōs, custṓdis, m., *guard* (26, 44)
cýathus, -ī, m., *small ladle, measure (of wine)* (34)

D

dē, prep. + abl., *down from, from, concerning, about* (16, 53)
déa, -ae, f., *goddess* (X)
dḗbeō, -ḗre, -uī, -itus, *to owe*; + infin., *ought* (26)
dēcḗdō, dēcḗdere, dēcéssī, dēcessū́rus, *to die* (53)
décem, *ten* (15, 38)
Decémber, Decémbris, Decémbre, *December* (36)
décet, decḗre, décuit, *it is becoming, fitting; should* (50, 52)
  Nōn décet pátrem dēspondḗre fī́liam, *That a father should betroth his daughter is not fitting, A father should not betroth his daughter* (50)

décimus, -a, -um, *tenth* (38)
dédicō, -ā́re, -ā́vī, -ā́tus, *to dedicate* (33)
dḗditus, -a, -um, *devoted, dedicated* (50)
dēdū́cō, dēdū́cere, dēdū́xī, dēdúctus, *to show into, bring, escort* (50)
dēféndō, dēféndere, dēféndī, dēfḗnsus, *to defend* (I, 35)
dēféssus, -a, -um, *tired* (2)
dḗfricō, dēfricā́re, dēfrícuī, dēfríctus, *to rub down* (43)
dēíciō, dēícere, dēiḗcī, dēiéctus, *to throw down;* pass., *to fall* (32)
deínde, adv., *then, next* (8, 13)
dēléctō, -ā́re, -ā́vī, -ā́tus, *to delight, amuse* (29)
déleō, dēlḗre, dēlḗvī, dēlḗtus, *to destroy* (38)
dēlíciae, -ā́rum, f. pl., *delight* (48)
Dḗlos, -ī, f., *Delos (small island off the eastern coast of Greece)* (39)
dēmíttō, dēmíttere, dēmī́sī, dēmíssus, *to let down, lower* (50)
dēmṓnstrō, -ā́re, -ā́vī, -ā́tus, *to show* (24)
dēnā́rius, -ī, m., *denarius (silver coin)* (31)
dēpṓnō, dēpṓnere, dēpósuī, dēpósitus, *to lay down, put aside, set down* (31)
dērī́deō, dērīdḗre, dērī́sī, dērī́sus, *to laugh at, get the last laugh* (33)
dēscéndō, dēscéndere, dēscéndī, dēscēnsū́rus, *to come/go down, climb down* (4, 23)
dēsī́derō, -ā́re, -ā́vī, -ā́tus, *to long for, desire, miss* (26)
dēsíliō, dēsilī́re, dēsíluī, *to leap down* (40)
dḗsinō, dēsínere, dḗsiī, dḗsitus, *to stop* (53)
dēspóndeō, dēspondḗre, dēspóndī, dēspṓnsus, *to betroth, promise in marriage* (50)
déus, -ī, nom. pl., **dī**, dat., abl. pl., **dīs**, m., *god* (35, 39)
Dī immortā́lēs! *Immortal Gods! Good heavens!* (33)
Prō dī immortā́lēs! *Good heavens!* (42)
dī mā́nēs, *the spirits of the dead* (54)
dēvértō, dēvértere, dēvértī, dēvérsus, *to turn aside* (14, 27)
dḗvorō, -ā́re, -ā́vī, -ā́tus, *to devour* (20)
déxtra, -ae, f., *right hand* (53)
dī (nom. pl. of **déus**) (33, 39)

dī́cō, dī́cere, dī́xī, díctus, *to say, tell* (20, 21)
dī́citur, *(he/she/it) is said* (41)
salū́tem dī́cere, *to send greetings* (36)
vḗra dī́cere, *to tell the truth* (40)
Dī́dō, Dīdṓnis, f., *Dido (queen of Carthage)* (38)
díēs, diḗī, m., *day* (5, 13, 25)
in díēs, *every day, day by day* (34)
díēs nātā́lis, diḗī nātā́lis, m., *birthday* (46)
diffícilis, -is, -e, *difficult* (34)
difficúltās, difficultā́tis, f., *difficulty* (35)
dígitus, -ī, m., *finger* (43)
dígitīs micā́re, *to play* morra (46)
dī́ligēns, dīligéntis, *diligent, painstaking, thorough* (35)
dīligénter, adv., *carefully* (19)
dī́ligō, dīlígere, dīlḗxī, dīlḗctus, *to love, have special regard for* (54)
dīmíttō, dīmíttere, dīmī́sī, dīmíssus, *to send away* (51)
discḗdō, discḗdere, discéssī, discessū́rus, *to go away, depart* (9, 22, 41)
discípulus, -ī, m., *pupil* (38)
dísco, díscere, dídicī, *to learn* (40)
dīs mā́nibus, *to the spirits of the dead* (54)
dissímilis, -is, -e, *dissimilar* (34)
díū, adv., *for a long time* (15, 35)
diūtíssimē, adv., *longest* (35)
diū́tius, adv., *longer* (35)
dī́ves, dī́vitis, *rich* (42)
dīvítiae, -ā́rum, f. pl., *wealth, riches* (48)
dī́vidō, dīvídere, dīvī́sī, dīvī́sus, *to divide* (IX)
dīvī́nus, -a, -um, *divine* (IX)
dō, dáre, dédī, dátus, *to give* (21)
dṓnō (dat.) **dáre**, *to give as a gift* (44)
poénās dáre, *to pay the penalty, be punished* (40)
sē quiḗtī dáre, *to rest* (23)
dóceō, docḗre, dócuī, dóctus, *to teach* (6, 21)
dóleō, -ḗre, -uī, -itū́rus, *to be sorry, be sad, be in pain, hurt* (18, 49)
dólor, dolṓris, m., *grief* (38)
dómina, -ae, f., *mistress, lady of the house* (17)
dóminus, -ī, m., *master, owner* (11)

dómus, -ūs, f., *home* (23, 25, 39)
  dómī, *at home* (26, 39)
  dómō, *from home* (23, 39)
  dómum, *homeward, home* (23, 39)
dṓnec, conj., *until* (33)
dṓnō, -ā́re, -ā́vī, -ā́tus, *to give; to present somebody* (acc.) *with something* (abl.) (34, 54)
dṓnum, -ī, n., *gift* (46)
  dṓnō (dat.) **dáre**, *to give as a gift* (46)
dórmiō, -ī́re, -ī́vī, -ītū́rus, *to sleep* (4)
dórmitō, -ā́re, -ā́vī, *to be sleepy* (39)
dúbium, -ī, n., *doubt* (30)
dū́cō, dū́cere, dū́xī, dúctus, *to lead, take, bring* (7, 19, 20)
  exséquiās dū́cere, *to carry out funeral rites* (53)
  in mātrimṓnium dū́cere, *to marry* (50)
dum, conj., *while, as long as* (1)
dúo, dúae, dúo, *two* (15, 38)
duódecim, *twelve* (38)
duodécimus, -a, -um, *twelfth* (38)
duodēvīgíntī, *eighteen* (38)
duodēvīcḗsimus, -a, -um, *eighteenth* (38)

E

ē or **ex**, prep. + abl., *from, out of* (2, 5, 9)
ḗbrius, -a, -um, *drunk* (34)
Écce! *Look! Look at...!* (1)
édō, ésse, ḗdī, ḗsus, irreg., *to eat* (33)
ēdū́cō, ēdū́cere, ēdū́xī, ēdúctus, *to lead out* (46)
éfferō, efférre, éxtulī, ēlā́tus, irreg., *to carry out, bring out* (30)
effúgiō, effúgere, effū́gī, *to flee, run away, escape* (11, 21, 29)
effúndō, effúndere, effū́dī, effū́sus, *to pour out;* pass., *to spill* (32)
égo, *I* (5, 27)
ēgrédior, ḗgredī, ēgréssus sum, *to go out, leave, disembark* (37, 39)
Ḗheu! *Alas!* (7)
Ého! *Hey!* (25)
ēíciō, ēícere, ēiḗcī, ēiéctus, *to throw out, wash overboard* (30)
élegāns, ēlegántis, *elegant, tasteful* (29)
ēmíttō, ēmíttere, ēmī́sī, ēmíssus, *to send out* (30)
émō, émere, ḗmī, ḗmptus, *to buy* (21, 31)
énim, conj., *for* (20)
ēnū́ntiō, -ā́re, -ā́vī, -ā́tus, *to reveal, divulge* (52)
éō, ī́re, íī or **ī́vī, itū́rus**, irreg., *to go* (7, 17, 19, 20, 21)
  cúbitum ī́re, *to go to bed* (19)
éō, adv., *there, to that place* (23)
éō mágis, *all the more* (52)
epigrámma, epigrámmatis, n., *epigram* (47)
epístula, -ae, f., *letter* (7)
épulae, -ā́rum, f. pl., *banquet, feast* (50)
équus, -ī, m., *horse* (10)
érgā, prep. + acc., *toward* (51)
ērípiō, ērípere, ērípuī, ēréptus, *to snatch from, rescue* (29)
érrō, -ā́re, -ā́vī, -ātū́rus, *to wander, be mistaken* (5, 18)
ērudī́tus, -a, -um, *learned, scholarly* (37)
ḗruō, ērúere, ḗruī, ḗrutus, *to dig up* (54)
ērúptiō, ēruptiṓnis, f., *eruption* (26)
ésse (see **sum** or **édō**)
Éstō! *All right! So be it!* (20)
ēsúriō, -ī́re, -ī́vī, -ītū́rus, *to be hungry* (19)
et, conj., *and, also* (1)
  et...et, conj., *both...and*
étiam, adv., *also, even* (1, 6, 13)
etiámsī, conj., *even if* (37)
Eúge! *Hurray!* (33)
Eúgepae! *Hurray!* (7)
Eurýdicē, -ēs, f., *Eurydice (wife of Orpheus)* (VII)
ēvā́dō, ēvā́dere, ēvā́sī, ēvā́sus, *to escape* (42)
ēvértō, ēvértere, ēvértī, ēvérsus, *to overturn, upset* (32)
ex or **ē**, prep. + abl., *from, out of* (2, 5, 9)
exanimā́tus, -a, -um, *paralyzed* (49)
excḗdō, excḗdere, excéssī, excessū́rus, *to go out, leave* (54)
  ē vī́tā excḗdere, *to die* (54)
excípiō, excípere, excḗpī, excéptus, *to welcome, receive, catch* (5, 16, 22)
éxcitō, -ā́re, -ā́vī, -ā́tus, *to rouse, wake (someone) up* (8)
  excitā́tus, -a, -um, *wakened, aroused* (25)

exclā́mō, -ā́re, -ā́vī, -ā́tus, *to exclaim, shout out* (10)
excū́sō, -ā́re, -ā́vī, -ā́tus, *to forgive, excuse* (33)
sē excūsā́re, *to apologize* (33)
éxeō, exī́re, éxiī or **exī́vī, exitū́rus,** irreg., *to go out* (5, 23, 44)
exérceō, -ḗre, -uī, -itus, *to exercise, train* (43)
exímius, -a, -um, *outstanding* (53)
éximō, exímere, exḗmī, exḗmptus, *to remove* (54)
expéllō, expéllere, éxpulī, expúlsus, *to drive out, expel* (39)
expergī́scor, expergī́scī, experrḗctus sum, *to wake up* (39)
expérior, experī́rī, expértus sum, *to test, try* (37)
éxplicō, -ā́re, -ā́vī, -ā́tus, *to explain* (19)
rem explicā́re, *to explain the situation* (19)
éxprimō, exprímere, expréssī, expréssus, *to press out, express* (45)
exséquiae, -ā́rum, f. pl., *funeral rites* (53)
exséquiās dū́cere, *to carry out funeral rites* (53)
exsíliō, exsilī́re, exsíluī, *to leap out* (44)
exspéctō, -ā́re, -ā́vī, -ā́tus, *to look out for, wait for* (15)
éxstāns, exstántis, *standing out, towering* (23)
exstínguō, exstínguere, exstī́nxī, exstī́nctus, *to put out, extinguish* (30)
éxstruō, exstrúere, exstrū́xī, exstrū́ctus, *to build* (54)
éxta, -ṓrum, n. pl., *the inner organs of sacrificial animals (heart, lungs, liver)* (53)
exténdō, exténdere, exténdī, exténtus, *to hold out* (18, 39)
éxtrā, prep. + acc., *outside* (23)
éxtrahō, extráhere, extrā́xī, extráctus, *to drag out, take out* (14, 21)
éxuō, exúere, éxuī, exū́tus, *to take off* (33)

F

fā́bula, -ae, f., *story* (20)
fácilis, -is, -e, *easy* (34)
fácile, adv., *easily* (35)
fáciō, fácere, fḗcī, fáctus, *to make, do* (1, 23)
íter fácere, *to travel* (13)
fáctiō, factiṓnis, f., *company (of charioteers), political faction* (27)
fā́ma, -ae, f., *fame* (X)
família, -ae, f., *family, household* (51)
familiā́ris, -is, -e, *belonging to the family/household* (51)
familiā́rēs, familiā́rium, m. pl., *members of the household* (54)
fáscēs, fáscium, m. pl., *rods (symbols of office)* (54)
fā́tum, -ī, n., *fate* (39)
fátuus, -a, -um, *stupid* (13)
fáveō, favḗre, fā́vī, fautū́rus + dat., *to give favor (to), favor, support* (27)
fax, fácis, f., *wedding-torch* (53)
fébris, fébris, gen. pl., **fébrium,** f., *fever* (54)
Februā́rius, -a, -um, *February* (36)
fḗlēs, fḗlis, gen. pl., **fḗlium,** f., *cat* (21)
fḗlīx, fēlī́cis, *lucky, happy, fortunate* (34)
fēlī́citer, adv., *well, happily, luckily* (35)
Fēlī́citer! adv., *Good luck!* (53)
fḗmina, -ae, f., *woman* (3)
fenéstra, -ae, f., *window* (30)
férculum, -ī, n., *dish, tray* (33)
férē, adv., *almost, approximately* (46)
fēriā́tus, -a, -um, *celebrating a holiday* (27)
fériō, -ī́re, -ī́vī, -ī́tus, *to hit, strike, kill* (16, 48)
férō, férre, túlī, lā́tus, irreg., *to bring, carry, bear* (5, 12, 17, 21)
Fer/Férte auxílium! *Bring help! Help!* (5)
férōx, ferṓcis, *fierce* (35)
ferṓciter, adv., *fiercely* (13)
férula, -ae, f., *cane* (39)
festī́nō, -ā́re, -ā́vī, -ātū́rus, *to hurry* (9)
fidḗlis, -is, -e, *faithful* (31, 34)
fídēs, fídeī, f., *good faith, reliability, trust* (52)
fī́lia, -ae, f., *daughter* (11)
fī́lius, -ī, m., *son* (11)
fī́niō, -ī́re, -ī́vī, -ī́tus, *to finish* (21)
fī́nis, fī́nis, gen. pl., **fī́nium,** m., *end* (29)
fī́ō, fíerī, fáctus sum, irreg., *to become, be made, be done, happen* (34)
Quid Séxtō fíet? *What will happen to Sextus?* (46)
flámma, -ae, f., *flame* (29)

flámmeum, -ī, n., *orange (bridal) veil* (53)
flámmeus, -a, -um, *flaming* (XII)
fléō, flḗre, flḗvī, flḗtus, *to weep, cry* (53)
flḗtus, -ūs, m., *weeping, tears* (54)
flōs, flṓris, m., *flower* (34)
foédus, -a, -um, *filthy, disgusting* (34)
fóllis, fóllis, gen. pl., **fóllium,** m., *bag* (43)
fórās, adv., *outside* (41)
fṓrma, -ae, f., *form, shape* (X)
fortásse, adv., *perhaps* (15)
fórte, adv., *by chance* (33)
fórtis, -is, -e, *brave* (18)
  fortíssimē, adv., *most/very bravely* (35)
  fórtiter, adv., *bravely* (35)
fortū́na, -ae, f., *fortune (good or bad)* (54)
Fórum, -ī, n., *the Forum (town center of Rome)* (25)
fóssa, -ae, f., *ditch* (12)
frágor, fragṓris, m., *crash, noise, din* (4)
frángō, frángere, frḗgī, frā́ctus, *to break* (54)
frā́ter, frā́tris, m., *brother* (11)
frātérnus, -a, -um, *brotherly* (54)
frīgidā́rium, -ī, n., *cold room (at baths)* (43)
frī́gidus, -a, -um, *cool, cold* (5)
fritíllus, -ī, m., *cylindrical box* (34)
frōns, fróntis, f., *forehead* (12)
frū́strā, adv., *in vain* (14)
frústum, -ī, n., *scrap* (33)
fúgiō, fúgere, fū́gī, fugitū́rus, *to flee* (18, 25)
fúī (see **sum**)
fū́mus, -ī, m., *smoke* (29)
fúndus, -ī, m., *farm* (39)
fū́nebris, -is, -e, *funeral* (54)
fū́nus, fū́neris, n., *funeral* (53)
fūr, fū́ris, m., *thief* (44)
fúror, furṓris, m., *frenzy* (48)
fū́rtim, adv., *stealthily* (4, 13)
fū́stis, fū́stis, gen. pl., **fū́stium,** m., *club, cudgel* (35)

G

Gā́dēs, Gā́dium, f. pl., *Gades (Cadiz, a town in Spain)* (21)
Gállī, -ṓrum, m. pl., *the Gauls* (X)
Gállia, -ae, f., *Gaul* (39)
gaúdeō, gaudḗre, gāvī́sus sum, *to be glad, rejoice* (14, 40)
gaúdium, -ī, n., *joy* (23)
gelā́tus, -a, -um, *chilled* (54)
gémō, gémere, gémuī, gémitus, *to groan* (3)
gēns, géntis, gen. pl., **géntium,** f., *family, clan;* pl., *peoples* (50, 54)
génus, géneris, n., *race, stock, nation* (39)
gérō, gérere, géssī, géstus, *to wear; carry on, perform, do* (10)
gladiā́tor, gladiātṓris, m., *gladiator* (47)
gládius, -ī, m., *sword* (21, 26)
  gládium stríngere, *to draw a sword* (26)
glīs, glī́ris, gen. pl., **glī́rium,** m., *dormouse* (28)
glṓria, -ae, f., *fame, glory* (27)
grácilis, -is, -e, *slender* (34)
Graécia, -ae, f., *Greece* (21)
Graécus, -a, -um, *Greek* (17)
  Graécī, -ṓrum, m. pl., *the Greeks* (I)
grammáticus, -ī, m., *secondary school teacher* (37)
grā́tia, -ae, f., *gratitude, thanks* (26)
  grā́tiās ágere + dat., *to thank* (26, 51)
grā́tīs, adv., *free, for nothing* (31)
grā́tulor, -ā́rī, -ā́tus sum + dat., *to congratulate* (50)
grā́tus, -a, -um + dat., *loved (by), pleasing (to), dear (to)* (54)
grávis, -is, -e, *heavy, serious* (35)
grúnniō, -ī́re, *to grunt* (29)
gustā́tiō, gustātiṓnis, f., *hors d'oeuvre, first course* (33)

H

habḗnae, -ā́rum, f. pl., *reins* (22)
hábeō, -ḗre, -uī, -itus, *to have, hold* (10, 20, 26)
  in ánimō habḗre, *to intend* (16)
  ōrātiṓnem habḗre, *to deliver a speech* (26)
  prō cértō habḗre, *to be sure* (47)
hábitō, -ā́re, -ā́vī, -ā́tus, *to live, dwell* (1)
haéreō, haerḗre, haésī, haesū́rus, *to stick* (14)
harḗna, -ae, f., *sand* (54)
harpástum, -ī, n., *heavy hand ball* (43)
hásta, -ae, f., *spear* (48)

haud, adv., *not* (43, 54)
haúriō, hauríre, haúsī, haústus, *to drain* (34)
hédera, -ae, f., *ivy* (34)
Hérculēs, Hérculis, m., *Hercules (Greek hero)* (34)
héri, adv., *yesterday* (20)
Hespéria, -ae, f., *Hesperia (the land in the West, Italy)* (39)
Heu! = Ḗheu!
Héus! *Hey there!* (50)
hīc, adv., *here* (9, 13, 54)
hic, haec, hoc, *this, the latter* (18, 19, 20, 25, 26, 31)
híems, híemis, f., *winter* (39)
hílaris, -is, -e, *cheerful* (54)
hiláritās, hilaritā́tis, f., *good humor, merriment* (53)
Hispā́nia, -ae, f., *Spain* (39)
hódiē, adv., *today* (2, 13)
hólus, hóleris, n., *vegetable* (32)
hómō, hóminis, m., *man* (18)
  hóminēs, hóminum, m. pl., *people* (15, 36)
hónor, honṓris, m., *honor* (IX)
  honṓris caúsā, *for the sake of an honor, as an honor* (52)
hṓra, -ae, f., *hour* (9)
  Quóta hṓra est? *What time is it?* (38)
Horā́tius, -ī, m., *Horace (Roman poet)* (39)
hórtor, -ā́rī, -ā́tus sum, *to encourage, urge* (51, 53)
hórtus, -ī, m., *garden* (3)
  hórtulus, -ī, m., *small garden* (53)
hóspes, hóspitis, m., *guest, host, friend, a person related to one of another city by ties of hospitality* (16)
hūc, adv., *here, to here* (36)
  hūc illū́c, adv., *here and there, this way and that* (23)
hūmā́nus, -a, -um, *human* (48)
húmī, *on the ground* (27)
húmilis, -is, -e, *humble* (34)
hyacínthinus, -a, -um, *of hyacinth* (53)
Hýmēn! (**Hýmēn!** (an exclamation chanted at weddings; later thought of as the god of weddings) (53)
Hymenaée! = Hýmēn! (53)

I

iáceō, -ḗre, -uī, -itū́rus, *to lie, be lying down* (26)
iáciō, iácere, iḗcī, iáctus, *to throw* (10, 20)
iáctō, -ā́re, -ā́vī, -ā́tus, *to toss about, drive to and fro* (39)
iam, adv., *now, already* (1, 8, 13)
  nōn iam, adv., *no longer* (2, 13)
iā́nitor, iānitṓris, m., *doorkeeper* (9)
iā́nua, -ae, f., *door* (9)
Iānuā́rius, -a, -um, *January* (36)
íbi, adv., *there* (5, 13)
id (see **is**)
ídem, éadem, ídem, *the same* (3, 31)
  ídem ac, *the same as* (39)
idéntidem, adv., *again and again, repeatedly* (13)
id quod, *that/a thing which* (50)
Ī́dūs, Ī́duum, f. pl., *the Ides* (36)
iēntā́culum, -ī, n., *breakfast* (37)
ígitur, conj., *therefore* (4)
ignā́vus, -a, -um, *cowardly, lazy* (5)
ígnis, ígnis, gen. pl., **ígnium**, m., *fire* (32)
ignṓrō, -ā́re, -ā́vī, -ā́tus, *to be ignorant, not to know* (40)
ílle, ílla, íllud, *that; he, she, it; the former; that famous* (11, 15, 16, 20, 22, 25, 26, 31)
illū́c, adv., *there, to that place* (23)
  hūc illū́c, adv., *here and there, this way and that* (23)
imā́gō, imā́ginis, f., *likeness, mask* (54)
ímber, ímbris, gen. pl., **ímbrium**, m., *rain* (23)
immā́nis, -is, -e, *huge* (49)
ímmemor, immémoris + gen., *forgetful* (22)
immíttō, immíttere, immī́sī, immíssus, *to send in, release* (49)
ímmō, adv., *rather, on the contrary* (31)
  ímmō vḗrō, adv., *on the contrary, in fact* (40)
immṓbilis, -is, -e, *motionless* (12)
immortā́lis, -is, -e, *immortal* (27)
  Dī immortā́lēs! *Immortal gods! Good heavens!* (33)
  Prō dī immortā́lēs! *Good heavens!* (42)
ímpar (see **pār**)
impédiō, -ī́re, -ī́vī, -ī́tus *to hinder, prevent* (11)
imperā́tor, imperātṓris, m., *commander, emperor* (47)
ímperō, -ā́re, -ā́vī, -ā́tus + dat., *to order* (51)
ímpetus, -ūs, m., *attack* (49)

impṓnō, impṓnere, impósuī, impósitus, *to place on, put* (54)
in, prep. + abl., *in, on, among* (1, 9, 28)
in ánimō habḗre, *to intend* (16)
in quíbus, *among whom* (28)
in, prep. + acc., *into, against* (3, 9)
in díēs, *every day, day by day* (34)
in mātrimṓnium dū́cere, *to marry* (50)
incḗdō, incḗdere, incéssī, *to go in, march in* (48)
incéndium, -ī, n., *fire* (30)
incéndō, incéndere, incéndī, incḗnsus, *to burn, set on fire* (38)
incéssus, -ūs, m., *bearing, walk(ing)* (54)
íncidō, incídere, íncidī, incāsū́rus, *to fall into/onto* (54)
incípiō, incípere, incḗpī, incéptus, *to begin* (49)
íncitō, -ā́re, -ā́vī, -ā́tus, *to spur on, urge on, drive* (10)
íncola, -ae, m./f., *inhabitant, tenant* (30)
incólumis, -is, -e, *unhurt, safe and sound* (14)
incúrrō, incúrrere, incúrrī, incursū́rus, *to run into*
índe, adv., *from there, then* (38, 40)
indígnē, adv., *undeservedly* (54)
índuō, indúere, índuī, indū́tus, *to put on* (8, 23)
indū́tus, -a, -um, *clothed* (43)
íneō, iníre, íniī or **inívī, ínitus,** irreg., *to go into, enter* (28)
íners, inértis, *lazy* (53)
īnfándus, -a, -um, *unspeakable* (38)
ī́nfāns, īnfántis m./f., *infant, young child* (30)
ī́nferī, -ṓrum, m. pl., *the underworld* (32)
īnfériae, -ā́rum, f. pl., *offerings and rites in honor of the dead at the tomb* (54)
ī́nferō, īnférre, íntulī, illā́tus, irreg., *to bring in* (39)
īnfírmus, -a, -um, *weak, shaky, frail* (4, 30)
ingénium, -ī, n., *intelligence, ingenuity* (52)
íngēns, ingéntis, *huge* (22)
ingravḗscō, ingravḗscere, *to grow worse* (54)
ingrédior, íngredī, ingréssus sum, *to go in, enter* (37)
iníciō, inícere, iniḗcī, iniéctus, *to throw into, thrust* (54)
innocéntia, -ae, f., *innocence* (21)
ínquit, *(he/she) says, said* (7)
ī́nscius, -a, -um, *not knowing* (45)
īnscrī́bō, īnscrī́bere, īnscrī́psī, īnscrī́ptus, *to write in, register* (51)
īnspíciō, īnspícere, īnspéxī, īnspéctus, *to examine* (21)
ī́nsula, -ae, f., *island, apartment building* (30)
intéllegō, intellégere, intellḗxī, intellḗctus, *to understand, realize* (49)
inténtus, -a, -um, *intent, eager* (38)
ínter, prep. + acc., *between, among* (33)
intérdiū, adv., *during the day, by day* (23)
intérdum, adv., *from time to time* (39)
intéreā, adv., *meanwhile* (10, 13)
ínterest, *it is important* (39)
interpéllō, -ā́re, -ā́vī, -ā́tus, *to interrupt* (14)
intérrogō, -ā́re, -ā́vī, -ā́tus, *to ask* (53)
íntrā, prep. + acc., *inside* (22)
íntrō, -ā́re, -ā́vī, -ā́tus, *to enter, go into* (8, 19)
intrōdū́cō, intrōdū́cere, intrōdū́xī, intrōdúctus, *to bring in* (49)
intróeō, introíre, intróiī or **introívī, introitū́rus,** irreg., *to enter* (52)
inū́rō, inū́rere, inússī, inústus, *to brand* (12)
invéniō, inveníre, invḗnī, invéntus, *to come upon, find* (12, 21)
invī́tō, -ā́re, -ā́vī, -ā́tus, *to invite* (28, 32, 51)
invī́tus, -a, -um, *unwilling* (21)
ínvocō, -ā́re, -ā́vī, -ā́tus, *to invoke, call upon* (34)
Iō! (a ritual exclamation) (53)
iócus, -ī, m., *joke, funny story, prank* (16)
per iócum, *as a prank/joke* (16)
ípse, ípsa, ípsum, *himself, herself, itself, themselves, very* (6, 10, 29, 31)
ī́ra, -ae, f., *anger* (11)
īrācúndia, -ae, f., *irritability, bad temper* (40)
īrācúndus, -a, -um, *irritable, in a bad mood* (40)
īrā́tus, -a, -um, *angry* (3, 33)
íre (see **éō**) (7, 17)
irrúmpō, irrúmpere, irrū́pī, irrúptus, *to burst in* (33)
is, éa, id, *he, she, it; this, that* (27, 31)
íta, adv., *thus, so, in this way, in such a way* (3, 13, 21, 50)
Íta vḗrō! adv., *Yes! Indeed!* (3, 13)

Itália, -ae, f., *Italy* (1)
ítaque, adv., *and so, therefore* (16)
íter, itíneris, n., *journey, route* (10, 13, 15)
íter fácere, *to travel* (13)
íterum, adv., *again, a second time* (8, 13)
Íthaca, -ae, f., *Ithaca (island home of Ulysses)* (39)
iúbeō, iubḗre, iússī, iússus, *to order, bid* (10, 19, 21)
iūcúndus, -a, -um, *pleasant, delightful* (54)
iúgulō, -ā́re, -ā́vī, -ā́tus, *to kill, murder* (48)
Iū́lius, -a, -um, *July* (36)
iúngō, iúngere, iū́nxī, iū́nctus, *to join* (53)
Iū́nius, -a, -um, *June* (36)
Iū́nō, Iūnṓnis, f., *Juno (queen of the gods)* (39)
iússa, -ṓrum, n. pl., *commands, orders* (32)
iúvenis, iúvenis, m., *young man* (50)

K

Kaléndae, -ā́rum, f. pl., *the Kalends (first day in the month)* (36)

L

lā́bor, lā́bī, lā́psus sum, *to slip, fall, stumble* (44, 53)
lábor, labṓris, m., *work, toil* (24, 48)
labṓrō, -ā́re, -ā́vī, -ā́tus, *to work* (3)
lácrima, -ae, f., *tear* (45)
lácrimō, -ā́re, -ā́vī, -ā́tus, *to weep, cry* (9)
laédō, laédere, laésī, laésus, *to harm* (46)
laétus, -a, -um, *happy, glad* (1)
laétē, adv., *happily* (35)
lámbō, lámbere, lámbī, *to lick* (49)
lā́na, -ae, f., *wool* (6)
lā́nam tráhere, *to spin wool* (6)
lángueō, -ḗre, *to be ill in bed* (54)
lánguidus, -a, -um, *drooping* (48)
lanísta, -ae, m., *trainer* (48)
lánius, -ī, m., *butcher* (31)
lantérna, -ae, f., *lantern* (37)
lapídeus, -a, -um, *of stone, stony* (33)
lápis, lápidis, m., *stone* (25)
larā́rium, -ī, n., *shrine of the household gods* (51)
Lárēs, Lárum, m. pl., *household gods* (51)
láteō, -ḗre, -uī, *to lie in hiding, hide* (49)
Latī́nus, -a, -um, *Latin* (39)
Látium, -ī, n., *Latium (the area of central Italy that included Rome)* (39)
lātrā́tus, -ūs, m., *a bark, barking* (25)
lā́trō, -ā́re, -ā́vī, -ātū́rus, *to bark* (12)
latrúnculus, -ī, m., *robber;* pl., *pawns (a game like chess)* (46)
lū́dus latrunculṓrum, *game of bandits* (46)
laúdō, -ā́re, -ā́vī, -ā́tus, *to praise* (18)
laúrus, -ī, f., *bay (tree), laurel* (53)
Lāvī́nius, -a, -um, *of Lavinium (name of the town where the Trojans first settled in Italy)* (39)
lávō, lavā́re, lā́vī, laútus, *to wash* (20, 54)
lectī́ca, -ae, f., *litter* (23)
lectīcā́rius, -ī, m., *litter-bearer* (23)
léctus, -ī, m., *bed, couch* (19)
lēgā́tus, -ī, m., *envoy* (18)
légō, légere, lḗgī, lḗctus, *to read* (1, 24)
léntus, -a, -um, *slow* (35)
léntē, adv., *slowly* (2, 13)
léō, leṓnis, m., *lion* (45)
lépidus, -a, -um, *charming* (54)
lépus, léporis, m., *hare* (31)
lévis, -is, -e, *light* (54)
lḗvis, -is, -e, *smooth* (54)
libénter, adv., *gladly* (36)
líber, líbrī, m., *book* (24)
Līberā́lia, Līberā́lium, n. pl., *the Liberalia (Festival of Liber)* (51)
lī́berī, -ṓrum, m. pl., *children* (10, 11)
lī́berō, -ā́re, -ā́vī, -ā́tus, *to set free* (49)
lībérta, -ae, f., *freedwoman* (54)
lībértās, lībertā́tis, f., *freedom* (21)
lībértus, -ī, m., *freedman* (29)
líbet, libḗre, líbuit or **líbitum est**, *it is pleasing to someone* (dat.) *to do something* (infin.) (53)
lícet, licḗre, lícuit + dat., *it is allowed* (20, 24)
lícet nṓbīs, *we are allowed, we may* (20)
lī́ctor, līctṓris, m., *lictor, officer* (54)
lígō, -ā́re, -ā́vī, -ā́tus, *to bind up* (35)
lī́men, lī́minis, n., *threshold, doorway* (51)
língua, -ae, f., *tongue, language* (39)

línquō, línquere, líquī, *to leave* (54)
línteum, -ī, n., *towel* (43)
liquā́men, liquā́minis, n., *garum (a sauce made from fish, used to season food)* (33)
líttera, -ae, f., *letter (of the alphabet)* (12)
  lítterae, -ā́rum, f. pl., *letter, epistle, letters, literature* (39)
lī́tus, lī́toris, n., *shore* (39)
locā́rius, -ī, m., *scalper* (48)
lócō, -ā́re, -ā́vī, -ā́tus, *to place* (54)
lócus, -ī, m.; n. in pl., *place* (33)
lóngus, -a, -um, *long* (15)
  lóngē, adv., *far* (35)
lóquor, lóquī, locū́tus sum, *to speak, talk* (37)
lū́bricus, -a, -um, *slippery* (54)
lucérna, -ae, f., *lamp* (54)
lū́cet, lūcḗre, lū́xit, *it is light, it is day; (it) shines* (6, 50)
lū́ctor, -ā́rī, -ā́tus sum, *to wrestle* (43)
lū́dia, -ae, f., *female slave attached to a gladiatorial school* (48)
lū́dō, lū́dere, lū́sī, lūsū́rus, *to play* (16)
  pílā lū́dere, *to play ball* (16)
lū́dus, -ī, m., *school, game* (26, 37, 46)
  lū́dī, -ṓrum, m. pl., *games* (24)
  lū́dī circḗnsēs, lūdṓrum circḗnsium, m. pl., *chariot-racing* (27)
  lū́dus latrunculṓrum, *game of bandits* (46)
lū́na, -ae, f., *moon* (33)
lúpa, -ae, f., *she-wolf* (II)
lúpus, -ī, m., *wolf* (5)
lútum, -ī, n., *mud* (26)
lūx, lū́cis, f., *light* (21)
  prī́mā lū́ce, *at dawn* (21)

M

mágis, adv., *more* (34, 35)
  éō mágis, adv., *all the more* (52)
magíster, magístrī, m., *schoolmaster, master, captain* (37, 42)
magístra, -ae, f., *female teacher, instructress* (X)
magníficus, -a, -um, *magnificent* (24)
magnópere, adv., *greatly* (31, 35)
mágnus, -a, -um, *big, great, large, loud (voice, laugh)* (4, 34)
máior, máior, máius, gen., **maiṓris**, *bigger* (34)
  maiṓrēs, maiṓrum, m. pl., *ancestors* (54)
Máius, -a, -um, *May* (36)
mā́lō, mā́lle, mā́luī, irreg., *to prefer* (47)
mā́lum, -ī, n., *apple* (32)
málus, -a, -um, *bad, evil* (21, 34)
  áliquid málī, *some harm* (44)
  mále, adv., *badly* (35)
mandā́tum, -ī, n., *order, instruction* (22)
mā́ne, adv., *early in the day, in the morning* (21)
máneō, manḗre, mā́nsī, mānsū́rus, *to remain, stay, wait* (9, 20, 23)
mā́nēs, mā́nium, m. pl., *spirits of the dead* (54)
  dīs mā́nibus, *to the spirits of the dead* (54)
mā́nō, -ā́re, -ā́vī, *to flow* (54)
mānsuḗtus, -a, -um, *tame* (49)
Mántua, -ae, f., *Mantua (town in northern Italy)* (39)
mánus, -ūs, f., *hand, band (of men)* (18, 25)
máppa, -ae, f., *napkin* (27)
máre, máris, gen. pl., **márium**, n., *sea* (38)
marī́tus, -ī, m., *husband* (53)
Mārtiā́lis, Marcus Valerius, m., *Martial (poet, ca. A.D. 40–104)* (47)
Mā́rtius, -a, -um, *March; connected with Mars (the god of war and combat)* (36, 48)
mā́ter, mā́tris, f., *mother* (6, 11)
mātrimṓnium, -ī, n., *marriage* (50)
  in mātrimṓnium dū́cere, *to marry* (50)
mātrṓna, -ae, f., *married woman* (52)
mātū́rē, adv., *early* (47)
máximus, -a, -um, *biggest, greatest, very great, very large* (23, 34)
  máximē, adv., *most, very much, very* (34, 35)
mē, *me* (4)
  mḗcum, *with me* (9)
médicus, -ī, m., *doctor* (33)
Mediolā́num, -ī, n., *Milan* (39)
médius, -a, -um, *mid-, middle of* (20)
  média nox, médiae nóctis, f., *midnight* (20)

Mégara, -ae, f., *Megara (a city in Greece)* (21)
Mehércule! *By Hercules! Goodness me!* (18)
mélior, mélior, mélius, gen., **melióris**, *better* (19, 34)
mélius, adv., *better* (35)
mémor, mémoris, *remembering, mindful, unforgetting* (39)
memorā́bilis, -is, -e, *memorable* (47)
memória, -ae, f., *memory* (30)
memóriā tenḗre, *to remember* (37)
mendī́cus, -ī, m., *beggar* (29)
mḗnsa, -ae, f., *table* (29)
secúndae mḗnsae, -ā́rum, f. pl., *second course, dessert* (33)
mḗnsis, mḗnsis, m., *month* (38)
mercā́tor, mercātṓris, m., *merchant* (22)
Mercúrius, -ī, m., *Mercury (messenger god)* (32)
merīdiā́nī, -ṓrum, m. pl., *midday fighters* (48)
merī́diēs, -ḗī, m., *noon, midday* (46)
merī́diē, adv., *at noon* (33)
méritum, -ī, n., *good deed;* pl., *services* (54)
mérita cōnférre, *to render services (to)* (54)
mérus, -a, -um, *pure* (34)
mérum, -ī, n., *undiluted wine* (34)
mḗta, -ae, f., *mark, goal, turning post* (27)
métus, -ūs, m., *fear* (26)
métū exanimā́tus, *paralyzed with fear* (47)
méus, -a, -um, *my, mine* (7)
mícō, micā́re, mícuī, *to move quickly to and fro, flash* (46)
dígitīs micā́re, *to play morra* (46)
mígrō, -ā́re, -ā́vī, -ātū́rus, *to move one's home* (39)
mī́les, mī́litis, m., *soldier* (20)
mī́lle, *a thousand* (15, 38)
mī́lia, mī́lium, n. pl., *thousands* (48)
mīllḗsimus, -a, -um, *thousandth* (38)
mī́mus, -ī, m., *actor of mime, buffoon* (54)
mínāx, minā́cis, *menacing* (48)
mínimus, -a, -um, *very small, smallest* (34)
mínimē, adv., *least* (35)
Mínimē (**vḗrō**)! adv., *No! Not at all! No indeed!* (3,13)
mínor, mínor, mínus, gen., **minṓris**, *smaller* (34)
mínus, adv., *less* (35)
mínuō, minúere, mínuī, minū́tus, *to lessen, reduce, decrease* (31)
mīrā́bilis, -is, -e, *wonderful* (49)
mī́ror, -ā́rī, -ā́tus sum, *to wonder* (49)
mī́rus, -a, -um, *wonderful, marvelous, strange* (23)
mísceō, miscḗre, míscuī, míxtus, *to mix* (34)
míser, mísera, míserum, *unhappy, miserable, wretched* (9)
miserā́bilis, -is, -e, *miserable, wretched* (30)
mī́tis, -is, -e, *gentle* (49)
míttō, míttere, mī́sī, míssus, *to send, let go* (9, 20, 31, 48)
módo, adv., *only* (18)
módus, -ī, m., *way, method, rhythmic/harmonious manner* (34, 53)
moénia, moénium, n. pl., *walls* (39)
mṓlēs, mṓlis, gen. pl., **mṓlium**, f., *mass, huge bulk* (24)
moléstus, -a, -um, *troublesome, annoying* (4)
moléstus, -ī, m., *pest* (3)
móllis, -is, -e, *soft* (54)
móneō, -ḗre, -uī, -itus, *to advise, warn* (39, 51)
mōns, móntis, gen. pl., **móntium**, m., *mountain, hill* (24)
Mōns Vesúvius, Móntis Vesúviī, m., *Mount Vesuvius (a volcano in southern Italy)* (26)
mṓnstrō, -ā́re, -ā́vī, -ā́tus, *to show* (22)
monuméntum, -ī, n., *monument, tomb* (54)
mórbus, -ī, m., *illness* (54)
mórior, mórī, mórtuus sum, *to die* (39, 45)
móror, -ā́rī, -ā́tus sum, *to delay, remain, stay* (36,37)
mors, mórtis, gen. pl., **mórtium**, f., *death* (21)
mortā́lēs, mortā́lium, m. pl., *mortals* (X)
mortíferē, adv., *mortally, critically* (53)
mórtuus, -a, -um, *dead* (16)
mōs, mṓris, m., *custom*, pl., *character* (52)
móveō, movḗre, mṓvī, mṓtus, *to move, shake* (14, 24)
mox, adv., *soon, presently* (6, 13)
mulíebris, -is, -e, *womanly, female, of a woman* (53)
múlier, mulíeris, f., *woman* (27)

múlsum, -ī, n., *wine sweetened with honey* (33)
multitū́dō, multitū́dinis, f., *crowd* (23)
múltus, -a, -um, *much* (31, 34)
múltum, adv., *greatly, much* (31, 35)
múltī, -ae, -a, *many* (3, 34)
múltīs post ánnīs, *many years afterward* (39)
Mulviā́nus, -a, -um, *at the Mulvian Bridge* (XII)
mū́nus, mū́neris, n., *gift, service, gladiatorial show;* pl., *games* (47, 54)
múrmur, múrmuris, n., *murmur, rumble* (15)
mū́rus, -ī, m., *wall* (23)
mūs, mū́ris, m., *mouse* (21)
Mū́sa, -ae, f., *Muse (goddess of song and poetry)* (VII)
mússō, -ā́re, -ā́vī, -ātū́rus, *to mutter* (11)
mū́tus, -a, -um, *silent* (54)
mū́tuus, -a, -um, *mutual*, (49)
mýrtus, -ī, f., *myrtle* (53)

N

nam, conj., *for* (8)
nārrā́tor, nārrātṓris, m., *narrator* (8)
nā́rrō, -ā́re, -ā́vī, -ā́tus, *to tell (a story)* (20)
nārrā́tus, -a, -um, *told* (20)
nā́scor, nā́scī, nā́tus sum, *to be born* (39)
nā́sus, -ī, m., *nose* (33)
nātā́lis, -is, -e, *of/belonging to birth* (46)
díēs nātā́lis, diḗī nātā́lis, m., *birthday* (46)
nā́tiō, nātiṓnis, f., *nation* (XII)
nā́tō, -ā́re, -ā́vī, -ātū́rus, *to swim* (40)
nātū́ra, -ae, f., *nature* (XI, 50)
nā́tus, -ī, m., *son* (54)
nā́vigō, -ā́re, -ā́vī, -ā́tus, *to sail* (38)
nā́vis, nā́vis, gen. pl, **nā́vium**, f., *ship* (38)
-ne (indicates a question) (3)
nē, conj. + subjunctive, *not to, so that...not, to prevent, to avoid* (51, 53)
nē...quídem, adv., *not even* (34)
nē quis, *that no one* (52)
Neā́polis, Neā́polis, acc., **Neā́polim**, f., *Naples* (15)
nec, conj., *and...not* (45)
nec...nec..., *neither...nor*
necésse, adv. or indecl. adj., *necessary* (6, 13, 52)

nécō, -ā́re, -ā́vī, -ā́tus, *to kill* (20)
néglegēns, neglegéntis, *careless* (28)
neglegénter, adv., *carelessly* (28)
neglegéntia, -ae, f., *carelessness* (28)
néglegō, neglégere, neglḗxī, neglḗctus, *to neglect, ignore* (50)
negōtiṓsus, -a, -um, *busy* (47)
nḗmō, nḗminis, m./f., *no one* (9)
nḗnia, -ae, f., *lament, dirge* (54)
néque, conj., *and...not* (6)
néque...néque, conj., *neither...nor* (5)
néque...néque...quídquam, *neither... nor...anything* (40)
nēquī́quam, adv., *in vain* (54)
Nerōnḗus, -a, -um, *of Nero* (43)
nésciō, -ī́re, -ī́vī, -ī́tus, *to be ignorant, not to know* (9)
níger, nígra, nígrum, *black* (33)
níhil, *nothing* (4)
nīl, *nothing* (34)
nímis, adv., *too much* (34)
nísi, conj., *unless, if...not, except* (18, 26)
nṓbilis, -is, -e, *noble* (50)
nóceō, -ḗre, -uī, -itū́rus + dat., *to do harm (to), harm* (26)
nóctū, *at/by night* (45)
noctúrnus, -a, -um, *happening during the night* (22)
nṓlō, nṓlle, nṓluī, irreg., *to be unwilling, not to wish, refuse* (5, 17, 21)
Nṓlī/Nōlī́te + infin., *Don't...!* (9)
nṓmen, nṓminis, n., *name* (1, 15)
nṓminō, -ā́re, -ā́vī, -ā́tus, *to name, call by name* (54)
nōn, adv., *not* (2, 13)
nōn iam, adv., *no longer* (2, 13)
nōn módo...sed étiam, *not only...but also* (X)
Nṓnae, -ā́rum, f. pl., *Nones* (36)
nṓndum, adv., *not yet* (6, 13)
Nṓnne...? *Surely...?* (introduces a question that expects the answer "yes") (19)
nōnnū́llī, -ae, -a, *some* (51)
nōnnúmquam, adv., *sometimes* (26)
nṓnus, -a, -um, *ninth* (16, 38)
nōs, *we, us* (8, 27)
nóster, nóstra, nóstrum, *our* (14, 27)

nṓtus, -a, -um, *known* (31)
nóvem, *nine* (15, 38)
Novémber, Novémbris, Novémbre, *November* (36)
nóvus, -a, -um, *new* (16)
  nóva nū́pta, -ae, f., *bride* (53)
nox, nóctis, gen. pl., **nóctium**, f., *night* (11)
  média nōx, médiae nóctis, f., *midnight* (20)
nū́bēs, nū́bis, gen. pl., **nū́bium**, f., *cloud* (15)
nū́bō, nū́bere, nū́psī, nūptū́rus + dat., *to marry*
nū́llus, -a, -um, *no, none* (9)
Num...? adv., *Surely...not...?* (introduces a question that expects the answer "no") (46)
númerō, -ā́re, -ā́vī, -ā́tus, *to count* (33)
númerus, -ī, m., *number* (11)
númquam, adv., *never* (20)
nunc, adv., *now* (6, 13)
nū́ntius, -ī, m., *messenger* (7)
nū́per, adv., *recently* (50)
nū́pta, nóva, -ae, f., *bride* (53)
nūptiā́lis, -is, -e, *of/for a wedding* (53)
núsquam, adv., *nowhere* (39)
nux, núcis, f., *nut* (53)

O

ō (used with vocative and in exclamations) (9)
ob, prep. + acc., *on account of* (39)
obdórmiō, -ī́re, -ī́vī, -ītū́rus, *to go to sleep* (21)
obḗsus, -a, -um, *fat* (18)
obscū́rō, -ā́re, -ā́vī, -ā́tus, *to hide* (30)
óbsecrō, -ā́re, -ā́vī, -ā́tus, *to beseech, beg* (40, 51)
obsérvō, -ā́re, -ā́vī, -ā́tus, *to watch, pay attention to* (6, 50)
obsídeō, obsidḗre, obsḗdī, obséssus, *to besiege* (38)
obsígnō, -ā́re, -ā́vī, -ā́tus, *to sign* (53)
obstupefáctus, -a, -um, *astounded* (48)
occī́dō, occī́dere, occī́dī, occī́sus, *to kill* (45)
occupā́tus, -a, -um, *busy* (7)
occúrrō, occúrrere, occúrrī, occursū́rus + dat., *to meet* (24)
Ōcéanus, -ī, m., *Ocean* (53)
octā́vus, -a, -um, *eighth* (36, 38)
óctō, *eight* (15, 38)
Octṓber, Octṓbris, Octṓbre, *October* (36)
óculus, -ī, m., *eye* (26)
officiṓsus, -a, -um + dat., *ready to serve, obliging* (54)
offícium, -ī, n., *official ceremony, duty* (51)
óleum, -ī, n., *oil* (32)
olfáciō, olfácere, olfḗcī, olfáctus *to catch the scent of, smell, sniff* (12, 18)
ṓlim, adv., *once (upon a time)* (18)
olī́va, -ae, f., *olive* (33)
olīvḗtum, -ī, n., *olive grove* (14, 15)
ṓmen, ṓminis, n., *omen* (53)
omíttō, omíttere, omī́sī, omíssus, *to leave out, omit* (39)
ómnis, -is, -e, *all, the whole, every, each* (6, 18)
ónerō, -ā́re, -ā́vī, -ā́tus, *to load*
ónus, óneris, n., *load, burden* (15)
opériō, operī́re, opéruī, opértus, *to hide, cover* (53)
opórtet, oportḗre, opórtuit, *it is fitting; ought* (50, 52)
  Festīnā́re tē opórtet, *That you hurry is fitting, You ought to hurry* (50)
óppidum, -ī, n., *town* (39)
ópprimō, opprímere, oppréssī, oppréssus, *to overwhelm* (30)
  oppréssus, -a, -um, *crushed* (25)
óptimus, -a, -um, *best, very good, excellent* (20, 31, 34)
  óptimē, adv., *best, very well, excellently* (34, 35)
  vir óptime, *sir* (20)
óptō, -ā́re, -ā́vī, -ā́tus, *to wish* (54)
ṓra, -ae, f., *shore* (39)
ōrā́tiō, ōrātiṓnis, f., *oration, speech* (26)
  ōrātiṓnem habḗre, *to deliver a speech* (26)
ōrā́tor, ōrātṓris, m., *orator, speaker* (22)
ṓrdior, ōrdī́rī, órsus sum, *to begin* (38)
órior, orī́rī, órtus sum, *to rise* (45)
ōrnāméntum, -ī, n., *decoration;* pl., *furnishings* (30)
ṓrnō, -ā́re, -ā́vī, -ā́tus, *to decorate, equip* (53)
  ōrnā́tus, -a, -um, *decorated* (32)
ṓrō, -ā́re, -ā́vī, -ā́tus, *to beg* (51)
Órpheus, -ī, m., *Orpheus (legendary singer and husband of Eurydice)* (32)

ōs, ṓris, n., *mouth, face, expression* (38)
os, ossis, n., *bone* (54)
ṓsculum, -ī, n., *kiss* (45)
osténdō, osténdere, osténdī, osténtus, *to show, point out* (48)
ṓvum, -ī, n., *egg* (32)

P

paedagṓgus, -ī, m., *tutor* (37)
paéne, adv., *almost* (30)
palaéstra, -ae, f., *exercise ground* (43)
Palātī́nus, -a, -um, *on/belonging to the Palatine Hill* (24)
pálla, -ae, f., *palla* (10)
pállium, -ī, n., *cloak* (32)
pā́lus, -ī, m., *post* (43)
pā́nis, pā́nis, gen. pl., **pā́nium**, m., *bread* (32)
pār ímpār, *odds or evens (a game)* (46)
párcō, párcere, pepércī + dat., *to spare* (49)
párēns, paréntis, m./f., *parent* (11)
pā́reō, -ḗre, -uī + dat., *to obey* (39)
pária, párium, n. pl., *pairs* (48)
páriēs, paríetis, m., *wall (of a house or room)* (30)
párō, -ā́re, -ā́vī, -ā́tus, *to prepare, get ready* (5, 20)
  parā́tus, -a, -um, *ready, prepared* (10)
  sē parā́re, *to prepare oneself, get ready* (22)
pars, pártis, gen. pl., **pártium**, f., *part, direction, region* (13)
párvulus, -a, -um, *small, little* (26)
párvus, -a, -um, *small* (30, 34)
pā́scō, pā́scere, pā́vī, pā́stus, *to feed, pasture* (31)
pássum, -ī, n., *raisin-wine* (33)
páter, pátris, m., *father* (6, 11)
  pátrēs, pátrum, m. pl., *senators* (52)
pátior, pátī, pássus sum, *to suffer, endure* (38)
patrṓnus, -ī, m., *patron* (25)
pátruus, -ī, m., *uncle* (22)
paúcī, -ae, -a, *few* (34)
paulā́tim, adv., *gradually, little by little* (34)
paulísper, adv., *for a short time* (20)
paúlus, -a, -um, *little, small* (54)
  paúlum, adv., *little* (35)
  paúlum, -ī, n., *a small amount, a little* (37)
paúper, paúperis, *poor* (42)
pavīméntum, -ī, n., *tiled floor* (44)
péctō, péctere, péxī, péxus, *to comb* (28)
péctus, péctoris, n., *chest, breast* (54)
  péctus plángere, *to beat the breast* (54)
pecū́nia, -ae, f., *money* (21)
pécus, pécoris, n., *livestock, sheep and cattle* (33)
péior, péior, péius, gen., **peiṓris**, *worse* (34)
  péius, adv., *worse* (35)
per, prep. + acc., *through, along* (6, 9)
  per iócum, *as a prank/joke* (16)
percútiō, percútere, percússī, percússus, *to strike* (35)
pérdō, pérdere, pérdidī, pérditus, *to destroy* (45)
pérferō, perférre, pértulī, perlā́tus, irreg., *to report* (52)
perīculṓsus, -a, -um, *dangerous* (17)
perī́culum, -ī, n., *danger* (14, 15)
peristȳ́lium, -ī, n., *peristyle (courtyard surrounded with a colonnade)* (46)
pérlegō, perlégere, perlḗgī, perlḗctus, *to read through* (54)
pérna, -ae, f., *ham* (31)
pernóctō, -ā́re, -ā́vī, -ātū́rus, *to spend the night* (17)
perpétuus, -a, -um, *lasting, permanent* (54)
  in perpétuum, *forever* (54)
persuā́deō, persuādḗre, persuā́sī, persuā́sus, *to make something* (acc.) *agreeable to someone* (dat.), *to persuade someone of something; to persuade someone* (dat.) (36, 51)
pertérritus, -a, -um, *frightened, terrified* (5)
perturbā́tus, -a, -um, *confused* (50)
pervéniō, pervenī́re, pervḗnī, perventū́rus + **ad** + acc., *to arrive (at), reach* (25)
pēs, pédis, m., *foot* (13)
péssimus, -a, -um, *worst* (34)
  péssimē, adv., *worst* (35)
pestiléntia, -ae, f., *plague* (33)
pétō, pétere, petī́vī, petī́tus, *to look for, seek, head for, aim at, attack* (5, 21)
pictū́ra, -ae, f., *picture* (1)
píla, -ae, f., *ball* (16)
  pílā lū́dere, *to play ball* (16)

pínguis, -is, -e, *fat, rich* (31)
pīrā́ta, -ae, m., *pirate* (21)
pírum, -ī, n., *pear* (33)
piscī́na, -ae, f., *fishpond* (3)
pī́stor, pīstṓris, m., *baker* (54)
pīstrī́num, -ī, n., *bakery* (37)
pláceō, -ḗre, -uī + dat., *to please* (34, 52)
plácuit, *it was decided* (52)
plácidē, adv., *gently, peacefully, quietly, tamely* (14, 49)
plángō, plángere, plā́nxī, plā́nctus, *to beat* (54)
péctus plángere, *to beat the breast* (54)
plaústrum, -ī, n., *wagon, cart* (15)
plḗnus, -a, -um, *full* (11)
plṓrō, -ā́re, -ā́vī, -ā́tus, *to lament, mourn* (54)
plúit, plúere, plúit, *it rains, is raining* (23)
plū́rēs, plū́rēs, plū́ra, gen., **plū́rium**, *more* (34)
plū́rimus, -a, -um, *most, very much* (34)
plū́rimī, -ae, -a, *most, very many* (34)
plū́rimum, adv., *most* (35)
plūs, plū́ris, n., *more* (34)
plūs vī́nī, *more wine* (34)
plūs, adv., *more* (35)
Plū́tō, Plūtṓnis, m., *Pluto (king of the underworld)* (32)
pṓculum, -ī, n., *cup, goblet* (33)
poéna, -ae, f., *punishment, penalty* (40)
poénās dáre, *to pay the penalty, be punished* (40)
poḗta, -ae, f., *poet* (25)
pollíceor, pollicḗrī, pollícitus sum, *to promise* (45)
pómpa, -ae, f., *funeral procession* (54)
Pompéiī, -ṓrum, m. pl., *Pompeii*
pṓnō, pṓnere, pósuī, pósitus, *to put, place* (10, 21)
pōns, póntis, gen. pl., **póntium**, m., *bridge* (23)
popī́na, -ae, f., *eating-house, bar* (33)
pópulus, -ī, m. *people* (47)
pórcus, -ī, m., *pig, pork* (28, 33)
pórta, -ae, f., *gate* (11)
pórtō, -ā́re, -ā́vī, -ā́tus, *to carry* (6)
póscō, póscere, popóscī, *to demand, ask for* (34)
póssum, pósse, pótuī, irreg., *to be able; I can* (5, 14, 21)
post, prep. + acc., *after* (20)
post, adv., *after(ward), later* (39)
múltīs post ánnīs, *many years afterward* (39)
pósteā, adv., *afterward* (33)
pósterus, -a, -um, *next, following* (52)
póstis, póstis, gen. pl., **póstium**, m., *door-post* (25)
póstquam, conj., *after* (20)
postrḗmō, adv., *finally* (46)
postrī́diē, adv., *on the following day* (26)
pótius quam, *rather than* (52)
praébeō, -ḗre, -uī, -itus, *to display, show, provide* (52)
praecḗdō, praecḗdere, praecéssī, praecessū́rus, *to go in front* (53)
praecípiō, praecípere, praecḗpī, praecéptus + dat., *to instruct, order* (51)
praecípitō, -ā́re, -ā́vī, -ā́tus, *to hurl* (18)
sē praecipitā́re, *to hurl oneself, rush* (18)
praeclā́rus, -a, -um, *distinguished, famous* (13)
praecúrrō, praecúrrere, praecúrrī, praecursū́rus, *to run ahead* (18)
praédō, praedṓnis, m., *robber* (26)
praéferō, praeférre, praétulī, praelā́tus, irreg. + acc. and dat., *to carry X* (acc.) *in front of Y* (dat.) (37)
praéter, prep. + acc., *except* (21)
praetéreā, adv., *besides, too, moreover* (15)
praetéreō, praeterī́re, praetériī or **praeterī́vī, praetéritus**, irreg., *to go past* (15)
praetéxta, tóga, -ae, f., *toga with purple border* (10)
praetextā́tus, -a, -um, *wearing the **toga praetexta*** (52)
prásinus, -a, -um, *green* (27)
prehéndō, prehéndere, prehéndī, prehḗnsus, *to seize* (44)
prétium, -ī, n., *price* (31)
prī́diē, adv. + acc., *on the day before* (36)
prī́mus, -a, -um, *first* (21, 38)
prī́mā lū́ce, *at dawn* (21)
prī́mō, adv., *first, at first* (40)
prī́mum, adv., *first, at first* (23)
cum prī́mum, conj., *as soon as* (40)
quam prī́mum, *as soon as possible* (40)

prī́nceps, prī́ncipis, m., *emperor, leader, leading citizen* (7)
príor, príor, príus, gen., **priṓris**, *first (of two), previous* (45)
príus, adv., *earlier, previously* (33)
prī́scus, -a, -um, *of olden times, ancient* (54)
procā́citās, procācitā́tis, f., *insolence* (39)
prócāx, procā́cis, *insolent;* as slang, *pushy* (31)
prōcḗdō, prōcḗdere, prōcéssī, prōcessū́rus, *to go forward* (33)
prō cértō habḗre, *to be sure* (47)
prócul, adv., *in the distance, far off, far* (15)
prṓdeō, prōdī́re, prṓdiī, prōditū́rus, irreg., *to come forth* (53)
Prō dī immortā́lēs! *Good heavens!* (42)
prṓferō, prōférre, prṓtulī, prōlā́tus, irreg., *to carry forward, continue* (52)
proficī́scor, proficī́scī, proféctus sum, *to set out, leave* (36, 37)
prófugus, -a, -um, *exiled, fugitive* (39)
prōgrédior, prṓgredī, prōgréssus sum, *to go forward, advance* (45)
prōmíttō, prōmíttere, prōmī́sī, prōmíssus, *to promise* (9)
prṓnuba, -ae, f., *bride's attendant* (50)
prṓnus, -a, -um, *face down* (35)
própe, prep. + acc., *near* (5, 9)
própe, adv., *near, nearby, nearly* (45)
propínquus, -ī, m., *relative* (50)
prōpṓnō, prōpṓnere, prōpósuī, propósitus, *to propose* (X)
própter, prep. + acc., *on account of, because of* (26)
prōrúmpō, prōrúmpere, prōrū́pī, prōrúptus, *to burst forth, burst out* (53)
prṓtinus, adv., *immediately* (54)
prōvíncia, -ae, f., *province* (XII)
próximus, -a, -um, *nearby* (33)
prū́dēns, prūdéntis, *wise, sensible* (34)
prūdénter, adv., *wisely, sensibly* (34, 35)
prūdéntia, -ae, f., *good sense, discretion, skill* (52)
pū́blicus, -a, -um, *public* (51)
puélla, -ae, f., *girl* (1)
púer, púerī, m., *boy* (3)
puerī́lis, -is, -e, *childish, of childhood* (51)
pū́giō, pūgiṓnis, m., *dagger* (42)
púgna, -ae, f., *fight, battle* (48)
púgnam commíttere, *to join battle* (48)
púgnō, -ā́re, -ā́vī, -ātū́rus, *to fight* (48)
púlcher, púlchra, púlchrum, *beautiful, pretty, handsome* (28)
pulchérrimus, -a, -um, *most/very beautiful* (32)
púlchrē, adv., *finely, excellently* (35)
pulchritū́dō, pulchritū́dinis, f., *beauty* (53)
púllus, -ī, m., *chicken* (32)
pulvī́nar, pulvīnā́ris, n., *imperial seat (at games)* (48)
púlvis, púlveris, m., *dust* (15)
pū́niō, -ī́re, -ī́vī, -ī́tus, *to punish* (21)
pū́pa, -ae, f., *doll* (46)
pū́rgō, -ā́re, -ā́vī, -ā́tus, to clean (6)
pū́rus, -a, -um, *spotless, clean, plain white* (51)
tóga pū́ra, -ae, f., *plain white toga* (51)
pútō, -ā́re, -ā́vī, -ā́tus, *to think, consider* (46)
Pȳ́ryamus, -ī, m., *Pyramus* (45)

Q

quā dē caúsā, *for this reason* (32)
quadrā́tus, -a, -um, *squared* (25)
quaérō, quaérere, quaesī́vī, quaesī́tus, *to seek, look for, ask (for)* (30)
Quā́lis...? Quā́lis...? Quā́le...? *What sort of...?* (4)
Quam...! adv., *How...! What a...!* (13, 29, 36)
Quam...? adv., *How...?* (36)
quam, adv., *than, as* (34, 36)
pótius quam, *rather than* (51)
quam, adv. + superlative adj. or adv., *as...as possible* (35, 36)
quam celérrimē, adv., *as quickly as possible* (34)
quam prī́mum, adv., *as soon as possible* (40)
Quam ob caúsam...? *For what reason...?* (28)
quámquam, conj., *although* (11)
Quándō...? adv., *When...?* (12, 21)
quandṓquidem, adv., *since* (54)
Quántus, -a, -um...? *How big...? How much...?* (41)
Quántī...? *How much (in price)...?* (31)
Quántum...! adv., *How much...!* (41)

quā́rtus, -a, -um, *fourth* (38)
quā́rtus décimus, -a, -um, *fourteenth* (38)
quási, adv., *as if* (49)
quáttuor, *four* (15, 38)
quattuórdecim, *fourteen* (38)
-que, enclitic conj., *and* (36)
quī, quae, quod, *who, which, that* (1, 3, 14, 28, 29, 36)
Quī...? Quae...? Quod...? interrog. adj., *What...? Which...?* (29)
Quid ágis? *How are you?* (18, 53)
quídam, quaédam, quóddam, *a certain* (10, 29)
quídem, adv., *indeed* (31)
  nē...quídem, adv., *not even* (34)
quíēs, quiḗtis, f., *rest* (23)
  sē quiḗtī dáre, *to rest* (23)
quiḗscō, quiḗscere, quiḗvī, quiētū́rus, *to rest, keep quiet* (13, 23)
quī́ndecim, *fifteen* (38)
quīngentḗsimus, -a, -um, *five-hundredth* (38)
quīngéntī, -ae, -a, *five hundred* (15, 38)
quīnquāgḗsimus, -a, -um, *fiftieth* (38)
quīnquāgíntā, *fifty* (15, 38)
quī́nque, *five* (15, 38)
quī́ntus, -a, -um, *fifth* (26, 38)
quī́ntus décimus, -a, -um, *fifteenth* (38)
Quirīnā́lis, -is, -e, *Quirinal (Hill)* (35)
Quis...? Quid...? *Who...? What...?* (1, 4, 29)
  Quid ágis? *How are you?* (18, 53)
quis, nē (see **áliquis**) (52)
quis, sī (see **áliquis**) (51)
quō, adv., *there, to that place* (43)
  Quō cum, *When...there* (43)
Quō...? adv., *Where...to?* (4)
quō...éō..., *the (more)...the (more)...* (36, 47)
Quṓcum...? *With whom...?* (12, 26)
quod (see **quī, quae, quod**)
quod, conj., *because;* with verbs of feeling, *that* (1, 13, 29)
Quō īnstrūméntō...? *With what instrument...? By what means...? How...?* (12)
Quṓmodo...? adv., *In what way...? How...?* (12)
quóniam, conj., *since* (42)
quóque, adv., *also* (2, 13)
Quot...? *How many...?* (15, 38)
Quótus, -a, -um...? *What/Which (in numerical order)...?* (38)
  Quóta hṓra est? *What time is it?* (38)

R

raéda, -ae, f., *carriage* (10)
raedā́rius, -ī, m., *coachman, driver* (10)
rā́mus, -ī, m., *branch* (4)
rápiō, rápere, rápuī, ráptus, *to snatch, seize* (40)
rebélliō, rebelliṓnis, f., *rebellion* (XI)
recípiō, recípere, recḗpī, recéptus, *to receive, recapture* (54)
récitō, -ā́re, -ā́vī, -ā́tus, *to read aloud, recite* (29)
  recitándī, *of reciting* (39)
recognítiō, recognitiṓnis, f., *recognition* (49)
rḗctus, -a, -um, *right, proper* (35)
  rḗctē, adv., *rightly, properly* (31, 35)
recúmbō, recúmbere, recúbuī, *to recline, lie down* (29)
recúperō, -ā́re, -ā́vī, -ā́tus, *to recover* (21)
  ánimum recuperā́re, *to regain one's senses, be fully awake* (21)
réddō, réddere, réddidī, rédditus, *to give back, return* (29)
redḗmptor, redēmptṓris, m., *contractor* (54)
rédeō, redī́re, rédiī or **redī́vī, reditū́rus,** irreg., *to return, go back* (7, 23, 49)
  rédiēns, redeúntis, *returning* (39)
réditus, -ūs, m., *return* (25)
redū́cō, redū́cere, redū́xī, redúctus, *to lead back, take back* (42)
réferō, reférre, réttulī, relā́tus, irreg., *to bring back, report, write down* (46)
refíciō, refícere, refḗcī, reféctus, *to remake, redo, restore* (32)
rēgī́na, -ae, f., *queen* (38)
rḗgnum, -ī, n., *kingdom* (32)
regrédior, régredī, regréssus sum, *to go back, return* (36, 37)
relínquō, relínquere, relī́quī, relíctus, *to leave behind* (16, 21)

remóveō, removḗre, remṓvī, remṓtus, *to remove, move aside* (21)
rénovō, -ā́re, -ā́vī, -ā́tus, *to renew, revive* (38)
repéllō, repéllere, réppulī, repúlsus, *to drive off, drive back* (5, 40)
répetō, repétere, repetī́vī, repetī́tus, *to pick up, recover* (43)
reprehéndō, reprehéndere, reprehéndī, reprehḗnsus, *to blame, scold* (6, 31)
requī́rō, requī́rere, requīsī́vī, requīsī́tus, *to ask, inquire* (54)
rēs, réī, f., *thing, matter, situation, affair* (19, 25)
  rem explicā́re, *to explain the situation* (19)
  rēs urbā́nae, rḗrum urbānā́rum, f. pl., *affairs of the city/town* (33)
  rē vḗrā, adv., *really, actually* (49)
rescrī́bō, rescrī́bere, rescrī́psī, rescrī́ptus, *to write back, reply* (50)
resérvō, -ā́re, -ā́vī, -ā́tus, *to reserve* (48)
resístō, resístere, réstitī + dat., *to resist* (42)
respóndeō, respondḗre, respóndī, respōnsū́rus, *to reply* (5, 21)
respṓnsum, -ī, n., *reply* (38)
retíneō, retinḗre, retínuī, reténtus, *to hold back, keep* (31)
rē vḗrā, adv., *really, actually* (49)
révocō, -ā́re, -ā́vī, -ā́tus, *to recall, call back* (7)
rēx, rḗgis, m., *king*
rī́deō, rīdḗre, rī́sī, rī́sus, *to laugh (at), smile* (3, 21)
rīdículus, -a, -um, *absurd, laughable* (43)
rī́ma, -ae, f., *crack* (45)
  rīmṓsus, -a, -um, *full of cracks, leaky* (23)
rī́sus, -ūs, m., *laugh, smile* (13, 25)
rī́te, adv., *properly* (53)
rī́vus, -ī, m., *stream* (5)
ríxa, -ae, f., *quarrel* (29)
ríxor, -ā́rī, -ā́tus sum, *to quarrel* (45)
rogā́tiō, rogātiṓnis, f., *question* (40)
rógō, -ā́re, -ā́vī, -ā́tus, *to ask* (12, 51)
  sē rogā́re, *to ask oneself, wonder* (21)
rógus, -ī, m., *funeral pyre* (54)
Rṓma, -ae, f., *Rome* (7)
  Rṓmā, *from Rome*
  Rṓmae, *in Rome* (39)
  Rṓmam, *to Rome* (7)
Rōmā́nus, -a, -um, *Roman* (1)
  Rōmā́nī, -ṓrum, m. pl., *the Romans* (III)
rósa, -ae, f., *rose* (34)
róta, -ae, f., *wheel* (15)
ruī́na, -ae, f., *collapse, ruin* (38)
rúmpō, rúmpere, rū́pī, rúptus, *to burst* (29)
rū́rsus, adv., *again* (36)
rūs, rū́ris, n., *country, country estate* (39)
  rū́re, *from the country* (39)
  rū́rī, *in the country* (39)
  rūs, *to the country* (39)
russā́tus, -a, -um, *red* (27)
rū́stica, vī́lla, -ae, f., *country house and farm* (1)
rū́sticus, -ī, m., *peasant* (13)

S

sácculus, -ī, m., *small bag (used for holding money)* (34)
sácra, -ṓrum, n. pl., *religious rites, sacrifice* (53)
sacrífico, -ā́re, -ā́vī, -ā́tus, *to sacrifice* (53)
saéculum, -ī, n., *age, era* (48)
saépe, adv., *often* (2, 13, 35)
  saépius, adv., *more often* (35)
  saepíssimē, adv., *most often* (35)
saévus, -a, -um, *fierce, savage* (39)
sal, sális, m., *salt, wit* (34)
saltā́trīx, saltātrī́cis, f., dancer (21)
sáltō, -ā́re, -ā́vī, -ātū́rus, *to dance* (21)
sálūs, salū́tis, f., *greetings* (36)
  salū́tem dī́cere, *to send greetings* (36)
  salū́tem plū́rimam dī́cere, *to send fondest greetings* (36)
salū́tō, -ā́re, -ā́vī, -ā́tus, *to greet, welcome* (7)
Sálvē!/Salvḗte! *Greetings! Hello!* (7)
sálvus, -a, -um, *safe* (5)
sā́nē, adv., *certainly, of course* (36)
sanguíneus, -a, -um, *bloodstained* (45)
sánguis, sánguinis, m., *blood* (33)
sátis, adv., *enough* (23)
  sátis témporis, *enough time* (23)

scápha, -ae, f., *small boat, ship's boat* (40, 42)
sceléstus, -a, -um, *wicked* (10)
scélus, scéleris, n., *crime* (41)
scíndō, scíndere, scídī, scíssus, *to cut, split, carve, tear* (33, 54)
scíssā véste, *with torn clothing* (54)
scíō, -íre, -ívī, -ítus, *to know* (16, 49)
scriblíta, -ae, f., *tart or pastry with cheese filling* (37)
scríbō, scríbere, scrípsī, scríptus, *to write* (1, 24)
sē, *himself, herself, oneself, itself, themselves* (11)
sécum, *with him (her, it, them) (-self, -selves)*
sēcrḗtō, adv., *secretly* (45)
secúndus, -a, -um, *second* (9, 38)
secúndae mḗnsae, -ā́rum, f. pl., *second course, dessert* (33)
sēcū́rus, -a, -um, *carefree, unconcerned* (35)
sed, conj., *but* (2)
sḗdecim, *sixteen* (38)
sédeō, sedḗre, sḗdī, sessū́rus, *to sit* (1, 21)
sélla, -ae, f., *sedan chair, seat, chair* (28, 42, 44)
sēmisómnus, -a, -um, *half-asleep* (9)
sémper, adv., *always* (4, 13)
senā́tor, senātṓris, m., *senator* (7)
senā́tus, -ūs, m., *Senate* (25)
sénex, sénis, m., *old man* (I, 43)
sḗniō, sēniṓnis, m., *the six (in throwing knucklebones)* (34)
séntiō, sentíre, sḗnsī, sḗnsus, *to feel, notice, realize* (45, 49)
sepéliō, sepelíre, sepelívī, sepúltus, *to bury* (39)
séptem, *seven* (15, 38)
Septémber, Septémbris, Septémbre, *September* (36)
septéndecim, *seventeen* (38)
septentriōnā́lis, -is, -e, *northern* (39)
séptimus, -a, -um, *seventh* (13, 38)
séptimus décimus, -a, -um, *seventeenth* (38)
septuāgḗsimus, -a, -um, *seventieth* (IX)
sepúlcrum, -ī, n., *tomb* (22)
séquor, séquī, secū́tus sum, *to follow* (36, 37)
séquēns, sequéntis, *following* (25)
serḗnus, -a, -um, *clear, bright* (50)
sérmō, sermṓnis, m., *conversation, talk* (54)

sḗrō, adv., *late* (21, 35)
sḗrius, adv., *later* (35)
sēríssimē, adv., *latest* (35)
sérva, -ae, f., *slave-woman, slave-girl* (50)
sérviō, servíre, servívī, servītū́rus + dat., *to serve* (53)
sérvitūs, servitū́tis, f., *slavery* (XI)
sérvō, -ā́re, -ā́vī, -ā́tus, *to save* (26, 30)
sérvus, -ī, m., *slave* (3)
seu = síve, conj., *or if* (34)
sex, *six* (15, 38)
séxtus, -a, -um, *sixth* (37, 38)
séxtus décimus, -a, -um, *sixteenth* (38)
sī, conj., *if* (5)
sī quis (= áliquis), *if anyone* (51)
si vīs, *if you wish, please* (26)
sīc, adv., *thus, in this way* (38, 39, 50)
síccus, -a, -um, *dry* (53)
Sicília, -ae, f., *Sicily* (38)
sígnum, -ī, n., *signal, sign* (27)
siléntium, -ī, n., *silence* (15)
sílva, -ae, f., *woods, forest* (5)
símilis, -is, -e + dat., *similar (to), like* (34, 50)
símul, adv., *together, at the same time* (9, 13)
símulac, conj., *as soon as* (24)
símulō, -ā́re, -ā́vī, -ā́tus, *to pretend* (21)
síne, prep. + abl., *without* (26)
sinístér, sinístra, sinístrum, *left* (50)
sínō, sínere, sívī, sítus, *to allow* (34)
sítus, -a, -um, *located, situated, buried* (33, 54)
sīs = sī vīs, *if you wish, please* (36)
sōl, sṓlis, m., *sun* (50)
sólea, -ae, f., *sandal* (32)
sóleō, solḗre, sólitus sum + infin., *to be accustomed (to), be in the habit of* (10, 40)
sōlitū́dō, sōlitū́dinis, f., *solitude* (39)
sollícitus, -a, -um, *anxious, worried* (4)
sṓlus, -a, -um, *alone* (3)
sólvō, sólvere, sólvī, solū́tus, *to loosen, untie, dishevel* (54)
sómnium, -ī, n., *dream* (21)
sómnus, -ī, m., *sleep* (21)
sónitus, -ūs, m., *sound* (21, 25)

sórdidus, -a, -um, *dirty* (19)
sóror, soróris, f., *sister* (11)
S.P.D. = salū́tem plū́rimam dī́cit (36)
spectā́culum, -ī, n., *sight, spectacle* (30)
spectā́tor, spectātṓris, m., *spectator* (27)
spéctō, -ā́re, -ā́vī, -ā́tus, *to watch, look at* (7)
spéculum, -ī, n., *mirror* (28)
spēlúnca, -ae, f., *cave* (45)
spḗrō, -ā́re, -ā́vī, -ā́tus, *to hope* (47)
spóndeō, spondḗre, spopóndī, spṓnsus, *to promise solemnly, pledge* (50)
spṓnsa, -ae, f., *betrothed woman, bride* (50)
spōnsā́lia, spōnsā́lium, n. pl., *betrothal ceremony* (50)
spṓnsus, -ī, m., *betrothed man, bridegroom* (50)
státim, adv., *immediately* (5, 13)
státua, -ae, f., *statue* (3)
stḗla, -ae, f., *tombstone* (33)
stércus, stércoris, n., *dung, manure* (21)
stértō, stértere, stértuī, *to snore* (25)
stílus, -ī, m., *pen* (25)
stírps, stírpis, gen. pl., **stírpium**, f., *thorn* (49)
stō, stā́re, stétī, statū́rus, *to stand* (10, 22)
stóla, -ae, f., *stola, a woman's outer-garment* (10)
strā́tum, -ī, n., *sheet, covering* (32)
strḗnuus, -a, -um, *active, energetic* (2)
  strḗnuē, adv., *strenuously, hard* (6, 13, 35)
strépitus, -ūs, m., *noise, clattering* (23, 25)
strígilis, strígilis, gen. pl., **strigílium**, f., *strigil, scraper* (43)
stríngō, stríngere, strī́nxī, stríctus, *to draw* (26)
  gládium stríngere, *to draw a sword* (26)
stúdeō, -ḗre, -uī + dat., *to study* (39)
stúdium, -ī, n., *enthusiasm, study* (41)
stúltus, -a, -um, *stupid, foolish* (23)
stúpeō, -ḗre, -uī, *to be amazed, gape* (23)
suā́vis, -is, -e, *sweet, delightful* (34)
sub, prep. + abl., *under, beneath* (1, 9)
súbitus, -a, -um, *sudden* (54)
  súbitō, adv., *suddenly* (3, 13)
submíssus, -a, -um, *quiet, subdued, soft* (50)
súbsequor, súbsequī, subsecū́tus sum, *to follow (up)* (44)
Subū́ra, -ae, f., *Subura (a section of Rome off the Forum, known for its night life)* (35)
súī (see **sē**)
sum, ésse, fúī, futū́rus, irreg., *to be* (1, 14, 20, 21)
súmmus, -a, -um, *greatest, very great, the top of...* (35)
  súmmā celeritā́te, *with the greatest speed, as fast as possible* (29)
sū́mō, sū́mere, sū́mpsī, sū́mptus, *to take, take up, pick out, assume (i.e., put on for the first time)* (22, 51)
súper, prep. + acc., *over, above* (53)
supérbus, -a, -um, *proud, arrogant* (48)
súperī, -ṓrum, m. pl., *the gods above* (39)
súperō, -ā́re, -ā́vī, -ā́tus, *to overcome, defeat* (42)
suppositī́cius, -ī, m., *substitute* (48)
súprā, prep. + acc., *above* (23)
súprā, adv., *above, on top* (21)
súrgō, súrgere, surrḗxī, surrēctū́rus, *to get up, rise* (6, 21)
surrípiō, surrípere, surrípuī, surréptus, *to steal* (44)
súus, -a, -um, *his, her, its, their (own)* (9, 27, 54)

T

tabellā́rius, -ī, m., *courier* (13)
tabérna, -ae, f., *shop* (25)
tablī́num, -ī, n., *study* (26)
tábulae, -ā́rum, f. pl., *tablets, records* (51, 53)
Tabulā́rium, -ī, n., *Public Records Office* (51)
tabulā́tum, -ī, n., *story, floor* (30)
táceō, -ḗre, -uī, -itus, *to be quiet* (9)
tácitē, adv., *silently* (9, 13)
taéda, -ae, f., *torch* (53)
taédet, taedḗre, taésum est, *it bores, makes one* (acc.) *tired of something* (gen.) (16, 50, 52)
  mē taédet + gen., *it tires me of..., I am tired of/bored with...* (50)
Talássius, -ī, m., *Talassius (god of marriage)* (53)
tā́lī, -ṓrum, m. pl., *knucklebones* (34)
tā́lis, -is, -e, *such, like this, of this kind* (23, 50)
  tā́lia, tā́lium, n. pl., *such things* (41)

tam, adv., *so* (30, 50)
támen, adv., *however, nevertheless* (6, 13)
támquam, conj., *just as if* (33)
tándem, adv., *at last, at length* (2, 13)
tángō, tángere, tétigī, tā́ctus, *to touch* (54)
tántus, -a, -um, *so great, such a big* (24, 50)
tántum, adv., *only; so much* (15, 50)
tárdus, -a, -um, *slow* (15)
tē (from **tū**) (4)
tégō, tégere, tḗxī, tḗctus, *to cover* (54)
tḗla, -ae, f., *web, fabric, loom* (41)
temerā́rius, -a, -um, *rash, reckless, bold* (5)
tempéstās, tempestā́tis, f., *storm* (38)
témplum, -ī, n., *temple* (40)
témptō, -ā́re, -ā́vī, -ā́tus, *to try* (9)
témpus, témporis, n., *time* (2, 8, 12, 15)
ad témpus, *on time* (37)
téneō, tenḗre, ténuī, téntus, *to hold* (9, 25)
memóriā tenḗre, *to remember* (37)
tepidā́rium, -ī, n., *warm room (at baths)* (43)
ter, adv., *three times* (48)
térgeō, tergḗre, térsī, térsus, *to dry, wipe* (43)
térgum, -ī, n., *back, rear* (35)
térra, -ae, f., *earth, ground, land* (26, 38)
térreō, -ḗre, -uī, -itus, *to frighten, terrify* (4)
terríbilis, -is, -e, *frightening* (39)
térritus, -a, -um, *frightened* (39)
térror, terrṓris, m., *terror, fear* (22)
tértius, -a, -um, *third* (25, 36, 38)
tértius décimus, -a, -um, *thirteenth* (38)
téssera, -ae, f., *ticket* (48)
testāméntum, -ī, n., *will, testament* (IX)
téxō, téxere, téxuī, téxtus, *to weave* (41)
thérmae, -ā́rum, f. pl., *public baths* (43)
Thérmae Nerōnḗae, -ā́rum, f. pl., *the Baths of Nero* (43)
Thísbē, Thísbēs, f., *Thisbe* (45)
Thrā́cia, -ae, f., *Thrace (country northeast of Greece)* (39)
tībī́cen, tībī́cinis, m., *piper* (54)
tígris, tígris, gen. pl., **tígrium**, m./f., *tiger* (49)
tímeō, -ḗre, -uī, *to fear, be afraid to/of* (5)
timéndus, -a, um, *to be feared* (48)
tímidus, -a, -um, *afraid, fearful, timid* (21)
tímor, timṓris, m., *fear* (35)
tóga, -ae, f., *toga* (8)
tóga praetéxta, -ae, f., *toga with purple border* (10, 51)
tóga pū́ra, -ae, f., *plain white toga* (51)
tóga virī́lis, tógae virī́lis, f., *toga of manhood, plain white toga* (10, 51)
tóllō, tóllere, sústulī, sublā́tus, irreg., *to lift, raise* (48)
tórus, -ī, m., *couch* (38)
tot, indecl. adj., *so many* (48, 50)
tṓtus, -a, -um, *all, the whole* (21)
trā́dō, trā́dere, trā́didī, trā́ditus, *to hand over* (7, 22)
tráhō, tráhere, trā́xī, tráctus, *to drag, pull* (6, 12, 25)
lā́nam tráhere, *to spin wool* (6)
trāns, prep. + acc., *across* (39)
trānsgrédior, trā́nsgredī, trānsgréssus sum, *to cross* (X)
trédecim, *thirteen* (38)
trémō, trémere, trémuī, *to tremble* (21)
trémor, tremṓris, m., *cause of fright, terror* (48)
trépidāns, trepidántis, *in a panic* (52)
trēs, trēs, tría, *three* (13, 15, 38)
trīclī́nium, -ī, n., *dining room* (31)
trídēns, tridéntis, gen. pl., **tridéntium**, m., *trident* (48)
trígōn, trigṓnis, m., *ball game involving three people, ball (used in this game)* (43)
trī́stis, -is, -e, *sad* (36)
Tróia, -ae, f., *Troy* (I, 38)
Troiā́nus, -a, -um, *Trojan* (I, 38)
Troiā́nī, -ṓrum, m. pl., *the Trojans* (I)
tū, *you* (sing.) (4, 27)
túbicen, tubícinis, m., *trumpet-player* (48)
túlī (see **férō**)
tum, adv., *at that moment, then* (4, 13)
tumúltus, -ūs, m., *uproar, commotion* (25)
túnica, -ae, f., *tunic* (8)
túrba, -ae, f., *crowd, mob; cause of confusion/turmoil* (23, 48)
túus, -a, -um, *your* (sing.) (9, 27)

U

Úbi...? adv., *Where...?* (10, 12)
úbi, adv., conj., *where, when* (1, 5, 13)
Ulíxēs, Ulíxis, m., *Ulysses, Odysseus (Greek hero of the Trojan War)* (38)
úlulō, -ā́re, -ā́vī, -ā́tus, *to howl* (33)
úmbra, -ae, f., *shadow, shade (of the dead)* (31, 33)
úmquam, adv., *ever* (31)
ū́nā, adv., *together* (33)
únda, -ae, f., *wave* (42)
Únde...? *From where...?* (12)
ū́ndecim, *eleven* (38)
ūndécimus, -a, -um, *eleventh* (17, 38)
ūndēvīcḗsimus, -a, -um, *nineteenth* (38)
ūndēvīgíntī, *nineteen* (38)
úndique, adv., *on all sides, from all sides* (23)
unguéntum, -ī, n., *ointment, perfume, oil* (34, 43)
únguō, únguere, ū́nxī, ū́nctus, *to anoint, smear with oil* (43)
ūnivérsus, -a, -um, *the whole of, the entire* (48)
ū́nus, -a, -um, *one* (15, 38)
  ū́nā, adv., *together* (33)
urbā́nus, -a, -um, *of the city/town* (33)
  rēs urbā́nae, rḗrum urbānā́rum, f. pl., *affairs of the city/town* (33)
urbs, úrbis, gen. pl., **úrbium**, f., *city* (7)
úrgeō, urgḗre, úrsī, *to press, insist* (52)
ut, conj. + indicative, *as, when* (16, 54)
ut, conj. + subjunctive, *so that, that, to* (50, 53, 54)
utérque, útraque, utrúmque, *each (of two), both* (45)
ū́tilis, -is, -e, *useful* (37)
útrum...an..., conj., *whether...or...* (52)
ū́va, -ae, f., *grape, bunch of grapes* (33)
úxor, uxṓris, f., *wife* (11)

V

váldē, adv., *very, very much, exceedingly* (19)
váleō, -ḗre, -uī, -itū́rus, *to be strong, be well* (40)
  Válē!/Valḗte! *Goodbye!* (9)
valedī́cō, valedī́cere, valedī́xī, valedictū́rus, *to say goodbye* (45)
valētū́dō, valētū́dinis, f., *health (good or bad)* (39)
vápor, vapṓris, m., *steam* (43)
várius, -a, -um, *different, various, varied, many-hued* (43, 53)
-ve, enclitic conj., *or* (34)
véhemēns, veheméntis, *violent* (35)
  veheménter, adv., *very much, violently, hard, insistently* (19)
vehículum, -ī, n., *vehicle* (13, 15)
véhō, véhere, véxī, véctus, *to carry;* pass., *to be carried, travel* (54)
  véctus, -a, -um, *having been carried, having traveled* (54)
vel, conj., *or* (37)
  vel...vel..., *either...or...*
vēlā́men, vēlā́minis, n., *veil, shawl* (45)
vélle (see **vólō**)
véndō, véndere, véndidī, vénditus, *to sell* (28)
vénetus, -a, -um, *blue* (27)
véniō, venī́re, vḗnī, ventū́rus, *to come* (7, 20)
véntus, -ī, m., *wind* (42)
Vénus, Véneris, f., *Venus (the goddess of love); the highest throw of the knucklebones* (34)
venústus, -a, -um, *charming* (34)
vérberō, -ā́re, -ā́vī, -ā́tus, *to beat, whip* (11)
verbṓsus, -a, -um, *talkative* (26)
vérbum, -ī, n., *word, verb* (39)
véreor, verḗrī, véritus sum, *to be afraid, fear* (37)
Vergílius, -ī, m., *Vergil (Roman poet)* (37)
versipéllis, versipéllis, gen. pl., **versipéllium**, m., *werewolf* (33)
vérsus, -ūs, m., *verse, line (of poetry)* (29)
vértō, vértere, vértī, vérsus, *to turn* (16)
vḗrus, -a, -um, *true* (40)
  ímmō vḗrō, adv., *on the contrary, in fact* (40)
  Íta vḗrō! *Yes! Indeed!* (3, 13)
  Mínimē vḗrō! *No indeed! Not at all!* (31)
  rē vḗrā, *really, actually* (49)
  vḗra dī́cere, *to tell the truth* (40)
  vḗrō, adv., *truly, really, indeed* (31)
vḗscor, vḗscī + abl., *to feed (on)* (49)
vésperī, *in the evening* (18)
véster, véstra, véstrum, *your* (pl.) (22, 27)

vestíbulum, -ī, n., *entrance passage* (43)
vēstígium, -ī, n., *track, footprint, trace* (12, 15)
vestīméntum, -ī, n., *clothing;* pl., *clothes* (33)
véstis, véstis, gen. pl., **véstium**, f., *clothing, garment* (29, 54)
scíssā véste, *with torn clothing* (54)
vétō, vetā́re, vétuī, vétitus, *to forbid, tell not to* (26)
vétus, véteris, *old* (34)
véxō, -ā́re, -ā́vī, -ā́tus, *to annoy* (4)
vexā́tus, -a, -um, *annoyed* (28)
vía, -ae, f., *road, street* (10)
Vía Áppia, -ae, f., *Appian Way* (11)
Vía Flāmínia, -ae, f., *the Via Flaminia (a road from Rome leading through the Campus Martius and north to Ariminum on the Adriatic Sea)* (54)
viátor, viātṓris, m., *traveler* (18)
vīcésimus, -a, -um, *twentieth* (38)
vīcī́nus, -a, -um, *neighboring, adjacent* (1)
víctor, victṓris, m., *conqueror, victor* (27)
victṓria, -ae, f., *victory* (XII)
vídeō, vidḗre, vī́dī, vī́sus, *to see* (4, 21, 49)
vídeor, vidḗrī, vī́sus sum, *to seem, be seen* (21)
vígilō, -ā́re, -ā́vī, -ātū́rus, *to stay awake* (19)
vīgíntī, *twenty* (36, 38)
vī́licus, -ī, m., *overseer, farm manager* (11)
vī́lla, -ae, f., *country house* (1)
vī́lla rū́stica, -ae, f., *country house and farm* (1)
víncō, víncere, vī́cī, víctus, *to conquer, win* (27)
vī́nea, -ae, f., *vineyard* (12)
vī́num, -ī, n., *wine* (25)
vī́nō ábstinēns, *refraining from wine, abstemious* (34)
víolō, -ā́re, -ā́vī, -ā́tus, *to do harm* (54)
vir, vírī, m., *man, husband* (3, 11)
vir óptime, *sir* (20)
vírga, -ae, f., *stick, rod, switch* (13)
vírgō, vírginis, f., *maiden* (45)
virī́lis, -is, -e, *of manhood* (23)
tóga virī́lis, tógae virī́lis, f., *toga of manhood, plain white toga* (10)
vīs, acc., **vim**, abl., **vī**, f., *force, amount;* pl. *strength* (30)
víscera, víscerum, n. pl., *vital organs* (53)
vī́sitō, -ā́re, -ā́vī, -ā́tus, *to visit* (23)
vispíllō, vispillṓnis, m., *undertaker* (54)
vī́ta, -ae, f., *life* (54)
ē vī́tā excḗdere, *to die* (54)
vī́tō, -ā́re, -ā́vī, -ā́tus, *to avoid* (13)
vítta, -ae, f., *ribbon, headband* (53)
vī́vō, vī́vere, vī́xī, vīctū́rus, *to live* (39)
vix, adv., *scarcely, with difficulty, only just* (24)
vócō, -ā́re, -ā́vī, -ā́tus, *to call, invite* (28)
vólō, vélle, vóluī, irreg., *to wish, want, be willing* (5, 17, 20, 21)
sī vīs, *if you wish, please* (36)
volúptās, voluptā́tis, f., *pleasure, delight* (48)
vōs, *you* (pl.) (8, 27)
vōx, vṓcis, f., *voice* (4)
vúlnerō, -ā́re, -ā́vī, -ā́tus, *to wound* (33)
vúlnus, vúlneris, n., *wound* (35)
vult (from **vólō**) (5, 17)
vúltus, -ūs, m., *face, expression* (45)

English to Latin Vocabulary

Verbs are usually cited in their infinitive form. For further information about the Latin words in this list, please consult the Latin to English Vocabulary list.

A

able, to be, **pósse**
about, **dē**
above, **súper, súprā**
absent, to be, **abésse**
abstemious, **vī́nō ábstinēns**
absurd, **rīdículus**
accidentally, **cā́sū**
accompanied, **comitā́tus**
accompany, to, **comitā́rī**
accomplish, to, **cōnfícere**
accuse, to, **accūsā́re**
accustomed (to), to be, **solḗre**
across, **trāns**
active, **strḗnuus**
actor, **ā́ctor**
actor of mime, **mī́mus**
actually, **rē vḗrā**
add, to, **áddere**
address, to, **álloquī**
adjacent, **vīcī́nus**
adopt, to, **adoptā́re**
adopt a plan, to, **cōnsílium cápere**
advance, to, **prṓgredī**
advise, to, **monḗre**
Aeneas, **Aenḗās**
Aeneid, the, **Aenḗis**
affair, **rēs**
affairs of the city/town, **rēs urbā́nae**
affect, to, **affícere**
affected, **afféctus**
afraid, **tímidus**
afraid, to be, **verḗrī**
afraid (to/of), to be, **timḗre**
Africa, **Ā́frica**
after, **póstquam**
after(ward), **post**
afterward, **póstea**
again, **íterum, rū́rsus**
again and again, **idéntidem**
against, **cóntrā, in**
age, **saéculum**
ago, **abhínc**
agreed, it is, **cṓnstat**
agreement, **cōnsḗnsus**
aim at, to, **pétere**
Alas!, **Ḗheu! Heu!**
Alba Longa, of, **Albā́nus**
all, **cū́nctī, ómnis, tṓtus**
All right! **Éstō!**
allow, to, **sínere**
allowed, it is, **lícet**
allowed, we are, **lícet nṓbīs**
almost, **férē, paéne**
alone, **sṓlus**
along, **per**
Alps, the, **Álpēs**
already, **iam**
also, **átque, et, étiam, quóque**
altar, **ā́ra**
although, **quámquam**
always, **sémper**
amazed, to be, **stupḗre**
amazement, **admīrā́tiō**
amazement (to), to be a source of, **admīrātiṓnī ésse**
among, **in, ínter**
amount, **vīs**
amount, a small, **paúlum**
amphitheater, **amphitheā́trum**
amuse, to, **dēlectā́re**
ancestors, **maiṓrēs**

ancient, **antī́quus, prī́scus**
and, **ac, átque, et, -que**
and...not, **nec, néque**
and so, **ítaque**
Androcles, **Ándroclēs**
anger, **ī́ra**
angry, **īrā́tus**
anoint, to, **únguere**
annoy, to, **vexā́re**
annoyed, **vexā́tus**
annoying, **moléstus**
another, **álius, álter**
another time, at, **áliās**
anxious, **sollícitus**
anyone, if, **sī quis**
apartment building, **ī́nsula**
apologize, to, **sē excūsā́re**
appear, to, **appārḗre**
Appian Way, **Vía Áppia**
apple, **mā́lum**
appoint, to, **creā́re**
approach, to, **adī́re, appropinquā́re**
approximately, **férē**
April, **Aprī́lis**
aqueduct, **aquaedúctus**
arch, **árcus**
arena, **arḗna**
arise, to, **coorī́rī**
armed, **armā́tus**
arms, **árma**
around, **círcum**
aroused, **excitā́tus**
arrive (at), to, **advenī́re, pervenī́re**
arrogant, **supérbus**
as, gen. + **caúsā, quam, ut**
as an honor, **honṓris caúsā**
as...as possible, **quam** + superl. adj. or adv.
as fast as possible, **súmmā celeritā́te**
as if, **quási**
as long as, **dum**
as quickly as possible, **quam celérrimē**
as soon as, **cum prī́mum, símulac**
as soon as possible, **quam prī́mum**
as yet, **adhū́c**
ashes, **cínis**
Asia Minor, **Ásia**
ask, to, **interrogā́re, requī́rere, rogā́re**
ask (for), to, **póscere, quaérere**
ask oneself, to, **sē rogā́re**
asparagus, **aspáragus**
assemble, to, **convenī́re**
assume, to, **sū́mere**
astonished, **attónitus**
astounded, **attónitus, obstupefáctus**
at, **ad**
at last, **tándem**
at length, **tándem**
at night, **nóctū**
at the house of, **ápud**
Athens, **Athḗnae**
atrium, **ā́trium**
attack, **ímpetus**
attack, to, **adorī́rī, pétere**
attendant, bride's, **prṓnuba**
attentively, **atténtē**
augur, **aúspex**
August, **Augústus**
Augustus, **Augústus**
avoid, to, **nē, vītā́re**
awake, to be fully, **ánimum recuperā́re**
away, to be, **abésse**

B

Babyon, **Bábylōn**
back, **térgum**
bad, **málus**
badly, **mále**
bag, **fóllis**
bag (used for holding money), small, **sácculus**
Baiae, **Báiae**
baker, **pī́stor**
bakery, **pīstrī́num**
bald, **cálvus**
ball, **píla, trígōn**
ball game involving three people, **trígōn**
band (of men), **mánus**

banquet, **convī́vium, épulae**
bar, **popī́na**
bark, a, **lātrā́tus**
bark, to, **lātrā́re**
barking, **lātrā́tus**
baths, **bálneae**
baths, public, **thérmae**
Baths of Nero, the, **Thérmae Nerōnḗae**
battle, **púgna**
battle, to join, **púgnam commítterre**
bay (tree), **laúrus**
be, to, **ésse**
be done, to, **fíerī**
be made, to, **fíerī**
Be of good mind! **Bónō ánimō es!/éste!**
bear, to, **férre**
bearing, **incéssus**
beast, **bḗstia**
beat, to, **plángere, verberā́re**
beat the breast, to, **péctus plángere**
beautiful, **cándidus, púlcher**
beautiful, most/very, **pulchérrimus**
beauty, **pulchritū́dō**
because, **quod**
because of, **própter**
become, to, **fíerī**
becoming, it is, **décet**
bed, **léctus**
bed, to go to, **cúbitum ī́re**
bedroom, **cubículum**
before, **ánte, ánteā, ántequam, ápud**
beg, to, **obsecrā́re, ōrā́re**
began, I, **coépī**
beggar, **mendī́cus**
begin, to, **incípere, ōrdī́rī**
believe, to, **crḗdere**
beloved, **cā́rus**
beneath, **sub**
beseech, to, **obsecrā́re**
besides, **praetéreā**
besiege, to, **obsidḗre**
best, **óptimē, óptimus**
bestow, to, **cōnférre**
betroth, to, **dēspondḗre**
betrothal ceremony, **spōnsā́lia**
betrothed man, **spṓnsus**
betrothed woman, **spṓnsa**
better, **mélior, mélius**
between, **ínter**
beware, to, **cavḗre**
bid, to, **iubḗre**
big, **mágnus**
big, such a, **tántus**
bigger, **máior**
biggest, **máximus**
bind up, to, **ligā́re**
bird, **ávis**
birth, of/belonging to, **nātā́lis**
birthday, **díēs nātā́lis**
Bithynia, **Bīthȳ́nia**
black, **níger**
blame, **cúlpa**
blame, to, **reprehéndere**
blaze, to, **ārdḗre**
blood, **sánguis**
bloodstained, **sanguíneus**
blue, **vénetus**
boat, small/ship's, **scápha**
body, **córpus**
bold, **aúdāx, temerā́rius**
bone, **os**
book, **líber**
bored (with), I am, **mē taédet**
bores, it, **taédet**
born, to be, **nā́scī**
both, **ámbō, utérque**
both...and, **et...et**
box, cylindrical, **fritíllus**
boy, **púer**
branch, **rā́mus**
brand, to, **inū́rere**
brave, **fórtis**
bravely, **fórtiter**
bravely, most/very, **fortíssimē**
bread, **pā́nis**
break, to, **frángere**
breakfast, **iēntā́culum**
breast, **péctus**

bride, **nóva nū́pta, spṓnsa**
bridegroom, **concubī́nus, spṓnsus**
bridge, **pōns**
briefly, **bréviter**
bright, **clā́rus, serḗnus**
bring, to, **addū́cere, afférre, dēdū́cere, dū́cere, férre**
bring back, to, **reférre**
Bring help! **Fer/Férte auxílium!**
bring in, to, **afférre, intrōdū́cere, īnférre**
bring out, to, **efférre**
bring to, to, **afférre**
bring together, to, **commíttere**
Britain, **Británnia**
British, **Británnicus**
Britons, **Británnī**
brother, **frā́ter**
brotherly, **frātérnus**
Brundisium, **Brundísium**
Brundisium, at, **Brundísiī**
Brundisium, from, **Brundísiō**
Brundisium, to, **Brundísium**
buffoon, **mī́mus**
build, to, **aedificā́re, exstrúere**
building, **aedifícium**
bulk, huge, **mṓlēs**
bunch of grapes, **ū́va**
burden, **ónus**
buried, **sítus**
burn, to, **ārdḗre, incéndere**
burst, to, **rúmpere**
burst forth, to, **prōrúmpere**
burst in, to, **irrúmpere**
burst out, to, **prōrúmpere**
bury, to, **sepelī́re**
busy, **negōtiṓsus, occupā́tus**
but, **at, aútem, sed**
butcher, **lánius**
buy, to, **comparā́re, émere**
by, **ā, ab**
By Hercules! **Mehércule!**
by night, **nóctū**
bystanders, **adstántēs**

C

Caesar, **Caésar**
cage, **cávea**
Caligula, **Calígula**
call, to, **appellā́re, vocā́re**
call back, to, **revocā́re**
call by name, to, **nōminā́re**
call together, to, **convocā́re**
call upon, to, **invocā́re**
can, I, **póssum**
candelabrum, **candēlā́brum**
candle, **candḗla**
cane, **férula**
captain, **magíster**
captive, **captī́vus**
capture, to, **cápere**
care, **cū́ra**
carefree, **sēcū́rus**
careful, be, to, **cavḗre**
carefully, **dīligénter**
careless, **néglegēns**
carelessly, **neglegénter**
carelessness, **neglegéntia**
carriage, **raéda**
carriage, light two-wheeled, **císium**
carried, having been, **véctus**
carry, to, **férre, portā́re, véhere**
carry away, to, **auférre**
carry forward, to, **prōférre**
carry on, to, **gérere**
carry out, to, **efférre**
carry out funeral rites, to, **exséquiās dū́cere**
carry X in front of Y, to, **praeférre**
cart, **plaústrum**
Carthage, **Carthā́gō**
carve, to, **scíndere**
castanet, **crótalum**
cat, **fḗlēs**
catch, to, **cápere, excípere**
catch sight of, to, **cōnspícere**
catch the scent of, to, **olfácere**
catch up to, to, **cṓnsequī**
cause of anxiety (to), to be a, **cū́rae ésse**

cause of confusion/turmoil, **túrba**
cause of fright, **trémor**
cave, **spēlúnca**
Cerberus, **Cérberus**
ceremony, official, **offícium**
certain, **cértus**
certain, a, **quī́dam**
certainly, **cértē, sā́nē**
chair, **sélla**
chance, by, **cā́sū, fórte**
changing-room, **apodytḗrium**
character, **mṓrēs**
chariot-racing, **lū́dī circénsēs**
charioteer, **aurī́ga**
charming, **lépidus, venústus**
Charon, **Chárōn**
chaste, **cástus**
Cheer up! **Bónō ánimō es!/éste!**
cheerful, **hílaris**
chest, **císta, péctus**
chicken, **púllus**
child, young, **ī́nfāns**
childhood, of, **puerī́lis**
childish, **puerī́lis**
children, **lī́berī**
chilled, **gelā́tus**
Christian, **Chrīstiā́nus**
Christians, the, **Chrīstiā́nī**
circus, in the, **circénsis**
Circus Maximus, **Círcus Máximus**
citizen, **cī́vis**
city, **urbs**
city, of the, **urbā́nus**
clan, **gēns**
clattering, **strépitus**
clean, **pū́rus**
clean, to, **pūrgā́re**
clear, **serḗnus**
client, **clíēns**
climb, to, **ascéndere**
climb down, to, **dēscéndere**
climb into (a carriage), to, **ascéndere**
cloak, **pállium**
closed, **claúsus**
closely, **atténtē**
clothed, **indū́tus**
clothes, **vestīménta**
clothing, **vestīméntum, véstis**
clothing, with torn, **scíssā véste**
cloud, **nū́bēs**
club, **fū́stis**
coachman, **raedā́rius**
coaxing manner, in a, **blándē**
cobweb, **arā́nea**
cold, **frī́gidus**
cold room (at baths), **frīgidā́rium**
collapse, **ruī́na**
collapse, to, **collā́bī**
comb, to, **péctere**
come, to, **venī́re**
come down, to, **dēscéndere**
come forth, to, **prōdī́re**
come near (to), to, **appropinquā́re**
Come on! **Áge!/Ágite!**
come to, to, **adī́re**
come together, to, **cóngredī, convenī́re**
come upon, to, **invenī́re**
commander, **imperā́tor**
commands, **iússa**
comment on, to, **commemorā́re**
common, **commū́nis**
commotion, **tumúltus**
companion, **cómes**
company (of charioteers), **fáctiō**
compel, to, **cṓgere**
complete, to, **complḗre**
compose, to, **compṓnere**
conceal, to, **cēlā́re**
concerning, **dē**
condemn, to, **condemnā́re**
confer, to, **cōnférre**
confine, to, **continḗre**
confused, **perturbā́tus**
confusion, cause of, **túrba**
congratulate, to, **grātulā́rī**
conquer, to, **víncere**
conqueror, **víctor**
consider, to, **putā́re**

consul, **cṓnsul**
consult, to, **cōnsúlere**
continue, to, **prōférre**
contractor, **redḗmptor**
contrary, on the, **ímmō vḗrō**
conversation, **collóquium**, **sérmō**
converse, to, **cólloquī**
cook, **cóquus**
cook, to, **cóquere**
cool, **frī́gidus**
Cornelius, belonging to, **Cornēliā́nus**
cottage, **cása**
couch, **léctus, tórus**
count, to, **numerā́re**
country, **rūs**
country, from the, **rū́re**
country, in the, **rū́rī**
country, to the, **rūs**
country estate, **rūs**
country house, **vī́lla**
country house and farm, **vī́lla rū́stica**
courier, **tabellā́rius**
course, first, **gustā́tiō**
course, second, **secúndae mḗnsae**
courteously, **cṓmiter**
cover, to, **operī́re, tégere**
covered, **aspérsus**
covering, **strátum**
cow, **bōs**
cowardly, **ignā́vus**
crack, **rī́ma**
cracks, full of, **rīmṓsus**
crash, **frágor**
create, to, **creā́re**
Cremona, **Cremṓna**
Crete, **Crḗta**
crime, **scélus**
critically, **mortíferē**
cross, to, **trā́nsgredī**
crowd, **catérva, multitū́dō, túrba**
crown, **corṓna**
crown, to, **corōnā́re**
cruel, **crūdḗlis**
cruelty, **crūdḗlitās**
crushed, **oppréssus**
cry, to, **flḗre, lacrimā́re**
cudgel, **fū́stis**
cultivate, to, **cólere**
cup, **pṓculum**
Cupid, **Cupī́dō**
custom, **mōs**
cut, to, **scíndere**
cylindrical box, **fritíllus**

D

dagger, **pū́giō**
daily, **cotī́diē**
dance, to, **saltā́re**
dancer, **saltā́trīx**
danger, **perī́culum**
dangerous, **perīculṓsus**
dare (to), to, **audḗre**
dark, it gets, **advesperā́scit**
daughter, **fī́lia**
dawn, at, **prī́mā lū́ce**
day, **díēs**
day, by, **intérdiū**
day, during the, **intérdiū**
day, early in the, **mā́ne**
day, every, **in díēs**
day, it is, **lū́cet**
day before, on the, **prī́diē**
day by day, **in díēs**
dead, **mórtuus**
dear (to), **cā́rus, grā́tus**
death, **mors**
debate, to, **ágere**
December, **Decémber**
decide, to, **cōnstitúere**
decided, it was, **plácuit**
decorate, to, **ōrnā́re**
decorated, **ōrnā́tus**
decoration, **ōrnāméntum**
decrease, to, **minúere**
decree, **cōnsúltum**
dedicate, to, **cōnsecrā́re, dēdicā́re**

dedicated, **dḗditus**
deed, good, **méritum**
deep, **áltus**
deep, the, **áltum**
defeat, to, **superā́re**
defend, to, **dēféndere**
delay, to, **cessā́re, morā́rī**
delight, **dēlíciae, volúptās**
delight, to, **dēlectā́re**
delightful, **iūcúndus, suā́vis**
deliver a speech, to, **ōrātiṓnem habḗre**
Delos, **Dḗlos**
demand, to, **póscere**
denarius (silver coin), **dēnā́rius**
depart, to, **discḗdere**
dependent, **clíēns**
desire, to, **cúpere, dēsīderā́re**
dessert, **secúndae mḗnsae**
destroy, to, **dēlḗre, pérdere**
detestable, **abōmindándus**
devoted, **dḗditus**
devour, to, **dēvorā́re**
Dido, **Dī́dō**
die, to, **dēcḗdere, ē vī́tā excḗdere, mórī**
different, **várius**
difficult, **diffícilis**
difficulty, **difficúltās**
difficulty, with, **vix**
dig up, to, **ērúere**
diligent, **dī́ligēns**
din, **frágor**
dine, to, **cēnā́re**
dining room, **trīclī́nium**
dinner, **cḗna**
dinner, to eat, **cēnā́re**
direction, **pars**
dirge, **nḗnia**
dirty, **sórdidus**
discretion, **prūdéntia**
discuss, to, **ágere**
disembark, to, **ḗgredī**
disgusting, **foédus**
dish, **férculum**
dishevel, to, **sólvere**
display, to, **praebḗre**
dissimilar, **dissímilis**
distance, in the, **prócul**
distant, to be, **abésse**
distinguished, **praeclā́rus**
ditch, **fóssa**
divert, to, **āvértere**
divide, to, **dīvídere**
divine, **dīvī́nus**
divulge, to, **ēnūntiā́re**
do, to, **ágere, fácere, gérere**
do harm (to), to, **nocḗre**
do nothing, to, **cessā́re**
doctor, **médicus**
dog, **cánis**
doll, **pū́pa**
done, to be, **fíerī**
Don't...! **Nṓlī/Nōlī́te** + infinitive
door, **iā́nua**
doorkeeper, **iā́nitor**
door-post, **póstis**
doorway, **lī́men**
dormouse, **glīs**
doubt, **dúbium**
down from, **dē**
drag, to, **tráhere**
drag out, to, **extráhere**
drain, to, **haurī́re**
draw, to, **stríngere**
draw a sword, to, **gládium stríngere**
dream, **sómnium**
drink, to, **bíbere**
drinking party, **commissā́tiō**
drive, to, **ágere, incitā́re**
drive back, to, **repéllere**
drive off, to, **repéllere**
drive out, to, **expéllere**
drive to and fro, to, **iactā́re**
driver, **raedā́rius**
drooping, **lánguidus**
drunk, **ḗbrius**
dry, **síccus**
dry, to, **tergḗre**
dung, **stércus**

dust, **púlvis**
dust (of the cremated body), **cínis**
duty, **offícium**
dwell, to, **habitā́re**

E

each, **ómnis**
each (of two), **utérque**
eager, **inténtus**
earlier, **príus**
early, **mātū́rē**
early in the day, **mā́ne**
earth, **térra**
easily, **fácile**
easy, **fácilis**
eat, to, **ésse**
eat dinner, to, **cēnā́re**
eating-house, **popī́na**
egg, **ṓvum**
eight, **óctō**
eighteen, **duodēvīgíntī**
eighteenth, **duodēvīcésimus**
eighth, **octā́vus**
either...or, **aut...aut, vel...vel**
elegant, **ḗlegāns**
eleven, **ū́ndecim**
eleventh, **ūndécimus**
embrace, **compléxus**
embrace, to, **ampléctī**
emperor, **Caésar, imperā́tor, prī́nceps**
encourage, to, **hortā́rī**
end, **fī́nis**
endure, to, **pátī**
energetic, **strḗnuus**
enough, **sátis**
enough time, **sátis témporis**
enter, to, **íngredī, inī́re, intrā́re, introī́re**
enthusiasm, **stúdium**
entire, the, **ūnivérsus**
entrance passage, **vestī́bulum**
entrust, to, **commíttere**
envoy, **lēgā́tus**
epigram, **epigrámma**
epistle, **lítterae**
equip, to, **ōrnā́re**
era, **saéculum**
eruption, **ērúptiō**
escape, to, **aufúgere, effúgere, ēvā́dere**
escort, to, **dēdū́cere**
establish, to, **cóndere**
Eurydice, **Eurýdicē**
even, **étiam**
even if, **etiámsī**
evening, in the, **vésperī**
ever, **úmquam**
every, **ómnis**
every day, **cotī́diē, in díēs**
evil, **málus**
examine, to, **īnspícere**
exceedingly, **váldē**
excellent, **óptimus**
excellently, **óptimē, púlchrē**
except, **nísi, praéter**
excited, **commṓtus**
exclaim, to, **exclāmā́re**
excuse, to, **excūsā́re**
exercise, to, **exercḗre**
exercise ground, **palaéstra**
exiled, **prófugus**
expel, to, **expéllere**
explain, to, **explicā́re**
explain the situation, to, **rem explicā́re**
express, to, **exprímere**
expression, **ōs, vúltus**
extinguish, to, **exstínguere**
eye, **óculus**

F

fabric, **tḗla**
face, **ōs, vúltus**
face down, **prṓnus**
facing, **cóntrā**
in fact, **ímmō vḗrō**
fair-skinned, **cándidus**
faith, good, **fídēs**
faithful, **fidḗlis**

fall, to, **cádere, lā́bī**
fall down, to, **concídere**
fall into/onto, to, **incídere**
fame, **fā́ma, glṓria**
family, **família, gēns**
family, belonging to the, **familiā́ris**
famous, **céleber, praeclā́rus**
famous, that, **ílle**
far, **lóngē, prócul**
far off, **prócul**
farm, **fúndus**
farm manager, **vī́licus**
fast, very, **celérrimē, celérrimus**
fast as possible, as, **súmmā celeritā́te**
fastest, **celérrimus**
fat, **obḗsus, pínguis**
fate, **fā́tum**
father, **páter**
fault, **cúlpa**
favor, to, **favḗre**
fear, **métus, térror, tímor**
fear, paralyzed with, **métū exanimā́tus**
fear, to, **timḗre, verḗrī**
feared, to be, **timéndus**
fearful, **tímidus**
feast, **convī́vium, épulae**
February, **Februā́rius**
feed (on), to, **pā́scere, vḗscī**
feel, to, **sentī́re**
female, **mulíebris**
female slave attached to a gladiatorial school, **lū́dia**
fever, **fébris**
few, **paúcī**
field, **áger, cámpus**
fierce, **férōx, saévus**
fiercely, **ā́criter, ferṓciter**
fifteen, **quī́ndecim**
fifteenth, **quī́ntus décimus**
fifth, **quī́ntus**
fiftieth, **quīnquāgḗsimus**
fifty, **quīnquāgíntā**
fight, **púgna**
fight, to, **pugnā́re**
figure out, to, **conícere**
fill, to, **complḗre**
filthy, **foédus**
finally, **postrḗmō**
find, to, **invenī́re**
find out, to, **cognṓscere**
finely, **púlchrē**
finger, **dígitus**
finish, to, **cōnfícere, fīnī́re**
fire, **ígnis, incéndium**
first, **prī́mus**
first, (at), **prī́mō, prī́mum**
first (of two), **príor**
first course, **gustā́tiō**
first day in the month, **Kaléndae**
fishpond, **piscī́na**
fit, to, **aptā́re**
fitting, it is, **décet, opórtet**
five, **quī́nque**
five hundred, **quīngéntī**
five-hundredth, **quīngentḗsimus**
flame, **flámma**
flaming, **flámmeus**
flash, to, **micā́re**
flee, to, **effúgere, fúgere**
flee for refuge, to, **cōnfúgere**
flesh, **cárō**
floor, **tabulā́tum**
floor, tiled, **pavīméntum**
flow, to, **mānā́re**
flower, **flōs**
follow, to, **séquī**
follow (up), to, **súbsequī**
following, **pósterus, séquēns**
following day, on the, **postrī́diē**
food, **cíbus**
foolish, **stúltus**
foot, **pēs**
footprint, **vēstī́gium**
for, **énim, nam**
for a short time, **paulísper**
for the sake of, **caúsā**
for the sake of an honor, **honṓris caúsā**
forbid, to, **vetā́re**
force, **vīs**

force, to, **cṓgere**
forehead, **frōns**
forest, **sílva**
forever, **in perpétuum**
forgetful, **ímmemor**
forgive, to, **excūsā́re**
form, **fṓrma**
former, the, **ílle**
fortunate, **fḗlīx**
fortune (good or bad), **fortū́na**
Forum, the, **Fórum**
found, to, **cóndere**
four, **quáttuor**
fourteen, **quattuórdecim**
fourteenth, **quā́rtus décimus**
fourth, **quā́rtus**
frail, **īnfírmus**
free, **grā́tīs**
freedman, **lībértus**
freedom, **lībértās**
freedwoman, **lībérta**
frenzy, **fúror**
friend, **amī́ca, amī́cus, hóspes**
friendly way, in a, **cṓmiter**
frighten, to, **terrḗre**
frightened, **pertérritus, térritus**
frightening, **terríbilis**
from, **ā, ab, dē, ē, ex**
from time to time, **intérdum**
front of, in, **ánte, ápud, cóntrā**
full, **plḗnus**
funeral, **fū́nebris, fū́nus**
funeral pyre, **rógus**
funeral rites, **exséquiae**
funeral rites, to carry out, **exséquiās dū́cere**
furnishings, **ōrnāménta**

G

Gades, **Gā́dēs**
game, **lū́dus**
game of bandits, **lū́dus latrunculṓrum**
games (in the Circus), **lū́dī, mū́nera**
gape, to, **stupḗre**
garden, **hórtus**
garden, small, **hórtulus**
garland, **corṓna**
garment, **véstis**
garum, **liquā́men**
gate, **pórta**
gatekeeper, **appā́ritor**
Gaul, **Gállia**
Gauls, the, **Gállī**
gentle, **mī́tis**
gently, **plácidē**
get, to, **accípere**
get ready, to, **comparā́re, parā́re, sē parā́re**
get up, to, **súrgere**
get well, to, **convalḗscere**
gift, **dṓnum, mū́nus**
girl, **puélla**
give, to, **dáre, dōnā́re**
give as a gift, to, **dṓnō dáre**
give back, to, **réddere**
give favor (to), to, **favḗre**
give trust (to), to, **cōnfī́dere**
glad, **laétus**
glad, to be, **gaudḗre**
gladiator, **gladiā́tor**
gladiatorial show, **mū́nus**
gladly, **libénter**
glory, **glṓria**
go, to, **ī́re**
go around, to, **circumī́re**
go away, to, **abī́re, discḗdere**
go back, to, **redī́re, régredī**
go down, to, **dēscéndere**
go forward, to, **prōcḗdere, prṓgredī**
go in, to, **incḗdere, íngredī**
go into, to, **inī́re, intrā́re**
go in front, to, **praecḗdere**
go out, to, **égredī, excḗdere, exī́re**
go past, to, **praeterī́re**
go to sleep, to, **obdormī́re**
goal, **mḗta**
goblet, **pṓculum**
god, **déus**
goddess, **déa**

gods above, the, **súperī**
gold, **aúrum**
golden, **aúreus**
good, **bónus**
good, very, **óptimus**
Good heavens! **Dī immortā́lēs! Prō dī immortā́lēs!**
Good luck! **Fēlī́citer!**
good sense, **prūdéntia**
Goodbye! **Válē!/Valḗte!**
Goodness me! **Mehércule!**
goods, **bóna**
grab, to, **corrípere**
grab hold of, to, **arrípere**
graciously, **cṓmiter**
gradually, **paulā́tim**
grape, **ū́va**
gratitude, **grā́tia**
great, **mágnus**
great, so, **tántus**
great, very, **máximus, súmmus**
greater, **máior**
greatest, **máximus, súmmus**
greatest speed, with the, **súmmā celeritā́te**
greatly, **magnópere, múltum**
Greece, **Graécia**
Greek, **Graécus**
Greeks, the, **Graécī**
green, **prásinus**
greet, to, **salūtā́re**
greetings, **sálūs**
Greetings! **Ávē!/Avḗte! Sálvē!/Salvḗte!**
greetings, to send, **salū́tem dī́cere**
grief, **dólor**
groan, to, **gémere**
ground, **térra**
ground, on the, **húmī**
grow worse, to, **ingravḗscere**
grunt, to, **grunnī́re**
guard, **cústōs**
guard, to, **custōdī́re**
guess, to, **conícere**
guest, **hóspes**
guest (at a banquet), **convī́va**

H

habit of, to be in the, **solḗre**
Hail! **Ávē!/Avḗte!**
hair, **capíllī, crī́nēs**
hair, with long, **capillā́tus**
half-asleep, **sēmisómnus**
halt, to, **cōnsístere**
ham, **pérna**
hand, **mánus**
hand ball, heavy, **harpástum**
hand over, to, **trā́dere**
handsome, **púlcher**
happen, to, **fíerī**
happen to Sextus?, What will, **Quid Séxtō fíet?**
happens, it, **áccidit**
happily, **fēlī́citer, laétē**
happy, **fḗlīx, laétus**
hard, **strḗnuē**
hare, **lépus**
harm, some, **áliquid málī**
harm, to, **laédere, nocḗre**
harm (to), to do, **nocḗre, violā́re**
harmonious manner, **módus**
have, to, **habḗre**
he, **is, ílle**
head, **cáput**
head for, to, **pétere**
headband, **vítta**
health (good or bad), **valētū́dō**
hear, to, **audī́re**
"heart," heart, **ánima, cor**
heat, **aéstus, cálor**
heaven, **caélum**
heavy, **grávis**
Hello! **Sálvē!/Salvḗte!**
helmet, plumed metal, **cássis**
help, **auxílium**
Help! **Fer/Férte auxílium!**
help, to, **adiuvā́re**
her (own), **súus**
herself, **sē**
herself, with, **sḗcum**
Hercules, **Hérculēs**

here, **hīc, hūc**
here, to, **hūc**
here and there, **hūc illū́c**
Hesperia, **Hespéria**
Hey! **Ého!**
Hey there! **Héus!**
hide, to, **cēlā́re, latḗre, obscūrā́re, operī́re**
high, **áltus**
highest throw of the knucklebones, the, **Vénus**
hill, **cóllis, mōns**
himself, **ípse, sē**
himself, with, **sḗcum**
hinder, to, **impedī́re**
hipbone, **cóxa**
hire, to, **condū́cere**
his (own), **súus**
hit, to, **ferī́re**
hold, to, **continḗre, habḗre, tenḗre**
hold back, to, **retinḗre**
hold out, to, **exténdere**
holiday, celebrating a, **fēriā́tus**
home, **dómum, dómus**
home, at, **dómī**
home, from, **dómō**
homeward, **dómum**
honor, **hónor**
honor, as an, **honṓris caúsā**
honor, for the sake of an, **honṓris caúsā**
hope, to, **spērā́re**
Horace, **Horā́tius**
horn-player, **córnicen**
horrible, **abōmindándus**
hors d'oeuvre, **gustā́tiō**
horse, **équus**
host, **hóspes**
hot room (at baths), **caldā́rium**
hour, **hṓra**
house, **dómus**
house of, at the, **ápud**
household, **família**
household, belonging to the, **familiā́ris**
household, members of the, **familiā́rēs**
household gods, **Lárēs**
How...! **Quam...!**
How...? **Quam...? Quō īnstrūméntō...? Quṓmodo...?**
How are you! **Quid ágis?**
How big...? **Quántus**
How many...? **Quot...?**
How much...? **Quántus**
How much...! **Quántum...!**
How much (in price)...? **Quántī...?**
however, **aútem, támen**
howl, to, **ululā́re**
huge, **immā́nis, íngēns**
human, **hūmā́nus**
humble, **húmilis**
humor, good, **hilā́ritās**
hundred, a, **céntum**
hundredth, **centḗsimus**
hungry, to be, **ēsurī́re**
hurl, to, **praecipitā́re**
hurl oneself, to, **sē praecipitā́re**
Hurray! **Eúge! Eúgepae!**
hurry, to, **festīnā́re**
hurt, to, **dolḗre**
husband, **cóniūnx, marī́tus, vir**
hut, **cása**
hyacinth, of, **hyacínthinus**

I

I, **égo**
Ides, the, **Ī́dūs**
idle, to be, **cessā́re**
if, **sī**
if anyone, **sī quis**
if...not, **nísi**
ignorant, to be, **ignōrā́re, nescī́re**
ignore, to, **neglégere**
ill, **aéger**
ill, to be, **aegrōtā́re**
ill in bed, to be, **languḗre**
illness, **mórbus**
immediately, **prṓtinus, státim**
immortal, **immortā́lis**

Immortal Gods! **Dī immortā́lēs!**
important, it is, **ínterest**
in, **in**
in fact, **ímmō vḗrō**
in front of, **ápud**
in return, **cóntrā**
in vain, **frū́strā, nēquī́quam**
Indeed! **Íta vḗrō!**
indeed, **quídem, vḗrō**
infant, **ī́nfāns**
ingenuity, **ingénium**
inhabitant, **íncola**
inn, **caupṓna**
inner organs of sacrificial animals, the, **éxta**
innkeeper, **caúpō**
innocence, **innocéntia**
inquire, to, **requī́rere**
inside, **íntrā**
insist, to, **urgḗre**
insistently, **veheménter**
insolence, **procā́citās**
insolent, **prócāx**
instruct, to, **praecípere**
instruction, **mandā́tum**
instrument..., With what, **Quō īnstrūméntō...?**
instructress, **magístra**
intelligence, **ingénium**
intend, to, **in ánimō habḗre**
intent, **inténtus**
interrupt, to, **interpellā́re**
into, **in**
invite, to, **invītā́re, vocā́re**
invoke, to, **invocā́re**
irritability, **īrācúndia**
irritable, **īrācúndus**
island, **ī́nsula**
it, **ílle, is**
Italy, **Itália**
Ithaca, **Íthaca**
its (own), **súus**
itself, **ípse, sē**
itself, with, **sḗcum**
ivy, **hédera**

J

January, **Iānuā́rius**
join, to, **iúngere**
join battle, to, **púgnam commíttere**
joke, **iócus**
joke, as a, **per iócum**
journey, **íter**
joy, **gaúdium**
July, **Iū́lius**
June, **Iū́nius**
Juno, **Iū́nō**
just as if, **támquam**

K

Kalends, the, **Kaléndae**
keen, **ā́cer**
keep, to, **retinḗre**
kill, to, **ferī́re, iugulā́re, necā́re, occī́dere**
kind, of this, **tā́lis**
kindness, **benevoléntia**
king, **rēx**
kingdom, **rḗgnum**
kiss, **ṓsculum**
kitchen, **culī́na**
know, not to, **ignōrā́re, nescī́re**
know, to, **scī́re**
known, **nṓtus**
knucklebones, **tā́lī**

L

lack, to, **carḗre**
ladle, small, **cýathus**
lady of the house, **dómina**
lame, **claúdus**
lament, **nḗnia**
lament, to, **plōrā́re**
lamp, **lucérna**
lamp-stand, **candēlā́brum**
land, **áger, térra**
language, **língua**
lantern, **lantérna**

large, **mágnus**
large, very, **máximus**
last, **postrḗmus**
last, at, **tándem**
last laugh, to get the, **dērīdḗre**
lasting, **perpétuus**
late, **sḗrō**
later, **post, sḗrius**
latest, **sēríssimē**
Latin, **Latī́nus**
Latium, **Látium**
latter, the, **hic**
laugh, **rī́sus**
laugh (at), to, **dērīdḗre, rīdḗre**
laughable, **rīdículus**
laughter, **cachínnus**
laurel, **laúrus**
Lavinium, of, **Lāvī́nius**
lay down, to, **dēpṓnere**
lazy, **ignā́vus, íners**
lead, to, **dū́cere**
lead back, to, **redū́cere**
lead on, to, **addū́cere**
lead out, to, **ēdū́cere**
leader, **prī́nceps**
leading citizen, **prī́nceps**
leaky, **rīmṓsus**
leap down, to, **dēsilī́re**
leap out, to, **exsilī́re**
learn, to, **cognṓscere, díscere**
learned, **ērudī́tus**
least, **mínimē**
leave, to, **ḗgredī, excḗdere, línquere, proficíscī**
leave behind, to, **relínquere**
leave out, to, **omíttere**
left, **siníster**
length, at, **tándem**
less, **mínus**
lessen, to, **minúere**
let down, to, **dēmíttere**
let go, to, **míttere**
letter, **epístula, lítterae**
letter (of the alphabet), **líttera**
letters, **líttera e**
Liberalia, the, **Līberā́lia**
lick, to, **lámbere**
lictor, **lī́ctor**
lie, to, **iacḗre**
lie down, to, **recúmbere**
lie in hiding, to, **latḗre**
life, **vī́ta**
lift, to, **tóllere**
light, **lévis, lūx**
light, it is, **lū́cet**
like, **símilis**
like, to, **amā́re**
like this, **tā́lis**
likeness, **imā́gō**
line (of poetry), **vérsus**
lion, **léō**
listen to, to, **audī́re**
literature, **lítterae**
litter, **lectī́ca**
litter-bearer, **lectīcā́rius**
little, **paúlus, párvulus**
little, a, **paúlum**
little by little, **paulā́tim**
live, to, **habitā́re, vī́vere**
livestock, **pécus**
load, **ónus**
load, to, **onerā́re**
located, **sítus**
locket, **búlla**
long, **lóngus**
long for, to, **dēsīderā́re**
long time, for a, **díū**
longer, **diū́tius**
longest, **diūtíssimē**
Look (at)...! **Écce...!**
look after, to, **cūrā́re**
look around, to, **circumspícere**
look around at, to, **respícere**
look at, to, **spectā́re**
look for, to, **pétere, quaérere**
look out for, to, **exspectā́re**
loom, **tḗla**
loosen, to, **sólvere**
loud (voice, laugh), **mágnus**

love, **ámor**
love, to, **amā́re, dīlígere**
loved (by), **grā́tus**
lower, to, **dēmíttere**
luck-charm, **búlla**
luckily, **fēlī́citer**
lucky, **fēlīx**
lying down, to be, **iacḗre**

M

made, to be, **fíerī**
magnificent, **magníficus**
maiden, **vírgō**
main room in a house, **ā́trium**
make, to, **fácere**
make something agreeable to someone, to, **persuādḗre**
man, **hómō, vir**
man, old, **sénex**
manhood, of, **virī́lis**
manner, in a kindly, **clēménter**
manner…?, In what, **Quṓmodo…?**
Mantua, **Mántua**
manure, **stércus**
many, **múltī**
many, very, **plū́rimī**
many-hued, **várius**
many years afterward, **múltīs post ánnīs**
March, **Mā́rtius**
march in, to, **incḗdere**
mark, **mḗta**
marriage, **mātrimṓnium**
marry, to, **in mātrimṓnium dū́cere, nū́bere**
Martial, **Mārtiā́lis, Márcus Valérius**
marvelous, **mī́rus**
mask, **imā́gō**
mass, **mṓlēs**
master, **árbiter, dóminus, magíster**
master of the drinking, **árbiter bibéndī**
matter, **rēs**
may, we, **lícet nṓbīs**
me, **mē**
me, with, **mḗcum**
means…?, By what, **Quō īnstrūméntō…?**
meanwhile, **intéreā**
measure (of wine), **cýathus**
meat, **cárō**
meet, to, **convenī́re, occúrrere**
Megara, **Mégara**
members of the family of Cornelius, the, **Cornḗliī**
members of the household, **familiā́rēs**
memorable, **memorā́bilis**
memory, **memória**
menacing, **mínāx**
mention, to, **commemorā́re**
merchant, **mercā́tor**
Mercury, **Mercúrius**
merriment, **hilā́ritās**
messenger, **nū́ntius**
method, **módus**
mid-, **médius**
midday, **merī́diēs**
midday fighters, **merīdiā́nī**
middle of, **médius**
midnight, **média nox**
Milan, **Mediolā́num**
mind, **ánimus**
mindful, **mémor**
mine, **méus**
mirror, **spéculum**
miserable, **míser, miserā́bilis**
miss, to, **dēsīderā́re**
mistaken, to be, **errā́re**
mistress, **dómina**
mix, to, **miscḗre**
mob, **túrba**
moment, at that, **tum**
money, **pecū́nia**
month, **mḗnsis**
monument, **monuméntum**
mood, in a bad, **īrācúndus**
moon, **lū́na**
more, **mágis, plū́rēs, plūs**
more, all the, **éō mágis**
moreover, **aútem, praetéreā**
morning, in the, **mā́ne**
mortally, **mortíferē**

mortals, **mortā́lēs**
most, **máximē, plū́rimī, plū́rimum, plū́rimus**
mother, **mā́ter**
motionless, **immṓbilis**
Mount Vesuvius, **Mōns Vesúvius**
mountain, **mōns**
mourn, to, **plōrā́re**
mouse, **mūs**
mouth, **ōs**
move, to, **commovḗre, movḗre**
move aside, to, **removḗre**
move one's home, to, **migrā́re**
move quickly to and fro, to, **micā́re**
move toward, to, **admovḗre**
moved, **commṓtus**
much, **múltum, múltus**
much, so, **tántum**
much, too, **nímis**
much, very, **máximē, plū́rimus**
mud, **lútum**
Mulvian Bridge, at the, **Mulviā́nus**
murder, to, **iugulā́re**
murmur, **múrmur**
Muse, **Mū́sa**
mushroom, **bōlḗtus**
mutter, to, **mussā́re**
mutual, **mútuus**
my, **méus**
myrtle, **mýrtus**

N

name, **nṓmen**
name, to, **appellā́re, nōminā́re**
napkin, **máppa**
Naples, **Neā́polis**
narrator, **nārrā́tor**
nation, **génus, nā́tiō**
nature, **nātū́ra**
near, **ad, própe**
near, to be, **adésse**
nearby, **própe, próximus**
nearly, **própe**
necessary, **necésse**
need, to, **carḗre**
neglect, to, **neglégere**
neighboring, **vīcī́nus**
neither…nor, **nec…nec, néque…néque**
neither…nor…anything,
  néque…néque…quídquam
Nero, of, **Nerōnḗus**
never, **númquam**
nevertheless, **támen**
new, **nóvus**
next, **deínde, pósterus**
night, **nox**
night, at/by, **nóctū**
night, happening during the, **noctúrnus**
nine, **nóvem**
nineteen, **ūndēvīgíntī**
nineteenth, **ūndēvīcḗsimus**
ninth, **nṓnus**
no, **nū́llus**
No! **Mínimē (vḗrō)**
No indeed! **Mínimē vḗrō!**
no longer, **nōn iam**
no one, **nḗmō**
no one, that, **nē quis**
noble, **nṓbilis**
noise, **frágor, strépitus**
none, **nū́llus**
Nones, **Nṓnae**
noon, **merī́diēs**
noon, at, **merī́diē**
northern, **septentriōnā́lis**
north wind, **áquilō**
nose, **nā́sus**
not, **haud, nōn**
Not at all! **Mínimē vḗrō!**
not even, **nē…quídem**
not knowing, **ī́nscius**
not only…but also, **nōn módō…sed étiam**
not to, **nē**
not yet, **nṓndum**
nothing, **níhil, nīl**
nothing, for, **grā́tīs**
nothing, to do, **cessā́re**
notice, to, **animadvértere, sentī́re**

November, **Novémber**
now, **iam, nunc**
nowhere, **núsquam**
number, **númerus**
nut, **nux**

O

obey, to, **pārḗre**
obliging, **officiṓsus**
obtain, to, **comparā́re**
Ocean, **Ōcéanus**
October, **Octṓber**
odds or evens (a game), **pār ímpār**
Odysseus, **Ulíxēs**
of course, **sā́nē**
offerings and rites in honor of the dead at the tomb, **īnfériae**
officer, **lī́ctor**
often, **saépe**
often, more, **saépius**
often, most, **saepíssimē**
oil, **óleum, unguéntum**
ointment, **unguéntum**
old, **vétus**
olden times, of, **prī́scus**
olive, **olī́va**
olive grove, **olīvḗtum**
omen, **ṓmen**
omit, to, **omíttere**
on, **in**
on account of, **ob, própter**
on time, **ad témpus**
once (upon a time), **ṓlim**
one, **ū́nus**
one (of two), the, **álter**
one...another, **álius...álius**
one...the other, the, **álter...álter**
oneself, **sē**
only, **módo, tántum**
only just, **vix**
open, to, **aperī́re**
open space, **ā́rea**
opposite, **cóntrā**
or, **an, aut, -ve, vel**
or if, **seu**
oration, **ōrā́tiō**
orator, **ōrā́tor**
order, **mandā́tum**
orders, **iússa**
order, to, **imperā́re, iubḗre, praecípere**
Orpheus, **Órpheus**
other, **álius**
other (of two), the, **álter**
others, the, **cḗterī**
otherwise, **áliter**
ought, **dēbḗre**
ought, one, **opórtet**
ought to hurry, You, **Festīnā́re tē opórtet**
our, **nóster**
out of, **ē, ex**
outside, **éxtrā, fórās**
outstanding, **exímius**
over, **súper**
overcome, **afféctus**
overcome, to, **superā́re**
overseer, **vī́licus**
overtake, to, **cṓnsequī**
overturn, to, **ēvértere**
overwhelm, to, **opprímere**
owe, to, **dēbḗre**
owner, **dóminus**
ox, **bōs**

P

pain, to be in, **dolḗre**
painstaking, **dī́ligēns**
pairs, **pária**
Palatine Hill, belonging to the, **Palātī́nus**
palla, **pálla**
panic, in a, **trépidāns**
paralyzed, **exanimā́tus**
parent, **párēns**
parsley, **ápium**
part, **párs**
pastry with cheese filling, **scriblī́ta**

pasture, to, pā́scere
patron, patrṓnus
pawns (a game like chess), latrúnculī
pay attention to, to, observā́re
pay the penalty, to, poénās dáre
peacefully, plácidē
pear, pírum
peasant, rū́sticus
pen, stílus
penalty, poéna
people, géntēs, hóminēs, pópulus
perform, to, gérere
perfume, unguéntum
perhaps, fortásse
peristyle, peristȳ́lium
permanent, perpétuus
person related to one of another city by ties of hospitality, hóspes
person who fights wild beasts in the arena, bēstiā́rius
persuade, to, persuādḗre
persuade someone of something, to, persuādḗre
pest, moléstus
pick out, to, sū́mere
pick up, to, repétere
picture, pictū́ra
pig, pórcus
piper, tībī́cen
pirate, pīrā́ta
place, lócus
place, to, aptā́re, locā́re, pṓnere
place, to that, éō, illū́c, quō
place on, to, impṓnere
plague, pestiléntia
plain, cámpus
Plain of Mars on the outskirts of Rome, the, Cámpus Mā́rtius
plain white, pū́rus
plan, cōnsílium
plan, to adopt a, cōnsílium cápere
play, to, lū́dere
play ball, to, pílā lū́dere
play *morra*, to, dígitīs micā́re
pleasant, cómmodus, iūcúndus
please, sī vīs, sīs
please, to, placḗre
pleasing (to), grā́tus
pleasing to someone to do something, it is, líbet
pleasure, volúptās
pledge, to, spondḗre
Pluto, Plū́tō
poet, poḗta
point out, to, osténdere
political faction, fáctiō
Pompeii, Pompéiī
poor, paúper
pork, pórcus
possessions, bóna
post, pā́lus
pour out, to, effúndere
praise, to, laudā́re
prank, iócus
prank, as a, per iócum
prefer, to, mā́lle
prepare, to, parā́re
prepare oneself, to, sē parā́re
prepared, parā́tus
present, to be, adésse
present somebody with something, to, dōnā́re
presently, mox
press, to, urgḗre
press out, to, exprímere
pretend, to, simulā́re
pretty, púlcher
prevent, to, impedī́re, nē
previous, príor
previously, abhínc, ánte, ánteā, príus
price, prétium
priest, officiating, aúspex
prisoner, captī́vus
procession, funeral, pómpa
promise, to, pollicḗrī, prōmíttere
promise in marriage, to, dēspondḗre
promise solemnly, to, spondḗre
proper, rḗctus
properly, rḗctē, rī́te
propose, to, prōpṓnere
proud, supérbus

provide, to, **praebḗre**
province, **prōvíncia**
public, **pū́blicus**
Public Records Office, **Tabulā́rium**
pull, to, **tráhere**
punish, to, **pūnī́re**
punished, to be, **poénās dáre**
punishment, **poéna**
pupil, **discípulus**
pure, **mérus**
pushy, **prócāx**
put, to, **impṓnere, pṓnere**
put aside, to, **dēpṓnere**
put on, to, **indúere**
put out, to, **exstínguere**
Pyramus, **Pȳ́ramus**

Q

quarrel, **ríxa**
quarrel, to, **rixā́rī**
queen, **rēgī́na**
question, **rogā́tiō**
quickly, **celériter**
quickly, more, **celérius**
quickly, very, **celérrimē**
quiet, **submíssus**
quiet, to be, **tacḗre**
quiet, to keep, **quiḗscere**
quietly, **plácidē**
Quirinal (Hill), **Quirīnā́lis**

R

race, **génus**
race track, **currículum**
rain, **ímber**
raining, it is, **plúit**
rains, it, **plúit**
raise, to, **tóllere**
raisin-wine, **pássum**
rash, **temerā́rius**
rather, **ímmō**
rather than, **pótius quam**
reach, to, **advenī́re, pervenī́re**
read, to, **légere**
read aloud, to, **recitā́re**
read through, to, **perlégere**
ready, **parā́tus**
ready, to get, **comparā́re, sē parā́re**
ready to serve, **officiṓsus**
realize, to, **intellégere, sentī́re**
really, **rē vḗrā, vḗrō**
rear, **térgum**
reason, **caúsa**
reason, for this, **quā dē caúsā**
reason...?, For what, **Quam ob caúsam...?**
rebellion, **rebélliō**
rebuke, to, **castīgā́re**
recall, to, **revocā́re**
recapture, to, **recípere**
receive, to, **accípere, excípere, recípere**
recently, **nū́per**
recite, to, **recitā́re**
reciting, of, **recitándī**
reckless, **temerā́rius**
recline, to, **recúmbere**
recline (at table), to, **accúmbere**
recognition, **recognítiō**
recognize, to, **agnṓscere**
records, **tábulae**
recount, to, **commemorā́re**
recover, to, **recuperā́re, repétere**
red, **russā́tus**
redo, to, **refícere**
reduce, to, **minúere**
refraining from, **ábstinēns**
refraining from wine, **vī́nō ábstinēns**
refuse, to, **nṓlle**
regain one's senses, to, **ánimum recuperā́re**
regard for, to have special, **dīlígere**
region, **pars**
register, to, **īnscrī́bere**
reins, **habḗnae**
rejoice, to, **gaudḗre**
relative, **propínquus**

release, to, **immíttere**
reliability, **fídēs**
religious rites, **sácra**
remain, to, **manḗre, morā́rī**
remake, to, **refícere**
remember, to, **memóriā tenḗre**
remembering, **mémor**
remove, to, **exímere, removḗre**
render services (to), to, **mérita cōnférre**
renew, to, **renovā́re**
repeatedly, **idéntidem**
reply, **respṓnsum**
reply, to, **rescrī́bere, respondḗre**
report, to, **perférre, reférre**
reprimand, to, **castīgā́re**
rescue, to, **ērípere**
reserve, to, **reservā́re**
resist, to, **resístere**
rest, **quíēs**
rest, the, **cḗterī**
rest, to, **sē quiḗtī dáre, quiḗscere**
restore, to, **refícere**
return, **réditus**
return, to, **réddere, redī́re, régredī**
returning, **rédiēns**
reveal, to, **ēnūntiā́re**
revive, to, **renovā́re**
rhythmic manner, **módus**
ribbon, **vítta**
rich, **dī́ves, pínguis**
riches, **dīvítiae**
right, **rḗctus**
right hand, **déxtra**
rightly, **rḗctē**
ring, **ā́nulus**
rise, to, **orī́rī, súrgere**
rise up, to, **coorī́rī**
road, **vía**
robber, **latrúnculus, praédō**
rod, **vírga**
rods (symbols of office), **fáscēs**
Roman, **Rōmā́nus**
Romans, the, **Rōmā́nī**
Rome, **Rṓma**
Rome, from, **Rṓmā**
Rome, in, **Rṓmae**
Rome, to, **Rṓmam**
room, **cubículum**
room (at baths), warm, **tepidā́rium**
rose, **rósa**
rouse, to, **excitā́re**
route, **íter**
rub down, to, **dēfricā́re**
ruin, **ruī́na**
rumble, **múrmur**
run, to, **cúrrere**
run about, to, **concursā́re**
run ahead, to, **praecúrrere**
run away, to, **aufúgere, effúgere**
run into, to, **incúrrere**
run to and fro, to, **concursā́re**
run together, to, **concúrrere**
run toward/up to, to, **accúrrere**
rush, to, **sē praecipitā́re**
rush up, to, **concúrrere**

S

sacrifice, **sácra**
sacrifice, to, **sacrificā́re**
sad, **trī́stis**
sad, to be, **dolḗre**
safe, **sálvus**
safe and sound, **incólumis**
said, (he/she), **áit, ínquit**
said, (he/she/it) is, **dī́citur**
sail, to, **nāvigā́re**
salt, **sal**
same, the, **ī́dem**
same as, the, **ī́dem ac**
same time, at the, **símul**
sand, **arḗna, harḗna**
sandal, **sólea**
savage, **saévus**
save, to, **servā́re**
say, to, **dī́cere**
say goodbye, to, **valedī́cere**
says, (he/she), **áit, ínquit**

scalper, **locā́rius**
scarcely, **vix**
scholarly, **ērudī́tus**
school, **lū́dus**
schoolmaster, **magíster**
scold, to, **reprehéndere**
scrap, **frústum**
scraper, **strígilis**
sea, **aéquor, áltum, máre**
sea, of/belonging to the, **aequóreus**
seat, **sélla**
seat (at games), imperial, **pulvī́nar**
second, **secúndus**
second, a/the, **álter**
second time, a, **íterum**
secretly, **clam, sēcrḗtō**
sedan chair, **sélla**
see, to, **vidḗre**
seek, to, **pétere, quaérere**
seem, to, **vidḗrī**
seen, to be, **vidḗrī**
seize, to, **arrípere, cápere, corrípere, occupā́re, prehéndere, rápere**
self, **ípse**
sell, to, **vḗndere**
Senate, **senā́tus**
Senate House, **Cū́ria**
senator, **senā́tor**
senators, **pátrēs**
send, to, **míttere**
send away, to, **dīmíttere**
send fondest greetings, to, **salū́tem plū́rimam dī́cere**
send for, to, **arcéssere**
send greetings, to, **salū́tem dī́cere**
send in, to, **immíttere**
send out, to **ēmíttere**
sensible, **prū́dēns**
sensibly, **prūdénter**
September, **Septémber**
serious, **grávis**
servant, public, **appā́ritor**
serve, to, **servī́re**
service, **mū́nus**
services, **mérita**
set down, to, **dēpṓnere**
set free, to, **līberā́re**
set on fire, to, **accéndere, incéndere**
set out, to, **proficī́scī**
seven, **séptem**
seventeen, **septéndecim**
seventeenth, **séptimus décimus**
seventh, **séptimus**
seventieth, **septuāgḗsimus**
several, **complū́rēs**
shade (of the dead), **úmbra**
shadow, **úmbra**
shake, to, **movḗre**
shaky, **īnfírmus**
shape, **fṓrma**
shawl, **vēlā́men**
she, **éa, ílla**
she-wolf, **lúpa**
sheep and cattle, **pécus**
sheet, **strā́tum**
shines, (it), **lū́cet**
ship, **nā́vis**
ship's boat, **scápha**
shop, **tabérna**
shore, **lī́tus, ṓra**
short, **brévis**
short time, for a, **paulísper**
should, (someone), **décet**
shout, **clā́mor**
shout, to, **clāmā́re**
shout out, to, **exclāmā́re**
shouting, **clā́mor**
show, to, **dēmōnstrā́re, mōnstrā́re, osténdere, praebḗre**
show into, to, **dēdū́cere**
shrine of household gods, **larā́rium**
shut, **claúsus**
shut, to, **claúdere**
Sicily, **Sicília**
sides, from/on all, **úndique**
sight, **spectā́culum**
sign, **sígnum**
sign, to, **obsignā́re**

signal, **sígnum**
silence, **siléntium**
silent, **mū́tus**
silent, to become, **conticḗscere**
silently, **tácitē**
similar (to), **símilis**
since, **cum, quandṓquidem, quóniam**
sing, to, **cánere, cantā́re**
sing together, to, **concínere**
sir, **vir óptime**
sister, **sóror**
sit, to, **sedḗre**
sit down, to, **cōnsī́dere**
situated, **sítus**
situation, **rēs**
six, **sex**
six (in throwing knucklebones), the, **séniō**
sixteen, **sḗdecim**
sixteenth, **séxtus décimus**
sixth, **séxtus**
skill, **ars, prūdéntia**
sky, **caélum**
slave, **sérvus**
slave-girl, **sérva**
slave-woman, **ancílla, sérva**
slavery, **sérvitūs**
sleep, **sómnus**
sleep, to, **dormī́re**
sleep, to go to, **obdormī́re**
sleepy, to be, **dormitā́re**
slender, **grácilis**
slip, to, **lā́bī**
slippery, **lū́bricus**
slow, **léntus, tárdus**
slowly, **léntē**
small, **párvulus, párvus, paúlus**
small, very, **mínimus**
small amount, a, **paúlum**
small boat, **scápha**
smaller, **mínor**
smallest, **mínimus**
smear with oil, to, **únguere**
smell, to, **olfácere**
smile, **rī́sus**
smile, to, **rīdḗre**
smoke, **fū́mus**
smooth, **lḗvis**
snap (the fingers), to, **concrepā́re**
snatch, to, **arrípere, rápere**
snatch away, to, **abrípere**
snatch from, to, **ērípere**
sniff, to, **olfácere**
snore, to, **stértere**
so, **íta, tam**
So be it! **Éstō!**
so many, **tot**
so much, **ádeō**
so that, **ut**
soft, **móllis, submíssus**
soldier, **mī́les**
solitude, **sōlitū́dō**
some, **áliquī, nōnnū́llī**
some…others…, **áliī…áliī**
someone, **áliquis**
something, **áliquid**
sometimes, **nōnnúmquam**
son, **fī́lius, nā́tus**
soon, **mox**
sorry, to be, **dolḗre**
soul, **ánima**
sound, **sónitus**
space, open, **ā́rea**
Spain, **Hispā́nia**
spare, to, **párcere**
spatter, to, **aspérgere**
spattered, **aspérsus**
speak, to, **lóquī**
speak to, to, **álloquī**
speak together, to, **cólloquī**
speaker, **ōrā́tor**
spear, **hásta**
spectacle, **spectā́culum**
spectator, **spectā́tor**
speech, **ōrā́tiō**
speed, **celéritās**
speed, with the greatest, **súmmā celeritā́te**
spend the night, to, **pernoctā́re**
spill, to, **effúndere**

spin wool, to, **lā́nam tráhere**
spirits of the dead, **dī mā́nēs, mā́nēs**
spirits of the dead, to the, **dīs mā́nibus**
splash, to, **aspérgere**
split, to, **scíndere**
spotless, **pū́rus**
sprinkle, to, **aspérgere**
sprinkled, **aspérsus**
spur on, to, **incitā́re**
squared, **quadrā́tus**
staff, **báculum**
stand, to, **cōnsístere, stā́re**
stand by/near, to, **adstā́re**
standing out, **éxstāns**
statue, **státua**
stay, to, **manḗre, morā́rī**
stay awake, to, **vigilā́re**
steal, to, **surrípere**
stealthily, **fū́rtim**
steam, **vápor**
stick, **báculum, vírga**
stick, to, **haerḗre**
still, **adhū́c**
stock, **génus**
stola, **stóla**
stone, **lápis**
stone, of, **lapídeus**
stony, **lapídeus**
stop, to, **cōnsístere, dēsínere**
storm, **tempéstās**
story, **fā́bula, tabulā́tum**
story, funny, **iócus**
strange, **mī́rus**
stream, **rī́vus**
street, **vía**
strength, **vī́rēs**
strenuously, **strḗnuē**
strigil, **strígilis**
strike, to, **ferī́re, percútere**
strong, to be, **valḗre**
stronger, to grow, **convaléscere**
study, **stúdium**
study, to, **studḗre**
study (room), **tablī́num**
stumble, to, **lā́bī**
stupid, **fátuus, stúltus**
subdued, **submíssus**
substitute, **supposití́cius**
Subura, **Subū́ra**
such, **tā́lis**
such a big, **tántus**
such a way, in, **íta**
such an extent, to, **ádeō**
such things, **tā́lia**
sudden, **súbitus**
suddenly, **súbitō**
suffer, to, **pátī**
summer, **aéstās**
summon, to, **arcéssere**
sun, **sōl**
support, to, **favḗre**
sure, to be, **prō cértō habḗre**
Surely…not…? **Num…?**
surname, **cognṓmen**
sweet, **suā́vis**
swift, **céler**
swim, to, **natā́re**
switch, **vírga**
sword, **gládius**

T

table, **mḗnsa**
tablets, **tábulae**
tail, **caúda**
take, to, **cápere, dū́cere, sū́mere**
take away (from), to, **adímere, auférre**
take back, to, **redū́cere**
take care of, to, **cūrā́re**
take off, to, **exúere**
take out, to, **extráhere**
take up, to, **sū́mere**
Talassius, **Talássius**
talk, **sérmō**
talk, to, **lóquī**
talkative, **verbṓsus**
tall, **áltus**

tame, **mānsuḗtus**
tamely, **plácidē**
tart with cheese filling, **scriblī́ta**
tasteful, **ḗlegāns**
teach, to, **docḗre**
teacher, female, **magístra**
teacher, secondary school, **grammáticus**
tear, **lácrima**
tear, to, **scíndere**
tears, **flḗtus**
tell, to, **dī́cere**
tell (a story), to, **nārrā́re**
tell not to, to, **vetā́re**
tell the truth, to, **vḗra dī́cere**
temper, bad, **īrācúndia**
temple, **témplum**
ten, **décem**
tenant, **íncola**
tenth, **décimus**
terrified, **pertérritus**
terrify, to, **terrḗre**
territory, **áger**
terror, **térror, trémor**
test, to, **experī́rī**
testament, **testāméntum**
than, **quam**
thank, to, **grā́tiās ágere**
Thank you! **Grā́tiās tíbi ágō!**
thanks, **grā́tia**
that, **is, ílle, quī, quod, ut**
that…not, **nē**
that famous, **ílle**
that no one, **nē quis**
that place, to, **éō**
that which, **id quod**
That you hurry is fitting, **Festīnā́re tē opórtet**
the (more)…the (more), **quō…éō…**
their (own), **súus**
themselves, **ípsī, sē**
themselves, with, **sḗcum**
then, **deínde, índe, tum**
there, **éō, íbi, illū́c, quō**
there, from, **índe**
therefore, **ígitur, ítaque**
thief, **fūr**
thing, **rēs**
thing which, a, **id quod**
think, to, **cōgitā́re, putā́re**
third, **tértius**
thirteen, **trédecim**
thirteenth, **tértius décimus**
this, **hic, is**
this way and that, **hūc illū́c**
Thisbe, **Thísbē**
thorn, **stirps**
thorough, **dī́ligēns**
thousand, a, **mī́lle**
thousands, **mī́lia**
thousandth, **mīllḗsimus**
Thrace, **Thrā́cia**
three, **trēs**
three times, **ter**
threshing-floor, **ā́rea**
threshold, **lī́men**
through, **per**
throw, to, **conícere, iácere**
throw down, to, **dēícere**
throw into, to, **inícere**
throw of the knucklebones, the highest, **Vénus**
throw of the knucklebones, the lowest, **cánis**
throw out, to, **ēícere**
throw together, to, **conícere**
thrust, to, **inícere**
thus, **íta, sīc**
ticket, **téssera**
tiger, **tígris**
time, **témpus**
time, on, **ad témpus**
time to time, from, **intérdum**
timid, **tímidus**
tired, **dēféssus**
tired (of), I am, **mē taédet**
tired of something, it makes one, **taédet**
tires, (it), **taédet**
to, **ad, ut**
to here, **hūc**
today, **hódiē**
toga, **tóga**

toga, plain white, **tóga pū́ra, tóga virī́lis**
toga of manhood, **tóga virī́lis**
toga with purple border, **tóga praetéxta**
together, **símul, ū́nā**
toil, **lábor**
told, **nārrā́tus**
tomb, **monuméntum, sepúlcrum**
tombstone, **stḗla**
tomorrow, **crās**
tongue, **língua**
too, **praetéreā**
too much, **nímis**
top, on, **súprā**
top of..., the, **súmmus**
torch, **taéda**
toss about, to, **iactā́re**
touch, to, **tángere**
toward, **ad, érgā**
towel, **línteum**
towering, **éxstāns**
town, **óppidum**
town, of the, **urbā́nus**
trace, **vēstī́gium**
track, **vēstī́gium**
train, to, **exercḗre**
trainer, **lanísta**
travel, to, **íter fácere**
traveled, having, **véctus**
traveler, **viā́tor**
tray, **férculum**
tree, **árbor**
tremble, to, **trémere**
trident, **trídēns**
Trojan, **Troiā́nus**
Trojans, the, **Troiā́nī**
troublesome, **moléstus**
Troy, **Tróia**
true, **vḗrus**
truly, **vḗrō**
trumpet-player, **túbicen**
trunk, **císta**
trust, **fídēs**
trust, to, **cōnfī́dere, crḗdere**
try, to, **cōnā́rī, experī́rī, temptā́re**
tunic, **túnica**
turmoil, cause of, **túrba**
turn, to, **vértere**
turn (around), to, **convértere**
turn aside, to, **dēvértere**
turn away, to, **āvértere**
turned, having, **convérsus**
turning, **convérsus**
turning post, **mḗta**
tutor, **paedagṓgus**
twelfth, **duodécimus**
twelve, **duódecim**
twentieth, **vīcḗsimus**
twenty, **vīgíntī**
two, **dúo**
two-wheeled carriage, light, **císium**

U

Ulysses, **Ulíxēs**
uncle, **pátruus**
unconcerned, **sēcū́rus**
under, **sub**
understand, to, **intellégere**
undertaker, **vispíllō**
underworld, the, **ī́nferī**
undeservedly, **indígnē**
unforgetting, **mémor**
unhappy, **míser**
unhurt, **incólumis**
unless, **nísi**
unspeakable, **īnfándus**
untie, to, **sólvere**
until, **dṓnec**
unwilling, **invī́tus**
unwilling, to be, **nṓlle**
uproar, **tumúltus**
upset, to, **commovḗre, ēvértere**
urge, to, **hortā́rī**
urge on, to, **incitā́re**
us, **nōs**
useful, **ū́tilis**

V

varied, **várius**
various, **várius**
vegetable, **hólus**
vehicle, **vehículum**
veil, **vēlā́men**
veil, orange (bridal), **flámmeum**
Venus, **Vénus**
verb, **vérbum**
Vergil, **Vergílius**
verse, **vérsus**
very, **ípse, máximē, váldē**
very much, **váldē, veheménter**
Via Flaminia, the, **Vía Flāmínia**
victor, **víctor**
victory, **victṓria**
vineyard, **vī́nea**
violent, **véhemēns**
violently, **veheménter**
virtuous, **cástus**
visit, to, **vīsitā́re**
vital organs, **víscera**
voice, **vōx**

W

wagon, **plaústrum**
wait, to, **manḗre**
wait for, to, **exspectā́re**
wake (someone) up, to, **excitā́re, expergī́scī**
wakened, **excitā́tus**
walk, to, **ambulā́re**
walk(ing), **incéssus**
wall, **mū́rus, páriēs**
walls, **moénia**
wander, to, **errā́re**
want, to, **cúpere, vélle**
war, **béllum**
warlike, **bélliger**
warm, **cálidus**
warn, to, **monḗre**
wash, to, **lavā́re**
wash overboard, to, **ēícere**
watch, to, **observā́re, spectā́re**
watch out, to, **cavḗre**
water, **áqua**
wave, **únda**
way, **módus**
way, in this, **íta, sīc**
way…?, In what, **Quṓmodo…?**
way and that, this, **hūc illū́c**
we, **nōs**
weak, **īnfírmus**
wealth, **dīvítiae**
weapons, **árma**
wear, to, **gérere**
wearing the **toga praetexta**, **praetextā́tus**
weave, to, **téxere**
web, **tḗla**
wedding, of/for a, **nūptiā́lis**
wedding-torch, **fax**
weep, to, **flḗre, lacrimā́re**
weeping, **flḗtus**
welcome, to, **accípere, excípere, salūtā́re**
well, **béne, fēlī́citer**
well, to be, **valḗre**
well, very, **óptimē**
werewolf, **versipéllis**
What…? **Quī…?, Quid…?**
What a…! **Quam…!**
What sort of…? **Quā́lis…?**
What time is it? **Quóta hṓra est?**
What/Which (in numerical order)…? **Quótus**
wheel, **róta**
when, **cum, úbi, ut**
When…? **Quándō…?**
When…there, **Quō cum**
whenever, **cum**
where, **úbi**
Where…? **Úbi…?**
where…?, From, **Únde…?**
Where…to? **Quō…?**
whether…or…, **útrum…an…**
which, **quī**
Which…? **Quī…?**
Which (in numerical order)…? **Quótus**
while, **dum**

whip, to, **verberā́re**
white, **albā́tus, álbus, cándidus**
who, **quī**
Who...? **Quis...?**
whole, the, **ómnis, tṓtus**
whole of, the, **ūnivérsus**
whom...?, With, **Quṓcum...?**
Whose...? **Cúius...?**
Why...? **Cūr...?**
wicked, **sceléstus**
wife, **cóniūnx, úxor**
wild beasts, involving, **bēstiā́rius**
will, **testāméntum**
willing, to be, **vélle**
win, to, **víncere**
wind, **véntus**
window, **fenéstra**
wine, **vī́num**
wine, undiluted, **mérum**
wine sweetened with honey, **múlsum**
winning manner, in a, **blándē**
winter, **híems**
wipe, to, **tergḗre**
wise, **prū́dēns**
wisely, **prūdénter**
wish, if you, **sī vīs, sīs**
wish, not to, **nṓlle**
wish, to, **optā́re, vélle**
wit, **sal**
with, **ápud, cum**
with difficulty, **vix**
without, **síne**
wolf, **lúpus**
woman, **fḗmina, múlier**
woman, married, **mātrṓna**
woman, of a, **mulíebris**
womanly, **mulíebris**
woman's outer-garment, **stóla**
wonder, to, **mīrā́rī, sē rogā́re**
wonder (at), to, **admīrā́rī**
wonderful, **mīrā́bilis, mī́rus**
woods, **sílva**
wool, **lā́na**
word, **vérbum**
work, **lábor**
work, to, **labōrā́re**
worried, **sollícitus**
worse, **péior, péius**
worst, **péssimē, péssimus**
wound, **vúlnus**
wound, to, **vulnerā́re**
wrestle, to, **lūctā́rī**
wretched, **míser, miserā́bilis**
write, to, **scrī́bere**
write back, to, **rescrī́bere**
write down, to, **reférre**
write in, to, **īnscrī́bere**

Y

year, **ánnus**
Yes! **Íta vḗrō!**
yesterday, **héri**
you, (sing.) **tū**, (pl.) **vōs**
young child, **ī́nfāns**
young man, **aduléscēns**
your, (sing.) **túus**, (pl.) **véster**
youth, **aduléscēns, iúvenis**

Index of Grammar

INDEX OF CULTURAL INFORMATION

CREDITS

Special gratitude is extended to Jenny Page of The Bridgeman Art Library, London, for her invaluable assistance in locating illustrative materials sought for *ECCE ROMANI.*

The publisher gratefully acknowledges the contributions of the agencies, institutions, and photographers listed below:

Chapter 28
(p. 6) (a) Bronze head of a Roman woman, first quarter 2nd century A.D., Louvre, Paris/Bridgeman Art Library, London; Bronze head of a Roman man, lst–2nd century A.D., Louvre, Paris/ Bridgeman Art Library, London

(b) Sardonyx cameo thought to be of Emperor Julian and his wife (A.D. 361–363), British Museum, London/ Bridgeman Art Library, London

(p. 7) Bas relief sculpture of a hairdresser, circa A.D. 50, Landesmuseum, Hesse/Bridgeman Art Library, London

(p. 8) "A Roman Boat Race" by Sir Edward John Poynter (1836–1919), The Maas Gallery, London/Bridgeman Art Library, London

(p. 9) Woman Having Her Hair Dressed by a Maidservant, South West corner of South Wall, Oecus 5, 60–50 B.C. (fresco) Villa dei Misteri, Pompeii/ Bridgeman Art Library, London

Chapter 30
(p. 27) "Marius Triumphing Over the Cimbri" by Saverio Altamura (1826–1897) Museo e Gallerie Nazionali di Capodimonte, Naples/Bridgeman Art Library, London

(p. 28) "Caius Marius Amid the Ruins of Carthage" by John Vanderlyn, The Albany Institute of History and Art, Albany

Chapter 31
(p. 32) Roman butcher's, stone frieze, 2nd Century B.C., Musée de la Civilisation, Paris/Bridgeman Art Library, London

Chapter 32
(p. 39) Preparations for a banquet: fragment of marble, limestone, and glass mosaic pavement from Carthage, Roman c. 180–190 A.D., Louvre, Paris/Bridgeman Art Library, London

(p. 45) "Psyche and Charon" by John Roddam Spencer-Stanhope (1829–1908), Roy Miles Gallery, London/Bridgeman Art Library, London

Chapter 33
(p. 53) Roman tableware. Photograph courtesy Elizabeth Lyding Will

(p. 58) "Orpheus Charming the Animals," Roman mosaic, Blanzy, Musée Municipal, Laon, France/Girandon/ Bridgeman Art Library, London

Chapter 34
(p. 61) Counters and dice, Gallo-Roman, second half of 1st Century B.C., Musée Alesia, Alise-Sainte-Reine/ Giraudon/Bridgeman Art Library, London

(p. 64) Dionysiac Mystery Cult, c. 60–50 B.C. (fresco) Villa dei Misteri, Pompeii/Bridgeman Art Library, London

Chapter 35
(p. 78) "Cicero and the Magistrates Discovering the Tomb of Archimedes" by Benjamin West (1738–1820), Christie's, London/Bridgeman Art Library, London

(p. 81) Statue of Julius Caesar of the Trajan Era, Campidoglio, Rome/Bridgeman Art Library, London

Chapter 36
(p. 90) "Neaera Reading a Letter from Catullus" by Henry J. Hudson, Bradford Art Galleries & Museums/ Bridgeman Art Library, London

(p. 93) "Penelope and Her Suitors" by John William Waterhouse, City of Aberdeen Art Gallery and Museums, Aberdeen, Scotland

Chapter 37
(p. 103) Stone relief of Roman classroom scene, photograph courtesy The Mansell Collection

Chapter 38
(p. 110) "Ariadne in Naxos" by Evelyn de Morgan (1850–1919), The De Morgan Foundation, London/Bridgeman Art Library, London

Chapter 39
(p. 124) Antony and Cleopatra by Rockwell Kent in *The Complete Works of William Shakespeare* ©1936, Doubleday and Co., Garden City

(p. 127) Augustus (63 B.C.–A.D. 14) and his wife Livia (39 B.C.–A.D. 14) seated classical marble statues, Ephesus Museum, Turkey/Bridgeman Art Library, London

(p. 129) Detail from "Vergil Reading the *Aeneid* to Augustus," by J.A.D. Ingres (1780–1867), courtesy of The Fogg Art Museum, Harvard University Art Museums, Cambridge; bequest of Grenville L. Winthrop

Chapter 40
(p. 138) "A Roman Scribe" by Sir Lawrence Alma-Tadema (1836–1912), private collection/Bridgeman Art Library, London

Chapter 41
(pp. 145–146) Drawings by Mary O. Minshall

Chapter 43
(p. 167) Photograph of a bronze oil flask and two strigils, reproduced by courtesy of The Trustees of the British Museum, London

(p. 171) Drawing of Hadrian's Baths at Lepcis Magna, reprinted by permission of the publisher George Braziller, Inc.

Chapter 44
(p. 179) "The Citharist from Stabia," scene from New Comedy, Roman Mosaic, Museo Nazionale di San Martino, Naples, Scala/Art Resource, New York

Chapter 45
(p. 181) Art by Mahmoud Sayah in *The Rubaiyat of Omar Khayyam*, Random House, New York, 1947

(p. 187) "Ovid Among the Scythians" by Eugene Delacroix (1798–1863) National Gallery, London/Bridgeman Art Library, London

Chapter 46
(p. 197) Photograph courtesy Alinari/Art Resource, New York

(p. 205) "Girls Playing Knucklebones," photograph courtesy Scala/Art Resource, New York

(p. 209) Claudius, marble head, A.D. 41–54, Louvre, Paris/Bridgeman Art Library, London

(p. 210) Bust of Trajan, marble, A.D. 53–117, Ephesus Museum, Turkey/ Bridgeman Art Library, London

(p. 211) Marcus Aurelius (A.D. 121–180), Emperor A.D. 161–180: Gold aureus, private collection/Bridgeman Art Library, London

Chapter 47
(p. 217) Photograph by Peter Clayton

(p. 220) Model reconstruction of the Colosseum, Rome, private collection/ Bridgeman Art Library, London

Chapter 48
(p. 223) "Ave Caesar! Morituri te Salutant" by Jean Leon Gerome (1824–1904), Yale University Art Gallery, New Haven, Connecticut, gift of C. Ruxton Love, Jr., B.A. 1925

(p. 232) Fragment of gilded glass showing a gladiator, Rome, circa A.D. 400, British Museum, London/ Bridgeman Art Library, London

(p. 234) Drawing photograph courtesy The Mansell Collection

Chapter 49
(p. 242) The nymph Cyrene overpowering a lion is crowned by Libya, British Museum, London/Bridgeman Art Library, London

Chapter 50
(p. 259) Photograph of Roman betrothal ring, courtesy The Trustees of the British Museum, London

(p. 262) "In a Courtyard in Pompeii" by Luigi Bazzani (1836–1927), Waterhouse and Dodd, London/ Bridgeman Art Library, London

Chapter 51
(p. 265) Gold bulla from the House of Menander, Pompeii, A.D. 79, Museo e Gallerie Nazionali di Capodimonte, Naples/Bridgeman Art Library, London

(p. 272) Caracalla, Roman marble cuirassed bust A.D. 212–217, Louvre, Paris/ Bridgeman Art Library, London

Carved amethyst cameo of Emperor Constantine II (Emperor A.D. 337–340) British Museum, London/ Bridgeman Art Library, London

Chapter 52
(p. 281) Melitene, priestess of the Mother of the Gods, Roman marble bust, consecrated A.D. 162, Louvre, Paris/Bridgeman Art Library, London

(p. 282) Detail of "Landscape with the Father of Psyche Sacrificing to Apollo" by Claude Lorrain (1600–1682), National Trust, Fairhaven/ Bridgeman Art Library, London

(p. 284) "Tarquin the Elder Consulting Attus Navius the Augur," by Sebastiano Ricci (1658–1734), Sotheby's, London/Bridgeman Art Library, London

Chapter 53
(p. 291) Drawing of Aurelius Hermia and his wife by Claudia Karabaic Sargent

Chapter 54
(p. 298) "Scene in a Classical Temple: Funeral Procession of a Warrior" by Joseph Charles Barrow by courtesy of the Board of Trustees of the Victoria and Albert/Bridgeman Art Library, London

Epilogue
(p. 309) Drawing of Roman soldiers destroying a German camp, courtesy Barnaby's

(p. 313) Marble statue of Socrates, British Museum, London

(p. 314) Roman Emperor as a Pharoah, Egyptian marble bust, 1st Century A.D., Louvre, Paris/Bridgeman Art Library, London

(p. 317) "Visit of a Sick Child to the Temple of Asclepius," oil on canvas by John William Waterhouse (1849– 1917), The Fine Art Society, London/Bridgeman Art Library, London

(p. 320) Harl 4425, "Seneca Bleeding in Bath," Roman de la Rosa (c. 1487– 1495), British Library, London/Bridgeman Art Library, London

(p. 322) "Philosophy," woodcut by Albrecht Dürer, in *The Complete Woodcuts of Albrecht Dürer*, ed.: Willi Kurth, Dover Publications, New York, 1961